UNDERSTANDING, ASSESSING,
AND REHABILITATING

JUVENILE

SEXUAL OFFENDERS

UNDERSTANDING, ASSESSING, AND REHABILITATING

JUVENILE

SEXUAL OFFENDERS

PHIL RICH

Foreword by Robert E. Longo

WILEY

JOHN WILEY & SONS, INC.

This book is dedicated first and foremost to the victims of sexual abuse. Their victimization is a personal and social tragedy.

The book is dedicated also to the leadership and staff of the Stetson School in Barre, Massachusetts, a residential treatment program fully committed to the best possible treatment of children and adolescents who engage in sexually abusive behavior. Stetson is a remarkable working environment and a combination of remarkable people in a remarkable field.

Foreword

I have worked in the field of treating sexual offenders since 1978 and have focused my work exclusively on children and adolescents with sexual behavior problems since 1992. During the past twenty-five years, I have tried to keep up with the literature in the field. There are a few good books on the market that are well written and comprehensive in describing the assessment and treatment process with juveniles who sexually abuse. Most of these books are now a decade old or better. After reading Phil Rich's book *Understanding, Assessing, and Rehabilitating Juvenile Sexual Offenders,* I found it to be the best and most current book on the market today.

Understanding, Assessing, and Rehabilitating Juvenile Sexual Offenders is a book I would recommend as a staple in the office of therapists, probation officers, and administrators, and in the staff libraries of treatment programs. Any professional who finds him- or herself working in some capacity with juveniles who sexually abuse will find this book to be of great interest and tremendous value in working with this highly specialized population.

The field of treating children and adolescents with sexual behavior problems began to grow during the early 1980s and experienced its most rapid growth in the 1990s. There are several emerging issues related to the assessment and treatment of juvenile sexual offenders, and *Understanding, Assessing, and Rehabilitating Juvenile Sexual Offenders* covers all of them. The most important is the issue of stopping the trickle-down phenomenon from the adult field of assessing and treating sexual offenders to the juvenile field. This has been an ongoing phenomenon for well over two decades and has been destructive to the work we try to do with children and adolescents. Unfortunately, we continue to view these children erroneously as mini-adults, mini-perpetrators, sexual mini-predators, and the like. Rich's book makes perfectly clear that working with youth is and must be very different.

Based on adult sex offender protocol, we often keep youthful sexual abusers in treatment longer than is necessary using adult-based models and treatment modalities that my even prove harmful to these patients. Many adult treatments are controversial and may include involuntary treatments for purposes of public safety, rather than rehabilitative reasons.

Unlike adults, children and adolescents are still advancing in many areas. Developmentally they are still growing physically, cognitively, and emotionally. Although these patients must be held accountable for their behaviors, from a developmental perspective, adolescents from the age of thirteen to eighteen are still dealing with their identities, and they may experience role confusion. Even healthy youths are fine-tuning their sense and understanding about what it means to be responsible and who they are as individuals. We do not give children of this age the full complement of adult responsibilities, and we should not think that we can arbitrarily single out particular behaviors, criminal or otherwise, in order to selectively treat them as adults.

The field of treating adult sex offenders does not take into account developmental stages and moral development. However, assessment and treatment planning for youth must take into account the patient's developmental abilities as well as potential developmental lags. Many if not most adolescents who have sexual behavior problems also have learning disabilities that must be taken into account. All systems, from judicial to mental health, need to take these and other factors into account when working with these cases.

What really struck me about this book that sets it apart from others is that Rich takes the time to give the reader a comprehensive look at youths with sexual behavior problems. In Section I, he gives the reader the necessary information to understand what is important about assessment and why having this information is so important to the assessment process. This book is honest, straightforward, and factual in its approach.

Rich begins by reviewing the research on juvenile sexual offenders and cautions the reader that the research on this population is not perfect. He explains why the research is often flawed and describes the complexities of youth, and of working with youth who sexually abuse, and thus shows why we have such a difficult time producing conclusive research with this population. He notes that the problems facing the field of juvenile sex offender assessment and treatment stem, in part, from the differing philosophies professionals hold regarding this specialized population. In fact, he notes, we can't even agree on what to label these young people, let alone agree on what the many disciplines should do in assessing and treating them.

Yet, with the varying philosophies, opinions, and clinical knowledge we have on this population, Rich manages to put it all together in this singular volume so that the reader has a sense of direction to take given the knowledge, and limitations of knowledge, within this discipline. In addition, *Understanding, Assessing, and Rehabilitating Juvenile Sexual Offenders* puts the research and literature into perspective. When readers are done with section I, they truly understand the complexities of juvenile sexual offending and have a foundation upon which to build their practice and work assessing these young people.

In section II, Rich outlines the assessment protocol for juvenile sexual offenders. Currently there are several scales being investigated: the J-SOAP, the ERASOR, the J-RAT, and the Protective Factors Scale. Although these tools all show promise, further research is necessary to further develop them and validate them, because none are researched enough to date to be considered reliable and valid in determining risk of juveniles who sexually abuse.

Rich addresses the fact that when assessing risk the practitioner need to take into account both static and dynamic risk factors. To date, the field still needs to develop and agree upon dynamic risk factors for children and adolescents who sexually abuse. Some of the aforementioned risk assessment scales include dynamic risk factors, but these are not comprehensive. Because children and adolescents are still in developmental stages, there are multiple treatment areas and concerns and thus multiples dynamic risk factors for which we can track progress.

This book also address the important point of diagnosis and assessment of comorbidity. The general literature on adolescents is growing with information about dual diagnosis and co-occurring disorders seen in working with youth. Juveniles with sexual behavior problems are no different. Comprehensive assessment must take into account the multitude of factors we are faced with in assessing youth, and comorbidity appears to be more commonly seen with this specialized population; thus it must be addressed in both assessment and treatment.

In section III, *Understanding, Assessing, and Rehabilitating Juvenile Sexual Offenders* describes the treatment and rehabilitation process of the juvenile sexual offender. As of the writing of this foreword, the field has yet to firmly establish what contitutes best practice in treating children and adolescents with sexual behavior problems. Although the number of programs for youthful offenders grew rapidly during the first half of the last decade, ideas and concepts about treating this specialized population have not necessarily advanced accordingly.

As I have noted, the trickle-down of clinical approaches used with adult sex offenders has occured with little regard for developmental and contextual issues that need to be taken into consideration in treating adolescents, or evidence that the areas of therapeutic focus are relevant for the juvenile sex offender population. Most often, treatment techniques and modalities used in treating adult sexual offenders have been directly applied to juvenile sexual abusers or modified only slightly to make materials more easily understood, without taking into conderation learning styles and multiple intelligences. High levels of confrontation still abound in many programs with little regard for the potential impact these approaches may have on youth with histories of abuse and neglect.

Unfortunately, many juvenile sexual offender treatment programs have generally adhered to a traditional adult sex-offender model. Questions about the appropriateness and effectiveness of these approaches in the treatment of juvenile sexual offenders make imperative the full development and testing of juvenile-specific intervention programs.

Rich clearly describes the importance of using a holistic or intergrated approach that blends traditional aspects of sexual abuser treatment into a holistic, humanistic, and developmentally consistent model for working with youthful sex offenders. As an author who has written about this approach and developed materials for patients that teach them about a holistic model, I applaud Rich's effort to support this model in his book.

Although there are still many concerns in the field regarding treating juveniles with sexual behavior problems, leaders have noted that the sequencing of treatment is important to overall programs efficacy and that current models using cognitive-behavioral treatment appear to be most promising regarding sex-offender–specific treatment. *Understanding, Assessing, and Rehabilitation Juvenile Sexual Offenders* takes this into account as well as pointing out that treatment programs must go well beyond treating just the "sexual" problems with these patients and clients. It emphasizes that treatment needs to address growth and development, social ecology, increasing health, social skills, emotional development, and resiliency, and incorporate treatment for the offender's own victimization and co-occurring disorder.

I have no doubt you will enjoy reading this well-written and easy-to-understand book. I trust it will remain one of your more popular references for treating juvenile with sexual behavior problems for many years to come.

Robert E. Longo, MRC; LPC
Corporate Director of Special Programming and Clinical Training
New Hope Treatment Centers
Summerville, South Carolina

Acknowledgments

I must first and above all else thank and extend my great appreciation to Kathleen Lovenbury and Kerry Cornwell, respectively the Executive Director and Program Director of Stetson School, for providing me with the support, encouragement, and time to write this book, as well as their warmth and their friendship. I am extremely grateful.

A very special thanks also to Tracey Belmont, my Editor at John Wiley & Sons, who probably understood what I was trying to say better than I did, and whose expertise and experience I absolutely counted on and to whom I am very appreciative. Tracey has taught me what it means to have a great editor. Thank you so much!

I also want to express my gratitude for the opportunities provided to me by Stetson School and its leadership, to whom this book is partially dedicated. In addition to Kathleen and Kerry, many thanks to the executive and program administration, clinicians, case managers, educational, residential, overnight, and nursing staff who unflaggingly provide the core of the program and enact the values of Stetson, and our secretarial, business, and support staff who allow us all to do our work. It is difficult to single out any group in particular, but I have learned a great deal from our clinicians especially, and have built many of our conversations into this book. A special thanks to Beth Danforth for the Jolly Ranchers, taken as needed.

I also must thank Peggy Alexander, Vice President and Publisher at John Wiley & Sons, for her willingness to publish my ideas and for extending to me the opportunity to contribute to the professional literature. Thanks also to copy editor Paul McCurdy and project manager Susan Dodson at Graphic Composition, Inc., who provided book management services.

A special thanks to those colleagues who graciously gave their time to review this book, prepublication. The field is stronger and better because of their professionalism and expertise. Thanks to all, and a particular thanks to Robert Longo for generously writing the foreword to this book.

Finally, and as always, I want to thank my wife and my very good friend, Bev Sevier, and my daughter and one of my favorite people, Kaye Sevier, for providing me with a wonderful home environment and a loving family—two very bright and very good-humored people who do a good job of putting up with me.

Contents

PART I

Understanding the Juvenile Sexual Offender

CHAPTER 1

Working With Juvenile Sexual Offenders: Framing the Ideas and the Tasks

THE ISSUES of sexuality, sexual conduct, and sexual offending among adolescents and children have never been more significant. Unfortunately, these issues and concerns threaten to become more significant still, as we see and tackle increasingly serious and more pervasive developmental, emotional, and behavioral problems in our children.

We live in a society in which children of all ages in the general population are increasingly more exposed to sexuality and violence on a daily basis. Under the most benign of circumstances, exposure is through the media, with an increasingly heavy focus on violence and a near endless (and still mounting) emphasis on the importance and prevalence of sex. In virtually every form of media, children are inundated with images of and ideas about sexuality and sexual behavior. In the United States, for instance, it is virtually impossible to watch prime-time television or see a movie directed toward adolescents that is free of implicit—and with increasing frequency explicit—sexual innuendo, content, and behaviors. In many cases television shows, movies, electronic games, and music recordings with explicit sexual and violent themes or overtones are aimed directly at teenagers and often have an audience that includes children from 6 years of age and up (U.S. Federal Trade Commission, 2000). Of course, most recently added to the list, and for many children perhaps the most available and flexible form of media, is the Internet and its often direct, graphic, invasive, and sometimes shocking sexual messages and content.

Under less benign and more direct circumstances, many children are exposed to sexual behaviors through the reality of their own lives and their own experiences in their communities and, in some cases, their own families. Some of these children witness sexual practices, behaviors, and violence in their own homes and communities through the lives of their parents, siblings, and other community members. For many other children, exposure is of the most direct form as they become victims of sexual abuse and violence. Sadly, in many cases when children are the victims of sexual abuse, the sexual offenders are *themselves* children.

Accordingly, we live in a society that is more and more focused on social interventions and on the treatment of both the sexually abused and those who abuse. Statistics of every kind tell us that of the multitude of sexual crimes committed in the United States each year, many are committed by teenagers and younger children, ranging from exposure to molestation and rape. Most times, children are the victims of these crimes committed by other children.

THE TREATMENT TASK

We approach social and behavioral problems with juveniles through treatment, with *sexual-offender-specific* treatment most distinguished from other therapeutic interventions by its *forensic* focus. That is, sexual-offender-specific treatment crosses the line between the treatment of criminal behavior and the treatment of mental health and behavioral disorders. Work with child and adolescent sexual offenders is even more complex as it deals with developmental and cognitive issues, personality development, family and community systems, a complex interplay between developing emotions and behaviors, the line between normative sex play and experimentation and the development of sexual offending behavior, psychiatric comorbidity, social learning, and often the echoes of personal trauma in the adolescent or child offender. Here, we are working with young people, troubled and troubling in behavior, still very much in the process of exploration, development, and maturation, and still very much influenced and directed by the messages embedded in the activities, relationships, social models, and larger social environment that surround them.

Relatively few individuals working in the field are well versed in all aspects of such treatment, and practitioners skilled in one area often lack knowledge and skills in another. Mental health practitioners are often overwhelmed by or simply unaware of the complex forensic, criminal, and social issues tightly wrapped up in the treatment of juvenile sexual offenders. Conversely, those well versed in forensics and criminal behaviors are often not familiar with developmental, family, mental health, or diagnostic considerations and issues. Either way, practitioners in forensic and mental health treatment may not be familiar with the special dynamics found in children and adolescents who, after all, are not merely underdeveloped adults. In addition to blending forensic psychology and adolescent mental health and behavioral treatment, there is a need to adopt the perspective offered by social psychology, which posits that individual psychology and behavior must be understood in the context of the surrounding society.

Given both the changing face of child and adolescent sexual experiences and behaviors and the prevalence of adolescent and younger sexual offending, the reality is that sexual-offender-specific assessment and treatment are being pushed onto practitioners who are poorly trained and ill prepared for the work. Current training models are often too simplistic or unintegrated, focusing on either (a) a forensic and correctional approach assuming that the clinical treatment of juvenile sexual offenders is dealt with elsewhere (in a specialized treatment program), or (b) a mental health approach that fails to recognize or incorporate a forensic mind-set and assumes that criminal issues either are not present or have been dealt with elsewhere (presumably in a prior correctional program). Here, we risk treating forensics and mental health treatment as different disciplines rather than combining the two into a single approach. Of course, specialists trained in forensic psychology, forensic social work, or forensic counseling do exist, but they are few and far between in the world of juvenile sexual offender (JSO) treatment, where the vast majority of practitioners are neither trained nor experienced in both aspects of treatment. In fact, we have few specific training programs that marry these distinct approaches into a single specialization: the forensic and mental health treatment of juvenile sexual offenders. Instead, we use the relatively few specialists trained and experienced in general forensic treatment to consult and educate or appear in court to provide expert testimony, rather than ensuring that those who treat juvenile sexual offenders are themselves fully trained in forensic mental health.

The task, then, is to develop practitioners who understand the complexities of the juvenile sexual offender, are trained in both forensics and mental health, and understand the world and behavior of the adolescent. These clinicians will understand the development of sociopathy and social deviance, the psychology and development of personality and behavior, the assessment and treatment of behavioral and mental health, and the influence of the social world on the ideas, attitudes, beliefs, expectations, social framework, and behaviors of children and adolescents. This requires that we understand the forensic principles that frame and shape this work, the interpersonal and intrapsychic dynamics that lead to and maintain sexual offending behaviors, and the issues and processes involved in the development of personal identity and mental health, and that we know how to apply our knowledge in such a complex environment.

THE APPROACH TO TREATMENT

Despite its forensic underpinning, the work of assessing and treating juvenile sexual offenders is not isolated from the mainstream of clinical work with developing or troubled children and adolescents of every kind. Rather, it is a subset of this larger field. As such, the work requires educated and trained clinicians and program managers who understand the tasks and methods of treatment, the development of normative and psychopathological adolescent behavior, and the influence of social psychology, at all times remaining informed and often directed by the forensic perspective.

Happily, work with juvenile sexual offenders has to some degree moved away from an isolated and limited form of treatment that depended and borrowed heavily from either an adult criminological model or a substance abuse treatment model. Instead, the field is developing into a far more sophisticated and informed practice that lies within, and not separated from, a broader clinical approach in which the adolescent is understood and recognized as a *whole* person, and not merely a sexual offender. At the same time, our work with juvenile sexual offenders requires that the mental health approach be informed and guided by a forensic mind-set that seeks to understand offending and related behaviors as meeting criminogenic needs (factors that contribute to criminal behavior), as well as needs related to personal identity, social attachment, and emotional satisfaction. In the treatment of the juvenile sexual offender, criminality, deviant behavior, public safety, social competency, personal development, and mental health are intertwined and inseparable. In addition, mental health treatment without forensics is naive; a forensic or criminogenic approach without mental health is unrealistic and punitive; and a combined forensic and mental health approach without the application of social psychology is hopeful but poorly informed and limited, and probably bound to fail.

THE THIRD DIRECTION

In our understanding and treatment of juveniles we have, over the years, alternated between a nurturing-guidance approach to a criminal justice approach and perhaps are beginning to swing back somewhere toward the middle. The risk, though, in any pendulum-like application of ideas is that we become reactive rather than proactive, because pendulum thinking is limited in its flexibility and responsiveness. What we can hope for is a new direction, unfettered by a single pivot point. It involves understanding and treating the adolescent as an adult-in-the-making with unique patterns of thinking and behavior that are not simply shadows of early adulthood; recognizing the criminogenic, antisocial, detached, and socially abhorrent and deviant needs embedded in sexually abusive behavior; and working with the emotional, cognitive, and behavioral components basic to mental health and the development of sound and resilient individuals.

THE GOAL OF THIS BOOK

This is a book for practitioners of behavioral and emotional assessment and treatment and for the designers and managers of assessment and treatment programs for juvenile sexual offenders. It is designed to provide both a broad overview of and a detailed look at treatment for juvenile sexual offenders, as well as presenting a specific set of tools for working with this group of troubled children and adolescents and a framework in which to practice.

The book explores basic ideas that will help readers develop an understanding of the problems, behaviors, and factors that contribute to sexual offending among adolescents and children and provides detailed ideas and methods for assessing juvenile sexual offenders and their risk for future reoffending. It also describes methods for treating juvenile offenders, going beyond the cognitive-behavioral approaches prevalent in the treatment of sexual offenders and marrying psychoeducational, cognitive-behavioral, and psychodynamic treatments into a larger model that in turn incorporates individual, group, and family treatment into an approach that treats the whole child.

However, I do not intend this book to be simply another version of how to assess and treat juvenile sexual offenders; there are already many well-written and developed books that address these ideas, many of which are listed as references. Instead, this book looks at the same issues, concepts, and models through critical eyes and presents a clear and direct pathway to assessment and treatment in a manner that will help practitioners to become familiar with or critique the ideas of the field and perhaps go beyond them to find or create ideas of their own design that meet their own clinical orientations and experiences.

This book addresses complex issues and ideas in straightforward terms, without falling short of the high ideals, integrity, and sophistication required to be instructive, knowledgeable, contemplative, and critical enough to induce original thinking in the minds of every practitioner. This book simplifies but is not simplistic, instead urging the reader toward discerning thinking. In addition, this book is both theoretically and empirically driven, with many references to historical and current research and publications, but is neither built upon nor driven by research. It describes many standard ideas, models, and methods but supports neither the status quo or de facto conclusions nor the practice of adopting existing ideas simply because they are in use everywhere else. If anything, this book actively cautions against adopting and using such models merely because they are standard treatment fare. Models and ideas should be developed and used because they work and because we can see they work, not because they are the standards in the field. This requires the application of critical thinking in every practitioner. This is a book for practice, then, and the development of the knowledge base and informed thinking that are required for effective practice.

UNDERLYING BELIEFS

For the individual sexual offender, the treatment questions are what happened, how, why, and what we can do to ensure that it does not happen again. However, the larger and more looming questions ask why so many children sexually abuse other children and how this situation comes about. What social forces have led to the development of so many adolescents and children who engage in sexually abusive behavior or behavior that is sexually inappropriate or, at least, sexually precocious? Although this book cannot possibly answer such complex issues, we can approach these questions, asserting the importance of developing informed practitioners who consider and struggle with such questions and think originally while engaging in the practice of assessment and treatment. Having strong and well-informed opinions can shape both our practice at the level of the individual juvenile and the way we think about juvenile sexual offenders and execute our practice at the broadest level. Accordingly, this book asserts the importance of both knowledge and original thinking in the practitioner and addresses the need for critical thinking in everything we do as treaters of juvenile sexual offenders.

Additionally, this book explores our beliefs about juvenile sexual offenders, as well as the source of the ideas and influences behind our thoughts and assumptions. I ask what shapes the way we assess sexual offending behaviors and provide treatment, as well as our choice of treatment interventions. Underlying each method is a belief system about what works best in the assessment and treatment of juvenile sexual offenders. But instead of simply adopting such methods and ideas as received wisdom, we can be most effective when we apply a critical eye even to the most accepted methods and practices. Informed by studies and opinions that support or refute the most common interventions and ideas, and by understanding the thinking that lies behind our beliefs and practice, we are most able to engage in informed treatment and are placed in the best position to decide which treatment methods and approaches to adopt. The willingness to challenge the status quo of treatment is an important tool in the development of inspired, informed, and original thinkers.

This book also adopts the perspective that insight into the motivation, the mind, and the behavior of the juvenile sexual offender is critical to effective practice. In each case, clinicians must understand how and why the juvenile committed a sexual offense and demonstrate this insight through clinical formulations that demonstrate knowledge of the case, as well as the ability to visualize and describe the juvenile's pathway to sexual offending, causation and motivation, psychological development, and the goal or need that the offense filled for the juvenile. This is very different from the model found in many programs today, in which treatment is conceived primarily as a cognitive process provided primarily through the teaching of concepts and techniques to juvenile offenders. This model typically requires clinicians to teach such concepts and test for their acquisition and retention but demands little clinical insight into motivation, the development of behavior, or the underlying psychology of the individual. Concerns about attachment, empathy, remorse, personal responsibility, sexual arousal, and other factors central to the treatment of juvenile sexual offenders are often addressed through treatment methods that require little insight in either the juvenile or the clinician. A model that emphasizes clinical insight is not mutually exclusive or antithetical to a cognitive-behavioral approach to treatment but instead underpins and adds to that treatment by ensuring that the clinician has a depth of understanding that shapes and directs all treatment.

Above all, this book takes the perspective that our response to the problem of juvenile sexual offending (and ultimately adult sexual offending, as we know that a good many, if not most, adult sexual offenders begin as juvenile sexual offenders) must be informed and measured, well founded, and fresh and creative, based on both knowledge and analytical thinking in practitioners and program managers. I wish to avoid the trap described by Chaffin and Bonner (1998), who suggested that our search for the truth has led us to a poorly informed conventional wisdom that has shaded into dogma.

THE SEARCH FOR THE PERFECT ANSWER

In forensic work in general, and perhaps in sexual offender work in particular, there seems to be an insistence on producing (or discovering) universal and simplistic tools that can provide noncomplex and parsimonious answers to extremely complex and convoluted issues. At the heart of this is the idea that our theory is too poor and that if only it were stronger and more informed, we would be able to understand and control more of our universe. This used to be called a *machine model* because it implies that the world and all the people in it simply unfold in a manner that is predictable and can be fully understood with enough information. This contrasts with a clinical perspective that more or less considers experience to be too rich for our theory to ever explain fully.

In clinical work we treat every case as unique, guided by theory, research, and experience, understanding that the situation and context are instrumental in the development and unfolding of individual experience. We depend on the work and ideas of others as a foundation on which to build our own work, illuminate and guide our way, provide a common language, shape our ideas, help us understand those interventions and practices that work, and define treatment methods and protocols. But in clinical work we do not abandon our intellect and experience and hand everything over to fixed ideas that claim to represent the way things really are as well as the reality of our clients' experiences and our own. This is especially important because so many certain ideas have later turned out to be not so certain—and even wrong.

THE PERILS OF RESEARCH

Research provides an opportunity to hypothesize and test out ideas, and much of what one reads and hears is based on research-driven studies aimed at producing the empirical evidence described throughout this book. However, the problem with research into juvenile sexual offending is that it is seriously flawed, fails to produce meaningful data, and often is not replicated by others or cannot be replicated.

In the natural sciences, experiments (i.e., research) can be replicated with relative ease. The same brick can be dropped off of the same tower under the same conditions time after time with the same results, and all variables can be controlled to see not only the effects but also the controlling factors. In addition, the experimenters can measure the results in quantifiable data. Not so in the social sciences. In fact, it is difficult to imagine running the *same* experiment with the same subjects and getting exactly the same results, let alone using *different* subjects and under different circumstances. That is why we use inferential statistics in the social sciences, why we require random samples that we believe represent the general population under study, and why we require large sample sizes so that we can be relatively sure that our data have true meaning. For many practical and ethical reasons, however, research into juvenile sexual offending typically does not meet these standards.

In fact, many research studies are too limited in size or design to be of any significant value other than pointing in a particular direction. It is enormously difficult, if not ethically impossible, to create experimental and control groups for study; subjects selected for study are usually not selected randomly; and it is virtually impossible to replicate experimental research designs. In addition, much research in our field seems geared toward proving an already-adopted perspective, and there is a self-fulfilling aspect to it. Moreover, when we read research that tells us one thing, we can usually cite research that tells us just the opposite. Nevertheless, those who support a particular perspective often present research that strengthens and justifies their position and ignore research that negates or refutes their point. In this vein, the same research data are often reported and passed on repeatedly as though they are flawless, creating the myth of known fact where none exists. Consequently, research is of great importance but has limited use at this time, and can just as easily hold treatment back as promote it.

So what do we know? Well, perhaps that no one *really* knows. We can only suppose and make calculated and educated guesses informed by research that is often weak at best and by our professional judgment and experience.

TERMINOLOGY AND LABELING: GETTING IT "RIGHT"

It is important to note that many professionals, including many central to this field, choose not to use and sometimes frown upon the term *juvenile sexual offender*. Accordingly, the term is used here in recognition of the view of many treatment professionals that the term mislabels and stigmatizes children and is even unnecessary. In this view the label is believed to cloud the fact that these are deeply troubled children who need our help more than our labels and who do not deserve the labels we place on them.

The underlying questions for assessment and treatment are, What is a sexual offense; why do kids sexually offend; and should we call their behavior sexual offending? Is it more correct to call these kids "sexual offenders," "sexual abusers," "children who sexually offend," "children who engage in sexualized behaviors," "children who sexually abuse others," or even "young males who are sexually acting out and displaying abusive or challenging behavior," as described on one business card? Where does one draw the line between the desire to avoid stigmatizing kids through negative labeling, euphemism, semantics, hairsplitting, and political correctness?

Does good and effective treatment practice even have anything to do with the labels or terms we use to identity the kids with whom we work? For those who believe that labels do matter there is the assumption that using the right treatment term aids treatment and that using the wrong term hinders or hurts treatment prospects. Of course, it is a little more complex than this. The view that negative labels are, or may be, harmful pulls on a sociological tradition asserting that negative labeling leads to both social stigmatization and negative self-image.

Those who wish to avoid harsh-sounding terms see such labeling as unnecessary and, under the worst circumstances, harmful; the sociological model of *secondary deviance* holds the view that deviant acts are committed in part as a *result* of being labeled deviant. Critics of strong labels additionally suggest that the tag is unnecessary and does not help treatment and thus should be avoided rather than risking harm to the still-developing personal identity of juveniles, as well as to the way others see and think about them. Additionally, those who are uncomfortable with or prefer not to use the term juvenile sexual offender sometimes consider the label to be incorrectly applied and assert that the term applies only to juveniles adjudicated on charges of sexual offense (i.e., charged with and found responsible for criminal sexual acts) and that we should refer to other children and adolescents entering treatment for sexually abusive behavior by other terms.

Alternatively, proponents of such labeling note that direct terms convey more precise meaning and that a label like juvenile sexual offender jolts juveniles who are sexually aggressive, as well as their families, into awareness. They argue that calling a spade a spade both provides a framework for treatment and a mind-set that helps the juvenile sit up and pay attention and avoids potentially whitewashing a harsh reality. The term not only focuses on why the juvenile has come into treatment but also fits a model of restorative justice in which there is a clear emphasis on the harm caused and the victims of such harm, rather than on the juvenile and his need for treatment alone.

Finkelhor (1979) described the decision to reject certain labels because they are pejorative and might lead to bias in examining the problem or treating the individual. He recognized that certain terms and labels have political and moral overtones but did not feel that this "disqualifies them from use in scientific investigation" (p. 18). Although Finkelhor is referring to the term *sexual victimization* (the polar opposite, one might say, of "sexual offending"), he wrote that in an effort to raise consciousness, it is appropriate to use terms that arouse feelings and stimulate responses. He also declared that "merely choosing another 'sanitary' term . . . does not solve any problems. It is still obvious to anyone but the most gullible that the researcher is interested in the phenomenon that is being called sexual abuse by people in the social and political arena" (p. 18). He advised that "the better course of action . . . is to use the value-laden term but to carefully caution readers about perceptual biases that it may introduce" (p. 18).

Vizard (2002) noted that in relation to labels that describe sexually aggressive behavior in children and adolescents, "virtually all these terms may be criticized on some basis or other" (p. 177). Why even bother discussing what may amount to hairsplitting, then? Because at times, terms and labels become a point of contention among professionals, and because one objective of this book is to help the reader recognize the ideas and issues that help us to understand and build the foundation for both knowledge about and treatment of sexually abusive behaviors in juveniles. Another reason is to make the strong point that there is no correct way to think about or understand treatment, and before we move on to exploring and thinking about sexual offenses and juvenile sexual offenders, we must understand that the basis of our work is not clear-cut, as we sometimes make it out to be. Our field continues to develop and emerge, but if the things that seem most obvious to us at any given time become the "correct" things, we may fail to recognize that the tide of treatment beliefs and interventions ebbs and flows.

It is also reasonable to think of changes in the field as evolutionary, recognizing that we adopt and sometimes discard new ideas, revisit old ideas, and inject into or remove from treatment those things that we learn along the way. Convictions about what is right risk limiting new and creative ideas that do not fit with conventional wisdom, relegating other ideas and practices to the realm of ineptitude or failure to understand the real issues.

In this book the term *juvenile sexual offender* is used synonymously with the many other terms—some far more subtle—used to depict and describe children and adolescents who are sexually aggressive, who sexually abuse or offend, or who engage in inappropriate sexual behaviors that victimize others. I am not sure whether the use of any of these terms, all of which are labels, is proper. On the other hand, I am sure that they all, to some degree, fail to express fully the complexities inherent in the sexually abusive and inappropriate behavior of children and adolescents. I frankly hope we never find the right term that we all *must* use, and at the same time I hope that we never miss seeing the troubled kid *behind* the label.

I encourage practitioners to decide for themselves the terms with which they are the most comfortable in describing the children and adolescents with whom they work. This book does not purport to present the right answers or the correct things to do. Instead, it presents a wide range of information and ideas intended to inform, educate, stimulate critical thinking, and above all help practitioners to arrive at their own conclusions and head in the directions that make the most sense to them, based on the clinical, theoretical, and empirical-research evidence of the field. My conviction is that we should not accept the first term or idea that comes our way, regardless of its source, but instead recognize the diversity of opinions, ideas, and perspectives in our field and the larger fields of forensics and mental health in which it is nested, any of which may be right. In fact, it may be true that there is a continuum of sexual behaviors along which children's sexual offending lies, and we should create a typology that allows us more neatly to use different terms to describe different kinds of children who engage in different kinds of sexual behaviors and abuse. Perhaps it is most useful to refer to juveniles who sexually offend as "juveniles at risk for becoming adult sexual offenders."

Nevertheless, the task of wrestling with what we mean when we speak about juvenile sexual offenders is important. The changing terminology reflects a healthy change in our thinking, supportive of the juvenile behind the sexually abusive behavior, in which the assessment and treatment pendulum may be swinging away from the criminal justice end of the spectrum and back toward the more understanding and sensitive end of the scale.

A NOTE ON PRONOUNS

Whenever a pronoun is required, I refer to sexual offenders as "he" because most sexual offenders are male, although there is awareness of the number, and perhaps the growing number, of females who commit sexual offenses against children and adults.

THE WISH

Many of the ideas in this book are neither original nor correct, but they are explored, framed, and laid out in a manner that, I hope, will bring the practitioner to a clear understanding of the ideas, issues, tasks, and methods of the work. Above all, this is a book with a goal (and a passion): to develop skills and informed, sophisticated, critical, and original thinking in those who assess and treat juvenile sexual offenders, or whatever we choose to call these troubled children.

CHAPTER 2

Sexually Abusive Behaviors, Victims, and Perpetrators

WHEN WE describe sexual abuse and sexual offending, we refer to things like rape and sexual molestation perpetrated by adults who know what they are doing and intentionally engage in such behaviors. Nowadays, we also include as sexual offenses the possession or dissemination of child pornography as well as acts of public nudity, sexual indecency, lewdness, and lasciviousness. But ideas that are taken for granted when it comes to adults are less clear when we discuss still-developing children and adolescents who engage in some of the same behaviors but whose motivations, intentions, and sometimes normative adolescent behaviors are not really understood, and especially in a time of great social change. This is of special concern when we realize the personal consequences to children and adolescents who engage in such behaviors, including both social sanctions and criminal culpability.

Because treatment may also result in criminal prosecution, public disclosure, social rejection, stigma, and shame, the perpetrators of sexual abuse (adult and adolescent) rarely seek out (or want) treatment, thus further complicating the ability to provide effective interventions. But if we intend to assess, treat, and help young offenders, we first need to have a clear understanding of what we mean by juvenile sexual abuse.

DEFINING SEXUALLY ASSAULTIVE BEHAVIOR

A fully defined and agreed-upon definition of the word *rape* does not exist, although many people imagine that they know exactly what it is when they hear the word. Many states define rape to include nonconsensual oral sex and digital or object penetration, as well as nonconsensual sexual intercourse. Similarly, the Center for Sex Offender Management (1999a, p.18) described

15

rape as forcible and sexual vaginal, anal, or oral penetration with penis, finger, or object. Still other definitions are so broad that they render virtually any unwanted or coercive sexual act as rape. Going far beyond the commonly understood meaning of rape as nonconsensual vaginal or anal sexual intercourse, these definitions are too broad to be useful. Some states smartly avoid the problem of describing rape at all and instead define any sexual act as abusive when accompanied by force, performed without consent, or when one party is a mentally incompetent individual or a child.

In the case of children, life is still more complex. Some sexually inappropriate behaviors in children and adolescents, such as obscene phone calls, voyeurism, lewd and sexual hand gestures, and even mooning and genital exposure, are often simply part of the juvenile lifestyle and developmental path. The same applies to something even as obviously inappropriate and antisocial as the theft of underwear for the explicit purpose of sexual gratification. These are each inappropriate, antisocial, and sometimes illegal behaviors, but should we prosecute juveniles or seek sexual-offender-specific treatment for them? And if so, when and under what circumstances?

In trying to unravel this web, the National Task Force on Juvenile Sexual Offending (1993) tried to address the heart of the problem in defining sexual abuse. In so doing, they also identified the elements of sexually abusive behavior:

> The laws regarding sexual behavior do not entirely define abuse: some behavior may be prohibited by law but not be abusive, while some abusive behaviors are not covered by law. It is the nature of the relationship; the inequality of the participants; presence of exploitation, coercion, and control; manipulation; and the abuse of power, combined with a sexual behavior, which constitute sexual abuse. Sexually abusive behavior is represented by a continuum of behaviors, some of which may not fall within the court's parameters for prosecution. . . . We live in a society that demonstrates a great deal of confusion about sexuality. In some cases, societal norms seem repressive while in other cases societal norms seem excessively permissive. Individuals may hold different values about sexual behaviors, influenced by religious, familial, and cultural norms or beliefs. We are often unprepared to substantiate what is "normal" and what is "deviant" sexual behavior in juveniles. We do know, however, that certain sexual behaviors are abusive because they cause harm to others and that some sexual behaviors are illegal in our society. (pp. 6–7)

If we can agree with the National Task Force on Juvenile Sexual Offending (1993) that sexual abuse is any sexual behavior that occurs (a) without consent, (b) without equality, or (c) as a result of coercion (p. 11), we can begin to distinguish more easily among sexual behaviors that are typical of kids (obnoxious and troubling as they may be), sexual behaviors that are inappropriate, and sexual behaviors that are offenses and assaults.

Prendergast (1993) presented a definition of sexual abuse that is less succinct, more ungainly, and probably a little too restrictive due to its very wording but that nonetheless provides a different slant on the same ideas. He asserted that three factors must be included in any definition of sexual abuse:

1. A bigger and more powerful person used his or her strength or authority over a smaller, weaker, and more vulnerable individual (*Without Equality*).
2. Force, implied force, or deliberate deception was used to engage in a sexual act (*Use of Coercion*).
3. The victim was too frightened, inadequate, or intellectually or emotionally immature either to realize what was happening or to resist, so that there was no real or true choice (*Lack of Consent*).

Although this trifactor definition of sexual abuse is clear, it remains cloudy regarding the role played by coercion in juvenile sexual offending because kids are constantly coercing one another to do things, and especially in sexual relationships, although it gives us some footing on which to stand as we build an understanding of sexually abusive behaviors.

TYPES OF SEXUAL OFFENSES

No matter what defines a sexual behavior as sexually abusive, such behaviors cover a broad range, including both hands-off and hands-on sexual offenses.

HANDS-OFF, NONASSAULTIVE, OR NO-TOUCH OFFENSES

Hands-off sexually abusive behaviors involve clearly sexual behavior that is abusive to others. In both juveniles and adults some of these behaviors may be prosecutable as criminal misdemeanors or felonies but are not likely to and may not be recognized as sexual offenses. Nevertheless, an individual adjudicated for public indecency or possession of child pornography may still be mandated to receive sexual-offender-specific treatment.

With juveniles, however, these behaviors are complicated by developmental issues and conduct-disordered behaviors that are not unusual in adolescence. Obscene phone calls, for instance, are not especially unusual in kids and clearly are *not* sexual offenses, even though they may be for adults who are not as prone to making obscene phone calls for the pure fun or risk of it. However, in the continuum of possibly developing sexual offenses, we are likely to pay attention to such behavior in juveniles and to be concerned that it may be a precursor to other sexually inappropriate behaviors that may later become part of a pattern of sexually abusive behaviors. The same goes for public exhibitionism (exposure of the genitalia, also called *flashing*), which may not be a sexual offense per se, depending on the circumstances under which exposure occurred, but may still lead to significant concerns about sexually abusive behaviors. Accordingly, behaviors like this are often included under the heading of hands-off, nonassaultive, or no-touch sexual offenses, which are sometimes subject to sexual-offender-specific treatment, particularly in the case of exhibitionism:

- Obscene phone calls
- Theft of clothing for sexual purposes, most typically for masturbation
- Voyeurism (watching another person naked or engaged in sexual behavior without their knowledge or permission for the purposes of sexual gratification)
- Threats of sexual harm
- Exhibitionism (public exposure of genitals or other sexual parts for sexual gratification or other sexual purposes)
- Public masturbation
- Distribution, public display, or depictions of sexually obscene material

Hand-On, Assaultive, or Touching Offenses

Hands-on sexual offenses include touching behaviors and unmistakably cross the line of sexually abusive and criminally prosecutable behaviors, ranging from mild sexual assault to extreme forms of sexual assault and violence. Even within a continuum with frottage (or its mental health equivalent, frotteurism) at one extreme and rape at the other, rape itself lies along still another continuum: from rape that is not accompanied by additional physical violence or force to rape that is violent, sadistic, and even homicidal in nature.

Unlike no-touch sexual offenses, which are unlikely to involve violence, touching offenses by definition always involve physical contact and assault. Accordingly, even within the touching-offenses continuum itself, there are offshoots at each point that range from no violence to threats of violence, actual violence, and sadistic violence. For example, although molestation is not as extreme a sexual crime as rape, variants in molestation may include coercion, threats of violence, actual violence, and even sadism.

- Frottage, also known and diagnosed as frotteurism, involves rubbing up against another person for sexual gratification, although this may not necessarily involve rubbing of the genitalia.
- Fondling and molestation include touching the genitalia, buttocks, breasts, or other body parts of another person for sexual gratification.
- Oral sex involves cunnilingus or fellatio.
- Digital penetration involves the use of fingers to penetrate the vagina or anus.

- Object penetration involves penetration of the vagina or anus with a physical object of some kind.
- Penile penetration, in which the vagina or anus is penetrated by the erect penis, is the most clearly associated with rape.
- Sexual torture and homicide involve the sadistic torture and death of the victim, sometimes accompanied by mutilation.

OTHER SEXUAL OFFENSES

Other sexual offenses that involve neither a direct nor an indirect sexual assault against a person include

- Creation of child pornography
- Possession and distribution of child pornography
- Bestiality, or sexual contact and interactions with an animal

Of course, there are a range of sexual behaviors that we may think of as unusual, inappropriate, unhealthy, abnormal, perverse, or deviant that are not necessarily sexual offenses. However, although in some cases such behaviors may be illegal, these fall into the category of personal and nonoffending behaviors, and although they may require treatment, such treatment will not involve sexual *offender* treatment.

Figure 2.1 presents and ties together the range of nonassaultive, assaultive, and other sexual behaviors, noting the possible range of acts of aggression that exist along a continuum for each sexual act.

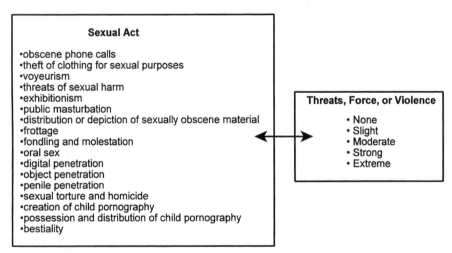

Figure 2.1
The range of sexual offenses: Nonassaultive, assaultive, and other, and the presence of aggression.

SEXUAL VICTIMIZATION

Perhaps the single factor that most clearly defines a sexual offense is the presence of a perpetrator and a victim. In this regard, there are situations in which there is a clear and easily recognizable victim, such as

- Rape
- Kidnapping and forced sexual contact
- Situations in which sex is required by one party of the other and is coerced through threats
- Sexual contact between adults and children (of any age and, potentially, until age 18)
- Sexual contact between children in which there is a significant age difference
- Situations in which there are other clear differences in power or control between the parties (e.g., the victim is retarded, elderly, infirmed, or in some way unable to resist or assertively refuse sexual contact or unable to give consent)
- Circumstances in which the victim is physically incapacitated or mentally incompetent

Although the occurrence of a sexual offense and the presence of a victim is sometimes completely clear (e.g., in cases of rape) at other times it can be difficult to discern whether there was a victim. This is especially true under circumstances in which the perpetrator denies any wrongdoing and the facts are not necessarily certain. This is perhaps most obviously demonstrated in cases of date rape, in which, by definition, a voluntary and consensual quality to the relationship existed until a certain point, but consent either was never given for a sexual relationship or was withdrawn. In such incidents, it can be difficult for the victim to prove that she or he was actually victimized.

However, there are many other reasons why it may be difficult to spot a victim clearly, notably in cases in which the victim may not step forward to report being victimized or even recognize his or her own victimization. It is more difficult to spot a victim in cases of peer sexual contact, regardless of age, unless one party experiences being the victim of a sexual assault *and* steps forward to report this. In still other cases, the victim may not even feel like a victim. For example, even when there is a clear age difference between the parties (adult and child, or children aged several years apart), the younger party may ostensibly have agreed to the sexual contact, may have wanted or even initiated the sexual contact, and may not feel like a victim.

Nevertheless, victimization is defined by several factors, some of which are obvious but not all of which necessarily make sense to the juvenile sexual offender—and sometimes not even to the victim. In the situation just described, in which the younger party may not feel like or recognize being a victim, the circumstances define the younger child as a victim and the adult or older child as a perpetrator of a sexual offense. This is because regardless of circumstance, the appearance of consent, or the experience of mutuality, the older party is considered a perpetrator due to the younger person's inability to give meaningful consent as defined by the law, our beliefs about children, and prevailing social values. Victims are victims, then, for one or more of several reasons, some of which are obvious and some of which involve moral, social, or legal realities.

- *Victim of sexual assault*, most typically involving unwanted sexual contact in which the victim clearly did not consent to the sexual interaction and made this clear in some way and experiences her- or himself as the victim of sexual assault
- *Child victim of adult*, involving an adult over the age of 18 engaged in sexual contact with a child below the age of consent and legally and socially unable to give consent regardless of any other circumstances or conditions
- *Younger victim of older child*, in which an older child of any age below age 18 engages in sexual contact with a younger child, in which the age difference is typically three years or more and two years in cases of very young children (below 7)
- *Inability to give consent*, in which an individual engages in sexual contact with someone who is clearly unable to give meaningful consent for any one of a number of reasons, including age of consent, intellectual-developmental delay, mental incompetence, unconsciousness, or drugged or otherwise inebriated or incapacitated state
- *Threatening coercion*, in which the perpetrator gains sexual access and compels sexual contact through the use of coercion or threats of consequences that may involve violence, threats of violence, or other threats of consequences of some kind
- *Non-threatening coercion*, in which the perpetrator gains access and sexual compliance with an individual below the age of consent primarily due to the presence of bribes, rewards, or other promises, and most typically when the perpetrator is an adult or older adolescent or the victim is significantly younger than the perpetrator

There are doubtless other variants of sexual victimization that range from mild to extreme and obvious to subtle, but the aforementioned general categories help to make clear the nature of sexual offending and the resulting categories of sexual victimization.

CONSENT VERSUS COERCION

As noted, the National Task Force (1993, pp. 8–9) has adopted a definition of sexual abuse as any sexual behavior that occurs (a) without consent, (b) without equality, or (c) as a result of coercion.

1. *Consent* is an agreement that includes
   - An understanding of the proposed behavior or interaction based on age, maturity, developmental level, functioning, and experience
   - Knowledge of social standards for the proposed behavior or interaction
   - Awareness of possible consequences and alternatives
   - Honoring agreement or disagreement
   - Voluntary decision
   - Mental competence
2. *Equality* is defined as two participants operating with the same level of power in a relationship in which neither is controlled or coerced by the other.
3. *Coercion* is defined as exploitation of authority and use of bribes, threats of force, or intimidation to gain cooperation or compliance.

Although listed as independent elements, these three factors are tied together, and each factor implies the other two. Although there are many examples in which lack of consent, inequality, or coercion is clear, at the other end of the spectrum the absence or presence (depending on the point of view) of these factors is less clear. There are times when the perpetrator claims consent was given, but equality was lacking because the consenting party was incapable of giving meaningful consent, or consent was the result of coercion, such as threats, blackmail, bribery, promises, or other forms of manipulation. Under such circumstances, true consent is either impossible, suspect, or highly unlikely. In some cases, although consent was given, it may be the product of planned and highly manipulative behaviors such as *grooming*, in which the perpetrator has spent much time building and developing a relationship in which there is the appearance of consent. False consent occurs when the consenting party is incapable of understanding moral norms, social expectations, possible consequences, the difference between right and wrong, and so forth due to age, intellect, mental condition, experience, and other factors that limit or make impossible meaningful and true consent.

Similarly, not every form of coercion involves threats or overt manipulation. Some involve power differentials in which the victim consents to or allows sexual contact because of a difference in power or perhaps is unaware that victimization is even occurring. One example is the employee who consents to a sexual relationship with a supervisor because of the power differential even though the employee really does not want sexual contact; another is the sexual relationship of a parent with a young child.

VICTIMS AND PERPETRATORS: THE STATISTICAL STORY

The statistics on sexual abuse in general and sexual abuse of children in particular are both disturbing and chilling. The statistics on children and adolescents who sexually offend are in some ways more disturbing, not only because of the offender's age but also because much of the abuse is directed against children.

A Cautionary Note

Data come from many sources and are often misleading and even misinformed. At times, data are drawn from relatively small research studies that describe percentages, which can easily hide the fact that the number of people included in the study is small. As a result, one has to ask 50% of what? For instance, 2% of a sample may not sound like much but in a sample size of 250,000 amounts to 5,000 people. On the other hand, a whopping 80% is only 16 people when drawn from a sample of 20 subjects. The characteristics of the sample population are important as well. When research is conducted among the general population, one can expect results to differ from those in research carried out among juvenile delinquents. It is important to know who was represented in the sample, then, as well as the sample size.

Data can also be confusing and even contradictory, especially when compared (as they should be) across different studies that examine the same population under the same conditions. Even when reviewing government sources of information, such as arrest rates, reported crimes, child abuse reports, and other demographics, different statistics and facts show up in the reports of different wings of the government. Such variances may stem from blatant mistakes in the data, typographical errors, or poor research design. Accordingly, it is evident that while providing useful and important data, we cannot depend on research for the "truth," and we must recall the words of Mark Twain, who reminded us that there are three kinds of lies: lies, damned lies, and statistics.

Nevertheless, we can use research and statistics to discover and recognize social patterns and events that go on beneath the surface of daily social life. As long as we understand their flaws and errors and do not allow them alone to determine our decisions, good research practice and resulting statistical information can provide us with an important and reasonable approximation of the world in which we live and thus help to inform and shape our perspectives, our understanding, and our responses. With this in mind, the statistics on sexual abuse and the perpetration of violence and sexual abuse educate, enlighten, and provide us with a generally accurate picture of child sexual abuse and juvenile sexual offending.

MALTREATMENT AND SEXUAL ABUSE

The 1999 National Child Abuse and Neglect Data System (NCANDS), reported by the United States Administration on Children, Youth, and Families (U.S. Department of Health & Human Services, 2001a), showed 2.9 million investigations of reported or suspected child maltreatment in the United States, with 826,000 substantiated incidents involving the neglect or abuse of a minor child, including 21% physical abuse and 11% sexual abuse. This amounts to over 93,000 cases of child sexual abuse. In terms of overall maltreatment, including all forms of physical abuse, sexual abuse, and neglect, 52% of child victims were girls and 48% boys. This is not true, however, in the case of child sexual abuse, in which female victims of sexual abuse far outstrip the number of male victims (1.6 girls per 1,000, compared to 0.4 boys). Still focusing on all types of child maltreatment, one or both parents were responsible for 92% of maltreatment; 61.8% of the perpetrators were women; and the most typical perpetrator was a mother (45%). Things shift radically in the case of child sexual abuse, however, where most perpetrators (by far) are men, and the focus swings to include nonparental perpetrators, as well as a large percentage of juvenile perpetrators.

In cases of child sexual abuse, parents were responsible for only 50% of abuse (as opposed to almost 92% of all forms of maltreatment), with the father alone responsible for 21% of the abuse, both parents for 12%, and the mother alone for 4% only (in contrast to 45% of all maltreatment). An additional 18% of child sexual abuse is perpetrated by other family members, 3% by substitute care providers, 18% by other known perpetrators, and 11% by unknown perpetrators.

Table 2.1 shows the shift in perpetration patterns from child neglect to child sexual abuse, with fewer female perpetrators and a smaller percentage of parental perpetrators across the continuum. In the case of child sexual abuse, 18% of perpetrators were other family members, and an additional 29% were other or unknown perpetrators, responsible for 47% of child sexual abuse (44,055 cases), many of which were perpetrated by other juveniles.

THE VICTIMS OF SEXUAL ASSAULT

Despite downward trends in reported crime rates, the American Academy of Child and Adolescent Psychiatry (1999) described sexual assault as a significant crime in the United States, reporting that one out of every three girls and one out of every seven boys will be sexually victimized before age 18 (p. 55S). Print and Morrison (2000) noted that sexual abuse victims are predominantly

Table 2.1

Comparison of Perpetrators of Child Neglect, Physical Abuse, and Sexual Abuse

	Perpetrators of Child Maltreatment (%)								
Type of Abuse	Female Parent Only	Male Parent Only	Both Parents	Female Parent and Other	Male Parent and Other	Family Relative	Substitute Care Provider	Other	Unknown
Neglect	51.7	12.4	18.5	8.2	1.0	2.5	1.3	2.7	1.7
Physical abuse	35.6	26.6	14.2	7.3	1.3	3.9	1.8	5.8	3.6
Sexual abuse	3.9	20.8	12.3	11.0	2.0	18.2	2.8	17.7	11.3

Source: Based on U.S. Department of Health and Human Services (2001a).

children, and in 1986 Fehrenbach, Smith, Monastersky, and Diesher stated that 62% of those sexually abused by adolescents were under age 12 and 44% were 6 years or younger.

The 1999 National Report of the Office of Juvenile Justice and Delinquency Prevention (2000a) reported that children under age 12 were the victims in one out of every three sexual assaults (32%). Snyder (2000a) confirmed these numbers, reporting that between 1991 and 1996 juveniles were the victims in almost 67% of all sexual assaults (40,802 children). Of these, as shown in Table 2.2, 33% (20,005 children) were aged 12–17, and 34% (20,737) were aged 11 or younger; 14% (8,539) were younger than age 6, meaning that approximately one in every seven victims was 5 years old or younger!

Based on incidents of sexual assault reported to the National Incident-Based Reporting System (NIBRS) between 1991 and 1996, involving 60,991 adult and child victims, forcible rape and sodomy combined were the most commonly reported sexual offenses, accounting for 50% of all sexual assaults, followed closely by forced fondling and molestation (Snyder, 2000a). Children of all ages (birth to 17 years) were the victims of 84% of fondling and molestation assaults, 80% of sodomy, 75% of sexual assault with an object, and 46% of forcible rape. Given the incidence of only 8% sodomy and 4% of sexual assault with an object in the overall population of sexual assault victims, and 42% vaginal rape, it is clear that children are subjected to a different form of sexual assault than are adults and that these forms of assault are related to the age of the victim and quite likely to the age of the perpetrator, many of whom are themselves children or adolescents.

In close agreement with the 1996 NCANDS data, girls in Snyder's (2000a) report were six times more likely than boys to be victims of sexual assault; 86% of all victims were girls, and female victims represented 69% of sexual assaults on children below age 6, 73% of victims under age 12, and 82% of all sexual assaults on juveniles. Furthermore, the likelihood of a female child's being sexually abused increased with age. Of all female victims, 69% were

Table 2.2

Victims of Sexual Offenses by Age and Percentage of Total Assault Victims

Victim Ages	Age Profile of Child Victims of Sexual Assaults (%)				
	All Sexual Assault	Rape	Sodomy	Sexual Assault With Object	Fondling
All Juveniles	66.9	45.8	79.8	75.2	83.8
0–5	14.0	4.3	24.0	26.5	20.2
6–11	20.1	8.0	30.8	23.2	29.3
12–17	32.8	33.5	24.0	25.5	34.3

Source: Adapted from Snyder (2000a).

Table 2.3

Percentage of All Sexual Assaults Directed Against Females by Age Group

Victim Age	Percentage of Female Victims
All ages	86.2
0–17	82
0–5	69.4
6–11	74.9
12–17	90.9

Source: Based on Snyder (2000a).

below 6, 75% were 11 or younger, and 91% were 18 or younger. Snyder's data are summarized in Table 2.3. Not shown is that the female proportion of *all* sexual offenses was 90% at age 13, and 95% at age 19.

Just as girls are more likely to be the victims of sexual assault, boys are more likely to be victims than are adults. At 18% of the total of sexual assaults for all ages, boys represented a higher percentage of sexual abuse victims than all adults of both genders combined (4% of total sexual assaults). For boys, the highest level of risk for both physical and sexual abuse is in early childhood, whereas for girls it is during adolescence. According to the NIBRS 1991–1996 data, boys are most likely to be sexually victimized at age 4, and girls at age 14, and Snyder (2000a) reported that female victimization rates during ages 14–17 are 10 times that of boys the same age. This fits with the idea that sexual offenders seek out and victimize the weakest, most vulnerable, and perhaps most accessible victims.

Perpetrators of Sexual Assaults

As shown in Table 2.4, of the 57,762 sexual offenders identified in Snyder's (2000a) study, family members were the perpetrators in 34% of all child sexual abuse cases, 49% of offenses against children below 6, 42% of offenses against 7- to 11-year-olds, and 24% of offenses against 12- to 17-year-old victims. Al-

Table 2.4

Percentage of Sexual Assaults Against Juveniles by Victim-Offender Relationship

Victim Age	Perpetrator of Sexual Abuse (%)		
	Family Member	Acquaintance	Stranger
0–17	34.2	58.7	7.0
0–5	48.6	48.3	3.1
6–11	42.4	52.9	4.7
12–17	24.3	66.0	9.8

Source: Based on Snyder (2000a).

Table 2.5

Percentage of Sexual Assaults by Gender

Victim Age	Sexual Offender by Gender (%)	
	Female	Male
All Ages	4	96
0–17	6	94
0–5	12	88
6–11	6	94
12–17	3	97

Source: Based on Snyder (2000a).

though most of the perpetrators against adolescents aged 7–17 were not family members, they were known to the victim. Similarly, the Office of Juvenile Justice and Delinquency Prevention (2000a) reported that the offender is most likely to be a family member in sexual abuse of children below age 6 and that in the sexual abuse of children below age 12 strangers are the least likely to be offenders.

In Table 2.5, the NIBRS data show that 96% of all offenders were male. Females offended against only 1% of adults and 6% of juveniles of all ages, although female offenders perpetrated 12% of sexual offenses against children below age 6. The NIBRS data also tell us that 23% of all sexual offenders were juveniles aged 7–17 (13,400 juvenile sexual offenders). Juveniles aged 12–17 represented 20% of all sexual offenders (11,264 adolescents), and juveniles 7–11 represented 4% of all offenders (2,079 preadolescent sexual offenders). Fourteen-year-old boys perpetrated the greatest number of sexual offenses, but most juvenile sexual offending was directed against other children, with young offenders assaulting only 4% of adult victims (Snyder, 2000a). As shown in Table 2.6, juveniles represented 17% of offenders who raped, 36.2% of sodomizers, 23.4% of offenders who used an object, and 27% of those who engaged in forcible fondling. According to Snyder, juvenile sexual offenders engage in anal and oral sexual assaults (sodomy, in

Table 2.6

Juvenile Sexual Offenders by Percentage of Total Offenders, Age, and Sexual Offense

	Age Profile of Perpetrators of All Sexual Assaults (% of All Assaults)				
Offender Age	All Sexual Assaults	Rape	Sodomy (Oral/Anal)	Sexual Assault With Object	Fondling and Molestation
All juveniles	23.2	17.0	36.2	23.4	27.0
Age 7–11	3.6	1.3	8.2	4.1	5.2
Age 12–17	19.5	15.7	28.1	19.3	21.8
Adult	76.8	83.0	63.8	76.6	73.0

Source: Based on Snyder (2000a).

Table 2.7

Percentage of Sexual Offenses Committed by Juvenile Sexual Offenders by Victim Age

		Percentage of Juvenile Offenders by Victim Age			
Offender Age	Percentage of Total Offenders	Adult Victims	Victims Below Age 6	Victims 6–11 Years of Age	Victims 12–17 Years of Age
All Juvenile Sexual Offenders (7–17)	23.2	4	40	39	27

Source: Based on Snyder (2000a).

NIBRS terms) far more than they engage in fondling, sexual assault with an object, or vaginal rape.

Although juvenile sexual offenders sexually assaulted only 4% of adult victims, they were responsible for 40% of the sexual assaults against children under 6: 13% of those who sexually offended children under age 6 were aged 7–11, and an additional 27% of offenders of children under age 6 were aged 12–17. Of those who sexually assaulted children aged 6–11, 39% were juveniles aged 7–17, and juveniles aged 12–17 were perpetrators in 27% of sexual assaults against juveniles 12 years and older (Snyder, 2000a). Figures published by the Office of Juvenile Justice and Delinquency Prevention (2000a) are similar: Approximately 43% of sexual assaults against children 6 years or younger and approximately 34% against victims 7–11 were committed by juveniles aged 17 or younger, and about 24% of victims aged 12–17 were offended by juveniles aged 17 or younger. Table 2.7 provides a brief overview of the NIBRS data.

These figures are consistent with those published by the National Task Force on Juvenile Sexual Offending (1993), which reported that the age range for juvenile sexual offenders is 5 to 19 years with the median age between 14 and 15, that boys represent 90% of juvenile sexual offenders, that girls are sexually victimized more frequently than are boys, and that most sexual assaults are directed against someone known to the juvenile perpetrator. The Task Force also asserted that more than 60% of offenses include penetration, which is somewhat supported by Snyder (2000a), who reported a combined 53% for forcible rape and sodomy. The Task Force reported the median age for victims at 7 and stated that more than 33% of sexual assaults by juveniles involve physical force. Hunter (2000) noted that the use of violence is more prevalent in juveniles who offend peers and that juveniles who sexually assault younger children rely more on their wits than on the use of force or threats.

However, it is clear that juveniles can and do use violence in the execution of criminal behaviors, and the office of the U.S. Surgeon General (U.S. Department of Health and Human Services, 2001b) reported that arrest of juveniles in 1998 accounted for one in every six violent crimes. Nevertheless, it is not clear what role is played by violence in sexual assaults overall, although violence is clearly a factor. Most likely, threats, overt force, and violence figure more prominently in the sexual abuse of older children and adolescents in which juveniles neither have as easy access nor are able to easily trick, bribe, coerce, or otherwise gain compliance from their victims.

JUVENILE SEXUAL ASSAULTS AND VIOLENCE

Prentky and Burgess (2000) have written that known adolescent sexual offenders may represent a relatively small proportion of juveniles who commit such offenses. However, not every juvenile sexual offender engages in or uses violence in the perpetration of his sexual offense—in fact, far from it. Nevertheless, in trying to understand and make sense of juvenile sexual offending from a social, as well as an individual, perspective, it is important to understand juvenile sexual assault in the larger context of adolescent and child violence.

Sexual abuse, including no-touch offenses, always contains an aggressive and potentially violent undercurrent. This is perhaps most evident in the fact that threats and actual violence are more often used in sexual assaults against older children, adolescents, and adults who are less likely to comply with demands for sexual behaviors. In fact, despite the circumstances under which violence occurs or its actual incidence, the presence or use of violence in juvenile sexual offending has clearly and repeatedly been cited by a number of authorities in the field as a significant element in juvenile sexual offending, including use of threats, intimidation, force, or violence (Hunter, 2000; National Task Force on Juvenile Sexual Offending, 1993; Righthand & Welch, 2001; Ryan, Miyoshir, Metzner, Krugman, & Fryer, 1996). Accordingly, the presence of and willingness to use violence in juvenile sexual offending cannot be separated from the use of violence in other forms of juvenile delinquency, in which juveniles accounted for 16% of all violent crimes in the United States during 1999 and 17% of total arrests for forcible rape (Snyder, 2000b; U.S. Department of Health and Human Services, 2001b).

Juvenile Victims and Juvenile Offenders

Based on the data, which may change from year to year but appears to be generally consistent, researchers can safely (and generally) say the following about the victims of child sexual abuse:

- Approximately 11% of all cases of child maltreatment involve child sexual abuse.
- 70% of child sexual abuse occurs in the child's home or in the home of another person.
- 71% of child sexual abuse is perpetrated by someone known to the child.
- One or both parents are responsible for 50% of child sexual abuse.
- The most frequent form of child sexual abuse, and especially of boys, involves anal or oral sex, with fondling, sexual assault with an object, and rape occurring in that order of frequency.
- Children and adolescents are the victims of 84% of all cases of forcible fondling.
- Children and adolescents are the victims of 79% of anal and oral sex.
- Children and adolescents are the victims of 75% of sexual assaults with an object.
- Children and adolescents are the victims of 46% of vaginal rape.
- Children below age 18 are victims in 66.9% of all sexual assaults.
- Children between 12 and 17 are victims in 32.8% of all sexual assaults.
- Children below age 12 are victims in 34.9% of all sexual assaults.
- Children below age 6 are victims in 14% of all sexual assaults.
- Adolescents and children are at greater risk of being sexually assaulted than are adults.
- Boys are at greater risk of being sexually assaulted than are adults.
- Girls are at greater risk for being sexually assaulted than are boys and are at the greatest risk for being sexually assaulted.
- Girls are six times more likely to be sexually assaulted than are boys.
- Female victims account for 86.2% of all sexual assaults (adult and child).
- Female victims account for 90% of all sexual offenses by age 13, and 95% by age 19.
- Female victims account for 86.2% of all sexual assault victims.
- Female victims account for 82% of all sexual assaults on juveniles.
- Female victims account for 73% of all sexual assaults on children under age 12.
- Female perpetrators account for 69% of sexual assaults on children below age 6.
- Girls are at the greatest risk for sexual assault during early to middle adolescence.
- Boys are at the greatest risk for sexual assault below age 6.

- 19% of sexual assaults against children involve more than one victim at the same time.

Based on a statistical picture of who is offending, the following facts are known about juvenile sexual offenders:

- Juveniles account for 17% of arrests for sexual assault, or about one in every six arrests.
- 14-year-old boys perpetrate the greatest number of sexual offenses.
- Boys are at the greatest risk of sexually offending.
- Adult and juvenile females sexually offend but at a far lower rate than boys and men.
- Juveniles account for about 24% of sexual assault against victims aged 12–17.
- Juveniles account for about 34% of sexual assaults against children aged 7–11.
- Juveniles age 7–17 account for 40% of sexual assaults against children aged below age 6.
- Most juvenile sexual offending is directed against children and adolescents (in that order), not adults.
- Most juvenile sexual offending is directed against girls (of every age).
- Juvenile sexual offending against boys is directed mostly at children below age 6 or 7 and secondarily against children below age 12.
- Most perpetrators of sexual abuse against children below age 6 are family members, so the juvenile offender is quite likely a sibling or close relative.
- Most perpetrators of sexual abuse against older children or adolescents are known to the victim, so the juvenile offender is likely to be a sibling, close relative, baby-sitter, or neighbor, or in some other way connected to the victim.
- Juvenile offenders are more likely to use threats, force, and violence in sexual assaults against older children and adolescents.

Having described this statistical picture of the juvenile sexual offender, it is important to recognize that there is no single profile or snapshot image. In fact, kids who commit sexual offenses do not all look alike and do not belong to a homogeneous group. The children and adolescents in this mixed group range widely in their psychological makeups, their behaviors and histories of sexual and nonsexual offenses, and their personal histories (Association for the Treatment of Sexual Abusers, 1996; Becker, Johnson, & Hunter, 1996; Righthand & Welch, 2001; Weinrott, 1996).

JUVENILE SEXUAL OFFENDERS ARE AT RISK

Juvenile sexual offenders and adult sexual offenders are at completely different developmental, emotional, and behavioral stages in their lives. Adult behavior is prompted by a different set of experiences, circumstances, internal
factors, and external environments and contexts from that of adolescents and
children. Although adolescents are en route to becoming adults, they are not
yet there, but the things they do and experience as adolescents certainly shape
and define the sorts of adults they become.

Nevertheless, adult patterns and motivations for sexual offending behaviors differ from those of adolescents and children who engage in sexual offending behaviors. Although many adults begin their sexually abusive behaviors as adolescents (and even as children), it is not true that every child or
adolescent who engages in offending behavior will become an adult offender.
The National Task Force on Juvenile Sexual Offending (1993) reports that "as
many as 60%–80% of adult sexual offenders reported offending as adolescents. . . . Although the retrospective data from chronic adult offenders *cannot*
be projected onto all sexually abusive youth as a prediction, it does define an
'at risk' condition and early intervention is clearly indicated" (p. 5). In fact,
the finding and widely held belief that adult sexual offenders often, and even
typically, began their careers as juvenile sexual offenders has been stated repeatedly by many in the field, who have restated or reasserted figures indicating that between 30% and 60% of adult sexual offenders experienced or engaged in sexually deviant or assaultive behavior as adolescents (Barbaree &
Cortoni, 1993; Barbaree, Hudson, & Seto, 1993; Brown & Kolko, 1998; Epps,
1999; Masson & Erooga, 1999; Wieckowski, Hartsoe, Mayer, & Shortz, 1998).
Robert Prentky, with colleagues and in his own research, reported that as
many as 50% of known adult sexual offenders committed sexually abusive
acts as juveniles, and 33% of adult offenders with no criminal charges for sexually offending disclosed sexual offenses as adolescents (Knight & Prentky,
1993; Prentky & Burgess, 2000; Prentky, Harris, Frizzell, & Righthand, 2000).
Gene Abel, cited by many for his research on adult and juvenile sexual offenders, reported that between 42% and 58% of adult sexual offenders disclosed the onset of deviant sexual interests or sexually deviant activities before age 18 (Abel, Osborn, & Twigg, 1993), and his Web site unequivocally
states that "men who have sex with children usually start that behavior before
they are 18" (Abel Screening, 2001). In a similarly retrospective fashion, Burton (2000) noted that in a study of 471 juvenile sexual offenders, 45% of the adjudicated juveniles admitted to sexual offending before age 12, and 47% reported having experienced sexual behavior problems as younger children.

Still, not every juvenile offender continues into adulthood as a sexual offender. Although incidents and patterns of sexual offending in some adolescents and children evolve into hardened patterns of adult sexual offending,

the behaviors of most adolescent and younger sexual offenders neither involve the sort of intentions or patterns of gratification that motivate adult offenders nor will develop into adult patterns. Although Weinrott (1996) stated that we have very little sense of how many juvenile sexual offenders progress to more serious forms of sexual aggression, Schram, Milloy, and Rowe (1991) asserted that "very few youth who commit sex offenses as juveniles go on to commit sex offenses as young adults" and concluded that "adolescent sex offense behavior does not necessarily lead to adult sexual offending behavior" (p. 33). In fact, although we have limited statistics regarding recidivism (sexual reoffenses) in juvenile sexual offenders, it seems likely that many, and even most, juveniles do *not* recidivate and that the sexually assaultive behaviors of many juveniles do not persist into adulthood (Association for the Treatment of Sexual Abusers, 2000; Center for Sex Offender Management, 1999, December; Knight & Prentky, 1993; U.S. General Accounting Office, 1996, September). Indeed, as Ryan (1999b) and the Association for the Treatment of Sexual Abusers (2000) noted, some children and adolescents who engage in sexually abusive behavior discontinue the behavior even without intervention or treatment.

Just as not all juvenile sexual offenders become adult sexual offenders, not all adult sexual offenders began as juvenile sexual offenders. Nevertheless, evidence exists to support the idea that many, if not most, adult sexual offenders began sexually offending when they were adolescents and that for some adolescents, sexual offending behavior develops and progresses from less to more serious offenses through adolescence and into adulthood. Barbaree, Hudson, and Seto (1993) described juvenile sexual offenders as a high-risk group, in part because of the general belief that for some individuals offenses are progressive (i.e., they progress from less serious to more serious offenses) and because these children often exhibit significant social and developmental adjustment problems—independent of their offense histories—that place them at risk. Consequently, we believe that children and adolescents who engage in sexually abusive behaviors are *at risk* of becoming adult offenders. Accordingly, it is important that we provide assessment and treatment and help now in order to help prevent them from becoming adult sexual offenders.

DISTINGUISHING SEXUAL OFFENDING FROM SEXUALIZED BEHAVIORS

It is important not to pathologize sexual behaviors, even inappropriate sexual behaviors, into sexual offending. Gail Ryan (1999b) speaks of the distinction among sexual behaviors, sexual relationships, sexual experiments, and sexual abuse when she noted that "it is not the sexual behavior that defines sexual abuse, but rather, it is the nature of the interaction and the relationship that give an accurate definition" (p. 424).

Like other areas of growth, the sexual behavior of children and adolescents develops over time. Many behaviors are healthy and normal for children at certain ages. Although we may not like it or agree, adolescents who initiate or participate in sexual activities are often following social norms or helping to set the pace. Sometimes, these behaviors may seem, or in fact *are*, exploitive of others, but such behaviors are not necessarily criminally or sexually abusive, nor unusual during adolescence. Our job is to understand the behaviors, distinguish between normative and disturbed behaviors, and either help shape values and behavior or provide treatment interventions as appropriate, without overstating or pathologizing those behaviors.

Many children below the age of puberty who engage in sexual activities with other children their age or younger may not be engaged in sexual offending behaviors at all or may not be intending to engage in sexually abusive behavior. Younger children may sometimes be engaging in mutual or otherwise nonabusive sexual play with others, and it is important to distinguish between sexual abuse and various forms of sexual play and sexual experimentation in this age range. On this point, Cantwell (1995) noted that "there is little agreement as to what is normal, normative, abnormal, pathological, or aggressive when discussing children" (p. 80) and added that sexual behavior in young children is not well tolerated by adults. Nonetheless, although some childhood behaviors are merely troubling, others are more serious and may be dangerous to the child and others. When a child engages in sexual behaviors, it can be difficult to decide when the behavior is natural and healthy and when it may reflect a problem or disturbance. At the same time, however, certain childhood behaviors should concern us and should not be ignored or written off merely as child's play.

The normative behaviors of childhood and adolescence are of concern when they are extensive, suggest preoccupation, or involve others and the behaviors are not mutual. That is, sexual behaviors in children present a special concern when they appear as prominent features in a child's life or when sexual play or behaviors are not welcomed by the other parties involved in the play. This is the point on which sexually harmful, aggressive, and offending behaviors hinges. Toni Cavanagh Johnson (1999), who specializes in childhood sexual development, listed 20 signs indicating concern in children up to the age of approximately 12. Although she stressed that sexualized behaviors in children are common, she also described a continuum of sexual behaviors in children up to age 12 and identified four specific groups. One group, *natural and healthy,* consists of children who engage in healthy, appropriate, and natural sexual experiences, but the other three contain elements of sexual behavioral problems. *Sexually reactive* children engage in more sexual behaviors than do their age-mates and have often been sexually abused or exposed to sexually explicit environments or materials. The category *children engaged in extensive mutual sexual behaviors* includes children who often engage in adult-like sexual behavior with a willing child partner, and Johnson believes that all children in this group have been sexually abused. The final group, *children who molest*, contains the most sexually disturbed children, who coerce or force other children into sexual acts, often aggressively, and whose behavior can be considered molestation (Johnson, 1999, 2000; Johnson & Feldmeth, 1993).

Just as children engage in sexual behaviors during their own development, many of which are normative, healthy, and appropriate, so too, of course, do adolescents. In fact, it has become increasingly common for teenagers to engage in a wide range of sexual behaviors, including oral sex and sexual intercourse, and adolescents are endlessly exposed to sexual ideas, behaviors, and expectations directed specifically to them through the media. Adolescents are considered to be engaging in abusive sexual behaviors only when there is an unwilling other party (through either clear force or significant coercion), a clear imbalance of power, or a distinct age difference. Even so, there are times when the line between force, coercion, and mutual consent can become blurry. Nevertheless, for an adolescent to be considered a sexual offender, there must be a victim, defined by lack of consent, a power differential, age, or other clear circumstances.

THE SEXUALLY REACTIVE CHILD

As noted, children (prepubescent, or up to about age 12) who engage in inappropriate sexual behaviors are often considered to be *sexually reactive*. That is, their sexualized behaviors, whether abusive or not, are the result of their own inappropriate exposure to sexual activities. Their sexualized behaviors with others may or may not be abusive, but their developmental stage and the pathway to their sexual behavior lead us to consider their behavior as more *reactive* than *proactive*.

The term is used here in a broader manner than it was used by either Johnson (1999, 2000; Johnson & Feldmeth, 1993), who included sexual reactivity as a subset along a continuum of increasingly troubled sexual behavior in children, or Rasmussen, Burton, and Christopherson (1992), who applied the term to younger and less sexually aggressive children. We use the term to describe prepubescent children who have been exposed to, or had direct contact with, inappropriate sexual activities, sexual behaviors, or relationships, and have thereafter themselves engaged in or initiated sexualized behaviors, activities, interactions, or relationships that include excessive sexual play, inappropriate sexual comments or gestures, mutual sexual activity with others, or sexual molestation and abuse of other children. This description includes a range of sexualized behaviors in children and considers sexually aggressive or abusive behavior to be one particular facet of sexually reactive behavior.

Any inappropriate sexual behavior in a child aged 11 or younger is reactive if that child was exposed to some earlier sexual experiences that were age inappropriate. In addition, a child between 12 and 13 years of age is sexually reactive if sexual behaviors follow exposure to an explicit sexual experience that occurred during the past 12 months. Using this model allows us to evaluate and treat sexually abusive behavior in children, recognizing it as a serious condition without overpathologizing it or treating it in the same manner as we do adolescent sexual aggression. It recognizes and treats sexual behaviors of all kinds in children as less intentional, less fixed, and less developed than equivalent behaviors in adolescents.

The sexually reactive category is not applied to adolescents aged 14 or older, even if their sexual behavior seems to be (or is) a reaction to a sexual experience. Children who do not engage in inappropriate sexual behaviors until adolescence are not classified as reactive because adolescents are considered to have the capacity for greater self-control and are thus held more responsible for behaviors. Referring to sexually abusive behaviors as reactive suggests that the adolescent is not responsible for his own behavior.

CONCLUSION

Epps (1997) pointed out that "in considering the abusive act, it is not always clear what constitutes sexually abusive behavior" (p. 37). In fact, because sexual offending always requires a *victim*, sexual misconduct, sexually inappropriate behaviors, and highly sexualized behaviors are *not* offenses unless there is an unwilling participant or victim, a clear imbalance of power, or a significant age difference; typically, a difference of three years (two to three years in younger children) represents victimization of the younger person.

Gail Ryan (1997b, p. 3) defined sexually abusive behavior simply as any sexual interaction with persons of any age that is perpetrated

- Against the victim's will
- Without consent
- In an aggressive, exploitive, manipulative, or threatening manner

Such a definition summarizes our beliefs about sexual offending, as well as both the subtleties and range of sexually abusive behaviors. However, although we can, in the end, define the behavior, it is not always possible to understand it, and we must be on our guard against either underresponding, overresponding, minimizing, or pathologizing situations.

There are definitely those individuals who mean to harm their victims in some way, but for the vast majority of juvenile sexual offenders, the act is simply a means to an end—some sort of sexual, social, or personal experience—rather than a vehicle for intentionally gaining control, dominating, or causing harm. As noted by Calder (2001), no single etiology can explain all instances of sexual aggression, but we can recognize juvenile sexual offending as a means through which troubled children and adolescents attempt to meet a whole range of needs. Nevertheless, in the process of meeting those needs, juvenile sexual offenders *do* control, dominate, and harm others. In treatment, we practitioners try to help kids see that these things are intrinsically connected to their behavior as abusers and to the way they attempt to meet their needs. Accordingly, we work with juvenile sexual offenders to try to change both their needs and their methods for meeting needs, as well as heightening and deepening their levels of awareness and concern.

Most juveniles who engage in sexually abusive acts are aware that they are acting in an illicit, illegal, or socially unacceptable manner and thus usually hide the behaviors. However, although aware of the legal and behavioral consequences, they seem unaware of the moral consequences or the full impacts of their behaviors on others and themselves. In fact, much of the time, kids just want what they want. Rather than intending to harm or engage in deviant behavior, the operating force is more typically a self-centered drive coupled with lack of awareness, intimacy, attachment, and social competency. In this context, awareness means knowledge that the behavior is intrinsically and morally wrong and harmful to others. Linked to this idea, intimacy and attachment difficulties suggest that juvenile offenders lack a sense of strong connection with others (or at least their victims) and so can act against others while considering only their own needs and desires. Treatment here aims to build or restore attachment bonds that connect juveniles with other people in a socially and personally meaningful way. With respect to social competence, many juvenile sexual offenders, including those who are gregarious and socially comfortable, seem to lack the intrinsic skills of social competency that tell us when to get our needs met in a socially appropriate manner and, more to the point, *how* to get them met. Presumably, many of the needs being met (or the needs that the juvenile is trying to get met) through sexual offending are not being met through other socially acceptable channels, or the child does not possess the necessary social skills and hence lacks social competence.

Beyond all this, although we can simply define sexual abuse, there is no one set of factors tying together all juvenile sexual offenders, except this: They are all kids living in a society of decreasing sexual taboos, changing norms and mores, and increasing sexual awareness and sexuality, trying to meet social, personal, and sometimes sexual needs in a secretive, emotionally empty, disconnected, antisocial, and dangerous manner.

Acknowledging that there is no single factor, set of factors, personality profile, or other clearly defining marks that identify juvenile sexual offenders, the next chapter discusses some of the personal and developmental characteristics often found in juvenile sexual offenders and explores ideas and explanations that can help us to understand the development of sexually abusive behaviors and why juveniles perpetrate sexual offenses.

CHAPTER 3

The Juvenile Sexual Offender: Commonalities and Characteristics

THE "AVERAGE" juvenile sexual offender, drawn from a broad statistical perspective, is a 14-year-old male with a low to average IQ. Girls are the most likely victims, followed by young boys, and approximately half of all juvenile sexual offending involves vaginal or anal penetration or oral sodomy. Many juvenile sexual offenders have engaged in sexually aggressive behavior by age 10 and by age 14 have had several victims, and many juvenile sexual offenders also have a history of nonsexual criminal or conduct offenses. Traumatic experiences, including physical and sexual abuse, are common in juvenile sexual offenders, and many have been exposed to pornography as early as age 7 (Brown & Kolko, 1998; Center for Sex Offender Management, 1999b; Miranda & Corcoran 2000; National Task Force on Juvenile Sexual Offending, 1993; G. Ryan, 1999b; G. Ryan, Miyoshi, Metzner, Krugman, & Fryer, 1996; Snyder, 2000a; Weinrott, 1996; Wieckowski, Hartsoe, Mayer, & Shortz, 1998).

These findings are mirrored in a voluntary and confidential self-report survey completed by 76 juvenile sexual offenders aged 10 to 18 in long-term residential treatment (Rich, 2002); 75% of students have IQs that range between 70 and 115 (borderline intellectual to high-average IQ), and 71% have IQs that fall between 77 and 122. By self-report, these offenders have together victimized 270 individuals, with an average of 3.5 victims each. Victims ranged in age from infancy to adulthood with an average age of 8, which is skewed upward because several respondents reported sexually abusive behaviors toward adults. In fact, the most common (modal) victim age was 6 years. For the adolescents (ages 13–18), the mean average age for the first sexual offense was 11, but the most common age for that first offense was 13. The first sexual offense for the younger children (ages 10–12) occurred at age 8. Of all respondents, 79% reported offenses that included actual or attempted vaginal or anal penetration or oral sodomy (fellatio or cunnilingus), whereas another 11% engaged in digital penetration or object masturbation. The remainder engaged in various forms of fondling and public exposure, and many residents reported multiple offenses. The split between male and female victims was a little different for this group than that more generally reported, with 55% female victims and 45% male, although female victims were slightly more common among the adolescent offenders. Ninety-seven percent of all students reported being exposed to at least one form of pornography, and 100% of kids aged 10–12. Only 9% of this younger group had experienced Internet pornography, compared to 57% of the adolescent group. Magazine pornography was most common, used by 90% of residents, followed closely by pornography on video. Among adolescents, Internet pornography came next. Among all of the respondents, 58% reported multiple use of pornography (more than 10 times), and 51% believed that pornography was a contributing factor in their sexual offenses. Finally, in keeping with the data described earlier, 71% of respondents reported being physically abused; 57% reported a history of sexual abuse; and 84% reported a history of being either physically or sexually abused or both.

THE SEXUAL OFFENDER PROFILE

A profile of the juvenile sexual offender would make identification and assessment a far easier and clean-cut process than it actually is. However, even though researchers have defined some of the characteristics and behaviors of juvenile sexual offenders and drawn a picture based on statistical and self-reported data, there is no known set of characteristics, behaviors, or other features that uniquely identifies and flags the actual or potential juvenile sexual offender. Despite characteristics that lend themselves to the possibility of sexual aggression in children and adolescents, there is no research evidence to support the notion of a typical profile for any particular kind of offender, including those at risk for arson, general violence, or school shootings (McCann, 2002, p. 125). As such, there is simply no meaningful or responsible way to describe a sex offender profile. When used in sex offender treatment, *profile* usually describes the offender's preferred victim type (if there is one), rather than defining characteristics common to sexual offenders.

Although a profile for the so-called prototypical sexual offender does not exist, there are characteristics that appear with some regularity in juveniles who sexually offend, although not with enough frequency or consistency to conclude that these are undeniable features found in offenders or unique features by which we can distinguish offending from nonoffending adolescents. In fact, the same characteristics show up in other children and adolescents who never go on to offend sexually, although many do engage in other conduct disordered or troubling behavior. Indeed, models that attempt to distinguish JSOs by these characteristics lack the discriminate power to separate such youth from other troubled juveniles who do not engage in acts of sexual aggression. Although we can describe features characteristic of many juvenile sexual offenders, they do not apply to *all* of them; indeed, many do not possess all or *any* of these characteristics. At this time, we can only identify a juvenile sexual offender after he has offended and been discovered. This is not to say that there are no flags to alert us to troubled children and adolescents before they act out in ways that are self-destructive, destructive to others, or generally antisocial, but that is beyond the scope of this book.

JUVENILE SEXUAL OFFENDERS ARE ALSO CHILDREN

Having examined what constitutes sexual abuse, the role of juveniles as both victims and perpetrators, and statistical data for juvenile sexual offenders, it is important to consider why juveniles sexually offend and the possible roots, development, and factors that drive such behavior. Here the goal is to understand motivation and cause and to explore theories and ideas that help explain juvenile sexual offending.

As we think about young people who are sexually abusive, the first thing to recognize is that they are kids. That is, they may be troubled and troubling, they may represent a danger to others and themselves, and they may be part of a culture that is harming society as a whole, and especially the children who will follow them into adolescence, but for the most part they are not hardened serial rapists, deviant sexual maniacs, or psychopaths. And in many cases, they will not grow into any of these things. Rather, they are the very products of our society.

Twenty years ago, this level of youthful sexual offending did not exist. Certainly juvenile sexual offenders existed, but not at the current levels and it is unlikely that they were always there and we just were not seeing them. Back then, we often overlooked sexual behaviors and sexual offenses in adolescents with a boys-will-be-boys attitude, the belief that they will grow out of it, or a lack of knowledge about what the behaviors meant or how to respond. If such offenses were detected at all, these youths were mixed in with a general population of conduct disordered juveniles and were perhaps undertreated or not treated at all. Gail Ryan (1999b) noted that programs for juvenile sexual offenders grew from 20 in 1983 to more than 800 by 1993. Although it is difficult to track all programs, today, there are at least 357 programs in the United States and Canada that specialize in the treatment of juvenile sexual offenders, and probably far more. In 1998, at least 6,422 children or adolescents were treated in community or residentially based sexual offender treatment programs, and this is likely a significant underestimate of programs and youth in treatment (Burton & Smith-Darden, 2001).

As statistics and practical experience tell us, many of these kids are more delinquent than they are sexual predators. In fact, most juvenile sexual offenders who are also delinquents will get into far more trouble and recidivate far more often as conduct disordered delinquents (and later, conduct disordered adults) than due to sexual offenses (the same is true for adults; see Hanson and Bussière, 1998). That is probably not because they are not getting caught for their sexual offenses but more likely because they are committing and engaging in far more nonsexual antisocial and criminal behaviors. Weinrott (1996) reviewed 23 studies of recidivism in juvenile sexual offenders, in which nine studies compared sexual offense recidivism against recidivism for nonsexual offenses. In all but one case, recidivism for nonsexual offenses far outweighed sexual reoffending, with a mean average for sexual recidivism of 8.3% against 30.8% recidivism for nonsexual offenses. Drawn from his review, Weinrott noted that there are two clear outcomes with respect to criminal behavior: (a) Most boys who sexually abuse younger children do not sexually reoffend during the 5- to 10-year period following apprehension, and (b) "there exists at least a fair likelihood that JSOs will subsequently come to the attention of police for non-sex offenses" (p. 84).

For those juvenile sexual offenders who are not conduct disordered in the typical sense (i.e., adolescents not considered to be engaged in otherwise delinquent behavior or diagnosable as conduct disordered), many are socially uncomfortable, lack important social skills, have a poorly developed sense of personal identity, and have poorly developed attachments to others in their lives. These kids may be at as much, or even more, risk for continued sexual offenses as the conduct disordered variety of juvenile sexual offender, if only because they may have no other outlet for their social needs, sexual preoccupations, and need to experience and demonstrate some mastery over the world (presumably, in part, through sexual offending, and in that case, most likely by offending children who are the most vulnerable and susceptible).

ADULT AND JUVENILE SEXUAL OFFENDERS

As described in Chapter 2, adult and juvenile sexual offenders share similar behaviors, and many adult sexual offenders describe a history of sexual offending that began in adolescence. Consequently, all juvenile sexual offenders are at risk for becoming adult offenders.

Nevertheless, although adults and juveniles who sexually offend share behaviors and some characteristics, their behaviors, motivations, and paths to offending should not be confused. Most often, juveniles engage in sexually assaultive behaviors for entirely different reasons than do their adult counterparts, and along developmental pathways that may or may not lead them further into sexual offending. Addressing the subject, Calder (2001, p. 3) listed some of the significant differences between adult and juvenile sexual abusers:

- Patterns of sexual interest and arousal are developing and not yet fixed in adolescents.
- Perpetration behaviors are less consistent and sophisticated in adolescent sexual offenders, in whom the sexual abuse process is still developing.
- Situational and opportunity factors appear to be more typical in juvenile sexual offenses, rather than the fixed, internal cognitive factors often found in adult offenders.
- Adolescent sexual abusers who have themselves been the victims of sexual abuse are far closer in time to their own abuse than are adults who were sexually abused as children or adolescents.
- Adolescents have less developed sexual knowledge.
- Adolescents live in a world with different values, beliefs, and expectations.
- The role of the family is more critical in adolescent life.
- Adults experience and expect a much greater degree of external control over their behaviors and interactions.
- Adolescents are more open and used to education and the acquisition of new skills.
- There is less research on juvenile sexual offenders and no integrated knowledge base from which to work.

In a position paper that addressed juvenile sexual offending, the Association for the Treatment of Sexual Abusers (2001) stated,

> Recent research suggests that there are important distinctions between juvenile and adult sexual offenders, as well as the finding that not all juvenile sexual offenders are the same. There is little evidence to support the assumption that the majority of juvenile sexual offenders are destined to become adult sexual offenders. Moreover, the significantly lower frequency of more extreme forms of sexual aggression, fantasy, and compulsivity among juveniles than among adults suggests that many juveniles have sexual behavior problems that may be more amenable to intervention. . . . In fact, recent prospective and clinical outcome studies suggest that many juveniles who sexually abuse will cease this behavior by the time they reach adulthood, especially if they are provided with specialized treatment and supervision. (p. 1)

Recognizing, then, that not all juveniles who engage in sexually aggressive behavior will become adult offenders and that some may not even need treatment to take a healthier path, assessment is designed to help identify what level of risk might be posed by a juvenile with a history of sexual offending and what level and type of treatment might be required to help avoid a tragic future.

COMMON THREADS

Bearing in mind that juvenile sexual offenders are a heterogeneous group of kids who range in interests, self-images, identity formations, personal skills, social competencies, and behaviors, many juveniles who sexually offend do share common, and often predictable, features. Such commonalities can often be found in family life, personal history, interpersonal connections, social competencies, academic functioning and motivation, and patterns of nonsexual behaviors. However, as already observed, these same commonalities, life experiences, and lifestyles can be found in other children and adolescents who do not engage in sexually abusive behaviors. Indeed, sexually abusive juveniles take a different pathway than do other kids who are similar in every respect but who do not sexually offend. Consequently, some researchers believe that there is an extra pathology that has led them to sexual offending, and it is this missing extra element (called, say, *Factor X*) that marks the juvenile sexual offender.

In reality, there are likely multiple Factor Xs. However, the concept illustrates the belief that there is some point of departure from the normative path of juvenile development (including the development of juvenile nonsexual antisocial behavior) and a point of demarcation that distinguishes juveniles who sexually offend from the rest of that population. Unfortunately, in such a model we risk once again looking for a magic bullet—the thing that will allow us to recognize in all (or most) juvenile sexual offenders the common thread that led them along a pathway to sexual offending—and we know that there is no such single common pathway. In the real world of adolescent development there are clearly multiple pathways, in part because juveniles engage in multiple types of sexual offenses at multiple levels of severity and intensity, driven by multiple motivations and influenced by multiple factors and variations in individual development that push different individuals along different passages through life. Aside from the unlikelihood that there is a single Factor X, the risk of the Factor X approach is that it leads to shortsighted visions of both evaluation and treatment and to cookie-cutter approaches to understanding and treating juvenile sexual offenders.

Nevertheless, it is reasonable to seek commonalities that allow us to spot danger signs for both the development of juvenile sexual offending and continued juvenile sexual offending in those instances where a sexual offense or sexually aggressive or abusive behavior has already occurred. This idea of an at-risk condition is potentially difficult, confusing, and controversial because in sexual-offender-specific treatment we treat only those juveniles who have already engaged in sexual offending, rather than those at risk to offend sexually. However, spotting common threads and potential at-risk conditions and circumstances allows us to adopt a primary prevention approach in which we can respond to and resolve at-risk conditions before they lead to any kind of juvenile behavioral or emotional dysfunction, whether sexual or nonsexual in expression.

HISTORY OF PERSONAL VICTIMIZATION AND MALTREATMENT

Among the 3,400 individuals studied in the National Health and Social Life Survey, Laumann (1996) reported a strong relationship between being touched sexually as a child and elevated rates of sexual activity, sexual dysfunction, and general sexual discomfort in adulthood. In fact, juvenile sexual offenders are more likely to have been sexually or physically abused than is the general population of kids, which may represent a significant factor in the development of the juvenile sexual offender. Lee, Jackson, Pattison, and Ward (2002) asserted that childhood sexual, physical, and emotional abuse and family dysfunction are general developmental risk factors for later sexually abusive behaviors; more specifically, they report that childhood sexual abuse is a predictor for pedophilia.

This does not mean that all or even most juvenile sexual offenders have been victimized in such ways or that such victimization is a necessary cause or inevitably leads to the development of sexual offending. On the contrary, such abuse does not appear to be directly related to the development of sexual offending; nor is it always present. It also fails to explain why so many juveniles and adults who have *not* been sexually or physically victimized become sexually abusive. In itself, then, a history of abuse is neither an explanation for sexually aggressive behavior nor a necessarily causative factor. In fact, most childhood victims of physical or sexual abuse do not go on to perpetrate such abuse against others, nor do most physically or emotionally deprived children become abusive, aggressive, or neglectful.

Nevertheless, Knight and Sims-Knight (in press) proposed that a history of physical abuse or witnessing domestic violence may contribute to the development of sexual violence in adolescents. Hunter, Figueredo, Malamuth, and Becker (in press) also supported the position that childhood exposure to violence, especially toward women, increases the risk of aggression and delinquency in juvenile sexual offenders. Addressing the fact that most victims do not later develop into perpetrators, Knight and Prentky (1993), Burton (2000), and Knight and Sims-Knight suggested that the connection between childhood abuse and later sexual offending may be linked to the victim-offender relationship; the frequency, type, and physical invasiveness of childhood abuse; and the developmental stage at which such abuse occurred in the life of the child. Hunter, Figueredo, Malamuth, and Becker (2003) similarly asserted that the characteristics of an adolescent's own sexual victim-ization will define his characteristics as a perpetrator of sexual aggression. Likewise, Knight and Sims-Knight hypothesized that childhood sexual abuse increases the risk for the development of aggressive sexual fantasies, and Wyre (2000) asserted that "the type of relationship with the abuser will often determine the nature of the experience for the child and influence whether or not the child is likely to be predisposed to abusing children" (p. 65).

Despite these assertions, there is little consistent or significant empirical support for these themes. In fact, Finkelhor (1979) argued that there is little ev-idence that the length of a sexually abusive relationship or the presence of se-rious sexual acts makes the experience more traumatic for child victims or that sexual experiences with relatives were more damaging than with other abusers. Finkelhor noted only two major factors in terms of the traumatic ex-perience: Experiences were much more negative for the victim if force was in-volved; and the older the partner, the more unpleasant was the experience.

In fact, the Office of the U.S. Surgeon General (U.S. Department of Health and Human Services, 2001b) reported that child abuse and neglect are weak predictors of violence and that sexual abuse does not predict violence. Glasser et al. (2001) maintained that few studies actually support the idea of a *cycle* of sexual abuse in which perpetrators are somehow re-enacting or resolving their own abuse, and the U.S. General Accounting Office (1996a) found no conclu-sive evidence to support the idea that childhood sexual abuse results in the de-velopment of adult sexual offenders. Similarly, Craissati, McGlurg, and Browne (2002) noted that "numerous questions remain unanswered regarding the nature of the relationship between sexual victimization in childhood and the subsequent perpetration of sexual assaults" (p. 225). Consequently, al-though histories of physical and sexual victimization are quite common in ju-venile sexual offenders, the link between victimization and perpetration re-mains speculative. Although we recognize that a history of childhood sexual abuse is a risk factor, we also know that "the vast majority of sexual abuse vic-tims do not become sexual abusers" (G. Ryan, 1999b, p. 134).

Accordingly, such experiences alone are inadequate explanations for juve-nile sexual offending, making clear that the issue of child maltreatment and its relationship to sexual aggression is far more complex (Center for Sex Of-fender Management, 2000; Righthand & Welch, 2001). Consequently, we be-lieve that childhood trauma, and in this case the experience of childhood sex-ual abuse, is only a single factor that combines with many others to produce sexually aggressive behavior.

MALTREATMENT

Among both those juvenile sexual offenders who have been sexually or phys-ically abused and those who have not, many have experienced a wider range of maltreatment that includes neglectful and generally inadequate parenting and child-rearing practices, as well as negative and dysfunctional living and child-rearing environments. In her review of the literature of child maltreatment in the histories of juvenile sexual offenders, Way (2002) reported high rates of childhood sexual and physical abuse, family violence, and neglect, including maltreatment beginning at an early age and of long duration, perhaps disrupting multiple stages of personality and emotional development, and Bailey (2000) found that child maltreatment is linked to short- and long-term psychopathology in its victims.

G. Ryan (1999a) noted that when physical violence, sexual abuse, and parental neglect are included as maltreatment factors, "almost the whole population (of juvenile sexual offenders) can be seen to have experienced some type of maltreatment" (p. 134). In their wide-ranging review of the professional literature on juvenile sexual offending literature, Righthand and Welch (2001) agreed, suggesting that childhood experiences of physical abuse and family violence are both common and seem to be associated with sexual offending, and Bailey (2000) reported that "juvenile sexual offenders often come from disadvantaged backgrounds with a history of victimization" (p. 206). Similarly, Weinrott (1996) observed that "however flawed the measures of personal victimization, it seems pretty clear that juvenile sexual offenders are likely to have encountered some form of abuse or parental neglect" (p. 23). Pithers, Gray, Busconi, and Houchens (1998) suggested that an important link to the development of adolescent offending of all types may be due in part to the insecure and damaged attachment that develops between children and parents as a result of neglect and maltreatment, and Bailey noted that physically abused and neglected infants typically develop insecure attachments with caregivers. Lee et al. (2002) agreed, stating that family dysfunction often goes hand in hand with childhood difficulties among sexual offenders and concluding that childhood sexual, physical, and emotional abuse and family dysfunction are general developmental risk factors.

Domestic Violence

Witnessing and experiencing family violence (rather than being physical abused) serve both as an aspect of maltreatment and as a likely risk factor in the development of later sexual offending. G. Ryan et al. (1996) noted that 63% of the 1,000 juveniles included in their study witnessed family violence, and in the survey conducted by Rich (2002), 68% of all students reported witnessing physical violence at home, including 82% of the 10- to12-year-olds. Bailey (2000) described exposure to repetitive or extreme violence in the family environment as a risk factor for aggressiveness and violence, and Skuse et al. (2000) reported that male victims of sexual abuse are more likely to become sexual abusers if they have witnessed family violence, although they pointed out that "it may be more appropriate to view a climate of violence as conferring an increased risk, whether or not the boy is a direct victim of the physical abuse" (p. 229). This assertion is echoed by Bentovim (2002), who described family violence as one of three distinguishing elements found in juvenile sexual offenders who are also sexual abuse victims. In the sample of juvenile sexual offenders studied by Smith and Monastersky (1986), 26% had witnessed domestic violence, and Lewis, Shanok, and Pincus (1981) reported that 79% of the incarcerated juvenile sexual offenders in their study had witnessed domestic violence. Print and Morrison (2000) concluded that "adolescents who sexually abuse others often have major care deficits and frequently grow up in families in which they experience and/or witness violence, lack of empathy and a lack of sexual boundaries" (p. 296).

MULTIPLE, LINKED CAUSES

The etiology of juvenile sexual offending is more likely linked to a catalytic combination of factors present in early development, childhood, and adolescence, including a history of childhood sexual or physical abuse, neglect, or broad maltreatment. Indeed, Knight and Sims-Knight (in press) wrote that the experience and outcome of child maltreatment are likely determined by the interaction of many forces in the child's environment, as well as predisposing personality traits in the child. Skuse et al. (2000) concluded that a history of childhood sexual abuse is most likely to be a significant factor only when other risk factors, not directly related to the abuse, are present. The idea that juvenile sexual offending is one possible result of multiple causes that come together in the social environment in which children develop and learn is discussed and developed further in Chapter 4.

TRAUMAGENIC AND LIFE-TRANSFORMING EXPERIENCES

Although many juvenile sexual offenders have histories of childhood abuse and neglect and are painfully aware of and actively or passively traumatized by their abuse and maltreatment, not all children experience their own abuse or neglect as harmful. In some cases, they may just take it for granted, imagining that the behaviors are somehow normal, expect the worst as part of their everyday lives, feel that their parents or other abusers have the right to treat them this way, or fail to recognize that they are being harmed physically or emotionally. If there is a pattern of abuse or neglect among other siblings or between parent figures, they may also come to see it as family values and "the way we do things in this family."

In other cases, and particularly in childhood sexual abuse, children and adolescents may not experience the relationship as traumatic, emotionally difficult, or painful and may even come to enjoy it in some way. There are many instances of child abuse by family members and acquaintances—whether older children, adolescents, or adults—that contain a strong element of bonding in the relationship and in which the sexual encounter is not experienced as dystonic or unpleasant. Sometimes it is the relationship itself that makes the experience syntonic; sometimes it is the bribes and rewards for compliance; sometimes it is the excitement and shared secret; and sometimes it is just a sense of connection that may not be there at any other time in the child's life or that is especially enhanced through the sexual activity. In some cases, it is the pleasure of the sexual experience itself. In many ways, the experience of such a situation is dependent on the psychology and resilience of the particular child, the quality and experience of the actual behavior and interaction, and the identity of and relationship to the perpetrator, as well as on the circumstances and contexts in which the abuse occurs. As noted already, it is possible that later sexual offending may be influenced not by childhood abuse per se, but by abuse that is more highly invasive, more frequent, and perceived by the child more negatively at the time of the abuse.

Either way, although such experiences may not be experienced as traumatic by the child, they nonetheless represent life-transforming experiences, or marked departures from the course of development that we believe all children should take on the path to becoming healthy and well-adjusted adults. In his work on childhood sexual abuse, Finkelhor (1979) observed that children who have been sexually victimized react and respond in different ways. Although many of the respondents in his study experienced childhood sexual experiences negatively, some said that the experiences had been rather positive. Here, Finkelhor reminds us that we are dealing with the sexual experiences of children and not adults, and that we may need a different framework for recognizing and understanding their experiences. He wrote that "sex for humans is as much in the head as in the body. Because what is in a child's head about sex cannot be assumed to be the same as what is in an adult's, we need to look critically at our assumptions about the trauma of children's sexual experiences" (p. 98). He noted that these ideas cast doubt on conventional assumptions about the nature and experience of trauma in reaction to sexual victimization.

Everstine and Everstine (1993) described trauma as a response and a reaction and distinguished between the event as *cause* and trauma as an *effect*. It is the individual's experience and perception of the event rather than the event itself that determines the nature and intensity of the traumatic response, if any. Therapists should be careful to recognize and understand the individual's experience of the situation and not project the experience or reaction that they imagine or expect the individual should have.

MENTAL HEALTH IN THE JUVENILE SEXUAL OFFENDER

Mental health is not necessarily the opposite of mental illness. Mental health implies a well adjusted and personally satisfying approach to life, including the capacity to function effectively, respond appropriately to situations, learn and grow from experience, and derive pleasure from social interactions. It reflects a balance among rational thinking, stable emotional processes, and connection to people and things. A lack of mental health neither automatically signifies a mental disorder nor justifies such a diagnosis.

The concept of *wellness* captures this quality of mental health. Here, wellness represents not simply the absence of illness, but a state of physical, mental, and social well-being. Perhaps more important, it implies a sense of well-being. Only when a lack of mental health becomes, or moves toward, the dysfunctional end of the spectrum of expected human behavior does the diagnosis of mental disorder become justified.

Various thoughts have been expressed on the presence of mental disorders among juvenile sexual offenders, but reports that 80% of juvenile sexual offenders have diagnosable mental disorders (Center for Sex Offender Management, 1999b) are misleading, given the inclusion of *Diagnostic and Statistical Manual of Mental Disorders–Fourth Edition, Text Revision* (DSM-IV-TR; American Psychiatric Association, 2000) diagnoses such as conduct disorder and oppositional defiant disorder. In fact, Righthand and Welch (2001) asserted that the most common *DSM* diagnosis found among juvenile sexual offenders is conduct disorder. However, for many offenders a diagnosis of either conduct disorder or oppositional defiant disorder is almost a given because the diagnoses are virtually a description of the very behaviors that underpin much juvenile sexual offending. Useful as these diagnoses are, they are generally not considered targets for psychiatric medication or other significant psychiatric interventions and can significantly inflate statistics that describe the incidence of mental disorders among an adolescent population.

To some degree, this is true also for the diagnoses of attention-deficit/ hyperactivity disorder and posttraumatic stress disorder that are frequently found among the population of juvenile sexual offenders. Both of these diagnoses are often made without adequately meeting the diagnostic criteria of the *DSM-IV-TR*. Even when diagnostic criteria are met, they are often minimally met and often too quickly made. In this context, then, the risk is that we will mistake a lack of mental health and the presence of mental disorders for mental illness and subsequently overreport diagnoses of mental disorders that do not truly represent serious mental illness. This may account for reports of diagnosable mental disorders in 80% or more of juvenile sexual offenders, in which we are really describing behavioral and affective difficulties rather than significant psychiatric illnesses in the population.

This is not to suggest that mental disorders and mental illnesses are not factors in the etiology of juvenile sexual offending, nor that they are uncommon. Rather, they are more likely collateral and contributing factors whose influence varies from case to case rather than factors that typically lead to or directly influence juvenile sexual offending. However, it is important that we recognize the coexistence of mental disorders and illness in juvenile sexual offenders as an active ingredient in the evaluation and treatment of juvenile sexual offenders where such psychiatric comorbidity exists (this is the subject of Chapter 9).

Nevertheless, although Weinrott (1996) asserted that the only two diagnostic categories for which sparse data even exist for juvenile sexual offenders are conduct disorder and depression, there is considerable evidence that children and adolescents who sexually offend experience significant mental health difficulties. Moreover, children and adolescents who violate the rights of others—managing to overcome social and personal barriers to sexually offending—lack the mental wellness required to prevent such behaviors and understand the consequences of such behaviors to themselves and others.

BEHAVIORAL DISORDERS AND PSYCHOPATHY IN CHILDREN AND ADOLESCENTS

Behavioral problems are commonly seen in children and adolescents who engage in sexually abusive behaviors (Center for Sex Offender Management, 1999b; Office of Juvenile Justice and Delinquency Prevention, 2000b; Righthand & Welch, 2001). As noted, conduct disorder is the most commonly made diagnosis for juvenile sexual offenders (Righthand & Welch).

However, it is also true that many juvenile sexual offenders do not exhibit conduct disordered behavior other than the sexually abusive behavior itself and do not otherwise meet the criteria for the *DSM-IV-TR* diagnosis. Although it can easily be argued that sexual offending *is* a conduct disorder, the diagnosis requires a pattern of conduct problems in several areas and is intended to describe juveniles who show a range of significant behavioral problems. Aside from the sexual abuse itself, many juvenile sexual offenders simply do not behave in ways typical of conduct disordered adolescents and are not delinquent in any other appreciable manner.

Juvenile sexual offenders, then, may or may not display broader conduct disordered behavior. At the same time, when a conduct disorder is present in juvenile sexual offenders, it is neither a necessary nor a sufficient condition to qualify or predict sexual abuse because not every juvenile sexual offender is diagnosed with a conduct disorder (not a necessary condition) and because most conduct disordered juveniles do not engage in sexually abusive behaviors (not a sufficient condition). Consequently, although it is an important factor, conduct disorder does not reflect the Factor X condition that so many seek in understanding juvenile sexual offending and predicting the potential for sexual offending and reoffending.

Other aspects of conduct disorder may appear in some children. In particular, severe, consistent, and persistent behavioral problems in adolescents are often considered precursors to the *DSM-IV-TR* diagnosis of antisocial personality disorder. This diagnosis, which can only be assigned to adults over 18 years of age,[1] is the equivalent of the more commonly used terms *psychopath* or *sociopath*,[2] although Robert Hare (1999) and others have asserted that the diagnosis is far too broad to capture the depth and seriously disordered qualities embodied in the idea of psychopathy. Hare believes that the psychopath can best be understood in terms of shallow affect, superficial and abusive interpersonal relationships, and risky behaviors, displaying a characterological disregard for and manipulation of others, lack of empathy and remorse, and a self-centered and criminal way of thinking and approach to life. Bowlby (1979) described the psychopath as a person who, neither psychotic nor "mentally subnormal," persistently engages in acts against society, acts against the family, or acts against the self. He maintained that "in such people the capacity to make and maintain affectional bonds is always distorted and not infrequently conspicuous by its absence" (p. 72).

Much controversy persists in the field of adolescent development about applying the concept of psychopathy to children or adolescents. To assign the diagnosis of antisocial personality disorder to an adult, the individual must have been diagnosed with conduct disorder since at least age 15; however, Hare (1999) and others have asserted not only that there are clear signs of psychopathy in adolescence and childhood but also, in some cases, that it is a legitimate diagnosis even in juveniles (Frick, 2002; Lynam, 2002). Hare continues to work toward the development of a checklist to screen for and diagnose psychopathy in adolescents, although the checklist is still in a research phase and is not yet routinely available. On the other hand, many feel that the diagnosis is unwarranted or inappropriate in juveniles, who are still in the process of experimentation and personality development. Moreover, in this view many adolescent behaviors—especially those that include shallow and superficial affect, inconsideration for others and lack of empathy, and risky lifestyle—are actually normative behaviors for adolescents, or at least typical in many cases. Seagrave and Grisso (2002) described in detail the risks and possible mistakes inherent in diagnosing adolescents as psychopaths, and these findings were supported by Hart, Watt, and Vincent (2002), whose only criticism of Seagrave and Grisso was that they did not go far enough in expressing their concerns.

---

[1] Dennis Doren (2002) asserted that under specific conditions, antisocial personality disorder can be diagnosed in individuals below age 18, although this is his interpretation only, and it does not appear to be supported by the *DSM-IV-TR* (American Psychiatric Association, 2000).

[2] Robert Hare (1999) saw little differences between the terms *psychopath* and *sociopath*, regarding the differences more as reflective of a psychological versus sociological view of etiology than as substantively different.

Right or wrong, we are likely to see the psychopath label applied to more adolescents in the coming years given the import and impact of Hare's work and given the importance of the psychopath label in the assessment and prediction of continued violence in adults. Of particular note, Hanson and Bussière's (1998) meta-analysis highlighted antisocial personality disorder as a relatively high risk factor in predicting both sexual and nonsexual recidivism in adult sexual offenders, and antisocial personality disorder or some variant often appears as a significant risk factor in civil commitment proceedings for sexual offenders in those states that have such laws.

Nevertheless, the presence of a conduct disorder in children or adolescents (which may be the result of still other disorders, family history, personal experiences, or other pre- or coexisting conditions) is not an adequate indicator of a later antisocial personality disorder. Even if it were, adult antisocial disorder (or psychopathy) in its own right is not an indicator of sexual offending, although it may well be a significant contributor in the risk for sexual re-offense.

Consequently, although potentially serious at-risk conditions deserving of treatment under any circumstances, conduct disordered behaviors themselves are probably not a direct cause of sexual offending, which may occur as a primary or secondary feature of the conduct disorder. It is just as (or more) likely that the conduct disorder itself is actually the product of a more serious underlying disturbance or precondition (Factor X) that is acted out through conduct disordered behavior. The antisocial behavior may be a learned response, later becoming a lifestyle adopted by children already disturbed by other factors present in their lives.

SOCIAL COMPETENCIES

Many researchers have observed or hypothesized that juveniles who sexually offend have deficits in social engagement and social skills. Indeed, there exists a strong belief that there is some underlying Factor X in juvenile sexual offenders that is associated to the twin strands of social relatedness and social skills. One strand of social competence involves the capacity to experience security, connection, and intimacy in social relationships; understand the experience of the other person in the relationship; and derive satisfaction and a sense of well-being from such relationships. Along the other strand, social competence involves the ability to demonstrate and experience mastery over the social environment through the development and expression of social skills that lead to goal accomplishment. Such goals are, presumably, connected to the development of successful and rewarding social relationships and the resulting sense of personal accomplishment, recognition, empowerment, and belonging.

SECURE ATTACHMENT, BONDING, AND SOCIAL CONNECTION

Many have noted and described attachment difficulties in juvenile sexual offenders. In a related vein, the literature is also drawn to dysfunctional families and to the incidence of difficulties in the children of such families. Righthand and Welch (2001) noted that "dysfunctional patterns of family life are routinely reported among children and adolescents who are sexually abusive, including family instability, disorganization, and violence" (p. xii). This idea is echoed by Smallbone and Dadds (2000), who asserted that "disruptive or dysfunctional family-of-origin experiences appear to exist commonly in the childhood backgrounds of sexual offenders" (p. 4). The idea of impaired attachment is reminiscent of the work of object- and attachment-relations theorists such as John Bowlby, Melanie Klein, and Donald Winnicott. It suggests that children (and later, adolescents) who have failed to form secure attachments will continue to have difficulties throughout their lives forming and experiencing meaningful relationships and that they may fail to understand appreciably or respond appropriately to relationships. This may include the failure to develop or experience empathy in relationships and the lack of true mutuality in relationships.

G. Ryan (1999b) noted that juvenile sexual offenders experience a high incidence of parental loss and that attachment disorders are the product of breakdowns in early child-parent relationships. In Bowlby's (1979) attachment theory, the affectional (or emotional) bond is based primarily on the relationship between one or both parents (usually the mother) and the young child. Bowlby maintained that an antecedent of psychiatric disturbance in children is always the result of either an absence of the opportunity for affectional bonding or long or repeated disruptions of previous bonds. In Ryan's view, such attachment disorders are manifested in part through a lack of empathy demonstrated or experienced by juvenile sexual offenders. Pithers et al. (1998) described the development of insecure attachments between children and their parents as a possible variable that may help explain later sexual offenses, as well as other delinquency and adult criminal behaviors. Becker and Kaplan (1988) saw inadequate and disturbed family relationships as possible factors in the development of sexual offending. These interconnected elements of impaired family relationships and social connection are also addressed by the National Task Force on Juvenile Sexual Offending (1993), which identified 22 areas as treatment targets. These include the treatment of family dysfunctions that support or trigger offending behaviors, attachment disorders, and boundary problems in juveniles, as well as working on the development of victim empathy.

Marshall, Serran, and Franca (2000) wrote that "we have developed theories that relate sexual offending both to chronic loneliness and deficits in intimacy" and that research has shown that "sexual offenders are often bereft of intimacy and experience loneliness to a greater extent than both other offenders and nonoffenders" (p. 17). Not only is there a great deal of theoretical and also some research support for the idea that a lack of connection and meaningful attachment is important in understanding juvenile sexual offending, but attachment disorders also seem fairly apparent in clinical work with juvenile offenders. That is, these young offenders often seem to lack empathy or concern for others, fail to understand (or care about) the consequences to others of their behaviors,[3] often experience little remorse for their behaviors, and have difficulty forming strong attachments to others. In addition, they often seem to lack a sense of guilt, an attribute described by Winnicott (1965) as vital in the development of healthy individuals.

EMPATHY AND INTIMACY

Bumby (2000) noted the common belief that "without empathy, sexual offenders remain likely to reoffend" (p. 146). In a model of social connectedness and attachment, empathy and intimacy are conditions derived from attachment. Both imply the ability to feel connected to others and the actual experience of connection. Whereas intimacy reflects closeness and shared meaning, empathy describes the ability to recognize and understand on an intuitive level the experience of another person. Both require a sense of connection to others and the experience of shared understanding. Intimacy reflects connection and understanding through shared experience and mutual closeness, and empathy is the ability to recognize the feelings and experiences of another, the desire to meet the needs of another, and the willingness to respond to those needs. In our field, we often work with kids who seem unable to experience or understand the impact of their actions on others or fail to care. In this regard, we see a lack of empathy at play or inability to feel for, understand, or care about their effects on other people.

SOCIAL SKILLS AND PEER RELATIONSHIPS

Individuals with effective social skills are able to exercise control and demonstrate mastery over the social environment. They can form and maintain meaningful friendships, possess effective problem-solving and decision-making skills, and experience a sense of personal control and effectiveness. In Erikson's (1963) model of psychosocial development, these individuals have had successful childhood experiences, mastered developmental tasks, and sequentially developed increasing social skills, high self-esteem and sense of

---

[3] Understanding the consequences of offending behavior for victims and families is also identified as a treatment goal by the National Task Force on Juvenile Sexual Offending (1993).

self-actualization, and positive personal identity. Over an extended period of time, these individuals have developed not only the social skills on which a sense of personal success is built but also the interoceptive skills (the ability to recognize and understand internal-emotional conditions) that allow success in the social environment. In a broad model, social skills include both the ability to engage successfully with others (the external social environment) and the ability to recognize, tolerate, and modulate internal states (the internal-psychic environment) through which social requirements are recognized and social interactions mediated.

Much has been written on the presence, and lack, of social skills in juvenile sexual offenders. Marshall, Hudson, and Hodkinson (1993) asserted that adolescent sex offenders are characterized by poor social relationships and signs of social isolation, an idea mirrored by Hawkes, Jenkins, and Vizard (1997), and Lane (1997a) observed that most sexually abusive youths exhibit a paucity of effective social competencies. Becker and Kaplan (1988) saw inadequate social skills resulting in isolation and nonsexual misconduct, and a number of other researchers have described low social skills as a risk factor for sexual reoffending (Beckett, 1999; Kenny, Keogh, & Seidler, 2001; Knight & Prentky, 1993; Worling, 2001).

Social skills and peer relationships are inevitably tied together, for it is through the development and enactment of social skills that relationships are formed and maintained. To this degree, social skills and later social attachment (i.e., friendships, rather than the primary mother-child relationship) go hand in hand and are perhaps intimately related. In his research, Beckett (1999) identified and focused on the assessment of emotional and social loneliness in juvenile sexual offenders as a potential high-risk factor, and Gilgun (1999) described and assessed social connections as either a strength or a vulnerability, or as protective or risk factors, further supporting the notion that social relationships and social skills are linked.

In its 1997 publication describing standards and principles for the management of sexual abusers, the Association for the Treatment of Sexual Abusers (ATSA) wrote that many sexual offenders have "deficits in basic social and interpersonal skills" (p. 29).[4] Similarly, Richard Beckett (1999) noted that "particularly for adolescent child abusers, poor social competency and deficits in self-esteem rather than paraphilic interests and psychopathic tendencies currently appear to offer the best explanation as to why they commit sexual assaults" (p. 224). In their development of a typology of juvenile sexual offenders, Hunter et al. (2003) contended that social-skills deficits are a particularly important factor in juveniles who sexually abuse children, as

---

[4] ATSA modified this position somewhat in its 2001 publication on Practice Standards and Guidelines, then reporting that "some sexual abusers have significant deficits in relationship and social skills" (p. 27), thus moving to a more restricted and cautious position.

opposed to juveniles who sexually abuse adolescent girls or women (who are more violent in their behaviors and less socially incompetent). To this end, the National Task Force on Juvenile Sexual Offending (1993) adopted as one of its 22 areas in the treatment of juvenile sexual offenders the development of internal sense of mastery and control.

ON SOCIAL COMPETENCE

Although yet to be proved or disproved, the literature supports the idea that deficits in attachment and social skills are related to the development of poor coping skills, relationships, and the ability to function effectively and prosocially. Moreover, such deficits are suspected to be linked to the development of sexually aggressive behavior.

At the same time, we must understand the qualities of children and adolescents who sexually offend in the larger context of adolescent development in general, as well as the development of the emotionally and behaviorally troubled nonsexually offending adolescent. If we look only at juvenile sexual offenders in the context of their sexual offending, we risk reaching erroneous conclusions.

Although Weinrott (1996) recognized and accepted the idea that social isolation and disconnection are believed to be the most common deficits among juvenile sexual offenders, he also wrote that these kids appear to be no more socially inept than other delinquent or psychiatric populations. As noted, however, although it is not unusual to see juvenile sexual offenders in whom lack of attachment, empathy, and social skills are very apparent, many juvenile sexual offenders in treatment do develop relationships and do have the ability to experience both remorse and empathy. In fact, in the larger context, adolescents are generally egocentric, and such attributes are developmentally normal for all teenagers.

It may also be that some of what we see and interpret as deficits in attachment and empathy in juvenile sexual offenders actually reflects a lack of moral development. In such a model, juvenile sexual offenders and other troubled juveniles may have never developed past the early preconventional stage of moral development described by Kohlberg (1976). This model focuses on the drives and motivations behind moral behavior, as well as on the development of an intrinsic versus extrinsic schema of right (or moral) behavior. In such a model of moral development, empathy and attachment are not the focus but nonetheless may well be key factors. Conversely, it may be that regressed moral development is actually the product of an attachment disorder.

Regardless, the ideas of moral underdevelopment or delay, social disconnection, lack of secure attachment bonds, and (perhaps resultant) lack of empathy and intimacy all seem to be strongly linked and are often present in

---

Factor Xs

- History of personal victimization
- Witness to family dysfunction
- Mental health issues
- Attachment difficulties
- Limited empathy
- Underdeveloped social skills
- Regressed moral development
- Limited social competence

Figure 3.1
Features commonly found in the population of juvenile sex offenders.

troubled juvenile behavior. Thus, we can say that many juvenile sexual offenders have experienced great difficulty in forming attached relationships, fail to experience empathy for others, have poorly developed social skills, and have a limited sense of moral correctness. Overall, it is safe to say that these juveniles are limited in their social competence. How much of this links directly to juvenile sexual offending rather than to other aspects of juvenile delinquency—as well as to normative adolescent development—is difficult to say.

CONCLUSION

Juveniles who sexually offend are a diverse group. They share in common their sexually abusive behaviors, but there are no common factors that single out juveniles as actual or would-be sexual offenders, and none with which we can predict recidivism with any definitive edge. However, in general, juvenile sexual offenders do share many attributes in terms of social histories, personal characteristics, and other nonsexual behaviors that are important points for primary, secondary, and tertiary interventions, as well as prevention, treatment, and social change.

Figure 3.1 summarizes some of the features that are commonly found among juvenile sexual offenders, or the most typical Factor Xs.

In the next two chapters we review the influences of the social and learning environment in the development and enactment of sexual and sexually abusive behaviors, as well as developmental predispositions and factors that may drive or signal potential sexual offending behaviors and help us to understand, both prospectively and retrospectively, the pathways along which juvenile sexual offending may develop.

CHAPTER 4

Sexual Learning and Personal Development in the Sociocultural Environment

SOCIAL LEARNING theory offers the idea that children learn, grow, and develop through interactions with their environment by absorbing, mimicking, and experimenting with what they see and experience. Consequently, in the social learning model, kids become the product of their environment.

Social psychology posits that individual psychology is shaped by social forces. Thus, personal (including biological) and social forces combine, catalyze, and influence one another. The social psychology model helps us to understand the interactional exchange that goes on between kids and their social environment, as well as how and from where they are getting their ideas, learning their behaviors, and finding direction. It also helps explain differences between kids and recognizes the complexity of each individual situation. Furthermore, from a sociological perspective, we recognize that the product acts on the producer. That is, social forces influence and produce individuals within the society who, in turn, act on and shape social forces. From this perspective, what we are given by society and what we contribute in return are linked. This interactional experience in which individuals are shaped by and in return reshape society can create a positive social experience that is personally empowering to its members, or a hostile social life that limits personal growth and the development of a healthy social environment.

For the sexual offender, Boeringer (2001) considers social learning, more than the factors of social attachment or social ineptness, to be significant in the development of sexual coercion and aggression.

DEVELOPMENTAL VULNERABILITIES, PREDISPOSITIONS, AND SUSCEPTIBILITY

A social environment and learning perspective, combined with individual differences, goes a long way toward explaining why some children and adolescents engage in troubling behaviors and others do not—even those with similar backgrounds, and particularly for those who have the *developmental vulnerabilities* described by Marshall and Eccles (1993). From their perspective, such vulnerabilities result from a developmental history that makes these individuals susceptible to a variety of influences and events that would not otherwise significantly affect other individuals. In keeping with the model of attachment disorders and disruptions described in Chapter 3, Marshall and Eccles consider these vulnerabilities to be the result of impaired attachment bonds.

The concept is similar to that of *threshold phenomena* postulated by Watkins and Bentovim (1992), in which individual, family, and social variables serve as the predisposing backdrop to potential violence and sexual aggression, either sparked into action by triggers that occur at a later developmental time or repressed and diffused through mediators that defuse and dilute the potential for violence. Itzen (2000) has written that the extent to which threshold phenomena predispose children to become sexual abusers is influenced by the range of such mediating and motivating (triggering) factors.

Bailey (2000) has written that "humans are in constant interaction with their environment, reacting to information they take in and adjusting to demands placed upon them. Within a vulnerable group of young people . . . unaddressed, traumatic and early damaging experiences set in motion a certain thinking pattern" (p. 209). These developmental vulnerabilities and predispositions make some individuals highly susceptible to the influences and messages of society, including the influences of those social scripts connected with sexual behavior. From Itzen's (2000) perspective, in a developmental and social learning model, threshold experiences such as childhood sexual abuse, maltreatment, and exposure to domestic violence will shape and influence the psychosocialization and psychosexualization process and contribute to the child's vulnerability to later possible triggers, such as sexual messages in the media, pornography, substance use, and so on.

Figure 4.1 describes a model of the interactions between early developmental experiences and ongoing life experiences, in which developmental vulnerabilities are understood as predispositional factors and later life events are considered as catalytic or determining factors that serve to activate or dampen the negative or antisocial potential that lies in the predispositional factors.

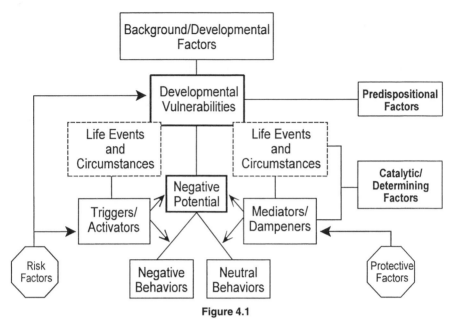

Figure 4.1

Interaction between predispositional factors (developmental vulnerabilities) and catalytic factors (later life events) in the enactment of troubled behaviors.

THE DEVELOPMENTAL MODEL

In addition to the developmental particulars of a single individual and resulting developmental vulnerabilities and predispositional characteristics, we can also understand individuality and the development of personality and behavior through an analysis of the social structure that surrounds the individual, and in which he or she grows and learns. When social learning theory crosses with human developmental theory, we see children passing through stages of emotional and cognitive growth within a social context.

A developmental model describes the growth of personality, highlights the needs that children and adolescents have as they pass through each stage, and describes what they will have to learn and accomplish at each point to be successful. A social learning model, on the other hand, describes the means by which children learn as they pass through those stages. It is in the social environment, healthy or not, that social learning and developmental success or failure takes place, and for this reason we refer to it here as the developmental-learning environment.

In any developmental model, at each learning stage the child is introduced to specific emotional (and in the young child, physical) tasks and is required to accomplish each task successfully to move on to the next stage with the requisite skills and groundwork laid. In Erikson's (1963) well-known model of psychosocial development, children pass through five stages en route to

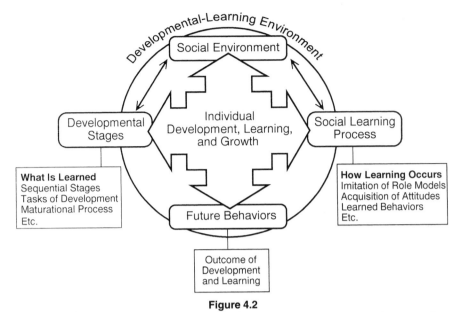

Figure 4.2
The developmental-learning environment: Social environment, developmental stage, and social learning.

adulthood. But unlike the stages of psychosexual development described by Freud in his model of psychic and personality development, in which an individual can remain emotionally regressed, or fixed, at an early point in psychic development, in Erikson's model the child moves on to the next stage of development, ready or not. This means that a child may move to a later stage of development without having built the foundations for success in the new stage—sort of like building a house on a poor foundation, followed by a poorly built first floor, then second floor, and so on. For children to achieve success in later life (i.e., later developmental stages), they must have achieved success in the earlier stages. To do so, and particularly in the earliest stages of their development when they depend the most on others to take care of and nourish them physically and emotionally, children must be raised in a healthy social environment. Way (2002) suggested that histories of childhood maltreatment in juvenile sexual offenders may have started at an early age and extended over a lengthy period, perhaps disrupting multiple stages of personal development.

Of course, there are many other theories that describe psychic and personality development and many variants within each, including psychodynamic, behavioral, cognitive, and physiological theories. Within each, however, the social environment, social learning, and the stages of physical, emotional, and cognitive development figure prominently, even if they go by different names. Illustrated in Figure 4.2, this triad of social environment, social learning, and sequential developmental stages interacts to form a system in which the child develops and through which he or she interacts within the system and within larger and surrounding external systems. It is through this triadic system that children grow from childhood through adolescence and into adulthood, in addition to and regardless of other physical, psychic, cognitive, behavioral, or emotional processes that may be in play. This developmental-learning environment through and in which children grow and achieve adolescence is in the hands of their adult caretakers, and indeed society as a whole: "The basis for adolescent and adult sexuality is laid down in childhood, and also the roots of all sexual perversions and difficulties. The prevention of all but the hereditary aspects of mental . . . illness . . . is in the province of those who care for infants and children" (Winnicott, 1964, p. 160).

THE DEVELOPMENTAL-LEARNING ENVIRONMENT

The social environment is the great mediator in many of the developmental tasks faced by the child and the context in which personal learning take place. It is within this developmental and learning environment that the vulnerabilities described by Marshall and Eccles (1993) develop and grow into risk factors or in which children develop the assets and strengths that serve as protective factors, and it is within this environment that children find (or fail to find) love, attention, emotional bonding and attachment, role modeling, structure, supervision, guidance, social relationships, physical and emotional security, wisdom and mentoring, information, ideas, and encouragement. These ideals foster trust, independence, self esteem, social mastery and competence, motivation, intimacy, knowledge, morals, satisfaction, and a healthy sense of personal identity, as well as the host of other personal attributes necessary to function successfully, effectively, and happily in the world. Just as their presence provides the greatest opportunities for children, their absence presents an environment in which a child will have great difficulty succeeding.

As we consider why some juveniles become sexually aggressive, it is important to think not solely in terms of individual and developmental characteristics and markers, but also in terms of the developmental-learning environment in which sexual aggression develops and is enacted. Like most things, sexual behaviors, expectations about sexual behaviors, and choices about sexual behaviors do not emerge out of nowhere. A biological-physiological, and even evolutionary, component to sexual behaviors also exists that has been described as "essentially unequaled in importance . . . the cornerstone of evolution" (O'Donohue, Penix, & Oksol, 2000, p. 124). However, these drives are essentially preconscious and therefore prechoice and are of far less concern than the role of expectation and intentional choice in sexual offending and in the treatment of the juvenile sexual offender. After all, as Eldridge (2000) pointed out, most sexual offenders offend because they want to. For many juvenile sexual offenders, a prime question is, Why did he make the sexual choices he made, and what are the roots of those choices?

What happens, then, when children with developmental vulnerabilities—one consequence of which may be impaired social skills and another poor judgment—come into contact with powerful, compelling, and attractive messages that suggest behaviors that are of an adult nature, involve moral and ethical decisions, require strong decision-making and problem-solving skills, contain strong elements of risk to self or others, or are of an antisocial nature?

JUVENILE SEXUAL BEHAVIORS IN THE CONTEXT OF THE SOCIOCULTURAL ENVIRONMENT

In striving to understand juvenile sexual offending, we must first recognize that sexual interests and behaviors are not unusual or atypical in teenagers and preteenagers. On the contrary, Huston, Wartella, and Donnerstein (1998) reported that sexual behaviors are prevalent among adolescents in the United States, and they noted that adolescents are intensely interested in sexuality, romance, and relationships. In addition to actual sexual behaviors and practices, children and adolescents are exposed to sexual ideas and portrayals on a regular and routine basis. Kann et al. (1998) reported that nearly half of all high school students have had sexual intercourse, and J. Kirby (2001) reported that two thirds have sex before graduating from high school. Kann et al. stated that 7% of students have engaged in sexual intercourse before age 13, and boys are significantly more likely than girls to have initiated sexual intercourse before 13 years of age. The authors reported that 16% of U.S. students have had sexual intercourse with four or more partners.

The American Academy of Pediatrics (2001c) reported that children most likely to engage in earlier sexual activity included those with social, behavioral, or emotional problems, low IQs, learning problems or low academic attainment, and histories of physical or sexual abuse. Also included as candidates for early sexual behaviors are children of low-income families and some ethnic minorities and families in which marital discord and low levels of parental supervision are prevalent. The work identified children at risk for early or coercive sexual behaviors as those who have been physically or sexually victimized or abused or who have witnessed sexual or physical violence and described children with social risk factors such as learning problems, patterns of substance abuse, and antisocial behavior as being at a potentially increased risk, a finding corroborated by Huston et al. (1998). J. Kirby (2001) included emotional distress and sexual beliefs, attitudes, and skills as additional factors that increase the risk for early sex (preadult). D. Kirby (2001) also maintained that attachment to social norms and connections plays an important part in the development of teen sexual values and behaviors, including both family values and attitudes toward sexuality and the perspectives, attitudes, and values of peers. Huston et al. suggested that early onset of sexual intercourse is most likely for adolescents who have loose or loosening ties to their families, are in conflict with their families, and are involved in peer groups with norms that support sexual activity.

There are parallels between normative teenage sexual behaviors and the behaviors of juvenile sexual offenders, just as there are parallels among other aspects of normal and abnormal development in other areas of teenage life. For instance, recognized as important and significant factors are the quality of family life and family dynamics, attachment and connection to others, the impact and effect of the social environment, and the acquisition of attitudes and values that shape decisions about sexual behaviors. Similar also is the recognition that "no single theory . . . can explain all findings on adolescent sex behavior" (D. Kirby, 2001, p. 280) because it is a complex phenomenon that defies simple explanations. Another similarity lies in the fact that behind adolescent behaviors are predisposing and latent factors that form early in development and mediating factors that later serve either to activate and bring into existence the potential contained in the predisposers or to dampen, deactivate, or redirect that potential.

However, social values, personal beliefs, and behaviors are developed and enacted in the same developmental-learning environment that gives rise to both prosocial and antisocial sexuality. It is in this environment that potential is transformed into action and the seeds of ideas and behaviors (predispositional factors) flower into life activities (enactment) through the mediating and triggering effects of the social environment. Societies that lean toward violence and sexuality can probably expect to find incidences of violence and sexual behaviors within the society that approximate the degree to which it leans. Societies that fail to teach prosocial values and behaviors or adequately engage, supervise, or mentor their children can probably expect to find children who build their norms, attitudes, values, ideas, and behaviors on what they find and based on whatever is available.

WHERE ARE CHILDREN LEARNING ABOUT SEX?

To a great degree, and especially in the younger years, the developmental-learning environment is centered largely on the family and in the home. As kids grow, and particularly once they enter the larger educational and social world outside of their homes, so too does their developmental-learning environment grow and expand. In some cases, such as in the dysfunctional or abusive family, this can be a relief and help normalize a child to some degree or flag authorities that external help is needed. For those children who are introduced to sex through inappropriate exposure within their own homes and families, or through sexual abuse in which they are victimized, it is evident where sexual learning, knowledge, and activity begins. But for those children who are not the victims of sexual abuse (i.e., for many juvenile sexual offenders), the acquisition of inappropriate sexual ideas, knowledge, and interests develops in the larger environment into which their lives expand. To a great degree, that environment is reflected in and shaped by the mass media.

In many ways, sex (and violence) seems to be mass-produced and marketed to everyone in much the same way as tobacco once was. Despite the tobacco industry's denial that marketing was aimed at teenagers and younger children, cigarettes were marketed in such a way that they became part of the fabric of society. Today, sex seems to be mass-produced and -marketed to everyone in much the same way, including children and adolescents, who for the most part are exposed to exactly the same material and messages as are adults.

The American Academy of Pediatrics (2001a) reported that the media and advertising industries constantly expose children and teenagers to sexual images and innuendos and that American children view an estimated 360,000 television advertisements before graduating from high school. Reviewing the results of its three-year National Television Violence Study, the Mediascope Press (2001) determined that in a study of 4,294 network television commercials, nearly 25% included sexual attractiveness as a base for the message.

SEX AND THE MEDIA

For the past 15 years, the American Academy of Pediatrics has expressed its concerns about the amount of time children and adolescents spend viewing television and about the content of what they view; it reported (2001a) that the average American child or adolescent watches an average of nearly 3 hours of television per day. Taking multiple forms of media into account (e.g., television, commercial or self-recorded video, movies, video games, print, radio, recorded music, computer, and the Internet), children and adolescents spend between 4 and 7 hours engaged in media use each day (American Academy of Pediatrics, 2001b; Brown & Keller, 2000; U.S. Department of Health and Human Services, 2001b).

According to the American Academy of Pediatrics (2001b), due to the amount of time that children are exposed to the media, it has replaced parents and teachers as "educators, role models, and the primary source of information about the world and how one behaves in it" (p. 1223). With respect to sexual education, Roberts (1982) noted that the media plays an important role in the development of sexual knowledge, attitudes, and behaviors in children and adolescents due to (a) the adult nature of programming watched by children; (b) children's limited access to or experience with countervailing information or ideas; (c) the realism with which sexual roles, relationships, and lifestyles are portrayed; and (d) the overwhelming consistency of the messages about sexuality that are communicated throughout the development in children and adolescents.

Indeed, many teenagers rank the media as their major source for sexual ideas and information, and there appears to be a strong link between exposure to sexual content in the media and sexual beliefs and behaviors (Brown & Keller, 2000; Kunkel, Cope-Farrar, Biely, Farinola, & Donnerstein, 2001). Mediascope Press (2001) reported that the media's portrayal of sex as normative contributes to teen sexual behaviors, and Brown and Keller (2000) noted that "the clash between the media's depiction of sexual relationships and the real-life experiences of youth contributes to their difficulties in making healthy sexual decisions" and that "the media saturated world in which children live is a world in which sexual behavior is frequent and increasingly explicit" (p. 255). Similarly, Mediascope Press asserted that sexually seductive messages embedded in the media provide little to no support for an actual understanding of sexual feelings and do not help define responsible sexual behaviors, and such messages contribute to both confusing and contradictory beliefs and behaviors in adolescents.

In fact, explicit sexual messages and portrayals of sexual behavior are commonplace and perhaps even the norm on television, in the movies, and in other forms of media. Watch a prime-time situation comedy or any music channel and note how many minutes elapse before reference is made to sex or sex is depicted in some way (usually in a highly positive or desirable fashion). Indeed, Kunkel et al. (2001) reported that during the 1999 television season, situation comedy was the genre most commonly filled with sexual references or behaviors, with 84% of situation comedies containing sexual content. On the other hand, Lichter, Lichter, and Amundson (2000) reported that music videos contain more sex per minute than does any other form of media, with 1.5 sex scenes per minute.

Children and adolescents, as well as adults, are consumers of such media. In fact, the U.S. Federal Trade Commission (2000) noted that 55% of the MTV audience is aged between 12 and 24 and that the channel is as popular with children aged 6 to 11 as it is with boys aged 12 to 17. The Commission also found evidence that R-rated movies, Mature-rated electronic games, and Explicit Content–rated music are often routinely and intentionally marketed to children and adolescents ages 12 to 18 (pp. iii–iv).

TELEVISION AND MOVIES

In movies and television there has been a steady increase over the past 20 years in sexual messages and the amount of explicit sexual content and increased access to a much wider range of sexual information and depictions (Huston et al., 1998; Kunkel et al., 2001), with an increase in sexual content of 12% between the 1997 season and the 1999 season and an increase of 28% in situation comedies (Kunkel et al.). Huston et al. reported 15 instances of sexual behaviors on TV per hour; the Kaiser Foundation study (Kunkel et al.)

found that 75% of all prime-time broadcast network include sexual content, with an average of 5.8 scenes per hour involving sexual talk of behavior; and Mediascope Press (2001) reported that teenagers are exposed to 14,000 sexual references and innuendos per year on television. The report by the Center for Media and Public Affairs on sexual imagery in popular entertainment (Lichter et al., 2000) found one scene of sexual material for every 4 minutes of programing on broadcast television in the 1998–1999 television season, with one scene involving hard-core sexual material (usually in talk, rather than action) every 10 minutes. The Kaiser report also noted an increase in the number of teenagers depicted engaging in intercourse, from 3% of all teenage characters during the 1997 season to 9% during the 1999–2000 season.

Movies, according to Huston et al. (1988), contain even more frequent and more explicit portrayals of sexual behavior than television. However, Lichter et al. (2000) reported that music videos contain more sex per minute than any other form of media, and of scenes with sexual content, 63% contain sexual images. Mediascope Press (2001) reported that between 1980 and 1990 music videos became increasingly more overt and erotic and that explicit sexual references increased by 15%. Huston et al. reported that 81% of the videos sampled in their study that contained violence also portrayed sexual imagery.

Print Media

Overt sexual messages and depictions are not limited to TV and movies. Magazines and catalogs produce sexually titillating and provocative material as well. Mediascope Press (2001) reported that many magazine advertisements and articles feature seductive models, with a significant increase in provocatively dressed female and male models between 1983 and 1993, and also noted an increase during that decade in magazine advertisements that depicted or implied at least one man and one woman in sexual intercourse (from 1% percent of magazine advertisements reviewed in 1983 to 17% in 1993). Huston et al. (1998) reported an average of two to five pages per issue devoted to sexual issues.

The Internet

There are 100,000 Internet sites dedicated to sex, and 200 new sex-related sites are added daily, according to Carnes, Delmonico, and Griffin (2001), who purported that sex on the Internet represents the third largest economy on the World Wide Web. Finkelhor, Mitchell, and Wolak (2000) described 24 million children and adolescents aged 10 to 17 using the Internet regularly in 1999, including 52% of 10-year-olds and 87% of 17-year-olds. They reported that 25% of these juveniles experienced unwanted exposure to explicit sexual material through Internet e-mail, general searches, misspelled Web links, and links to sites from other Web sites and that 20% of children received unwanted sexual solicitation through the Internet.

MEDIA AND THE SEXUAL MESSAGE

Lichter et al. (2000) reported that television shows and movies rarely show any negative consequences of sex. Of 3,228 scenes studied, 98% depicted no physical consequences at all, and 85% showed no emotional consequences; 96% of the scenes showed no moral judgment, and sexual activity was generally associated with positive portrayals. The authors described this as the glamorization of sex without consequences.

The consistent, glamorized, and highly desirable sexual message across media genres, in which most portrayals of sex are positive and many depict or imply intercourse between unmarried individuals, is not balanced by educational messages about the dangers of unwanted and inappropriate sexual behaviors (Huston et al., 1998; Mediascope Press, 2001; Roberts, 1982). Kunkel et al. (2001) reported that in the 1999–2000 television season, only 2% of all scenes with sexual content depicted any risks or negative consequences attached to sexual behavior, and only 1% of all shows portrayed sexual patience, or the willingness to defer sex. The report noted that programs that placed emphasis on sexual risk or responsibility were very infrequent.

Prendergast (1993) observed that "society is preoccupied with sex and uses sex to prove everything, especially manhood. Both boys and girls are affected by this factor, especially as they enter adolescence. Boys develop the need to prove their manhood. What they see on television . . . portrays sex as the ultimate proof of reaching adulthood and being accepted as normal and healthy" (p. 6). Given the barrage of sexual messages, ideas, and depictions found in the media and given the media's role as a legitimate social mirror (an argument that media representatives have often made in defense of the industry), it should come as no surprise, then, that kids—even the prepubescent ones—want to experiment with and engage in sexual behaviors.

SEXUAL BEHAVIOR AND PORNOGRAPHY

The actual relationship between exposure to pornography and sexual aggression in children and adolescents is unknown. Nevertheless, it is easily available on the Internet, and Huston et al. (1998) noted that while many of the TV depictions of sexuality are not pornographic, many children and adolescents have access to explicitly erotic or pornographic materials. As already described, commonly accepted statistics indicate that many juvenile sexual offenders have been exposed to pornography by age 7, and the previously cited self-report study (Rich, 2002) indicated that 97% of all students aged 10 to 18 had been exposed to at least one form of pornography and that 100% of the kids aged 10 to 12 had seen pornography.

THE MEDIA'S IMPACT ON SEXUALLY AGGRESSIVE BEHAVIOR IN JUVENILES

Sexual abuse cannot be separated from violence. Whether passive or active, sexual offending always involves aggression.

The American Academy of Pediatrics (2001b) wrote that children learn by observing and trying out behavioral scripts and asserted that repeated exposure to violent behavioral scripts can lead to increased feelings of hostility, expectations that others will behave aggressively, desensitization to the pain of others, and increased likelihood of interacting and responding to others with violence. The Academy estimated that by age 18 the average child will have viewed 200,000 acts of violence on television alone, and the National Television Violence study (Mediascope Press, 1997) found that 61% of almost 10,000 hours of television broadcast between 1995 and 1997 portrayed violence, much of it in an entertaining or glamorized manner, with the highest proportion of violence found in children's shows.

In fact, the American Academy of Pediatrics (2001a) asserted that the connection of media violence to real-life aggressive behavior and violence has been substantiated, with as much as 10% to 20% of actual violence attributable to media violence. The U.S. Federal Trade Commission (2000) also reported that

> a majority of the investigations into the impact of media violence on children find that there is a high correlation between exposure to media violence and aggressive and, at times violent, behavior. In addition, a number of research efforts report that exposure to media violence is correlated with increased acceptance of violent behavior in others, as well as an exaggerated perception of the amount of violence in society. (p. ii)

The Office of the U.S. Surgeon General (U.S. Department of Health and Human Services, 2001a) also asserted statistically significant evidence for the relationship between viewing television violence in childhood and later aggression, describing the influence of the mass media "best viewed as one of the many potential factors that help to shape behavior, including violent behavior" (p. 2).

THE MEDIA IN THE DEVELOPMENTAL-LEARNING ENVIRONMENT

As Kunkel et al. (2001) wrote, the reach of television (and other media) makes it "a significant social force, even though some in the audience may be influenced more strongly or weakly than others by TV's sexual content, depending upon individual differences in their lives" (p. 1).

However, when juveniles are exposed to themes of sexuality and violence, is it any wonder that some children incorporate into and replicate these behaviors into their own lives? In asking one young child why, in an act of sexual aggression, he attempted anal rather than vaginal penetration on a younger girl, he told us that this is what he had learned from a pornographic video. Presumably, had he seen an act of vaginal penetration, he would have taken that route instead. A similar situation was related to us by another child who described having repeatedly viewed a scene of anal penetration in a Japanese pornographic animated cartoon to which he had access and then having acted out this scene with his younger siblings.

However, Huston et al. (1998) reminded us that media effects are not unidirectional and that adolescents select media that provides information and entertains, helps them to cope with problems and emotions, builds identity, and forms the basis for identifying with other youths and cultural norms. Nonetheless, it is not that adolescents have no choice about what they watch but that we should not expect them necessarily to exercise good choices, especially when they may already be demonstrating poor decision-making skills and worrisome behaviors in other areas of their lives.

DON'T SHOOT THE MESSENGER: THE MEDIA AS MESSENGER

Of course, the sociocultural environment extends beyond the media. In the larger context, the media is merely a tool of society, as well as a reflector and shaper of social values and direction. At the same time, the role that the media plays in sexual values, behavior, and aggressiveness cannot be overlooked, especially when researchers ask from where children get their ideas and information.

A MOLECULAR MODEL OF SOCIOSEXUAL RISK FACTORS

At the same time that we recognize that media alone is not the problem, to imagine that it is not part of the problem is to overlook and deny the idea that multiple factors interact to form social behaviors and that the media is one of those factors. Arguing that the media is not a part of the problem is much the same as arguing that attachment deficits, antisocial values and beliefs, sexual victimization, history of maltreatment, or lack of social competence are not problems in the development of juvenile sexual offending because each—in its own right and when examined alone—is not an adequate explanation of cause. That route again takes us back to a single factor theory of cause, in which we are forced to look for the magic bullet, or the single or most powerful element that guarantees behavior. Illustrated in Figure 4.3, a multifactor

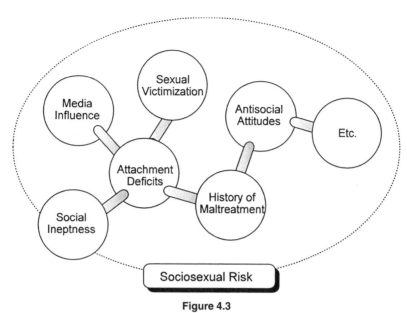

Figure 4.3
A molecular model in which social behavior is the result of interactions and connections among different elements, rather than the result of a single element.

model is molecular in that it combines atoms or elements, each of which has a particular valence (or attractiveness for other elements or factors), into a complex and phenomenological model of etiology.

The media contributes to the problem because it serves as a powerful—and often indiscriminate and unchecked—provider of messages and information. Immature and impressionable minds may misunderstand complex information and be drawn to and sold on certain ideas. When impressionability is combined with vulnerability and predisposition, such as when children with poor attachment, low social adequacy, and a host of other developmental vulnerabilities come into contact with and believe the idea that sex is a potential leveler of the playing field, the potential exists for inappropriate sexual behavior. To the mind of the offending juvenile, sexual behavior can level the playing field by replacing powerlessness with dominance and control, loneliness with the illusion of intimacy, lack of social competence with the impression that sexual behavior equals social competence and mastery, sexual naïveté and inquisitiveness with knowledge, rage with revenge, adolescent angst with momentary calm, sexual frustration with sexual fulfilment, or a host of other imagined or real benefits that are based on the psychological makeup of each particular juvenile sexual offender.

Just as the media can serve as a potent trigger in an interaction between predispositional developmental vulnerabilities and the social learning environment, so too there are many other triggers and mediators in the social environment that serve to activate or dampen predispositional factors, helping troubled kids to overcome developmental vulnerabilities or stimulating them into life. Mediators help children and adolescents make sense of information, develop healthy decision-making and problem-solving skills, provide support and guidance, avoid risk, and form prosocial values. Minimally, they serve to dampen or neutralize the potential for troubled behaviors; at their best, they can help build on developmental strengths that may also exist, as well as help turn vulnerabilities into strengths. These protective factors buffer the child against antisocial and troubled behaviors that may be harmful to self or others.

THE PUBLIC HEALTH APPROACH

Given the complexity of the problem with sexual abuse and the relative success of the public health approach to other social problems, sexual abuse has recently been targeted for intervention using this approach.

In a mental health orientation, primary treatment is aimed at the individual experiencing the problem; secondary treatment is aimed at heavily interacting and comorbid systems such as the family; and tertiary treatment is directed at the larger and surrounding systems such as the schools, community, and subculture. As shown in Figure 4.4, the public health model takes a converse approach, adopting an intervention rather than a treatment model. In this approach, *primary* intervention is aimed at the larger community, and indeed society itself, applying methods to recognize and stop the problem at its cause, thus preventing its development in the first place. In all cases, this means early intervention, and in the case of human behavior, this means identifying possible problems in early childhood and intervening in the systems that surround the

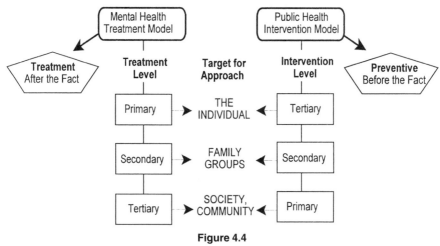

Figure 4.4
The public health approach to social and individual health.

child (i.e., the child's developmental-learning environment). Primary intervention represents the most sweeping and broadest level of action, potentially affecting all members of the society. *Secondary* intervention is directed at groups far smaller than the greater community or society, typically targeting groups of individuals or related systems that are likely to be at risk for the behavior. *Tertiary* intervention is aimed at the individual who is at the greatest level of actual risk or has already been infected or affected by the illness.

Described in recent reports developed and distributed by the U.S. Surgeon General (U.S. Department of Health and Human Services, 2001b, 2002), a public health model

1. Identifies the problem
2. Defines the problem
3. Identifies potential causes
4. Identifies risk and protective factors
5. Designs, develops, and evaluates interventions
6. Disseminates successful models
7. Continues to evaluate interventions that have demonstrated effectiveness

The public health approach recognizes multiple potential or likely causes for the problem and its transmission to others, as well as multiple types and intensities of intervention aimed at multiple targets. These potential problems are identified as risk factors, whereas those factors that can eliminate, shield, or lessen the impact of the risk factors and the risk environment are described as protective factors.

PROTECTIVE AND RISK FACTORS

In its report on youth violence, the office of the U.S. Surgeon General (2001b) described a *risk factor* as anything that increases the probability that a person will suffer harm and a *protective factor* as something that decreases the potential harmful effect of a risk factor. In this context, risk factors, which are not necessarily causative, increase probability, and protective factors buffer against those probabilities. Risk factors are neither static nor contained to one area or part of the environment.

In other words, risk factors are precisely that: factors that contribute to and flag the possibility or probability of risk. However, in both the public health and sociocultural models, risk factors are not the result of a biological condition but instead stem from environmental and social conditions that create, nurture, and maintain antisocial behaviors. Further, as in a molecular model, risk factors combine and interact with other risk factors to create situations that any single risk factor might not have sufficient energy to produce on its own. Consequently, in a model of social etiology and change, risk factors found in the sociocultural environment are the target for intervention.

Protective factors are conceptualized only in relation to risk factors. That is, although they have an independent existence, their role is to protect against, or mitigate the effects of, risk factors. Protective factors are the personal characteristics and social ties, values, beliefs, and supports that bolster individuals against negative and antisocial influences, increase social skills and promote positive personal identity, and help to develop individuals who have the strength to recognize and overcome adversity prosocially. In its call to action to promote sexual health and responsible sexual practice, the office of the Surgeon General (U.S. Department of Health and Human Services, 2002) described "a number of . . . variable risk and protective factors that shape human sexual behavior" (p. 6), including biology, parents and family members, schools, friends, the community, the media, religion, health care professionals, the law, and the availability of necessary services. In its earlier report (U.S. Department of Health and Human Services, 2001b), the office of the Surgeon General described five specific levels for both risk and protective factors: (a) the individual, (b) the family, (c) the school, (d) the peer group, and (e) the community. This mirrors the levels of interventions used from primary to tertiary in a treatment model (individual to community) and the public health model (going from community to individual).

Bentovim (2002) reported that childhood sexual abuse victims who go on to become sexual offenders are distinguished by primary risk factors such as histories of physical abuse, the witnessing of family violence, and disruptions in parental care. However, he described the protective factors of positive attachments and adequate care as neutralizers to the impact of living in a climate of abuse and violence. Figure 4.5 provides an overview of both risk and protective factors that serve as aggravating or mitigating elements in the development of antisocial or dysfunctional behavior. Note that in many cases the protective factors represent either the absence of a risk factor or the polar opposite condition.

The U.S. Surgeon General (U.S. Department of Health and Human Services, 2001b) also identified different risk factors at play, or with more potency, at different points in the development of the child and adolescent. In this regard, risk and protective factors are not only both static and dynamic but developmental as well; that is, they appear at different times and have different valences at different points in the developmental process. The construct of risk factors does have limitations, however. On assessment, many individuals are found to have been exposed to risk factors—many of which may still be at play in their social environment—but clearly have not succumbed. The reason is that although risk factors increase in potential when grouped together, no single risk factor or set of combined risk factors has enough impact to bring about a *certain* outcome. Similarly, no set of risk factors is strong enough to

Risk Factors	Protective Factors
• Being male	• Being female
• Low socioeconomic status	• Active parental interest
• Uninvolved parents	• Parental monitoring
• Poor or absent parental supervision	• Close family relationships
• Poor parent-child relationship	• Prosocial parental values
• Antisocial parents	• Parent self-control
• Parent substance abuse	• Appropriate sanctions for poor behaviors
• Harsh, lax, or inconsistent parent discipline	• Respectful parents
• Abusive or neglectful parents	• Supportive family relationships
• Family conflict	• Intact family relationships
• Broken home	• Stable care with stable caregiver
• Disrupted early care	• Positive relationship with adult
• Attentional difficulties and hyperactivity	• Positive peer relationship
• Antisocial attitudes or behaviors	• Positive sibling relationship
• Aggression and violence	• Modeling of prosocial behaviors
• Academic difficulties	• Modeling or prosocial values and attitudes
• Negative school experiences and attitudes	• Involvement in conventional activities
• Weak social ties	• Relative academic success
• Antisocial peers	• Positive social orientation
• Substance use	• Prosocial peer group

Figure 4.5

Examples of risk factors and protective factors in the development or mitigation of antisocial or dysfunctional behavior.

predict any specific antisocial behavior with certainty. In addition, although clearly having the potential to affect every individual in the risk pool—let us say all children and adolescents who share many of the characteristics described in this and the previous chapter—it is nonetheless true that risk factors reflect *probability* more than they do certainty. That is, risk factors take on real meaning only in groups large enough for statistical inferences to be drawn and thereby point to the possibility (or even the probability) of a certain kind of behavior being enacted by some individuals within that group, without knowing exactly who that individual might be. Thus, for specific individuals, the presence of one or more risk factors may be interpreted only as placing the individual at risk for certain behaviors, and not as a sure thing.

CONCLUSION

Although some believe that we live in a society that is sexually uncomfortable and that represses sexual ideas and discussion, it is probably truer to say that we live in a society filled with open sexual messages, few of which address sexual constraint or reflect sexual reality. In fact, the research and ideas presented in this chapter highlight our culture as sexually oriented—and much more so than even a generation ago.

We have seen also that children do not grow up in a vacuum. Instead, they develop in the context of a social environment and social interactions, or a developmental-learning environment, which in our society is filled with messages about social attitudes, values, and behaviors and in which risk factors are everywhere and protective factors are sometimes missing. It is no surprise, then, that some kids become sexually active at a young age and that some kids take this path to become offenders. Moreover, Itzen (2000) noted that through sexualized or violent events and experiences witnessed or directly experienced in childhood and early adolescence, some boys develop predispositions that not only make them more vulnerable to the triggering effects of pornography and sexual media but also predispose them to internalizing attitudes, beliefs, and themes of dominance and power. Paraphrasing Itzen, some of these boys later externalize these ideas by perpetrating violence against women and children (p. 423).

Some children are never exposed to significant risk factors, and the absence of risk itself represents a strong protective factor. For those kids who are exposed to risk factors, however, other protective factors may serve to protect and buffer them against risk, which may help explain why not every kid who is exposed to risk factors becomes dangerous to self or others. Of this, Bentovim (2002) wrote that "having a sufficient set of protective factors may be sufficient to prevent a young person with moderate levels of risk from abusing" (p. 350), and he described one good adult relationship, one good sibling relationship, one good peer relationship, and stability in care by the same caregiver as significant, and perhaps sufficient, protective factors.

In our struggle to understand how children who engage in sexually abusive behaviors learn the mechanics of sex and from where they find the motivation to engage in such behavior, we must look beyond the possibility or probability that all were sexually victimized. For those children and adolescents already predisposed to antisocial relationships, poor judgments, and behavioral problems, we can also look to the media as a transmitter of social values and a primary source of sexual ideas, information, ideas, instruction, and incentive (the *four "I"*s of sexual knowledge), but we must also go beyond the notion that the media alone is the culprit. Although we can investigate from where the information and ideas are coming, ultimately the motivation to offend is the critical factor in understanding and treating the juvenile sexual offender. Just as children and adolescents do not develop in a vacuum, neither does the development of sexual offending behavior. In concert with natural physiological, psychological, and sociological developments, the emotional and cognitive drives and sexual interests behind that first episode of sexual aggression develop due to a complex interaction of social, interpersonal, and intrapsychic cues. Bearing in mind the risks and factors present in the social environment, the next chapter explores some of the pathways along which sexual offending lies in terms of both motivation and the differences in causation and motivation.

CHAPTER 5

Pathways to Juvenile
Sexual Offending

MANY THEORIES exist as to why juvenile sexual offenders *are* sexually aggressive and to explain the pathways that lead to such behavior. This is a confounding situation, as earlier chapters noted that no clear factors distinguish juvenile sexual offenders from other juveniles, other than the fact that they are sexually abusive. Many of the characteristics shared by the JSO population were discussed in Chapters 3 and 4, as well as the developmental-learning environment in which the juvenile sexual offender grows into his ideas, attitudes, values, relationships, and behaviors. These try not only to recognize similarities and commonalities among all juvenile sexual offenders but also to differentiate the offender from the non-offender, as well as explaining the pathways that lead to sexual offending.

In fact, seemingly common developmental pathways, personal experiences, and risk factors seem to lead to different outcomes in different children. The reason is that sexually aggressive and assaultive behaviors develop not in a vacuum but in the context of the lives of individual children and adolescents and the internal and external influences and factors that shape emotion, thinking, social interactions and relationships, behavior, and personality. Addressing this point, both G. Ryan (1997a) and Calder (2001) emphasized the need to recognize and understand human behavior in the context of individual development and life experiences, or with a phenomenological view in which we recognize that individual action is influenced by many factors, rather than single or universal causes.

DEVELOPMENTAL PATHWAYS TO OFFENDING

Developmental pathways can be thought of as channels through which children and adolescents pass en route to sexual offending and by which their movements are directed along the journey. The metaphor implies that under the right circumstances juveniles who enter these channels are routed in a rather rigid and predictable movement from an initial entry point to the end point of sexual aggression. Through these channels, children's behaviors are directed to a near-certain outcome unless an intervening factor reroutes them.

Statistically, pathways are no more than strongly correlated links among stimuli, events, or behaviors. However, more than just entities in a corelationship, these markers are linked in a manner that suggests a particular direction (hence the concept of a path or a channel leading from one point to another), which likewise suggests a causal relationship. That is, an earlier marker not only points to the next but actually leads to, or causes, the next marker to come into existence. In statistics we learn that correlation does not imply causation or that just because two items tend to appear together with some regularity and consistency, it does not mean that one causes or is caused by the other. However, in a developmental pathway model, such correlation implies causality or directionality at the very least. After all, what is a pathway if it doesn't lead somewhere?

In a pathway model, one event, aided by various other factors (mediators), channels the development of behavior and its antecedents in a clear direction. In such a model, the path can be described from beginning to end as it unfolds, and the outcome of the path can be predicted by its originating point because the points along the pathway are linked in a causal manner, or each step is caused by, or is the result of, the preceding marker. Retrospectively, we should be able to hypothesize and recognize a predictable starting point to the path. In the causal pathway model we should be able to predict movement in either direction.

The developmental pathway model thus provides a means for recognizing starting points along a journey, a predictable end point (or result), and other mediating influences along the way. It can help us picture the sort of metaphorical paths along which children and adolescents are channeled in their journey toward sexual offending. Nevertheless, in real life not all situations may fit the mold. As mentioned earlier, although there are many common features in the lives and development of juvenile sexual offenders, there are also countless permutations of markers, mediators, activators, dampeners, risk factors, and protective factors, all of which combine in unique ways to define the lives of different individuals. A developmental pathway model is a useful way to illustrate how a youth may journey, but it may not apply to every case. In addition, in developmental psychopathology we recognize the principles of equifinality in which diverse developmental pathways can lead to similar outcomes and multifinality in which the same developmental pathway can lead to different outcomes for different people (Hart, Watt, & Vincent, 2002).

Despite the lack of a single factor model or unifying theory, researchers continue to try to statistically ferret out and discover models that can help explain the development of sexual offending and identify critical factors and pathways. Recognizing the complexity of the problem and considering the richness of individual experience and the uniqueness of the environment, as well as commonalities found in the developmental experiences of many juvenile sexual offenders, researchers weave together complex pathways that attempt to explain the linear development and eventual enactment of sexually abusive behaviors.

In their exploration of such pathways, Hunter et al. (in press) reported that (a) childhood exposure to violence against women and (b) male-modeled antisocial behavior increase the risk of sexual aggression and nonsexual delinquency, with psychosocial deficits and egotistical-antagonistic hypermasculinity[1] playing an important mediating role in sexual offenses against children. The authors believe that these factors support the idea of social learning, in which boys internalize and mimic socially deviant behaviors in their social environment and elsewhere. Further, they have written (Hunter et al., 2003) that hostile masculinity is a strong predictor of sexual aggression in boys.

Knight and Sims-Knight (in press) proposed a three-factor model of causal pathways that they described as the basis for a unified model of sexual aggression causation:

1. *Physical or verbal abuse* leading to callousness and lack of emotionality, in turn leading to disinhibition of sexual drives and sexual fantasy and finally to sexual coercion
2. *Sexual abuse* contributing directly to the disinhibition of sexual drive and sexual fantasies and also leading to sexual coercion
3. *Early antisocial behavior,* including aggression, resulting from both physical and verbal abuse and callousness and lack of emotion, which affects sexual coercion and hostile sexual fantasies.

The authors noted that these pathways combine with existing personality predispositions to produce three latent traits that predict sexual aggression: arrogant, deceitful personality/emotional detachment; impulsivity/antisocial behaviors; and sexual preoccupation/hypersexuality.

Malamuth (2002) proposed two major factors in the development of sexual

---

[1] Hypermasculinity is an exaggerated sense of what it means to be a male, accompanied by strong male-identity needs and often-stereotyped male behaviors and often juxtaposed against a view in which females are considered to be less dominant than males or subservient to male needs.

offending: (a) *compulsive, deviant, and impersonal sexuality* and (b) *hostile and dominant antisociality*. In his model, these two factors represent constellations of characteristics that distinguish between sexually aggressive and nonsexually aggressive males and include hostility and negativity towards women, sexual promiscuity, frequent use of pornography, and attitudes in which sexual offenders consider coercive sex as a means to exert control over women. Malamuth considers these factors, which emerge in sexual offenders, to have earlier antecedents, so that they can be recognized as the products of a developmental path.

As actual cases of juvenile sexual offending follow one of the defined pathways in many ways, far from scientifically pinpointing every detail, researchers often build clinical and social factors into their models, recognizing and allowing for individual variation without explaining the mechanism of such variation. For instance, Hunter et al. (in press) suggested that differences in individual psychology and the specific environment allow individuals to choose survival and adaptation strategies most pertinent to their situation, and thus move along different pathways to sexual aggression. Rather than explaining *why* individuals select such pathways, however, or explaining why there is more than one pathway, the allowance of individual psychology and indeterminate social conditions fits the statistical model to the phenomenology of the individual (not vice versa). The model in this case merely *points* to possible pathways, rather than explaining why an individual took (or was forced along) that particular pathway. Knight and Sims-Knight (in press) built into their model a similar perspective by noting that many complex and interactive factors are determined by many forces in the child's experience. In effect, these researchers are simply pointing to possible pathways to sexual aggression, without knowing exactly why some children sexually offend and others do not.

CONCERNS WITH STATISTICALLY DEFINED PATHWAYS

These researchers, among others, believe not only that it is possible to describe the developmental pathways that lead to sexual aggression but also that these will be adequate and accurate explanations for understanding and describing the etiology and perpetration of sexual abuse. There is little doubt that research on developmental pathways is of great importance to better understanding juvenile sexual offenders (and others) and is hitting on real factors that can also be seen through clinical observation (and, in fact, thus supports and validates clinical practice). Nevertheless, we must ask whether the developmental pathways or factors that are hypothesized to be present for all sexual aggressors are actually there or whether we are manufacturing them. That is, are researchers actually discovering and uncovering objective realities, or only substantiating what they are speculating is there in the first place?

Are they merely confirming a clinical reality that is already observable to them (and others) and thus inventing the answers they seek through the application of the right set of research questions and the right set of statistical processes?

What appears to be moving toward the right answers and unified models of knowledge, then, may actually fall into the category of socially constructed reality. Here, reality is what we make of it, rather than an independent thing waiting to be discovered and experienced. Berger and Luckmann (1967) argued that reality is subjective but is transformed into a reality that has the appearance of objectivity.

Many theories and explanations for sexual offending exist. Of these, Calder (2001) noted that no one theory is generally accepted about why children and adolescents sexually offend, and Weinrott (1996) commented that most explanations either are too simplistic or fail because they are applied universally. In a similar vein, Marshall and Eccles (1993) pointed out that an overarching or single theory of sexual offending is probably not possible and proposed instead that specific theories be developed for specific sexual behaviors, each of which emphasizes different processes that contribute to the specific behavior.

G. Ryan (1997c) described sexual aggression as "a multidimensional model without a clearly defined cause" (p. 19). To this end, it is more likely that the real explanation for juvenile sexual aggression consists of a complex and idiosyncratic overlap between individual psychological, sociological, and possibly physiological processes, mediated and shaped by the developmental-learning environment.

Thus, as useful as statistical procedures such as factor and path analysis may be in uncovering and exploring reality, they are just tools. We should be on guard against theories that purport to explain everything—especially when our experience tells us that juvenile sexual offending is a complex and multidimensional phenomenon that lacks single explanatory theories and defies universal answers.

ACTIVATING DRIVES OR THEORIES OF ACTION

Theories of the underlying dynamics that fuel behavior vary. Nevertheless, theories about the development and emergence of behaviors fall into one of several categories, each of which tries to explain the behavior in terms that allow us to, at a minimum, better understand one aspect of human functioning. Through such theories we can understand how behavior and ideas develop over time and what lies behind them, how the mind works to direct action, and how to understand human dysfunction and bring about subsequent change in personal and psychological functioning.

Physiological theories suggest that the cause of sexual aggression is biological in origin. In the physiological model of sexual abuse, research is directed toward physical functions that affect and shape sexual response, and treatment is directed toward physical processes that stimulate and control aggression, sexual arousal, disinhibition, and related behavior.

Behavioral theories suggest that behavior and thought are products of the environment in which children grow and develop and that behavior can be understood and treated through understanding and remediating the environment. From a behavioral perspective, sexual aggression is a learned behavior in which sexual arousal and aggression are linked to, or conditioned by, environmental stimuli. Treatment is aimed at modifying behavior through a process of reconditioning or, at the least, unconditioning.

Cognitive theories consider irrational, negatively biased, and learning-impaired thinking that shapes thoughts, attitudes, and assumptions to be the source of emotional distress, behavioral problems, and other functional problems (Thase & Beck, 1993). These theories concentrate on recognizing and changing problematic, self-defeating, and biased patterns of thinking and hold cognitive change as the essential ingredient in both behavioral pathology and rehabilitative treatment. In a cognitive model, distorted attitudes and ideas allow individuals to perpetrate acts of sexual aggression, and various thinking errors allow the behavior to be cognitively assimilated in ways that further support and perpetuate the behavior, thus creating or contributing to a cycle of sexual assault.

Cognitive-behavioral theories are a hybrid of cognitive and behavioral theories. The essential idea is that cognitions (thoughts) are central in defining beliefs that underlie action and result in behavior, faulty or otherwise. Thus, thoughts (or thinking processes and patterns of thinking) dictate and drive behavior, which can be treated, redirected, and rehabilitated through changes in the way that people think and in their resulting attitudes, perspectives, mind-sets, and cognitive schemata. Cognitive-behavioral therapies, until recently, have been the treatment of choice in most sexual-offender-specific treatment programs.

Social learning theories, sometimes also called social cognition, are similar to cognitive-behavioral theories and suggest that children learn how and what to think, as well as how to behave, from role models in their developmental-learning environment. As children grow into adolescence and adulthood, role models and the source of social learning changes, based on earlier social learning, but attitudes, values, and belief systems continue to be influenced and shaped through a process of social learning until they freeze or harden into established patterns of thought, attitudes, values, and behavior in adulthood.

Developmental theories suggest that as individuals grow from infancy through childhood, into adolescence, and then into adulthood and eventually old age, they pass through distinct stages of physical, cognitive, and emotional development that set the stage for psychological and personality development, self-image, and personal identity. Like social learning theories, models of psychological development hold that human development takes place within the developmental-learning environment. Sexual aggression in such a model is the composite outcome of damaged and incomplete developmental growth and of a developmental-learning environment that has failed to meet the prosocial and positive personality development needs of the individual.

Psychodynamic theories suggest that thoughts and emotions and all of their manifestations, including attitudes, relationships, interactions, and behavior, are the result of instinctual drives and unconscious mental processes. Central to these theories is the idea that early experiences, consciously remembered or not, as well as physical and emotional drives intended to meet or fulfill unconscious and instinctual needs, drive all interactions. In a psychodynamic model, unconscious psychological defense mechanisms may contribute to sexually aggressive behaviors in individuals who were victimized or anxious about their own sexual development.

Attachment and object relations theories assert that the early mother-child relationship serves as the basis for all intrapsychic, interpersonal, and interactional experiences and for the experience of social interactions and dependencies. The ability to form affectional ties and bonds (attachment theory) serves as the basis for all later relationships and experiences of the self. Sexual aggression and assault result from impaired attachments and a resulting lack of affectional bonds, intimacy, and empathy or from the attempt to engage in an attached relationship of sorts or live out relationship needs.

Systems theories grew out of the constructs of biologically based general systems theory. These theories are ecological in that they recognize that individuals operate within a larger system and can only be understood within the context of that system and that systems operate and can be best understood only within the context of the larger systems that surround them and of which they are a part and in constant interaction. Pathology or health of individuals within the system reflects health or pathology within the larger system. In a systems model, dysfunctional sexual behavior of an individual results from interactions and experiences within the system and represents the failure of the larger system itself, and most typically the familial system.

Trauma theories are not typical of psychological theories of action in general but are important to note here because the trauma of prior sexual and physical victimization is often seen as important in understanding childhood sexual reactivity and juvenile sexual offending. In trauma models, traumatic experiences and other significant life-transforming events not only disrupt normative and expected emotional and personality development but also potentially affect and reshape neural pathways in the brain, thus creating a very different experience of the world, relationships, and self for the victim of trauma, depending on the age at which trauma occurred. In these models, when the individual was a victim of abuse, sexually aggressive behavior is considered to be trauma reactive and is sometimes viewed as a recapitulation of the trauma, in which the earlier experience gives rise to its later reenactment by the victim.

Theories of psychopathy, although derived from other theories, are considered significant in the case of sexual aggression. In a model of psychopathy, the individual experiences only self-interest, lacks concern for or understanding of the needs of others, has shallow and superficially experienced emotions, and acts with neither regard for others nor remorse. Although some researchers use the terms *psychopath* and *sociopath* to describe subtypes of the same phenomenon or different types of individuals, the two terms are typically used interchangeably to describe the same construct: an under-socialized individual who nonetheless often has effective social skills, is emotionally cut off, experiences little to no conscience, and is substantially different from the rest of society. These theories suggest that when psychopathic individuals engage in sexual aggression, it is merely another facet of a personal needs–driven and entitled narcissism in which there is neither recognition of nor concern for the victim of the behavior, and in which personal needs and drives are disparate or out of tune with the needs or concerns of the larger society. Here, sexually deviant behavior is the result of an abnormal personality.

In fact, although some of these theories are often considered to be mutually exclusive (e.g., psychodynamic and behavioral theories), many overlap, enhance, and complement one another. In fact, as described in Chapters 11 through 15, even psychodynamic and cognitive-behavioral therapies may be seen as extensions of one another and can be blended into a model of integrated treatment. There is no reason to doubt that a "real" theory of human functioning embraces elements of many theories, and human functioning and individual psychology is the product of the interplay of many different aspects of physical and emotional development, difference, and social interaction. Here, theories merge in a larger model in which physiology, individual psychology, and social interrelatedness combine into *biopsychosocial theory,* as portrayed in Figure 5.1.

FROM INTENT TO ACTION

Some of the early and developmental steps along the pathway to juvenile sexual offending, as well as forces of action that may initiate and propel the journey, have already been presented. It is also important to recognize the factors that finally intercede to carry intent into the final steps of action along those pathways or that prevent and redirect action. In trying to understand what brings to life behaviors that are as deviant, harmful, and socially repugnant as

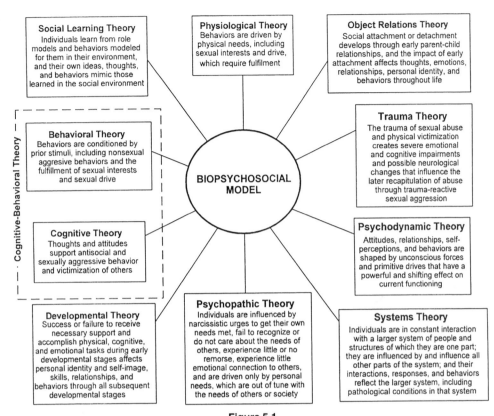

Figure 5.1
A composite model of biopsychological theory.

sexual offending, we need to understand several related concepts that combine to transform intent to act into action.

1. *Utilitarian Purpose* describes the immediate or surface objective of the behavior, or its immediate function—the thing or outcome that it is designed to achieve. In the case of sexual offending, for instance, the purpose may be to feel socially competent and capable or to know what it is like to have sexual intercourse.

2. *Intended Action* describes the act required to meet the utilitarian purpose and accomplish that goal. Thus, in sexual offending the intended action is to engage in some form of sexual act, with or without consent.

3. *Underlying Intent* describes the underlying, or true, goal to be accomplished, even if this is unknown to the actor. In sexual offending, whereas the utilitarian purpose may be to experience sex, the underlying intent may be to experience power over another, to experience a sense of social mastery or other form of accomplishment, or to live out a sadistic sexual (sado-sexual) act.

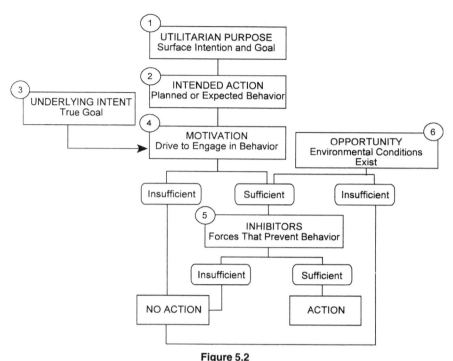

Figure 5.2
From intent to action, mediated by motivation and inhibitors.

4. *Sufficient Motivation* describes the required amount of pressure or drive to engage in the act and overcome other forces or pressures that may otherwise inhibit or prohibit the behavior.
5. *Sufficient Inhibitors* represent various internal and external forces that act to prevent or reduce sufficient motivation and thus serve to prevent the action from occurring.
6. *Available Opportunity* must exist, and environmental conditions must allow for access to the behavior; in the case of sexual offending, this means access to a victim and the ability to assault that victim sexually.

The relationship and interaction between these six factors is mapped in Figure 5.2.

David Finkelhor (1984) described four preconditions to the occurrence of sexual abuse: (a) the offender must be motivated to abuse (this reminds us of Eldridge's [2000, p. 315] comment that "most sex offenders do sexual things . . . because they want to"), (b) to overcome internal inhibitions, (c) to overcome external inhibitions, and (d) to overcome victim resistance.

MOTIVATION FOR SEXUALLY ABUSIVE BEHAVIOR AMONG CHILDREN AND ADOLESCENTS

If we assume that all behavior is purposeful, then what is the end toward which the behavior is directed? In the case of juvenile sexual offending, what idea or purpose is the juvenile attempting to accommodate when he engages in such behavior for the first time, and subsequent times if he continues? In other words, what fuels the immediate behavior?

Whereas several years ago power and domination were considered the central reason for sexual offending, we recognize today that sexual offending is a far more complex and multifaceted behavior and crime. At a glance, four obvious avenues along which juvenile sexual offending and sexually aggressive behavior may lie are apparent: (a) the experience of sexual activity itself as a primary goal, with coercion or aggression used as a means to accomplish that end; (b) aggression and violence as a means unto itself, in which sexual behavior is secondary to a larger conduct disorder (the power and control route); (c) experimentation and exploration, with a naive or nonexistent recognition of the larger consequences; and (d) mental illness or cognitive impairment in which the individual is not competent to make decisions or make judgments about right or wrong actions. These avenues may be expanded to create a broader picture of why some juveniles become sexual offenders.

- *Power seeking.* From this perspective, power is the primary motivator for the behavior of the sexual offender. Sexual gratification is viewed as a secondary gain that reinforces the primary behavior.
- *Taking charge.* The "I-take-what-I-want" and "I-have-the-right" behavior and attitude of the sexual offender may indicate that the perpetrator has come to see the world in terms of victims and victimizers. As many sexual offenders have themselves been victimized at some time in the past, the sexual offense behavior may prove a means for establishing control and ensuring that the perpetrator is not cast in the victim role again. In a world of victims and victimizers, this casts the offender in the role of victimizer rather than victim.
- *Thinking error.* The sexual offense is seen as just one example of criminal behavior, and all criminal behavior is seen as the result of thinking disorders.
- *Coping mechanism.* Sex is used in the service of nonsexual needs as an antidote to a state of emotional turmoil in which the perpetrator feels helpless, frustrated, angry, powerless, or like a victim of society. In this scenario, sexual offending may be the only means by which the offender can fight off feelings of depression, anger, and so on and may be viewed as an antidote against feeling bad.

- *Frustration and emotional release.* Engaging in sexual control or violence relieves and discharges emotions.
- *Social learning.* The offender has been exposed to, experienced, or learned a distorted and confused view of sexual relationships and has incorporated these experiences and beliefs into his thinking, behavior, and interactions.
- *Mental illness or cognitive limitation.* The offender is experiencing a mental illness or cognitive deficit that is contributing significantly to his perceptions, beliefs, interactions, and behaviors.
- *Physical compulsion.* Here, the offender feels physically compelled to act out highly sexualized feelings and is perhaps unable to control overwhelming physical (and mental) drives.
- *Experimentation.* In some cases in younger or developmentally delayed offenders, sexual offending behaviors are the result of curiosity, naïveté, and classic experimentation, in which case the offending behavior may be situational or the result of behavior that is not intended as an offense.
- *Self-reinforcing cycle.* The sexual behavior is the result of a repetitive and dysfunctional cognitive-behavioral cycle in which the personal history, triggering events, thoughts and feelings, thinking errors (cognitive distortions), and the sexual behavior itself serves as the preconditions for the very same set of thoughts, emotions, and behaviors to occur again, in a cycle of sexual abuse. This is a typical model used to treat adult and juvenile sexual offenders, and it is sometimes referred to as the sexual assault cycle.

Although these perspectives add detail, they remain general. Let us consider some of the specific reasons why juveniles and children engage in sexual offending behaviors, first by reason, and then by type of motivation.

MOTIVATORS AND MAINTENANCE FACTORS

Larger models and general perspectives aside, what is the immediate purpose for sexual offending among kids? In some cases the immediate motivator is in effect only for the first offense, such as sexual curiosity. After that, continued offending often takes on a new form. Motivators for the ongoing offenses become *maintenance* factors, or motivators that serve to repeat and maintain the behaviors. In these cases, the motivators or maintainers are applicable only in the case of repeated sexual misconduct, as patterns begin to develop and emerge, such as sexual obsession or compulsivity. Forty-six specific immediate motivators or maintenance factors for sexual offending are shown in Table 5.1, listed in alphabetical order, and are then clustered into the categories that can help identify and explain the variance and myriad of reasons that can prompt juvenile sexual offending. Motivators and maintainers are not neat

Table 5.1

Forty-Six Motivators for Juvenile Sexual Offending

Motivator	Rationale for Engaging in Sexually Abusive Behavior
Affection: Demonstrating	To demonstrate affection
Affection: Seeking	To receive affection
Anger	To dispel general anger or anger toward the specific victim
Antidote	To cope with and get rid of dystonic feelings about life, self-worth, frustration, or feelings of powerlessness
Cognitive/Intellectual Deficit	Mental retardation, borderline intellectual functioning, or another cognitive impairment
Compulsion: Addictive	Repeatedly due to internal pressures that resemble patterns of addiction and through which the juvenile feels a measure of internal relief
Compulsion: Nonaddictive	Repeatedly due to internal pressure to relieve sexual preoccupation, a mental disorder such as obsessive compulsive disorder, or for other nonaddictive reasons that drive obsessive thinking and behaviors
Emotional Discharge	To dispel and express pent-up emotional feelings
Emotional Satisfaction	The act is ego syntonic (feels good) and meets emotional needs
Experimentation: Curious	Primarily to learn about sex and sexual-related matters and ideas, rather than engaging in sexual abuse for its own sake or as part of a conduct disorder
Experimentation: Exploitive	Primarily to learn about sex and sexual-related matters and ideas, consciously taking the opportunity to explore and take advantage of others for this purpose
Experimentation: Naive	Primarily to learn about sex and sexual-related matters and ideas, in which the juvenile may not be aware of the antisocial nature of the behavior of abuse and use of others
Fantasy Fulfillment (Deviant)	As a means to live out an ongoing deviant sexual or relationship fantasy
Fantasy Fulfillment (Nondeviant)	As a means to live out an ongoing nondeviant sexual or relationship fantasy
Feel Normal	To feel like everyone else or feel better about himself, the juvenile uses sex as a means to experience feeling like what he imagines a normal person must feel
Hypersexuality	To relieve strong and frequent sexual urges that are not easily satiated in other ways
Incompetence	Inability to distinguish easily between right and wrong and make decisions that demonstrate a full understanding of the world
Intimacy	To establish a strong and shared connection or feel close to another person
Loneliness	As a means to connect and engage with others
Mental Illness	Although the juvenile may or may not be incompetent, the sexual abuse is a symptom of the mental illness
Mutuality: Actual	The actual consent of the other party is given although the other party is incapable of giving true consent for any number of reasons, including significant age difference
Mutuality: Imagined	Mistaken but genuine belief that the relationship is mutual, however inappropriate or unlikely

Table 5.1

continued

Motivator	Rationale for Engaging in Sexually Abusive Behavior
Opportunity: Impulsive	An impulsive act that seemed right at the time
Opportunity: Predatory	An emerging opportunity that has been anticipated and even planned or set up by the offender
Opportunity: Situational	No prior specific planning, but in response to an opportunity that presents itself
Paraphilia (Sexual Fetish)	Sexual pleasure or relief can be gained only through the expression of deviant sexual interests in a particular class of individual, objects, sexual acts or situations, or combination of deviant arousal factors
Peer-Cohort Encouragement	Direct pressure or indirect influence or impact of peers or other cohorts
Power, Control, and Domination	To exert control directly or indirectly over another individual, whether the actual victim or another individual over whom the offender exerts control through the victim
Psychosis	Psychotic mental illness in which the juvenile is motivated by reasons that are not rational and thus may not be competent at the time
Re-enactment of Pornography	To act out a sexual image or idea previously experienced in pornography
Relationship Building	To form a relationship with another person, however misplaced
Revenge	To get revenge or retaliate directly or indirectly for a perceived injustice, whether directed against the actual victim or whether as a means of getting revenge against another individual connected to the victim
Role Modeling	To emulate the effects and impact of another important or influential individual in the juvenile's life who has previously engaged in either sexual abuse or sexual or social behaviors
Sadism and Cruelty	To gain sexual pleasure through the use of intentional cruelty and the infliction of harm to the victim
Sexual Arousal: Deviant	Specific sexual arousal to paraphilic interests that involve the actual victim or the act of sexual abuse in some way
Sexual Arousal: Nondeviant	Current physical sexual arousal that is not of a sexually deviant nature and the juvenile's willingness to get sexual relief wherever he can
Sexual Gratification	To gratify sexual needs
Sexual Identity Exploration	To explore gender or sexual preference ideas or confusion that the juvenile is not comfortable with or capable of exploring in other ways; the social-skills deficit lies in the inability to recognize otherwise or express thoughts, feelings, or ideas appropriately
Sexual Impulsivity	Primitive sexual urges over which the juvenile has little ability or willingness to exert control
Sexual Obsession	Repeated and recurrent sexual ideas and thoughts that the juvenile feels compelled to act on to gain relief
Sexual Preoccupation	Frequent sexual thoughts, daydreams, and feelings that the juvenile eventually or repeatedly decides or feels compelled to act out

Table 5.1

continued

Motivator	Rationale for Engaging in Sexually Abusive Behavior
Social Competence or Mastery	To feel capable in an area over which the juvenile has some control, demonstrate skills he believes are common in others his age or older, and experience mastery over some part of his environment, even through coercion and force if necessary
Social Expectations	The juvenile's belief that sexual behaviors are expected of him and cannot be accomplished in other ways
Social Messages	The influence of social messages that the juvenile has misperceived or misunderstood, in which social ideas he experiences as attractive and normative are lived out
Substance Use Driven	The active influences of drugs or alcohol, in which substance use acts as a disinhibitor or stimulant and contributes to judgment impairment, and in some circumstances the indirect effects of substance use
Trauma-Reactive Recapitulation	The impact of his own sexual or physical victimization, in which the abuse of others somehow serves as a relief mechanism or as a primitive/psychological urge to re-enact the abuse or continue the behaviors

and clean, however, and are certainly not mutually exclusive; in some instances and for some young offenders, more than one motivator or maintenance factor may apply at any given time, and a number overlap with one another.

Motivator/Maintenance Categories

- Aggression
- Cognitive impairment
- Coping mechanism
- Sexual experimentation
- Sexual opportunism
- Relationship building
- Sexual deviance
- Sexual preoccupation
- Social environment
- Social-Skills deficit

Figure 5.3 clusters the various motivating reasons by category, which helps differentiate among juvenile sexual offenders and thus creates a rudimentary typology that can be useful in risk assessment and treatment planning. Typologies are complex undertakings, however. Nevertheless, for some, including the Association for the Treatment of Sexual Abusers (2000), the development of a complete typology represents an ultimate goal in the identification, assessment, and treatment of juvenile sexual offenders.

Category 1: **Aggression** Anger Power, Control, and Domination Revenge	**Category 6:** **Relationship Building** Affection: Demonstrating Affection: Seeking Intimacy Loneliness Mutuality: Actual Mutuality: Imagined Relationship Building
Category 2: **Cognitive Impairment** Cognitive/Intellectual Deficit Incompetence Mental Illness Psychosis Substance Use Driven	**Category 7:** **Sexual Deviance** Fantasy Fulfillment (Deviant) Paraphilia (Sexual Fetish) Sadism and Cruelty Sexual Arousal: Deviant
Category 3: **Coping Mechanism** Antidote Emotional Discharge Emotional Satisfaction Trauma-Reactive Recapitulation	**Category 8:** **Sexual Preoccupation** Compulsion: Addictive Compulsion: Nonaddictive Fantasy Fulfillment (Nondeviant) Hypersexuality Re-enactment of Pornography Sexual Arousal: Nondeviant Sexual Gratification Sexual Impulsivity Sexual Obsession Sexual Preoccupation
Category 4: **Sexual Experimentation** Experimentation: Curious Experimentation: Exploitive Experimentation: Naive	**Category 9:** **Social Environment** Peer-Cohort Encouragement Role Modeling Social Messages
Category 5: **Sexually Opportunistic** Opportunity: Impulsive Opportunity: Predatory Opportunity: Situational	**Category 10:** **Social Skills Deficit** Feel Normal Social Competence or Mastery Social Expectations Sexual Identity Exploration

Figure 5.3

Forty-six motivators for juvenile sexual offending clustered by category.

Figure 5.4 illustrates a hypothetical pathway to juvenile sexual offending. Included on the right-hand side of the diagram and along the horizontal dashed lines are the "stage instructions" for what is occurring during any particular point (the impact of static and later dynamic risk factors, modulators, actuators, etc.) as the pathway emerges and evolves with the individual as he ages from early childhood toward or into adolescence.

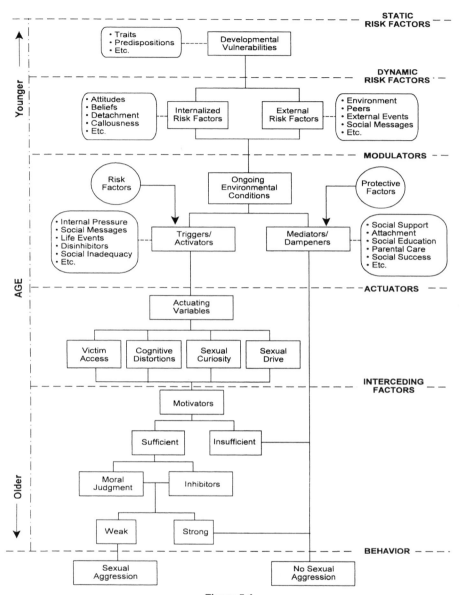

Figure 5.4

Hypothetical developmental pathway to sexual aggression.

SEXUAL DEVIANCE

Steele and Ryan (1997, p. 59) described deviancy as "any quality, conduct, or thought that significantly diverges from a standard or norm." Sexually abusive behaviors qualify as deviant if they violate social norms that govern behavior and relationships. *Sexual deviance* refers to sexual interests and arousal considered to be outside of normative sexual practices, or sexual paraphilias, the essential features of which are "recurrent, intense sexually arousing fantasies, sexual urges, or behaviors generally involving (1) nonhuman objects, (2) the suffering or humiliation of oneself or one's partner, or (3) children or other nonconsenting persons" (American Psychiatric Association, 2000, p. 566). The concept of sexual deviancy, or sexual perversion, is basically divided into three categories:

1. Sexual interest in and arousal to age-inappropriate individuals or to individuals who are otherwise sexually off-limits and in whom sexual interest is considered not only improper but also outside of the norm
2. Sexual practices that cause or aim to cause physical or emotional harm and in which sexual pleasure is derived in part from the infliction of pain or suffering
3. Sexual interests in fetish objects, which typically means inanimate objects but can also include arousal to specific characteristics of humans (such as sexual arousal to deceased individuals, or necrophilia)

In the case of the second two categories, society can be forgiving and quite nonjudgmental. For example, even though we might think of causing or receiving pain for the purpose of sexual pleasure as sexually deviant, we can live with it as long as no consenting adults are harmed against their will. In many cases, sexual acts like this (e.g., one sexual partner spanking or tying up the other in sexual play or the acceptance of mutual, mildly sadomasochistic sexual relationships) are described in mildly pornographic material and even in the mainstream media. The same is true in the case of many common sexual fetishes that do not involve especially far-out sexual interests or behaviors, including cross-dressing, which seems to have become increasingly more accepted as only mildly paraphilic and is relatively commonplace in sexual discussions and media portrayals. However, in the case of the first category, the behavior is almost always considered to be deviant if the object of sexual desire is clearly outside of the boundaries of social convention or expectation or is considered unnatural.

For example, we believe that it is deviant not only for an adult to have sexual contact with a prepubescent child but also for an adult (or older adolescent) to *want* to have sex with a child. In other words, regardless of actual behavior, it is considered deviant simply to be sexually aroused by children. In fact, when it comes to certain sexual behaviors and interests, sexual arousal alone is considered deviant, absent of behavior. The same is true when the other two categories of paraphilia involve more extreme or dangerous urges or behaviors. In adult offenders, deviant sexual arousal patterns are considered a significant and high risk factor (Hanson & Bussière, 1998) for sexually abusive behaviors, but the role of sexual deviancy in juveniles is far less understood, and the significance of deviant arousal, even when it can be recognized and measured in adolescents, is also largely unknown (Beckett, 1999;

Graham, Richardson, & Bhate, 1997; Masson & Erooga, 1999; Prentky et al., 2000).

Sexual deviance in sexually reactive children and juvenile sexual offenders requires some explanation. In the first place, how does one differentiate between deviant and normative sexual arousal in children and adolescents? Part of the problem here is that adolescent behaviors sometimes *appear* deviant with respect to an adult point of view but may not actually be deviant when compared to the behaviors of other adolescents, and Weinrott (1996) noted the paucity of studies devoted to measuring deviant arousal in juvenile sexual offenders. In fact, much of what we do know or assume comes from studies conducted with adult sexual offenders.

In many instances, for juveniles who sexually offend, the offending behavior is always considered to be sexually deviant, as in Wieckowski et al.'s (1998) study of child and adolescent offenders. However, this defines the concept of sexual deviancy so widely as to make it unusable. In their study of factors related to sexual arousal in juvenile sexual offenders, Murphy, DiLillo, Haynes, and Steere (2001) distinguished sexual abuse linked to sexually deviant arousal from sexual abuse related to conduct disorder, social anxiety, and other drives that lie behind and motivate the abuse. By linking sexual arousal in adolescent offenders with stimuli associated with child sexual abuse, sexual assault of a peer or adult, and forms of nonstandard sexual behaviors (e.g., voyeurism, frottage, and exhibitionism), they described juveniles who become aroused by deviant images that go beyond the sexual act or interaction itself. Consequently, although little is known about the sexual arousal preferences of juvenile sexual offenders, they concluded, as have others (e.g., Kahn & Chambers, 1991; Righthand & Welch, 2001; Schram et al., 1991; Worling, 2002; Worling & Curwen, 2000), that there is evidence to suggest that in some cases deviant arousal does play a role in the development and enactment of the sexual crimes committed by some juveniles.

Indeed, some adolescent offenders are driven, or at least influenced, by true sexual deviance. These youths develop a fixed pattern of unusual sexual interests and repeated sexual offenses, most clear when the victims are children many years younger than they *and* the offenders report a pattern of sexual arousal to these children. Still, even in these cases the concern is that sexual deviancy will increase as adolescents near young adulthood and patterns of sexual interest and arousal become fixed, thereby establishing the basis for lifetime deviant arousal. To this end, the National Task Force on Juvenile Sexual Offending (1993) called for understanding the role of and reducing deviant sexual arousal in juvenile sexual offending.

Although it is clear that sexual deviancy does occur in and prompts some juvenile sexual offending, especially in older adolescents, the Association for the Treatment of Sexual Abusers (2000) also noted significantly lower frequencies of extreme forms of sexual aggression and fantasy among juvenile offenders compared to adults. Accordingly, true sexual deviance—that is, patterns of sexual arousal that are driven and can only be expressed and satisfied by behaviors that are far outside of sexual expectations regarding normative and natural sexual interests—is probably not significant in the case of most sexually reactive children and juvenile sexual offending.

SUBSTANCE USE

Although described earlier as a possible motivating factor in juvenile sexual offending, there is generally little evidence to support substance abuse as a cause of or significant factor in juvenile sexual offending (Center for Sex Offender Management, 1999b, 2000; Hanson & Bussière, 1998; Righthand & Welch, 2001; Weinrott, 1996). Monahan (1995) described an illusory correlation as a supposed link between two events that are actually unrelated or weakly related. Given the current lack of supporting evidence, to consider substance use as a causative factor in the development and enactment of sexual offending behavior in juveniles qualifies as an illusory correlation at this time. Nevertheless, although the use of substances does not appear to be significantly related to juvenile sexual offending, it is important to recognize the impact that the use of alcohol and drugs may have on the juvenile sexual offender, particularly as a disinhibiting influence or when clearly used in a prior sexual offense.

TYPOLOGIES

Typologies of juvenile sexual offenses and juvenile sexual offenders can help us better understand and organize the different pathways to sexual offending taken by different children under different conditions. However, the development of such a typology is unlikely, at least in the immediate future. Far from being comprehensive, overarching, and all-inclusive, most of the existing typologies for juvenile sexual offending are of limited utility, explanatory value, and depth in construction. Typically, offense-related factors are classified by only one or a few dimensions that fail to capture the complexity of sexual offending or provide for mutually exclusive categories that clearly discriminate between particular offense characteristics or forms. In other cases, typologies are marred by an exaggerated sense of meaning in which too many aspects of the sexual offense are crammed into a typology built on only one or two dimensions. Existing typologies are largely useful only in reviewing specific (rather than global) aspects of offending.

For instance, a typology that distinguishes between adult male sexual offenders who are fixated child molesters (never developed any sexual interest in adults) and those who are regressed molesters (have adult sexual interests but periodically regress back to pedophilic behavior) is a useful description of two types of offenders. However, other than offering a basic description and a possible direction for treatment or management, the typology fails to tell us anything else about the individual at all, or about the offenses. To have utility beyond a simple description (which may not even capture the characteristics of all child molesters, even across these two dimensions), a typology must be far more complex and detailed.

On the other hand, some typologies of juvenile sexual offending have very little value at all. In the case of the well-known and often-cited *Phase typology* (O'Brien & Bera, 1986), the typology takes on far too much with far too few resources and lacks sophistication, discrimination, and even face validity. In the seven categories of *Naive Experimenter, Undersocialized Child Exploiter, Pseudo-Socialized Child Exploiter, Sexual Aggressive, Sexual Compulsive, Disturbed Impulsive,* and *Group Influenced,* the typology attempts to incorporate and describe the characteristics, history, motivation, and typical offense patterns of the offender; the situational characteristics in which offenses occur; the victim profile; and the tactics used to gain compliance. This grossly simplifies the phenomenon of JSO types, tries to explain too much in each label, and fails to provide exclusive categories. That is, juvenile sexual offenders in one category might also share characteristics with offenders in other categories or not quite fit into the category provided. Consequently, the typology lacks the power to meaningfully identify juvenile sexual offender types (if such a thing exists) or to recognize unique differences among types.

For an organizational scheme to meet the demanding tasks of both complexity *and* simplicity (even though this may seem a contradiction), as well as exhaustiveness and discrimination, and thus to meet the goal of a comprehensiveness and detailed classification system, one needs a taxonomy rather than a typology. Whereas a *typology* usually represents a series of designated labels along a continuum of sorts and is incapable of complexity, a *taxonomy* is a more complex, systematic, and comprehensive undertaking. In effect, a taxonomy is a multilayered typology with ever-deepening levels of subclassification below the originating typology, similar to an organizational flow chart. A taxonomy provides clearly and logically derived categories for classifying items that are like one another but unlike other items (which go into other categories). By creating multiple subclassifications nested below or within larger categories, it is eventually possible to create a taxonomy that adequately, meaningfully, and comprehensively categorizes all occurrences and shades of a phenomenon (in this case, juvenile sexual offending) into discrete and increasingly smaller taxa (classification compartments) that are both separate from and related to all other taxa and thus are able to account for every variation and nuance. The zoological classification system of kingdom, phylum, class, order, family, genus, and species is an example of a systematized complex and complete taxonomy, as is the Dewey decimal system for organizing books and periodicals into related and ever-smaller logically derived categories. In any discipline this is a huge task. In the study of human behavior, it is presently—and may always be—beyond our capacity.

Nevertheless, if we consider typologies useful ways to store basic information and identify basic traits and similarities, there are a number of simple ways to categorize juvenile sexual offenders, discriminating only among discrete variables rather than the whole enchilada. It may be useful, in this case, to develop different typologies to deal with offender characteristics, offender history, offender motivation, typical offense patterns and behaviors, situational characteristics or modis operandi, preferred victims, and levels of force or coercion used. If we want to go further than a simple one-level or unidimensional typology, we can find ways to begin to combine these typological categories into multidimensional and multilevel typologies.

CONCLUSION

In sum, there is no profile or set of unique identifiers that defines or distinguishes juvenile sexual offenders, and juvenile sexual offenders are not at the same developmental, cognitive, or behavioral levels in their lives as are adult offenders. Factors that influence and direct adult sexual offending are not necessarily—and in many cases are unlikely to be—at play in juvenile sexual offending. However, although there is no profile of the juvenile sexual offender, we can say with some certainty that there are features that pertain both to personal characteristics and developmental history often shared by juvenile sexual offenders. Offenders have typically experienced a level of maltreatment or abuse beyond that experienced by the general population, are likely to have developed vulnerabilities and predispositions that make them particularly sensitive and susceptible to negative and antisocial messages and environmental stimuli, live in environments that have relatively many risk factors and relatively few protective factors, and may have significant deficits in attachment and empathy, experiencing little intimacy with others and having few effective relationship-building skills.

Despite many differences in individual qualities, behaviors, and perceptions of the world, juvenile sexual offenders often

- Have poor coping skills
- Have limited internal rules for social behavior
- Possess poorly developed or primitive senses of morality
- Experience significant emotional problems
- Exercise limited self-control and act out their emotional experiences through negative or otherwise inappropriate behaviors
- Have little insight into the needs and feelings of others
- Place their own needs and feelings ahead of the needs and feelings of others

- Exhibit a poorly defined sense of personal boundaries and taboos
- Have developed strong and not easily corrected cognitive distortions about others, themselves, and the world
- Have deficits in social skills or at least lack the ability to use social skills appropriately

Finally, when it comes to overcoming internal inhibitions to antisocial behaviors, including sexual abuse, for many juvenile sexual offenders there seem to be few internal inhibitions to overcome in the first place, which makes overcoming them that much easier. This lack of internal prosocial judgment may result from lack of attachment and remorse often found among juvenile sexual offenders or, in a Freudian model, a poorly developed superego (i.e., social conscience and connectedness). Nevertheless, these characteristics, including lack of superego, are not unusual in any child or adolescent. In fact, many of these attributes and characteristics are common in young children, who are still early in the emotional evolution and development of their personalities. However, the presence of many of these factors in many juvenile perpetrators makes us suspect that the pathway to sexual offending is developmental, with its roots found in the earliest stages of childhood and fed and fueled by negative experiences throughout childhood and into adolescence, or at least an absence of adequate positive (protective) experiences.

PART II

Assessment of the Juvenile Sexual Offender

CHAPTER 6

Evaluation of the Juvenile Sexual Offender and the Assessment of Risk

As THE CORNERSTONE of both treatment and the evaluation of possible future dangerousness, assessment is an area both central and critical to the treatment of the child or adolescent sexual offender. Accordingly, it is important not to treat assessment as a cut-and-dried process that is well understood by all practitioners, universal in construction, or simply applied. It is equally important that we neither take sexual offender assessment for granted nor treat the assessment of risk as just another form of mental health evaluation. In fact, the assessment of risk is a forensic concern involving criminality and public safety as well as the future behavior, treatment, and freedom of the individual being evaluated. Given the importance of assessment, this and the following two chapters address the underlying principles, design, and application of the sexual offender assessment process, including conducting the evaluation and writing the assessment report. This chapter lays the groundwork for a detailed understanding of the process of risk assessment and the ideas and models on which assessment is built, with a focus on the similarities and differences between the two major forms of risk assessment: actuarial and clinical.

THE ASSESSMENT OF JUVENILES

The first thing to know is that there are many types of assessments, although broad and general principles can be applied to any form (or purpose) of assessment. Second, although all assessments can be said to follow the same basic rules, the assessment of children and adolescents often takes significant detours from the path followed in the assessment of adults. For instance, the locus of personal control for children and adolescents usually lies outside themselves, and they are almost always heavily involved with adult caretakers and others who make daily decisions on their behalf, provide supervision, and exercise control over their lives.

Juveniles live within and experience different family and community systems than adults and are subject to a different set of rules and obligations. Children and adolescents are also substantially different from adults in the development of their bodies, in their cognitive and personality development, in their formation of attitudes and acquisition of information, and in their emotional and behavioral maturity. Juveniles experience the world in ways that are significantly different than those of adults and are stimulated, pleased, influenced, and motivated by different things. Children and adolescents are also more experimental, with fewer fixed ideas than adults and fewer fixed personality characteristics. Their interests are still developing, and ideas, attitudes, emotions, and behaviors that may be considered outlandish, inappropriate, hostile, antisocial, or even deviant in adults may not represent any of these things in juveniles. In fact, many of these may be considered part of the normative development of older children and adolescents.

Accordingly, the assessment of juveniles focuses in part on understanding the systems within which children and adolescents live, learn, and function and on which they depend for structure, guidance, and nurturance. Assessments of juveniles take into account the still-developing nature of the child or adolescent and recognize that juveniles are far closer than adults to both positive and negative developmental influences, social learning and experimentation, and early childhood experiences. Whereas, for instance, we are unlikely to describe an adult's sexual offending as reactive to past trauma, we may describe a child or adolescent's sexual behavior in that manner.

In thinking about models of sexual offending and in assessing sexually abusive behaviors in children and adolescents, we must recognize that different intrapsychic and social mechanisms are in place than exist for adult offenders. We must also recognize that most of the work and energy spent in researching and studying sexual offending and developing tools for assessing risk for sexual dangerousness and recidivism has focused on the world of the adult sexual offender. Although we do not know that much about how to assess risk most accurately for future dangerousness in adults, we know even less about how to assess risk for sexual reoffending in juveniles. Therefore, a clear-minded and well-educated approach is required for the meaningful assessment of juvenile sexual offenders. At the same time, the words of Martin Calder (2000b) bear repeating: "There is no ideal risk assessment methods or framework. Risk assessment is a feature of both the initial and the comprehensive assessments, as risk needs to be continuously reassessed as circumstances change and/or more information becomes available" (p. 27).

THE KEY: SEXUAL OFFENDER ASSESSMENT AND THE EVALUATION OF RISK

Regardless of the specific purpose, mental health and psychosocial assessments are intended to help better understand the individuals being evaluated, including their social functioning, emotional stability, behavioral responses and control, cognitive abilities, interests and attitudes, thought processes, and mental status. Such assessments are often used to make determinations about necessary help, treatment planning, safety and risk management, and placement decisions, and in many ways "the assessment process (and ongoing reassessment) is a clinical intervention in itself" (Lundrigan, 2001, p. 196).

David Will (1999) described three broad purposes of sexual offender assessment: (a) assessment of risk, or the likelihood of ongoing dangerous behavior; (b) development of a clinical formulation on which treatment can be based and developed; and (c) assessment of the motivation of the individual to accept and engage in treatment (p. 87). Graham et al. (1997) described the purpose of assessment in slightly different terms: (a) identification of abnormal, antisocial, or deviant patterns of thoughts, feelings, and behavior; (b) identification and understanding of the learned experiences and processes that might have led to abuse-related behaviors and their maintenance; (c) identification of situational contexts in which sexual abuse has occurred; (d) evaluation of the likelihood of repeat behaviors; (e) determination of the adolescent's motivation to accept help toward more effective control of his behavior; and (f) elicitation of information necessary for the formulation of an intervention or treatment strategy (p. 54). Although the second description is more detailed, in both cases the assessment is a tool by which to learn about and describe the juvenile, including the likelihood that he will repeat the abusive behavior, to make decisions about the type of treatment to be provided, and to determine his willingness to engage in treatment.

Graham et al. (1997) wrote that "assessment of sexually abusive youth involves the same kind of history taking and information gathering process as in any other kind of comprehensive clinical assessment" (p. 52). However, risk assessment is distinct from other types of evaluation. Whereas other forms of assessment may yield a wide range of information that can be used to extrapolate or lead to larger conclusions, the risk assessment is unique because it is *specifically* and *solely* intended to assess the likelihood of future behavior. In fact, the term *risk assessment* describes the expected *outcome* of an assessment, rather than the type or form of assessment itself, or the process of assessment.

Although we want to gather as much information as we can to understand the offender, the offense, and the offense history and to shape and guide treatment decisions, Hudson and Ward (2001) noted that in addition to leading to a clinical formulation and thus informing treatment, the heart of the sexual offender assessment "is in the assessment of risk" (p. 370). Thus, although a thorough sexual offender assessment will review the antecedents to the offending behavior, the etiology of other problem behaviors, comorbidity (the existence of other mental health or behavioral pathologies), developing personality traits, strengths and weaknesses, and other factors related to the development and enactment of behaviors, it is also concerned with the risk for future *potential* behavior. In attempting to evaluate the likelihood that such an offense will occur, risk assessment involves predictions of, or the potential for, *low* risk, *moderate* risk, or *high* risk to reoffend. The outcome of such an assessment, as well as the assignment of a risk level, becomes the basis for making decisions regarding the treatment, placement, and supervision of the offender and thus is a critical part of the process of treatment and rehabilitation, and sometimes criminal or civil incarceration.

Prentky and Burgess (2000) noted that in general, forensic examiners have moved increasingly toward the idea of "risk" assessments, rather than assessments of dangerousness, in part because risk implies or suggests "the presence of a potential hazard, and the probability of occurrence of that hazard" (p. 100). Boer, Hart, Kropp, and Webster (1997) defined risk assessment as "the process of evaluating individuals to (1) characterize the risk that they will commit violence in the future, and (2) develop interventions to manage or reduce that risk" (p. 1). In short, in sexual offender assessments, what we want to know is, What is the possibility or likelihood that this juvenile will reoffend? The answer is central to many issues, from the type and intensity of treatment provided to the juvenile offender to the length and location of treatment (ranging from outpatient to residential to incarceration) and aftercare plans and community supervision. For these and other reasons that include both public safety and the care, treatment, rehabilitation, and even incarceration of the child or adolescent sexual offender, the key to treatment is the assessment. In turn, the key to the assessment is the method, approach, and design that underlies the assessment process.

RISK ASSESSMENT: THE ULTIMATE GOAL OF THE SEXUAL OFFENDER EVALUATION

A juvenile sexual offender assessment involves a process designed to

1. Understand the details and circumstances of the offending behavior
2. Understand how the offending behavior occurred and how it developed over time
3. Predict the likelihood that the offending behaviors will continue or repeat if untreated
4. Make recommendations regarding treatment

Typically, a broad sexual offender assessment is psychosexual as well as psychosocial in that it explores and examines psychosocial (psychological and social) history and development, and sexual interests and the development of sexual behaviors, and the likelihood of future sexual offending behaviors.

A risk assessment is more limited and narrowly defined, however, because its sole purpose is to assign a level of risk or dangerousness. This assignment of risk can be made in one of two ways: It can result from a broad sexual offender evaluation that examines a range of information before the examiner draws conclusions and assigns a risk level, or it can result from a more limited evaluation that examines only specific facts without taking into consideration larger issues or factors, gathering information outside of the evaluation format itself, or making judgments as to the relevance, reliability, or validity of certain information. This means that the general purpose and desired outcome of a sexual offender assessment is a determination of how dangerous an individual (who has formerly sexually offended) may be in the future and whether he is likely to offend sexually again.

Why is risk assessment the most salient and critical feature in the assessment of a juvenile sexual offender? The answer is not intended to demean the other goals of the assessment, but it highlights why the child is coming into the assessment process—and presumably treatment—in the first place. For the juvenile sexual offender, all treatment decisions are (or should be) built on the assessment of sexual behaviors and the possibility that the child will engage in sexually abusive behaviors again. If we were not concerned with ongoing or repeated sexual offending, we would not provide sexual-offender-specific treatment. In fact, the purpose of this treatment is to eliminate the likelihood that such behavior will recur. All other treatment goals, no matter how important and significant for the juvenile, are secondary to the goal of eliminating sexual offending behavior and producing a healthier and safer child or adolescent. To this end, Wood and Cellini (1999) described the prediction of risk as one of the most important decisions that can be made about a sexual offender.

RISK PREDICTION VERSUS RISK POTENTIAL

The literature on risk assessment often refers to prediction, potential, or both. Whereas *prediction* attempts to foreshadow and foretell the future, *potential* reflects the possibility or likelihood that something will occur. *Prognosis* is based on *potential* and is a form of *prediction*. Risk assessments generally make *predictions* (or prognostications), based on the *potential* for a behavior to occur, on the basis that the behavior is likely if things remain unchanged. Despite the insistence sometimes presented by the authors of risk assessment tools that risk assessments are not attempts to predict (but, rather, only to attempt to assess potential), the distinction is generally slight and somewhat semantic.

More to the point, the violence assessment literature is filled with references to the prediction of risk (e.g., Boer et al., 1997; Epps, 1997; Hanson, 2001; Hanson & Thornton, 1999; Hoge & Andrews, 1996; Monahan et al., 2001; Prentky & Burgess, 2000; Prentky & Edmunds, 1997; Quinsey, Harris, Rice, & Cormier, 1998; Wood & Cellini, 1999), supporting the view that risk assessment equals risk *prediction*.

Nevertheless, there is no certain way to determine whether a reoffense will occur, and it is only possible to assess the likelihood of reoffense based on history and information presented and collected during the course of the assessment. This is true because the recurrence of a dangerous behavior is influenced by a wide range of factors, which become mediating influences on whether a reoffense will actually occur. Accordingly, risk assessment and prognosis are measures of *potential*, rather than certainty.

THE ASSESSMENT SEQUENCE

Risk is difficult to measure because we do not really understand what critical factors and variables shape the path along which sexual reoffending may lie. Although there are many versions of risk assessment and many short cuts to the assessment of risk, a thorough process involves several distinct steps, as illustrated in Figure 6.1.

1. Information gathering
2. Assembly or organization of information into a meaningful whole
3. Analysis and interpretation of information in order to provide meaning
4. Diagnosis of condition
5. Formulation of cause, development, and action
6. Prognosis of imminent or eventual outcome if things remain the same

Where *psychosocial* assessment starts in the present, peers back in time, and explores and understands the individual through current and historical factors, *risk* assessment is intended to predict future behavior or describe the potential that certain types of behavior will reoccur at some point in the future. To this degree, psychosocial evaluation is *diagnostic,* and risk assessment is *prognostic.*

- *Interpretation* means translating data so that the information demonstrates coherence and conveys meaning.
- *Diagnosis* is a means to distinguish a problem. In medical and mental health, diagnosis involves a classification system that assigns a specific name to a defined set of symptoms that suggest a particular condition or disorder. The diagnostic process involves recognizing, identifying, and understanding the relationship between symptoms, resulting in a diag-

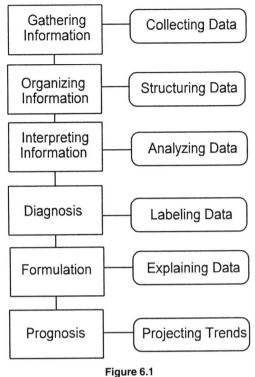

Figure 6.1
The steps, process, and purpose of assessment.

nosis. The diagnosis is in effect a shorthand term that conveys much information about the condition or disorder.

- *Formulation* represents a visualization of the diagnosis and contributing factors and reduces the history, facts, and symptoms into a brief summary that provides meaning, conjectures causes, outlines current issues, and informs prognosis.

- *Prognosis* is a judgment in advance or an attempt to forecast a future event or the possibility that a future event will occur. In medicine and mental health, prognosis is a calculated best-educated guess or prediction about the course or likely outcome of an illness if unchecked or untreated. It is also a judgment in advance of the possible or likely course of events and the chances of recovery or successful outcome.

THE BROAD ASSESSMENT OF RISK

No matter what the purpose, assessment can be a one-step process, completed with the administration of a single checklist or the application of a statistical equation, or it can be a multifaceted and multistep process that involves different forms of information gathering, assessment, and interpretation that result in a final measure, statement, or prognostication of some kind. In the one-step evaluation, information collection, organization, interpretation, formulation, and prognosis are yielded through the structure of the evaluation format itself. The multistep process is more complex, typically involving a number of different means for gathering information, and the outcome—the measure or final assessment—is the result of putting together and synthesizing data from different sources.

The same is true of the sexual offender risk assessment. It can be a one-step process, completed by administering a checklist or evaluation format, or it can be the product of a multistep process that involves different forms and facets of assessment that result in an assignation of risk level. This book advocates strongly for a broad and far-reaching process of evaluation that is built on the psychosocial assessment of the juvenile and results in the final assessment of risk and that in the process incorporates record review, clinical interviews with the juvenile, collateral interviews with other informants (e.g., parents, other caregivers, prior therapists and other mental health practitioners, teachers, social service workers, probation officers, etc.), and clinical observations and also may include other measures such as actuarial assessment (a thorough one is not currently available for juveniles), psychological testing, psychiatric evaluation, and physiological testing such as polygraph and plethysmograph examination. This is consistent with the literature on the assessment of juvenile sexual offenders, although much of this literature focuses only on the general aspects of evaluation and fails to address in significant detail the importance or methods of risk assessment in juvenile sexual offenders (see, e.g., American Academy of Child and Adolescent Psychiatry, 1999; Association for the Treatment of Sexual Abusers, 1997; Calder, 2000a; Center for Sex Offender Management, 1999b; Epps, 1997; Graham et al., 1997; Lane, 1997a; Loss & Ross, 1988; Mussack & Carich, 2001; National Task Force on Juvenile Sexual Offending, 1993; O'Connell, Leberg, & Donaldson, 1990; Perry & Orchard, 1992; Righthand & Welch, 2001; Ross & Loss, 1991; Salter, 1988; Will, 1999).

In the model described in this chapter, risk assessment, no matter how it is administered, is part of, and not separate from, the clinical assessment. In other words, the clinical assessment both subsumes the risk assessment process and thereby *produces* the assignment of risk, and is the overarching method by which actuarial and purely subjective methods can be integrated through a clinical process. This model, by which the assignment of risk is an outcome of the assessment, and not merely one part, is also described by Epps (1997), who asserts that the assessment of risk is based on and aimed at the synthesis of psychosocial, statistical, factual, and environmental information, resulting in "clinically defensible decisions" regarding treatment, placement, and other factors (pp. 37–38). In this vein, a wide-ranging clinical assessment of sexual offending behavior will not be limited to a single means for gathering or analyzing data but instead may include many assessment tools and measures and will base the assignment of risk on a number of factors.

Minimally, a broad clinical sexual offender assessment will include a psychosocial assessment *and* a risk assessment (which is actually a by-product of the psychosocial assessment), combining them to produce the JSO assessment, including both a psychosocial history and an assessment of current and future risk.

THE DELICATE NATURE OF RISK ASSESSMENT

However we conduct risk assessment, we must recognize the dangers of *false positives*, in which we assign high risk where no such risk actually exists (very damaging for the individual whom we have just declared a potential public menace), and *false negatives*, in which we assign low risk in a case where the individual is actually quite dangerous (very damaging to the public safety and to possible future victims). Both must be our concern in our choice of an assessment approach and method, as both are extremely damaging to the fabric of our society, public safety, and our treatment of individuals in the social services or juvenile or criminal justice systems. In fact, in the world of risk assessment, many clinicians and risk assessment instruments often err on the side of safety, preferring to assign *high* risk rather than *low*, effectively preferring to label the innocent guilty rather than let the guilty go free.

ACTUARIAL AND CLINICAL ASSESSMENTS

In something as delicate and potentially damaging as an assessment of future risk, we must choose a method for assessing the potential for future behavior in circumstances where we cannot truly know what an individual may or may not do. Typically, this involves making either an assignment of risk based on a broad range of information gathered and observed about the individual or an assessment of risk based on a few facts and variables believed to be statistically salient and linked to factors that are likely to result in future dangerous behavior. Although not necessarily mutually exclusive, these are two quite different methods for assigning risk, and they are most typically considered either *actuarial* or *clinical* in construction and administration. The two approaches and accompanying sets of beliefs are also the subject of a long-standing debate in the field of risk assessment.

ACTUARIAL ASSESSMENT

Risk assessments that are based on limited and predetermined facts and observations—as well as governed by set rules, computations, or algorithms and based on statistical properties—are typically known as statistical or *actu-*

arial risk assessments. Most actuarial assessments are *static* as they are based on risk factors that are historical and therefore not susceptible to change over time (as opposed to *dynamic* risk factors, which can change over time). In the case of every current actuarial assessment tool for sexual reoffense, the evaluator must be aware that these tools have been developed based on research, normative data, and beliefs about adults and not juveniles and that they are not suitable or appropriate for the assessment of juveniles. In fact, no complete actuarial tool yet exists for children or adolescents, although the Juvenile Sex Offender Assessment Protocol (J-SOAP), developed by Robert Prentky and associates (Prentky et al., 2000), is becoming an actuarial tool as the developers research and develop greater statistical and psychometric properties.

CLINICAL ASSESSMENT

By *clinical* we mean the direct interactions of the assessor or clinician with the individual, including direct contact, observations, collateral interviews and contacts, and other interactions that allow the mental health or forensic professional to form judgments and design assessment and treatment interventions based on that direct contact and direct knowledge. In this context, clinical judgment involves *direct* experience and an intuitive approach to the individual, which some would call flawed and the weakness of clinical work[1] and others would call the art of assessment and therapeutic practice. Borum, Fein, Vossekuil, & Berglund (1999) referred to the use of clinical judgment as "using our heads" (p. 324).

Unlike the actuarial assessment, a clinical assessment depends on observations and judgments made by the evaluator rather than on set rules or statistically based computations. Far less defined than actuarial assessments, a clinical assessment can be narrow in scope and dependent on limited information, facts, or observations, or it can be thorough, far ranging, and complex. The main marker of a clinical assessment is that the final assessment of risk is based on a set of clinical processes and decisions rather than on statistically based processes and rules that determine outcome.

CLINICAL ASSESSMENT VERSUS ACTUARIAL ASSESSMENT

Actuarial evaluations compute *probability* and yield a statement of future risk based on a series of invariant rules and facts that involve statistical calculation and facts usually not subject to interpretation. However, interpretation is ex-

---

[1]For example, Paul Meehl (1996) wrote, "I should like to see clinical psychology become as scientific as possible and am impatient with those who appear to revel in its irrational components" (p. 73).

actly the thing to which we are referring when we talk about clinical assessment. Clinical assessments are evaluations ultimately determined by human judgment (Litwack, 2001) but based on a gathering and interpretation of facts, assertions, and beliefs about any individual case.

However, it is common to hear and read that, when available, actuarial assessments are more accurate and more highly predictive than are unstructured (or unaided) clinical assessments. For instance, Steadman et al. (2000) stated that "actuarial predictions are almost always more accurate than *unstructured* [italics added] clinical ones" (p. 84), and Hanson and Thornton (2000) wrote that "when actuarial tools have been available, they have proved more accurate than clinical judgment" (p. 132). Indeed, Quincey et al. (1998) advocated for the complete elimination of clinical practice in assessment: "What we are advising is not the addition of actuarial methods to existing practice, but rather the complete replacement of existing practice with actuarial methods" (p. 171). Of these ideas, Litwack (2001) noted,

> It is frequently claimed, often as if it were hardly worth discussing, that actuarial assessments of dangerousness have proven to be superior to clinical assessments. However, the actual picture that emerges from the research is far more complex. And, apart from their relative merits vis-à-vis clinical assessments, far more is currently claimed regarding the utility of actuarial tools for assessing dangerousness than is merited by actual research findings. (p. 411)

Litwack (2001) asserted that there is little actual empirical support for the claim that actuarial assessments of risk are superior to clinical assessments and described empirical evidence that clinical assessment is actually more effective. Similarly, Boer et al. (1997) determined that there are "presently no well-validated actuarial scales of risk for sexual violence" (p. 3), and Melton, Petrila, Poythress, and Slobogin (1997) wrote that "the bottom line is that the research has not delivered an actuarial equation suitable for clinical application in the area of violence prediction" (p. 285). Litwack concluded, therefore, that "it is premature to substitute actuarial for clinical assessments of dangerousness" (p. 410).

In fact, despite a movement toward acceptance of the actuarial assessment for risk assessment over the use of the clinical assessment, it is nonetheless true that such assessments alone provide limited and narrow answers that are far from proven under the best of circumstances. Alone, the actuarial assessment has neither the range nor the flexibility to serve as the primary basis on which predictions of future sexual offending should rest. They may or may not be more accurate than clinical assessments but also provide a statistical approach that, depending on their bandwidth, either captures a wide range of individuals (and risks many false positives) or a narrow range (including possible false negatives). Either way, they generally cannot take into account the vagaries and changes in life, human functioning, or situation-specific responses and potentially balance statistical power, parsimony, and elegance against the uncertainty of real life, individual characteristics, and unique circumstances.

For this reason, Doren (2002) asserted that no actuarial instrument can assess true risk of reoffending because "existing actuarial instruments do not yet include enough of the relevant considerations to maximize our predictive effectiveness" (p. 113), and he concluded that reasons for clinical adjustments to actuarial assessments still exist. In part, this is because actuarial assessments are based largely on what *has* happened (static factors) and cannot be based on things that *might* happen (dynamic factors) and that may change the predicted statistical outcome.

CLINICAL BASIS OF ACTUARIAL ASSESSMENT TOOLS

In the context of the actuarial assessment, fact should serve as the objective basis for the assessment and assignation of risk level rather than interpretation, which will always have a subjective basis and can therefore be swayed. A pure actuarial assessment is based on noninterpretable facts.

In practice, this is not the case. In many instances, clinical judgment, not factual reality, is at the root of key measurements in actuarial assessment instruments. Witt (2000) commented that "even today, only a few risk assessment instruments are truly actuarial" (p. 791), and Campbell (2000) observed that most risk assessment procedures rely on clinical judgment and noted that actuarial procedures eventually fall back on clinical judgment. It is not that actuarial tools are not valuable instruments for assessment, but that they are not the objective or proven predictive tools one would expect of an actuarial assessment, and themselves are heavily dependent on clinical judgment or input.

WEAKNESSES OF ACTUARIAL ASSESSMENTS

Although extremely useful, and especially if used in conjunction with and as part of a larger and more comprehensive clinical assessment process, actuarial assessments are significantly flawed. Indeed, Boer et al. (1997) described actuarial assessments as "passive predictions of limited practical use" (p. 4).

- Although sometimes based on objective facts, in many instances actuarial assessment depends on clinical judgment or interpretation to produce pseudofacts (clinical variables that have the appearance of fact but actually have no objective or consistent existence).
- Actuarial assessments are limited in scope to facts or pseudofacts and are unable to infer or search out important data that do not fit into the structure of the assessment or do not take the form of fact or pseudofact.

- Actuarial assessments are rigid and lack the ability to provide meaning or render judgments about data.
- Actuarial assessments lack the ability to formulate and are thus able to present only a simple picture without any explanation.
- In the case of risk for sexual reoffense, actuarial assessments are not based on truly valid variables as there is no clear profile of either adult or adolescent sexual offenders or the variables that unequivocally contribute or lead to sexual offending, and this results in the selection of variables that in themselves are the product of judgment and not fact.
- The ability to determine the effectiveness and utility of an actuarial assessment is based entirely on its predictive power, which cannot be fully evaluated without adequate and meaningful recidivism studies.

WEAKNESSES OF CLINICAL ASSESSMENTS

Like so many things, the strengths of the clinical assessment are also its weaknesses. The ability to form individual judgments based on observation, interactions, record review, interviews, mental status exams, and so on also leads to the very distinct possibility of poor evaluations if administered by poorly trained or inexperienced clinicians or administered without the benefit of a clearly defined assessment process or tool. Accordingly, clinical assessments can be

- Conducted by untrained or inexperienced clinicians
- Subject to inappropriate clinician bias based on a priori expectations, uninformed or incorrect data, or clinician attitude and values
- Based on variables that are meaningless or without empirical support
- Unreliable and inconsistent when administered by different clinicians or even the same clinician over time
- Vaguely designed, unstructured, or poorly constructed
- Idiosyncratic and incapable of replication
- Incomplete or lacking in detail
- Unproven and inaccurate
- Confusing and lacking in clear formulation

Of course, clinical judgment is always flawed and never free of the possibility of error. This is a potentially significant problem because the goal in risk assessment is to avoid false negatives and false positives. This is not, however, a reason to negate clinical judgment. It *is* a reason to provide and ensure adequate training, supervision, and monitoring for clinicians and to develop tools that reduce the potential weaknesses and limitations of clinical assessments and strengthen their ability to make appropriate, well-informed, and meaningful judgment and assignations of risk. Such a tool is the empirically based, structured clinical assessment instrument (more or less, the opposite of unaided clinical judgment), described in Chapter 7.

THE ADVANTAGES OF THE CLINICAL ASSESSMENT

Despite some objections in the current literature, the approach taken in this book is that in the assessment of juvenile sexual offenders a broad clinical assessment is preferred over other methods because it gathers the most data on which to base opinion and prognosis and may one day include an actuarial assessment if one becomes available. Whereas actuarial assessments are far more limited in their ability to include clinical data in the actual assessment, clinical evaluations have the option of including actuarial and other assessment data.

Under any circumstances, no actuarial assessments are currently available for children and adolescents (although, as mentioned, the J-SOAP is striving to fill this need). However, even if such an instrument becomes available, there is considerable debate about the efficacy of statistical risk assessments, as well as questions about whether they are actually any more accurate than clinical risk assessments, as mentioned. Indeed, Hart (1998) described reliance on actuarial decision making as professionally unacceptable (p. 126), and Monahan et al. (2001) wrote that actuarial assessments are "best viewed as . . . tools that support, rather than replace, the exercise of clinical judgment" (p. 134). They asserted that "this reliance on clinical judgment—aided by an empirical understanding of risk factors for violence and its interactions—reflects, and in our view, should reflect, the standard of care at this juncture in the field's development" (pp. 134–135).

Borum et al. (1999) described a conceptual shift away from an actuarial model in which risk is seen as dispositional (residing within the individual), static (unchanging), and dichotomous (present or not present) to a new risk assessment model in which risk is seen as contextual (dependent on situations and circumstances), dynamic (changeable), and continuous (varying along a continuum of probability). Given its flexibility and its ability to expand out to embrace all relevant data and assessment tools, the clinical assessment is the preferred way to combine both the statistical (actuarial) world and the experienced (clinical) world.

COMPREHENSIVE EVALUATIONS

Litwack (2001) asserted that good clinical practice will entail, and even require, the results of appropriate actuarial assessments and other relevant data and asserted that clinicians should take actuarial estimates of risk into account when relevant and meaningful statistical data are available. Similarly,

Prentky and Burgess (2000) wrote that "treatment cannot, or at least should not, proceed without the benefit of an informed, comprehensive sex offender specific assessment" (p. 97), which according to them includes a series of clinical assessments, among them a psychosocial history and actuarial assessment (where one exists). The clinical interview, they asserted, is a "critical component of all assessments" (p. 75).

Advocating also for inclusive evaluations, Hanson (1997, 2000) wrote that actuarial assessment tools alone are effective screening measures but have limited overall utility, and he did not recommend their use in isolation. Regarding static actuarial assessments, Hanson and Thornton (2000) noted that they cannot be used to select treatment targets, measure change, evaluate treatment benefit, or predict when or under what circumstances sexual offenders are likely to recidivate, asserting also that a multistep assessment of risk takes into account "the complexity of the real situations in which risk assessments take place" (1999, p. 17). In a similar vein, Hudson and Ward (2001) wrote that "assessment ought to reflect etiology, at least in the sense of the proximal causes for offending behavior" (p. 365).

THE IMPORTANCE OF THE BASE RATE

Without sufficient knowledge about the behavior under assessment, the population that engages in the behavior, the variables that influence the behavior, and a high incidence of the behavior (the *base rate*, or the rate of measured and known frequency of a behavior), it can be difficult to draw valid or reliable conclusions about risk. For this reason, Borum et al. (1999) described the impossibility of high rates of accuracy in statistical assessment when the base rate is low and noted that even if actuarial methods are superior to clinical evaluation, such methods can be applied only when "appropriate equations exist, have been adequately validated, and are applicable to the question and population at issue" (p. 326). Adequate known base rates for sexual reoffenses barely exist for adults and do not exist for adolescents.

Nevertheless, base rates are as important to clinicians in determining risk as they are to statisticians. To make an assessment of risk for reoffense without being familiar with and understanding the rate at which sexual offenders reoffend is ill advised and serves only to weaken and make meaningless the assessment process and assignment of risk. For instance, a base rate of 95% (i.e., 95% of sexual offenders reoffend) will lead to significantly different assessments of risk than would a base rate of 5%. In fact, researchers generally agree that the recidivism rate for treated juvenile sexual offenders is somewhere between 7% and 13% (see Chapter 11), which at least gives an approximate base rate on which to understand and assess risk.

THE ULTIMATE MEASURE OF RISK ASSESSMENT: RECIDIVISM

Aside from its importance in establishing a base rate, Prentky and Burgess (2000) described recidivism as "the centerpiece for the evaluation of treatment effectiveness" (p. 229). Equally, the final arbiter of any assessment of risk is its success in actually predicting risk. In any individual assessment, there is no way to judge the accuracy of the evaluation without knowing whether the individual reoffended over time. As the clinical assessment is always conducted on an individual-by-individual basis, this means that assessment of the assessment is also individualized: That is, did the assessment turn out to be correct for the individual assessed? For the actuarial assessment, accuracy is judged not by the accuracy of individual assessments but by the recidivism rate of the pool of assessed individuals as a whole. In this case, the questions are, What percentage of the individuals assessed turned out to behave as predicted by the actuarial assessment, and is this percentage high enough to support or validate the actuarial assessment tool as an accurate and reliable measure?

However, in either case, recidivism studies face several obvious problems:

- The length of the study is important because recidivism rates will vary based on the length of the study period during which recidivism is tracked, and recidivism rates will increase with the length of the follow-up period (Hanson & Bussière, 1998). Should offenders be tracked for 1 year, 5 years, 10 years, or the remainder of their lives?
- The definition of recidivism is also significant. Recidivism rates will be lower for narrow definitions of relapse than for broad definitions (Hanson & Bussière, 1998).
- The hidden quality of sexual offending makes any study of recidivism difficult because an individual may have relapsed and no one, except the offender and victims, may be aware of the re-engagement in sexual offending. Accordingly, the study may not reveal the actual number of recidivists but depends only on those relapses that become public through one means or another.
- Finally, and of great significance in the assessment of juvenile sexual offenders, is the fact that there are few studies of recidivism in juvenile offenders. For instance, in the meta-analysis conducted by Karl Hanson and Monique Bussière (1998), of the 61 included studies, encompassing 28,972 sexual offenders, only six studies followed adolescents, and three more examined both adolescents and adults. Noting this lack of data, James Worling and Tracey Curwen (2001) reported that most research regarding the prediction of sexual offense recidivism has been based on adult offenders. Even in the development of the J-SOAP, the only actuarial-like assessment tool for adolescent offenders, Prentky et al.

(2000) cautioned that their research was conducted on a very small sample (96) of adolescent offenders, among whom only three adolescents actually recidivated sexually (p. 82), although work is currently underway on an additional sample of 153 adolescents (Prentky, R. A. personal communication, March, 2002).

The "surprisingly sparse" (Epps, 1997, p. 35) research on recidivism among juvenile sexual offenders and the low known base rate for adolescent sexual recidivism significantly limit the ability to develop and judge actuarial assessments. This is less of an issue in the development of clinical risk assessment instruments because they do not depend on base rates (nevertheless, meaningful clinical assessment requires knowledge of the base rate), but the largely unaddressed issue of recidivism is still a significant factor in evaluating the efficacy (or accuracy) of the clinical assessment over time. Not only do we not know enough about the factors involved in juvenile sexual offending in the first place (Hunter & Lexier, 1998), but we also know little about sexual recidivism in youthful offenders, let alone who will recidivate and why. This makes it difficult to make risk assessment an exact science and to assess the validity and reliability of risk assessment tools, the risk assessment process, or individual assessments of risk.

Aside from these problems, the accuracy of any given assessment at the time it was administered cannot necessarily be proved or disproved, even by recidivism base rates. In fact, at the time of the assessment, the risk may indeed have been high but the course of treatment that followed, the course of external supervision, or the course of life itself may have deterred or changed the course of the potential offending behavior. The individual may not ever reoffend, even though the designation of high risk given at the assessment was appropriate *at the time* (reflecting the contextual, dynamic, and continuous nature of behavior). The converse is also true. An assessment of low risk may be appropriate and most relevant at the time of the assessment even though the individual may later reoffend. This illustrates that risk assessment assesses *potential*, not certainty. It also illustrates the difficulty of measuring the effectiveness of a risk assessment tool, whether actuarial or clinical. Aside from our lack of knowledge about risk factors, as well as the true and complete history of individuals, our inability to unerringly predict future behavior is due also in large part to the presence and highly active role and nature of dynamic individual and life circumstances, which constantly shift and veer the direction of the future.

CONCLUSION: THE NECESSITY OF CLINICAL JUDGMENT

The paucity of adolescent recidivism studies, and even our lack of knowledge about the true (genuinely valid) variables and factors that result in sexual offending, makes it difficult meaningfully to create or judge tools for risk as-sessment. In fact, no system of assessment is foolproof, and each method of risk assessment has strengths and weaknesses (Wood & Cellini, 1999). This is especially true for actuarial assessments, and even advocates of the actuarial system recognize that no single actuarial tool can be certain to include all fac-tors that contribute to risk or even to be measuring the right (valid) variables. The role of clinical intervention and judgment, then, becomes central in the as-sessment of juvenile (and perhaps adult) sexual offenders, as it allows us to use our training and experience as the guiding principle that assesses the in-dividual and determines judgment, ideally shaped by a structured process and guided by the research and empirical evidence.

In summary, the evaluation of the juvenile sexual offender and the assess-ment of risk for sexually reoffending are intertwined. It is only by examining and coming to understand the psychosocial history of the individual (includ-ing cognitive beliefs and attitudes, behavioral patterns, emotional stability, context and environment, and other factors related to personal development and social functioning) and being guided by an examination and under-standing of the presence of risk factors in the individual (factors that are be-lieved to be connected to risk for sexually abusive behavior) that the assess-ment of risk can be most meaningfully made. This is the process by which assessed risk emerges from the assessment of the whole individual and is combined with an assessment of risk factors is a decidedly clinical process.

CHAPTER 7

The Purpose and Construction of the Structured Clinical Assessment Tool

BOER ET AL. (1997) commented that actuarial assessments are passive tools that disengage professionals from the evaluation process because they require, by design, minimal professional intervention and judgment. On the other hand, one essential hallmark of clinical work is that it places the practitioner in direct contact with the subject to be assessed. This method has both strengths and weaknesses, but the goals of both efficacy (the ability to prove effective) and efficiency (the ability to complete the job with the least wasted energy) demand that we develop the strengths and work toward eliminating the weaknesses. In clinical assessment, one way to do this is to build the evaluation process and method on sound underlying theory and shape the evaluation through a defined structure.

This chapter explores and outlines the principles behind instruments that define, guide, and add both consistency (reliability) and empirical relevance (validity) to the clinical assessment of risk in the juvenile sexual offender.

THE CLINICAL ASSESSMENT OF THE JUVENILE SEXUAL OFFENDER

As described in Chapter 6, the clinical evaluation is a broad method used to gather and assess information through the process of face-to-face interviewing, observation, and live interaction. This process typically involves the psychosocial assessment, which is designed to explore and understand critical factors, events, and points in the physical, psychological, and social development of the individual, as well as the social and contextual issues and systems in which the individual has lived and grown, and which shape and maintain behavior.

When the psychosocial assessment format is applied to a specific problem or pathology, it takes on a special shape because it is designed to address the issue of particular concern, such as substance abuse, fire setting, or delinquency. In the case of the juvenile sexual offender, the psychosocial assessment takes on a larger and even farther reaching role, including other important features and exploring areas of special interest and concern. Of central importance, the psycho*sexual* format is added to the basic evaluation format, and the psychosocial assessment now pays special attention to the development of sexual interests and the nature and enactment of sexual behaviors, including sexual offending. In addition, as described in Chapter 6, a comprehensive clinical assessment of juvenile sexual offending includes an assessment of risk, or the possibility that the juvenile will engage in future acts of sexual offending. In this case, the psychosocial assessment basic to any evaluation of mental or behavioral health is expanded to become a clinical assessment of sexual offending, minimally including exploration, explanation, and assessment of risk.

The clinical assessment may also include a series of tools designed to explore and yield information about many facets of the individual's personality, functioning, thinking, attitudes, and propensities. Multiple aspects of the individual's life are examined and included in the development of a clinical formulation (a perspective that helps summarize and explain the individual and his or her behavior), leading to the final outcome of the assessment. In the case of sexual-offender-specific assessment, this outcome also provides an assessment of risk, as well as potentially providing recommendations about treatment, placement, and other important decisions concerning the juvenile sexual offender. As depicted in Figure 7.1, there are many types of assessments and assessment tools, both clinical and nonclinical, all of which can be used in the sexual offender assessment, subsumed under and incorporated into the clinical assessment of risk.

THE CLINICAL ASSESSMENT TOOL

An assessment instrument is a designed format, or tool, created to provide structure, definition, clear process, and consistency to an operation or set of operations. An actuarial assessment is always guided by such an instrument, following a clear set of questions and rules, and this is one its strengths. In contrast, clinical assessment is not necessarily guided or shaped by any structure, rules, or particular method, and this is one of the major weaknesses of the clinical evaluation.

However, clinical assessments need not be unstructured or loosely defined but can be carefully constructed to ensure that the underlying basis for the evaluation is founded in both theory and empirical practice and that it pro-

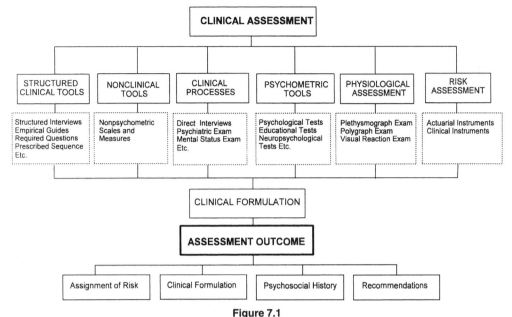

Figure 7.1
The inclusive nature and process of the clinical assessment.

vides consistency and direction for the assessment. To this end, the application of a formal clinical assessment tool provides organization, structure, and definition and ensures consistency to the clinical process. The Structured Clinical Interview for *DSM-IV-TR* Axis I Disorders (SCID; First, Spitzer, Gibbon, & Williams, 1997) is an example of a tool used to guide clinical judgment and define and sequence a semistructured interview that results in a psychiatric (*DSM*-based) diagnosis. The SCID itself does not define or determine the diagnosis but leads and informs the clinician, ensuring that a consistent path is followed as diagnoses are considered and rendered. This is one example of a guided clinical instrument used to aid judgment without replacing it. Unlike actuarial assessment, which triggers an algorithm that arithmetically leads to a statistical assignment of risk, in clinical risk assessment an instrument used to guide a clinical process invokes a series of questions to be explored and answered by the clinician. This in turn leads to a clinical assessment of risk. Here, Doren (2002) noted that one of the strengths of the structured and empirically guided approach to risk assessment is that "evaluators can give weight to the different risk considerations based on the case dynamics" (p. 108).

UNSTRUCTURED AND STRUCTURED CLINICAL ASSESSMENTS

Practitioners in the medical and mental health professions depend on clinical judgment and recognize that the future may be *shadowed* by the past, but not foretold. That is, the individual who comes into the emergency room feeling depressed and with suicidal ideation is clearly at risk but may or may not be at high risk. Our clinical assessment, based on both fact *and* presentation, will determine our best guess—our prognosis—about the potential for suicidality. Here is where the cutting line can be found between plain clinical judgment (or *unstructured* clinical assessment) and structured or empirically based clinical assessments.

The determination that an individual may commit suicide within the immediate future is based not on expressed suicidal ideation alone but on a series of factors that include both historical facts (e.g., past attempts), empirically based beliefs about suicidality (the factors that are likely to predict suicide attempts and the factors that are likely to offset or reduce the likelihood of a suicide attempt), and clinical judgment based on experience (the clinician's assessment of the individual's current presentation, taking into account affect, cognition, thinking processes, and behaviors, as well as the circumstances surrounding this individual's life at that moment and in the imminent future—i.e., dynamic case factors). Out of this develops a prognosis for low, moderate, or high risk for suicide in the imminent future.

An unstructured version of this process allows the clinician to determine what questions to ask and in what order and depends entirely on the clinician's experience and ability to conduct an adequate, meaningful, and well-informed assessment. Such a process, however, requires highly trained clinicians. In addition, even with a high level of training and expertise, we cannot be certain of consistency between clinicians (interrater reliability) or even that the same clinician will do different assessments over time (test-retest reliability). On the other hand, a highly structured version of an assessment of suicidality, while neither negating nor discounting experience, nevertheless provides a defined, guided, and even delimited protocol that determines the information to be gathered, how questions are to be asked, and potentially even the sequencing of questions. It may also provide a way to rate or score answers, thus yielding a result that is relatively standard regardless of who conducts the assessment.

In fact, most of the criticism of clinical risk assessments seems to be directed toward unstructured assessment, and Doren (2002) asserted that the empirically guided approach to clinical assessment is a more accurate and reliable method of assessing risk. Doren (2001) also reported that unaided clinical judgment results in more assessments of high risk for sexual reoffending than does actuarial-based assessments, and this overestimate is one of the common criticisms of unstructured assessment. In their study of recidivism among juvenile sexual offenders, Schram et al. (1991) found that without the benefit of a structured evaluation process, risk for sexual reoffense was significantly overestimated by treatment staff, thus creating false positives.

CLINICAL EVALUATION AND THE BASE RATE

Regarding clinical process, Meehl (1996) considered it important to express clinical "intuition" as specifically as possible, thus validating the basis of the clinical response. He suggested that the experienced clinician, in fact, forms opinions and renders decisions based on empirically known risk factors, compares these to expected frequencies among a similar population, and makes decisions built on the base rate, thus acting as an actuarian. Meehl argued that creating and using an actuarial table is simply an advancement and more accurate version of this system.

However, this point drives home the importance of knowing the base rates for the behavior being assessed. Without knowing the frequency at which the predicted behavior actually occurs in any given population and having the benefit of knowing how this individual compares to other individuals who present with similar symptoms and situations, it is impossible to make anything other than a purely individualized, or unstructured, assessment. In part, such deficits in knowledge or clinical awareness result in false positives and false negatives.

FROM UNSTRUCTURED TO STRUCTURED ASSESSMENT

Wood and Cellini (1999) described four methods for assessing risk: (a) *professional judgment*, which is unstructured and unguided by anything other than the clinician's own experience and beliefs, and which is referred to elsewhere as subjective or impressionistic (Grove & Meehl, 1996); (b) *anchored and guided judgment* shaped by and anchored to a set of empirically derived factors believed to be associated with risk; (c) *actuarial assessment*, or an arithmetic and statistical process of assigning risk without human judgment (also referred to by Grove & Meehl as mechanical and algorithmic); and (d) *adjusted actuarial assessment*, or the recalculation of the actuarial assessment of risk through the intervention of clinical judgment.[1]

Campbell (2000) described the anchored and guided empirical assessment, or the guided clinical risk assessment, as an evaluation based on em-

---

[1] There is some dispute in the field about whether actuarial assessments can, or should, be adjusted. Some feel that the data should not be tampered with under any circumstances. Others believe that the data not only can be adjusted by clinical judgment but *should* be under certain circumstances. For instance, in the rare case in which factual information that is available outside of the assessment schema clearly changes the statistically predicted outcome, the assessment must be adjusted to reflect more accurate and certain information. One example is the broken-leg scenario that could not be known in advance or predicted by the statistical assessment, thus rendering an otherwise statistically certain outcome impossible. On this subject, Doren (2002) offered some very clear perspectives and ideas about when and how to make clinical adjustments to actuarial assessments.

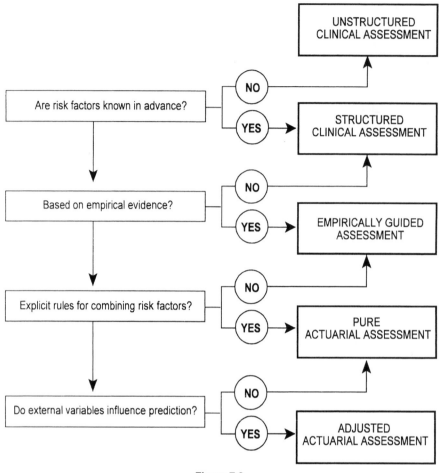

Figure 7.2

Basic factors and rules relevant to the possible level and form of assessment. From Hanson (2002).

pirically validated risk factors "arriving at recidivism estimates based on an offender's status on these factors" (p. 120).

Hanson (2000) described empirically guided clinical judgment in similar terms, with each offender rated on a list of established risk factors followed by the evaluator's formulating "an overall assessment of risk based on the observed combination of risk factors" (p. 5), and he presented risk assessment models that range from unstructured clinical assessment to pure and clinically adjusted actuarial predictions (Hanson, 2001, 2002). Figure 7.2 shows Hanson's model along with rules for determining which level or form of assessment is available or most appropriate.

STRUCTURED, EMPIRICALLY BASED CLINICAL ASSESSMENTS

When the clinical assessment is clearly organized and shaped by a defined guide, it becomes a structured (or guided or aided) assessment and assumes the same format as every other clinical assessment organized by the guide. Thus, the structured assessment tool works to ensure consistency across assessments. When the structure contains not just a format for the assessment but also specific questions built on underlying principles relevant to the assessment, the tool takes on the additional quality of being theory driven. When those same questions are based (or anchored) on more strongly developed and empirically validated underlying principles, the instrument guiding the assessment becomes a *structured, empirically based assessment tool,* as illustrated in Figure 7.3.

Due to the format provided by the tool and the questions that must be answered, a structured and empirically based assessment tool requires that specific data be gathered in every assessment and also may specify that certain other data are *not* included, thus ensuring that the assessment conforms to an underlying empirical model. Such a tool can also include a specific sequence of algorithmic questions that allow the clinical process to branch in different directions based on the way that certain questions are answered, and even a rating or scoring system that directly affects and determines the outcome of the assessment. Minimally, use of a tool like this ensures consistency and builds the assessment on empirically derived principles believed to be important to the assessment, thus moving the tool closer to being both reliable and valid.

In using a structured, empirically based tool, the specific information gathered in the assessment process and the manner in which the outcome is formulated is defined by the structure of the tool. On the other hand, the manner in which the information is gathered, how it is interpreted, and the formulation derived are determined strictly by the clinician (based on the rules of the assessment instrument). Thus, there remains a balance between what is gathered (the tool determines that), how it is gathered, and how it is interpreted

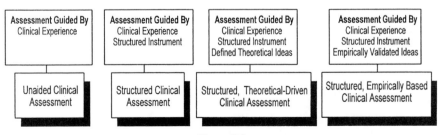

Figure 7.3
From unaided clinical judgment to structured, empirically based assessment.

(both determined by the clinician). Examples of structured tools currently used in mental health examinations include the SCID mentioned earlier and the Children's Interview for Psychiatric Syndromes (Weller, Weller, Fristad, & Rooney, 1999), both structured and empirically based instruments used to aid, guide, and shape the clinical process, but not intended to replace it.

BUILDING A STRUCTURED CLINICAL TOOL

Clinical assessment instruments that are both structured and empirically based result in a well-defined and highly structured tool built on profession-ally accepted and empirically based principles and variables. The structured clinical tool modeled in Figure 7.4, built to shape and guide the assessment procedure and its outcomes, produces a meaningful, understandable, and comprehensive assessment of risk built on an in vivo (clinical) assessment and understanding of the individual, as well as factors and variables supported in the empirical and research literature. Despite its lack of statistical certainty, such a tool has face validity—that is, because it is built on empirically sound principles, the risk factors incorporated in it have the appearance of measur-ing the right variables, rather than variables that are irrelevant to the assess-ment of risk.

Without underestimating the skills, knowledge, effort, and energy re-quired to create a meaningful and useful clinical assessment tool, it is impor-tant to note that no matter how much the tool is based on research and the lit-erature, it is *not* a psychometric tool (i.e., a psychological test instrument statistically designed and tested and having proven statistical validity). Ac-cordingly, it does not require the energy, time, and resources that go into the research, development, testing, validation, and analysis required for the cre-ation of an actuarial (or actuarial-like) tool. Although guided and shaped by the literature and empirically validated principles, clinical assessment tools need not have any statistical properties whatsoever and are generally not psy-chometric tools.

In fact, to a large degree, a clinical assessment tool (whether empirically based or not) is in most cases a complex, organized, and well-informed check-list designed to ensure that the clinical assessment follows a particular model, incorporates specific data, and pursues and answers particular questions. Il-lustrating this point, Boer et al. (1997) referred to the Sexual Violence Risk–20 (SVR-20) checklist as "an assessment method or procedure, rather than a test or scale" (p. 25), or a forensic assessment instrument described by Webster, Douglas, Eaves, and Hart (1997) as an aide-mémoire. Similarly, Borum, Bartel, and Forth (2002) described the use of tools for structured professional judg-ment or guided clinical assessment as a method for conducting a systematic risk assessment by referring to a checklist of factors that have a demonstrated

---

Strengths of the Structured, Empirically Based Assessment Tool

- Face Valid
- Empirically Based
- Responsive to and Informed by Professional Literature
- Flexible and Adaptive
- Structured, Organized, and Well Defined
- Focused and Directive
- Consistent and Reliable Process
- Clear Standards and Procedures for Practice
- Uniform Process for Outcome
- Outcome Based on Formulation
- Built on Formulation and Clinical Interpretation
- Multifaceted
- Multiple Sources of Data
- Capable of Replication
- *In Vivo*

Figure 7.4
A model combining the strengths of actuarial- and clinical-based assessments.

relationship to recidivism, based on the literature. The structured, empirically based clinical assessment, then, is a synthetic instrument derived from the research and literature, incorporating ideas believed to be important and valid into a formal, organized, and coherent instrument for use in a defined and organized assessment.

The lack of psychometric properties and statistical rigor are weaknesses of a clinical tool and may limit the willingness of others in the field to use the instrument, as well as limiting its use in research and as expert evidence in criminal or civil proceedings. A poorly developed tool may also (and probably will) fail to do the job it sets out to accomplish (i.e., the assessment of juvenile sexual offenders) and may even cause potential harm and lead to false positives or false negatives. Furthermore, as a derived tool, rather than the result of original research, a clinical instrument cannot prove its point by demonstrating statistics that support its reliability, validity, or efficacy over time. This is not to say that a structured, empirically based clinical assessment tool cannot become a psychometric tool over time, however, or undergo later transformation into a statistical instrument.

That being said, building a useful and meaningful structured clinical tool requires a significant understanding of the mechanics of such tools, as well as a commitment to understanding the research, clinical literature, and empirical factors that must be incorporated into the instrument.

CONSTRUCTION OF THE TOOL

The structured clinical instrument is both an aid to the assessment process and a reflection of that process. The instrument outlined in Figure 7.5 helps structure and define what is included in the assessment process and ensures that the outcome will be based on a consistent and uniform methodology. In addition, the empirical tool ensures that the assessment is built on professionally and empirically valid ideas and data.

Nevertheless, there are two continua along which the structured tool can lie. It can rest anywhere along a continuum that runs from highly empirical and research based at one end to an extreme where the tool is low in empirical validity, based loosely on empirical ideas, and without a great deal of proven or tested validity at the other end. Similarly, the tool can rest somewhere between the two extremes of high structure and low structure. A highly structured tool may create structure for virtually every aspect of the assessment process by assigning scores to data, sequencing the order in which the assessment is administered, rigidly defining the questions asked, and so on.

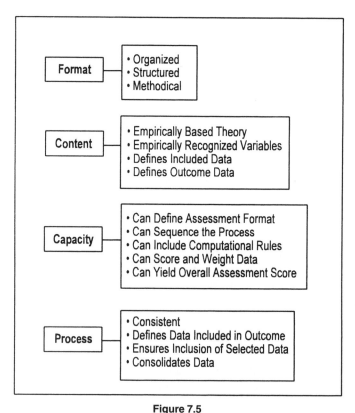

Figure 7.5
Outline and strengths of a structured, empirically based clinical assessment instrument.

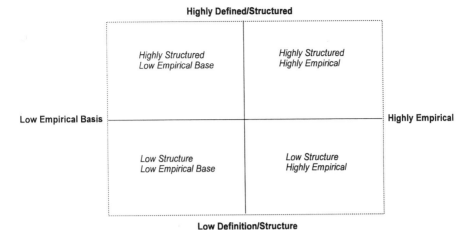

Figure 7.6
Continua of structure and empiricism among clinical instruments.

At the other end of this continuum, a low-structure tool provides only an out-line and generally organizes the assessment without requiring rigid compliance. When the two continua are combined, they form a matrix with four cells, each of which identifies a type of structured assessment tool, as illustrated in Figure 7.6.

MEASURING RISK FOR REOFFENDING VERSUS RISK FOR OFFENDING

Although it is not clear whether it is possible to effectively and accurately measure the risk for sexually assaultive behavior in an individual who has never offended, it is far easier to measure the risk in an individual who has *already* offended. Consequently, risk assessments are almost always based on static (historical) factors. These are behaviors and events that have already oc-curred in the life of an individual and that represent a major element in the assessment of risk. It is not that an individual who has never offended cannot be assessed for the possibility of a future offense, but more that history is an important precursor to future behavior. Accordingly, without a history of of-fending, the basis for predicting a future offense is minimal. We can make ed-ucated guesses, and the more we know about human nature (or psychology), the individual we are assessing, and the events in that individual's life, in-cluding past behaviors and events, the more likely we are to be able to make an accurate calculated guess; in medicine and mental health, educated guesses like this are called professional judgment or prognostication.

Thus, risk assessments of juvenile sexual offenders measure the risk for a reoffense, and not a first-time offense. In cases where we are trying to assess the potential for violence to self or others in individuals with no history of violence, it is more difficult to read into past and current behaviors, ideas, attitudes, and events in order to determine the possibility of future injury to others or self.[2] However, dangerous behaviors are more likely to occur in individuals who already have indicators in their lives of dangerous thoughts or ideas.

VALIDITY: MEASURING THE RIGHT THINGS

What are the right things to look for in a risk assessment? In the actuarial assessment, we must condense the assessment, through statistical procedures, to the relatively few variables that we think, when combined, most predict risk of dangerousness. In fact, Boer et al. (1997) considered this to be one of the weaknesses of the actuarial assessment because such a process ignores "factors that may be important but idiosyncratic to the case at hand," focusing on largely stable and static variables and excluding factors that are "entirely logical but of unknown validity" (pp. 4–5).

Aside from the issue of imposing potentially artificial and narrow limitations on the number of variables included in assessments, the level of significance assigned to any given variable is questionable because we do not really know the nature of the critical, or "correct," factors in assessing future risk, or even past sexualized behaviors. In fact, although many elements have been identified as important and significant—and sometimes contributory—factors in the development of sexual offending behaviors, there is no clarity or certainty. For instance, juvenile sexual offenders who also engage in a range of other conduct disordered and oppositional behaviors do *not* appear to be significantly different from juvenile delinquents or other conduct disordered adolescents who do not engage in sexual offending behavior (Righthand & Welch, 2001).

In statistical research, validity refers to the idea that the particular measure being studied and assessed is related to the concept that is being studied. For instance, although weight displayed on a weight scale is a valid measurement of whether an individual has gained (or lost) weight, it is not a valid measure of whether that person has been eating too much chocolate or not enough vegetables. If we study the wrong variables, we risk making significant errors in assessment, correlation, and causation. Accordingly, it is important to ensure, as best as we can, that the factors we examine have at least face validity—that is, they appear to be related to sexual offending behaviors.

---

[2] For instance, it is critical to be able to predict school violence prior to any occurrence in any individual student, and some have turned to the threat assessment model developed by the U.S. Secret Service to address risks of such targeted but otherwise unexpected violence (Borum et al., 1999; McCann, 2002: Reddy et al., 2001).

Hanson and Bussière's (1998) study shed some light on factors related to sexual offending and rates of recidivism and provided the basis for selecting some face-valid variables on which to build assessment tools. The study also illustrated that some actuarial and clinical assessment tools base their assessment of risk on factors that have *no* demonstrable validity.

SELECTING RISK FACTORS

To ascertain the right factors in assessing risk of sexual reoffending, we can conduct research that informs us about the sort of factors that emerge with frequency and relative certainty in individuals who sexually offend and about the base rate of those who actually reoffend. In an ideal research world, we can then make statistical inferences about key factors—or the factors that are most valid in measuring sexual offending—and develop a valid tool for predictive analysis. However, given the absence of certainty about risk factors and conditions that give rise to sexual reoffenses, an empirically based clinical assessment tool must be built on those factors that are the *most* represented in the literature, with the most empirical support and the most face validity in clinical experience. The literature on juvenile sexual offending is full of risk factors believed to be associated with or responsible for juvenile sexual offending or important to note in assessing the offender. The list presented in Figure 7.7, which consolidates many of the variables presented, contains 136 factors, many of which are interchangeable or approach the same general idea from a different perspective, and many of which are not supported at all in empirical research as verifiably related to risk assessment.

In fact, there are still more variables related to juvenile sexual offending identified in the literature, many of which are poorly defined and others of which have little validity. Bearing in mind the vast quantity of ideas out there, a primary task in developing a clinical risk assessment tool is deciding which factors to include in assessment.

UNDERSTANDING RISK FACTORS: STATIC AND DYNAMIC

Historical behaviors and experiences are *static* risk factors because they have previously occurred and will remain unaltered over time. *Dynamic* risk factors are those associated with current behaviors, thoughts, feelings, attitudes, interactions, and relationships toward which treatment is generally directed.

Static factors, such as age and offense history, predict recidivism but are immutable to outside influences; in the absence of new information, static factors remain fixed. In contrast, dynamic risk factors can and often will change over time. An important characteristic of dynamic risk factors is that *reductions* in such factors are associated with *reduced* recidivism. For this reason, dynamic factors are sometimes referred to as *criminogenic* needs because

Affect states before, during, and after the offense
Alcohol abuse
Arrests prior to age 16
Attitude toward victim
Behaviors before, during, and after the offense
Characteristics of the victim that attracted the offender
Cognitive problems
Criminal arrests, convictions, and incarceration
Degree of accepted responsibility
Denial
Deviant sexual arousal and interests
Duration of sex offense history
Evidence of empathy, remorse, and guilt
Evidence of support systems in the community
Family environment
Frequency and duration of offense
History of predatory behavior
Honesty and self-initiated disclosure
Insight into moral correctness of offending behavior
Internal motivation for change
Level of aggression
Medical history
Multiple types of offenses: sexual and nonsexual
Nonoffending sexual history and past victimization
Offense characteristics other than sexual aggression
Past trauma
Planning
Preferred victim
Prior sexual experiences
Psychiatric problems
Quality of peer relationships
Remorse (quality of)
School stability
School behavior problems
School suspensions or expulsions
Sexual/aggressive history
Sexual history
Social attachments
Social development
Social skills deficits
Stability of current living situation
Support systems
Treatment history
Understanding of sexual assault cycle/relapse prevention
Victim characteristics
World view and perspective

Age difference between abuser and victim
Anger management
Attachment bonds
Attitudes
Behaviors before, during, and after the offense
Caregiver stability
Cognitive distortions
Cooperation with evaluation process
Cultural and ethnic background
Degree of aggression/violence in offense
Depression and suicidal ideation
Documented offenses
Educational history
Evidence of poor anger management
External motivation for treatment
Family relationships and structure
Guilt
History of predatory behavior
Hypermasculinity
Intellectual capacity
Internal motivation for treatment
Level of force used in sexual assaults
Medical/neurological issues
Nature and extent of the offending behavior
Number of sex offenses
Other exploitive or addictive behaviors
Past victimization
Power and control
Premeditation or impulsivity
Progressive aspects of sexual offenses
Psychopathology
Relationship between abuser and victim
Response to confrontation
School suspensions or expulsions
School/employment stability
Self-concept
Sexual arousal preference
Sexual history and adjustment
Social competence
Social learning
Social support systems
Stability of living conditions
Temperament
Understanding of consequences of behavior
Verbal interchange with the victim
Violence

Age of victim
Antisocial behavior
Attempts to avoid detection
Behavioral problems
Characteristics of the sexual offense
Cognitive limitations
Coping ability
Current degree of access to victims
Degree of remorse and regret
Developmental history
Drug abuse
Empathy
Evidence of sexual preoccupation
Family background
Family system functioning
History of conduct disorder
Honesty and forthrightness
Impulsivity
Intent and motivation
Length/progression of sexual aggression
Locus of control: internal or external
Mental status
Nondeviant sexual history
Number of victims
Parental alcohol abuse
Peer relationships
Precipitating factors to offense
Prior charged sex offenses
Psychiatric history
Psychosocial history
Relationships
Risk factors/triggers
School achievement
School history
Self-expression and anger management
Sexual arousal
Sexually abusive behaviors
Social competencies
Social relationships
Specifics of offenses
Stability of school
Trauma history
Understanding of effects of the victim
Victim access
Vocational stability

Figure 7.7

A selection of 136 risk factors for juvenile sexual offending proposed in the literature.

they contribute directly to criminal behavior; criminogenic needs are considered to be dynamic because as they change, the likelihood of criminal behavior changes also. In addition, dynamic factors also include situational variables that may change over time, including family factors and other environmental conditions that may affect and influence individuals and their behavior.

Static factors are useful for making assessments of an offender's overall risk level because risk level is often associated with past behavior. Knowledge of dynamic factors, however, is required to identify targets for intervention, assess changes in risk, and predict the possibility of possible reoffenses. Dynamic factors are the targets of treatment programs because treatment aims at changing these factors (static factors, by definition, cannot be changed, so it is pointless to address treatment toward them). Accordingly, a clinical assessment tool designed for both broad assessment and treatment planning must necessarily take into account both static and dynamic risk factors. Examples of both static and dynamic risk variables are shown in Figure 7.8.

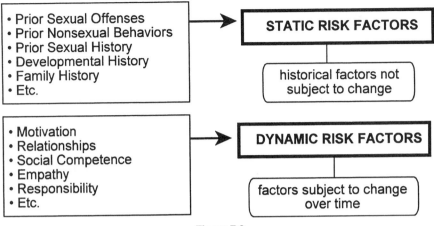

Figure 7.8
Static and dynamic factors of risk.

DOMAINS OF RISK

Even if we can be sure of the risk factors that are most significant and most likely to predict reoffending, we also know that no single factor—even one with relatively high predictive strength—is capable of predicting recidivism. Even combined groups of risk factors do not tell us a great deal about the risk for reoffending (Calder, 2000b; Hanson & Bussière, 1998).

Accordingly, risk assessment must consider multiple aspects of risk, and the final assignment of risk is based on the interrelationship among all of the individual factors or groups of factors. In a statistical model, scores are assigned to each factor (according to scoring rules), adding to a total score that assigns the level of risk. However, in a clinical model, the evaluator examines each risk factor as an element of risk, taking into account the actual sexual offenses and other static factors, the relationship among all factors, and the personal and contextual factors that lend themselves to a more complete understanding of the offender and the circumstances that shaped, contributed, or led to the sexual offending. Recognizing that there are multiple risk factors and that they must be examined and pieced together, it is useful to create categories of risk that incorporate and contain these multiple factors and allow the assessment to remain highly organized and coherent. In this model, similar elements of risk are grouped together into larger risk *domains*, and within each domain individual risk elements are explored and assessed. Figure 7.9 provides two examples of risk domains that organize and categorize similar individual risk factors.

Each risk domain represents an area of activity, attitude, skill, behavior, personality, history, or environment relevant to the development of a complete

Risk Domain: Responsibility This domain describes the offender's ability/willingness to accept responsibility for behaviors, and apparent motivation and/or interest in treatment.	**_Risk Domain: Antisocial Behaviors_** This domain describes generally antisocial nonsexual behaviors, attitudes, and issues, including school behaviors.
1. <u>Denial</u>: *ability to acknowledge or propensity to deny offending and other related behavior* 2. <u>Minimization</u>: *tendency to minimize or reduce the significance of offending and other antisocial behaviors* 3. <u>Responsibility</u>: *ability to accept responsibility for personal behaviors* 4. <u>Honesty</u>: *ability or tendency to be honest about offending and other related behaviors* 5. <u>Selfdisclosing</u>: *ability or willingness to reveal the truth about offending behaviors, related issues or history, and/or other matters that may be private and difficult to discuss with others* 6. <u>Selfinitiating</u>: *willingness to be honest, forthright, and direct without coercion, undue prompting, or excessive questioning, or without being asked at all* 7. <u>Participation in evaluation</u>: *willingness to engage fully in the evaluation process* 8. <u>Internal motivation</u>: *personal motivation for treatment, regardless of external sanctions or coercion* 9. <u>Concern for victim</u>: *measurement of offender's concern for his victims and harm possibly caused by offending and other related behaviors*	1. <u>Nonsexual conduct</u>: *behavior and conduct in general, other than sexual offending behaviors* 2. <u>Violence</u>: *level of violence exhibited by offender in general* 3. <u>Sadism</u>: *intentional acts of physical or emotional cruelty directed toward other people* 4. <u>Intimidation/aggression</u>: *level of anger, threats, yelling, or aggression in general* 5. <u>Oppositionality</u>: *general level of oppositional or non-compliant behavior* 6. <u>Cruelty to animals</u>: *intentional acts of cruelty directed toward animals* 7. <u>Fire setting</u>: *intentional acts of fire setting or arson* 8. <u>Destruction of property</u>: *general respect for property and/or acts of property destruction* 9. <u>Response to authority</u>: *general level of respect for and response to authority figures in the home, school, and community* 10. <u>Legal problems</u>: *arrests, past or present criminal charges, and/or other history of difficulties with the police or the law in general* 11. <u>Deceitfulness</u>: *level of honesty, lying, intentional omission of the truth, and manipulation in general* 12. <u>School behaviors</u>: *response to and behaviors in school, including suspensions and expulsions as well as general school behaviors*

Figure 7.9

Example of risk domains and risk factors (elements).

picture of the individual offender and identified as a possible area of risk. Included within each domain are individual risk factors (risk elements in this model) that together provide a sense of the risk for reoffense attached to that domain. In an actuarial instrument, the grouping of individual risk factors into larger risk domains (or categories) is determined through a statistical procedure such as factor or cluster analysis, but in the development of a clinical tool, groupings are more likely to be logically derived in a best-fit model; that is, which elements of risk seem most alike and can most easily be fit together under the broader descriptions that define each of the larger risk domains?

Once risk domains are used to group and organize similar factors (i.e., risk elements), the evaluator is able to assess each individual risk element with relative ease, leading to a complete assessment of risk in each given risk domain. Such a model allows the evaluator to concentrate on many individual areas of possible risk without becoming overwhelmed or disorganized by the sheer amount of information that must be examined and creates a series of smaller assessments within and across each risk domain, which together add up to the complete assessment of risk. As a result, the final assessment of risk is ac-

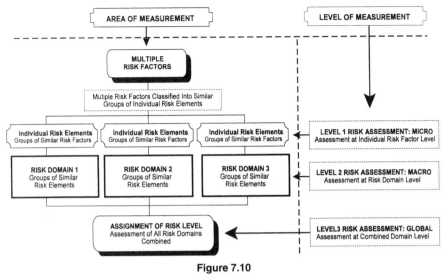

Figure 7.10
Assessment of risk factors and domains at micro, macro, and global levels.

tually the outcome of a series of smaller assessments in distinct risk domains. The advantage of subsuming individual elements of risk under larger risk domains is that it allows the evaluator to examine many individual potential risk factors before rendering a clinical judgment about risk in any given risk domain. That is, macro decisions about risk are always informed by micro decisions at a lower level, adding up to the overall assessment of risk as the assessment is completed, as illustrated in Figure 7.10.

The Juvenile Risk Assessment Tool (J-RAT; Rich, 2001a, 2001b; Stetson School, 2000c) follows this model. The J-RAT is an empirically based, structured clinical assessment instrument used to assess risk for sexual reoffense, and it evaluates 118 individual risk elements incorporated into 12 risk domains, shown in Figure 7.11. These domains, in addition to the individual elements subsumed under each, cover a wide range of static and dynamic factors that have significant face validity and consequently ensure and provide the structure for a comprehensive (and consistent) assessment of risk for sexual reoffending in the adolescent being evaluated.

The J-RAT is designed and intended to be used in conjunction with a structured psychosocial assessment, which may include a wide range of tools, such as record review, clinical interviews with the offender and other informants, psychological and physiological testing, and so forth. However, the instrument itself contains more information than simply the assessment of risk in these different domains. As a clinical tool, informed by a psychosocial assessment process, the J-RAT contains other significant information about the offenses and the juvenile offender and provides a summarizing written formulation that both clarifies and justifies the risk level assigned.

Domain 1:	Responsibility	9 elements
Domain 2:	Relationships	8 elements
Domain 3:	Cognitive Abilities/Skills	4 elements
Domain 4:	Social Skills	8 elements
Domain 5:	Past Trauma	6 elements
Domain 6:	Personal Characteristics and Qualities	8 elements
Domain 7:	Comorbidity and Other Treatment	7 elements
Domain 8:	Substance Abuse	4 elements
Domain 9:	Antisocial Behaviors	12 elements
Domain 10:	Pattern of Sexual Offending Behavior	26 elements
Domain 11:	Family Factors	20 elements
Domain 12:	Environmental Conditions	6 elements
Total		**118 elements**

Figure 7.11

Risk domains used in the Juvenile Risk Assessment Tool. From Stetson School (2000c).

ASSIGNING RISK

Even though information for a clinical assessment of risk is obtained from the psychosocial assessment and other means, the clinician is still faced with the task of actually assigning risk, which is most often rendered in the form of low, moderate, or high risk (some models may additionally use low-moderate and moderate-high categories to allow for greater distinction and nuance). In the most straightforward model, a technical manual defines and describes each risk factor to ensure clarity and offers guidance on how to rate each factor from low risk to high. Regardless of how it is done, the task of assessment involves the clinician's ability both to recognize the meaning of each risk factor and to assess the significance of each of those factors in the life of that particular individual (in terms of the likelihood that any particular factor is a risk factor for that particular individual). In addition, the clinician must also recognize that some factors bear greater weight than others in the assessment of risk.

Weighting Risk Domains

Through the process of discovery that occurs during the clinical assessment or predetermined and a priori rules or ideas that shape the evaluation, the clinician may choose to place emphasis (weight) on one specific risk domain, or even on a specific single risk factor. For instance, although the juvenile may be highly functional (and consequently at low risk) in many areas, the clinical assessor may place added weight on any single area in the individual's life that suggests high risk, such as the nature of the actual prior offense if it was severe enough or otherwise suggests tremendous dysfunctionality. In this way the clinician has the option of neutralizing areas of low risk because of the presence of extremely high risk in other areas. In a numerically scored assessment, the assignment of a higher (high-risk) score will automatically counteract or neutralize lower (low-risk) scores. However, in assessments that assign nominal (low, moderate, or high risk) rather than numeric scores, it will be up to the clinician to render a decision about overall level of risk, possibly by weighting some assessment areas over others. That is, despite risk assignments of low risk in particular domains, the clinician may still decide to assign an overall high risk level due to a single high-risk category that, in the clinician's opinion, is critical and elevates risk.

For example, Ted Bundy was a serial sex offender and murderer who might have been (mistakenly) assessed at low or no risk in many areas of his life, including social competence, conflict management, stability, global assessment of functioning, cognitive skills and intellect, and other areas that may have completely missed the underlying, serious psychopathology. However, once revealed, knowledge of one factor alone—the severity of his sexual crimes—would have resulted in an assignment of high risk, regardless of the level of risk in any other area of assessment. Furthermore, although the severity of crime is a static factor, the weight placed on such a factor would likely be so high that it would negate any positive assessment of other static or dynamic variables, including those that might be considered treatable. This provides an example of weighting, in which more emphasis and weight are assigned to one risk domain, or even a single risk element, thus ranking its importance in the overall assessment.

NUMERICALLY SCORED RISK DOMAINS

In developing a clinical tool, it is possible to assign a numerical score to a risk element and domain in which the weighting is assigned through a higher or lower score. This makes the task of assigning a risk level for each domain and completing the entire risk assessment easier for the clinician because the risk level can be based on the overall score. In a hypothetical example, a total score of 1–19 indicates low risk, 20–39 moderate risk, and 40 and above high risk.

By using a numerically scored assessment instrument, clinical judgment is to some degree taken away from the individual assessor. In this version of the structured clinical tool, the *developer* of the instrument applies the most clinical judgment (and foresight) by determining and building numerical scores into the design of the tool. The *clinician* using the instrument applies judgment in deciding which numerical score to apply in each area, but the overall risk level in any domain and the overall assessment lie outside of the evaluator's judgment.

The difficulty in assigning numerical scores is that it is complex and somewhat arbitrary. For instance, although a violent rape may earn a higher numerical score than sexual exhibitionism, does a single rape warrant a lower score than multiple rape of the same victim or single rapes of multiple victims? Assigning numerical scores results in a more structured assessment with more control applied by the designer of the instrument, but it also requires careful consideration and reduces the ability of the clinician conducting the assessment to use clinical judgment.

NOMINALLY SCORED RISK DOMAINS

Clinical assessment tools that do not provide numerical scores typically assign risk in the form of low, moderate, and high risk. In this case, the clinician must decide for each of the risk elements, the composite risk domains, and the overall risk assessment whether to assign a rating of low, moderate, or high, based on his or her clinical judgment and knowledge of the factors. Such assessments are not as highly structured as are numerically scored instruments and in this regard are more clinical and less objective in both construction and administration. However, as is always true in the use of clinical evaluation and judgment, there is no clearly defined scientific or reliably proven way to assess the risk for reoffending.

Either way, whether numerically or nominally scored, the assessment is a clinical process that requires the clinician conducting the assessment to determine risk based on the overall risk assessment process. If well designed, the assessment tool will generally yield the same results from any assessor who is familiar with the tool and the principles of assessment and is provided with the same information.

In describing the three-point scoring for the SVR-20 assessment, Boer et al. (1997) noted that "although admittedly crude, such simple coding is readily comprehended by other decision-makers and easily translated into action" (p. 34). They also wrote that

> it is not possible to specify a method for reaching a summary or final decision that is appropriate for all situations. . . . For clinical purposes, it makes little sense to sum the number of risk factors present in a given case and then use fixed, arbitrary cutoffs to classify the individual as low, moderate, or high risk. It is both possible and reasonable for an evaluator to conclude that the individual is at high risk for violence based on the presence of a single factor. (p. 36)

However, in the absence of single highly weighted factors, "it is reasonable for assessors to conclude that the more factors present in a given case, the higher the risk for violence. Even here, though, assessors must be cautious" (p. 36).

ADDITIONAL CLINICAL INFORMATION

The clinical assessment tool is merely a shell used to record and organize information and reflect on and assign a level of risk. The data that inform and activate the assessment risk tool are collected through the psychosocial assessment, and as previously described the tool itself is really no more than a sophisticated checklist that allows the clinician to cover a great deal of territory, assess multiple specified risk areas, and organize data in a prescribed manner. The use of such a tool ensures that the assessment of risk is comprehensive, follows a clearly defined model, and provides a consistent means for arriving at a clinically defined assessment of risk for sexual reoffense. The organized aspect of the instrument keeps the evaluator focused on empirically based risk factors that apply to all risk assessments, whereas the clinical aspect allows the evaluator to consider the many factors that impinge on the life and behavior of a particular adolescent.

Despite the fact that assessing risk is not simple, the clinical assessment tool has the capacity to go beyond the function of only assigning a risk level. A well-developed clinical assessment can also elicit additional information that not only helps explain and justify the level of risk assigned but also identifies and highlights (a) characteristics of prior sexual offenses, such as types of victims and elements present in prior offenses; (b) likely scenarios and conditions under which risk is highest, as well as possible victim types in the event that the juvenile does reoffend; and (c) possible motivators for the offense and extenuating circumstances. In addition, a detailed clinical risk assessment includes a written clinical formulation that summarizes and explains the risk assessment level assigned and also presents a perspective about the juvenile sexual offender that helps explain his behavior, describes personal development and characterological and psychological traits, central issues and problems for the offender, and the prognosis if things go unchanged. Finally, the risk assessment can highlight recommendations for placement, treatment, and supervision that will be useful in the process of disposition and treatment planning.

REASSESSMENT OVER TIME

As noted, it is conceivable that such weight is placed on a single risk factor due to a history of severe and heinous crimes that no amount of treatment or rehabilitation will change or reduce the designation of high risk. However, in many cases, and especially in the case of children and adolescents, great emphasis is placed on treatment and rehabilitation and the accompanying belief that it *is* possible to reduce risk level. Accordingly, ongoing assessments of risk for juveniles are not simple repeats of past assessments but are aimed at changes in dynamic variables. If this were not so, an initial assessment of high risk would suffice, and no amount of treatment would affect the later assignment of risk or the decision to release an individual from treatment. Indeed, this is one of the major drawbacks to static actuarial assessment. Accordingly, it is important to reassess individuals over time, in order to assess both the

Domain 1. Responsibility . . . . 6 elements
Domain 2. Relationships . . . . 8 elements
Domain 3. Social Skills . . . . 7 elements
Domain 4. Cognitive Ability/Skills . . . . 4 elements
Domain 5. Impact of Past Trauma . . . . 3 elements
Domain 6. Personal Characteristics . . . . 8 elements
Domain 7. Comorbidity . . . . 4 elements
Domain 8. Conduct . . . . 10 elements
Domain 9. Psychosocial Stressors . . . . 8 elements
Domain 10. Interactions and Contact . . . . 6 elements
Domain 11. Ongoing Sexual Behaviors/Offending . . . . 9 elements
Domain 12. Family Factors . . . . 10 elements
Domain 13. Prior Sexual Offending . . . . 3 elements
Domain 14. Progress in Sex Offender Specific Treatment . . . . 19 elements

Total . . . . **105 elements**

Figure 7.12
Risk domains of the Interim Modified Risk Assessment Tool, which largely measures dynamic
risk factors or response to treatment. From Stetson School (2000b).

impact of treatment or the passage of time and the current level of risk to reoffend. To this end, Lundrigan (2001, p. 189) noted that "comprehensive assessment must be viewed as ongoing."

In addition to the development of the clinical risk assessment tool described in this chapter, it is possible to develop structured and empirically
based clinical assessment tools designed to evaluate changes over time as well
as ongoing risk level. Such tools are designed to measure the response to
treatment, typically measuring dynamic factors only. The Interim Modified
Risk Assessment Tool (IM-RAT; Stetson School, 2000b) is a significantly modified version of the J-RAT that reviews 14 risk domains and 105 individual risk
elements that together reflect current information, behaviors, interactions, relationships, attitudes, and stressors, as well as the juvenile's ability to engage
in significant aspects of treatment. Shown in Figure 7.12, the IM-RAT is directed strictly toward assessing dynamic factors (criminogenic needs).

CONCLUSION: CLINICAL RISK ASSESSMENT AS THE ROUTE TO TREATMENT

The trouble with assigning risk is that it varies under different circumstances.
That is, risk is fluid and contextual and to a great degree varies and depends
on the circumstances and context of the individual's life at any given time. In
fact, under some circumstances the offender may not be at any significant
level of risk at all; under other circumstances he may be at high risk.

If we were not to provide treatment and rehabilitation, it might be just as
well simply to classify an offender at the appropriate level of risk (low, mod-

erate, or high) and leave that designation in place. Assigning a risk level and assuming a constant level of risk is certainly the broadest and safest approach to risk management and the management of the sexual offender and fits with the larger perspective of the Association for the Treatment of Sexual Abusers (ATSA) that "although many, if not most, sexual abusers are treatable, there is no known 'cure.' Management of sexually abusive behavior is a life long task for some sexual abusers" (ATSA, 2001, p. v). However, this perspective may not be the best approach, or even the most accurate perspective, to take in the treatment of adolescent and child sexual offenders. Indeed, ATSA believes that juvenile sexual offenders are more responsive to treatment than are adult offenders and reflects the belief that adolescent offenders are amenable to treatment and can be successfully treated.

This chapter has highlighted and described the use of structured and empirically based clinical tools in the assessment of juvenile sexual offenders in the belief that for the juvenile sexual offender assessment is not aimed just at defining a level of risk but at developing a clinical understanding of the youth on which to build and develop realistic, appropriate, and meaningful treatment interventions. The process of clinical assessment is more likely to serve as that platform than even the best and most informed actuarial assessment, and the development and use of structured clinical assessment tools provide a significant, and perhaps the best, means for ensuring thorough and professionally informed evaluation and risk assessment.

CHAPTER 8

Conducting the Juvenile Sexual Offender Assessment

CHAPTERS 6 and 7 addressed the underlying theory, use, and construction of the juvenile sexual offender evaluation and risk assessment. By contrast, this chapter focuses on the actual administration of the assessment, including the comprehensive nature of the assessment, types of assessment and assessment venues, the role of clinical formulation in the assessment process, and guidelines for practice, clinical interviews, and the writing of the assessment.

BASIC PRINCIPLES AND PURPOSE

Assessments are not intended to provide complete details of everything that actually occurred during the sexual offense. In fact, it is virtually impossible to gather every detail about what happened, when, and why and to gain a full understanding of the "truth."

A comprehensive assessment refers more to the range of information covered than the depth of that information. Assessments should address and reach deeply into the individual's history, social environment, thinking, and behaviors. It is this data set that will inform the clinician not only about the individual but also about the individual's possible level of risk with respect to future offenses. In addition, a comprehensive assessment will give the clinician maximum information in making inferences and drawing conclusions about the juvenile, with respect to both understanding the youth and making informed decisions and recommendations about treatment needs and interventions.

A comprehensive assessment also delves into and reveals details about the juvenile's personal characteristics, skills, and abilities, including level of honesty, self-disclosure, motivation, responsibility, and attachment and relatedness to others. In addition, clinical assessment explores and evaluates the circumstances that surrounded and continue to surround the life of the juvenile offender, and hence surround and probably give rise to his behaviors. In other words, assessment is not necessarily intended for the purposes of disclosure or the admission of sexual offenses, although this is ideal. Instead, the purpose is to make sense of the juvenile sexual offender and his behaviors. In fact, for treatment purposes, we are more interested in understanding the individual than his behavior alone, for without such an understanding we are unlikely to know how to treat the behavior. Even if the assessment was intended to gather a complete confession of all wrongdoing and antisocial behavior, including sexual offending, the assessment goes far beyond the ability and willingness of the offender to admit and describe the truth.

In reality, in many (if not most) situations, juvenile offenders are unable to describe why the offense occurred with respect to both their motivation and the complex sequence and interaction of events, circumstances, emotions, cognitions, and behaviors that influenced and led to the offense. Unlike other crimes, juvenile sexual offending is often not motivated or prompted by any blatant reason that juveniles can easily recognize or grasp themselves.

Remember, *risk* assessment is concerned only with the question of whether recurring sexual offense is likely, regardless of history. But *broad* assessment, which includes assessment of risk, is aimed not only at risk for future behaviors but also taking stock of the individual and understanding his life in its context. It is thus concerned with far more than simply the behavior in question.

ASSESSMENT AND THE DISCLOSURE OF SEXUAL OFFENSES

Disclosure (i.e., the juvenile's willingness to describe fully, admit to, and take responsibility for his sexual offending behaviors) follows assessment. Thus, the attainment of full disclosure is usually a goal of treatment and takes place in the rehabilitation phase of sexual-offender-specific treatment. If all the work was done during assessment, there would be no need for treatment at all. In fact, many things not disclosed during an initial assessment *do* emerge later, in treatment, as they should. To this end, Baker, Tabacoff, Tornusciolo, and Eisenstadt (2001) wrote that "clinical experience strongly suggests that the true number and extent of sexual crimes may be revealed only after several months of treatment" (p. 80). They pointed out that for any number of reasons, juvenile sexual offenders do not fully disclose and also noted that the same may be true for the families of juvenile sexual offenders who may also deny, minimize, or even hide sexual offenses. They asserted that adolescent offenders (and their families) withhold information until a therapeutic alliance has been established and warned clinicians that "they probably do not have the full picture of the youth's early life and experiences or of his ability to commit certain offenses. Part of the clinical process, therefore, needs to focus on encouraging youth and their families to make full disclosures of offenses and victims" (p. 88). Over 53% of the juveniles included in their recent study reported additional sexual offenses or victims only after treatment had begun. Similarly, Mussack and Carich (2001) noted that "it is unreasonable to expect a sexual abuser to disclose his or her entire history of sexually deviant behaviors during an initial assessment. Further disclosures are likely during the course of therapy if intervention is at all effective" (p. 12).

Nevertheless, although assessment is a distinct process in its own right, the assessment phase also often marks the beginning of treatment and in itself can be therapeutic, although this is not always the case.

ASSESSMENT TYPE AND VENUE

We start to climb a slippery slope when we attempt to define assessment as a single entity or process, even though we can define its general purposes. The report of the National Task Force on Juvenile Sexual Offending (1993) asserted that assessment should be an ongoing process and outlined six phases of assessment: (a) pretrial/investigative, (b) presentence/risk prognosis, (c) postadjudication/disposition, (d) needs/treatment planning and treatment evaluation, (e) release/predischarge, and (f) monitoring/follow up (p. 28). In a similar vein, Hoge and Andrews (1996) described several key points in the decision-making process that can be (and are) informed by the assessment process: investigation/processing, intake/preadjudication, adjudication, and disposition (pp. 17–18).

There are different outcomes for assessment that are based primarily on the immediate purpose of the assessment, as well as the venue. That is, assessment can be part of the pretreatment process or the in-treatment process. In the first case, assessments can be used as investigative tools to inform and guide authorities such as social services or the police as to the appropriate course of action. Sometimes the assessment may lead to all further action being dropped. In many instances, however, such investigation leads to either an arrest and referral to the juvenile court system or a referral to social services and treatment that bypasses the juvenile court completely (sometimes referred to as court diversion). In the event of an arrest, and still on the pretreatment side of the line, assessments may also be used for preadjudication purposes, assisting the court in learning about the juvenile before a decision is made as to guilt (or responsibility) or innocence. Still on this side of the line, assessment can be used to guide the postadjudication disposition as well—that is, what the court can or should do in the event that the child or adolescent has been adjudicated as responsible or guilty. In cases of court diversion, assessments lead directly to decisions made by social service agencies (usually state agencies) as to the next and most appropriate course of action.

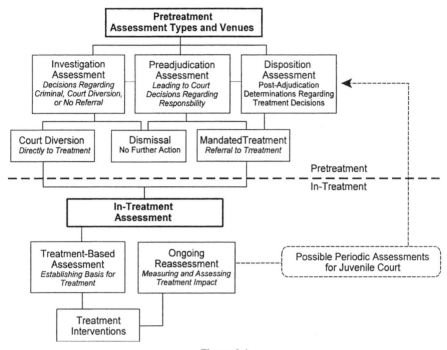

Figure 8.1
Assessment types and venue.

The other side of the assessment line involves in-treatment evaluation. That is, any further assessment is now specifically designed for the purposes of gathering facts, understanding the child, and establishing treatment. This is not true in those cases where the youth never goes to court, is found not responsible by the court, or social services declines or is unable to provide further services. In these instances, pretreatment evaluations either lead to the conclusion that no treatment is necessary or are simply dead ends because the social or legal system decides against or is unable to provide further treatment.

Even the distinctions drawn here are not always clear. For instance, in-treatment assessments are sometimes used to keep the court informed and, in effect, cross the line back to pretreatment as the outcome of the evaluation may lead to the court's making new judgments of what is or is not appropriate for the juvenile. On top of that, some assessments focus on a more narrowly defined aspect of the juvenile, such as psychological evaluations that build a picture of the individual through psychometric and other psychological tests in absence of any clinical data, or attempt actuarial risk assessment that concentrates on static rather than dynamic factors. Beyond this, assessments for many juveniles tend to be repeated over and over by different practitioners who enter the picture at different junctures in the process and apply different approaches and methods to the assessment process. Figure 8.1 illustrates JSO assessment types and venues both prior to and during the treatment process.

ASSESSMENT AS "PASSIVE" TREATMENT

Treatment rarely (and should never) occurs without assessment, although it is conceivable that assessment may not be followed by treatment. However, this book is concerned only with those juveniles for whom further treatment is recommended and will be provided. For these children and adolescents, it is artificial to think of clinical assessment and treatment as separate and distinct processes.

In the case of in-treatment assessment (assessment administered specifically for the purposes of establishing or evaluating treatment, rather than determining whether treatment should be provided), to some degree the assessment itself is part of the treatment process, if only because it most directly guides and sets that process into motion. To this degree, such assessments represent a *passive* form of treatment to be followed by or incorporated into active treatment. The point is raised here because the assessor should be aware of the power of the assessment process and of the fact that it not only gathers information but also, through the clinical interview, provides information. After all, the clinical interview is not a unidirectional process, like a one-way mirror. In fact, this is a significant factor in understanding the use of the clinical assessment to measure pathology and risk. In the very act of observing, the clinician gives much information to the client through the interview process because two-way communication is in the nature of the exchange. The client learns about the process, the sort of information asked and expected, and the method and approach of the clinician, as well as about what may lie ahead. This can be a positive or negative thing. For the client who can engage in treatment, this may provide a means for early engagement in the treatment process, even if later treatment is not with the clinician conducting the evaluation. The more devious client may have the opportunity to outwit the clinician and the entire assessment process by presenting himself in a way that obscures significant issues. The most manipulative and aware client may learn how to present himself in a positive and socially desirable light (*fake good*) and avoid telling the truth through what he is learning from the unaware clinician. The forensically experienced clinician is trained to be aware of this two-way interaction (which is a natural facet of the clinical interview) and of the two-way information "bleed" and remain in control of both information gathered and information given.

In this regard, assessment sets the pace for and becomes the first step in the treatment process. For instance, some studies on the treatment of depression have found that the initial (psychosocial) assessment itself is nearly as useful in terms of treatment as both antidepressant medication and ongoing therapy. The same phenomenon has been found in various other studies that gauge the impact of the initial clinical interview. As such, although assessment is not treatment, it remains a passive version of treatment yet to come, establishing expectations and process, as well as sometimes introducing the therapeutic relationship and laying the first steps of the therapeutic alliance. For the assessor who will also be the therapist in ongoing treatment, "the process of assessment is also an initial intervention that furnishes an important opportunity . . . to establish the therapist professionally as someone who is trustworthy and competent" (Thomas & Viar, 2001, p. 170).

ASSESSMENTS ARE COMPREHENSIVE

The Office of Juvenile Justice and Delinquency Prevention (Righthand & Welch, 2001) stated that comprehensive clinical assessments of juvenile sexual offenders are required to assess risk and facilitate treatment and emphasized that any attempt to explain or treat juvenile sexual offenders must be based on the specific factors pertinent to that juvenile's offenses and individual psychology. In a similar vein, the 1993 National Adolescent Perpetration Network report (National Task Force on Juvenile Sexual Offending, 1993) stated that a comprehensive assessment must be administered to juvenile sexual offenders, which require both records review and interviews with all relevant informants, including multiple interviews with the child or adolescent offender.

A number of writers have tried to define the elements of a comprehensive assessment. Thomas and Viar (2001) stated that the major goal of assessment is to develop the most complete understanding of the circumstances surrounding the problem so that necessary interventions can be addressed, and Welldon (1997) has noted that the assessment "requires a wide understanding of all factors concerning that particular person; his psychological growth, his family . . . his own subculture, and other circumstances" (p. 16). Graham et al. (1997), Will (1999), Houston (1998), Perry and Orchard (1992), and others described the assessment as having multiple goals and purposes and being used to gather extensive information whose inclusion forms the basis for both insight into the case and significant decision making. At a minimum, comprehensive assessments provide a platform from which to

- Understand relevant environmental, social, and personal factors in the life of the juvenile
- Recognize learned experiences that have influenced and shaped the juvenile's thinking and behavior
- Identify specific factors relevant to the sexual offense, including patterns and images of sexual arousal

- Estimate and assess the risk for reoffending, identifying factors that may contribute to reoffense
- Assess motivation and capacity for treatment in the juvenile
- Build a clinical formulation from which to develop and launch the treatment plan

To meet these goals, comprehensive risk assessments must identify *broad risk indicators,* or those factors that indicate risk for or the likelihood of reoffending and that contributed to and paved the way for sexual offending and perhaps even led directly to the behavior. As illustrated in Figure 8.2, these include, at a minimum:

- *Environmental risk factors,* or those risk factors that lie outside of the juvenile but affect and influence his thinking and behavior
- *Characterological risk factors,* which are already or are currently becoming incorporated into the juvenile's personality
- *Behavioral risk factors,* which are encompassed in or exacerbated by the juvenile's behavior
- *Cognitive risk factors,* incorporating ideas, attitudes, beliefs, and other patterns of thinking that influence and shape the juvenile's behavior
- *Developmental risk factors* that contribute to and shape personality, behavior, and responses to stimuli
- *Sexual risk factors,* or sexual experiences and interests that contribute to sexual offenses

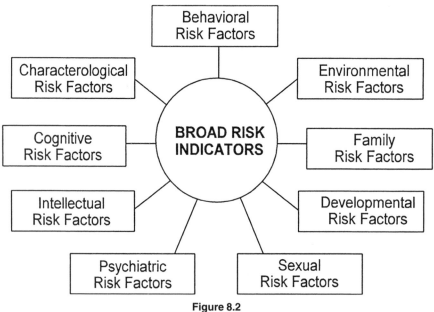

Figure 8.2
The constellation of risk factors.

- *Psychiatric (or comorbid) risk factors* that may hinder the juvenile's ability to participate in or benefit from sexual-offender-specific treatment
- *Intellectual risk factors,* which reflect cognitive deficits or abilities that may help explain the juvenile's behavior or hinder treatment
- *Family risk factors,* or those conditions within the family structure that have helped define and shape the juvenile's behavior and may continue to serve as risk factors

Conducting such a broad assessment is a complex and complicated task. This is why comprehensive assessments require the use of organizing and defining clinical instruments such as those described in Chapters 6 and 7. Of course, these tools provide only data and are unable to provide meaning. That part is up to the clinician. Structured clinical tools do, however, provide a means for organizing, examining, and piecing together complex and multi-faceted pieces of information so that the clinician can recognize elements, patterns, connections, and circumstances that ultimately lend themselves to insight and the development of clinical formulation.

To this end, assessment implies not simply gathering information but also developing insight and understanding in the clinician. This means collecting adequate information and organizing it in such a way as to allow the pieces to fit together and thus provide meaning behind what may otherwise seem like meaningless antisocial and often heinous behavior.

THE ROLE OF THE CLINICIAN IN ASSESSMENT OF THE JUVENILE SEXUAL OFFENDER

As described in Chapters 1 and 4, in forensic work in general there seems to be an insistence on producing simple tools that can provide parsimonious answers to extremely complex and convoluted issues. The same thinking is applied to the assessment of sexual offenders, especially in the form of producing mechanical methods for assessing and assigning risk for future behaviors. In fact, when assessments are removed from the clinician's domain and transferred to the psychometrician, we may lose the heart of the human interaction that is central to understanding, formulation, and subsequent treatment. As assessors, the role of clinicians is to observe, draw conclusions, and take actions informed by their explorations and formulations. Rather than take the position that fact-based (statistical) information about human interactions—removed from clinical observation and interpretation—can result in accurate assessments of future behavior, perhaps it is more important to note and improve the level of training provided to clinicians in their understanding of the meaning, process, and application of assessment, diagnosis, and prognosis.

CLINICAL FORMULATION: THE DEVELOPMENT OF INSIGHT

Clinical formulation represents the simple, concise, and condensed version of the clinician's visualization of the diagnosis, the factors leading to it, and the client profile. When accompanied by a forensic mind-set, it serves to reduce the history, facts, symptoms, and presentation into a brief summary that provides meaning, conjectures causes, outlines current issues, and informs prognosis.

The formulation combines the detective work of the discovery process (the gathering and examination of facts and information), the inventive work of piecing together information into a discernible whole (interpretation), and the development of hypotheses that suggest causes (etiology) and the likely outcome if untreated (prognosis). Clinical formulation helps clinicians understand the factors and motivations that shape and explain behavior, as well as prognosticate the further development or resolution of pathology. The formulation should describe

- The motivations of the offender and the reasons behind his behavior and thinking patterns
- Past and present factors that influence and shape the offender's thinking, attitudes, behaviors, and interactions
- Why the child or adolescent offended in the first place
- The prognosis, if things go unchanged
- Central issues or problems for the offender, as well as the treatment problem to be addressed and resolved
- Interventions that might be useful or will be used to attack the problem and bring about change

In effect, this list represents a different or alternate version of the comprehensive assessment described earlier. But in terms of understanding and formulating *why* the child or adolescent sexually offended in the first place, it is useful for the clinician to

- Envision the sequence of events that led to the first offense as a chart (or actually draw a chart)
- Picture the first sexual offense in a circle somewhere in the middle of the page
- Picture other sexual offenses flowing from (or following) that first offense
- Chart the factors, events, and circumstances that led to that first event
- Chart the factors and sequence or events—or the pathway—that indirectly led to the first offense
- Chart the pathway that led directly to the first offense

Figure 8.3 shows what a simple chart might look like. If the clinician is able to create such a chart (in the mind's eye or on paper), she or he will have de-

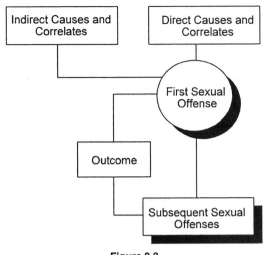

Figure 8.3
Formulating the first and subsequent offenses.

veloped a formulation that can help understand the motivations, the events, the sequence, and other factors that led directly to the offense and may also help the clinician understand the way in which the offense gratified the offender and met his needs. This becomes the pathway to understanding later offenses (if there are any) and thus helps to assess both future risk and treatment needs.

Without a formulation, the clinician is working in the dark. Formulation implies the ability to put together the pieces. How can we prevent further inappropriate behaviors and bring about change if we do not know what led to the behavior in the first instance or how all the factors fit together to produce the behavior? The cognitive-behavioral dysfunctional cycle model (described and discussed in detail in Chapter 16), in which behaviors are seen as the eventual outcomes of a series of events, emotional responses, and cognitive patterns, is a simplistic approach to developing insight like this. It attempts to look back at the stimulus for behavior, sequentially working through the emotional experiences and the thought processes that followed in an effort to generate insight about a particular behavior. In teaching clients how to process their behaviors using a cycle model, we are trying to generate insight of some kind in the client, thus allowing him to recognize dysfunctional patterns and precursors that kick dysfunctional behavioral responses into action, and thus to avoid them.

To this end, "our task as therapists is to identify, as accurately as possible, the unique risk factors that exist for each client, and to help our clients internalize those factors so that they become a part of their conscious awareness" (Prentky & Burgess, 2000, p. 97). The goal of the comprehensive assessment, however, is far broader. In assessment we pursue the development of insight into not just a single behavior dating back perhaps a few moments, a few days, or a few weeks, but insight into a whole set of behaviors that combine to form complex interactions, with precursors that date back to early development and include a myriad of influences that include external, social factors as well as emotional and cognitive responses that are internal to the client.

ASSESSMENT TOOLS AND TYPES

As shown in Figure 7.1, the sexual offender assessment can include and incorporate many types of assessment tools.

- *Psychosocial assessment* refers to gathering information about the developmental, psychological, and social history of individuals and is often referred to as a psychosocial history, with the emphasis on gathering information about and understanding the individual in the context of his or her life.
- *Psychosexual assessment* is a specific and more limited form of psychosocial assessment that is often overlaid and woven into the psychosocial history and explores and examines the development of sexual knowledge, sexual interests, and sexual behaviors.
- *The clinical interview* involves the process of meeting face to face with the client or other individuals who will serve as informants to the assessment for the specific purposes of gathering information about things that occurred and the juvenile in assessment, and sometimes the person providing the information. In conducting the clinical interview, the clinician is able to make assessments about the quality and meaning of that information and the source of the information.
- *The Mental Status Examination* is a typically brief and basic screening assessment used to evaluate the general mental clarity and condition of an individual at the time of the assessment.
- *Risk assessment* is intended to predict future dangerous behavior or related conditions if the current condition goes untreated or to signify the potential for such behavior.
- *Psychological evaluation* includes standardized methods and measurements of psychological states and traits, including feelings and thoughts, attitudes and values, behaviors, intellectual functioning, and cognitive and thought processes.
- *Educational testing* measures academic achievement, the acquisition of information, and cognitive states and intellectual functioning, as well as other measures related to learning, cognitive processing, and retention of learned information.

- *Neuropsychological tests* examine and screen for the possibility of neurological problems that may have an impact on psychological (cognitive, emotional, and behavioral) functioning.
- *Psychometric tests* are psychological, neuropsychological, and educational tests based on statistical concepts and quantitative measures that allow meaningful comparison both between the individual tested and other individuals in the general or specific population and among psychological test measures (not all evaluations are psychometric in nature).
- *Measures of function and interest* are typically nonpsychometric questionnaires and scales that identify and measure interests, attitudes, functioning, and so forth.
- *Psychiatric evaluations* are conducted by a psychiatrist (a physician who specializes in the diagnosis and treatment of mental disorders) and often focus on, but are not limited to, assessment of disturbances in emotions, behaviors, or thinking that may be helped through the prescription of psychiatric medication but also may include a wide psychosocial assessment that follows a medical perspective.
- *Physiological measures* attempt to measure honesty, sexual arousal, sexual interests, and other psychological conditions through physical correlates such as changes in blood pressure, galvanic skin response, respiration, physical (including visual) reaction time, and changes in penile tumescence.

These measures and processes can each be tied into a comprehensive assessment process, illustrated in Figure 8.4.

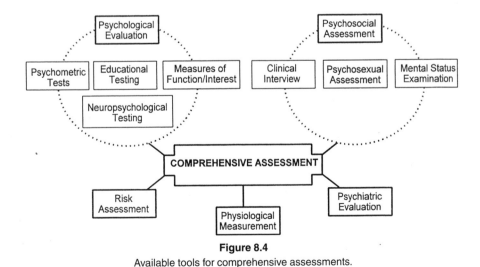

Figure 8.4
Available tools for comprehensive assessments.

A NOTE ABOUT PSYCHOLOGICAL TEST TAKING AND MEASUREMENT

A psychological evaluation is intended to tell us something significant about an individual, reflecting mood or emotion, intellect and related cognitive processes, attitudes or beliefs, interests, functioning, mentation and thinking processes, self-perceptions and perceptions about others, character traits, or other aspects of personal psychology and behavioral functioning. However, not all psychological tests are psychometric. That is, psychological evaluations do not uniformly demonstrate strong statistical properties, and some show no such properties at all. A psychometric test is constructed in such a way as to meet statistical standards for recording and measuring information against a statistical base, and psychological tests that are also psychometric are based on the statistical likelihood that the psychological construct being measured by the test is accurate.

Regardless of psychometric properties, in almost every case, psychological tests attempt to tell us something about the way an individual functions at the time of the test. In the case of psychometrically based testing, we can draw conclusions about current behaviors and make reasonable inferences about future behaviors if things remain unchanged. But here again clinical judgment and prognosis enter the picture. Although some tests measure psychological traits that are imagined to be relatively stable over time, such as personality testing, the reality is that tests that evaluate the psychology of an individual measure aspects of their *current* behaviors, yielding a profile of who that person is, that person's characteristics and interests, and how that person sees the world and reacts to things at the moment. Although psychological testing results may even make prognostic guesses about how the individual is likely to react to things or what that person is likely to do in the future, they do not attempt to predict the *actual* behaviors in which the person might engage in the future, nor can they.

Here is where most psychometric measures and risk assessment part ways. Psychological tests measure who the person is at the moment (whether correctly or not), and risk assessments predict or assess the potential for what that person is likely to do in the future (whether correctly or not). Psychological tests do imply that future behaviors of an individual rest on the current psychological profile of that individual, but for the most part their primary function is to yield a measurement of the individual at the time of the assessment. Risk assessments have no other purpose, however, than to peer into the future.

Even the best psychological tests are flawed. First of all, the strength of well-developed psychological tests rest on their statistical rigor. That is, they are based on the responses of a large sample of individuals drawn from a population similar in some way to the individual being tested. Their conclusions are statistically based, and one can draw strong inferences about the individual from the test. However, although they may work well statistically, we can never be sure of how well they work on any particular individual.

Second, many psychological tests are amenable to manipulation by the individual being assessed. The best developed tests recognize the importance of noting the way that the test taker responds to test items and accordingly build in scales to measure things such as intentional deceit, social desirability (the goal of looking good), intentionally understating symptoms (fake good), unintentional debasement or self-degradation, exaggeration, intent to appear more symptomatic than is actually the case (fake bad), and random or inconsistent patterns of answering. Some tests also attempt to recognize the presence and effect of conditions such as depression or anxiety on the test taker at the time of the test and arithmetically adjust scores accordingly. Nevertheless, it is possible for a test to show validity and reliability for any given individual (i.e., it appears to offer an accurate portrait of the test taker) and yet still offer an inaccurate view of the individual, whether that individual intentionally or unintentionally manipulated his or her responses.

Third, psychological tests are often either transparent or so convoluted that answers may not be true representations of the items to be measured. In the case of transparent items, it is obvious what the question is getting at and therefore easy to answer in one direction or another. Here, we depend upon the test taker's honesty and motivation (or gullibility, depending on what the item is asking) in giving an accurate and true answer. Conversely, individual questions can be worded with such complexity that the individual does not understand the meaning of the question and therefore unintentionally answers incorrectly or gives up and simply answers randomly. Another variant of complexity is the number of questions asked and the length of the test. Some psychological tests are limited to a few questions believed by the test developer to be central, but others contain hundreds of questions and can simply lose the test taker in the process. With respect to comprehension (most often related to complexity), tests often specify a grade level related to reading skills, but in this respect grade level may not reflect the level of comprehension.

Fourth, test questions are sometimes poorly constructed. In some cases, wording is difficult to understand or contains slang or other terminology that is outmoded or not relevant to the individual test taker. In other cases, the choices presented (e.g., choices limited to "yes" or "no") do not allow accurate answers. Fifth, the results of the psychological test may reflect any number of variables that have nothing to do with the test itself. For instance, an individual who is depressed, easily distracted or inattentive, emotionally upset, or unmotivated at the time of the test may skew the results, although based on the actual answers, these factors may not be apparent to the psychologist scoring and evaluating the results. Accordingly, to be most accurate, the results of the psychological test often require clinical interpretation with particular consideration to the individual test taker's personal characteristics and the conditions in his or her life at the time the test was taken. This last point reflects both the need for clinical oversight and understanding in the process of psychological testing and the possibility that a poorly trained, inexperienced, or overzealous psychologist may misinterpret the results of testing. In other words, and for all the reasons just described, the psychological test results may not accurately reflect the individual being tested. Ideally, the psychologist administering and evaluating the testing will know the individual and that individual's history, as well as factors that may support the results of the testing or skew it in other directions that are misleading or inaccurate.

For these reasons, the results of psychological testing should not necessarily be taken at face value. With particular respect to the use of psychological testing in risk assessment, Prentky and Burgess (2000) noted,

> A vast array of difficult inventories, questionnaires, and scales are used by different clinicians to assess sexual offenders. By any rigorous psychometric standard, *very few* of the inventories and questionnaires should be used. To begin with, the psychometric properties . . . for most of these scales are unknown. . . . Additionally, very few of these instruments have been validated on sexual offender samples and very few have normative data from sexual offender samples. . . . In general, risk assessment studies that have included psychometric instruments, find that psychometric data are not particularly useful in predicting recidivism in sexual offenders. Since most psychometric instruments were never designed to assess reoffense risk, this finding is not surprising. (p. 85)

PRACTICE GUIDELINES FOR COMPREHENSIVE ASSESSMENT

Prentky and Burgess (2000) wrote that a central task of the assessment phase of treatment is to identify accurately the most critical factors that contributed to the offense, and they further noted that treatment should not proceed without the benefit of an informed and comprehensive sexual-offender-specific assessment. They pointed out that "unfortunately, there are no standardized or even commonly accepted models for conducting such an assessment" (p. 98).

In fact, the clinical assessment is not a defined psychometric evaluation with required, prescribed, or sequential steps that must be followed. This means that the informed and effective clinician is free to proceed in the manner that most suits the situation and the clinician's own preferred style, rather than follow a prescribed format that limits flexibility, does not take in vivo interactions into account, and is rigid and shallow. Houston (1998) described this process as idiographic, meaning that the focus is on the individual, and framed within a nomothetic process, or the larger framework that governs the way that all assessments are designed and carried out.

Although each assessment is individually focused, it is nevertheless possible and desirable to define a clear protocol for gathering information, defining timelines, and establishing the preferred method for conducting the assessment. Usually, this will be a function of the individual program rather than the set way practiced by every program and every clinician. However, guidelines for the comprehensive assessment of juvenile sexual offenders are available. For instance, the American Academy of Child and Adolescent Psychiatry (AACAP, 1999) adopted a set of practice parameters for the assessment (and treatment) of children and adolescents who sexually abuse. Similarly, the Association for the Treatment of Sexual Abuse (ATSA) (1997, 2001) published guidelines for the assessment of juvenile sexual offenders. These noted the depth required of an assessment:

> The evaluation focuses on both the risks and needs of the sexual abuser, as well as identifying factors from social and sexual history which may contribute to sexual deviance. Evaluations provide the basis for the development of comprehensive treatment plans and should provide recommendations regarding the intensity of intervention, specific treatment protocol needed, and amenability to treatment, as well as the identified risk the abuser presents to the community. (Association for the Treatment of Sexual Abusers, 1997, p. 12)

Incorporating the ideas of AACAP and ATSA, other material in the literature, and ideas presented elsewhere in this book, 21 principles emerge to guide the administration of the comprehensive assessment:

1. The clinical assessment of juvenile sexual abusers requires the same level of comprehensiveness required in all clinical evaluations of children and adolescents.
2. The clinician must ensure that questions raised by the evaluation fall within his or her level of expertise.
3. Although clinical assessments are used for different purposes, the focus is usually on understanding the behaviors, development and causation, motivation for treatment, required level of care, development of treatment plans, and the risk for sexual reoffending.
4. Informed consent for the assessment is required, which in the case of juveniles must include consent of legal guardians.
5. All parties must be aware of any limits to confidentiality, especially if there is any possibility or likelihood that evaluation results will be shared with external agencies such as the police, the court, and social services.
6. There is no known profile or set of characteristics that differentiates juvenile sexual offenders from nonoffending juveniles.
7. The clinician must be aware of the individual's cognitive functioning, including reading, writing, and comprehension skills and abilities, and provide alternative means for gathering information directly from the juvenile if cognitive, intellectual, or language skills are poor.

8. The clinician should adopt a nonjudgmental and patient stance in the evaluation and should remain persistent and focused.

9. The clinician should be aware that information provided directly by the juvenile may not be true, complete, or sufficiently detailed and should recognize that the juvenile may lie, deny, distort, or minimize and that the same may be true of informants in the juvenile's family.

10. The clinician must be prepared for the evaluation and ensure a thorough review of existing documentation prior to the assessment, including police reports, victim statements, reports from social service and child protection agencies, mental health assessments, treatment progress reports, psychological tests, and so forth.

11. The clinician must be aware that information available in prior reports may be incomplete, incorrect, or not fully understood and must avoid simply passing along inaccurate or poorly understood information.

12. Information should be gathered from multiple sources, including family members, probation and parole officers, and current or former treatment practitioners such as therapists and psychiatrists, teachers, and treatment staff in former treatment programs or hospitals.

13. The assessment should employ multiple evaluation methods, if available and appropriate, including clinical interviews, psychological and educational testing, and physiological testing.

14. Neither psychological nor physiological testing can be used to prove or disprove that an individual will engage in sexual offending behavior.

15. Clinical interviews are used to gather specific data, as well as to observe, supplement, question, review, and clarify information obtained from other sources.

16. The clinician should seek multiple types of information, including early developmental history, intellectual and cognitive skills, social functioning and relationships, development and acquisition of social skills, psychiatric disorders and mental status, behavioral history, history of substance use, history of trauma and victimization, history of sexual development, attitudes and beliefs, personal characteristics, level of denial or acceptance of responsibility, family structure and current relationships, family history (general, mental health, substance abuse, criminality, etc.), and actual sexual offending behaviors.

17. If possible, the clinician should assess sexual interests and patterns of arousal in the juvenile, recognizing that such assessment does not necessarily indicate the presence of sexual deviance or prove that the juvenile will engage in future sexual offenses.

18. The clinician must recognize that evaluations without broad and supporting collateral information should be interpreted with caution, and

such caution should be noted in the written evaluation report if the assessment was conducted and completed in absence of such information.

19. Assessment of treatment needs and the development of treatment goals should be based on an understanding of the juvenile's needs, including both strengths and weaknesses, as well as an assessment of risk based on the juvenile's history and current level of functioning.

20. Placement and treatment recommendations must be based on the assessment of risk and public safety, the treatment needs of the juvenile, and the juvenile's motivation to engage in treatment and should not be made on the basis of whatever treatment services and resources are actually available or drop below the level of treatment that the clinician believes is required.

21. The written report must be accurate, complete, transparent, and free of speculation and judgment. In the written evaluation, the clinician should

   • Document all records reviewed and informants interviewed
   • Note any limitations on the assessment, including lack of collateral or supporting information that may affect the ability to make informed judgments about the juvenile, the reported offenses, or the risk for future sexual offending
   • Specify that consent was given for the evaluation and describe any limits to confidentiality explained to the juvenile and legal guardian
   • Employ a nonjudgmental and impartial style and ensure that all data presented are both objective and accurate
   • Avoid making speculative statements, except when stating clinical formulations and when ample evidence exists to support the hypotheses of the formulation
   • Document any denial of offenses that the juvenile may make, as well as his explanation, if any, for allegations he claims are false
   • Make assessments of future risk only when adequate information is available on which to base the risk assessment

PROVIDING STRUCTURE FOR THE PSYCHOSOCIAL ASSESSMENT AND WRITTEN REPORT

Although clinical assessments may take many formats and routes, with no particular "how" to the assessment, there clearly are guidelines that define the "what" of the assessment, or the information to be gathered. In addition to understanding the sexual offense itself and sexual history in general, these factors include a thorough understanding of the individual's functioning, developmental history, relevant family history and patterns of interactions, cognitive and emotional functioning, and comorbid psychiatric or substance abuse issues that may influence and shape thoughts, emotions, and behavior.

Beyond simply framing questions, however, just as risk assessment can be based on a structured process, so too can the broad psychosocial evaluation. Here, the framework is largely organized in the form of the final written evaluation report with specific headings that both define and organize the data to be included under each heading. This framework identifies the questions to be asked, organizes the data, and provides the actual format for the final written report. Although there are many such formats, the following framework provides a thorough and comprehensive set of psychosocial questions to be asked and a good starting point for anyone wishing to develop his or her own framework. With 31 active headings, this format leads to a comprehensive written report, often between 12 and 17 single spaced pages.

1. *Purpose*, describing the reason for the assessment
2. *Explanations of Process*, explaining the use and process of the assessment, as well as noting that there is no way fully to ascertain future risk and that risk assessment is based on a combination of current and past behaviors exhibited by the juvenile that place him at a particular level of risk
3. *Consent*, documenting that the process and purpose of the assessment was described to the juvenile (and legal guardians, if a minor), that the limits of confidentiality were discussed, and that consent was given for the assessment
4. *Informants*, identifying those individuals interviewed during the course of the assessment
5. *Records*, noting documents reviewed for the assessment
6. *Reason for Referral*, explaining the specific reason the juvenile is being referred for assessment and usually providing a brief recap of the sexual charges or allegations
7. *Identifying Information*, including information such as age, grade, race, religion, physical appearance, and other information that helps identify the juvenile or by which he identifies himself
8. *Placement and Treatment History*, including current or former placement such as home, foster care, or residential placement, and current or former treatment including outpatient, day treatment, inpatient, or residential treatment and the general dates and reasons for treatment
9. *Presentation and Cooperation*, explaining the juvenile's level of participation and engagement in the evaluation
10. *Legal Status and State Agency Involvement*, explaining current legal standing, custody and guardianship, pending charges, court dates, and the like, and state agency involvement, if any

11. *Significant Life Events,* presenting a basic chronology of significant life events from birth to current evaluation

12. *Family History* (may include several subheadings), including family structure and relationships (genogram), current family environment and living arrangements, family trauma, family stability, significant history of other family members, and other important family dynamics

13. *Family Mental Health and Substance Abuse History,* including all significant use of alcohol or drugs by immediate or other significant family members

14. *Developmental History,* including birth; developmental milestones; early health issues; behaviors and interactions in infancy, preschool, and elementary school; and other early behaviors or difficulties

15. *Relevant Medical Information,* including significant or notable medical or health conditions, including enuresis and encopresis

16. *Past Psychiatric Medications,* including reasons and dates

17. *Current Medical and Psychiatric Medications,* including reasons for current medications

18. *Cognitive Functioning and Psychological Evaluations,* including IQ score and history of prior or current psychological testing, dates, and general results

19. *School Functioning,* including current grade level and any grade retentions, general academic functioning, learning disabilities, history of special education and reasons, behaviors and difficulties in school and the development of problem behaviors, excessive tardiness or absence, school disciplinary action, and so forth

20. *Social Functioning,* including peer and adult relationships outside of the school environment and social relationships and functioning in general

21. *Problematic Nonsexual Behaviors,* providing a general overview of the development and history of nonsexual behavioral or emotional problems, including age of onset, extent and frequency of problems, and most recent occurrence of conduct disorder and oppositionality, violence and aggression, arrests and legal problems, school problems or difficulties, fire setting, running away, and other significant behavioral concerns

22. *History of Substance Use,* including current or prior history of substance use and abuse, with special emphasis on whether alcohol or drugs were involved in problem behaviors or sexual offending behaviors

23. *Victimization or Trauma History,* including physical or sexual victimization or abuse and trauma or life-transforming events experienced by the juvenile

24. *Psychiatric Comorbidity and Diagnostic History,* including current or prior significant coexisting psychiatric conditions and generally including a review of the major categories of mental disorders notated and defined in the *DSM-IV-TR* (American Psychiatric Association, 2000)

25. *Psychiatric Assessment,* noting outcome and significant details of psychiatric evaluation (with psychiatrist), if conducted

26. *Sexual Development and Nonoffending Sexual Interests and Behaviors,* including all prior nonoffending sexual experiences and encounters, early interest in sexual activities, exposure to sexual activities, history of masturbation, sexual interests and fantasies, and use of pornography or other sexual materials

27. *Sexual Offending History,* including description of offenses, the juvenile's description of and attitude toward the offenses, and the family's response to offenses

28. *Risk for Reoffending,* in which a risk level is assigned based on a clinical assessment of risk developed through the psychosocial assessment, a companion risk assessment instrument (as proposed by this book), or an actuarial-like assessment if one is available (if a risk assessment tool is used, the completed instrument should be attached to or accompany the broad assessment report, and the risk assignment should be explained in this written report)

29. *Current Diagnosis* if following a clinical model that utilizes *DSM-IV-TR* diagnoses

30. *Diagnostic/Clinical Formulation,* representing the simple, concise, and condensed version of the clinician's visualization of the diagnosis, the factors leading to it, and the client profile (this is a formulaic reduction of the history, facts, symptoms, and presentation that reduces the entire complex picture into a brief summary that provides meaning, conjectures causes, outlines current issues, and informs prognosis)

31. *Recommendations,* providing recommendations for treatment goals and interventions to be provided or considered further over the course of treatment (these are not treatment goals, which will result from the first treatment plan that will later be developed for the juvenile if he continues in treatment)

32. *Signature, Credential, and Date*

EXPLAINING CONFIDENTIALITY AND PURPOSE OF THE ASSESSMENT

Confidentiality is always a prime issue in therapy. However, in the case of therapy for the sexual offender, it is of special concern as, in many cases, not all communication is considered or will be treated as privileged or confidential.

There are instances where disclosures of past, current, or intended sexual or physical victimization of others must be reported by law (e.g., mandated reporter regulations involving child or elder abuse, where the provider is required to report the information). In other cases, the primary purpose for a psychosexual or risk assessment is to predict risk, determine responsibility, or assess competence and results *will* be communicated to a court or state agency. In still other cases, it may be the policy of the clinician or the assessing treatment agency to report all disclosures that involve crimes and major rule infractions or suggest risk for self-harm or harm to others. The clinician or program may thus report behaviors or disclosures to state social service or youth authority agencies, the courts, or parents. Going further, in some instances, licensed mental health clinicians may not even have the legal right to withhold certain information revealed to them by their clients, which is usually defined by the professional license granted to them by the state in which they practice. Not all licensed clinicians are granted the right to privileged communication, even if they want to maintain confidentiality.

Accordingly, it is vital that juvenile sexual offenders and their legal guardians are informed and understand that they may not be entitled to confidentiality, and in some cases disclosures *will* be reported within the program or to external agencies. Although this may dampen, reduce, and even shut down communication, it is nevertheless critical that juveniles who sexually offend understand that confidentiality is (usually) not guaranteed. In addition to ensuring that limits of confidentiality are well understood, it is also important that individuals being assessed, and their legal guardians, understand the assessment process. As presented in the assessment framework above (item no. 2), it is advisable that the written assessment report itself contain an explanation and description of the psychosocial and risk assessment process.

TYING IT ALL TOGETHER: FROM PSYCHOSOCIAL ASSESSMENT TO PROGNOSIS

Before moving on to the actual process of administering the evaluation, it is worth looking at the assessment process again. Figure 8.5 pictures the assessment process traveling from (a) information gathering, (b) assembling or organizing information into a meaningful whole, (c) analysis and interpretation of information in order to provide meaning, (d) diagnosis of condition, (e) formulation of cause, development, and action, to (f) prognosis (or risk) of imminent or eventual outcome if things remain the same.

CONDUCTING THE JUVENILE SEXUAL OFFENDER ASSESSMENT

Assessment is a process with several distinct stages. The process of evaluating a sexual offender begins with a review of all prior records and concludes

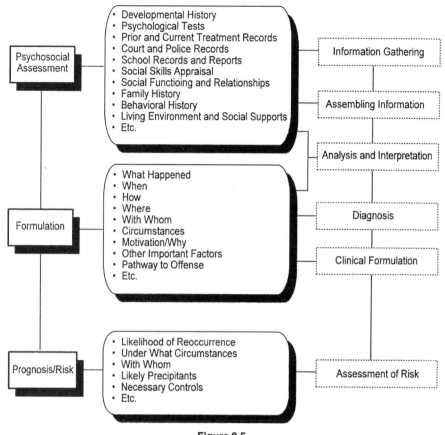

Figure 8.5
The process of clinical assessment.

with the establishment of a diagnosis, a determination of risk level, the identification of specific treatment needs geared to the offender under evaluation, and the development of treatment goals and interventions that will serve to supervise, treat, or rehabilitate the sexual offender and that can be demonstrated in observable and measurable outcomes.

LENGTH OF THE ASSESSMENT PERIOD

The period of days or weeks over which the assessment takes place will vary depending on the purpose, the venue, and the context. For instance, a court-requested or clinic-based outpatient assessment may offer fewer opportunities to meet with the juvenile offender and may also significantly limit the amount of time available for individual interviews and the number of available interviews, compared to an evaluation of a juvenile in an outpatient treatment program or residential program.

Accordingly, the period available for the active phase of the assessment (i.e., direct or repeated interviewing of the offender and other informants) may last anywhere from one day to several weeks. Consequently, the assessment process must be carefully planned and paced to fit the context in which the evaluation will occur, as well as the time available per session and during which the entire evaluation must be completed. Under any circumstances, much of the work of the assessment occurs in the clinician's office, outside of direct interviews, and involves a great deal of collateral work (work other than offender interviews).

PHASES OF ASSESSMENT

The process of the assessment can be broken down into three distinct stages, which may overlap with one another. For example, even though the clinician may be well into the active, or middle, stage of the assessment, it may be important to return to the original documents for further review or to review new documents that may emerge. Likewise, during the final phase, the clinician may find it necessary to return to the active phase and reinterview an informant, and may be quite likely to reread certain materials. Nevertheless, for the most part, the assessment process can be visualized as having separate and distinct tasks.

Phase 1. Preassessment: Preparing for the Evaluation
This phase of assessment provides the groundwork for the active assessment (that part of the process during which information is directly gathered through interviews, clinical contact, and observation). Accordingly, the assessor must

- Read all pertinent information: victim reports; witness reports; court and probation reports; inpatient, or residential, day treatment, and outpatient treatment summaries, court and psychological evaluations; police reports; state and referral agency reports and evaluations; etc.
- Identify important holes in the record and request and gather additional records or information missing from the record
- Identify important informants: parents, foster parents, prior therapists, teachers, probation officer, etc.
- Gather signed release of information forms allowing discussion with informants

Phase 2. Active Assessment: Conducting the Assessment
This phase involves the assessment proper, including interviews, contacts, discussions, and meetings with all relevant informants (i.e., those who can provide a perspective or information about the offender that is relevant to the assessment process). During this phase, the assessor must

- Notify all informants of confidentiality limits and the purpose of the evaluation
- Ensure that all appropriate forms (including release of information) are signed by the legal guardian and offender
- Interview important informants
- Interview the juvenile sexual offender (one or multiple times, depending on availability)
- If able, monitor and remain aware of daily interactions and functioning and patterns of behavior, mood, thinking, or interactions that develop or emerge during the course of the assessment period; this will be easier to do for juveniles in residential programs but can also be accomplished with juveniles in outpatient settings, although it requires far more effort, coordination, and communication

Phase 3. Concluding the Evaluation: Writing the Assessment Report
The assessment concludes with a written report that

- Summarizes pertinent historical and current data
- Formulates hypotheses about the development of sexual offending behavior
- Formulates a description of the psychological profile of the juvenile
- Formulates a description of the environment in which sexual offending behavior occurred, gave rise to or helped maintain the offenses, or otherwise shaped and influenced the juvenile's emotions and behavior
- Identifies a diagnosis that classifies any comorbid psychiatric (or substance abuse) symptoms
- Assigns a level of risk for sexual reoffending
- Proposes treatment needs and identifies suggested treatment goals

INTERVIEWING AND INTERACTING WITH THE JUVENILE OFFENDER

Few offenders, adult or adolescent, seek treatment of their own volition. Offenders often refuse or are afraid to participate honestly in the assessment process for many different reasons, ranging from shame, embarrassment, and fear of consequences to manipulation, planning and exploitation. Rather than state their refusal outright, offenders will frequently participate in the process only in the most minimal of ways, often attempting to deceive the assessor through active lies, lies of omission, and claims of forgetfulness or by providing only the information that the offender believes is already available and therefore hoping to fool or manipulate the assessor.

The ultimate goal of the assessment is to get to the truth behind the behaviors and best understand the individual, as well as the motivation for the sexual offending behavior. As stated earlier, during the assessment period, the truth may not include every detail of the offenses (and is not likely to) but is more likely to involve the history, thinking, relationships, other behaviors, and even some of the sexual offenses, all of which provides the context in which the sexual offending occurred and helps us determine how great the risk is that this particular offender will offend again and what treatment is most appropriate given this determination.

INTERVIEW GUIDELINES

There is no single, correct way to interview and work with an offender, whether adult or adolescent. Unless they follow a structured interview schedule or protocol, clinical interviews are not rigid processes that must be followed in a prescribed sequence or manner but instead allow the experienced clinician to follow the path created at the time of and during the interview itself. Accordingly, in the end the assessor must choose which style or approach to take with each individual offender under assessment. Nevertheless, there are guidelines to direct the clinician working with and assessing the juvenile sexual offender:

1. Be prepared prior to beginning the interview process, and have an already well-formed sense of information about the case. Carefully read the materials in the record.
2. Concentrate on building a safe environment for the child or adolescent. This is difficult because many of the steps taken by the clinician during the assessment are challenging and difficult for the juvenile. However, an important clinical skill involves the ability to make a difficult assessment environment as comfortable and safe as possible for the youthful offender.
3. Realize that for many clinicians conducting both assessment or treatment, work with sexual offenders is quite different from the traditional model, and it contains interventions and approaches that may conflict with other forms of treatment. For instance, there is limited confidentiality regarding the sexual offending behavior and related information, and clinical work with offenders is often more challenging and direct than that with other client populations.
4. Recognize that sexual offender treatment is difficult and often painful for the juvenile. It is a challenging environment for children and adolescents who are not, under the best of circumstances, able to handle difficult emotional situations or stress. The goal is *not* to make the assessment and treatment environment uncomfortable but to recognize that it is emotionally uncomfortable by nature. Conversely, recognizing that treatment is necessarily difficult, it is also *not* the assessor's job to make the environment less challenging or stressful. Instead, the

task is to help the juvenile offender learn to deal and cope with the stress instead of trying to avoid it.

5. Ensure that the juvenile offender and his legal guardian are aware of his rights, as well as the limitations on his rights and confidentiality, and are informed of the general purposes of the evaluation and that it may be shared with others.

6. Test the honesty, self-disclosure, and self-initiation of the juvenile. Facilitate an environment that will allow the offender to be honest and forthright, and provide opportunities for self-initiated and honest disclosure.

7. Expect denial and minimization of the offenses, ranging from complete denial to minimization of the frequency, duration, number, or type of offenses, or the significance of the offending behavior. Ensure that the juvenile understands the consequences of not participating honestly in the assessment. Part of the assessment measures the level of the juvenile offender's participation, compliance, honesty, and self-disclosure. If the child or adolescent is not compliant or honest, the assigned risk for reoffense level is bound to move closer to the high-risk end based on dishonesty, manipulation, or inability to work in treatment.

8. Pursue details of the sexual offending behavior. The assessor should gather more than just the "facts"; one goal is to understand the sexual offending behavior and behavioral cycle as completely as possible, and usually only the juvenile can answer questions that involve pre-, during, and postoffense details.

9. Remember that juvenile offenders are often evasive and will take the path of least resistance. There are times when it is most appropriate to ask leading and closed-ended questions ("When did you . . . ," "Why did you . . . ," "When you first . . . ," "How did you . . . ," etc.), rather than open-ended questions ("Have you ever . . . ") that can be easily denied.

10. Be aware that sexual offenders often provide minimal information that is sometimes based on what they think the assessor already knows. In this way, the juvenile can appear to be participating openly, but may not be. Accordingly, the assessor should ideally not reveal information already known about the offense or other important information relevant to the assessment.

11. If information from the record or other informants *is* shared with the juvenile, use it primarily to help the juvenile piece together an accurate history, jog his memory (not provide information for the juvenile), or prompt him to be more open. However, assessments are dynamic, so this guideline is likely to change over the course of the assessment process.

12. Do not pass judgment. Although some of the tenets of traditional therapy are suspended in work with sexual offenders, the principals of acceptance, support, and nonjudgment are not. A safe environment means a nonjudgmental environment.
13. Build a relationship. Again, this is basic to any therapeutic relationship, including the assessment relationship.
14. Remain in emotional control. Some juveniles are easily able to arouse strong feelings in others, including anger.
15. Confront dishonesty and challenge misinformation, missing information, or contradictions. This may mean that the assessor *must* disclose part of what is already known; consequently, this sort of intervention strategy may be more appropriate during the later stages of the assessment.
16. Stay in control of the process. If the juvenile refuses to work with the assessment or in some other way shortcuts or sabotages the assessment, the clinician must decide how best to remain in control of the process. This may mean allowing a refusal, insisting on meeting anyway, or assigning consequences for nonparticipation. The juvenile should be informed that lack of participation is a factor in the assessment outcome.
17. Seek additional clarification as needed from other sources, such as outside informants, previous records, or other staff.
18. If unclear, seek help, consultation, or just plain discussion; discuss the assessment with a supervisor, other clinicians, or other relevant staff. Do not go it alone if you do not have to. Even if you do not need help, talking the case out with someone else can help process the case, provide insight, and move the clinician toward a greater understanding of the case.

Structuring the Interviews: Length, Frequency, and Duration

Just as there is no correct method for conducting a clinical assessment or a clinical interview, there is no correct length for each individual offender interview, the number of interviews necessary to gather all relevant information, or the frequency of multiple interviews.

Typically, a single interview will last 1 to 1½ hours. Typically, three to five interviews are adequate to gather important data, including personal history, psychosexual development and behaviors, details of the sexual offense and the context in which it occurred, and the character and approach of the child or adolescent. Multiple interviews allow the clinician to observe and experience changes in the juvenile's affect and willingness or ability to be honest and confiding with the clinician. They also allow the juvenile offender the opportunity to reveal more information and provide more insights and to feel more comfortable in the relationship over the course of the interviews. In addition, multiple interviews allow the clinician to switch gears in each interview, gathering different types of information, addressing different aspects of the assessment, and shifting the focus of the interviews over time. Interviews can be scheduled daily until completed, twice a week, or weekly. The appropriate frequency is up to the clinician and will depend on the intensity, the method, and sometimes the timetable governing the assessment process. Consecutive daily interviews are far more intense for the juvenile than are weekly interviews, and perhaps for the clinician as well, but intensity may not be what is desired in any given assessment. The assessment process itself, including the definition provided by a structured risk assessment tool, clinical experience, and often external requirements, shapes and defines the scheduling and frequency of individual interview sessions.

COLLATERAL INTERVIEWS

Collateral interviews with other informants, such as parents, prior treatment providers, probation officers, school personnel, and others are aimed at gathering a complete picture of the juvenile's psychosocial development, functioning, and interactions and at understanding as much as possible about the child or adolescent, the family history and living environment, and the sexual offending and other related behaviors from the perspective of other individuals.

These interviews are less formal than interviews with the juvenile; that is, they are more likely to have a collegial feel to them, even with parents, who usually do not expect the clinician to engage them in an interrogative-style interview. However, the level of formality falls along a continuum. Interviews with parents, for instance, are likely to be more formal and more similar to interviews with the juvenile than are interviews with other professionals. For all interviews the clinician should be prepared and decide in advance what she or he wants to know. To this degree, an interview checklist with questions will help clinicians ensure that they are organized and ask all the questions for which they want answers *before* the interview. It can be frustrating for the clinician to realize later that he or she forgot to ask one or more specific questions. It can also appear to the informant at the other end of the phone that the clinician is poorly organized or—even worse—unqualified. Organization makes all the difference in all forms of work, and clinicians who are organized in their collateral interviews are likely to be both more efficient and more effective; that is, they get the information they want the first time. As some of the collateral informants are also likely to be involved in the later treatment process (e.g., parents, social service case workers, and probation officers), these early interviews also set the pace for later relationships that will be key in both treatment and communication.

ACCURACY IN REPORTING

One of the unfortunate realities in assessment seems to be that inaccurate, incorrect, incomplete, or otherwise faulty information gets passed on through reports and sometimes seems to pass from report to report. In part, the role of the assessing clinician is to ensure accuracy in reporting and to identify areas where there are information gaps, where important information is missing or unavailable, or where information is vague and uncertain. The clinician may even note that the assessment cannot be fully completed or that an assessment of risk is uncertain due to missing data. Clarity and accuracy are hallmarks of a good evaluation.

The clinician should refrain from using definitive statements in assessments and report writing unless the clinician definitively knows that the statement is an accurate representation of the facts as they happened. This includes statements such as "The adolescent *did* do such and such," "The child *was* told by his teacher," or "The individual sexually assaulted three victims." If the clinician cannot verify or vouch for the accuracy or correctness of a statement or the actuality that a particular event took place as reported, terms should be used such as "It is reported that . . . ," "It appears that . . . ," "The client states that . . . ," "The offender reports that . . . ," "The victim alleges that . . . ," "The adolescent allegedly . . . ," and so on.

It is acceptable to make clinical speculations in written reports and assessments as long as the clinician makes clear that this is his or her clinical opinion, based on facts, details, circumstances, statements, and other factors. However, even under these circumstances, clinicians should avoid overly broad speculation and sweeping statements. It is critical that professional reports do not overreport, assume, assign guilt or responsibility, or definitively make statements that are unproven or unverified.

The written evaluation report may be heavily scrutinized at a later point in time. The clinician should ensure its accuracy and that due care was taken in stating fact, speculation, and formulation, clearly distinguishing between fact and speculation.

- Do not speculate without making clear that you are doing so.
- Provide evidence or support for speculative statements.
- Do not make definitive statements unless you know that they are correct.
- Qualify uncertain statements.
- Cite the source of information.
- Use quotation marks to indicate that you are using the actual words of a particular informant.
- Use terms such as "alleged" and "reported" when you are reporting unsubstantiated facts.
- Avoid overly broad and sweeping statements.

CONCLUSION AND SUMMARY

In the end, the process of developing and administering a clinical assessment process is based on the needs, approach, and beliefs of the individual clinician or agency providing the assessment. However, the clinical assessment process can be significantly aided and improved through the use of structured and empirically based assessment tools, and especially in the process of assessing risk for sexual reoffense. Without use of such a tool in something as critical as the assessment of risk, the evaluating clinician faces the distinct possibility of not only inadequate assessments but also the judgment of other professionals that the assessment was poorly informed, incomplete, inadequate, and even unprofessional. Clinical assessments of risk should always be based on the use of a structured and empirically based instrument especially designed for the purpose at hand. Anything less falls into or toward the category of unguided clinical judgment. In the world of forensic assessment and treatment, this is an unacceptable mode of assessment.

In the context of broad psychosocial sexual offender assessment, the assessment of risk is only one part of the entire evaluation. Nevertheless, risk assessment remains critical to the process and outcome of evaluation and is best served through the use of a structured and empirically guided instrument. The same is true of the psychosocial assessment itself. By providing a framework for the assessment, in the form of a report format, clinicians overlay structure and define the ideas and principles behind the assessment. Although the structure for an assessment report cannot be as tight or defined as that provided by an assessment instrument that employs a checklist-style format, with specific and exact questions to be asked and a clear format by which to answer those questions, a format for psychosocial assessment can accomplish similar goals by ensuring comprehensiveness, consistency, and structure to all assessments so that they reflect beliefs about the evaluation of the juvenile sexual offender and incorporate elements critical to those beliefs.

Finally, the clinical assessment process provides depth in administering and completing a comprehensive sexual offender evaluation. Providing training and supervision to the clinician and a clear framework and method for conducting, completing, and writing the juvenile sexual offender assessment strengthens our ability to ensure the most effective and complete evaluations.

CHAPTER 9

Diagnosis and Assessment of Comorbidity

BEYOND THE assessment of risk based on factors such as sexual and nonsexual behavioral history, cognitive reasoning, attitudes and beliefs, and so on, the assessment of psychiatric comorbidity plays a role also in the risk for reoffense. Comorbidity is the co-occurrence of a psychiatric disturbance or disorder that may affect or influence the individual's functional ability. When the behavior, attitudes, emotions, and thinking involved in juvenile sexual offending overlap and coexist with a psychiatric condition, there is an intersection between sexual offending and mental health.

Hodgins (2001) noted that individuals with major mental disorders (defined as schizophrenia, major depression, bipolar disorder, delusional disorder, and atypical psychosis) are more likely than those without to be convicted of criminal offenses and that among people with major mental disorders there is a subgroup characterized by antisocial behavior from childhood on. Similarly, in the MacArthur study of mental disorder and violence, Monahan et al. (2001) described the common perception of increased risk for violence among those diagnosed with mental disorders, noting that among mentally ill patients, "violence is not a rare event" (p. 33). Regardless, other than antisocial personality disorder and sometimes psychosis, comorbidity is usually not linked to risk assessment in adults or the risk for sexual reoffending. Similarly, although the presence of psychiatric diagnoses has often been cited in juvenile sexual offenders (discussed in Chapter 3), little detailed research has been reported on this subject.

Because assessments of risks should be understood in relationship to a base rate, this means comparing the individual to a larger group. Based on the limited amount of material available, the base rate (for adult offenders at least) suggests that sexual offending is not linked to psychiatric difficulties.

The important Hanson and Bussière (1998) metaanalysis found no significant correlationship between adult sexual offending and psychiatric disorders (or psychological variables), and other studies have reported similar findings. Perhaps because of such findings, little has been written on the subject of sexual offending and psychiatric disorders, and a general belief exists that in adult sexual offending at least, psychiatric disorders are not substantially linked. However, the motivation for and influences on sexual offending may simply be easier to recognize and understand in adult offenders than in juvenile offenders. In the adult population, psychiatric diagnoses (or psychological factors) may be far less instrumental in sexually abusive behaviors that by adulthood take on a different aspect and design than that found in the juvenile offender. In adults, sexual offending is more often the result of criminality, psychopathy, or severe sexual deviance than the result of a mental disorder. For this reason, for instance, the act of rape is recognized and treated as a criminal behavior under the control of the rapist rather than a behavior caused or influenced by a mental disorder.

In the primordial swamp of juvenile sexual offending, motivation, influence, purpose, and pattern are much less clear. In this case, relatively primitive instincts and drives, still-forming personality traits, simplistic ideas, developmental vulnerabilities, and motivation are swimming around freely, mutating, coalescing, and forming into more concrete shapes; thus it is possible that the impact of psychiatric comorbidity is much greater than in the adult. How *much* greater and how *much* of a factor in the population of juvenile sexual offenders remain questions for research. Whether it is statistically true that psychiatric comorbidity is connected to sexual offending behaviors, a significant thrust of this book is on clinical assessment, which means trying to understand the risk, protective, and other factors in the lives of the individual under assessment while also understanding the characteristics of the larger population.

In fact, among juvenile sexual offenders, one often finds factors that are significant in terms of mental health. Nevertheless, this does not mean that psychiatric disorders lead to sexual offending—merely that they coexist. In some cases, there may be a common root for both the sexual offending behaviors *and* the psychiatric disorder, or perhaps the offense gave rise to the development of a later psychiatric disorder. In still other cases, although comorbidity exists, there may be no causal relationship of any kind between the offending and the psychiatric difficulty. It is the assessor's job to recognize the existence of psychiatric disorders and establish what relationship, if any, exists between them. To do this, the assessor must have a clear grounding in psychopathology, as well as forensic work, in the event that comorbidity exists between mental health and criminal behaviors.

THE MENTAL HEALTH CONTINUUM

The difference between mental health and mental illness lies along the continuum illustrated in Figure 9.1 and is marked by an increase toward functionality at the one end and an increasing movement toward dysfunctionality at the other. On the mental health end lies wellness, or the idea that health cuts across all areas of life. Symbolizing healthy body, mind, and spirit, wellness is defined by six features that capture many of the developmental accomplishments previously described as frequently conspicuous in juvenile sexual offenders by their absence:

1. *Self-Acceptance:* a sense of personal satisfaction and a healthy self-image regardless of whichever direction life may have taken
2. *Purpose:* a set of values and goals that gives direction and meaning to life
3. *Environmental Mastery:* the ability to manage the tasks and demands of everyday life
4. *Personal Growth:* a sense of accomplishment, personal competency, and continued development
5. *Positive Relationships:* successful relationships that provide meaningful ties to the larger world
6. *Autonomy:* a sense of independence and self-determination

At the other end of the continuum lies mental illness. This term refers to major psychiatric conditions that significantly interfere with the ability to think clearly, overcome pervasive emotional disturbances, or respond appropriately to environment stimuli and that often trigger simultaneous disturbance in more than one of these domains (cognitive, affective, and physical). Mental illness is often evident in the inability to make sense of or respond rationally to external or internal stimuli, respond appropriately to external demands or expectations, make competent decisions, and judge right from wrong. Almost by definition, a mental illness represents a significant departure from the ability to make well-formed judgments and take appropriate

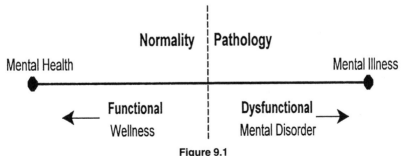

Figure 9.1
The mental health continuum: From mental health to mental disorder.

action due to a failure of mental process. Diagnoses of major mental illness often include pervasive and significant depressive and anxiety disorders, schizophrenia and other psychotic conditions, and other affective or mental conditions that are debilitating, affect multiple domains, and cannot be overcome by willpower, pep talk, behavioral change, or fear of consequences.

Rather than adopting the use of the term mental illness (or mental health, for that matter), the *DSM-IV-TR* (American Psychiatric Association, 2000) uses the term *mental disorder* to denote the boundary between mental health (normality) and mental illness (pathology). The *DSM-IV-TR* describes mental disorders as significant behavioral or psychological syndromes or patterns associated with distress, functional disability, or increased risk of death, pain, disability, or loss of freedom. It excludes deviance and social conflicts as disorders, describing these as mental disorders only when they arise as a symptom of a specific dysfunction in an individual. Hence, rather than defined as mental disorders, rape generally remains a criminal behavior and civil disobedience a sociopolitical conflict. Accordingly, anchored on the line between mental normality and mental pathology, the *DSM-IV-TR* describes all things on the pathological side of the line as mental disorders, thus covering a broad range of pathologies that are based on ability to function rather than the specific symptoms of a major mental illness (which exists only at the extreme end of the continuum). Simply put, if mental health is significantly enough impaired, then by definition it becomes a mental disorder. Accordingly, we can think of comorbidity in sexual offending as a coexisting mental disorder that affects functioning and can be recognized as a separate syndrome or complex in its own right.

MENTAL HEALTH IN AMERICA

Mental disorders are defined by symptoms and functional impairments. According to the U.S. Surgeon General's report on mental health (U.S. Department of Health and Human Services, 1999), 20% of Americans experience a mental disorder during the course of a single year, and 15% of those experiencing a mental disorder also experience a co-occurring diagnosis of substance abuse. Regier et al. (1988) reported that 15% (25.6 million) Americans over the age of 18 meet the criteria for at least one substance abuse or mental disorder. Although not as well documented in children and adolescents, the Surgeon General's report states that almost 21% of all children aged 9 to 17 experience signs and symptoms of a psychiatric disorder with at least mild functional impairment during any given year. Approximately 11% (4 million youths) experience significant functional impairment, and about 5% of all children and adolescents experience extreme functional impairment during the course of any given year. Anxiety disorders represent 13% of diagnosed disorders in children and adolescents, followed by disruptive disorders (10.3%) and mood disorders (6.2%). Levin, Hanson, Coe, and Taylor (1998) reported diagnosable broad mental health disorders in 12–20% of children and adolescents and serious emotional disturbance in 9–13% of children aged 9 to 17.

MENTAL HEALTH IN THE JUVENILE SEXUAL OFFENDER

Correlation is a statistical measurement, whereas comorbidity, which is not a statistical property, is a statement of coexistence of two or more phenomena. The question is, Does psychiatric comorbidity occur with high enough frequency in juvenile sexual offenders to demonstrate the properties of correlation?

Correlation measures the link between two or more phenomena. Significant correlation means that when one factor is present, the other factor will invariably be present as well, regardless of whether a causal or dependent relationship actually exists.[1] This means that unless it is sufficiently common for a mental disorder also to be present in sexually aggressive children and juveniles, no significant correlation can be said to exist. Although there is a dearth of studies on the presence of mental disorders in juvenile sexual offenders, it is commonly believed that mental disorders do exist with some regularity in the population of juvenile sexual offenders, as well as in the delinquent juvenile population in general. Cocozza and Skowyra (2000) and Eileen Ryan (2001) reported that research on mental disorders among youth in the juvenile justice system is scarce and flawed, and they described inconsistent definitions and measurements of mental illness, as well as biased and nonrandom samples. Nevertheless, Cocozza and Skowyra reported that juvenile delinquents experience substantially higher rates of mental disorders than do youth in the general public and noted that with regard to broad mental disorders in youths, "research has found that most youth in the juvenile justice system qualify for at least one diagnosis" (p. 6). They estimated that 20% of children in the juvenile justice system have a serious mental health problem. Grisso, Barnum, Fletcher, Cauffman, and Peuschold (2001) concurred, also reporting a greater proportion of mental health problems in the delinquent population, with diagnosis rates as high as 70–80% when all mental disorders are included and 40–50% when disruptive behavioral and substance abuse disorders are excluded. Bilchik (1998) reported that 150,000 youths who come into contact with the juvenile justice system each year suffer from a diagnosable mental disorder.

In fact, the idea of a comorbid mental disorder is an almost a priori assumption in the assessment and treatment of almost all behaviorally and emotionally troubled children and adolescents kids, sexually aggressive or

---

[1] This is true in the case of positive correlations. Negative correlations indicate that where one factor exists, the other is invariably absent.

not. There is, then, a face valid and clinically supported argument that co-morbidity is common among juvenile sexual offenders, and because this belief is so widely held, observed, and practiced, there is thus a priori evidence of a correlation between juvenile sexual offending and mental disorders.

However, just as correlationship does not imply causation (i.e., two factors can routinely coexist without any actual process of influence among the two), comorbidity is not necessarily a cause of juvenile sexual offending. In many cases of delinquency, a diagnosable mental disorder may be merely peripheral, or independently coexisting, without any significant impact or influence on aggressive or antisocial behavior. Regardless, then, of high correlation, when comorbidity of psychiatric disturbance and sexual offending does exist, it does not imply that an influential relationship exists between these two phenomena. Nevertheless, clinicians should consider whether a significant causal or interactive relationship exists between a mental disorder and behavior in the individual under assessment or in treatment. Not doing so would be an omission in assessment, and an even greater omission—and error—in treatment. Lexcen and Redding (2000) asserted that because of the level of mental disorders among juvenile offenders, mental health assessment is a requirement, especially as Redding (Reppucci & Redding, 2000) also asserted that such disorders can contribute substantially to delinquency (thus asserting causality, at least in some cases). Grisso and Barnum (2000) also recognized the need for mental health evaluations of youths entering the system. These are necessary not only to respond and provide treatment to kids in mental and emotional distress but also to assess for comorbid mental disorders that may have played a role in their behaviors as well as the influence of a mental disorder on risk.

Minimally, as shown in Figure 9.2, where comorbidity does exist, the clinician must assess the impact of the psychiatric condition. In addition, in an area often related or integral to comorbidity, the clinician must also assess cognitive capacity, or intellect, thinking, and the capacity to reason and judge right from wrong. This includes:

Psychiatric Comorbidity		
Assessment of Symptoms and Impact	Assessment of Cognitive Abilities and Skills	Comorbid Interaction
• Diagnosis • Impact of symptoms on behavior • Need for prior treatment • Response to past treatment • Need for medication to manage symptoms	• Intellectual capacity • Judgment • Insight • Comprehension	• Impact of diagnosis on cognition • Impact of cognition on diagnosis • Nature of interaction between diagnosis and cognition

Figure 9.2
Assessment of comorbidity.

- The nature of the diagnosis
- The significance of the diagnosis in terms of its impact on sexual offending or other antisocial behaviors
- The history of and response to prior treatment
- The need for psychiatric medication to manage symptoms
- Intellectual capacity, or the ability to learn complex information and apply thought processes that support judgment, comprehension, and insight
- Judgment, or the capacity to understand individual situations and variables and draw reasoned, sound, and appropriate conclusions
- Insight, or the capacity to understand personal motivations, the motivations and expectations of others, interactions with others, and triggers and precipitants to ideas, emotions, and behavior
- Comprehension, or the ability to understand social cues and expectations and the capacity to respond correctly to such cues
- The effect of the interaction, if any, between psychiatric diagnosis and cognitive ability and functioning

THE NATURE OF MENTAL DISORDERS IN JUVENILE OFFENDERS

Little concrete and specific data exist about the presence and types of mental disorders among juvenile sexual offenders and the juvenile offender population in general. This is due in part to a lack of consistent, well-defined, and broad research and in part due to the great difficulty in discerning true mental disorders in these populations. That is, although it relatively easy to spot the presence of a florid mental illness, mental disorders can often be more difficult to recognize or tease out because they lie hidden in the background of day-to-day functioning. In many instances, we may not recognize that a mental disorder exists because the juvenile does not readily present or volunteer symptoms and sometimes because symptoms are masked by more obvious and more commonplace disorders such as conduct, oppositional, impulsive, or attentional disorders, or even depressive disorders. And because a sizable number of juvenile sexual offenders are not delinquent or antisocial in other ways (i.e., they do not otherwise meet the criteria for a conduct or oppositional disorder), it can be even more difficult to recognize mental health conditions that are not grossly pathological. In fact, for these and other reasons, diagnosis and differential diagnosis require considerable training, skill, and experience in the clinician. Even more important questions are, What mental disorders are most prevalent; What mental disorders are most significant in terms of the mental health continuum; and What role, if any, do mental disorders play in the development and enactment of sexual offending behaviors?

The second largest category of mental health disorders in children and

adolescents aged 9 to 17 are behavioral disorders, including conduct, oppositional defiant, and attention-deficit disorders, described by the Surgeon General as a collection of antisocial behaviors "rather than a coherent pattern of
mental dysfunction" (U.S. Department of Health and Human Services, 1999,
p. 164). It is not surprising that these disorders are the most prevalent among
juvenile sexual offenders as well, with behavioral disorders accounting for
perhaps half of all mental disorders among juvenile sexual offenders
(Kavoussi, Kaplan, & Becker, 1988; Righthand & Welch, 2001; Will, 1999), with
relatively few experiencing a major mental illness, such as major depression,
bipolar disorder, or schizophrenia. Because the prevalence of mental disorders among troubled kids is inflated by the inclusion of disruptive disorders,
Cocozza and Skowyra (2000) noted that "it is not uncommon for 80 percent or
more of the juvenile justice population to be diagnosed with conduct disorder" (p. 6). As already described, Grisso et al. (2001) noted that behavioral
diagnoses increase the rate of mental disorders among troubled juveniles by
as much as 30–40%, and elsewhere Grisso (1998) wrote that conduct disorder
is the most prevalent diagnosis among juvenile delinquents, representing as
much as 50% of the diagnoses. This should come as no surprise, as conduct
disorder describes the behavior that constitutes juvenile delinquency. It is difficult to say, however, whether the behavior leads to the diagnosis or the disorder causes the behavior. Similarly, although a diagnosis of conduct disorder
has great bearing on juvenile sexual offending, it is equally true that such behaviors often create the diagnosis.

CONDUCT DISORDER

The frequent diagnosis of conduct disorder among juvenile offenders is potentially of some philosophical concern because it implies that children who
misbehave in certain ways and beyond a certain limit have a mental disorder.
The same is true also of children who act out defiantly (oppositional defiant
disorder). This is why Cocozza and Skowyra (2000) reported that virtually
100% of juveniles in trouble qualify for a diagnosable mental disorder. If the
same were true for adults, suddenly every adult criminal would be diagnosed
with a mental disorder, rather than just criminal behavior. However, whether
or not we agree, descriptions of mental disorders among troubled juveniles
include behavioral disorders, and we must take that into account when we try
to make sense of such statistics.

The diagnosis of conduct disorder, although behavioral and antisocial in
nature rather than signifying a major mental illness, is not insignificant because it signals the possibility of *later* significant mental health difficulties, including personality, substance abuse, affective, and anxiety disorders, especially with earlier onset. Accordingly, the diagnosis, which differentiates
among mild, moderate, and severe forms of the disorder, as well as childhood

versus adolescent onset, should be made only when there is a persistent and repetitive pattern associated with major functional impairment and when the behavior is symptomatic of an underlying dysfunction within the individual rather than in reaction to the environment (American Psychiatric Association, 2000). In addition, not only because the diagnosis sometimes serves as a gateway diagnosis to later more significant mental disorders, but also because the diagnosis is often currently comorbid with other psychiatric diagnoses, Grisso (1998) noted the importance of looking beyond, and not stopping at, the diagnosis of conduct disorder, which is frequently the obvious diagnosis made among this population.

SERIOUS MENTAL HEALTH DISORDERS

Most of the psychiatric comorbidity in juvenile sexual offenders, then, is constituted by disruptive and antisocial behaviors, rather than mental dysfunction. Filtering these behavioral diagnoses out, we can focus on the more limited occurrence of other psychiatric diagnoses that more closely fit the concept of a mental disorder in that they have a damaging or crippling effect on the ability to function due to often severe disruptions in affect, anxiety, or thought process. Cocozza and Skowyra (2000) used the term *serious mental health disorder* or *serious emotional disturbance* to distinguish between children whose behavior qualifies them for a mental disorder (including behavioral disorders) and youths who experience more complex and significant difficulties with mental health that move further toward the mental illness end of the spectrum. Using these more significant diagnoses as cutoff criteria, the frequency of comorbidity in juvenile sexual offenders drops drastically, although Cocozza and Skowyra reported that one in every five kids (20%) in the juvenile justice system experiences a serious mental disorder, and Grisso (1998) reported percentages that vary widely but also suggested that significant mental disorders (excluding behavioral disorders) are not infrequent among youthful offenders. Most agree that serious disorders such as schizophrenia and other psychotic disorders are the least prevalent, and Grisso suggested rates of between 1% and 6%. This estimate is far higher than prevalence rates in the general population, which for schizophrenia is between 0.5% and 1.5% (American Psychiatric Association, 2000).

AFFECTIVE AND ANXIETY DISORDERS

Affective and anxiety disorders are widespread and represent a fair amount of the diagnoses ascribed to adolescents in general. E. P. Ryan (2001) reported that depression in juveniles is generally underdiagnosed in the general population, with as many as 70–80% of depressed adolescents not receiving treatment as a result. She noted that major depression is even more prevalent among juvenile offenders and that a significant proportion of juvenile offenders suffers from depression or bipolar disorder. Sometimes, depression in children and adolescents is considered to be masked, emerging as irritation, agitation, and even aggression, rather than depressed mood and listless behavior. However, this requires further investigation. Depressive disorders include major (or clinical) depression that ranges from mild to severe and can include psychotic features; dysthymia, or a long-lasting, chronic, mild depression; and bipolar disorder, which can include both depression and agitated, manic, and even psychotic thinking and behaviors.

It can be argued that depression can influence criminal behavior, especially if the depression takes on an agitated form—as some believe it does in adolescence—as a means for alleviating depression or just feeling better. However, it seems unlikely that depression itself has a significant effect on the development and enactment of highly antisocial behavior. If anything, the opposite seems more likely. This may be less true of dysthymic disorder, which must last for one year or more in children and adolescents (and two years in adults) to be diagnosed and thus starts to approach the level of a personality disorder given its enduring quality. Here, one can see how feeling mildly depressed almost all of the time can create a deadening of other emotions and interactions, lessen motivation, and make the child more susceptible to ideas that might otherwise be unacceptable, especially if he thinks they might lead to an improvement in mood. However, as with depression, a direct link between the mental disorder and the behavior seems tenuous, and there is no evidence in the limited literature to support a significant link between dysthymia and sexual aggression.

The manic phase of a bipolar disorder can be more obviously linked to behavioral aggression and the acting out of manic, and sometimes psychotic, ideas. However, bipolar disorder is flat much of the time in that there are discrete episodes of manic thoughts and behaviors, and it is unlikely that sexual offending occurs exclusively within these windows of mania. Further, bipolar disorder is not easily understood or recognized in children (E. P. Ryan, 2001), and many consider the disorder to be rare in children and adolescents. Whereas depression and dysthymia may begin at any age and are common diagnoses in children and adolescents, the average age of onset for bipolar disorder is 20 (American Psychiatric Association, 2000). On the other hand, cyclothymia (frequent mood swings that are a form of bipolar disorder and have onset in adolescence or early adulthood) is often evident in adolescents. On the face of it, chronic mood swings such as those found in cyclothymia may be a more appropriate way to recognize and respond to what is often, perhaps incorrectly, diagnosed as bipolar disorder in juvenile sexual offenders. In addition, such mood swings may have a greater influence on both judgment and behavior than either depression or bipolar disorder in the same way that dysthymia might, in which acting out behavioral impulses may serve as a means to gain relief, and in which there may be little regard for consequences. In the case of cyclothymia, there is an additional factor of impaired judgment during episodes of frequent and near-manic mood swings (hypomania) that are never absent for more than two months. Thus, in cyclothymia it is more likely that the effects and presence of mood swings are more pervasive and routine than the more limited frequency of bipolar manic episodes.

On the other hand, anxiety, which encompasses a range of disorders, is often difficult to recognize in juveniles and may easily be masked or mistaken for depression, oppositionality, or agitated acting out. However, with the exception of posttraumatic stress disorder (PTSD) and obsessive-compulsive disorder (OCD), which are anxiety disorders, there is no clear connection between the disorder and antisocial behavior. In the case of PTSD (discussed later in this chapter) that follows an experience of sexual victimization, there is the possibility of recapitulation of some kind, or the need to re-enact or somehow relive the sexual abuse as a means to control the symptoms. An individual with OCD may feel a compulsion to act out an obsessive thought, which in this case would be sexual behavior with another person. Nevertheless, although there is considerable evidence that juveniles who have been sexually victimized are at greater risk to engage later in sexually aggressive behavior, whether this is related to the diagnosis of PTSD is not clear. Similarly, there is little evidence to support the idea of sexually aggressive behavior as the outcome of an obsessive-compulsive mental disorder, other than in the possible case of an autistic spectrum disorder (discussed later in this chapter).

ATTENTION-DEFICIT/HYPERACTIVITY DISORDER

The diagnosis of attention-deficit/hyperactivity disorder (ADHD) has been controversial for some time in terms of both overdiagnosis and appropriate treatment. Nonetheless, there is little question that many kids in general, and certainly many juvenile sexual offenders, suffer from this disorder.

Given the relatively high incidence of ADHD diagnoses in juvenile sexual offenders, the first issue is not which treatment is most appropriate or most effective, but whether the diagnosis is correct. Too often, children and adolescents are diagnosed with ADHD on the basis of skimpy and poorly defined observations, and pharmacological treatment begins with little further evaluation (Zametkin & Ernst, 1999, reported an eightfold increase in the prescription of stimulant medication during the 1990s). Indeed, ADHD is one of the most commonly diagnosed disorders in children and adolescents, but in practice many children diagnosed with ADHD do not meet all of the diagnostic criteria (Jensen et al., 1999; U.S. Department of Health and Human Services, 1999). In reality, clinicians often cite fidgeting, inattentiveness, distractibility, silliness, and other behaviors that are or can be symptoms of ADHD as evidence that

ADHD is the correct diagnosis, rather than any number of other diagnoses that may also account for some of the same behavioral symptoms, including mental retardation and borderline intellectual functioning, oppositional defiant disorder, learning disorders, depression, boredom, or disinterest.

Regarding the possible influence of ADHD on juvenile sexual offending, it is true that attention and hyperactive disorders can lead to out-of-control and sometimes highly antisocial behaviors. The ADHD symptom of impulsivity (i.e., action without forethought or regard for consequences) is often considered to be the aspect of hyperactivity that is most likely to impact sexual offending. Even so, impulsivity alone does not cause sexual offending, which requires that many internal and external obstacles be overcome and is a form of antisocial behavior that mere impulsivity cannot explain. In many cases sexual offending is not an impulsive act at all but requires planning and patience. On the other hand, some sexually abusive acts are both reactive and impulsive, as well as tension reducing for the perpetrator. This suggests that this component of ADHD may play a role in influencing sexual offending behavior in some juveniles. Nonetheless, such behaviors are more likely the result of a coexisting conduct disorder than an attention-deficit disorder.

POSTTRAUMATIC STRESS DISORDER

Posttraumatic stress disorder is also often overdiagnosed in children and adolescents on the basis that agitation and emotional and behavioral problems in juveniles who have been abused or maltreated must be the result of the earlier abuse. Linked to this notion is the idea, discussed in Chapter 3, that developmental difficulties, abuses, and negligence, as well as exposure to domestic violence and other developmental insults, automatically add up to trauma in the child whether the child experiences it that way or not.

Although abusive and distressing childhood experiences are traumagenic in that they sow the seeds for the experience of trauma, they are not necessarily perceived or experienced as traumatic by the child. The risk for the clinician is assuming that a diagnosis of PTSD is justified when faced with current behavioral or emotional difficulties in the juvenile *and* a history of trauma, or at least a traumagenic history. This is tantamount to the idea that if the only tool you have is a hammer, everything looks like a nail. We must have a broader set of tools in our clinical tool belt. By jumping to conclusions, we risk overlooking the fact that many behavioral and emotional difficulties are not pathological but actually part of the typical course of adolescence. Second, we fail to recognize that the same symptoms may be evidence of a different diagnosis if they are evidence of a mental disorder at all. Third, if we do not recognize the severe nature of PTSD and its often severe symptomatology, we lower the bar to making the diagnosis and risk overpathologizing the normal and expected sequelae to trauma—this is like treating the appearance of grief following the death of a loved one as a mental disorder, rather than a normal occurrence. When a diagnosis of PTSD is made, even under circumstances in which the child or adolescent has no recollection of a trauma or does not experience a particular event as traumatic, clinicians will sometimes search for the "missing" trauma, in these situations working hard to convince the juvenile that he was, indeed, traumatized.

In fact, many children who have been maltreated never develop true signs of PTSD despite stress and behavioral and emotional problems that may result from difficult early life circumstances. That is, kids can experience stress following a trauma or traumagenic experience without developing a mental disorder. Despite the likelihood of a direct link between early abuse or maltreatment and later problems, and sometimes the development of personality difficulties and disorders, this does not add up to the specific diagnosis of PTSD. Just as deficits in attention do not automatically equal ADHD, it is also true that symptoms of posttraumatic stress do not automatically equal PTSD. In the same way that mental health and mental illness exist as points along a continuum, behavioral and emotional difficulties lie along a continuum with behaviors of concern at one end and mental disorders at the other, as shown in Figure 9.3. We should be careful not to overpathologize behaviors that are problematic but do not necessarily reach the proportion of a mental disorder.

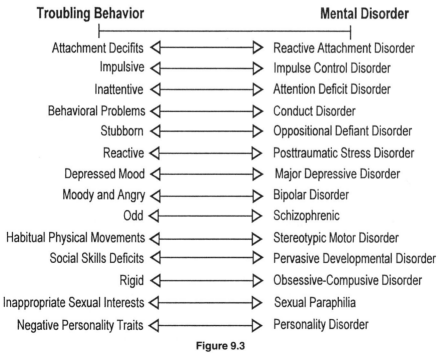

Troubling Behavior		**Mental Disorder**
Attachment Decifits	⟵⟶	Reactive Attachment Disorder
Impulsive	⟵⟶	Impulse Control Disorder
Inattentive	⟵⟶	Attention Deficit Disorder
Behavioral Problems	⟵⟶	Conduct Disorder
Stubborn	⟵⟶	Oppositional Defiant Disorder
Reactive	⟵⟶	Posttraumatic Stress Disorder
Depressed Mood	⟵⟶	Major Depressive Disorder
Moody and Angry	⟵⟶	Bipolar Disorder
Odd	⟵⟶	Schizophrenic
Habitual Physical Movements	⟵⟶	Stereotypic Motor Disorder
Social Skills Deficits	⟵⟶	Pervasive Developmental Disorder
Rigid	⟵⟶	Obsessive-Compusive Disorder
Inappropriate Sexual Interests	⟵⟶	Sexual Paraphilia
Negative Personality Traits	⟵⟶	Personality Disorder

Figure 9.3
From problem behavior to mental health pathology.

A second risk for clinicians is assuming that PTSD has played a role in the sexual offending behavior. As described, one possible influence of true PTSD in the occurrence of juvenile sexual offending might lie in the special case of a PTSD following sexual victimization. In this case, the juvenile who has been sexually victimized may be recapitulating or somehow attempting to exorcise a traumatic memory that causes clinical distress or attempting to experience a sense of mastery over a social environment that he experiences as dangerous. These explanations seem strained, however, as it clear that most individuals who are experiencing PTSD, including those who are the victims of sexual abuse, do not engage in the victimization of others as a means of reducing or eliminating symptoms. Although earlier sexual victimization is clearly common among juvenile sexual offenders, the connection between that earlier abuse and later sexual aggression is more likely due to the development of attachment difficulties, antisocial behaviors, and pathological personality development than the result of PTSD, as well as the development of reactive and impulsive behaviors in some juveniles, and especially children. As with ADHD, the level of impulsivity and reactivity sometimes attached to PTSD in children and adolescents may be far more instrumental in the development of sexually abusive behaviors than other aspects of posttraumatic stress. Combined with the emotional numbing often associated with PTSD, which may allow juvenile sexual offenders to remain cut off from the experiences of their victims, comorbid impulsive and reactive behaviors may contribute to juvenile sexual offending.

Reactive Attachment Disorder

Some clinicians have used the *DSM-IV-TR* diagnosis of reactive attachment disorder of infancy and childhood (sometimes referred to as RAD) to describe the phenomenon of apparent attachment disorders and difficulties in some juvenile sexual offenders. In general, however, the diagnosis is more appropriately aimed at young children who exhibit serious and obvious deficiencies in social (and particularly parental) relationships. The diagnosis is less relevant to the far more complex and far less obvious aspects of social disconnection and lack of secure bonding present in the troubled older child and adolescent. Although such disturbances of attachment and intimacy are the result of earlier childhood experiences, the behavior does not follow the experience in the immediate or direct manner that would normally define reactivity. The sexually aggressive and other troubled behaviors displayed by juveniles may, more appropriately, be considered the long-term sequelae of insecure attachments. Here, lack of attachment is transformed over time into acting out behaviors that if unchecked, may turn into persistent and lifetime antisocial behaviors and serious relational difficulties. It is this lack of attachment, not RAD, that

Cognitive Skills
Comprehension . . . the ability to understand the details of a situation in all of its complexity
Judgment . . . . the ability to form an opinion that takes into account appropriate perspective and contextual factors and adequately reflects the relevant input
Decision Making . . . the ability to recognize the problem, discern between different choices, and understand possible outcomes
Insight . . . . the capacity to understand situations, events, and other phenomena with depth, in a penetrating manner, and sometimes intuitively

Figure 9.4
Descriptions of specific cognitive skills related to competence.

may be a significant contributor to juvenile sexual offending, although there is no specific *DSM-IV-TR* diagnosis to address this concept.

COGNITIVE IMPAIRMENT AND MENTAL RETARDATION

Two other diagnostic types not uncommon among juvenile sexual offenders are the categories of impaired intellectual functioning and autistic-like experiences of the world. In the first case, juvenile sexual offenders frequently exhibit average to low-average intelligence (IQs between 85 and 115, where 100 represents average IQ), but it is not uncommon to see borderline IQs in juvenile sexual offenders (IQs of between 70 and 85), as well as IQs in the range of mental retardation (below 70). For the cognitively impaired juvenile, it is especially important to understand the impact that borderline or diminished IQ may have on comprehension, judgment, decision making, and insight, concepts described in more detail in Figure 9.4. These factors together add up to individual competence, or the ability to respond or function with the knowledge and skills required to form and act on appropriate and adequate decisions. Additionally, individuals with lower IQs tend to have less ability to deal with abstract ideas and to understand more easily and respond to concrete ideas, information, and situations. This has implications for both assessment and treatment.

Cognitive impairment has a direct and recognizable impact on the individual's ability to form opinions, make decisions, understand consequences, and take action. Individuals with low IQs are not necessarily more likely to act out sexually or to be at greater risk for sexual offending. However, individuals with low IQs who have been sexualized by one means or another do not have the protective factor afforded by higher intelligence and thus may not have the intellectual capacity required either to recognize or sort through the many factors involved in decisions to act out sexually. In some extreme cases, usually involving lower IQ, the individual may not be fully aware of social norms and expectations, have any insight into the victim's experience, recognize or think about the consequences, or even be truly aware that he is committing a serious infraction.

AUTISTIC SPECTRUM DISORDERS: PERVASIVE DEVELOPMENTAL DISORDERS

Juveniles with autistic-spectrum disorders have extremely poor social skills, often to the point of being seriously undersocialized, and lack the ability to understand the way that others respond to and interact with their environment. For diagnoses such as these to be attached to sexual offenses, however, the juvenile often has a relatively high level of behavioral and cognitive functioning, at least compared to the classic autistic child who is disengaged from and uninvolved with the outside world. Typically, this involves a diagnosis of Asperger's syndrome (in the *DSM-IV-TR*, Asperger's disorder), considered by many to be high-functioning autism. This disorder often involves an average to high IQ and a significant deficit in social skills, social understanding, and ability to recognize the manner in which others think and experience the world. Individuals with autistic-spectrum disorders are often considered unable to intuitively understand the minds of other people (the way that others think and feel) or form abstract mental representations of the world that both inform judgment and guide behaviors. This deficit in social understanding, in which the child is unable to form a *theory of mind* (or understand how others think), is considered a hallmark of the disorder and is present at birth and throughout the life span.

Other significant features of autistic-spectrum disorders include emotional and behavioral rigidity and difficulty accepting change, obsessive and compulsive attention to details, significantly impaired reciprocal social interactions, and lack of intimacy and shared enjoyment. Finally, with this disorder children often appear physically awkward and exhibit idiosyncratic mannerisms and behaviors that not only further isolate them from others and make them appear different but often suggest other mental disorders such as OCD, stereotypic vocal or motor disorders, schizophrenia, and schizotypal or schizoid personality disorder. Indeed, many of the symptoms of pervasive developmental disorders appear similar to the secondary symptoms of schizophrenia.

Although such pervasive developmental disorders keep the individual separate from others, the higher functioning autistic-like child is not necessarily prevented from wanting and seeking contact and relationships with others, especially after entering adolescence, which creates both an unwanted separation from others and a frustration that can lead to severe depression, anger and agitation, and sometimes bizarre and dangerous behavior by the time the child reaches mid-adolescence. Not infrequently, they fail to appreciate or recognize subtlety and instead act out their thoughts, impulses, needs, and interests in ways that are devoid of understanding, without regard for others, grossly antisocial, and sometimes dangerous. In particular, for many kids who suffer from a high-functioning pervasive developmental disorder, acting out is a means to relieve the tremendous emotional and intellectual tension that may build up as a result of social isolation and ineptness.

Juveniles with autistic-spectrum disorders—even those with average or high intelligence—may act with the same lack of insight as the cognitively impaired child does and may also act out behaviorally without recognizing or caring about social consequences. As the child with a pervasive developmental disorder can be extremely fixed on and preoccupied with his own interests and ideas (obsessions) and often feels the need to act these out (compulsions), this can present a real risk in those juveniles who have been sexualized through earlier experiences or who may have developed a sexual preoccupation. This is especially true for those juveniles who have already acted on these ideas at least once.

Although pervasive developmental disorders are recognized more frequently now, more subtle forms of the disorder (such as high-functioning autism) are often not recognized until later in life—and even then not until diagnosticians familiar with the symptomatology become involved. Yet this is an important diagnosis in understanding the interaction between the diagnosis and sexual offending, the influence of the disorder on behavior, and the approach to and course of treatment. Because evidence of the disorder is present from infancy on, clinicians who conduct assessments should seek out developmental and elementary age histories in all children.

Psychotic Disorders

Psychosis is characterized by a failure to recognize and respond appropriately to reality and an accompanying lack of reality testing in which individuals experiencing a psychosis are unable to distinguish between their internal reality and the external reality. The essential features of psychosis remain the same despite different causes, and psychosis most typically results from schizophrenia or related conditions, a deep depression that spills over into a psychotic condition, or a bipolar episode in which mania and expansiveness become so great that they form a psychosis. By definition, psychosis involves delusions, hallucinations, disorganized thinking, or disorganized behavior and is often accompanied by other unusual experiences and behaviors. Psychosis is a rare disorder in general, but psychoses and psychotic-like conditions (or atypical psychoses) are nonetheless present among some juvenile sexual offenders.

Psychosis itself is so varied and individualized that it cannot be said to necessarily contribute to juvenile sexual offending, other than in a manner strictly defined by the specific case. However, due to disconnections from reality, misattribution and the inability to understand or respond appropriately to social interactions, and the countless and unpredictable ideas of psychotic imagination and experience, it is easy to see how a psychotic condition may take over a person's thoughts and actions and result in behavior that is dangerous to self and others. Additionally, the incidence and likelihood of violence are greater among individuals with major mental illnesses, especially psychosis. For this reason, more than in any other mental disorder, incompetence may play a significant role in determining the personal responsibility of the individual in perpetrating a crime. For juveniles who have been sexualized in some way or have otherwise become preoccupied by sexual thoughts and who also have a history of poor boundaries and conduct problems, psychosis may be an important factor on which a sexual offense, or reoffense, turns.

On the other hand, although violence and agitated behavior may be more common among individuals with psychosis, it is the combination of other factors working together that brings this propensity to life. No single factor, including psychosis, is itself "either necessary or sufficient for a person to behave aggressively toward others" (Monahan et al., 2001, p. 142). The same is true of the interaction between sexual offending and psychosis.

Impulse-Reactive Disorders

Although there is a *DSM-IV-TR* category for impulse-control disorders, in this case the term describes underlying disorders that—although often implied by and evident in other behavioral diagnoses—are diagnostic elements in their own right. By impulse and reactive disorders we mean often thoughtless behaviors that are not preplanned and frequently occur in reaction to an unexpected situation, spontaneous thought, or other unplanned event. As stated, many sexual offenses are the result of planning and predation, but many are also the result of reactive responses and impulsive acting out without thought or regard for consequences. In reactive disorders there is little motivation or planning for the behavior, which is more of a primitive response to the stimuli. In impulsive disorders there is a similar reactive quality, although it is more of a spontaneous (rather than primitive or intuitive) version in which motivation is more clearly understood as "it seemed like a good idea at the time." Together, these two propensities form a clinical syndrome often subsumed by and present in other disorders, and especially the behavioral disorders.

Paraphilias

Paraphilias describe sexual fetishes that are outside of the norm of sexual thoughts and practices in the general population. As discussed in Chapter 5, sexual deviance is often not a factor in juvenile sexual offending. That is, the offense, which may itself be deviant, is neither driven by nor motivated by a sexual fetish. However, in those cases where a paraphilia exists, the occurrence of a sexual offense is the direct result of the fetish *plus* other factors that allow the perpetrator (juvenile or adult) to overcome the various internal and social inhibitors and barriers that prevent sexual victimization. This means that although the comorbid paraphilia may be a key factor, the sexual offense itself cannot occur without an accompanying comorbid condition such as conduct disorder, cognitive impairment, psychosis, or significant personality disorder that allows the paraphilia to be played out in real life with a victim or party incapable of giving consent. Regardless, the presence of paraphilic comorbidity is of concern especially when it involves patterns of sexual arousal that are clearly deviant (e.g., sexual arousal to children) and in which sexual satisfaction can only be achieved through inappropriate behavior (sex with children or animals) or involves harm of some kind to another person (e.g., rape or sadism).

Paraphilias are difficult to discern in adolescents because sexual interests are still forming, and sexual interests (like other things) that may be deviant in adulthood may not be in adolescence but may represent only a passing interest. Caution is recommended, then, in diagnosing any paraphilia in a juvenile below the age of 16, primarily because paraphilias suggest well-defined sexual interests and formed fetishes that often develop only in later adolescence and early adulthood. Regarding specific paraphilic interest in prepubescent children (pedophilia), the *DSM-IV-TR* does not allow the diagnosis to be made prior to age 16, in effect defining this as the age at and beyond which sexual fetishes and interests can be considered well formed and meaningful. Doren (2002) asserted that the diagnosis can be made in cases where sexual interest in young children is clear prior to age 16. However, this is his own interpretation of the *DSM-IV-TR* wording that guides the diagnosis, and he cautioned the clinician against making this diagnosis without clear and strong evidence that pedophilia exists. It is likely that pedophilic interests *do* exist in juveniles under 16, such as among adolescents who have perpetrated multiple sexual offenses against multiple very young children. On the other hand, many adolescents sexually offend children because they are the most available, most accessible, and easiest to control rather than because of any specific sexual interest in children.

PERSONALITY DISORDERS

With the exception of mental retardation, most of the aforementioned disorders represent those affective, cognitive, behavioral, and sometimes physiological diagnoses that are most often the focus of treatment and are diagnosed on Axis I of the *DSM-IV-TR*'s five-axis diagnostic classification. On the other hand, personality disorders, along with mental retardation, are classified on Axis II. Rather than reflecting or approximating mental illness, personality disorders represent dysfunctional character traits, a maladaptive personality style, and an impaired sense of connection to the world.

Personality is the means by which we interact with the world and by which we experience others, they experience us, and we experience our place in the world. It represents the interactional layer between self and the world through which everything is filtered, including all incoming information and outgoing communication. A personality disorder signifies a significant, pervasive, and chronic problem with that interactional membrane. The *DSM-IV-TR* describes personality disorders as enduring, maladaptive, and dysfunctional patterns of perceiving, relating to, and thinking about the environment and oneself that are exhibited in a wide range of social and personal contexts (American Psychiatric Association, 2000).

Hart, Watt, and Vincent (2002) noted that there is no clear consensus on whether personality disorders exist in children and adolescents, suggesting that defined and stable personality does not develop until at least late adolescence. Nevertheless, many juvenile sexual offenders, of all ages, exhibit strong and clear traits of personality disorders in the making. This means that they exhibit many dysfunctional traits that underlie their experience of the world, their sense of identity, and how they fit into the world. Actually, this may not be far from the description of normal adolescence, but in the developing personality disorder these traits are the result of developmental vulnerabilities (described in Chapter 4), including gross cognitive distortions, deficits in social skills, social disconnection and lack of attachment, and maladaptive behaviors leading to an ineffectual and dysfunctional whole. In these cases, the clinician's job is to recognize, divert, and alter the current and future path of that fledgling personality disorder before it solidifies into something more permanent.

With respect to their possible influence on sexual offending, comorbid personality disorders are considered of greatest concern when they are self-absorbed or clearly antisocial in nature (*DSM-IV-TR* Cluster B personality disorders). Special attention is paid to antisocial personality disorder, which is the *DSM-IV-TR*'s equivalent of psychopathy (or sociopathy), and Seagrave and Grisso (2002) described the "immeasurable consequences" wreaked by psychopaths on their targets (p. 219). As described in Chapter 3, antisocial personality disorder features a marked disregard for and callousness toward others and social conventions, shallow emotions, a drive to meet personal needs and desires, lack of empathy and remorse, and sometimes impulsivity. In addition, for the *DSM-IV-TR* diagnosis to be made, the individual must be at least 18 years old, and clear traits of the disorder must have emerged during adolescence or childhood in the form of a conduct disorder, thus establishing a pervasive and enduring history of antisociality.[2] However, Seagrave and Grisso also warned against assessing juveniles as fledgling psychopaths

---

[2] This does not mean that conduct disorder always evolves into antisocial personality disorder. On the contrary, the *DSM-IV-TR* states that conduct disorder remits by adulthood in the majority of cases.

for many of the reasons described in Chapter 3, and Hart et al. (2002) noted that "the assessment of juvenile psychopathy is like an Impressionist painting: fine from a distance; but the closer you get, the messier it looks" (p. 241).

Nonetheless, adolescent personality traits suggestive of personality disorders, whether full-fledged or rudimentary, are of concern, especially those driven by egocentricism and callous disregard for others and underpinned by lack of authentic attachment. Combined with sexualization, strong sexual urges, and possible paraphilias, as well as a history of prior sexual offenses, the comorbid diagnosis of an aggressive personality disorder, and especially antisocial personality disorder (which cannot be diagnosed prior to age 18), is of special concern.

OVERPATHOLOGIZING

As noted earlier, as we look for and assess mental disorders, discover and diagnose them, and distinguish among similar diagnoses, we should be careful not to diagnosis a mental disorder where one does not exist. The *DSM-IV-TR* provides "V" codes for problems and concerns that are not considered to be mental disorders. These can be used (with or without additional mental disorders) to describe behaviors, relationships, moods, thoughts, experiences, and other factors that are problems or are of concern but nonetheless are not mental disorders.

ABNORMAL PSYCHOLOGY

It is quite common for juvenile sexual offenders to have more than one diagnosis and for concurrent psychiatric diagnoses to overlap with one another to create more complex diagnostic pictures and syndromes. Sometimes these individual diagnoses are so complex (e.g., pervasive developmental disorder or atypical psychosis) that when combined, they create even more complex diagnoses that are very difficult to understand and sometimes even challenge the diagnostic categories and labels provided by the *DSM-IV-TR*. When they coexist or overlap with already complex physical conditions such as Klinefelter's syndrome,[3] cerebral palsy, or seizure disorders, diagnoses can become even more complicated because the many different psychological and physiological functions overlap, interact, and potentiate one another. In fact, some mental disorders, such as autism and mental retardation, are themselves more rightly considered physical or organic conditions than mental ones.

Additionally, when psychiatric diagnoses combine with developmental or

---

[3] Klinefelter's syndrome is a chromosomal variation in which males have an additional X chromosome (and are sometimes referred to as XXY males), which often has a strong component of sexual underdevelopment and can also include serious language deficits, cognitive impairment, impulse-control difficulties, and problems with self-esteem.

social problems (e.g., attachment disorders, social skills deficits, identity problems, or relational difficulties) that are evident in their effect but not diagnosable as mental disorders, the problem of diagnostic classification and accuracy becomes even greater. This is partly because the *DSM-IV-TR* is a medical text that does not recognize or diagnose social or communication problems such as interpersonal problems that exist within families or problems with social development.[4] In complex and interactive diagnostic situations, diagnostic classification becomes stretched. In this regard, sometimes symptoms do not fit into any neat and clean category, either requiring forced-fit diagnoses, the use of Not Otherwise Specified (NOS) diagnostic labels, or the use of invented diagnostic labels and descriptions. Here I use the term *abnormal psychology* to describe the individual whose diagnosis falls outside of the normal diagnostic scheme.

Once used to describe mental illness in general, the term *abnormal psychology* is now used less frequently outside of introductory college courses. Abnormal psychology refers to complex psychological pictures such as those described previously, which sometimes emerge in a subset of the population of juvenile sexual offenders and which defy any clear diagnosis. These juveniles may display some of the symptoms of a standard diagnosis, but not all. In this case the NOS diagnostic category must be invoked. This diagnostic label is available in every *DSM-IV-TR* category to capture diagnoses that resemble but do not quite meet the criteria for the main diagnosis or that fall somewhat outside of it. The problem with NOS, though, is that it either fails to offer specificity or can be used illegitimately or incorrectly by clinicians not accustomed to the process of diagnosis.

It is difficult to understand juvenile sexual offenders even under the best circumstances. As described in previous chapters, we do not fully understand their development and can find no true commonalities among all juvenile sexual offenders. Nonetheless, we can understand their functions and dysfunctions, the general causes and correlates of their behaviors, and the areas in which treatment and rehabilitation are required, as well as methods by which to provide such treatment. Sometimes we provide cognitive-behavioral treatment, sometimes psychodynamic, and sometimes a combination. Whatever treatment we apply, it is aimed at (or should be) the diagnosis and assessment, which requires that we understand the individual and can make a diagnosis. In discussing abnormal psychological profiles, however, we are describing those juvenile sexual offenders who fall outside of the norm, even among juvenile sexual offenders and who are far from the "neat and clean" young of-

---

[4] Axes IV and V of the *DSM-IV-TR* do pay attention to social issues and relationships and are used to inform the medically oriented diagnoses on Axes I and II. Nevertheless, they merely provide explanatory or collateral information to support or further explain Axis I or II diagnoses, which constitute the diagnosis proper. As noted, V codes can also be used to describe problems that are not necessarily mental disorders in their own right.

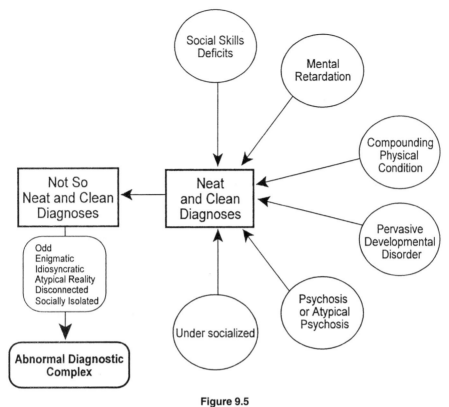

Figure 9.5
The impact of compounding and mixed diagnostic variables.

fenders with whom we most frequently work, and whom, to some degree, we can understand.

These unusual offenders are outliers with diagnoses that are more like complexes of mixed diagnoses, making it difficult not only to understand causation and risk but also to know what kind of treatment to apply. In these diagnostic syndromes made up of sometimes multiple partial diagnoses (i.e., symptoms that do not quite fit any diagnostic category), we have kids with significant cognitive impairments, kids with gross deficits in social skills, kids who are undersocialized, kids with autistic-spectrum disorders, kids who are psychotic, kids who are not actually psychotic but appear psychotic, and kids who have such strange or bizarre interpretations of reality as to make it very difficult to understand how their minds work, what they are thinking, or what motivates them, and who might be more appropriately treated in psychiatric facilities if such facilities existed (which they typically do not). As shown in Figure 9.5, for these juveniles the more commonplace "neat and clean" diagnoses are affected and transformed by many additional factors into far more complex diagnostic complexes.

Juvenile sexual offenders whose psychology cannot be easily understood represent an additional challenge, both to a formal diagnostic system and to the formulation of treatment. These are juveniles who, like psychotic individuals, often live in a world of their own that is difficult to penetrate or understand from the outside. Juvenile sexual offenders in this group are not necessarily motivated by or even interested in the same things as is the "average" juvenile sexual offender. Consequently, here more than in any other diagnostic category besides psychotic disorders, we are least likely to understand the influence of comorbidity on juvenile sexual offending and may have the greatest difficulty in both determining individualized treatment goals and assessing future risk. Still, it is important to recognize that this group of atypical juvenile sexual offenders exists and to realize that they may not understand or be amenable to the standard types of sexual-offender-specific treatment described in this and other books that address such treatment. For these kids, ongoing assessment and treatment must be individualized and built on a custom-made clinical formulation.

INFLUENCE OF MENTAL DISORDERS ON JUVENILE SEXUAL OFFENDING

Recognizing that no single factor is responsible for sexual offender behavior, it is probably true that mental disorders for the most part do play an influential role in juvenile sexual offending, though in an often indirect and somewhat passive manner. That is, they are part of the makeup of the psyche behind the behavior and hence drive and influence ideas, emotions, and eventual behaviors but, with few exceptions, probably remain minor players. That is, if we were to treat only the psychiatric disorder, we would not necessarily be getting to or treating the causes of juvenile sexual offending or rehabilitating the juvenile offender.

In fact, given the range of variables that constitute developmental pathways to juvenile sexual offending, mental disorders are at best probably low influencers, for the most part serving more as agitating or aggravating factors than as direct agents. This is even more true if we recognize that behavioral, impulsive, and many anxiety disorders represent more the *outcomes* of developmental difficulties than mental illness, which we can safely limit to mental disorders such as pervasive psychotic disorders, major depression, bipolar disorder, and others that are largely considered to have a biological base and are closer to the mental illness end of the continuum. In other words, although mental disorders may contribute to sexual aggression in some cases, in and of themselves they generally seem to be of relatively little influence. The mental disorders that are of the greatest concern are those that develop as *part* of the developmental pathway, such as conduct disorders; those that pair social-skills deficits with obsessive-compulsive and sometimes disinhibited behavior, such as autistic-spectrum disorders; and those that confuse thinking and impair judgment, such as pervasive psychotic disorders.

Mental disorders, then, do influence sexual offending behavior. Although they often act in the background as passive aggravators, some act more powerfully, obviously, and directly than others. It is also true that it is not the single diagnosis that is most likely to influence behavior, but more the diagnostic complex that is built out of overlapping diagnoses that are comorbid with one another *and* comorbid with developmental and other personal factors. Together, these combinations make the presence of comorbid mental disorders significant and therefore important to detect and diagnose. Here, we can recognize mental disorders as an overarching risk factor without losing sight of the fact that the presence and influence of a mental disorder as a risk factor will be quite different in each individual.

CONCLUSION

Understanding comorbid psychiatric diagnoses and their relationship and possible impact on sexual offending behaviors is critical in both understanding the behavior and making assessments of future risk. However, little specific research is available on the presence and types of mental disorders in juvenile sexual offenders or the influence of mental disorders on sexual aggression. The research that is available often overgeneralizes, is limited in scope, varies in construction from study to study, and fails to use definitions of mental health that are consistent across all studies. Moreover, mental health, mental disorders, and mental illness are often confused with one another or lumped together in an all-inclusive spectrum of mental disorders that fails to distinguish among mild mental disorders, major mental illness, and everything in between. This not only inflates the presence of psychiatric comorbidity but also fails to help us recognize the impact and influence of different types of mental disorders on behavior, particularly those of a more serious psychiatric nature. It is not that the behavioral variety of mental disorders is insignificant, but that they are often the result of problems that started long before the juvenile engaged in sexually abusive behavior and that probably led to sexual offending. We should search for the influence of the more serious mental disorders—those that, unlike behavioral disorders, are more typically treated with psychotropic medications. We can neither accomplish this nor understand the interaction between diagnoses and the development of diagnostic complexes when all mental disorders are treated equally and described as comorbidity.

Nevertheless, comorbidity is important both as a possible causative factor that can help explain prior sexual offenses and as a risk factor that can help predict the possibility of reoffense. In this sense, we can recognize and treat comorbidity in juvenile sexual offenders as an additional and general at-risk condition. Nevertheless, comorbidity may not be an important and relevant causative or risk factor in every case, although the presence and strength of comorbidity and its influence on past and possible future behavior should be assessed at all times.

On a final note, many forensically trained clinicians do not look for serious psychiatric disorders but focus more on those surface attributes that are presented. Although many are increasingly more aware of and sensitive to the issues of mental health, many are not trained as mental health specialists and are inadequately trained in diagnosis and abnormal psychology. On the other hand, many mental health clinicians are unaware of the world of forensic work and do not recognize the criminogenic behavior, needs, and drives that usually accompany the mental health of juvenile sexual offenders. Furthermore, many mental health clinicians are not themselves adequately trained in or comfortable with mental health assessment and diagnosis.

The task, then, is to develop practitioners who understand the complexities of the juvenile sexual offender, who are well trained in both forensics and mental health, and who understand the world and behavior of the adolescent. To this end, Grisso (1998) wrote that clinicians working with juvenile offenders must have specialized knowledge and experience about the sort of children and adolescents with whom they are working, and he broke such knowledge into four specific categories: (a) adolescent development, (b) theories about adolescent offenders, (c) adolescent assessment, and (d) adolescent psychopathology.

PART III

Treatment and Rehabilitation of the Juvenile Sexual Offender

CHAPTER 10

Forensic Mental
Health Treatment

THE JUVENILE sexual offender treatment environment is, by definition, forensic. This means that the moment that a child enters treatment through the criminal or juvenile justice system, he has entered a world that includes legal as well as social concepts, assessment, remedies, and sanctions. In understanding the treatment of juvenile sexual offending, then, the place to start is with the role of forensics and the nature of forensic mental health. This chapter advocates that treating juvenile sexual offenders is both a forensic and a mental health speciality. Accordingly, all treatment provided to the juvenile offender lies in the domain of forensic mental health treatment.

OVERVIEW

Forensics broadly involves matters pertaining to the court and the systems of criminal and civil justice, or the law in general. This frequently involves any behavior that violates adult or juvenile criminal laws and also includes matters pertaining to civil law that require evaluation, assessment, or psychological input, such as child custody cases, adoption, or miscellaneous law suits. Practically, forensics applies to the investigation and assessment of facts and evidence in court, or the application of scientific knowledge and technology to legal matters. The treatment of the juvenile sexual offender is a forensic speciality that crosses the lines between understanding criminal behavior, assisting the process of legal discrimination and decision making regarding the behavior, assessing the behavior for future occurrence, and treating the behavior. With juveniles, such work requires an additional understanding of the developmental and personal psychology of children and adolescents and surrounding social systems and social forces that shape and define the emotions, cognitions, and behaviors of the child.

Forensics includes science and art, covering matters of fact and legal jurisprudence as well as causes and consequences of legal issues, whether in the courtroom or outside. Forensic psychiatry, psychology, and social work deal with the psychology of the individual as it pertains to criminal behavior, as well as broader aspects that involve sentencing recommendations, child custody, malpractice, and legal mediation. Additionally, there is the need to understand the legal process, including competency, assessments of dangerousness or risk, legal procedures and criminal jeopardy, confidentiality and privileged communication, and due process rights and protection. Given the twin purposes of informing and serving the law and serving and treating the individual, Bluglass (1990) described the forensic practitioner's ability to deal with and reconcile the differences between legal interests and the interests of mental health as both important and crucial. In this vein, McCann (1998) warned that "the role of a mental health professional in forensic contexts is distinctly different from that in clinical settings. Failure to acknowledge this difference can be disastrous for anyone who applies the values and roles of one to the other" (p. 181).

Barker and Branson (2000) described 10 functions attached to criminal or civil forensic work:

1. Evaluation of individuals facing legal consequences
2. Investigations pertaining to the legal system
3. Provision of court testimony, possibly as an expert witness
4. Recommendations to courts or other legal authorities
5. Facilitation of and involvement in the outcomes of court proceedings
6. Mediation between individuals involved in the legal system
7. Provision of testimony regarding professional standards in malpractice cases
8. Education of professional colleagues about the influence of law on their practice
9. Development of standards for the regulation and practice of forensic work
10. Strict adherence to ethical standards of forensic practice

FORENSIC EVALUATION

Grisso (1998) asserted that all evaluations are forensic if intended for direct use or for assistance in decision making in a legal environment and that they require a different way of thinking than do nonforensic evaluations, which are typically applied in the purely clinical context. He noted that "clinicians can never merely transport their clinical skills to the juvenile court and carry out their evaluations as though they were in a clinical setting. Every evaluation for juvenile court is transformed by the legal context in which it is being performed" (p. 24).

In the forensic evaluation, clinicians assess the individual in a manner relevant to both the legal and the mental health systems, communicating ideas and outcomes in ways that are understandable and meaningful to both systems and in a manner that ensures that the legal system is able to apply results in a way commensurate with legal standards (Grisso, 1998). To this end, Minne (1997) declared that forensic clinicians must understand the law and its language and learn how to translate clinical formulations into language that is comprehensible to the court. Grisso pointed out that unlike other evaluations, forensic evaluations are used and interpreted by nonclinical decision makers and typically require a different way of thinking for the clinical evaluator, a different language, and far more documentation. As much is potentially resting on the outcomes of forensic evaluations, both for the individual under assessment and the public, the requirement for thorough and detailed assessment and documentation of the assessment and its conclusions is especially important.

Forensic evaluations are also different from standard mental health evaluations because the rules and practices of confidentiality—and for some clinicians, privileged communication—do not apply. Often, the evaluation is prepared expressly for the court, but the court almost always may have full access to the evaluation anyway. This lack of confidentiality must be imparted to the individual being evaluated and may have a significant bearing on his or her willingness to engage in or be truthful during the evaluation. The same is true for family members and other collateral informants, who may be unwilling to participate or be honest in the evaluation.

The forensic evaluation begins and ends with an assessment of the circumstances and situation of the subject. Regardless of the depth of the evaluation, it ends with a formulation about the case, an assessment of risk in the case of criminal behavior and public safety, and usually (but not always) a set of recommendations that guide and inform the court or the legal process. However, as Millon (1996) wrote, the primary task for the forensic assessor is "clarifying the personality characteristics of the person being examined. This focus on understanding the person who has been charged with a crime, or is a participant in a complicated civil suit, is essentially that of appraising traits and characteristics, not symptoms or disorders" (pp. vii–viii). Here, then, the forensic evaluation lays the groundwork for the treatment that often follows—especially in the case of the juvenile—and is the starting point in the far wider process of forensic mental health and the role of the forensic practitioner.

FORENSIC MENTAL HEALTH

Forensics deals with the legal aspects and ramifications of behavior. Mental health, on the other hand, deals with increasing the level of mental acuity and functional capacity and health in individuals. Forensic mental health deals with the intersection of legal and mental health processes, incorporating a full understanding of both, including the criminogenic factors that influence, shape, and drive illegal behaviors and the kind of mental health issues that affect, drive, or result from criminal behavior.

One way to define forensic mental health is to describe all mental health services applied within a forensic setting as forensic in nature. Here, mental health services are provided due to or as the result of a criminal or criminally oriented process, as in the case of assessment and treatment of juvenile and adult sexual offenders, or are attached to behaviors that have criminal consequences and could have criminal charges if discovered. In this case, given mandated reporting requirements that affect all mental health practitioners, the possibility of criminal prosecution is almost certain to be triggered. When we do this kind of work, it is critical that we have both mind-sets—the forensic and the mental health—in place. The mental health clinician who has limited or no knowledge of forensics is at risk of missing some major and important shaping dynamics and motivations. On the other hand, the forensic clinician with limited knowledge about or experience in mental health is going to miss underlying drives and dynamics that may result in cookie-cutter and simplistic approaches to dealing with potentially complex issues of comorbidity and mental health functioning in general.

Grisso (1998) wrote that forensic clinicians working with juveniles must have specialized knowledge of adolescent development, adolescent offenders (or juvenile antisocial behavior and offenses), adolescent psychopathology, and the assessment of adolescents. The practitioner must also understand, at least to some degree, the legal considerations and processes that are in play and serve as the background in forensic work, including due process rights and other legal protections that often apply to juveniles as well as adults. The forensic mental health clinician, then, understands the development of sociopathy and social deviance, the psychology and development of personality and behavior, behavioral and mental health assessment and treatment, and the influence of the social world on the cognitions, relationships, behaviors, and social frameworks of children and adolescents. In working with juvenile sexual offenders, this requires that we understand the forensic principles that frame and shape this work, the interpersonal and intrapsychic dynamics that lead to and maintain sexual offending behaviors, and the issues and processes involved in the development of personal identity and mental health, and that we know how to apply our knowledge in such a complex environment.

FUNDAMENTAL SKILLS IN FORENSIC TREATMENT

Building on Grisso's (1998) model of fundamental knowledge, we can briefly describe the basic knowledge and mind-set required of the forensic practitioner.

ADOLESCENT DEVELOPMENT

Grisso (1998) asserted that "nothing about the behavior of adolescents can be understood without considering it in the context of youth's continued biological, psychological, and social development" (p. 27). Especially important is the recognition of adolescence as a time of emotional turmoil, behavioral experimentation, identity development, and serious self-doubt for many (if not most) adolescents, or a period of Sturm und Drang (from the German for "storm and stress") as originally characterized in 1904 by G. Stanley Hall (1970). Although not all adolescents experience this storm and stress, Arnett (1999) nevertheless described this turmoil as a part of life for many adolescents. In particular, he described conflicts with parents, mood disruptions, and risky behaviors as a normal aspect of development for many adolescents, and this reminds forensic practitioners that what might otherwise seem especially troubled and disturbed behavior among adolescents may be completely normal and expected developmental experiences.

JUVENILE ANTISOCIAL BEHAVIOR AND OFFENSES

The forensic practitioner must understand theories that help explain the development and patterns of delinquent and antisocial behaviors, be aware of statistics that pertain to juvenile crime and delinquency, and be familiar with the causes and correlates of antisocial and aggressive behaviors in children and adolescents. There are three general populations against whom we are comparing the juvenile offender: the nonoffending normative child or adolescent, the sexually abusive child or adolescent, and the non–sexually offending juvenile delinquent. Without having a broad understanding of each of these populations, we cannot meaningfully understand the behavior of the juvenile sexual offender or the etiology of the behavior. This also means recognizing the behavior of the juvenile sexual offender in the context of the social environment in which he was raised, developmental vulnerabilities in the individual, and developmental pathways to sexual offending.

ADOLESCENT PSYCHOPATHOLOGY

Understanding the nature and diagnosis of mental disorders, or psychopathology, in children and adolescents is critical for assessment and treatment. The ability to recognize psychiatric comorbidity and the presence of a mental disorder that may influence cognition, emotion, or behavior is an essential skill for any mental health practitioner, forensic or not, as well as the ability to distinguish among diagnoses (differential diagnosis) and understanding their prevalence, development, and prognosis. Equally important is the ability to distinguish between mental disorders and nonmental disorders without failing to recognize that both may result in functional deficits and impairments in the child or adolescent. This fundamental skill was the subject of Chapter 9.

Adolescent Assessment

As described in detail in earlier chapters, assessment is a complex process that can be conducted in several different ways based on different methods and different guiding principles and beliefs. In the case of forensic assessment, which always involves the legal system at some level, there is much more at stake for the juvenile and the public. Grisso (1998) warned forensic examiners used to working with adults that the evaluation of youthful offenders must have a far broader focus than the clinical (nonforensic) evaluation, and the American Academy of Child and Adolescent Psychiatry (1999) noted that such assessments require the same comprehensive evaluation required of any other evaluation of children or adolescents. They wrote that forensic evaluations of juvenile sexual offenders must include an understanding of normal sexual development, as well as interactions with family, ethnic, social, and cultural influences and the epidemiology and phenomenology of sexually abusive youths. Twenty-one principles to guide juvenile assessment were described in Chapter 8.

The Legal Background

Many issues not normally related to either assessment or treatment are attached to forensic treatment. These include legal jeopardy and legal protections, confidentiality or the lack thereof, and the consequences to the public of untreated or ineffectively treated sexual offenders. Forensic practitioners must be aware of this context and must take great care to ensure that both the juvenile and his legal guardian are aware of the evaluation and treatment process and the lack of confidentiality almost always involved. In addition, practitioners must be aware of the status or course of any legal procedures that have been initiated, ranging from no legal process to pre- and postadjudication. As assessment or treatment can occur, and often does, under any of these circumstances, it is important for the clinician to be aware of the legal status and any implications it may have for treatment.

The first case applies to nonadjudicated offenders, or juvenile sexual offenders who have not been charged with a sexual crime, possibly because a court diversion process has been applied through the social services system that may be managing the case. These youths may later be charged with an offense, particularly in light of information that results from the assessment or treatment process and the no-confidentiality position often adopted by sexual offender treatment programs. Preadjudication refers to cases in which charges have been filed and are in process, although no court decision has yet been made (in which case adjudication is the equivalent of a guilty finding), and assessment or treatment may occur within that stage of preadjudication, in which the case is active and open even if it appears dormant (which may continue for several months, and sometimes throughout treatment). Postadjudication means that assessment and treatment are occurring following a guilty finding (in the case of the juvenile, adjudication), which may affect the stakes faced by the juvenile, especially if on probation (served instead of a sentence in prison or otherwise incarcerated setting) or parole (following release from a prison or otherwise incarcerated setting, although the sentencing term has not yet expired). Figure 8.1 provides an overview of the varied levels of criminal (or noncriminal) venue at which assessment and treatment occur.

In addition, there are sometimes important questions about competence to agree to an assessment or disclose information that might jeopardize freedom, as well as competence to stand trial or competence regarding knowledge that the criminal behavior was right or wrong. These complex issues are far beyond the scope of this book as they affect not only the work of the forensic practitioner but also the environment in which the work occurs and are critical issues in preserving both the integrity of individual rights (including the rights of minors) and public safety.

FORENSIC TREATMENT

Besides producing the assignment of risk, the forensic evaluation also includes an understanding of causality and motivation, formulation of treatment needs, and placement and treatment recommendations. In the broader model of forensic treatment, however, forensic work continues beyond evaluation and recommendations incorporating the entire process of treatment into the forensic orbit. Here, forensic work is the sun about which the various treatment planets (or modes and aspects of treatment) orbit, and the treatment solar system involves every aspect of forensic assessment and treatment. In this model, illustrated in Figure 10.1, forensic assessment lies at the center of a series of ever-widening concentric circles, each of which expands out to include an additional forensic-treatment responsibility from assessment through the end of treatment, forming a whole system of forensic mental health treatment. Consequently, the term *forensic treatment* encompasses the

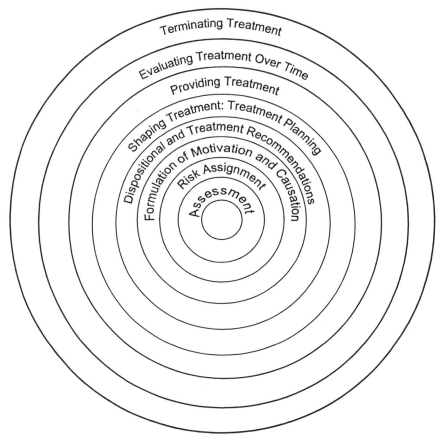

Figure 10.1
Widening circles of forensic mental health responsibilities.

range of behavioral, cognitive, emotional, and psychiatric treatment provided to these children, from soup to nuts.

The Soup and Nuts

Here only a brief description of the tasks encompassed in a model of forensic treatment is necessary.

1. *Assessment:* Conducting the comprehensive psychosocial assessment required both to understand the juvenile and to make recommendations, as well as to assign a level of risk in the case of the juvenile sexual offender

2. *Risk Assignment:* The outcome of the risk assessment portion of the assessment, in which a level (from low to high) is assigned for the risk of sexual reoffending

3. *Formulation of Motivation and Causation:* The clinical formulation that summarizes the case and the factors at work, as well as hypothesizing the developmental pathway and factors possibly relevant to the offense

4. *Dispositional and Treatment Recommendations:* Recommendations made following, or as part of, the assessment regarding sentencing and/or required treatment

5. *Shaping Treatment—The Treatment Plan:* Initiates treatment and serves as the map of the expected and projected treatment process, including recommended treatment goals, treatment interventions, and treatment modalities

6. *Providing Treatment:* The broad course of treatment itself of varying lengths, shaped, guided, and reviewed by the process of treatment planning; in a model of rehabilitation, essentially the equivalent of the process of rehabilitation

7. *Evaluating Treatment Over Time:* Represents the in-treatment process inclusive of both ongoing treatment planning and re-evaluation of risk over time and as treatment progresses, with a focus on the dynamic risk factors that are the targets in the treatment of juvenile sexual offenders

8. *Terminating Treatment:* Marks the final point in formal treatment, or at least the final point in a particular treatment setting, where treatment ends and the juvenile goes on to another treatment program or treatment is ended completely

FORENSIC THERAPY AND THE THERAPEUTIC RELATIONSHIP

Another way to define forensic mental health is as the application of mental health ideas and techniques in treating and rehabilitating behaviors that are forensic in nature. This most typically applies to psychotherapy, which is a central component in any form of mental health that is implemented in the direct interaction between the clinician and the client or, in the case of group or family therapy, the group of clients.

Both Cordess (2001) and Welldon (1997) described forensic psychotherapy as a new discipline, referring in particular to the application of psychodynamic treatment principles to forensic therapy. Of special note, however, is Welldon's description of forensic therapy as going beyond the special relationship between client and therapist. She described the transformation and extension of that relationship to the triangular relationship that exists in forensic therapy of client, clinician, and society. This sums up the relationship between mental health treatment and the forensic imperative, in which in the ideal model of forensic treatment, the health and well-being of both the juvenile client and the community are served in the best possible manner without sacrificing one for the other.

THE FORENSIC BACKDROP

Clinicians in nonforensic mental health treatment hope that individuals in assessment or treatment will be reasonably honest or at least will not intentionally hide information because they fear criminal consequences or other legal action due to their disclosures. Naturally, there are situations in nonforensic mental health in which illegal behaviors are disclosed, such as child or elder abuse, the planned commission of a crime, or activities involving illegal substance use. Typically, however, the vast majority of mental health practitioners provide nonforensic treatment, not addressing, being concerned with, or thinking about forensics or criminal behavior in their work. Instead, they begin the process of clinical formulation and treatment believing that the client is a compliant and open participant in the treatment process who has no illicit reason to hide pertinent information. However, forensic work always involves behaviors that have criminal (or civil) impact. The forensic orientation, accordingly, recognizes that the criminal perpetrator is unlikely to tell the truth and that malingering and deception are typically viewed as significant issues to be constantly addressed (McCann, 1998). Thus, the forensic practitioner is always seeking indirect links and clues that lead to and expose the truth, and these often include psychological, behavioral, and physical data.

Additionally, unlike nonforensic treatment, in forensic work, and especially sexual offending, a great deal is at stake for the individual, the family, the community, the legal system and public safety, and the clinician. There is a tremendous stigma attached to sexual offending: public notions of perversion, attacks against defenseless individuals and most typically women and children, the images and reality of often heinous crimes, and the socially reprehensible quality of the behavior or crime. In addition, under such circumstances the perpetrators (even the terminology is different here—*perpetrator* instead of *client*) have a great deal at stake in terms of not only stigma but also legal consequences and personal freedom, and this is as true for juvenile sexual offenders as it is for adult offenders. Sexual offender registration laws, which combine stigmatization with loss of free and unfettered movement in the community, make this even more pertinent; in these cases, "doing the time" does not exonerate, absolve, or purge the individual of the criminal behavior or put him back on an equal footing with everyone else in society. Of note, registrations often have no lower age limit and apply equally to juveniles as to adult sexual offenders.

Accordingly, forensic mental health practitioners engage in assessment and treatment of criminal behavior knowing that clients often will not openly, honestly, or fully disclose information, that evidence or clues may have to be found that point to or prove the truth, and that entire systems may exert pressure on the practitioner in one direction or another (sometimes to minimize behavior and sometimes to come up with black-and-white indictments of the individual). In other words, the process—not surprisingly—resembles the adversarial court process itself.

Many of the features in play during the forensic assessment of juvenile sexual offenders are also present during treatment. It is not that most kids are criminally minded and intend to fool the clinician and maintain the sexual offending behavior, plan to continue the behavior, or even want to continue the behavior. In most cases, the opposite is probably true, as least insofar as most kids believe they have learned their lesson and will never do it again. This raises the questions of who actually needs treatment, where and under what circumstances it should be provided, how we know whether it is effective, and when it ends.

Another question in forensic work is *how* one becomes a sexual offender. In a model of healthy personal development, people develop internal or intrapsychic barriers and perspectives that prohibit the development (or at least the enactment) of sexually abusive behaviors, as well as the attitudes and beliefs that support such behaviors. Within the psychology of juvenile sexual offenders, however, either these inhibitions have failed to develop fully, or other elements are present that allow them to overcome the external and internal barriers that normally inhibit inappropriate sexual or criminal behavior. Furthermore, juvenile sexual offenders have already committed a serious act, have already changed as a result of committing that act, and have already developed a set of internal beliefs, attitudes, and cognitive constructs that both lend themselves to continued problem behaviors and interactions *and* make it difficult to treat the behavior.

Addressing these factors, as well as the complex interactions among them, is the target for forensic mental health treatment. Accordingly, the tasks of forensic therapy involve (a) assessing the subjective mental health states of individuals in all of their complexity, (b) finding effective ways of addressing the pathological aspects of these states, and (c) evaluating changes in mental representations and ways of being, feeling, thinking, and behaving (Cordess, 2001, p. 326). Perhaps more than anything else, forensic mental health is a mind-set or approach to treatment informed by an understanding of the interplay between criminogenic processes and mental health, or those factors related to criminal thinking, social adjustment, and behaviors.

THE FORENSIC MIND-SET

Forensics involves criminal behavior and proceedings. In addressing and treating forensic problems, clinicians conduct evaluations and provide mental health treatment *within* the context of the criminal behavior. To be effective in this area, forensic clinicians must understand the nature and circumstances of criminal and deviant behavior, recognizing this backdrop of criminal behavior as the context in which they work.

It is critical for forensic clinicians *not* to assume that the ongoing (and troublesome) behaviors of their clients, even within treatment, are neutral occurrences. Rather, it is important to know the background of the client, evaluate the client forensically and in the context of past behavior, and treat the forensic client in that knowledge. Accordingly, some things that we know about the juvenile sexual offenders with whom we work should be applied in our ongoing treatment with these kids. Although not true of every kid in treatment, in working with juvenile sexual offenders we generally *know* that

- Our clients are emotionally troubled and often confused
- Most of our clients are capable of breaking significant social rules, and many are willing to do so again
- Virtually all of our clients have already engaged in sexually abusive behavior at least once
- Our client population, as a whole, is highly sexualized
- Some of our clients think about sex a great deal of the time
- Most of our clients do not understand their own sexual motivations and interests
- Our clients are not necessarily motivated by treatment issues, but more often by factors beyond our immediate knowledge, and sometimes beyond even their knowledge
- Some of our clients are obsessive and compulsive, and even addictive, about sex
- Some of our clients are in denial about their sexual and sex-related behaviors
- Some of our clients will go to great lengths to engage in sexualized behaviors
- Some of our clients will engage in somewhat odd and even bizarre sexual behaviors if given the opportunity
- Some of our clients know the staff that work with them better than the staff know them and use this knowledge in a planful and sometimes predatory fashion to get their sexual (and other) needs met
- Some of our clients are impulsive, and others antisocial
- Some of our clients are masters of deceit
- Some of our clients are great manipulators
- Some of our clients will grow up to become significantly disturbed or dangerous adults

We *know* these things about our general client population. If we do not consider these items relevant or believe them to be overgeneralizations, we do not know our client population well and are at great risk for making significant mistakes in evaluation, judgment, and treatment.

However, the risk in assuming a forensic mind-set like this is that we become mistrustful and suspicious of every child and thereby unable to assess individual behaviors adequately or appropriately. On the other hand, the risk in *not* assuming this forensic mind-set is that we will miss significant treatment opportunities and that offenders will have the opportunity to engage in ongoing sexualized thoughts or behaviors that minimize the likelihood of effective treatment. In the practice of treatment, the forensic clinician is advised to assume the mind-set of both a forensic investigator and a clinician. As forensic clinicians, our job is not to prove innocence or guilt or to make personal or legal judgments about the individuals with whom we work. Nor is the clinical forensic mind-set an all-or-nothing attitude that views clients as either good or bad. Instead, it is a realistic and informed mind-set that allows us to make interpretations of behavior in full knowledge that

- Behavior has meaning
- Behavioral patterns are more likely to persist than to easily change
- Client behavior is initially more likely to be motivated by intra- and interpersonal factors than by treatment factors
- Clients who have already engaged in criminal and sexual offending behaviors are more likely than others to reoffend
- Odd or unusual behaviors are possible evidence of antisocial or sexualized thoughts, attitudes, or activities

With this in mind, all significant negative or unusual behaviors in our clients should be interpreted as possible indicators of sexualized or other antisocial thoughts or activities. Again, this is not an all-or-nothing perspective; rather, it is merely informed. Clinical formulation helps clinicians understand the factors and motivations that shape and explain behavior, as well as prognosticate the further development or resolution of pathology. A forensic mind-set provides a context for that formulation and prognosis when working in the forensic treatment environment.

CONCLUSION: SYNTHESIZING FORENSICS AND MENTAL HEALTH

McCann (1998) saw the roles of forensic practitioner and mental health clinician as mutually exclusive and wondered whether the two roles could cross. In the end, he recommended that clinicians avoid engaging in the dual roles of therapist and forensic evaluator. He wrote that "the ultimate client in clinical settings is the identified adult, adolescent, or child client or family. In forensic settings, practitioners generally serve the judicial system" (p. 18). He further noted that the goals of each role are completely different and that the clinical techniques that are used serve different end purposes. Similarly, Greenberg and Shuman (1999) considered the two roles to be inherently different and impossible for any one person to fill. They write that by failing to recognize inherent conflicts and a dual relationship, clinicians who practice as

Area	Mental Health Treatment	Forensic Evaluation
1. Client	Patient is the client	Attorney or court is the client
2. Confidentiality	Protected in favor of the patient	Little to no confidentiality
3. Perspective	Supportive, accepting, and empathic	Neutral, objective, and detached
4. Competence	Clinical assessment and treatment	Forensic evaluation procedures and psycholegal issues relevant to the case
5. Expert Skills	Appropriate therapeutic interventions	Appropriate psycholegal assessment tools
6. Applied Scrutiny	Assumed patient honesty	Need to ascertain truthfulness
7. Assessment Structure and Completeness	Less structure required or provided, less complete information necessary	Rigid and high structure, and thorough information required
8. Relationship	Allied	Adversarial
9. Goals	Treatment	Accurate assessment
10. Judgment	Nonjudgmental	Evaluative and judgmental

Figure 10.2
Irreconcilable differences between mental health care and forensic evaluation. (based on Greenburg and Shuman, 1999)

forensic evaluators and therapists in the same case risk harm to their profession, their clients, and the legal process. In particular, they described 10 areas of practice basic to each role that they considered to be irreconcilably different, as shown in Figure 10.2.

Nevertheless, in the treatment of juvenile sexual offenders, both roles must be synthesized into a model of forensic mental health if we are to provide effective treatment for kids and serve the public good. The fact is that we are unlikely ever to have a situation in which juvenile sexual offenders are always assessed independently of treatment or in which mental health treatment occurs in absence of a forensic backdrop. Still, McCann, Greenberg, and Shuman raise an important point, which is that the two practices—forensics and mental health—are driven by different sets of needs, ideas, and end purposes.

In forensic mental health we must find a way to unite these two sets without giving up the values of one for the other and without moving over too far or aligning too closely with one side or the other, thus potentially losing perspective. In such a case, we risk being seen as either naive mental health clinicians who fail to recognize the criminogenic model or aligned with the often punitive and always judgmental (by design) legal and correctional system, failing to recognize the basic principles, ideas, and practices that lie at the heart of all therapeutic models. In fact, McCann, Greenberg, and Shuman are discussing more the clear schism between forensic *evaluation* and mental health *treatment* than a model of forensically informed treatment and thus fail to take into account the reality that there is often not a clear dividing line, at least in the treatment of juveniles. Here, I am suggesting not only that forensic principles do not cease to exist at the line where evaluation ends and treatment begins but also that in the treatment of the juvenile sexual offender there is no such line because treatment is based on and driven by both criminogenic and mental health factors, and forensic principles therefore continue to play an instrumental and active role throughout treatment.

On a final note, McCann (1998) commented that the application of findings from mental health evaluations to forensic settings requires an objective and neutral stance. This should be the guiding principle at all times and throughout every phase of assessment and treatment for the forensic clinician.

CHAPTER 11

Overview of Treatment

ASSESSMENT REPRESENTS the first step in forensic practice, but beyond assessment lies treatment. Whereas assessment is the process of exploration, evaluation, and formulation, treatment focuses on understanding and treating maladaptation and pathology and helping to increase functionality, personal capacity, and sense of well-being. In the case of the juvenile sexual offender, whereas assessment formulates an understanding of his psychology and behavior and evaluates the potential or likelihood for future dangerous behavior, treatment is the process by which interventions are applied to resolve or rehabilitate that pathology. In a narrow model of treatment in any field, we aim only to address and resolve the particular problem that brings the individual into treatment. In a broad model, the goal is to address the particular pathology *and* the contiguous and underlying issues connected to the pathology, thus restoring the individual to a higher state of functioning than treating only the limited issues that brought the client into treatment.

In other words, a limited treatment model treats symptoms alone and not causes, whereas a broad model evaluates and treats factors that contribute to or cause symptoms. Models of sexual offender treatment fall into both categories, although with children and adolescents most models typically fall toward the broader end of the spectrum.

The ultimate purpose of treatment is rehabilitation, or the restoration of health. Many juvenile sexual offenders have never been in good health, emotionally or behaviorally, so rehabilitation is more a process of creation than renewal or restoration. Either way, the broadest purpose of the treatment is increased functional ability and enhanced sense of well-being, and in the case of sexual aggression, public safety. This is no simple task, however. In fact, as complex and critical as evaluation is, it is far easier to evaluate, formulate, and diagnose individuals than to treat them effectively.

Before addressing and describing the specific tools and tasks involved in rehabilitation, it is first important to understand the models and ideas of treatment that drive rehabilitation. Built on an understanding of the juvenile offender and the development of sexually abusive behavior, models of and ideas about treatment are in many ways straightforward. Nevertheless, in development and application they require a thorough understanding of the principles by which they are thought to work and the philosophies and beliefs that fuel them because the approach to treatment is made complex by differing ideas about how the human mind and behavior work, how they can best be understood, and the best way to treat them in order to bring about improvement and change. Practicing therapy and applying treatment without an understanding of these complexities renders the practitioner less capable of forming informed opinions and making discerning decisions about treatment and treatment technique, susceptible to accepting the most common ideas in treatment at face value, and unable to exercise critical thinking about models of treatment and rehabilitation. The goal is to produce clinicians who are effective and informed at the level of the client as an individual (micro level) and as a juvenile sexual offender (macro level) so that their skills, experiences, and ideas help to move the field forward.

A NOTE ON TERMINOLOGY

Because the chapters in this part deal with treatment, the term *client* is frequently used instead of *juvenile* or *juvenile sexual offender* because this term is typically used in any treatment environment. In working with offenders, however, it is not always clear who the client is—the juvenile sexual offender, the probation department or social agency, the community or society at large, or all parties.

THE PROVISION OF TREATMENT

Treatment may be comprehensive and aimed at all of the primary areas identified in the assessment as pathological, maladjusted, or problematic, or it may favor one treatment area more than others or address a single domain. In its short history, the treatment of juvenile sexual offenders has tended to fall more closely into this last category and to focus largely on cognitive-behavioral approaches. This approach approximates the narrower form of treatment described earlier; happily, however, juvenile sexual offender treatment programs are now moving increasingly toward the broader end of the treatment spectrum. Programs of treatment are more often including treatment in the affective-psychiatric domain, including psychotherapy, individual and group work that is psychodynamically oriented, and expressive treatments. This is a shift from the largely cognitive-behavioral approach adapted from substance-abuse treatment models that focuses largely on cognitive distortions, relapse prevention planning, and skill development.

Nevertheless, cognitive-behavioral treatment remains a mainstay of juvenile sexual offender treatment. The shift to a broader perspective, however, is due in part to an increasing recognition that cognitive-behavioral therapy is not the only appropriate form of treatment for juvenile offenders and that well-rounded and effective treatment requires a more comprehensive approach than any single model can provide. On its own, cognitive therapy works well for those individuals for whom it was primarily designed (cognitively capable, seeking change, and committed to treatment) but is not aimed at the development of internal motivation in clients, fails to help develop understanding (or insight) in the individual, and does not aim at the recognition or resolution of affective or psychiatric precursors or comorbid conditions. At best, cognitive-behavioral therapy is an important tool in a well-rounded program of treatment that provides language, direction, and skill development. At worst, it provides little more than a guidebook or a road map that is often not followed by clients once they leave treatment (or even during treatment).

In terms of resting on the cognitive-behavioral model, Drake, Ward, Nathan, and Lee (2001) noted that many treatment programs regard cognitive distortions (thinking errors) as isolated and independent variables to be treated independently, rather than as the result of an underlying set of beliefs. A broad treatment model, within which a cognitive-behavioral approach is integrated, will address the presence and structure of cognitive distortions as well as the presence of underlying worldviews and dynamics that give rise to and maintain them (in addition to the multiple other needs of the juvenile offender).

The difficulty in developing a broader model for the treatment of juvenile sexual offenders lies in part in the prevailing but largely unfounded idea that there is not a more effective model for offenders than cognitive-behavioral treatment. In fact, Vizard (1997) noted that one of the problems in discussing treatment models (and by extension, the application of new models) is this division in the field, with few practitioners feeling able to advocate for an eclectic or integrated treatment approach. She noted, as have many others, that despite strongly held views about the efficacy of the cognitive model, neither research evidence nor clinical experience supports the use of one theoretical model to the exclusion of others. The single model approach in current use is based largely on work with adult offenders and does not take into account "the physical, emotional, and social developmental factors which are an integral part of the psychopathology of child and adolescent sexual abusers" (Vizard, 1997, p. 49). However, even in the area of adult sexual offending, there is little significant evidence of the efficacy of either cognitive-behavioral therapy or a single model approach.

Broadly, then, a comprehensive model of treatment for juvenile sexual offenders will include a range of components and modalities, each of which fills a particular treatment niche, that together form an integrated whole. Treatment will, however, be influenced and shaped to a great degree by the treatment venue, with respect to community-based (outpatient) treatment or residential treatment, length of time in treatment, and the individual program's capacity to provide a range of treatment services. The choice of treatment venue should reflect the level of treatment services believed to be required for any particular juvenile. In this case, the operating principle is that not all juvenile offenders require the same types of treatment services, nor the same level or intensity of treatment. This only works, however, if juveniles in need of treatment are matched to the appropriate treatment environment, which in turn has the capacity to provide the appropriate types of treatment services.

Regardless of the treatment that is actually available in any given community, the amount of funds available for such treatment, the placement decisions of a court or social service agency, or even political considerations, recommendations for treatment venue (typically outpatient or residential) and required services should always be based on the outcome of the assessment and the judgment of the clinician. To this end, in its *Practice Standards and Guidelines*, the Association for the Treatment of Sexual Abusers (2001) asserted that its members "shall not knowingly recommend an inadequate treatment program or level of risk management because existing resources limit or preclude adequate and appropriate services" (Standard 16.03, p. 16).

TREATMENT SERVICES IN THE REAL WORLD

How does treatment look in the real world in terms of the treatment services that are actually being provided? Burton and Smith-Darden (2001) surveyed over 800 community-based and residential treatment programs for sexual offenders including 357 programs for male and female juvenile sexual offenders (adolescent and child) serving 6,422 children and adolescents in 1998.

Treatment Population: Age and Gender
Among juveniles (child and adolescent), adolescents represent the bulk of those in treatment for sexually aggressive behaviors, accounting for 82% of treatment services. Among all surveyed programs, 69% treat boys, which means, surprisingly, that the other 31% of programs treat female offenders. However, despite the number of programs that serve female juvenile sexual offenders, 93% of the total number of kids in treatment were boys, and 85% were adolescent boys. For those 7% of the overall population who are female offenders, the bulk of treatment occurs in the outpatient setting. This is not

true in residential treatment, a more intensive and more secure level of care, where 90% of the population are boys.

Treatment Venue

Of the programs surveyed, 68% were community-based (outpatient) and 32% residential. However, adolescents are treated residentially far more frequently than are children: 88% of residential programs treat adolescents, compared to 12% treating children. Seventy-nine percent of programs for children are community-based outpatient programs, and the remaining 21% are residential. For adolescents, 65% of programs are outpatient, compared to 35% residential. Nevertheless, residential programs provided 41% of total care, compared to 59% outpatient programming.

As noted, a substantial percentage of programs treat female juvenile sexual offenders, but this is more true of outpatient treatment than residential. Although 61% of outpatient programs treat boys and 39% treat girls, 88% of residential programs serve boys. Excluding residential care for children, 90% of residential programs serve adolescent boys.

Length of Treatment

For both male and female adolescents in either outpatient or residential care, the average length of time in treatment is about 18 months. For children, for whom outpatient care is far more common (79% of programs), the typical length of care is 13 months outpatient and 10 months residential.

Treatment Provided

Each week juveniles in outpatient care attend on average one 55-minute session of individual therapy, a little more than one 80- to 90-minute group, and a little fewer than one 60-minute family session. In each week in residential care, juveniles attend on average between one and two 50- to 55-minute individual therapy sessions, between three and four 75- to 85-minute groups, and a little fewer than one 60- to 70-minute family session.

In terms of other services or treatments among programs surveyed, 83% focused on the sexual assault–dysfunctional behavioral cycle, 30% provided art therapy, 37% experiential therapy, 18% drama therapy, 13% sex education, and 8% eye movement desensitization and reprocessing (EMDR).[1] Although work on the sexual abuse cycle is provided relatively consistently in both outpatient and residential treatment, cycle work is offered more to girls on an outpatient basis than it is residentially. In general, though, far more of all services are offered to adolescents in residential care than in outpatient treatment. However, the opposite is true for children who with the exception of sex education (and

---

[1] Eye movement desensitization and reprocessing is an increasingly popular treatment for trauma and increasingly used to treat disorders other than clearly defined trauma-induced disorders (Greenwald, 1999; Shapiro, 1995).

for boys, cycle work) receive considerably more of each of the treatment services in outpatient care.

PSYCHOSOCIAL TREATMENT

In general, psychosocial treatment is any active form of treatment that provides direct treatment services to clients. This stands in contrast to case management services, which fill an important function for many clients, or the model of milieu therapy that is commonly found at the heart of residential treatment. Both of these forms of treatment are inactive because although they play an often vital role in treatment, they nevertheless typically serve as adjuncts to more active and prominent forms of treatment. It is these more active forms that are typically considered psychosocial therapies.

Psychosocial treatment can take many forms, including individual psychotherapy, group and family therapy, expressive and experiential therapies, and types of treatment such as psychoeducation, occupational therapy, and forms of treatment-oriented and focused guidance and counseling. However, the term *psychosocial treatment* is descriptive only and is not directed toward any specific form of treatment other than those that are treatment goal driven, fill a specific therapeutic function, are provided by a clinician, or are provided by paraprofessional/nonprofessional treatment staff in accordance with a treatment or service plan. Psychosocial interventions can accordingly be varied, including psychotherapy, skill development training, therapeutic recreation, art therapy, psychodrama, and so forth. They are active forms of treatment intended therapeutically to improve client functioning. However, it is important to recognize that the contextual background common to all forms of psychosocial treatment with juvenile sexual offenders is forensic.

Individual Psychotherapy

Like many terms applying to current mental health practice, *psychotherapy* is generic rather than specific, referring only to a particular practice and not a particular model or set of specific techniques for practice. The American Psychiatric Association (1996) described psychotherapy as a treatment for mental disorders and emotional and psychological distress that relies on the unique relationship between therapist and client using verbal means and techniques to achieve changes. The APA described therapy as fundamental to the practice of psychiatry and essential in the treatment of mental disorders. Although recognizing several major forms of therapy, all of which have been demonstrated as effective, the APA described the two most practiced versions as psychodynamic therapy, derived from psychoanalytic theory, and cognitive therapy, derived from learning theory.

In either case, individual therapy is administered through the relationship between the clinician and the client, and in modern application both therapy types contain elements of the other. In both cases, effective therapy requires the active participation of the client, and many have suggested that such participation is the key to therapeutic success (Asay & Lambert, 1999; Lambert, 1992; Lambert & Bergin, 1993; Tallman & Bohart, 1999). In addition, many, if not most, believe that a critical and essential factor in therapy is the client-clinician relationship, or the therapeutic alliance (Asay & Lambert, 1999; Bachelor & Horvath, 1999; A. T. Beck, 1979; J. S. Beck, 1995; Dryden, 1989; Hubble, Duncan, & Miller, 1999; Lambert & Bergin, 1993; Maione & Chenail, 1999; Meichenbaum, 1985; Thase & Beck, 1993).

Although there are only two primary forms of therapy, within each therapeutic genotype there are many practicing models of psychotherapy, and some that integrate the ideas of both. Most of these therapeutic variants and practice models involve talk between the clinician and the client, and for that reason psychotherapy is often referred to as the talking cure, although there are considerable variations on this theme as well. Some therapies feature highly directive, interactive, and talkative therapists, whereas others have the therapist working quietly and nondirectively in the background, talking only when necessary to prompt a response, set a direction, or clarify or mirror the client's ideas. Nevertheless, a key element in therapy is the use of dialogue and verbal exchange between the client and the clinician. However, in some therapies talk is focused on particular tasks to be accomplished in treatment and in others is centered more on the interchange between the clinician and the client, or the process of therapy. These have respectively been described as prescriptive and exploratory (Kerr, Goldfried, Hayes, Castonguay, & Goldsamt, 1992).

Prescriptive, or content-based, therapies tend to view the talk process less as simply talk and more as a means for imparting information and directing the client to work on certain tasks that are considered to be the route to change. Therapies like this include cognitive therapy (A. T. Beck, 1979), reality therapy (Glasser, 1965), and solution-focused brief therapy (Cade & O'Hanlon, 1993). Exploratory, or process-based, therapies, on the other hand, consider the talk itself to be therapeutic, often leading to insight, emotional relief, and the capacity to change. The exchange between clinician and therapist is the medium through which treatment is implemented and *is* the treatment. To this degree, process-based therapies are insight oriented and are usually psychodynamic in nature, focusing on the processes and dynamic interchanges that occur within and behind the client's emotional and thought processes and on his or her interactions with others (including the therapist).

Some psychodynamic, process-based therapies can be more supportive, pragmatic, and counseling oriented than psychoanalytical, using talk and exploration to prompt and guide change, such as motivational interviewing (Miller & Rollnick, 2002; Procahska, 1999). In supportive psychodynamic therapies, talk is a means to both support and counsel the client in order to bring about general change, using the therapeutic process to encourage and foster the development of self-motivated and inner-directed change. Pinsker (1998) asserted that the supportive relationship is essential to all psychotherapy, which cannot proceed without such a relationship, but a supportive relationship alone does not constitute psychotherapy.

Although the difference is clear between certain kinds of psychotherapy, some therapies cannot easily be pigeonholed because they contain elements of different kinds of therapy. Ultimately, it may not really matter into which therapeutic category we place a psychotherapy as long as we understand its theory, structure, and methods.

Psychoeducational Treatment

Although the term is used also in psychological-educational testing and evaluation, in the context of treatment psychoeducation can be a form of psychosocial treatment. Here, the modality involves an instructional approach to teaching juvenile sexual offenders tools, concepts, and methods considered important to their treatment and rehabilitation, including social and coping skills, anger management and conflict resolution, stress management and relaxation, activities of daily living, and other ideas and skills considered important to the development of self-efficacy, prosocial attitudes and behaviors, enhanced self-esteem, and positive self-identity. The teaching of cognitive distortions also can be seen as a target for psychoeducation, although this treatment subject usually falls into the arena of cognitive therapy.

Although psychoeducation is not therapy but a primary mechanism for delivering information and teaching important psychosocial and psychoeducational skills and ideas, it can take on a strong counseling flavor at times, especially if provided on a one-to-one basis. The practice of effective psychoeducation requires strong instructional skills, experience, and knowledge in the psychoeducational instructor, as well as counseling and clinical skills, in much the same way that classroom teachers need these skills to be effective instructors and classroom managers. Psychoeducation can thus begin to resemble therapy at times, especially at the corners of cognitive therapy or insight-oriented treatment when those practices take on a more instructive edge, as they tend to in working with juvenile offenders. On the other hand, many clinicians find themselves at times running psychotherapy groups and family psychotherapy sessions that turn out to be more psychoeducational in nature than therapeutic. Nevertheless, unlike therapy (especially the process-oriented brand), the skill development principle behind psychoeducation requires that it focus on delivering ideas, information, and skills in a largely factual and semi-instructional format, with little emphasis on the meaning of interactions, intention, or process in general. The focus is on teaching important basic concepts to juvenile sexual offenders.

Psychoeducation can be delivered individually but is most frequently a group process. These groups often are provided as supplements to clinically oriented groups but are often run independently as skill development groups with the focus on a particular skill or topic. Frequently, such groups are curriculum driven, and many excellent and well-designed curricula are available for purchase that can shape and drive such groups, allowing group leaders to apply their psychoeducational teaching skills to prepared materials without having to design group content themselves (de Anda, 2002; Goldstein, 1999; Goldstein, Glick, & Gibbs, 1998; Vernon, 1998).

Workbooks and Psychoeducational Materials
Usually key to psychoeducation are workbooks or other work materials that are also often essential and intrinsic to cognitive-behavioral therapy. Material in these workbooks is often an extension of material covered in group and individual sessions and is usually intended to teach and develop basic and intermediate psychoeducational concepts and help participants develop relapse prevention skills. Through workbook assignments completed outside of psychoeducational sessions, clients continue to develop psychoeducational learning. Such work is often expected and required of juvenile sexual offenders, especially in residential treatment. In fact, client treatment compliance, participation, and progress are often based at least in part on activities completed through workbooks and similar materials.

Psychoeducation and Families
In addition to working directly with juveniles, psychoeducation is also used to work with family members. In many treatment settings, including medical treatment, a frequent function of case management is to provide psychoeducation to family members. By teaching family members concepts about the difficulty faced by the client and explaining information relevant to the situation or circumstances, treatment staff can reduce the anxiety of family members, help them to understand the nature of the disorder and how to treat it, and empower family members to be active helpers and instrumental in treatment. In the treatment of juvenile sexual offenders, psychoeducation is used to help parents and other family members learn more about treatment and the process that their child is going through in treatment, as well as learning ways to manage family life better. In addition, through psychoeducation, families not only can learn more about the treatment and its underlying concepts but also can function more effectively as treatment supports during both treatment and posttreatment, including the development and implementation of relapse prevention plans.

Effective Psychoeducation
In general, the psychoeducational component is intrinsic to the treatment of both juvenile and adult sexual offenders in the belief that psychological con-

cepts are basic to helping them understand, recognize, and overcome their offending behaviors, as well as the roots of the behaviors. Because children and adolescents are still developing, it is even more important to teach information and ideas that will become part of the way in which they understand themselves and the world around them and how they develop as individuals. In much the same way that we teach sex education and drug awareness to students in all walks of life, we teach the psychoeducational concepts of sexual offending behavior to juvenile sexual offenders as important building blocks in their development and thinking.

Psychoeducation is an important process and should be delivered by staff who are skilled psychoeducational trainers and facilitators of learning. Psychoeducation should not be considered a process that can be implemented by any available staff, and certainly not be treated as a nonclinical and routine job to be assigned randomly to anyone available, especially in the residential setting where staff are available around the clock. These skills should not be taken for granted, and staff members should be trained in psychoeducational techniques and in the concepts and skills they will be teaching through the psychoeducational process.

GROUP TREATMENT

Group treatment is utilized in the treatment of all sorts of mental disorders, including juvenile sexual offending. In terms of both financial costs and the application of treatment to many clients at the same time, group treatment has many attractive qualities. Group treatment is at the heart of juvenile sexual offender treatment and is often the preferred and predominant mode (O'Boyle, Lenehan, & McGarvey, 1999; Print & O'Callaghan, 1999; Sawyer, 2000), based on the belief that group treatment is an effective means for delivering treatment messages; developing new ideas, behaviors, and skills; and generally bringing about change in participants.

Marshall, Anderson, and Fernandez (1999) used *only* group therapy in treatment because they believe that individual therapy "is both less efficient and less effective" (p. 35). Perry and Orchard (1992) wrote that group therapy is the preferred form of treatment because it offers therapy to the greatest number of clients (the economy model); because it builds on peer interactions, including support and confrontation, which the authors considered to be more powerful than interactions with the therapist; and because group membership allows clients to address similar issues, feelings, ideas, and experiences. In their view, slightly less severe than that expressed by Marshall et al., individual and family therapy are second stringers serving only as adjuncts to group treatment.

Not everyone agrees that group therapy is effective or even that it should serve a preeminent role in treatment. Although Sawyer (2000) reported that most practitioners and authors believe that sex offenders should be treated in groups, Dishion, McCord, and Poulin (1999) disagreed. They hypothesized that behavioral problems in high-risk adolescents escalate as a result of group interventions and suggested that certain group interventions actually increase adolescent problem behavior and negative life outcomes. They noted that "there is reason to be cautious and to avoid aggregating young high-risk adolescents into intervention groups" (p. 762), advising practitioners to be open to the possibility that group intentions may inadvertently harm rather than help.

Nevertheless, group work is a central feature in treatment that is provided in virtually all programs for juvenile sexual offenders, sometimes instead of individual therapy, sometimes as a primary treatment mode in which individual therapy is adjunctive, and sometimes as a separate treatment mode that is provided in addition to individual therapy, which also serves as a primary mode of treatment. As with all forms of treatment, group treatment can serve a broad purpose or a more limited one. In the most comprehensive version of group treatment, multiple groups are provided as part of a broad and varied group program that focuses on many different subjects and activities. Although groups in juvenile sexual offender programs tend to focus on issues most relevant to sexual offending and related issues, group topics can range widely, including sexual behaviors, relationships, trauma, fire setting, grief and loss, and substance abuse. Groups also often focus on the development of social skills, communication skills, anger management, and self-esteem. The subjects dealt with in group treatment can be limitless and are typically dependent on the design of the treatment program, specific client needs, and the creativity of the clinician.

DYADS AND TRIADS: SMALL GROUP TREATMENT

In addition to individual therapy and group therapy (typically consisting of at least four group members), therapy can be provided in dyads and triads, or small groups. In therapy with younger children, the model of dyadic therapy is often known as *pair therapy* and is used more for social-developmental treatment and sometimes in conjunction with play therapy, but the idea is not so different. In fact, with younger sexually reactive children, dyadic or paired-play therapy may often be an appropriate and effective form of therapy through which to accomplish certain therapeutic tasks, as well as develop interactional and communication skills and develop other skills that children need in order to engage effectively in either individual or group therapy.

Dyads and triads allow clients to interact with one another and the therapist in a way that is sometimes safer and more engaging than in groups and more comfortable than in individual therapy. Participants have a more focused interactional experience both as listeners and speakers and receive the attention they might need but not get in group. Having only two or three clients in therapy also allows children who are not quite sure what to do or how to behave in individual therapy to have the comfort and modeling capacity of one or two peers, and this enables a therapeutic connection to be built between the clinician and clients and between the clients themselves in ways not otherwise possible.

The dyad or triad combination works differently than either individual or group therapy, although traces of each are embedded within its structure. Not much has been written on this treatment modality, but it holds promise as a form of treatment, even if only as a therapy mode adjunctive to individual and group therapy or a means to prepare juveniles better to participate more actively and effectively in individual and group therapy.

EXPRESSIVE, EXPERIENTIAL, AND PLAY THERAPY

By providing both expressive and experiential therapy, treatment programs are able to transcend the talk therapy typically associated with and at the heart of treatment. Both forms of therapy offer additional ways to work with children and adolescents and treat difficult issues through expressive, creative, energy-releasing, and esteem-building interactional activities.

Experiential therapy, or experience-based therapeutic activity, provides another important means for kids to engage in a positive treatment activity through a largely nonverbal process for catharsis (emotional release), creativity, stress reduction, and relaxation. These therapies include activities that build initiative, physical skills and physical health, and cooperation. In group activities, experiential therapy builds teamwork, a sense of trust and cooperation, and, depending on the nature of the activity, a sense of fairness, mutual respect, and graciousness in winning or losing. Just as art therapy is distinguished from art by its therapeutic focus and inquiring perspective, so too are therapeutic recreation and other experiential therapies made distinct from other forms of recreation and sport by their focus on learning and personal development, rather than simply being fun, exciting, energy-releasing activities. Although adjunctive to other traditional therapeutic approaches, experiential and recreational development are essential treatment components that provide children and adolescents with the opportunity to develop play, problem-solving, social, and coping skills

- When words fail, expressive therapy can provide an important alternative form of communication.
- All clients can participate in expressive therapy, and at their own skill levels and levels of interest.
- Expressive therapy facilitates creativity.
- The methods of expressive therapy—art, music, drama, and movement—can be enjoyable and personally rewarding.

- Expressive therapy provides direct access to both fantasy and the unconscious.
- The products of expressive therapy, and particularly art therapy, may be tangible, are often accessible to large numbers of people, and can often be examined in more detail at a later time.
- Expressive therapy can be diagnostic or projective, allowing us a glance into the inner world of clients who are otherwise unable or unwilling to share their ideas, feelings, and experiences.
- Expressive therapy provides a combination of both individual and group experiences that draws on the traditions of both group work and personal creativity and self-expression.

Therapeutic recreation, in particular, provides children and adolescents with positive leisure experiences that improve their quality of life and their sense of independence, competence, self-determination, and satisfaction. Such services incorporate personal initiative, choice, involvement, enjoyment, and supportive and social networks, all of which have important implications for physical, social, and psychological well-being. The development of a broad repertoire of leisure skills is necessary to take part in meaningful experiences that have lifelong value. Engaging in meaningful activities is an effective way both to help and energize children and to increase their personal satisfaction and motivation.[2]

Play therapy is often an important and relevant form of therapy for sexually reactive children. It is a nonverbal therapy that resembles both expressive and experiential therapy: It has an expressive purpose but an experiential form. Play therapy can be shaped to fit different developmental levels and chronological ages. At the psychodynamic end of theory, children (typically ages 3–11) express unconscious ideas, wishes, fears, and conflicts through play that they are otherwise unable to express through words because they lack the introspective awareness, cognitive development, and verbal skills required for verbal therapy. In a more cognitive model, children lack the developmental ability to form clear cognitions or express them, even if they have developed cognitive awareness. Through play therapy, children can instead demonstrate their ideas and experiences and, with the help of a play therapist, develop the skills to master and overcome problems. At the least theoretical end of the play therapy spectrum, the therapeutic use of play is normative, expressive, and healing; allows a level of emotional and energy release; and, with the help of a play therapist, serves the child's growth and skill development. As is true also for both expressive and experiential therapies, play therapy serves both a diagnostic purpose for the therapist through the child's projection of internal experiences into the play and a cathartic or expressive experience for the child.

[2] Many thanks to Erin Bell for her words and ideas regarding therapeutic recreation.

FAMILY THERAPY

Family work is considered of great importance in the treatment of juvenile sexual offenders. Not every treatment program or practitioner views or understands family treatment in the same way, and some apply a more general model whereas others employ a model of family therapy more in line with the practices typically associated with systemic forms of family therapy.

To a great degree we see juvenile sexual offenders as the products of their environment, which includes the family environment in which they grew up and in which behaviors were learned and played out. All forms of family therapy attempt to treat this family system and to recognize those elements of family life that may have influenced, led to, or served to maintain attitudes and behaviors connected to juvenile sexual aggression. More to the point, in family therapy we seek out those elements that are still present and evident in the family system of relationships, roles, communication, and structure, identifying these as the targets for change in family work. Specifically, in family therapy we see the family as a system in need of help, rather than a family suffering because of the identified patient (the juvenile sexual offender). Our role is to help open up or build new channels of communication, to identify or aid in the self-identification of dysfunctional patterns of family behavior, to empower individual members, and, in some instances, to educate and direct so that the family may become more effective and independent. In family therapy, the *family*—not the child—is the client. Accordingly, the family is the focus of treatment, rather than the individual within the family.

Family therapy is not recommended in all cases. Nevertheless, families should always be considered as potential targets for treatment. In the assessment of the juvenile, the goal is to understand the family environment in which the child was raised, lived, and learned, and the family in which the child was living at the time of the sexual offense, whether the victim was a family member or not. The goal of family assessment, however (which is often part of initial family therapy), is that of understanding the family as it exists now.

Accordingly, clinicians should aim for family therapy as an important component of treatment whenever relevant and appropriate, and particularly when the juvenile will be returning to live with the family or will continue to be an active family member even if he will not be returning home. After an initial exploration of the family environment, it is important that clinicians develop a clear sense of the goals and targets of family therapy. Clinicians should be able to address the purpose of family therapy in any given case and describe what they are attempting to do, change, or bring about in the family environment through family therapy.

Family Meetings Versus Family Therapy and Education

Family meetings are important because they serve to provide important information and to clarify, explain, and define expectations and requirements. But a family meeting is not the same as family therapy, and the two types of family interventions should not be confused for one another. No less than any other form of therapy, family therapy requires therapeutic technique and design. In family meetings called to discuss the case, set behavioral contracts, develop relapse prevention plans, and so forth, a different set of skills is required, most typically those of chairmanship, facilitation, and psychoeducation. It is important to distinguish between the two types of interventions, even if both are provided by the clinician. One is for communication and management (family meetings), the other for bringing about change (family therapy).

Process and Content: Dynamics and Task

All treatment interventions contain elements of content and process. *Content* represents the tasks or the purpose of the treatment intervention. For instance, if a group is formed to educate and treat students for substance abuse, the content is substance abuse education, discussion, and relapse prevention plan strategies. Content reflects the task to be achieved; the identified things to be accomplished; the specific attitude, feeling, belief, or behavior to be changed through treatment; and facts that can be relatively easily described and taught.

Process, on the other hand, is a reflection of the psychodynamic aspect of treatment. In groups, this means a focus on the underlying and normally hidden dynamic interactions, methods of communication, and messages delivered in the group, and the process by which group members communicate and learn. Process reflects the underlying dynamics, relationships, interactions, and experiences that impede, facilitate, or in some other way influence the accomplishment of the task.

Many groups in group therapy are driven by psychoeducational and cognitive-behavioral ideas that focus on thinking errors, cognitive distortions, abuse cycles, and relapse prevention planning (content driven). Other groups are driven by group dynamics and interactions (process groups) and focus specifically on the daily and in-group interactions experienced by group members, using this as the fuel of the group. Both content and process are important elements of treatment.

Content and process are found not only in groups but in individual and family work as well. Individual therapy that is cognitive-behavioral or oriented toward reality therapy is more likely to be *content* based, working toward concrete behavioral changes more than insight or interpersonal understanding. *Process* therapy is psychodynamic and focuses on analysis, the development of insight and interpersonal awareness, and the emergence of formerly unconscious motivations, attitudes, emotions, and experiences.

However, content and process are two sides of the same coin. It is impossible to imagine a treatment intervention that lacks both elements.

PHARMACOLOGICAL TREATMENT

Psychiatry and pharmacology (sometimes referred to as psychopharmacology in the case of psychotropic[3] medication) go hand in hand. Although not all sexual offenders are treated with medication, it is a psychiatrist's job to consider the possibility that psychiatric medications will assist with one or more aspects of the problem. For most children and adolescents, psychiatric medication is used to treat comorbid emotional, attentional, and thought disorders, rather than behavioral disorders such as conduct and oppositional disorder or inappropriate sexual behaviors. Such behaviors are more typically treated via interactional or psychoeducational therapies, such as psychotherapy, cognitive-behavioral treatment, and experiential therapy. This is in keeping with the manner in which mental disorders are treated in children and adolescents in the general population. However, it is generally believed that pharmacotherapy (psychopharmacology used in combination with other forms of interactive therapy) is of great use with respect to both comorbidity and overall functioning. Based on the use of psychiatric medications, both among the general population and juvenile sexual offenders, there is support for and belief in the practice among treatment providers.

Little is available on the percentage of treated juvenile sexual offenders prescribed psychiatric medication or changes in the number of prescriptions written for this population over the past decade. However, Rich (2002) reported that as many as 73% of clients at a large residential treatment for juvenile sexual offenders were prescribed psychiatric medication for diagnoses that ranged from depressive and anxiety disorders to attention-deficit disorders, obsessive compulsive disorders, and schizophrenia. This may not be an unusually high percentage for juveniles in treatment as many outpatient and residential treatment facilities provide psychiatric care. Burton and Smith-Darden (2001) reported that on average 36% of outpatient and 58% of residential treatment programs for juvenile sexual offenders provide psychopharmacology.

In fact, the use of psychotropic medication in the treatment of children and adolescents in the general population is increasing, and this may also reflect increasing prescriptions for juvenile sexual offenders. Olfson, Marcus, Weissman, and Jensen (2002) noted significant increases in the overall annual use of psychiatric medications in the general population of children under 18, with an increase from 1.4% to 3.9% between 1987 and 1996. The rate of prescribed

---

[3] Psychotropic medications are medications that act on the mind and work to alter emotions, behavior, or perception.

stimulant use in 1996 was the highest among 6- to 14-year-old boys, and children and adolescents were almost four times more likely to be prescribed an antidepressant than in 1987. Of children and adolescents who were prescribed an antidepressant, 34% were also prescribed another class of psychotropic medication, most commonly combining stimulants and antidepressants (Olfson et al.). Prescriptions for neuroleptic (antipsychotic) medication remained stable over that decade, supporting the idea that psychosis is a relatively rare phenomenon in juveniles. Reporting similar findings, Waters (2000) reported that almost three million antidepressant prescriptions were written for juveniles in 1999, with a 52% increase since 1994, and that 1.8 million juveniles were prescribed selective serotonin reuptake inhibitors (SSRIs) or 6% of all SSRI prescriptions.

However, despite the widespread use of psychopharmacology in treatment with juvenile sexual offenders, and indeed many troubled kids, the effectiveness of such medications is neither clear nor universally accepted. Olfson et al. (2002) warned that "an important challenge ahead lies in determining the appropriateness (and ultimately the effectiveness) of the care provided to the large number of children and adolescents who receive prescribed psychotropic medications" (p. 520). Similarly, Murlow et al. (1999) reported a significant paucity of information about the effects of such medication in children and adolescents, noting that the safety and efficacy of new antidepressant medication for children and adolescents are unclear. Waters (2000) wrote that "in more than 10 years of research, researchers have never been able to show that SSRIs and many other powerful drugs provide significant and special benefits to most of the depressed children given them" (p. 43). In addition, many indicators suggest that psychotherapy is as effective as psychopharmacology (Duncan, Miller, & Sparks, 2000; "Mental Health," 1995; Seligman, 1995), and Fisher and Greenberg (1997) considered that most of the treatment effects often attributed to medication are actually the product of the placebo effect.

For these and related reasons, and despite its widespread use and acceptance, as well as its often central role in the treatment of juvenile sexual offenders, Righthand and Welch (2001) wrote that many questions remain concerning the psychopharmacology approach to treatment.

PHARMACOLOGY AND SEXUAL AROUSAL

Medications are also used to reduce or eliminate sexual drive in sexual offenders. The primary pharmacological treatment for paraphilic disorders utilizes antiandrogen medication, which chemically reduces or blocks the action of testosterone. This form of treatment, sometimes referred to as *chemical castration*, typically includes hormonal medications such as medroxyprogesterone (Provera and Depo-Provera), cyproterone (Androcur), and leuprolide acetate (Lupron). However, although these medications appear to be effective in achieving their goals and certainly are appropriate for some adult sexual offenders, they are nevertheless not intended as the sole intervention (Association for the Treatment of Sexual Abusers, 2000; Kafka, 1995). More important, these medications are typically used only with adult offenders because they have potentially serious effects on the body and may significantly affect normal growth and development in adolescents. Consequently, antiandrogens are rarely used with juvenile sexual offenders.

Antiandrogens are not psychotropic. That is, they have no effect on the mind and are not used in the treatment of psychiatric diagnoses. But psychotropic medications are used to treat deviant sexual arousal, with both adult and adolescent clients, including lithium, tricyclic antidepressants, and neuroleptic (antipsychotic) medication such as benperidol (Anaquil, Frenactil) and thioridazine (Mellaril). However, SSRIs such as fluoxetine (Prozac) and setraline (Zoloft), most typically prescribed for depression and anxiety disorders, are also believed to be effective in treating sexual arousal, even in the absence of a concurrent mood disorder (Kafka, 2001), and these are the most commonly prescribed psychotropic medications used to treat and dampen sexual arousal. In addition, Kafka and Hennen (2000) also described a successful trial with the psychostimulant methylphenidate (Ritalin), concluding that when used in combination with SSRIs, and under specific conditions, these may also prove useful in reducing sexual arousal. Nevertheless, Rösler and Witztum (2000) wrote

> we are of the opinion that in the present state of the art in research on psychotropic medications, especially SSRIs, there is an urgent need for good methodological research . . . in order to establish whether or not SSRI medication plays a beneficial role in the treatment of paraphilias. . . . Until proven otherwise, psychotropic medications do not play a crucial role in the treatment of paraphilias. (pp. 51–52)

Unlike antiandrogens, psychotropic medications (and particularly SSRIs) are prescribed to some male juvenile sexual offenders in order to diminish sexual drive, whether effective or not. However, the hypersexual and compulsive sexual drive described by Kafka (2001) as the target for treatment may for many adolescents simply be a description of everyday reality, lying squarely within developmental and social norms and symptomatic of adolescence rather than hypersexuality, compulsivity, or a paraphilic-like disorder.[4] The risk then is that we might tamper with normal biological, psychic, and emotional development in adolescents because we mistake normative behaviors and urges in adolescents for what are deviant urges and behaviors in adults.

---

[4] Kafka (2001) described paraphilic-like disorders as repetitive, impulsive-compulsive, and addictive sexual behaviors accompanied by intrusive sexual fantasies and urges (which in adolescent boys sound like normative experiences).

Under such circumstances, with the best intentions in mind, we may move toward medications too quickly, unnecessarily, and without full or adequate knowledge of the processes by which medications work in adolescents or the unintended consequences they may produce. In so doing, we may fail to treat the real problem of juvenile sexual offending (which, in most cases, is probably not hypersexuality or deviant sexual arousal).

With respect to the use of SSRIs among juveniles, Hunter and Lexier (1998) cautioned that questions remain about the benefits of these medications to juveniles in reducing sexual drive, including appropriate candidates and appropriate dosages. In a similar vein, the Center for Sex Offender Management (1999b) warned that very little information exists about the safety and effectiveness of these medications among juveniles.

THE ROLE OF PSYCHOPHARMACOLOGY

Even though psychiatrists commonly prescribe medications and clinicians often encourage their use and clearly believe they are of value, in truth we do not know how useful medications are either in treating the mental disorders we diagnose as comorbid or in dealing with sexually aggressive behaviors. With children whose psychiatric conditions are unmistakable, we do have the opportunity to see whether medication helps (although in some cases even positive effects may be attributable to a placebo effect rather than a true medication effect). But many children do not have symptoms that are that well defined in the first place, and for these juveniles it is much harder to discern a medication effect.

Because we are relatively quick to prescribe medications, it is often unclear how well these same kids might do without medication. In some instances where medications are clearly reported to work, with ADHD for example, it may be that a well-designed and implemented program of social skills development, parenting skills, and daily structure would do as well. Without well-designed and well-understood treatment programs and well-designed and well-implemented research studies, we may never know how well medications actually work, where their effect begins and ends in the case of medications combined with other forms of treatment, and whether they are truly necessary in all of the cases for which they are prescribed. For instance, Elkin et al. (1989) found that clients treated with psychotherapy alone (no medications) did as well as clients treated with both psychotherapy and medication, suggesting no difference in treatment. Despite the common use of medications, as well as a common belief in their value, they may not be as helpful as we think. In fact, the American Academy of Child and Adolescent Psychiatry (1998) wrote that although both medication and therapy are effective treatments for depression in youth, psychotherapy is the likely treatment of choice. Nonetheless, medications often seem to be of great use among kids who suffer from clearly defined and more severe mental disorders.

Finally, studies that cast doubt on the efficacy of medications and describe the unnecessary or flawed prescription of medications may also need to consider the accuracy and appropriateness of diagnoses applied to clients. If medications are prescribed in cases where the real issue is poor mood and limited social skills rather than clinical depression (for instance), it is little wonder that the medication did not work. Perhaps we need to look more closely at the correct and accurate application of the diagnoses that result in psychopharmacology, as well as at psychopharmacology itself.

CONCLUSION: THE EFFECTIVENESS OF TREATMENT

Treatment is only useful if it works. Certainly there is an abundance of evidence that psychotherapy is effective.[5] That does not mean it works equally well in every application and for every disorder, and research has been directed toward the use of psychotherapy in the mental health population more than in the forensic population.

There is a great deal of support for the idea that treatment for juvenile sexual offenders works and much optimism that it can work. On the other hand, Hollin (2001) cautioned that "it would be wrong to assume that the case for treatment is proven; it is evident that a great deal more work needs to be carried out on the effectiveness of treatment" (p. 11). However, this is both an overstatement and an understatement. Optimistically, Hollins implied that treatment works and implicitly overstated the idea that we have any substantial proof that this is true. His comment also significantly understated the paucity of available and robust evidence that supports treatment efficacy, as well as the amount of work that needs to be accomplished to prove the case.

In fact, unlike assertions that psychotherapy is an effective treatment, declarations about the effectiveness of sexual offender treatment are made in absence of any significant hard data, about either the effectiveness of sexual-offender-specific treatment (measured by the percentage of treated juveniles who reoffend sexually) or treatment formats and approaches that work (compared to those that work less effectively or not at all).

It is difficult, for many reasons, to develop data regarding either the effectiveness of treatment for sexual offenders or the effectiveness of different types of treatment. In terms of recidivism (a measure of treatment effectiveness), follow-up over a sufficient amount of time is very difficult because it

---

[5] See, for instance, Asay and Lambert (1999); Hubble, Duncan, and Miller (1999); Lambert and Bergin (1993); Luborsky, Singer, and Luborsky (1975); Maione and Chenail (1999); "Mental Health" (1995); and Seligman (1995).

often requires multiagency approval and coordination, as well as the cooperation of the family; because the living situations of many children and adolescents in treatment are not static, including children who move from state to state; and because as children age into adults their living situations become even more difficult to follow and they sometimes vanish from sight, so that their cooperation is required as well. In addition, for follow-up studies to be of real use, they should operate for at least 5 years, and ideally 10 or more, as we know that many adult and lifetime sexual offenders began as juvenile sexual offenders. It is also difficult to capture accurate information about relapse, or actual sexual reoffense, as opposed to only those reoffenses that are discovered because sexual offenders are unlikely to divulge offenses that they are otherwise able to keep hidden. In addition, the question of treatment effect on recidivism raises difficult logistical and ethical issues. For a study to be valid, it must have a control group so that treated subjects can be compared to untreated or undertreated subjects, and these two groups must be cohorts; that is, they must be alike in almost every respect in order to measure the differences in treatment effect, rather than age, background, IQ, or other personal factors. Additionally, in the ideal study we will select subjects randomly, rather than possibly including subjects who are already in better shape than others, and thus more likely to show good results. On top of all this, many studies are small in terms of the numbers of subjects included, and studies are almost always inconsistent from one to the next, making it impossible to replicate or confirm them independently. As if these obstacles were not enough, having a comparison group that has not received treatment raises ethical questions because this may mean intentionally not treating or undertreating group members and then releasing them into the community.

Much of the required evidence of treatment effectiveness in general, as well as the effectiveness of specific treatments, is absent in our work with juvenile sexual offenders. As little to none of this work has been undertaken in a scientifically rigorous manner, much of what we believe to be true about treatment and treatment outcome is largely anecdotal, observational, or based on weak and sometimes a priori studies that yield limited data. Where data do exist, they are not scientifically established and often do not match clinical experience. Nonetheless, it neither stops assertions from being made nor dampens enthusiasm for any one perspective over another.

In general, we know that juvenile sexual offenders who do get into continued trouble are more likely to get into trouble for continued nonsexual offenses and antisocial behaviors than for sexually abusive behaviors (Association for the Treatment of Sexual Abusers, 2000; Center for Sex Offender Management, 1999b; Knight & Prentky, 1993; Schram, Milloy, & Rowe, 1991; U.S. General Accounting Office, 1996a; Weinrott, 1996). We also generally believe that the recidivism rate for treated juvenile sexual offenders is somewhere between 7% and 13% over follow-up periods of 2 to 5 years (Hunter,

2000). In their study, which used a control-comparison group, Worling and Curwen (2000) came up with a more optimistic result. They compared a group of 58 treated juvenile sexual offenders against a comparison group of 90 untreated, undertreated, or otherwise-treated juvenile sexual offenders, with an average follow-up of 6 years. They found 5% sexual recidivism in the treated group compared to 18% in the comparison group, as well as reduced rates of nonsexual recidivism in the treated group. Even if we increase the percentage of recidivism in treated juvenile sexual offenders to 20%, by taking into account undiscovered sexual reoffenses, things still look relatively good. Pushing the envelope to 25% lifetime recidivism for treated offenders (meaning that they sexually offend again at some point in their lives) still means that 75% of treated offenders do not reoffend, or that the odds are better than 3 in 4 that treatment is a useful way to reduce the recurrence of sexually abusive behaviors in treated juveniles.

This optimistic belief in the effectiveness of treatment may be a necessity because in light of limited data we must have hope and a belief that treatment will work, as well as confidence that the evolution of treatment ideas and methods is constantly pushing us toward increased effectiveness even if we cannot prove it. Prentky and Burgess (2000) asserted that the logical and obvious conclusion, uninfluenced by either emotion or data, is that treatment is unlikely to be effective for all offenders but likely to be effective for some. They wrote that it is "logical that some, but not all, offenders would benefit from treatment. Stated otherwise, treatment undoubtedly will restore some offenders to a nonoffending lifestyle and will fail to touch other offenders" (p. 217).

We also believe that juvenile sexual offenders are still children who remain open to corrective emotional and cognitive experiences that will help reframe their ideas and worldviews, address their emotional and behavioral difficulties, and help them to engage prosocially and in ways that yield greater personal satisfaction and a sense of self-efficacy. For this reason alone, we see rehabilitation for most juvenile sexual offenders as an obvious choice over either incarcerating them, simply accepting the idea that we cannot treat them, or believing that they will just grow out of it and hoping for the best. The question is not whether to treat or whether treatment is really effective, but *what* the best treatment is.

CHAPTER 12

Rehabilitation: Treatment in Practice

THERE IS little difference between the rehabilitation and treatment of juvenile sexual offenders. I have used the term *rehabilitation* to distinguish between descriptions of treatment models and interventions and the actual application of treatment. In this sense, rehabilitation represents the application of treatment ideas, or treatment in practice. Rehabilitation also serves to describe the goal behind treatment: to restore to good health or reinstate functionality. As previously mentioned, for many juvenile sexual offenders rehabilitation is less about restoring health to a former level than developing a new level of health and functioning not formerly experienced by the youth. Nonetheless, rehabilitation serves the goal of renewing or developing prosocial skills and competencies in the child or adolescent, thus restoring his role in the community at large.

Rehabilitation suggests a pathology that separates individuals from their society and thus is a term that would not typically be applied to a depressed client or someone experiencing psychosis. More typically, it is applied to substance abusers and criminals whose behaviors have separated them from the social world. That is, they live in a world outside of conventional society and engage in behaviors that are unsafe to themselves and others. Rehabilitation in mental and behavioral health suggests a return to the prosocial world, and distinguishes between treatment ideas and treatment practice. Nonetheless, the terms *treatment* and *rehabilitation* are used interchangeably throughout the remainder of this book.

THE BACKDROP FOR TREATMENT AND REHABILITATION

Sexually abusive behavior has evoked special outrage and fear in the community because it causes so much harm to individuals and families. It is often

240

aimed at the weakest members of society and even in its least destructive form represents the offender's use of another person's body for his own gratification and needs. In its most extreme forms, it is an outrageous and heinous act of brutality against a callously selected victim that leaves permanent scars on the individual and society, causing all to feel vulnerable and damaged. Among adult offenders, at least, it is often tied to predatory and planned behaviors, and certainly in the case of multiple episodes, sexual offending is rarely related to spontaneous behavior or situational impulsivity.

Accordingly, social consequences may be more extreme for sexual offenders than for other criminals, including the potential for lifetime inclusion on publicly available sexual offender registries even for juvenile offenders, and in a number of states the possibility of indeterminate civil commitment following release from prison. All treatment for sexual offenders, whether adult or juvenile, must be framed by an understanding of the consequences of sexual offending to individuals and society and the social response. The Association for the Treatment of Sexual Abusers (2001) has defined and revised its guidelines for working with sexual abusers, which provide a backdrop for treatment and also reflecting current thinking that lies behind such treatment. It is important to recognize that these principles are designed largely for adult sexual offenders, rather than juveniles. Nonetheless, they are important guidelines, and the assessment and treatment of juvenile sexual offenders should be defined and applied in a manner informed by ATSA (2001, pp. v–vi) principles:

- Community safety takes precedence over any consideration and ultimately is in the best interest of sexual abusers and their families.
- Inadequate or unethical treatment damages the credibility of all treatment providers and presents an unnecessary risk to the community.
- Although many, if not most, sexual abusers are treatable, there is no known cure. Management of sexually abusive behavior is a lifelong task for some sexual abusers.
- Many sexual abusers will not comply with treatment or supervision requirements without external motivation. Internal motivation improves the prognosis for completing a treatment program but in and of itself may not be sufficient for treatment engagement and compliance.
- Criminal investigation, prosecution, and a court order requiring specialized sexual abuser treatment are important components of effective intervention and management.
- It is imprudent to release untreated sexual abusers into the community without providing specialized evaluation, treatment, or supervision.
- ATSA members should work cooperatively with probation and parole officers, child welfare workers, the client's support persons, and therapists who work with victims.

THE GOALS OF REHABILITATION

Gail Ryan (1999b) described two necessary components in the treatment of sexually aggressive juveniles: *offense-specific* interventions that focus on elements and patterns directly related to sexual offending and *holistic preventative* interventions that focus on increased self-control and efficacy, as well as more general issues. The struggle, she maintained, "is to combine the specific and the holistic into comprehensive models that can differentially diagnose and treat offenders while respecting the unique developmental and contextual realities of each individual" (p. 427), but she noted that not every sexually abusive juvenile requires the same treatment or will respond in the same way. She identified three essential goals as *communication*, or the development of a language that facilitates interaction and learning; the *development of empathy*; and *accountability*. She asserted that these three goals represent "the bottom line in creating a treatment program within which the youth can grow, change, give up defensive patterns, and internalize a sense of personal competence" (p. 429).

Ryan (1999b) also asserted that sexual-offender-specific treatment must address six active areas in the lives of juvenile offenders:

1. Consistent awareness of sexual abuse in their daily lives
2. Recognition of patterns associated with abuse cycles
3. Demonstration of competencies that interrupt those patterns
4. Awareness of risks for relapse
5. Demonstration of empathy in daily interactions
6. The ability to create and maintain safe and reciprocal relationships

Goals and Objectives

In educational and other planning models, goals are often conceptualized as the larger and more general targets at which treatment (or education) is aimed. Objectives, on the other hand, are more focused, are often described in terms of action steps (i.e., what will actually be accomplished), are more precise, and often are more measurable. It is useful in any program of treatment to define at least three levels of goals, evolving from most abstract to most concrete: (a) purpose (or broad goals), (b) specific goals, and (c) objectives. These are often followed by the action steps or interventions by which objectives are actually obtained.

Purpose and Broad Goals

In the most general terms, the ultimate goals of any sexual-offender-specific treatment program are to

- Prevent further sexual victimization of members of society
- Prevent reoccurrence of other aggressive or abusive behaviors
- Teach replacement behaviors

SPECIFIC GOALS

Based on the recommendations of the National Task Force on Juvenile Sexual Offending (1993), 17 specific treatment areas can be identified as important in any model of treatment and rehabilitation:

1. Personal responsibility for behaviors
2. Behavioral self-control, including interruption of patterns of dysfunctional behavior
3. Prosocial behavior with the concomitant reduction of antisocial behavior
4. Rational thinking and healthy attitudes, recognizing and eliminating cognitive distortions and attitudinal mind-sets that support sexually abusive behavior
5. Healthy and appropriate self-expression
6. Healthy and appropriate relationships with both peers and adults
7. Improved self-esteem and sense of personal identity
8. Improved mental health with resolution of comorbid psychiatric conditions
9. Addiction-free lifestyle with regard to both addictive and compulsive sexual behaviors and substance use
10. Intellectual improvement and development, recognizing and addressing cognitive impairments and developmental delays where present
11. Healthy sexual attitudes, fantasies, and identity and the reduction or elimination of deviant sexual arousal
12. Trauma resolution in the event of personal victimization in the youth's own history
13. Improved social skills and increased social competence and sense of self-efficacy and social mastery
14. Development of relapse prevention plans that recognize situational, emotional, and cognitive factors that might contribute to a sexual reoffense, as well as defined methods to avoid high-risk situations and escape patterns of sexually inappropriate or otherwise antisocial behavior
15. Improved family functioning in which family dysfunction, communication, attitudes, or roles contributing to or helping to maintain sexually aggressive and antisocial behaviors are addressed and remediated
16. Victim recognition and awareness with focus on the development of empathy and clarification of the harm caused to the victim and others

17. Victim and community restitution in which the juvenile sexual offender undertakes reparation and makes amends

OBJECTIVES OF TREATMENT

Operationalizing the aforementioned goals leads to nine concrete objectives that are the aim of the rehabilitation process in the treatment of juvenile offenders. Hence, the juvenile will

1. Understand, identify, and interrupt thoughts, feelings, beliefs, and behaviors that contribute to abuse
2. Develop responsibility for personal choices and behavior without minimization or justification
3. Understand the impact of past trauma on self-image, functioning, difficulties, and behaviors
4. Develop awareness, sensitivity, and compassion for others
5. Learn and understand normative and deviant sexual development
6. Identify, interrupt, and control deviant sexual arousal and deviant sexual fantasy
7. Learn and use adaptive coping and social skills
8. Build and engage in noncoercive relationships
9. Develop and use a relapse prevention plan

Without defining *how* to provide treatment or by what particular methods and techniques, these ideas, goals, and objectives provide a clear understanding of the targets for treatment but are flexible enough that individual programs and practitioners may decide how best to meet these treatment goals and general outcomes.

INTEGRATED AND MULTIFACETED TREATMENT

In order to meet disparate goals, treatment must be *multimodal* because not all treatment services can be provided through a single mode of treatment, *multidisciplinary* in that no one mental health or related discipline can provide the range of identified treatment services, and *multitheoretical* because it is unlikely that a variety of goals can be accomplished through a single-therapy model.

A comprehensive model of treatment will include multiple treatment components wrapped into an integrated and multifaceted model, as described in Chapter 15. However, as important as the treatment components themselves are, it is essential that they be geared toward the specific population for which they are intended within the broader population of juvenile sexual offenders, including cognitively impaired clients (typically borderline or mentally retarded youths), children versus adolescents, female clients, juveniles with autistic-spectrum disorders, and clients with psychotic or psychotic-like conditions. Specific components include

- *Sexual-offender-specific,* consisting of multimodality treatment elements aimed directly at the sexual offending behaviors that brought the juvenile into treatment, including cognitive distortions, insight development, safe behaviors, healthy sexuality, situational awareness, victim awareness, empathy development, and relapse prevention planning
- *Sexual-offender-relevant,* directed toward significant collateral treatment needs often connected to sexual offenses, such as social skill development, conflict management, stress management skills, relationship building and communication skills, and decision making and problem solving
- *Clinical collateral,* which addresses other specific issues on a case-by-case basis, such as sexual orientation, fire setting, trauma and loss, aggression and violence, substance abuse, and other specific treatment needs identified through the assessment and treatment plan
- *General treatment,* related to the general needs of all juveniles, including therapeutic recreation, self-awareness, social awareness, and community learning and service.
- *Psychiatric treatment,* aimed at comorbid psychiatric conditions where relevant, such as depression, anxiety, psychosis, autistic-spectrum disorders, and others discussed in Chapter 9
- *Educational-academic,* for those clients in residential treatment for whom the continued provision of academic-educational services is critical, with a focus on the remedial and special educational needs often evident in juvenile sexual offenders; even for those clients not in residential treatment, a solid and sound education aimed at the learning styles, needs, and capacity of each child or adolescent is critical both for success in treatment and the ability to function appropriately and achieve personal goals after treatment is complete

These multimodal, multidisciplinary, and multitheoretical components are integrated in the sense that they are part of a larger treatment program, and not simply a loosely strung together bunch of treatments. This implies coordination among the parts, communication among members of the treatment team that deliver each component, and a coherent model and vision that ensure that each modality is a single component of a larger model.

SEXUAL-OFFENDER-SPECIFIC TREATMENT

Sexual-offender-specific (or sexual-abuse-specific) treatment refers to therapeutic interventions aimed directly at the individual's sexual offending and related behaviors. These include the actual sexually abusive behaviors as well as the thoughts, feelings, attitudes, beliefs, and circumstances that contributed to, resulted in, and maintained the behaviors.

- To be effective, sexual-offender-specific treatment includes both specific interventions explicitly aimed at sexual offending behavior and interventions aimed at collateral or other contiguous conditions and factors that directly contribute to, influence, or maintain sexual offending behavior.
- Explicit abuse-specific treatment directly addresses sexually offending thoughts, beliefs, and behaviors, which are an essential and central component of the treatment process.
- Other components of sexual-offender-specific treatment can be thought of as collateral but are also aimed at the presenting problem of sexual offending behaviors.
- Whether aimed at explicit sexual offending behaviors or comorbid and collateral conditions, all sexual-offender-specific treatment is intended to extinguish and eliminate sexual offending behavior

TREATING THE WHOLE PERSON

A holistic treatment model is one in which the whole person is treated and not just his abuse-specific behaviors, including

- The sexual offenses that brought the youth into treatment in the first place
- Comorbid psychiatric conditions that may be affecting the youth
- Behavioral and relationship issues that shape and influence self-perception and interpersonal relationships
- Issues of developmental trauma and life-changing experiences that may have a profound effect on the youth's development and current behavior
- Issues of self-identity, self-concept, and self-esteem
- Social skills and the experience of social mastery and personal competency
- Family, environmental, and other systemic issues that may affect and strongly influence thinking, behavior, and relationships

The philosophy and driving force behind any form of holistic treatment for juvenile sexual offenders are those of forensic mental health and are built on several key ideas:

- The juvenile sexual offender is fully responsible and accountable for his sexually abusive behaviors.
- Juvenile sexual offenders cannot be treated strictly for their sexual offending behavior as though such behavior is separate from the rest of their behavior or can be understood out of context.

- Individual attitudes, experiences, and behaviors are intertwined with social life and especially with the family and the environment in which the child was raised, learned, and lived.
- Treatment must be directed toward the actual sexual offending behaviors as well as other personal characteristics, comorbid conditions, the environment in which the child has lived and learned, and other systemic variables that shape, facilitate, and maintain feelings, attitudes, beliefs, and behaviors.
- To be effective, sexual-offender-specifc treatment must be directed toward a range of emotional and behavioral conditions, including the environment that perhaps influenced the individual and in which sexual offending behavior developed and was carried out.

Nevertheless, no matter how it is conceptualized, the main task in sexual-offender-specific treatment is to treat sexual offending behavior. Children and adolescents do not enter sexual offender treatment because they are depressed, anxious, or even conduct disordered. Although these are legitimate targets for treatment—and, indeed, in the treatment of the whole person are *essential* targets—they are nevertheless secondary to the primary purpose. That focus is always on the treatment and resolution of the direct and indirect factors that led to sexual offending even if offender-specific interventions periodically drop into the treatment background while other related treatment issues become targets of treatment.

UNDERSTANDING AND FRAMING TREATMENT

Working with and treating juvenile sexual offenders is difficult and sometimes confusing, and it is easy to lose track of what to work on and how best to judge movement, progress, and success in treatment. Accordingly, it is useful for clinicians to have a framework for evaluating and making sense of treatment.

CLIENT COMFORT AND DISCOMFORT IN TREATMENT

It is to be expected that youths will be uncomfortable in the treatment environment. We are asking children and adolescents to be self-revelatory, expressive, and, in particular, to discuss behaviors that may be a combination of embarrassing, shameful, secret, deviant, pleasurable, and confusing. To understand fully not just what happened and when, but also the causes and motivations behind sexual offending behavior, youths will in most cases have to go to difficult emotional places and sometimes feel extreme emotional discomfort and even pain. It is the therapist's job, through the treatment alliance, to encourage, help, and support the clients through this process. Without such support, the process is untherapeutic and may fail.

As treatment progresses, clinicians should observe an increase in youth comfort and ability to talk about and explore difficult issues. In fact, one measure of treatment impact will be the youth's eventual ability to discuss his sexual interests, behaviors, and motivations openly and in detail with the clinician as well as in group and family treatment.

Pacing and Treatment Over Time

The goal is to accomplish all treatment goals in the shortest time possible. But with such a large array of treatment issues and targets, and the youth's developing personality and psyche, gains and changes from the treatment process, as well as the acquisition and retention of new ideas and behaviors, take place only over time.

Accordingly, although the guideline is to approach and tackle treatment issues as soon as possible, in reality treatment must be paced. A youth may be willing to reveal or learn only so much at any given point in treatment, which is why it is essential to revisit the same ideas and situations over time. A later look at the same situation, event, behavior, or relationship may reveal many more complex factors with the further development of the clinician-youth relationship and as the youth himself has progressed in treatment.

Treatment in any long-term environment has a serial quality. That is, earlier treatment is connected to later treatment through the many sessions and experiences shared by the youth and the clinician. Accordingly, although there may be episodic periods during which something particular is happening in treatment (or not happening), these must be recognized as episodes in a larger and unfolding picture that can only be fully seen and assessed over time. This means that clinicians must work to connect earlier treatment sessions to later ones, building later treatment experiences on earlier ones.

Pacing in the treatment of multiple areas also means that treatment in one area may well be dependent on treatment in another and that one type of target or treatment must precede another. In some cases, the provision of one type of treatment intervention may depend on work being done in other treatment areas; thus, pacing always implies a sequence of treatment. It also means that treatment is progressive, developing and changing over time. For instance, addressing trauma during individual therapy may not take place until a groundwork and therapeutic relationship are first built. Pressure on the therapist to address issues prematurely may result in failure, at least in that treatment area. Pacing treatment means not only finding a starting point, a middle point, and an end point to specific treatment targets but also arriving at critical treatment points at the right time, at the right speed, in the right order, and in the right frame of mind (for the juvenile).

In this context pacing, means making informed and reasonable decisions about *what* treatment goals should be applied at any given moment in treatment, and *how* and with what level of *intensity* to provide treatment interventions. In the final analysis, treatment is provided and paced according to treatment needs and readiness for treatment, as well as ability and willingness to accept treatment. The client who is neither ready for nor able to accept treatment must be engaged in a form of *pre*treatment that prepares him for treatment (which, of course, is a form of treatment itself). Before sexual-offender-specific treatment can be seriously considered, the offender must demonstrate at least a minimal level of behavioral and emotional control and a willingness and ability to work on sexual-offender-specific treatment issues and must have engaged in the precursory work that has prepared him for sexual-offender-specific treatment.

12 STEPS IN THE TREATMENT OF JUVENILE SEXUAL OFFENDERS

Loosely based on the 12-step model of Alcoholics Anonymous, a 12-step model for the treatment of juvenile sexual offenders provides an overview of the tasks that juveniles must accomplish during treatment and of the sequence and pacing of these tasks. In practice, many of the steps occur at the same time, and individuals go back as well as forward. However, the 12-step model shown in Figure 12.1 provides an illustration of sequenced and paced treatment tasks. For instance, it is not possible to work on Step 9 (victim restitution) meaningfully without having accomplished the treatment work that builds the foundation for successfully (and hence, meaningfully) engaging in this later treatment task.

THREE PHASES OF TREATMENT

Continuing to develop a framework on which treatment is built and through which it can be assessed, the clinician must keep in mind specific treatment tasks throughout the process. In fact, there are a number of ways to conceptualize treatment, and in doing so it is useful to imagine a sequence of treatment needs, goals, and processes in and through which the tasks of treatment are accomplished.

In the simplest of models, treatment can be conceptualized in three phases: *pretreatment*, in which the treatment tasks involve learning about and understanding the case and preparing from treatment; *active treatment*, which is treatment proper and involves treatment planning and the application of treatment interventions and constant reassessment and evaluation of treatment over time; and *posttreatment*, or the termination of active treatment and transition to an aftercare model of continued supervision or other form of treatment. This three-phase model is depicted in Figure 12.2.

1. Overcoming denial. "We admitted that our lives had become unmanageable." *In this first step the individual is able to recognize and admit that he has a problem.*

2. Recognizing need for help. "We came to believe that a power/help greater than ourselves could restore us." *The individual recognizes that he cannot handle or overcome this problem on his own.*

3. Accepting help. "We made a decision to turn our will and lives over to the care of others who can help." *Having accepted that help is required, the individual is ready to accept help and work with, and not against, helpers.*

4. Becoming honest with oneself. "We made a searching, fearless, moral inventory of ourselves." *The individual is able to engage in honest, and often painful, self-appraisal.*

5. Becoming honest with others. "We admitted to ourselves and to another human being the exact nature of our wrongs." *The individual is able and willing to be honest and authentic with helpers.*

6. Willing to change. "We are entirely ready to have these defects of character removed." *The individual has reached a point where the need to change is apparent and has been internalized and is willing, if not able, to change.*

7. Ready to change. "We humbly asked for help in removing our shortcoming." *The individual is now willing and able to effect real change.*

8. Ready to explore the damage caused to others. "We made a list of all persons we had harmed, and we are willing to make amends to them all." *The individual begins honestly to appraise who has been damaged by his behavior and how.*

9. Willing to make restitution and seek forgiveness in the spirit of healing others and self. "We make direct amends to people harmed, wherever possible, except when to do so would injure them or others." *The individual is willing and able to make makes amends and pay restitution to others as part of the spiritual healing process.*

10. Able to accept personal flaws and fully accept responsibility. "We continue to take personal inventories and promptly admit to being wrong." *The individual demonstrates humility, recognizes and acknowledges personal flaws and poor behaviors, and accepts personal responsibility.*

11. Building a life based on meaningful relationships, awareness of others, and self-awareness. "We seek to improve spiritual and emotional connections through personal reflection." *The individual is aware of and considers his own actions and is tuned into himself and the impact of his behaviors on self and others.*

12. Living a spiritually changed life. "We practice these principles in all our affairs." *Individuals have changed in significant aspects of their lives.*

Figure 12.1
12 steps in the treatment of juvenile sexual offenders.

10-STAGE TREATMENT ROAD MAP

Treatment can be further conceptualized in more complex and active stages if only to help clinicians recognize the JSO treatment road map that lies ahead for them. As with all stage models, the tasks of any one stage overlap with the tasks of each contiguous stage, and there is no set length of time that any one individual will spend in each stage. The road map illustrates sequence and the connection between each stage, as well as the general focus at each leg of the treatment journey, rather than the length of time in any given treatment stage. However, unlike a pure sequential model, youths in treatment move back and forth through these stages, often necessarily regressing at times before moving ahead once again. In addition, the model is conceptual only, and in reality many of the treatment tasks occur *throughout* treatment and are not limited to any one stage or period of time.

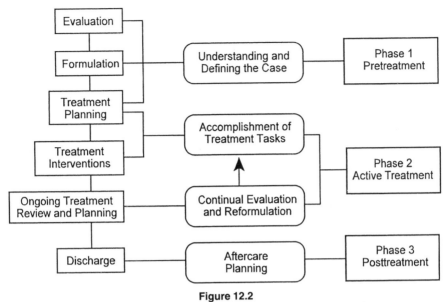

Figure 12.2
Simple three-phase model of treatment.

- *Stabilization and containment.* Some juveniles may not need the level and type of treatment encompassed by this stage, as the tasks of the stage are more often linked to younger children or emotionally troubled juveniles whose behavior is out of control, unpredictable, highly provocative, or in other ways difficult to manage behaviorally and connect with emotionally. These children and adolescents often exhibit behaviors that require great tolerance, patience, and nonreactivity on the part of providers, as well as sometimes physical containment or management with psychiatric medication. This stage may not be a significant or even noticeable feature for many juveniles in treatment, but for others it may last for 12 to 20 months. Further treatment goals cannot be meaningfully addressed or accomplished until clients are behaviorally and emotionally stable enough to proceed further. In sexual-offender-specific treatment, containment means ensuring that no sexual acting out occurs in order to pave the way for later sexual-offender-specific treatment. Sexual-offender-specific treatment is always focused on safety, but in many ways safety is the primary feature of this stage.
- *Engagement and attachment.* The tasks of this stage, built on the processes that occur during Stage 1, involve the youth's ability to form attachments with treatment staff and begin to engage in treatment that is more in-depth than simple stabilization and containment. If the tasks of Stage 1 are accomplished, the groundwork is fully laid for the accomplishment

of Stage 2 tasks, or the development of the therapeutic relationship and alliance.

- *Acceptance of responsibility.* The juvenile must move, at least in a rudimentary way, through denial and begin to acknowledge and accept responsibility for his sexually aggressive behaviors.
- *Learning new language and ideas.* Treatment focuses largely on psychoeducational and cognitive-behavioral ideas and language that will help juveniles recognize the way in which their thinking, attitudes, and beliefs affect and influence sexually aggressive and other antisocial and self-defeating behaviors (Chapters 13 and 16).
- *Developing awareness.* Through psychodynamic and experiential treatment, juveniles are helped to become more aware of themselves, their motivations and influences, the needs of others, and their impact on others.
- *Applying new ideas to behavior.* In this more advanced stage, juveniles must demonstrate their ability to retain what they have learned and demonstrate changes in their behaviors and interactions with others.
- *Commitment to change.* The final stages focus on preparation for discharge from treatment and require first a recognition that change is necessary and then a commitment to such change. If the tasks of earlier treatment stages have been accomplished, this is a natural step.
- *Development and application of a behavioral or relapse prevention plan.* The creation of the final and therefore most active relapse prevention plan (described in detail in Chapter 17) is the focus of this stage.
- *Discharge from active treatment.* This stage represents the end of active treatment, at least in the current treatment mode (i.e., another form of treatment may continue, but the role and function of the current treatment team are ending). Aftercare plans are developed, and in this stage it is critical that the juvenile is fully engaged in and committed to aftercare planning, as well as family members and outside agencies.
- *Maintaining a safe lifestyle.* In this posttreatment stage, the life of the treated juvenile takes its next form, including behavioral monitoring and supervision, ongoing therapy (individual, family, or group), and other forms of interventions to be applied in the posttreatment setting and designed to ensure a healthy and safe lifestyle.

It is important to recognize that treatment does not occur in a neat and clean manner, one step following the other. In practice, many of the treatment tasks not only overlap but occur simultaneously, each influencing the others. For this reason, it is wise to wrap these ten stages of treatment into the three phase treatment model previously described, as shown in Figure 12.3.

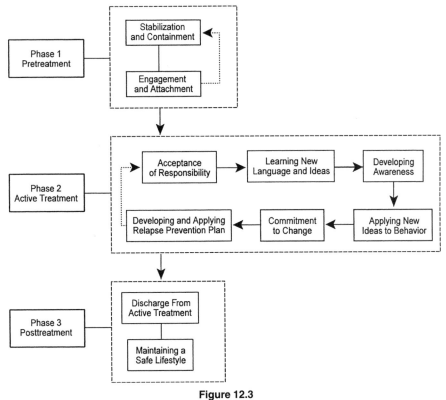

Figure 12.3
Stages of treatment incorporated into a three-phase treatment model.

SPECIFIC TREATMENT TASKS

In a sequential model of treatment, therapeutic tasks are completed in a particular order, and later treatment tasks are built on the completion of an earlier set of tasks. However, as Figure 12.3 shows, the stages (tasks) of active treatment are interdependent on and influence one another and in reality occur simultaneously. Rather than suggesting that one treatment task is truly dependent on another, it is more useful to describe the types of treatment tasks that must be accomplished during the active phase or stages of treatment without asserting that one precedes another. Tasks to be accomplished in sexual-offender-specific treatment include

1. Understanding sexual motivation and cause
2. Acquisition of psychoeducational and cognitive-behavioral concepts
3. Development of self-concept and personal identity
4. Disclosures of sexual offenses
5. Development of social skills
6. Provision of family therapy and resolution of family factors

7. Victim awareness and clarification
8. Relapse prevention planning
9. Diagnosis and resolution of comorbid conditions
10. Provision of psychopharmacology (where necessary)
11. Appropriate and adequate education

Understanding Sexual Motivation and Cause

During the course of treatment, clinicians must form an understanding of how each youth works psychologically and what motivates his interactions and behaviors, particularly those behaviors, causes, and motivations involved in the history of sexual offending. However, it is not enough simply to know the facts of what happened in any given sexual offense, even in great detail. The clinician must also understand the distant (distal) and immediate (proximal) causes of the offense and contributory elements such as personality factors, personal experiences of the youth, and factors in the youth's environment such as family relationships and friendships, sexual material available to the youth, and other passive or direct influences on the youth that contributed to his sexual offending behavior. Over time the clinician must explore and re-explore the actual offense and motivations for the offense; in this regard, the clinician's job is to go further and deeper in an attempt to understand what factors led to the sexual offense and may still be present. Without such an understanding, the clinician can neither make informed treatment choices nor assess the likelihood of future reoffending or the circumstances under which reoffenses may occur.

In fact, it is vital that clinicians recognize the seriousness and depth of the sexual issues and often already deeply ingrained patterns of sexual thought, attitudes, and behaviors experienced by their clients. It is equally important that clinicians not underestimate the treatment issues they are facing or the behaviors in which some juvenile offenders will continue to engage if given the opportunity. In light of the very harmful behaviors in which we know juveniles can engage, clinicians should be scrutinizing and thinking about client behavior at every opportunity and developing a growing awareness of the youth. Thus, over time, formulation should indicate the clinician's evolution in thinking about each client and his treatment.

Acquisition of Psychoeducational and Cognitive-Behavioral Concepts

Youths must learn the important cognitive-behavioral concepts that will help them recognize their thinking and behavioral patterns and learn how to regulate and manage their thinking and behaviors safely and appropriately. It is equally important for the clinician to assess whether a youth has actually learned, understood, and retained information about behavioral cycles, thinking errors, emotional regulation, choices and responses, relapse prevention planning, and other ideas involved in cognitive-behavioral therapy and can apply them in real life. Many youths are able to recite and describe ideas like behavioral cycles without any real understanding of how to apply them to their own life. However, if clinicians depend on the acquisition of such cognitive-behavioral skills alone, it is unlikely that the youth will actually do well in treatment over the long run. Most cognitive-behavioral techniques and methods have been developed for adults and may fail to bring about far-reaching changes in the still-developing psyche of the child or adolescent.

Development of Self-Concept and Personal Identity

An area strongly related to social skills is the development of positive self-image and sense of personal competence and social mastery. Like all youths, juvenile sexual offenders pass through the normative process of personal development on their way to adulthood. Many are struggling with self-concept and the development of personal identity even if they are not aware of this internal struggle. For youths with poor social skills, the development of a healthy self-image is even more strained and distant in that they achieve little sense of satisfaction, personal efficacy, or personal attractiveness from their peer relationships and interactions.

Disclosures of Sexual Offenses

Disclosure is the process by which the offender describes his sexual offenses and related behaviors to the clinician, group members, and family members, depending on the treatment model and mode. Disclosure is a complex treatment area without any correct answers or procedures. However, it is important that juvenile sexual offenders engage in this process and are able to do so openly and in accord with the expectations of the treatment model in use. The quality and the quantity of disclosure change over time, as do all elements of client participation in treatment, with the expectation that the youth is increasingly able and willing to engage in more detailed, complete, and honest disclosures of his sexually abusive behaviors. In fact, it is not unusual for juveniles in treatment to disclose additional details or victims many months into treatment, and even well into the second year. The disclosure process keeps the door open at all times, providing a constant channel for greater honesty and increased responsibility.

Disclosure is an important part of both assessment and ongoing treatment. Without disclosure, it is not possible for the juvenile to engage actively in treatment. Youths unable to engage in disclosure may be in a state of denial in which they either completely deny the offense or are in cognitive denial in which they minimize the significance of their offenses. Disclosure is also an important means to engage juveniles in group treatment, in which they expose their offenses to others and receive varying levels of support, challenge, confrontation, encouragement, and other forms of feedback. In family therapy, disclosure is often an important means for the juvenile and family members to recognize the enormity of the behavior and overcome any denial of the reality of the behavior. In fact, juvenile sexual offenders who do not openly or honestly engage in disclosure choose not to do so for many reasons that do not always imply guilt or criminal motivation. Nonetheless, they are never fully engaged in the treatment process unless they have undertaken a full disclosure, at least with their clinician. Disclosure holds the juvenile sexual offender accountable for his behavior. This helps keep the behavior alive in his mind daily, an important consideration in treatment and in the development and use of the relapse prevention plan and resignation from an abusive lifestyle.

The intention behind the disclosure process is not to shame the juvenile, although working with shame and guilt are important aspects of treatment for the juvenile sexual offender. The distinction between the two concepts of guilt and shame are described thoughtfully by Tagney and Doaring in their book (2002). The treatment of juvenile sexual offenders does not include shame-based treatments, humiliation (e.g., holding the juvenile out for criticism or ridicule), or angry and accusatory confrontations (with the exception of victim clarification work, described in chapter 18, in which case the victim may well bring in angry feelings which should be managed through the victim clarification process). Instead, the object of the disclosure process is different under different circumstances and at different points during treatment.

Disclosures occur in many different ways and venues, usually structured by the clinician. Disclosures also take several different forms, from introductory and minimally detailed disclosures to later, more detailed disclosures. However undertaken, first and foremost, the offender must be *able* and *willing* to disclose. Second, the clinician must ask,

- Why is it important for the offender to disclose?
- When in treatment is it important for the offender to disclose?
- Is it important to disclose in individual, group, or family therapy or in all three treatment modes?
- Is it important for the offender to do certain kinds of preparatory work prior to openly disclosing to others?
- What should the level of disclosure be, and in how much detail?
- How should the offender describe his offenses?
- Is it important to have the offender move from limited and vague disclosure to more detailed disclosure (progressive disclosure)?
- What is the "correct" way to introduce and build toward disclosure?

- What should the pacing be for disclosures, and at what speed and in what detail?
- How many times should the offender disclose, and when is the disclosure process over?

There are no correct answers to these questions, which must be left to the practitioner or treatment team to decide. However, as important as the offender's readiness and ability to disclose is the audience's ability to hear and respond to the disclosure, whether it be a group of peers, family members, victims, or the therapist. The audience's response is critical to disclosure as an effective and appropriate tool for treatment and growth. Pacing in the case of disclosure, then, means ensuring that the offender is ready and able to disclose *and* that the audience is ready and able to hear the disclosure.

DEVELOPMENT OF SOCIAL SKILLS

It is clear that many juvenile sexual offenders (though not all) do not have adequate or effective social skills and may have significant deficits in major social skills areas. Clinicians should not discount the potential impact of poor social skills in a history of sexual offending, especially when the offending behavior may have helped to bolster the youth's sense of personal competence, social mastery, and normalcy in a society that places increasing emphasis on sexual behavior as a measure of social effectiveness and desirability. Thus the development or enhancement of healthy social skills is an important, and perhaps critical, component in treatment and rehabilitation.

PROVISION OF FAMILY THERAPY AND RESOLUTION OF FAMILY FACTORS

In family assessment (often part of initial family therapy), the goal is to understand the family environment in which the child was raised and was living at the time of the sexual offense. Ongoing family therapy is aimed at understanding recent and current patterns of behavior, attitudes, relationships, communication, and roles within the family, and the goal of family therapy is to change the family environment in some way and improve family functioning. However, family therapy is not called for in all cases. Nevertheless, families should always be considered as a potential target for treatment, particularly when the youth will be returning to live with the family or will continue to be an active family member even if he is not returning home.

Formulation is as important in family therapy as in any other form of clinical treatment. Thus, if provided, clinicians must develop a clear sense of the purpose and targets of family therapy and be able to describe their goals to the family and others.

Victim Awareness and Clarification

When the victim is another family member, victim clarification (Chapter 18), or the process by which the offender understands the impact of his behaviors on his victims and others and begins to make amends to them, is an important goal of family therapy. Even though many youths engage in victim awareness projects, such as writing victim empathy letters and engaging in community service projects, it is not clear whether children accomplish true victim clarification. That is, youths must grasp not only the meaning of being a perpetrator of a sexual offense but also their victims' experience; and when the victim is a family member, they must also engage in victim clarification and restitution work. Although this is not always possible or desirable, it should be a goal for all clinicians in their family work.

Relapse Prevention Planning

Relapse prevention planning is a subset of cognitive-behavioral treatment that merits additional focus in any treatment framework. It is critical for juvenile sexual offenders to have a postdischarge aftercare plan that includes detailed steps for avoiding relapse, or sexual reoffense. This relapse prevention plan should be detailed, realistic, and capable of meeting the needs of youths both before and after discharge. Ideally, the plan should include the input and support of family members as well. Pacing also affects the relapse prevention planning process, in that to have meaning and be of real use the juvenile must see the need for it, have developed the prerequisite skills to understand the ideas on which it is built, and be committed to abstinence from sexually aggressive behavior. Relapse prevention plans can fail if such work has not been completed prior to the development of the final plan or if no real significance is attached to them.

For juveniles in community-based treatment, it is important to have at least a rudimentary relapse prevention plan in place throughout treatment as the youth is continuing to live and interact in the environment outside of treatment sessions. Although the plan cannot be meaningfully developed until treatment is in a more advanced stage, it is nevertheless important to have a relapse prevention plan in place at all times, recognizing that advanced and more meaningful relapse prevention skills can only develop over time.

Diagnosis and Resolution of Comorbid Conditions

The clinician must be focused on the existence of psychiatric factors in the youth's psychological makeup that may be influencing and affecting both behavior and treatment. These include problems in affective, thinking, behavioral, and personality functioning that rise to diagnostic proportions. For the clinician, this means maintaining a constant awareness of and assessing mental status reflected in the youth's emotional, cognitive, and behavioral functioning, as well as assessing relationships and daily functioning (the global assessment of functioning) and capturing this information in the *DSM-IV-TR* diagnosis. Trauma, disorders of attachment and empathy, unrestrained impulsivity, compulsivity, rage, and conditions along the autistic spectrum (such as Asperger's syndrome) are examples of comorbid conditions that may remain less obvious and in the background but must be recognized by the clinician if treatment has any chance of real success.

PROVISION OF PSYCHOPHARMACOLOGY

Clinicians should ensure that they are aware of and understand the psychiatric medications that are prescribed to address psychiatric symptoms and that they are capable of evaluating the effectiveness of such medications as evidenced in changes in the presentation of youths taking medications.

APPROPRIATE AND ADEQUATE EDUCATION

The juvenile's education is critical and central to effective treatment. If a child has educational deficits and learning disabilities, he may not be able to engage actively, understand, respond adequately to, or make use of treatment interventions, especially those that are cognitive in nature or assume a common way of learning. For instance, a child with a receptive and expressive language disability, problems with central auditory processing, or nonverbal language deficits may have great difficulty grasping certain treatment concepts. These learning problems often have nothing to do with IQ and represent more complex neurological and learning problems in which conventional educational techniques are ineffective. This is especially pertinent in cognitive-behavioral treatment, as it is largely a psychoeducational method. The same is true for juveniles with borderline or retarded intellectual functioning, where intellectual capacity *is* a clear factor in the ability to understand and use new ideas.

The inability to grasp treatment concepts or apply them frustrates both the youth and the clinician, who may wrongly conclude the client is unmotivated or "just doesn't get it." For the child, it becomes one more example of the inability to learn and understand material, and perhaps further contributes to a lifetime experience of failure, reinforces his feelings that he is stupid and inadequate, and makes him disinterested in and apathetic about treatment. In fact, it may even contribute to conduct disordered and antisocial behavior.

Furthermore, educational difficulties are a two-way street in treatment. In the first place, untreated educational difficulties fail to help treatment work and work to help treatment fail, perhaps reinforcing and strengthening emotional, cognitive, and behavioral difficulties. In the second place, an effective education is a protective factor, strengthening skills, raising self-esteem, and demonstrating the capacity to succeed. Consequently, even where treatment is effective, the failure to receive an adequate education outside of the treatment environment may ensure that treatment gains do not stick in the real world and are soon lost.

Educational and learning difficulties may be undiagnosed, and it may well be the clinician or the treatment team that eventually recognizes the problem. For these clients, concepts may have to be taught in a different way, and referrals should be made to the school component for further educational testing and the development of special education services. Equally true, the clinician may have to change his or her approach to all treatment with the youth, gearing treatment interventions to the needs of the client to ensure success rather than contributing to failure. This will have a significant impact on the therapeutic alliance, serving to weaken it where difficulties go unrecognized and strengthening it where the child is recognized, understood, and helped.

MONITORING AND ASSESSING TREATMENT PROGRESS

Clinicians must avoid providing the same version of treatment for every juvenile. Some youths do well with talk therapy, others with more reality-based therapy, and others may require more cognitive or behavioral approaches, or even more aversive treatment. This also means that clinicians must ensure that they have the range of knowledge and skills necessary to provide individualized and diverse treatment.

Under any circumstances, it is important that clinicians routinely remind themselves of the critical nature of their work and not fall into rote patterns of behavior where they take for granted the processes they use to provide treatment or the juvenile's engagement in treatment. On the contrary, clinicians must be vigilant about the effectiveness of treatment and constantly consider the type of treatment being provided on a case-by-case basis. Moreover, they must constantly assess the direction, impact, and effectiveness of treatment on their clients.

Targets for Sexual-Offender-Specific Treatment

Sexual offense treatment focuses on treating sexually oriented behaviors and attitudes, as well as the juvenile's engagement in treatment interventions that specifically address these targets. Figure 12.4 shows a checklist that allows clinicians to review participation and progress in treatment areas directly related to sex offender specific treatment. In addition to identifying treatment targets and expectations, the tool also helps clinicians to stay on track in their treatment of sexual behaviors.

Sexual-Offender-Specific Treatment Checklist

Treatment Goal
- Willingness/ability to disclose sexual offenses to clinician
- Willingness/ability to disclose sexual offenses in group
- Willingness/ability to disclose sexual offenses to family
- Willingness/ability to provide detailed disclosures
- Willingness/ability to discuss sexual issues and behaviors
- Willingness/ability to discuss sexual interests and fantasies
- Completion of timeline
- Sufficient detail in timeline
- Ability to understand motivation to offend
- Willingness/ability to recognize thinking errors
- Willingness/ability to correct thinking errors
- Willingness/ability to recognize offense cycle
- Willingness/ability to interrupt offense cycle
- Willingness/ability to recognize triggers
- Willingness/ability to use appropriate coping skills
- Development of relapse prevention plan
- Use of relapse plan
- Concern for victim
- Participation in victim clarification

Observed Behaviors
- Sexual fantasies
- Sexual arousal
- Peer interactions
- Staff interactions
- Physical contact with others

Level of Disclosure
- Adequacy or depth in detail of sexual offense disclosures
- Sexual offense disclosures match known/alleged offenses
- Self-initiating in sexual offense disclosures
- Consistency over time in disclosures of sexual offenses

Figure 12.4
Targets for treatment in sexual offender-specific work.

THE TREATMENT PLAN AND TREATMENT GOALS

Virtually every treatment program requires a treatment plan, and many regulatory agencies that monitor such programs also require treatment plans or the equivalent. Treatment plans are critical maps that shape, review, and plan treatment and are indispensable when treatment is provided or reviewed by a multidisciplinary treatment team. Aside from a review of the youth's participation and progress in treatment over time, the treatment plan is built on the development of treatment goals. The plan should identify short- and long-term targets for treatment and establish meaningful and achievable goals for the youth. These goals should be the focus of treatment during the period the

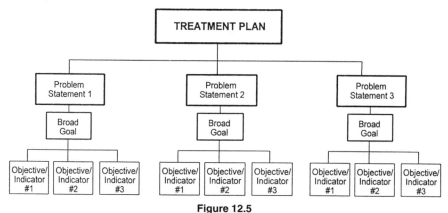

Figure 12.5
Levels of the treatment plan.

treatment plan is in effect and should accurately and meaningfully identify the major areas in need of treatment during any particular period.

Treatment goals define the orientation and direction of treatment, as well as all behavioral and clinical interventions. To be effective, however, treatment goals must have practical meaning for both the youth and the staff working with him and are based on problems central to treatment. Consequently, during any given treatment period, goals should be focused on key issues, with fewer goals in place rather than many. Of special importance, treatment goals must make sense to the youth, and he must be capable of accomplishing them. If both conditions are not met the youth and clinician will fail in treatment.

Typically, treatment goals are built on an identified problem, followed by a broad goal toward which treatment will be directed. Each treatment goal should be based on a particular presenting problem, as illustrated in Figure 12.5. The goal is operationalized through a series of measurable objectives, or indicators, which typically also define actual treatment interventions (or actions that will be taken to meet the objective). Whereas broad treatment goals define the generally sought outcome, objectives and indicators specify how goal achievement will be recognized and measured. Goals evolve and develop over time in treatment, with new goals replacing those that are accomplished or existing goals modified to accommodate continued treatment efforts to resolve an ongoing problem.

Interpreting Behavior

The behavior of youths is meaningful and will tell clinicians a lot if they observe, evaluate, and interpret those behaviors carefully. If clinicians fail constantly to watch behaviors and assess their meaning, they will miss a great deal of information about what is going on for a youth, as well as the effectiveness of treatment and the risk for problem behaviors.

Assessing Skill Acquisition

Clinicians must assess whether youths are adequately learning the concepts being taught and are able to apply these to their daily lives, as well as adequately plan for their future through the development of relapse prevention plans. Clinicians should be seeking evidence of treatment success in this area, as well as treatment *in*effectiveness, and switching treatment approach, focus, or methods if necessary. If successful, youths should be able to recognize and identify triggers, stressors, and high-risk situations, as well as the development of problem areas through their decisions, daily interactions, and thoughts and feelings.

Assessing Risk

The behavior of youths is largely a projection of their thoughts and feelings and thus allows clinicians to see what is going on inside of each youth. It is critical that clinicians look for and correctly interpret behaviors that indicate a disturbed psyche, and behavioral patterns at any given time may signal pending aggression, sexual assault, or self-harming behaviors. In this case, observing behaviors also means assessing risk at any given time. In addition, as described in earlier chapters, it is highly recommended that clinicians use a defined instrument specifically designed to assess risk so that reassessment is based on a consistent model and structure, rather than on clinical judgment alone.

Tools for Reviewing and Monitoring Treatment Effectiveness

In residential treatment and community-based (outpatient) multidisciplinary treatment, there will be routine planned communication and established meetings among team members designed to discuss cases. This treatment team is one of the most powerful of all tools in the residential setting, which is usually built on the idea of *milieu therapy* or the residential milieu but is also an extremely effective tool in the outpatient setting. The treatment team provides a significant means for the clinician to explore and review cases, get advice and direction, and receive feedback regarding the effectiveness of treatment.

In addition, clinicians in agencies are usually required to prepare interim treatment summaries and may use formatted reports and structured assessment tools to document, measure, and review treatment progress. If these tools are not seen for what they are—means to review, plan, assess the effectiveness of treatment, and make treatment corrections and changes—they will become rote and stale instruments that simply record information rather than inform and direct treatment. Clinicians must use each tool as a means for reviewing, assessing, discussing, and planning treatment. If clinicians do not have such meetings or tools at their disposal, they must develop or locate them, or their work will be based largely on clinical judgment alone, without benefit of guidance, structure, and multidisciplinary communication and input.

OUTCOMES

Outcome is the bottom line in treatment. The outcomes of treatment are those factors that determine whether treatment was successful. However, outcome is difficult to measure, partly based on the difficulty of obtaining recidivism data and difficulty developing rigorous research studies that can gather meaningful data. However, besides the scientifically driven method there are other forms of outcome that can be studied. For instance, it is possible to gather outcomes not about long-term abstinence from sexual aggression, but about changes in behavior, affect, attitudes, social skills, and relationships that can be seen and experienced during the treatment process. In a simple model, an outcome study may seek evidence of change from the beginning of treatment to its conclusion based on the accomplishment of quantifiable treatment goals, assessed clinically by therapists and other treatment staff, or evaluated by the subjective judgment of family members. Evidence of change may also be sought post-discharge based on the reports of after care providers or other professionals in the life of the juvenile. In the event of a formalized outcome study that seeks to monitor change in predefined areas, evidence of change can be made through comparisons to earlier psychological or physiological testing that serves as a baseline against which to measure evidence of later change.

Given the current inability to gather true empirical data with respect to recidivism and significant problems with classic research designs, alternative outcome measures may be necessary. It is important for treatment providers to develop some form of outcome measurement—if not for the sake of establishing that treatment reduces recidivism (which is the ultimate goal), then for the purpose of measuring the practitioner's own ability to define and meet treatment goals.

ROLE OF PSYCHOLOGICAL AND PHYSIOLOGICAL TESTING

Although neither psychological or physiological testing can be used to establish whether a juvenile sexual offender will offend again or to form a profile of the average juvenile sexual offender, it can nonetheless be used effectively in assessment and treatment. Psychological evaluation can establish a means for gathering and developing important psychological data and help us learn about the psychological makeup of an individual compared to a larger population. In addition, as noted, testing can also provide a psychometric and non-clinical (objective) baseline against which to measure later change. Not only can this provide reasonable information about any given individual, but an adequate research design can also help establish whether such changes in a large group of treated offenders can be attributed to the effects of the treatment. Psychological testing, then, can serve multiple purposes in any program of treatment.

Although the application of physiological measurements with juveniles remains open to question and is not in wide use, it is gaining acceptance. Many support the role of physiological testing in adolescents as useful and important, both to learn more about the individual and to establish baseline data against which to make later measurements. These tests include the penile plethysmograph (PPG), which is rarely used in work with juveniles but is nevertheless receiving greater attention and support for use with older adolescents. The polygraph examination, or the psychophysiological detection of deception (PDD), also in more widespread use with adolescents, is a useful way to test for honesty and deception and often increases the youth's willingness to be more honest, even on hearing that a "lie detector" will be introduced into treatment. Finally, visual reaction-time testing, typically the Abel Assessment for Sexual Interest (AASI), is an additional physiological test that is used to measure sexual interest and involves viewing time, or the amount of time (computerized measurements made in milliseconds) that examinees spend viewing photographed material that may be of sexual interest. Although the AASI can be used with children down to age 12, it has received widely mixed reviews.

THE TREATMENT RELATIONSHIP

The first task in the treatment of children and adolescents who are sexually aggressive is to build the therapeutic alliance. In any therapeutically interactive treatment, this relationship *is* the treatment or, at least, one of the factors common to all effective treatment (Chapter 14). Treatment ideas, techniques, and interventions are used to build and support the relationship, which in turn is used to address treatment issues and goals identified along the way. The treatment relationship is not a chronological event that occurs as the first step in a sequence but is an evolving and living relationship that is the medium for treatment, an integral part of the treatment itself, and the framework in which treatment techniques are applied. The treatment relationship is continually renewed and redefined throughout treatment, extinguished only at the moment that treatment ends.

In fact, many of the tasks of therapy can be accomplished only through the development of a meaningful relationship between the clinician and the youth. An enriching therapeutic relationship can foster a climate that will allow youths to explore difficult areas in their lives and express themselves more fully and more openly. Such relationships can only be built over time and are a key to the pacing of treatment and what can be accomplished during any given period in the therapeutic relationship. The role of the clinician is to establish a climate that allows for youth change and prepares the youth to feel emotionally uncomfortable while changing. In this respect, the role is not to help the youth feel comfortable, but to help the youth feel *un*comfortable, yet supported, while working on difficult and critical issues.

Norcross (2000) and Blanchard (1998) described the therapist as a central agent of change, and Bachelor and Horvath (1999) wrote that the important therapeutic relationship is formed early in therapy and is established through the climate of trust and safety fostered by the clinician through responsiveness, listening, and the communication of understanding, regard, and respect. Here, contrary to ideas that juveniles are bullied, coerced, or confronted into getting better, the therapeutic alliance is the environment in which the juvenile is able and willing to enter and engage in treatment. Dryden's (1989) description of the therapeutic alliance includes the relational bonds that develop between the clinician and client, of special importance in working with attachment disordered kids. This includes (a) the emotional and stylistic fit between the clinician and the youth, (b) the attitudes of the therapist and the impact of those attitudes on the client, and (c) the client's feelings and attitudes toward the therapist, including the youth's sense of trust, feelings of safety in the relationship, and the degree of faith in the therapist as a change agent. It also includes issues of transference and countertransference, which point to the fact that both the client and therapist bring to the counseling relationship tendencies to perceive, feel, and act toward others in ways that are influenced by their prior interactions with significant others.

Margison (2002) wrote that the balance between *responsiveness* and *detachment* is central to the therapeutic alliance. In such an engaged and supportive relationship, and with such difficult clients, it is important for clinicians to recognize and adhere to clear boundaries. Day and Sparacio (1989) described the structure of the relationship itself as central to the development, awareness, and limits of such boundaries.

CONCLUSION

Outlined in Figure 12.6, the treatment framework against which the therapeutic relationship works is intended to help clinicians gain a broad overview of the tasks of treatment that must take place both over time *and* simultaneously. In the combined forensic and mental health environment of sexual-offender-specific treatment, it is especially important for clinicians to have a clear sense of what they are trying to treat and why and of the importance of treating each area if they are to stand a good chance of treating the right tar-

General Framework for Treatment
- Defined Purpose/Broad Goal
- Defined Specific Goals
- Defined Objectives

Available Treatment Components
- Sexual Offender Specific
- Clinical Collateral Treatment
- Psychiatry
- Sexual Offender Relevant
- General Treatment
- Education

Attention to Treatment Tasks
- Psychoeducation/Cognitive-Behavioral
- Understanding Sexual Motivation/Cause
- Victim Awareness and Clarification
- Social Skills Development
- Comorbid Conditions and Diagnosis
- Education
- Relapse Prevention Planning
- Family Factors and Family Therapy
- Disclosures of Sexual Offenses
- Self-concept and Personal Identity
- Psychopharmacology (Psychiatric Medication)

Monitoring and Assessing Treatment Progress
- The Treatment Plan
- Range of Treatment
- Assessing Skill Acquisition
- Treatment Goals
- Interpreting Behavior
- Reassessing Risk

Tools for Reviewing and Monitoring Treatment Effectiveness
- Treatment/Multidisciplinary Team
- Reassessment Tools
- Consistent Documentation
- Other Means for Review

Outcomes
- Outcome Measures

Figure 12.6
Overview of treatment framework.

gets and bringing about change. In the relatively long-term environment in which the treatment of juvenile sexual offenders often takes place, it is also important to understand the nature of treatment over time and the capacity to build later treatment on earlier treatment, constantly revisiting and assessing targets for and the impact of treatment.

CHAPTER 13

Principles and Practices:
Psychodynamic, Cognitive,
and Behavioral Treatment

ALTHOUGH THE two primary modes of psychosocial treatment are cognitive-behavioral and psychodynamic, the two terms lack specificity because variants exist in either case. Instead, the names serve as generic labels that describe the ideas and methods typically attached to each therapeutic model. Consequently, both labels represent *genotypes* of therapeutic form, rather than specific name-brand schools of therapy or the well-defined ideas and clearly prescribed treatment techniques with which those schools are often associated.

In actuality, treatment models do not automatically come with a packaged set of techniques. Although this may be true of a highly defined model, such as those attached to specific schools of psychotherapy or those outlined in single-therapy treatment manuals, for the most part therapeutic models are not bound by technique. Ogles, Anderson, and Lunnen (1999) specified that *models* and *techniques* are not the same and defined a treatment model as a collection of beliefs or theories about change that sometimes includes techniques that serve to operationalize the theory. However, they emphasized that models can rest at the theoretical stage and "need not necessarily include technique" (p. 218), thus allowing generic models to provide guiding theory without attaching specific rules or methods to enact the theory. They argued that although models are essential to the advancement of psychotherapy, technique is not. Accordingly, the genotypic therapies are empty frameworks built around defined ideas, requiring the therapist to fill in the details or apply technique.

In practice, few models in either genotype are pure, and many clinicians who practice one form of treatment integrate the ideas and methods of the other genotype into their approach. In addition, several important factors are common to both treatment models, which makes it difficult to know whether the common factors or the specifics of the model are actually helpful in treatment. Finally, many therapists adopt an eclectic approach, and although often aligning themselves with one genotype or the other, they freely use whichever techniques seem most helpful for any given case.

THE TREATMENT BACKDROP

Despite the widely practiced eclectic model, cognitive-behavioral therapy receives the most support as the treatment of choice for sexual offenders, and psychodynamic treatment is considered less effective or not effective at all. Not all clinicians share this opinion, however. Many have written about expanding sexual-offender-specific treatment to include a diversity of treatment approaches and methods, and many programs provide a broader array of options than simply the cognitive-behavioral version (Longo, 2002; Rasmussen, 2002; Sirles, Araji, & Bosek, 1997).

Nevertheless, many of the leading and most authoritative figures in the field concur with the Association for the Treatment of Sexual Abusers (1997), which stated that cognitive-behavioral approaches appear to be the most effective treatment method. ATSA's *Practice Standards and Guidelines* (2001) stated that "abstract treatment programs are much less likely to be effective in reducing rates of offending, and some may even increase the risk of reoffending" (p. 18). They stressed that cognitive-behavioral treatment is "more likely to be effective than treatments that are unstructured, insight-oriented, and abstract" (p. 23). Many others also assert the superiority of cognitive-behavioral treatment or report that it is the most commonly used and accepted treatment practice (Grossman, Martis, & Fichtner, 1999; Hollin, 2001; Lundrigan, 2001; McIvor, 2001; Perkins, Hammond, Coles, & Bishop, 1998; Sirles, Araji, & Bosek, 1997), and Cooke and Philip (2001) not only reported that the treatment of choice is cognitive-behavioral but unequivocally stated that psychodynamic models have no impact on reducing recidivism.

This interest in the cognitive-behavioral model is in part due to a desire to get to sexually aggressive behavior as quickly and as directly as possible and treat the thoughts and attitudes that are believed to drive the behavior. Cognitive-behavioral therapy seems an obvious match for this goal.

Unproven Assumptions

Despite such strong and widely accepted assertions, no significant evidence exists proving that cognitive-behavioral therapy is effective in treating sexual offenders or that it is any more effective than any other type of treatment. In fact, assertions that any one form of treatment is better than any other not only are unproven but also appear to be inaccurate, and a number of studies have shown the equivalency of treatment regardless of treatment model or orientation (Hellerstein et al., 1998; Hubble, Duncan, & Miller, 1999; Keijsers, Schaap, & Hoogduin, 2000; Wampold et al., 1997).

Besides a lack of evidence supporting one therapy over any other, there is at best weak evidence that shows cognitive-behavioral therapy to be effective. Laws, Hudson, and Ward (2000), for instance, made it very clear that no substantial or definitive evidence exists to demonstrate the effectiveness of cognitive-behavioral relapse prevention models. However, they pointed out that the field has nonetheless adopted such models as if they *were* proven, treating their ideas as received wisdom. In fact, they asserted that the uncritical and indiscriminate acceptance of the unproven model has "been its undoing" (p. 5). Similarly, Marshall, Anderson, and Fernandez (1999), strong advocates for cognitive-behavioral treatment, acknowledged that evidence proving the efficacy of cognitive-behavioral therapy is weak. In 1989 Furby, Weinrott, and Blackshaw concluded that no evidence exists to support the idea that treatment for sexual offenders is effective, and Quinsey, Harris, Rice, and Cormier (1998) reported similar conclusions. In fact, several studies have shown that when used as the sole means of treatment, the underlying techniques of cognitive-behavioral therapy are not only ineffective but may be correlated to *negative* treatment outcomes (Ablon & Jones, 1998; Castonguay, Goldfried, Wiser, Raue, & Hayes, 1996; Kerr, Goldfried, Hayes, Castonguay, & Goldsamt, 1992).

The issue is not that treatment models are not proved and therefore should not be used. On the contrary, we should use and continue to research and develop further all the tools we have. Rather, adopting such models based on unproven assumptions and unwarranted claims of efficacy is the problem. In contrast to a best practice model, this not only perpetuates faulty data and ideas but also risks killing innovation and deadening criticism. Despite little evidence that any therapy is ineffective or any more effective than any other therapy, the resounding support that the cognitive-behavioral model receives at the highest and most respected levels in the treatment community makes it difficult to adopt a different perspective or even integrate different ideas.

Consequently, clinicians who practice psychodynamic therapies with sexual offenders, especially if they exclusively practice this form of therapy, are considered to be providing the wrong kind of treatment, focusing on the wrong things, and failing to address the cognitive change and behavioral skill development needed by juvenile sexual offenders. To some degree this may be true, because any unimodal or single-therapy treatment may fail to meet the complex needs of juveniles in treatment.

THE TREATMENT MODELS

Bearing in mind that most treatment actually consists of an eclectic blend, any discussion of treatment models is largely academic. It is rare that any single form of treatment is practiced exclusively, including cognitive-behavioral therapy despite its wide acceptance in the field. Also bear in mind that many common factors seem to underlie all forms of effective treatment, such as the qualities introduced into therapy by the client and the nature of the therapeutic relationship that develops between the client and therapist. More than any particular treatment ideology or set of techniques, it may be these common factors (discussed in Chapter 14) that make treatment effective and account for why psychotherapy is effective regardless of the treatment model used.

Psychodynamic Therapy

Psychodynamic treatment uses verbal therapy to discover, bring to the surface, and express hidden issues, thereby bringing insight to the client and discharging unconscious dynamic forces of their ability to influence and shape the client's moods, ideas, relationships, and behavior. Generically speaking, such therapies focus on an understanding of hidden or unconscious motivators and experiences that shape and drive emotion, cognition, relationships, and behaviors. Problems are resolved and personal growth fostered through the recognition and external expression of these formerly hidden dynamics, thus relieving them of their power. In addition, psychodynamic therapies are almost always associated with the supportive alliance between therapist and client, although this is considered by many to be an essential ingredient in cognitive therapies as well.

There are many schools of psychodynamic treatment, and these are associated with very specific constructs (almost all of which are abstract and empirically unprovable) and well-defined treatment methods, including psychoanalysis, analytical psychology, Gestalt therapy, self psychology, ego psychology, client-centered therapy, existential therapy, and object relations therapy. Although all are based to some degree on classic notions of the unconscious and the structure and development of the psyche, these therapies take many widely divergent paths in beliefs and, where defined, in technique. Some are more verbal than others, some are more action oriented, and some are more therapist directed. What they have in common is the belief that human emotion, cognition, sociality, and behavior are the result of a complex interplay of physical and social development from infancy to adulthood; the internal structure of the mind can be compartmentalized into different structures that serve different functions; and instinctive and socially learned drives motivate and influence the individual in every area. Much of this interactional process occurs on an unconscious level, hidden from the individual, who nevertheless experiences or acts out its influence. In the pathological condition, these interactional processes are filled with conflict of one kind of another, either between the mind and the environment (extrapsychic) or between the internal structural components of the mind (intrapsychic), leading to disturbances in mood, cognition, relationships, or behavior.

Bateman (2002) noted that contemporary psychodynamic therapy is based on an interactive therapist-client relationship. Utilizing the therapeutic relationship, psychodynamic treatment is thus aimed at developing client insight, thereby leading to cognitive and behavioral change. In the treatment of juvenile sexual offenders, it is one means by which we can clinically understand and influence the psychological, behavioral, and interactional functioning of the juvenile. It is not associated with any particular school of thought or set of techniques, and it is not a pure model free of the influences, ideas, and methods of cognitive therapy. In addition, embedded into psychodynamic therapy are therapeutic factors common to both psychodynamic and cognitive-behavioral therapy. Here, the term *psychodynamic* describes a set of principles and associated techniques that allows us to understand and work with cognition and emotion and, through them, with behavior. As such, psychodynamic treatment need not be an esoteric or mysterious art form, even though its ideas are often abstract and involve constructs and conditions that cannot actually be seen to exist. In fact, psychodynamic therapies range widely in approach and style and are defined by the degree to which each of several distinct attributes are applied in practice.

Attributes Common to Psychodynamic Therapy

Two primary sets of attributes are common to all psychodynamic therapy. One is connected directly to the therapeutic process itself, or the focus of the therapy, whereas the other pertains to the therapist's style and approach. The specific application of the generic psychodynamic model results from the interaction between these two sets of attributes. The application of each attribute can be measured along a scale ranging from high to low, as shown in Figure 13.1. Therapeutic process measures the level of abstractness and focus on the unconscious employed by the therapist, ranging from psychoanalytical (high abstraction) to pragmatic (low). Interactivity measures the style and nature of the clinician-client interaction, with a highly interactive relationship at one end and a more distant connection at the other.

Together, process and therapist attributes combine to define the approach and emphasis of the psychodynamic therapy that is provided, as illustrated in Figure 13.2. Although many permutations may exist, to a greater or lesser degree psychodynamic therapy is always focused on exploring hidden and interactional dynamics and is characterized by the importance of the therapist-client relationship.

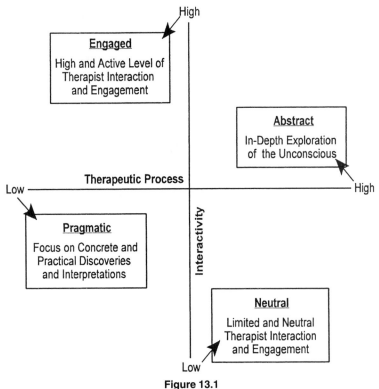

Figure 13.1
Measurement of psychodynamic attributes.

Attributes of the Therapeutic Process

1. *Exploratory.* At the high end of the scale the focus is on the unconscious and its impact on thoughts, feelings, behaviors, and relationships. At the low end the focus is more on exploring and discovering common elements and relationships in cognitions, emotions, and behaviors.

2. *Dynamic.* Treatment focuses on the interactions between the parts. The high end of the scale reflects the interplay between processes and structures that make up the mind (or psyche) itself, or *intrapsychic* dynamics. In more pragmatic therapies at the low end, the focus is on the dynamic interaction between the client and people in his or her environment, or *extrapsychic* or social-interactional processes.

3. *Expressive.* The high end emphasizes catharsis or abreaction (purging or release of emotions and the discharge of unconscious material). The low end focuses on the discussion of feelings and experiences.

4. *Connective.* The focus at the high end is to connect all cognitions, emotions, behaviors, and relationships to unconscious processes, whereas the focus at the low end is to recognize connections between experiences, ideas, feelings, and behaviors.

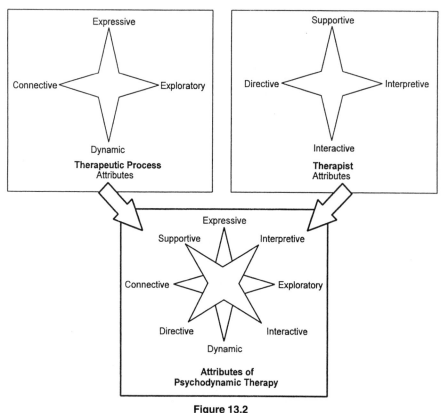

Figure 13.2
Process and clinician attributes common to psychodynamic therapy, combined in a generic model of psychodynamic practice.

Attributes of the Clinician

1. *Supportive.* At the high end the therapist is demonstrably and actively supportive. At the low end the clinician expresses a more general and underlying level of support.
2. *Interactive.* The clinician engages actively and mutually with the client at the high end and is more reserved, removed, and only mildly interactive at the low end.
3. *Directive.* At the high end the therapist provides a great deal of direction or advice or both. At the low end the therapist is generally nondirective and avoids giving advice.
4. *Interpretive.* Therapists at the high end actively clarify, attribute meaning, and interpret psychological and behavioral material. At the low end therapists offer little interpretation of meaning or clarification.

The Psychodynamic Model at Work With Juvenile Sexual Offenders: Interpersonal Functional Therapy

In treating juvenile sexual offenders, deeply psychodynamic therapy is of little practical use. If the goals are self-awareness and insight and resulting cognitive and behavioral change, more pragmatic versions of psychodynamic therapy are called for. Such therapy is focused less on deeply unconscious mental processes and conflicts and more on understanding the roots and effects of everyday interactions and is aimed at producing useful information and results. This more pragmatic therapy is better suited to the capacity of the child and adolescent to engage in therapy *and* find it useful and is geared more toward the discovery of information and ideas that are of immediate use to the client. With the juvenile sexual offender, pragmatic therapies are likely to place great emphasis on the counseling relationship and on the therapist's role as a guide and less emphasis on unconscious ideas that may or may not lie beneath behavior.

Psychodynamic therapy with juvenile sexual offenders will be high in therapeutic attributes (interaction, support, direction, and interpretation) and low on process attributes (exploratory, dynamic, expressive, and connective). The application of psychodynamic therapy with these individuals will be interpersonal, concentrating on building the therapeutic alliance, developing shared goals, and helping the client to recognize how he is affected by his experiences and interactions and how these shape his cognitions, emotions, and behaviors. From there, the clinician can help the juvenile sexual offender recognize and more fully experience his impact on others, the nature of his relationships, and his personal goals and how to accomplish them. This is a tall order, of course, but it is no less achievable with psychodynamic therapy than with any other therapy.

Providing a moderate to low emphasis on the process attributes, which are central to psychodynamic treatment, does not mean that they are neglected. Rather, the focus is on the lower, more concrete end of the scale closer to conscious awareness and immediate recognition where insight and self-awareness have more meaning and more practical value. This emphasis on high relationship and practical application of psychodynamic ideas lends itself to an interpersonal, or client-centered, functional form of psychodynamic therapy, shown in Figure 13.3, with an emphasis on self-awareness and personal development.

This form of psychodynamic therapy attacks targets not so different than those of cognitive-behavioral therapies. That is, although aiming at the discovery of hidden processes, the most pragmatic forms of psychodynamic therapy aim at ideas and attitudes (cognitions) and transactions and interactions (behaviors) that are not deeply buried, are close to consciousness, and are relatively easy to access, sometimes simply through the process of pointing them out or otherwise helping the juvenile see them for himself. In this regard, effective psychodynamic treatment may be tapping into the very same factors common to both forms of treatment.

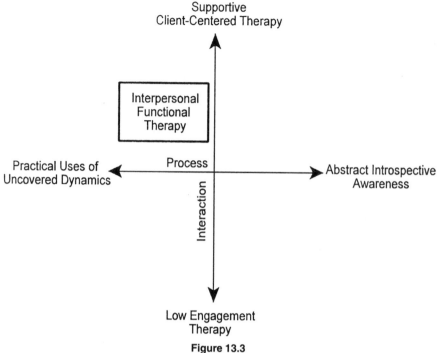

Figure 13.3
Interpersonal functional psychodynamic therapy for juveniles.

Psychodynamic Concepts as Explanatory Structures

Although psychodynamic theory can be overwhelming, it is nonetheless capable of helping to conceptualize and understand the psychology of individual personality and its disorders (Bateman, 2000). Psychodynamic ideas about the structure and the development of the mind, although theoretical, are also of great use in understanding the juvenile sexual offender; in fact, these ideas are often built into mainstream thinking about the development of juvenile sexual offending.

Although a completely abstract idea, incapable of being proved empirically, the idea that the mind is compartmentalized into separate structures or functions (e.g., the id, ego, and superego) is a useful way to recognize that there are primitive psychic elements beneath the conscious mind that later develop (both biologically and psychologically). It also helps us to recognize that there are instinctual and subliminal drives at work that are deeply buried in the structure of the mind. Psychic structure is a useful way for us to understand the psychology and developmental roots of dominant ideas and behaviors, especially in seriously troubled children. The younger or more troubled the kid, or both, the more likely it is that these more primitive structures will have power and control over later mental structures that have failed to develop well. These children often seem motivated by pre- or nonverbal forces that are neither rationally driven nor susceptible to cognitive interventions. When we see these children in their most emotionally and behaviorally volatile states, we are seeing a rampant display of primitive drives and ideas at work. Having a psychodynamic developmental language helps us both to understand the behavior and devise the most effective strategies to work with these kids.

Indeed, these ideas are central to much mainstream thought about the development and, hence, the treatment of sexual offenders. As we learned in earlier chapters, ideas like this are deeply incorporated into etiological and developmental models of juvenile sexual offending despite the focus of cognitive treatments. Most traumagenic models are built on the idea of disrupted psychic and neurological development as a result of emotional and mental (psychic) damage to the developing child, and attachment theory is built almost entirely on the highly psychodynamic concepts of object relations theory, an offshoot of psychoanalysis. Disrupted attachment, impaired interpersonal bonding, and lack of empathic development are central to ideas about sexual offending and are built on the psychodynamic principle that the developing mind integrates representations of the external world into its own structure. Moreover, psychodynamic ideas are central to understanding unconscious or preconscious underlying drives, the development of libido and normative sexual development and activity, the impact of the physical world on mental processes and the mind, personality development, and the developmental stages and tasks of emotion and personality formation.

Treatment Modalities

The principles and practices of psychodynamic therapy are not limited to individual therapy. Just as the psychodynamic or cognitive models serve as the underlying model for most individual treatment, so too do they apply to other therapeutic modalities. Either form of treatment is equally applicable to group therapy and family therapy, although psychodynamic theory is more easily applied to expressive treatments such as art and play therapy.

In group settings psychodynamic therapy operates on the basis that hidden, or unconscious, forces are at work among group members. These groups, often known as process groups, focus on the underlying and often invisible dynamics in group process, learning and the development of insight through the experience of being in the group, and the process of interaction, idea exchange, communication, and role modeling within the actual group.

In family therapy a psychodynamic process follows a similar idea, looking for the dynamic among family members that influences or is responsible for the structure, communication, and roles of the family. A psychodynamic approach to family therapy posits that dynamic interactions not only affect the structure of the family as a whole unit but also shape the cognition, behavior, and interactions of individual family members outside of the family. Psychodynamic constructs such as these include the individuation and differentiation of family members and patterns of family enmeshment, both processes considered important in adolescent development.

COGNITIVE-BEHAVIORAL THERAPIES

Cognitive-behavioral therapies understand and treat all psychological and behavioral problems as the result of dysfunctional, incorrect, and irrational cognitions. Unlike traditional psychodynamic treatment, cognitive-behavioral therapy deals with cognitive factors that are more immediately accessible and obvious to the client and the therapist and works on recognizing, understanding, and changing the cognitive distortions that are believed to result in maladaptive emotions and behaviors that are self-defeating and sometimes harmful to others. Cognitive-behavioral therapy focuses on the idea that behaviors are driven by thoughts, ideas, attitudes, beliefs, and values. In this model behavior can be reshaped and reformed by reshaping and reforming cognition. In essence, maladaptive, dysfunctional, or pathological behaviors, as well as dysphoric emotional states, result from and are driven by irrational and inaccurate ideas, negative attitudes and damaged values, and faulty thinking in general.

Cognitive-behavioral therapy combines the ideas and practices of both cognitive therapy and behavioral therapy, and its root ideas can best be illustrated by first understanding the basic ideas and treatments of both cognitive and behavioral therapy. However, although cognitive and behavioral therapy are both still practiced as independent models, to a great degree cognitive-behavioral therapy has subsumed many of the theories and practices of both, and especially those of cognitive therapy. This is far less true of behavioral therapy, however, which in its most extreme and active form is still practiced as a distinct treatment. Nevertheless, although techniques of behavioral modification are certainly used in the treatment of sexual offenders, and particularly adults, cognitive-behavioral therapy has incorporated many of the less intrusive and aversive behavioral techniques. As shown in Figure 13.4, cognitive-behavioral therapy incorporates cognitive and behavioral treatment but in practice may be closer to one treatment form than the other.

We shall return to a discussion of cognitive-behavioral therapy after first describing the ideas and practices of cognitive therapy and behavioral therapy.

COGNITIVE THERAPY

Cognitive therapy refers to the specific treatment model developed by Aaron Beck, which although initially developed as a treatment has evolved into a general model of therapy, contributed to by other important influences such as Donald Meichenbaum and Albert Ellis. Although adopted by many thera-

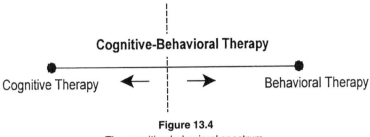

Figure 13.4
The cognitive-behavioral spectrum.

pists in various forms, the basic premise of cognitive therapy is that psychological difficulties, including emotional and behavioral problems, are always considered the result of distorted, dysfunctional, or otherwise inaccurate or irrational thinking.

Cognitive therapy is a straightforward and direct approach to treatment, focusing on the here and now and conscious understanding rather than delving into the unconscious or symbolic meaning. A. T. Beck (1979) wrote that psychological difficulties "are not necessarily the result of mysterious, impenetrable forces but may result from commonplace processes such as faulty learning, making incorrect inferences on the basis of inadequate or incorrect information, and not distinguishing adequately between imagination and reality" (pp. 19–20). In many ways this sums up what we believe about juvenile sexual offenders. From Beck's perspective, such psychological difficulties can be eliminated through a process of re-education, or cognitive therapy, in which discriminations are sharpened, misconceptions are corrected, and adaptive attitudes are learned (p. 20).

Unlike behavioral therapy, cognitive therapy recognizes the importance and central role of emotions in shaping experience and often serving as a primary source of distress. However, cognitive therapy attempts to treat emotional distress, as it does behavioral dysfunction, through the restructuring of underlying ideas, attitudes, and beliefs, or cognitive schemata. Cognitive therapy is interactive, as well as structured and problem centered, and attempts through various means to teach clients how to recognize, identify, and change cognitions believed to be irrational, maladaptive, and dysfunctional. To this end, cognitive therapy focuses on the development of emotional and behavioral self-regulatory skills, as well as broad and adaptive social skills, often using behavioral techniques to teach and apply new skills. Depending on client skills and style, as well as the clinician's approach, cognitive therapy may adopt an *intellectual* approach that identifies and replaces misconceptions, an *experiential* approach that exposes clients to experiences that are strong enough to change misconceptions (the corrective emotional experience), or a *behavioral* approach in which the intentional adoption of new behavior leads to changes in self-view and view of the others (A. T. Beck,

1979). Judith Beck (1995) described 10 underlying principles on which cognitive therapy is built:

1. Is based on an evolving formulation of the client
2. Requires therapeutic alliance
3. Emphasizes collaboration and active participation
4. Is goal oriented and problem focused
5. Emphasizes the present
6. Is educative and emphasizes relapse prevention
7. Aims to be short-term and time limited
8. Structures therapeutic sessions
9. Teaches clients to identify, evaluate, and respond to their dysfunctional thoughts and beliefs
10. Uses a variety of techniques to change thinking, mood, and behavior

Despite its focus on the conscious rather than the unconscious, in its most meaningful form cognitive therapy has a great deal in common with psychodynamic, or process-oriented, therapy. In much the same way that Aaron Beck considers the heart of cognitive therapy to be a more direct, but insight- and introspection-driven, approach to the same deeply ingrained problems addressed by psychodynamic therapy, Meichenbaum (1977) considered cognitive therapy to be an integration of psychodynamic, system-oriented, and behavioral therapy, rather than a model focused solely on cognition. In addition, despite its earlier leaning away from the clinician-client relationship, the therapeutic alliance is emphasized in contemporary practice as a critical starting point and factor throughout treatment (A. T. Beck, 1979; J. S. Beck, 1995; Meichebaum, 1985; Thase & Beck, 1993).

Figure 13.5 describes some of the similarities and differences between the two therapeutic forms. Like psychodynamic therapy, effective cognitive therapy requires client recognition that a problem exists and the desire to change, the willingness to engage in meaningful treatment, and the ability to understand and learn concepts and demonstrate insight into self and others: "Cognitive techniques are most appropriate for people who have the capacity for introspection and for reflection about their own thoughts and fantasies" (A. T. Beck, 1979, p. 216).

Difficulties With the Cognitive Model of Change
Cognitive therapy assumes that insight, reality testing, and learning are exclusively cognitive processes that can be adjusted and relearned through a renewed cognitive process. In fact, an essential and central belief in cognitive therapy is that these and other related and implied concepts such as attachment and connection to others, intimacy, remorse, self-esteem, personal identity, and personality formation are just cognitive processes that can be retrained or restructured, thus making up for any deficiencies in their earlier learning and acquisition.

Similarities	Differences
Both Cognitive and Psychodynamic Therapy . . .	*Unlike Psychodynamic Therapy, Cognitive Therapy . . .*
• Are introspection and insight oriented	• Focuses exclusively on immediate and conscious experience
• Consider the therapeutic relationship between the client and the clinician to be critical	• Clearly identifies and names problems
• Seek a clinical formulation around which the treatment plan develops	• Uses behavioral techniques to model, practice, and instill change
• Seek structural changes in the way in which clients view themselves and in their interactions with the world	• More clearly operationalizes (or puts into words) its approaches and concepts
• Focus on identifying and working through problems	• Is able to measure operational constructs

Figure 13.5
Similarities and differences between cognitive and psychodynamic therapy.

This does not square easily with a developmental model, however, which suggests that these concepts are learned in a particular sequence, through a series of internal psychic and external interactional processes in a complex developmental-learning environment, rather than simply learned through the intellect. It also does not fit easily with a neurological model, in which the brain is elastic and learning occurs in different ways at different points during its development, or a neurotrauma model in which early maltreatment can damage and dampen the brain's ability to learn, adapt, and respond appropriately. To suggest that one can unlearn and relearn at a much later point in life—and in a learning environment recreated by the clinician—seems to overlook and grossly simplify the process by which individuals (particularly emotionally damaged ones) grow and learn.

In this light, it may be that in many cases cognitive therapy is a *corrective* rather than a *relearning* experience in which revised cognitions serve as a new language by which to process phenomena and a framework to help prop up a house resting on a sometimes damaged foundation. This, plus the fact that cognitive therapy is best suited for individuals capable of at least a moderately high level of cognitive sophistication, suggests that it may not be successful on its own in treating juvenile sexual offenders. To this degree, like psychodynamic therapy, cognitive therapy should be considered one important tool to be integrated into a multimodal and pantheoretical approach to treatment.

BEHAVIORAL THERAPY

As noted, cognitive-behavioral treatment aims to bring about behavioral change by addressing cognitions, or ideas, attitudes, and beliefs. But some treatment falls closer to the behavioral end of the spectrum, in which the emphasis is on behavioral change with little or no regard for cognitive or emotional change. Behavioral treatment, built on the science, theory, and technique of behavior modification, focuses strictly on physical and physiological events and stimulation and resulting behaviors rather than emotional or cognitive states (mentation) or constructs. At the farthest end of the behavioral spectrum, there is no recognition that cognitions or emotions even exist as actual phenomena apart from behavior; and even if they do, they are of no consequence. More than either cognitive or psychodynamic therapy, behavioral therapy is closely associated with particular techniques and practices.

Strictly behavioral treatment, such as aversive therapy and other relatively intrusive therapies, is usually not used in the treatment of adolescents, with the exception of penile plethysmography (PPG). The PPG measures tumescence, or growth, of the penis when the individual is exposed to sexual materials or ideas, partly to measure sexual arousal and hence sexual interests and partly to measure sexual arousal to deviant materials, hence *deviant* sexual arousal. When applied to adults the PPG is often used for behavioral conditioning (or reconditioning). Previously used only in treating adults, the use of the PPG is becoming slightly more common with older adolescents (usually 15 and older), especially those for whom deviant arousal is a suspected or known concern. Keep in mind, however, that deviant sexual arousal is not considered an easily operationalized construct in juveniles under 16.

Behavioral Techniques
Aversive behavior therapy pairs unwanted behavior with an unpleasant or painful stimuli or response, thus reducing or eliminating the pleasure associated with the behavior. The treatment step beyond aversive therapy is to find stimuli considered normative and appropriate and recondition the sexual offender to the new and socially appropriate stimuli. Aversive techniques most typically include olfactory condition (coupling sexual images with foul odors) and occasionally faradic conditioning (mild electric shock). The addition of other physical tools such as biofeedback or the plethysmograph can strengthen the possibility and likelihood of reconditioning. Less aversive but still intrusive behavioral techniques cross into the category of cognitive-behavioral treatment, although they remain closer to the behavioral end of the scale. Nevertheless, unlike aversive behavioral therapy, which typically employs real behavior and real physical consequences (e.g., viewing real videos or photographs followed by exposure to a noxious odor), less aversive techniques require and depend on an active cognitive process in addition to behavioral consequences.

Masturbatory training is an intrusive behavioral technique that includes orgasmic (or masturbatory) reconditioning and masturbatory satiation, both of which couple cognition with behavior. Orgasmic reconditioning requires the client to masturbate to nondeviant material for as long as possible and to switch to deviant fantasies only to maintain sexual arousal. The goal is to ejaculate to the nondeviant fantasy, thereby exchanging the deviant fantasy for the normative one. In masturbatory satiation, the client continues to masturbate after ejaculation for up to one hour, intentionally employing only deviant fantasies. In this postejaculation latency period, in which it is usually difficult or impossible to reach orgasm again, continued masturbation to deviant thoughts becomes tiresome, unpleasant, and potentially painful, thus becoming aversive and intended to decondition the deviant fantasy. Verbal satiation is a less physically uncomfortable variant in which after ejaculation, instead of continuing to masturbate, the sexual offender verbally describes his deviant fantasies for an extended period of time (20–30 minutes) until they become tedious and lose their sexual power. This also is intended to decondition the deviancy and provide reinforcement for the nondeviant fantasy that (hopefully) accompanied ejaculation.

Covert sensitization is a still less intrusive technique that involves pairing a fantasy or mental image with an imagined unpleasant consequence. In this regard, covert sensitization is a form of cognitive-behavioral therapy in that there is no actual behavior but rather a cognitive substitute for behavior. Here, a target behavior is imagined (e.g., sexual arousal to a child) and then paired with an unpleasant thought, feeling, or sensation intended to decondition pleasure from the imagined act and ideally to make the act itself unpleasant, undesirable, and dystonic. A more intrusive and aversive variation couples the imagined (covert) act with a real-life (overt) stimulus, such as a foul odor, thus linking the idea to an actual unwanted consequence. Either way, the goal is to make the imagined thought a stimulus to be avoided.

Aside from the fact that aversion therapy has not "been convincingly demonstrated to be effective in producing long-lasting changes in sexual behavior" (Marshall et al., 1999), many of these techniques are considered questionable for use with juveniles, especially younger juveniles. Regardless of whether behavioral techniques are useful in the treatment of juveniles, attached to their use with juveniles are questions of social acceptability, age appropriateness, and ethics, especially as such techniques involve the use of graphic sexual images and sometimes unpleasant and noxious physical consequences.

BEHAVIORAL VERSUS COGNITIVE THERAPY

Aaron Beck (1979) described the similarities and differences between cognitive and behavioral therapy, noting that both are very detail conscious and highly structured, that both seek to alleviate and change overt symptoms, that both deal with the here and now, that neither attempts to deal with the unconscious, and that in both treatments the clinician is very active and controlling. The primary differences lie in the belief of cognitive therapy that cognitions of various kinds are the active players in behavioral change, whereas in behavioral treatment there is no recognition that cognitions exist. In behavioral treatment physical conditioning and physiological processes are the central ingredients, but in cognitive therapy clients are trained to recognize cognitions and choose to act or not act on them. In other words, in the cognitive model, behavioral change is possible because of cognitive reconditioning in which the client is an active thinker, whereas in the behavioral model change is the result of physiological reconditioning.

The Cognitive-Behavioral Model

Built largely on the principles of cognitive therapy and incorporating ideas and techniques of behavioral therapy, cognitive-behavioral therapy is a hybrid of the two models. A. T. Beck (personal communication, July 8, 2002) described cognitive-behavioral therapy as a category inclusive of cognitive therapy and behavioral models of reinforcement, distinguishing between the two ends of the cognitive-behavioral spectrum (heavily cognitive at one end, heavily behavioral at the other; see Figure 13.4).

Meichenbaum (1977) described cognitive-behavioral therapy as not just a talking cure but a proactive and enabling form of intervention, with a strong emphasis on the therapeutic alliance and the interaction between the client and the therapist. His model of stress inoculation training (Meichenbaum, 1985) is an example of how the cognitive-behavioral process helps the client to become a better observer and a more accurate interpreter of both self and incoming information, teaching stress management and social skills, as well as learning to apply various self-help skills.

Marshall, Hudson, Jones, and Fernandez (1995) considered cognitive-behavioral theory to be the unifying model that ties together the specific developmental factors that result in both cognition and behavior. They see the individual's capacity to respond appropriately or inappropriately to any given situation as the result of developmental vulnerability or resilience, which they consider to be the bridge between history, cognition, and behavior. They see this construct as lying along a continuum between strong resilience at one end and extreme weakness at the other. Here, vulnerability and resilience, as described in Chapter 4, represent the developmental predisposition to experience emotions, form cognitions, and respond behaviorally in a predictable and particular manner. Vulnerabilities will result in poor judgment and ineffectual or inappropriate behaviors, whereas resilience provides protection against difficult situations and guides appropriate problem solving and decision making. In effect, resilience reflects the individual's capacity to handle and respond appropriately to difficult situations, including temptation, and to resist transitory opportunities and internal emotional states that might result in maladaptive or dangerous behavior. Although these characterological factors develop largely in early childhood and especially through the parent-child relationship, they continue to develop throughout life and can be affected and changed as a result, either momentarily or more permanently. Here is where cognitive-behavioral therapy comes into play in the treatment of juvenile sexual offenders.

In their model (Marshall et al., 1995), both vulnerability and resilience can be understood as outcomes of various cognitive processes that include ideas, attitudes, beliefs, and the development of social skills. With specific reference to the sexual offender, they wrote, "The degree to which there is a failure to learn any or all of these skills, attitudes, and emotional capacities results in a corresponding degree of vulnerability. Such an individual would, therefore, be more likely to create, recognize, or give in to, opportunities to sexually offend" (p. 28). The goal of treatment, then, in this cognitive-behavioral model is to build resilience and diminish vulnerability. This is accomplished through the work of teaching the required skills, attitudes, and emotional capacities, thus restructuring cognitions, in part through directly engaging the cognitions of the client (cognitive therapy) and in part through the development and implementation of behavioral strategies and interventions (behavioral therapy).

This yields a potentially rich program of treatment that takes into account many factors relevant to the individual. From this broad perspective, cognitive-behavioral therapy is oriented toward both the individual client and the development of insight. It also focuses on the importance of the client-therapist relationship (the therapeutic alliance) and the active role of the clinician in understanding the client and designing and guiding treatment and follows a model of behavioral learning and practice that, in the case of sexual offenders, sometimes includes aversive or other techniques of behavioral conditioning.

THE COGNITIVE-BEHAVIORAL PATH

The basic cognitive-behavioral model follows a simple pathway. In the cognitive therapy model (A. T. Beck, 1979; J. S. Beck, 1995), fundamental (core) beliefs about self and others lead to automatic thoughts or cognitive responses mediated by intermediate beliefs that involve attitudes and assumptions. Automatic thoughts in turn lead directly to emotional, physiological, and behavioral responses. The model on which rational emotive behavioral therapy (REBT) is built is even simpler (Ellis, 1993, 1996), literally following an A-B-C <D-E> model. An *Activating* event leads to a rational or irrational *Belief* that results in a *Consequence*, such as an emotion or behavior. D and E represent the process of treatment, in which irrational beliefs are *D*isputed by the client and an *E*ffective new philosophy is created.[1] These are simple models with optimistic outcomes (especially in REBT). They suggest that cognitions (or experience of self and the world) and resulting emotions and behaviors can be changed through the application of new thinking and practice.

Cognitive-Behavioral Therapy in Application

Although there is little doubt about the ability to recondition behavior through physical means, the criticism remains that the primarily cognitive portion of cognitive-behavioral treatment banks significantly on the ability to teach and learn new cognitive concepts that will overcome years of pathological development in the troubled adolescent or adult. In the case of a child still in the early stages of the developmental process, the cognitive concepts of cognitive-behavioral therapy may be inapplicable anyway, given the lack of the child's formal cognitive development. In children, then, cognitive-behavioral therapy is generally applied more as a child-centered behavioral therapy, in which behavioral and not cognitive interventions are used to reshape and reform behaviors and interactions. When cognitive concepts are taught to children, they are presented as simple ideas and lessons about life, morality, and personal management taught in a psychoeducational format rather than as insight-oriented cerebral concepts learned through cognitive restructuring. For instance, rather than talking about physical boundaries in therapy, it is more effective to teach children about the concepts by demonstrating what breaking into someone's personal space looks and feels like, coupled with teaching simple rules about how to recognize and respect someone else's physical boundaries. Providing positive or negative consequences (or reinforcers) for appropriate or inappropriate boundary behavior will further strengthen the cognitive-behavioral lesson. Another example involves recognizing and changing cognitive distortions. With children, rather than using abstract ideas about cognitive-behavioral chains, it is more effective and appropriate to use simple language, coupled with modeling and activity exercises, to teach them how their ideas affect their behaviors and how to recognize "stinkin' thinkin'."

Even though cognitive-behavioral therapy can and should be individualized, it nonetheless is often built and depends on simple ideas that *do* follow a cookie-cutter approach even if this is not the intention. The model attributes psychological and behavioral problems to a path that connects irrational thinking to dysfunctional behaviors, and psychological well-being

---

[1]The ABCs of rational emotive therapy have also been described in more behavioral terms: A as the activating stimulus, C as the conditioned response, and B as the blank in the client's mind that serves as the bridge between A and C.

(and readjustment) to a similar path that links rational thinking to adaptive behaviors. An underlying belief of cognitive-behavioral therapy is that individuals can switch from the first path to the second, primarily through choice, accompanied by cognitive and behavioral techniques. The underlying model, in any version of CBT, does not significantly recognize or allow for the multiple and complex developmental difficulties and individual differences that contribute to or cause pathological problems in the first place, instead believing that developmental difficulties can be overcome and undone through thinking and behavioral exercises.

Without overly depending on behavioral reconditioning to alter the path from cognition to behavior (thus largely bypassing cognitive processes), cognitive-behavioral therapy depends on the ability of individuals to change the way they think through relearning and behavioral practice. Although it is true that many individuals can and do benefit from cognitive-behavioral interventions, it may be that in such cases the etiology of the problem being addressed, or the individual in question, is more amenable and easily accessible to cognitive restructuring. Here, as A. T. Beck (1979) noted, cognitive-behavioral therapy is best suited for motivated and cognitively able individuals, and thus a true cognitive-behavioral therapy model may be most appropriate only for those individuals who are ready, willing, and able to change. Unfortunately, the majority of juvenile sexual offenders are not ready, willing, or able to engage meaningfully or successfully in the process of cognitive-behavioral therapy. The cognitive-behavioral approach is thus more often applied as a psychoeducational and standardized process of cognitive-behavioral change, absent of many of the essential features required of a true model of cognitive-behavioral therapy.

CONCLUSION

In cognitive-behavioral therapy, ideas are concrete, easily defined, and measurable and can be tested for change over time. Unlike psychodynamic work, which aims for subtle shifts in consciousness (and unconsciousness), rather than the elimination of psychic structures, cognitive-behavioral therapy clearly seeks to change or eliminate dysfunctional cognitions, the presence of which can be later inferred by emotional and behavioral changes, as well as self-report. In this regard, psychodynamic therapy is generally deductive, meaning that it is virtually impossible to operationalize or empirically prove ideas. Cognitive-behavioral therapy, on the other hand, is inductive, which theoretically allows ideas to be set out and empirically proved—an attribute that has important implications for evidence-based practice.

Because cognitive-behavioral therapy is concrete and can be operationalized, it is easier to design replicable research studies in which expected treatment changes can be attributed to the treatment and that are open to scrutiny.

This makes cognitive-behavioral therapy a strong candidate both for the increasingly important evidence-based model of treatment and for the development of treatment manuals, which is an integral part of the CBT model.

However, in spite of obvious and significant differences, many factors are common to both psychodynamic and cognitive therapy. Given the commonalities, it may be that the only real difference between the two therapeutic genotypes is in their conceptualization and application of ideas, as well as an orientation toward empirically based practice or clinically based practice. Arguing for an integrated model of treatment, Bateman (2000) asserted that psychodynamic and cognitive-behavioral therapy only *seem* different; in actual practice, "competent practitioners usually disregard theoretical and political polemic" (p. 13). Among other reasons, this is because in the face of individual client and situational variables that call for clinical judgment, clinicians are not likely to rely on or use only theoretically pure techniques (Beutler, 2000a, 2000b; Faulkner & Thomas, 2001; Garfield, 1996). The techniques that clinicians actually use are more likely to be drawn from multiple sources, and the most effective therapeutic factors are most likely common to both forms of psychotherapy. In fact, despite their differences, many studies of treatment outcome find little to no difference between therapeutic types. That is, not only is psychotherapy considered to be an effective form of treatment, but it is also equally effective regardless of the form of therapy practiced.

Despite their design fit with the CBT model and much acclaim that we are on the right track with cognitive-behavioral models, there is little proof that cognitive-behavioral therapy is effective for sexual offenders. In those instances where cognitive-behavioral treatment has been shown to be effective, research suggests that positive outcomes may be the result of treatment elements common to most forms of therapy. These largely include the therapeutic alliance, therapeutic regard for the client, and the active participation of the client in the treatment process. It is equally true that no evidentiary support exists to validate the efficacy of psychodynamic therapy, in part because its methods are not conducive to standardized research. When psychodynamic therapy is effective, it is perhaps also the case that common features contribute more to successful outcome than to technique. Duncan (2001) noted that no solid evidence exists to demonstrate that any "specific treatment models have unique effects, or that any single therapeutic approach is superior to another" (p. 31).

The next two chapters look further at empirically based models and common therapeutic factors but also move toward an integrated treatment model that incorporates the strengths of the cognitive-behavioral and psychodynamic models into an interpersonal functional therapy that is informed and guided by empirically and clinically based practice.

CHAPTER 14

Common Factors and Evidence-Based Treatment

UNLIKE MANY other speciality fields within the allied mental healths, the field of sexual offender treatment has moved not just within the United States, but even internationally toward adopting a single approach to treatment, developing a language common to all, and applying the same ideas in every setting, with many of its most authoritative figures and organizations speaking with only one voice.

In fact, the pull toward the empirically more attractive but nonetheless unproved cognitive-behavioral model often seems more a struggle between treatment ideologies than a rich and creative search for best practice. More than the development of treatment models that focus on understanding and improving the role of the therapist, the therapeutic environment, and therapeutic practice, the adoption of a singular model seems to represent an extension of the long-standing antagonism between clinician and researcher described by Goldfried and Wolfe (1998). They argued that research-driven findings do not generalize to the way that therapy is conducted in the real world and that the movement toward a scientific, or medicalized, treatment model compromises the validity of research and its claims.

The research-driven agenda strongly pulls work with juvenile sexual offenders toward empirically validated treatments. The goal is to discover what treatments are most effective for different ailments, based on empirically established evidence of their efficacy. Once empirically proven, treatments are standardized so that they are always practiced that way, and other nonvalidated treatments are no longer used or recommended. This approach has been subject to great support and great criticism, as it both offers a seal of approval to certain treatments that meet the criteria and, in effect, designates all others as nonproven. In so doing, several assumptions are made:

- The only proof of efficacy is empirical.
- Empirical proof can be legitimately gathered only through quantitative, classic-design research methods.
- Empirically proven treatments actually work and are the best treatment.
- Empirically validated treatments work because of the single theory behind the treatment model and the associated treatment techniques rather than other explanations for its effectiveness.
- Lack of proof is a tacit assumption that a treatment is not effective.

Ironically, in defense of cognitive-behavioral therapy, which is intended as an evidence-based treatment but lacks evidence of efficacy in the treatment of sexual offenders, Marshall et al. (1999) defended the idea that a lack of evidence does not mean that treatment is ineffective.

Norcross (2000) critically asserted that the shift toward empiricized and standardized treatment not only is unrealistic and untenable but also contains an effort to eliminate the individual therapist as a variable in effective treatment. To a great degree, the movement characterized by the cognitive-behavioral shift *is* a movement toward single-theory and nonclinical models in which the role of the clinician is reduced to technician. Indeed, Quinsey et al. (1998) unequivocally argued that standardized treatments can be taught to and provided by intelligent laypersons rather than clinicians, noting that the same is true for the actuarial assessment of risk. This same trend toward research-driven and -validated treatment over clinical practice is also reflected in the risk assessment corner of the world of sexual offender treatment (a sentiment clearly expressed by Quinsey et al.) and is repeated yet again in the debate over the etiology and development of sexually aggressive behavior.

Treatment for juvenile sexual offenders must be built around the idea that it is effective and believable, giving us, the juvenile, and the community reasons to hope that treatment helps. This requires that we adopt a treatment model that incorporates a range of ideas and approaches linked to a clear understanding of what works in treatment, why it works, and evidence that it does indeed work, without getting caught up in a struggle to prove one set of ideas over another.

A COMMON FACTORS MODEL

Psychotherapy is an effective treatment. In an influential and well-respected study published in *Consumer Reports* magazine (Mental Health, 1995), 87–92% of 4,000 individuals attending some form of therapy reported improvement of symptoms. However, besides supporting the value of therapy, the study also concluded that no specific modality of psychotherapy did any better than any other form, serving to support and confirm the long-standing notion that under similar conditions and for the same problems, all psychotherapies are about as effective as one another, a finding reported by many others (Elkin et al., 1989; Hubble, Duncan, & Miller, 1999; Kazdin & Bass, 1989; Lambert, 1992; Lambert & Bergin, 1993; Luborsky et al., 2002; Luborsky, Singer, & Luborsky, 1975; Miller & Berman, 1983; O'Neill, 2002; Smith, Glass, & Miller, 1980; Stiles, Shapiro, & Elliott, 1986). In other studies designed to identify the relationship of treatment elements to treatment outcome, effective therapists used both psychodynamic and cognitive-behavioral elements in their treatment (Ablon & Jones, 1998; Castonguay et al., 1996; Kerr et al., 1992); it is the elements common to both forms of treatment that are most probably responsible for efficacy in treatment, rather than technique or ideology. Regardless of theoretical focus or technique, all forms of therapy take place within the context of the therapeutic relationship (Castonguay et al., 1996).

Norcross (2000) asserted that the clinician-client relationship accounts for as much of treatment outcome as do the particular treatment techniques, and Lambert (1992) and associates (Asay & Lambert, 1999; Lambert & Bergin, 1993) noted that most of what happens in successful treatment is related not to treatment model or technique but to factors that are common to all therapy. According to Lambert (1992), of the four elements most commonly associated with treatment efficacy, model and technique account for only 15% of the variance in treatment outcome, with most treatment successes resulting from client factors (40%), therapeutic alliance (30%), and the expectancy effects of placebo and hope (15%).

In describing therapies that cut across and integrate therapeutic forms, Holmes and Bateman (2002) noted that "common factors such as the therapeutic relationship, the creation of hope, explanations, a pathway to recovery, and opportunities for emotional release remain important explanatory variables for the similar outcomes of different therapies in the same conditions" (p. 8). The essential elements in these common factors, accounting for 70% of treatment outcome (Lambert, 1992), are the highly interpersonal factors introduced by the therapist and the client together, embodied in the therapeutic alliance that forms between them and in which the work of treatment is accomplished.

Extratherapeutic Client Factors

Factors outside of therapy contribute a great deal to successful outcome. Lambert and colleagues (Lambert & Borgin, 1993) reported that 40% of therapeutic success is related to the client and what the client brings to treatment, as well as his or her environment and even chance. Included here are client attitudes toward treatment, as well as the client's perception of the therapist as self-confident, skillful, and active; a willingness to discuss problems; and the client's pretreatment predisposition to change (Keijsers, Schaap, & Hoogduin, 2000). Tallman and Bohart (1999) described the capacity of the client as the "'engine' that makes therapy work" (p. 91), writing that it is the client who makes treatment effective, rather than the therapist or the technique. In work with juvenile sexual offenders, the attitude and beliefs that the youth brings into treatment, including his belief that he needs help or conversely his denial of facts of problems, contribute to the effect that treatment will have on him. Thus, the first steps in the treatment of a juvenile sexual offender usually involve his ability to acknowledge a problem.

THE THERAPEUTIC ALLIANCE

Lambert (1992) found that the therapeutic relationship, or factors contributing to the therapeutic alliance, account for 30% of the variance in treatment outcome, regardless of treatment orientation. This idea is supported by many in the field, including cognitive-behavioral therapists, who believe that the client-clinician relationship is a critical factor in any form of therapy (Bachelor & Horvath, 1999; A. T. Beck, 1979; J. S. Beck, 1995; Dryden, 1989; Hubble, Duncan, & Miller, 1999; Maione & Chenail, 1999; Meichenbaum, 1985; Thase & Beck, 1993). Included here are items such as caring, warmth, acceptance, affirmation, empathy, encouragement, positive regard, and genuineness. In addition, Lambert and Begin (1993) described reassurance, structure, advice, cognitive learning and cognitive mastery, changing expectations for personal effectiveness, and modeling and success experience as important factors in the therapeutic alliance. Hellerstein et al. (1998) showed therapeutic alliance to be an important factor in not just effective treatment but also long-lasting and significant change and suggested that more attention should be paid to this aspect of treatment in the training of psychotherapists. The therapist's ability to form a supportive and trusting relationship with the juvenile sexual offender will be critical to the juvenile's ability to engage in honest treatment, to feel connected and related to the therapist, to believe that he is not alone and that his clinician and others are working with him and are on his side, and to engage further in the therapeutic process, thus having a direct effect on the extratherapeutic client factors described earlier. To treat juvenile sexual offenders without the benefit of a strong clinical relationship and a working therapeutic alliance means that treatment success becomes the full responsibility of the juvenile and is not likely to result in successful outcomes.

PLACEBO, EXPECTANCY, AND HOPE

According to Lambert (1992), this factor accounts for 15% of treatment results and involves the client's expectation that therapy is a credible means for personal improvement and symptom relief and that he or she can change, partly through the process of treatment. This is a particularly important area for general research because there is a strong belief that the power of the placebo unlocks the capacity for spontaneous self-healing. Fisher and Greenberg (1997) strongly asserted that the placebo effect is more important in treatment with psychotropic medications than the effects of the actual medication itself and that the therapeutic alliance contributes significantly to the therapeutic effect of psychiatric medication.

For juvenile sexual offenders, this factor is linked to the aforementioned client factor and therapeutic alliance and represents the juvenile's willingness to accept the need for treatment and come to believe that he can be helped and can be successful. The instrumental idea is that the juvenile must believe he can get better; conversely, if he does not believe that things will improve, then the chances for treatment success are reduced. Accordingly, the treatment process must foster, build, and help maintain in the juvenile offender a belief that he needs help, hope that he will get better, and expectancy that he will succeed.

THERAPEUTIC MODEL AND TECHNIQUE

Norcross (2000) asserted that treatment technique accounts for only 12% to 15% of the variance across therapies, and Lambert (1992) estimated that only 15% of treatment outcome is the result of technique. Kazdin and Bass (1989) wrote that either techniques do not play a powerful role or, if they do, research methods are not powerful enough to detect them. Thus, factors related to the client and the therapeutic relationship appear not only far more important in determining treatment outcome, but in positive treatment outcomes appear to be the operating variables common to all treatment, rather than the specific ideas and techniques of treatment associated with a particular therapeutic form or genotype. In the treatment of juvenile sexual offenders, then, the use of a cognitive-behavioral or a psychodynamic model is far less important than the manner in which they are used and their ability to improve client factors, develop the therapeutic alliance, and enhance expectancy and hope. On its own, technique in the treatment of juvenile sexual offenders is a way of teaching and reframing ideas, developing awareness, and delivering corrective experiences. No technique is likely to produce effective results without being coupled to the larger framework of common factors that produce favorable treatment outcomes.

EVIDENCE-BASED AND MANUALIZED TREATMENT

Despite support for a common factors model, there has been an increasing movement toward treatments that have been proven in some way to work. This shift has also been evident in the treatment of sexual offenders. Unlike treatment practices based on clinical evidence only, or the opinion of the clinical community in absence of other empirical proof, evidence-based treatments are ostensibly held to a higher and more rigorous standard of scientific proof. Indeed, as noted, cognitive-behavioral therapy's ability to fit the empirically validated model is one of its great attractions.

Evidence Base

Chambless et al. (1998) described two types of empirically validated treatment as *well established* and *probably efficacious*. Both require a clear set of expected treatment outcomes against which effectiveness can be measured: the demonstration of treatment efficacy through scientifically designed research studies and a demonstration that the treatment accomplishes expected goals as well as or better than other treatment models that seek the same outcomes. To be considered well established, treatment must show statistical superiority over alternative treatments or equivalence to other well-established treatments, must use treatment manuals, must clearly define the client sample, and must demonstrate similar effects with at least two independent research teams. Probably efficacious treatments meet a lower standard of proof of effectiveness but follow similar guidelines.

Treatment Manuals

Validated treatment requires the development and use of treatment manuals that are single theory in design (i.e., not eclectic) and involve a clearly defined set of steps to be followed and techniques to be used in the treatment of a specifically defined disorder. In this manner, treatment validation not only supports particular treatments but also standardizes the treatment so that it must be practiced only in the manner prescribed by the model and described in the treatment manual. In effect, manuals serve as guided workbooks for clinicians to ensure consistency and adherence to the treatment model. It is generally only possible to manualize treatments that can be concretely defined and operationalized, including expected technique, progress, response, and outcomes. Woody and Sanderson (1998) wrote that treatment manuals describe validated treatments in enough detail to allow a trained clinician to replicate the treatment, but they added that no treatment manual is adequate in the absence of solid theoretical grounding and training.

Measuring Outcome

The idea that we want to use treatments that work seems basic, but the reality is that it is very difficult to know whether mental health treatment of any kind is actually effective given the many variables that affect outcome. Accordingly, highly designed research controls for every possible variation, at least in theory. An additional problem in outcome measurement lies in the definition of the treatment outcome. In the relatively straightforward case of depression, the primary goal is to eliminate or minimize the client's depression. But do we also want the quality of the client's life to improve? Although a likely by-product of achieving the primary goal, it is also very difficult to measure; thus, it is not typically included as a measurement of treatment efficacy.

In the case of the juvenile sexual offender, the goal is to prevent sexual re-offense, which is hard to measure, especially in the short run. Unlike the treatment of depression, where we can see the result of treatment unfolding before our eyes, we cannot see the desired outcome effects of juvenile sexual offender treatment unfold. Treatment effect in this case will not truly be tested until treatment has ended, and more likely long after treatment has ended. Moreover, because the ultimate goal is the lifelong elimination of sexual aggression, we need to study the outcome of treatment in juvenile sexual offenders for many years following the completion of treatment.

As empirical validation requires treatment outcomes that can be concretely defined, independently observed, and objectively measured, and because we cannot assess effectiveness in terms of the extinction of sexual aggression, we instead substitute different outcome goals as the goals of treatment. Different treatment programs may conceptualize these in different ways, but they are most likely to focus on behavioral and attitudinal changes, the remission or reduction of any existing comorbid psychiatric symptoms, and the mastery and demonstration of psychoeducational and cognitive-behavioral concepts, including the development and use of a relapse prevention plan of some sort. For the most part, in a cognitive-behavioral treatment model, outcome goals will often involve the acquisition of specific information, the completion of behavioral tasks, and a demonstration of reduced deviant sexual arousal where aversive behavioral techniques were used in conjunction with a plethysmograph.

These substitute measures may not even be related to the actual goal of eliminating sexual aggression. In fact, as we already know, no such evidence exists in the field of sexual offender treatment, making it difficult to assess any form of sexual-offender-specific treatment as effective, including the empirically attractive cognitive-behavioral model. This makes it hard to understand how cognitive-behavioral treatment, or indeed any treatment of juvenile sexual offenders, can ever be considered to be empirically validated, even assuming that empirically validated treatment is achievable and meaningful.

LIMITATIONS OF EVIDENCE-BASED TREATMENT

The validated treatment model represents a movement that de-emphasizes and curtails clinical judgment and practice, instead stressing the importance of independently gathered and concrete (empirical) evidence of efficacy.

Although the model has been widely accepted and adopted by many professional organizations, such as the American Psychological Association (APA), it has nonetheless led to great controversy in the field and is once again evidence of the split between a research-driven, scientistic perspective and a clinical point of view.

Duncan (2001) described the "certain seductive appeal to the idea of having a specific psychological intervention for any given type of problem" (p. 31) and considered the whole notion of validated treatment as critically flawed. The validated treatment model is driven by a particular philosophy that provides useful information but also stifles treatment, limiting and potentially ignoring innovation and other ideas outside of its framework. Martin Seligman (1995), a former president of the APA, wrote that evidence-based studies are not the only way, or the best way, of learning which treatments work, and he noted that the conditions under which treatment is actually practiced in the field themselves yield important validation of psychotherapy not accounted for by validated treatment. Similarly, Henry (1998) stated that the validated treatment model ignores the empirical results generated by decades of psychotherapy research and serves only to entrench an outmoded model of experimental research. Garfield (1996) criticized validated treatment because it overlooks limitations in research methods, as well as the variations in each case and the importance of the therapeutic relationship.

Asay and Lambert (1999) asserted that no matter how well intended, not only do findings not support the empirically validated approach, but they "scream of scientific or theoretical arrogance" (p. 23). Silverman (1996) called the movement toward validated treatment *methodolatry*, asserting that treatment manuals oversimplify treatment and provide a cookbook, paint-by-numbers approach to treatment. Indeed, by design, evidence-based models reduce or eliminate clinical interpretation and downplay or ignore the role of common therapeutic factors. Addressing the manualized approach to treatment, Beutler (2000a) noted that the most effective clinicians violate manualized treatments, and he further remarked (2000b),

> The tasks facing the modern clinician are often incompatible with selecting a specific structured manual that is built around a specific diagnosis. The art of psychotherapy is taking simple principles of relationship and interpersonal influence and applying them in creative ways to fit the endless permutations and complexities that characterize the people who seek our services. If a clinician is just a technician, that clinician will never cope with the complex problems that are presented in clinical practice. (¶ 47)

COMMON FACTORS OR SPECIFIC MODELS

Validated treatment models are based on the belief that specific therapeutic models and defined techniques are largely responsible for the success of therapy, rather than either unique or common factors (Ogles, Anderson, & Lunnen, 1999). In fact, one of the criticisms of the manualized approach to treatment is that it is technique dependent, incapable of innovation or flexibility and unable to integrate clinical judgment.

Of this, Beutler (2000a) wrote that effective manuals must resolve single-theory models in the face of multitheory practice and the idea and general belief that all treatments are more or less equivalent in treatment effect: "Procedures that enhance the quality of healing relationships are immanently more powerful than the theory-based techniques to which contemporary manuals are addressed. Indeed, the power of any set of techniques may well be to enhance the quality of the therapeutic relationship" (p. 1006).

EMPIRICALLY AND CLINICALLY DERIVED EVIDENCE

Rather than informing or guiding clinical practice and clinical judgment, empirically validated and manualized treatment *directs* treatment. Accordingly, it is another variant of the idea that practice is better served by research than clinical experience and that clinical judgment and ideas are not to be trusted. Of the greatest concern is the lack of any substantial evidence for this position, especially in the treatment of sexual offenders, as well as the apparent dismissal of other research that both is critical of the empirically validated approach and supports the idea of a common factors model. It is again reminiscent of "received wisdom" shading into dogma, in which one perspective dominates the other, rather than a search for integrated solutions that recognize and blend both perspectives.

Even if better outcome data existed, the forensic nature of juvenile sexual offender treatment renders it unlikely that we can ever meet the standards for empirically validated treatment described by Chambless et al. (1998) and Woody and Sanderson (1998). First, we would have to develop complex design studies that require cohort groups of juvenile sexual offenders and a process to ensure a nonbiased selection and grouping of research subjects. Second, research studies would have to be replicated by an independent research team, requiring a duplication or very close variant of the very same research design. These are both extremely difficult, if not impossible, conditions to meet in designing research for juvenile sexual offenders. Perhaps of greater concern, there are significant ethical implications to providing placebo treatment or pseudotreatment to a cohort of juvenile sexual offenders and then releasing them untreated into the community so that we can use them as a comparison group. This does not mean that we should abandon outcome studies or give up the quest for evidence of treatment effectiveness, but it does mean that we need to reimagine the ways in which we think about evidence of efficacy, as well as how to collect evidence that is consistent, accurate, and meaningful (reliable and valid).

To begin, we should recognize that there are at least two sources for evidence: empirical and clinical. In the first case, we should not assume that the only way to gather empirical evidence is through quantitative research designs; rather, we should consider alternate means such as qualitative research and descriptive social statistics. For instance, social demographics can provide evidence over time that supports effective treatment of today's juvenile sexual offenders. For example, if treatment for today's juvenile offenders is effective, then we should see, in 10 years, an increasingly aging population of adult sexual offenders, with fewer newer and younger adult offenders entering the data stream. In the second case, clinical practice itself yields evidence of treatment outcome, and there are means for designing research to assess clinical outcomes independently. In fact, the evidence-gathering process must be melded with treatment itself. The act of gathering proof that treatment works and about how it works should not control us or force fit treatment into a research model designed more for the natural sciences than the science of human behavior and interaction.

It should tell us something about our current research models when we read over and over that, in almost every aspect of the treatment of juvenile (and adult) sexual offenders, research is lacking. In 1987 Davis and Leitenberg wrote that the most important thing they could conclude about juvenile sexual offenders was that research was still in an early stage. Fifteen years later, little progress seems to have been made, despite our drive and inability to apply the scientific method to the problem. This situation seems to require new and innovative research methods, called for by the critics of current research methods, standards, and output, who criticize the process of research and the attitude of some in the research field, but not the goal or purpose of research. Like treatment itself, outcome studies and research on juvenile sexual offenders in general must find ways to become integrated, both informing and informed by clinical practice, as well as meeting high standards of reliability, validity, and rigor that yield objective and observable (i.e., empirical) results.

THE ATTRACTIVENESS OF THE COGNITIVE-BEHAVIORAL MODEL

However we define it and enumerate its weaknesses, not enough evidence-based treatment in the treatment of juvenile sexual offenders exists. However, cognitive-behavioral treatment is highly attractive to the evidence-based model. It is easy to set up and easy to implement, and it provides a clear framework within which therapists can focus on the psychoeducational aspects of cognitive treatment and by which client participation and progress can be easily measured. The same cannot be said about psychodynamic therapy, which is more abstract, requires more training and supervision of clinicians, cannot be practiced or necessarily well understood by anyone other than a clinician, and frequently does not yield easily observable results.

In sexual-offender-specific treatment, the cognitive-behavioral framework incorporates a shared set of general concepts about what the offender must learn if he is to get better, or at least be safe in the community. This allows clinicians to share common beliefs about the language, concepts, and goals of sexual-offender-specific treatment and incorporate them into a common model. It also provides a means to teach and test for the adoption and retention of new ideas in juvenile sexual offenders. Through this model we can discover whether the juvenile can recall and recite ideas, respond to specific questions, identify high risk situations, recognize and name thinking errors, and describe at-risk behaviors and ways to recognize and avoid future problems.

However, using cognitive-behavioral therapy in juvenile sexual offender treatment is a weak effort to meet an empirical standard. Although it looks like a good candidate on the surface, the difficulty of obtaining evidence of treatment effect (the elimination of sexual aggression) is too prohibitive, combined with the fact that cognitive-behavioral therapy as commonly practiced in juvenile sexual offender treatment is often more psychoeducational than it is cognitive-behavioral.

COGNITIVE-BEHAVIORAL THERAPY IN PRACTICE

In application, cognitive-behavioral therapy lies along a distinct continuum, as shown in Figure 14.1. On the one hand, cognitive-behavioral therapy is conceptualized and practiced as a rich process built on the same foundation as many other psychosocial treatments, including psychodynamic therapy, and is custom fit to its clients and matched in terms of readiness, willingness, and cognitive capacity. At the other end of the continuum, cognitive-behavioral therapy resembles a psychoeducational treatment process, which depends on workbooks, assignments, and single-minded techniques and concepts and applies one-size-fits-all ideas and methods to all clients. At this end of the continuum, in juvenile sexual offender treatment, group therapy is often the

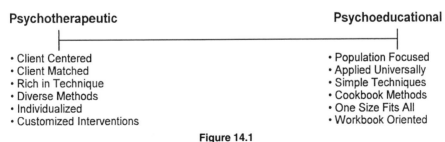

Psychotherapeutic   **Psychoeducational**

- Client Centered   - Population Focused
- Client Matched   - Applied Universally
- Rich in Technique   - Simple Techniques
- Diverse Methods   - Cookbook Methods
- Individualized   - One Size Fits All
- Customized Interventions   - Workbook Oriented

Figure 14.1
Two applications of cognitive-behavioral therapy.

preferred mode for cognitive-behavioral work, where ideas are disseminated en masse, with little recognition of the cognitive levels of or differences among group members, and with little room for or emphasis on discussion, exploration, or the establishment of the therapeutic relationship.

Even when cognitive-behavioral therapy is the focus of individual sessions, the same ideas and methods are taught to all clients, who are expected to come up with the same basic results. Failure is often seen as a deficit in the client, rather than a failure of the treatment model or the result of a mismatch between treatment model and client. Under these circumstances, cognitive-behavioral therapy more resembles social skill instruction and development than a psychotherapeutic process.

In practice, most cognitive-behavioral treatments for juvenile sexual offenders are built around a standardized relapse prevention model rather than a psychotherapeutic model of cognitive-behavioral therapy. Burton and Smith-Darden (2001) reported that the combined relapse prevention–cognitive-behavioral model is used by 79% of outpatient and residential treatment programs for male juvenile sexual offenders, compared to between 2% and 5% that use a psychotherapeutic cognitive-behavioral model. The basic cycle and relapse prevention models (Chapters 16 and 17) are highly standardized and geared more toward psychoeducational learning than cognitive dissembling and restructuring and the individualized approach to treatment emphasized by the cognitive-behavioral literature (J. S. Beck, 1995). However, given that the cognitive-behavioral approach in the treatment of juvenile sexual offenders is so often focused on relapse prevention, and as we have no definitive evidence that any relapse prevention model works, in its current form it is unlikely that cognitive-behavioral therapy can provide the empirical evidence base that is sought.

CONCLUSION: TOWARD INTEGRATION

Using a limited, primarily psychoeducational cognitive-behavioral model, we can nonetheless provide a central core for an integrated model of abuse-specific treatment, sharing common ideas and a common language as a means to teach and test for the adoption and retention of new ideas, and as a base for social-skills development. Cognitive-behavioral treatment provides both a concrete means for at least partially accomplishing such goals and a means for the juvenile to demonstrate his understanding of the external situations and interactions and the internal cognitive processes that influence and maintain sexual offending behavior and lead to repeated antisocial behaviors. Although far from the goals of empirically validated treatment, these ideas represent the heart of sexual-offender-specific treatment as it is currently provided, focusing on the cognitive-behavioral chain (or dysfunctional behavioral cycle), relapse prevention planning, and related concepts and tools.

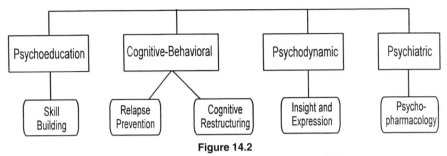

Figure 14.2
The treatment spectrum, from psychoeducation to psychodynamic.

As we turn toward an integrated treatment model, we can build on the strengths and the center provided by cognitive-behavioral treatment by adding and combining other treatment elements that augment, enhance, and expand on the central role that cognitive-behavioral therapy can play in the integrated treatment spectrum, as shown in Figure 14.2.

This integrated model will weave together many seeming opposites:

- Empirical and clinical evidence
- Research and practice methods
- Single-theory techniques and common therapeutic factors
- Cognitive-behavioral and psychodynamic therapies
- Skill development and psychotherapy insight
- Forensic and mental health perspectives
- Sexual-offender-specific treatment and the treatment of the whole child
- Individual and social psychology
- Old ideas and new ideas

Besides genuine limits to our knowledge, other obstacles to more effective and provable treatment exist. First, black-and-white thinking about what does and does not work is not helpful, nor is our failure to recognize or admit that we do not actually know what works (and what does not). Second, we have a limited ability to use what we have learned actually works over the last century of providing treatment. That is, instead of discarding what does not work and retaining what does, we want to discard the whole model. A third obstacle lies in the tension between clinical practice and the scientific method. The insistence that one is superior to the other and should drive treatment is a philosophically arrogant and naive position that ensures division in the field and a divided—rather than integrated—model of treatment. Finally, seeking Holy-Grail solutions, including unified theories and single-theory models, and using research designs that do not seem able to produce the evidence we seek are not helpful. Perhaps in order to find answers, we need to ask better and more refined questions for which answers are possible.

CHAPTER 15

An Integrated Approach
to Treatment

AN INTEGRATED approach to the treatment of juvenile sexual offending is geared toward the needs of the juvenile offender and the needs of the community and recognizes that no single model, theory, or set of techniques can possibly accomplish such a complex task.

This approach is informed not only by the techniques and ideas found in both the cognitive-behavioral perspective model and the psychodynamic sphere but also by a forensic perspective, an awareness of the forces of social psychology and the social environment, and a recognition of both the normative and the pathological developmental and mental health issues faced by children and adolescents who engage in sexually aggressive behavior. Integrated into this forensic treatment are ideas about (a) what to recognize and attack in treatment; (b) how to address the range of issues faced by juvenile sexual offenders, including those of both normative adolescent development and pathological maladaptation, and knowing how to tell the difference; (c) how best to treat the sexual and related nonsexual behaviors in our clients in a manner sensitive to and supportive of their needs, in full awareness of criminogenic tendencies and motivators and in a manner that protects the community from current or future sexual predators; and (d) how to use an array of treatment interventions and techniques that most match the problem, the individual client, and the treatment environment at the time of the intervention.

INTEGRAL COMPONENTS

The concept of sexual-offender-specific treatment is often vague. However, the assumption is that a specific model directs abuse-specific treatment, rather than just unconnected treatment approaches aimed at sexual offend-

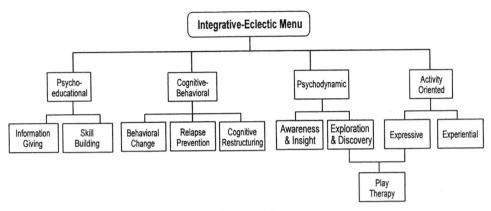

Figure 15.1
An integrative-eclectic menu approach to treatment.

ing behaviors. An important component in any integrated model of sexual-offender-specific treatment is that it has a vision and a framework that makes it specific to sexual offending behaviors and elaborates on this vision in operational terms. That is, what about the model is specific to the treatment of sexual offenders, and what about the treatment is specific toward the elimination of sexually aggressive behaviors? In a model of treatment for children and adolescents, an additional question concerns how the model differentiates the treatment of youthful sexual offenders from the treatment of adult sexual offenders. Vision and the definition of a model must not only define what we mean by sexual-offender-specific treatment but also describe philosophy and provide the framework that describes both the approach to treatment and the treatment that will be provided.

No specific treatment intervention or theory predominates in an integrative model. Instead, different ideas and techniques are knitted and blended together into a single pantheoretical and multi-intervention model that spans psychoeducation, cognitive-behavioral therapy, and psychodynamic treatment and includes activity-oriented treatments, each of which is inclusive of more specific elements incorporated into the larger model. This pantheoretical frame, shown in Figure 15.1, incorporates a multimodel approach to treatment and an integrated but eclectic menu from which to draw specific treatment interventions.

THE IMPORTANCE OF COGNITIVE-BEHAVIORAL TREATMENT

The easily defined ideas of a cognitive-behavioral model provide a central core around which to build a framework for sexual-offender-specific treatment. With clearly defined goals, an uncomplicated view of pathology, a direct and simple model of change, and concepts that are easily taught to clinicians and others involved in providing treatment, cognitive-behavioral therapy is an attractive model. In addition, cognitive-behavioral models frequently use structured workbooks and other written materials that strengthen the treatment framework and make it even more concrete, allowing and often requiring clients to complete homework outside of therapy sessions. This model holds clients responsible to a great degree for their own improvement and also provides a means to check on their participation in and motivation for treatment, which is especially true in the treatment of sexual offenders. Rather than engaging in treatment by choice or internal motivation, most adult and juvenile sexual offenders are externally required to attend treatment. Accordingly, it is frequently the case that such clients will avoid treatment work or engage minimally, often only to the degree necessary to meet external requirements.

At its best, cognitive-behavioral treatment provides an important organizing framework, explanatory constructs, and a language for both the juvenile sexual offender and the clinician, as well as collaterals (family members, probation and parole officers, state agency social workers, and other invested parties) who are thus able to join in, observe, or judge the effectiveness of treatment based on the apparent assimilation and demonstration of new ideas. This ability to provide a common language is a powerful means for naming and organizing ideas; describing emotional, cognitive, and behavioral problems and pitfalls; and creating a structured plan for both correct behavior and a way to recognize, avoid, or escape trouble before it escalates out of control.

The primary weakness of a cognitive-behavioral treatment, however, is the same as for any single-theory model: the idea that the model on its own is capable of the treatment task, or that it can work for everyone. Second, most cognitive-behavioral treatment in juvenile sexual offender treatment programs is intended to provide a corrective experience aimed at ensuring public safety as much as (or more than) alleviating symptoms of personal distress or a comorbid psychiatric disorder. As noted earlier, this fuels a psychoeducational approach to treatment and rehabilitation, in which the product of treatment is often behavioral compliance and the ability to reflect learned concepts and identify cognitive-behavioral sequences of events, rather than actual change. At this end of the continuum, treatment focuses more on teaching and didactics than psychotherapy, which is a significant problem in any wide-ranging program of treatment aimed at broader goals of change, rehabilitation, and lifetime improved functioning.

At its worst, cognitive-behavioral therapy as practiced in the treatment of juvenile sexual offenders is frequently workbook oriented, unable to change direction, and dogmatic in its opinions (which are delivered to the juvenile sexual offender, not derived from his experience); treats everyone the same way; and is deemed successful by the client's ability to recall and replay information and ideas rather than demonstrate actual change. When practiced in psychoeducational form, without a psychotherapy focus, cognitive-behavioral therapy can be useful but can also result in the parroting of concepts that may be mistaken for the actual acquisition of information.

THE CENTRAL POSITION OF COGNITIVE-BEHAVIORAL THERAPY

When incorporated into a more comprehensive treatment model that combines a variety of treatment approaches, cognitive-behavioral treatment is enhanced. In a broad-based treatment model, cognitive-behavioral therapy serves a central role in the integrative framework, providing clear and well-defined language, concepts, and expected outcomes for treatment.

INTEGRATING COGNITIVE-BEHAVIORAL AND PSYCHODYNAMIC THERAPY

Although cognitive-behavioral therapy is oriented toward the psychoeducational end of the treatment spectrum and psychodynamic therapy is focused on a more insightful, exploratory, and deeper area of psychological functioning, the two modalities are not incompatible. On the contrary, they appear to represent different views of the same phenomena—that is, psychological experience and behavioral functioning—that approach and treat the same problems in different ways. By combining them and allowing outlying psychoeducational and activity treatments to serve as additional feeds, we can define a model of change that results from integrating both approaches, depicted in Figure 15.2.

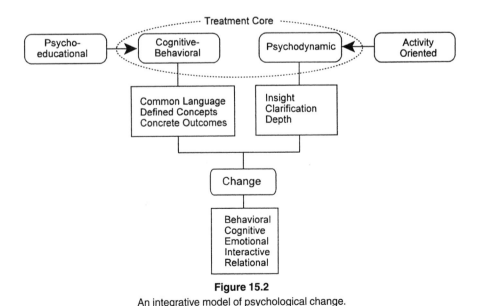

Figure 15.2
An integrative model of psychological change.

AN INTEGRATED PROTOTYPE

Ablon and Jones (1998) defined a prototype for both psychodynamic and cognitive-behavioral therapy in order to distinguish between the forms and recognize effective treatment elements unique to either treatment type. Each prototype contains elements most associated with that type of therapy, and in the study researchers observed the use of both sets of prototypical elements by both psychodynamic and cognitive-behavioral therapists, and the relationship between positive, neutral, or negative treatment outcomes. The prototypes shown in Figure 15.3 are not line-by-line comparisons, but instead represent the list of attributes and foci most associated with each treatment model.

Psychodynamic Prototype	Cognitive-Behavioral Prototype
The therapist . . .	*The therapist . . .*
• Is empathic and sensitive to patient feelings	• Is supportive
• Is nonjudgmental and accepting	• Exerts control over topics introduced into the session and structures sessions
• Is emotionally neutral	• Is didactic and explains the rationale behind technique and approach to treatment
• Recognizes transference-countertransference issues as important	• Ensures that the clinician-patient dialogue has a specific focus
• Uses the therapeutic relationship to learn about the patient's relational style	• Discusses and defines treatment goals for therapy sessions
• Focuses content on memories, self-image, feelings, experiences, dreams, and fantasies	• Sets therapeutic activities or tasks to be completed outside of the session
• Communicates with the patient in a clear and coherent style	• Focuses conversation on cognitive themes and related ideas and beliefs
• Facilitates the patient's ability to speak freely	• Emphasizes current and recent life experiences
• Points out the patient's use of defensiveness	• Seeks specific information and elaboration
• Points out feelings regarded by the patient as unacceptable	• Gives explicit advice and direction
• Links patient's current feelings and perceptions to past experiences or behavior	• Presents experiences or events in different perspectives
• Identifies recurrent themes in the patient's experience	• Encourages the patient to try or adopt new behaviors
• Helps the patient gain insight or new understanding	• Ensures that the patient understands what is expected and is committed to the work

Figure 15.3
Psychodynamic and cognitive-behavioral prototypes. Based on Ablon and Jones (1998).

By combining the two sets of attributes and treatment foci, we arrive at a single prototype in which the functions and approach embodied in both the psychodynamic and cognitive-behavioral prototypes are integrated into a single prototype with 31 therapist characteristics organized into five categories: (a) interactive style, (b) use of therapy, (c) therapeutic focus, (d) executive function, and (e) facilitation. The integrated prototype is characterized by a clinician who is flexible and able to use and combine supportive and task-focused approaches, switches gears and style to match the client and the treatment situation, and uses the methods and approaches typically associated with both therapeutic forms. These attributes reflect the totality of an integrated prototype. At any given time and in any given case, the therapist demonstrates particular characteristics and uses a selected focus. But it is the totality of the integrated prototype from which the clinician draws.

Interactive Style
- Confident and self-assured
- Empathic and sensitive
- Emotionally neutral
- Supportive, nonjudgmental, and accepting
- Informed by affective issues (transference and countertransference)

Use of Therapy
- To recognize the cognitive framework
- To understand the client's phenomenological experience
- To understand the way the client relates to others
- To reframe experiences and events
- To instruct

Therapeutic Focus
- Emotional experiences
- Cognitive themes, ideas, and beliefs
- Psychological defensiveness
- Avoidance of difficult feelings
- Recurrent themes in the client's experience
- Current and recent life experiences
- Connections between current and past experiences
- Insight or new understanding
- Meaning and clarification

Executive Function
- Defines and controls structure, including content
- Ensures focused discussion
- Seeks clarification
- Sets therapeutic activities or tasks to be completed outside of the session

Facilitative

- Communicates clearly
- Facilitates the client's ability to speak freely
- Explains treatment rationale
- Discusses and defines treatment goals
- Ensures that the client understands what is expected
- Ensures that the client is committed to the work
- Gives explicit advice and direction
- Encourages the client to try or adopt new behaviors

In this model it is the clinician who recognizes and identifies treatment issues, oversees and adjusts treatment, and facilitates the manner in which different treatment interventions are applied and when to apply them, as well as serving as the arbiter of treatment progress and effectiveness. In a multidisciplinary model, the treatment team shares these central roles and functions; nevertheless, in almost all models of juvenile sexual offender treatment the advanced-degree clinician carries these responsibilities and provides the individual, group, and family therapy central to treatment and evaluates treatment effectiveness.

IMPLICATIONS OF THE COMMON FACTORS IN AN INTEGRATED MODEL OF TREATMENT

Just as the underlying structure and approach of the cognitive-behavioral model provides direction and language for an integrated model of juvenile sexual-offender-specific treatment, so too does the common factors model described in the previous chapter.

Extratherapeutic Factors

Here we must consider the strengths that individuals bring to their treatment, as well as the developmental vulnerabilities that are so common in juvenile sexual offenders. In addition, both risk and protective factors found in the client's environment play a central role. Gilgun considered these factors in developing the *Clinical Assessment Package for Client Risks and Strengths* (CASPARS; Gilgun, 1999; Gilgun, Klein, & Pranis, 2000), which measures client and environmental factors in an attempt to understand and integrate them into treatment and thus to improve the likelihood of positive treatment outcome: (a) emotional expressiveness, (b) peer relationships, (c) family relationships, (d) the embeddedness of the child and family in the community, and (e) sexuality. The CASPARS was adapted for specific use with juvenile sexual offenders (the *Assessment of Student Assets and Vulnerabilities*; Stetson School, 2000a) and now measures items connected to dynamic risk factors in treatment.

THE TREATMENT ALLIANCE

Treatment alliance is key. Blanchard (1998) described the therapist as the primary tool for initiating change in sexual offenders, writing also that "when the fundamentals of relationship-building are not applied to sexual offenders, little movement or growth will take place" (p. 32). More than just a relationship between the juvenile in treatment and the clinician, the therapeutic alliance is inclusive of the qualities brought into treatment by the therapist (but not the techniques[1]) and the juvenile, as well as other factors that structure, frame, and define the content of the relationship. Dryden (1989) described the therapeutic alliance in terms of three main components: (a) *Bonds* include the nature of the relationship and the connection between the clinician and the juvenile; (b) *Goals* define the reasons for and the ideal outcome of the relationship, thus providing a starting and ending point and a boundary for the relationship; and (c) *tasks* include the specific and goal-directed activities to be carried out by both the client and the therapist.

TREATMENT STRUCTURE

Combined with Day and Sparacio's (1989) model, the therapeutic alliance is framed within a therapeutic structure that provides safety and protection for both the clinician and the client. Structure provides order and consistency to the therapeutic relationship and process, defines roles, and communicates expectations for both the clinician and the juvenile. Modifying Day and Sparacio, and always recognizing that structure cannot substitute for clinician competence, effective therapeutic structure is

1. Flexible and open to modification
2. Guided by a clear rationale that can be explained
3. Nonpunitive
4. Not overstructured and rigid
5. Without unnecessary or purposeless rules
6. Guided by the client's readiness for structure
7. Sensitive to the juvenile's needs, readiness, tolerance level, and resistance
8. Related to the juvenile's emotional, cognitive, and behavioral predisposition

---

[1] It can sometimes be difficult to distinguish between therapist qualities and the application of technique. This is especially true when technique is inextricably linked to clinician presentation, engagement, and attitude as in client-centered therapy, in which *technique* is more or less embodied in the attributes of the therapist and the therapeutic relationship is an extension of technique, or vice versa.

Expectancy, Hope, and Motivation

In juvenile sexual offending this factor is connected to the therapeutic alliance. It is also closely connected with motivation and other extratherapeutic attributes brought into treatment by the juvenile offender because expectancy and hope can serve as treatment factors only when there is a desire for treatment and motivation for change. Unlike the nonforensic mental health client seeking therapeutic help, the juvenile sexual offender is often (usually) not seeking help, is unmotivated to change, and does not believe that he needs help or needs to change. This is usually not because juvenile sexual offenders are committed to their current lifestyle or intend to become career sexual offenders or criminals but because they often simply do not think that they need help and believe that they can change on their own if they want to (which is sometimes true). It is also because they may not be ready to change, and much of the time because they are also normal children and adolescents who are not looking for intrusive adult and authoritarian intervention in their lives.

Laws, Hudson, and Ward (2000) declared that "one of the major deficiencies of RP [relapse prevention treatment] has been its assumption that clients participating in this intervention are highly motivated to change their behavior" (p. 16). Similarly, in describing cognitive therapy, A. T. Beck (1979) wrote that cognitive-behavioral treatment is most appropriate for people who are introspective and reflective. Neither is usually the case of juvenile sexual offenders, who are virtually always in treatment only because someone in authority put them there. Further, in most cases, juvenile sexual offenders are not especially introspective and in many cases may not be capable of self-reflection based on cognitive development, emotional condition, behavioral disposition, psychiatric comorbidity, or more likely some combination. The model of ready, able, and willing—the ideal model for anyone in treatment—is unlikely to apply to most juvenile sexual offenders, at least when they begin treatment.

Part of the work of the treatment team, then, is to spark motivation in the juvenile offender and help him to overcome the first obstacle to treatment. That is, to get treatment, you have to want it; and for treatment to be effective, you have to expect it to be. These conditions are based on the idea that the client is not in denial about the problem. Expectation and hope for treatment effectiveness in forensic mental health are linked to motivation and the recognition that a treatment problem exists. It is unlikely that any treatment can be successful with clients who are hostile or difficult. Effective therapy requires clients who participate (Power, 2002).

TREATMENT MODEL AND TECHNIQUE

Technique and model are also important. The common factors model supports the idea that a range of techniques is useful, although secondary to the therapeutic relationship rather than the driving force that shapes the therapeutic relationship.

In an integrated model techniques must be chosen that fit the treatment task *and* the individual juvenile sexual offender. To use a cognitive-behavioral strategy that might be relevant for an adolescent of average intelligence would be the wrong approach with a cognitively impaired client, for instance. Using a cognitive-behavioral approach with a child who has just received terrible news is another example of a poor choice of approach. Selecting a psychodynamic approach to work with juvenile sexual offenders to explore the reasons for cognitive distortions, rather than using a cognitive-behavioral technique to deal with the actual distortion, is one more example of mismatched technique. Finally, using either an abstract or a rationally based cognitive intervention with an acting-out 10-year-old is out of touch with both reality and the need for an intervention that will immediately help the situation. "If a person is just a technician, he or she will never transcend the use of techniques. . . . Only an artist can apply these scientific principles to the complexity of lives and find creative and new ways of making them relevant and workable in complex environments" (Beutler, 2000a, p. 1006).

BLENDING THE ELEMENTS

Holmes and Bateman (2002) described integrative therapies as "'dappled' in the sense that they bring together elements from single tradition therapeutic modalities in an organized and systematic way, in order to enhance therapeutic efficiency" (p. 1). They described integration as wedding together strands of different therapies into a new and coherent whole, as opposed to eclecticism which can be idiosyncratic, without theory, and beyond definition.

Such an integrated model is described in Figure 15.4, in which common therapeutic features act together, are mediated by the treatment needs of individual juveniles as well as general treatment needs that apply to all juvenile sexual offenders, and in turn influence and direct the actual treatment interventions selected, drawn from the integrated menu of treatment techniques. In such a model, the therapeutic alliance is built on a real and engaged connection between clinician and the troubled and often emotionally detached juvenile sexual offender; is experienced as supportive and motivating by the juvenile; is defined by clear structure, boundaries, goals, and tasks; and is dependent on selected treatment techniques that meet the needs of each juvenile. This is as true for cognitive-behavioral therapy as it is for psychodynamic treatment, which is built on the premise that treatment is based on an ever-

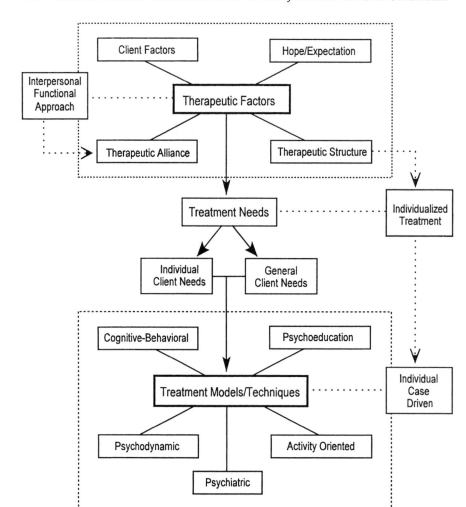

Figure 15.4

The relationship among common treatment factors, individualized treatment, and the selection of treatment interventions.

evolving formulation of the client, requires a sound therapeutic alliance, and emphasizes collaboration and active participation (J. S. Beck, 1995, pp. 5–6).

CONCLUSION: AN INTEGRATED MODEL

The development and application of an integrated model is not a huge leap for many clinicians. In fact, many programs and clinicians already follow an eclectic model of treatment. In these cases, it is a matter of recognizing and defining the model and using that definition as a means to understand and apply multimodal treatment. In other cases, it means developing and using a

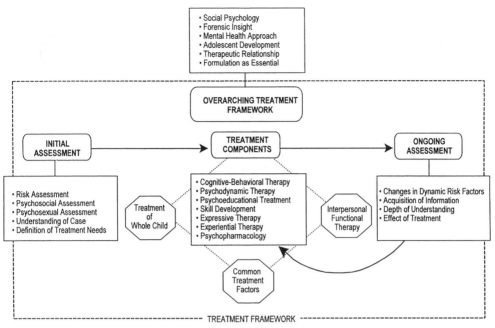

Figure 15.5
Integrated model of treatment.

broader range of treatment models and ideas and expanding treatment beyond a single-theory model. This will mean giving up the idea, in Blanchard's (1998) words, "that there is a right way and a wrong way to treat sexual offenders—a neat prescription that will have perfect application to all types of offenders" (p. 51).

Figure 15.5 illustrates the complete model, integrating the ideas discussed throughout this book. Encompassed within this framework lies the treatment continuum, from initial assessment to treatment interventions and ongoing re-evaluation until the course of treatment is complete. Nested within the integrated model are further levels of integration in each individual element.

The overarching framework combines forensic ideas with the ideas of social psychology, individual mental health, human development, and the therapeutic relationship and thus defines and informs the treatment that is provided within that frame. Initial assessment integrates psychosocial and forensic risk assessments in a model of comprehensive risk assessment that requires clinical insight and formulation, and not merely an assignment of risk level. Initial evaluation is followed by the provision of treatment itself, which integrates the range of treatment modalities, theories, and techniques available to the clinician. The model is integrative because multiple treatment techniques are intentionally combined and used side by side to reach a common goal; are driven by the treatment of the whole child, rather than his sexual aggression alone; and are based on common therapeutic factors in which treatment effectiveness is built on the client's own strengths and the therapeutic relationship. In this model, technique is used to teach, demonstrate, provide corrective experiences, and create opportunities for discovery, insight, and expression but does not otherwise define or drive treatment. Finally, ongoing assessment is an active element that is both part of the treatment process and a process in its own right. Information about the course and progress of treatment is constantly collected and evaluated; assessments are made about the breadth of treatment and the depth of treatment effectiveness; and decisions that are made about the ongoing course of treatment are implemented in a feedback loop that returns to the active treatment process.

Having reached an understanding of the children and adolescents who engage in sexually abusive behavior, of the assessment of risk, and of the development of a framework by which treatment is conceptualized and provided, it is time to turn to the process of rehabilitation, or the methods by which treatment ideas are transformed into action.

CHAPTER 16

Thinking Errors and Behavioral Cycles

REGARDLESS OF the treatment environment or model in which the treatment of juvenile sexual offenders occurs, emphasis is placed on the instruction of concepts considered important to the juvenile's ability to maintain safety in the community. This psychoeducational component is intrinsic to the treatment of both juvenile and adult sexual offenders in the belief that such concepts are basic to helping offenders understand, recognize, and overcome their offending behaviors and the roots of the behaviors. With children and adolescents, who by definition are still developing, it is even more important to teach information and ideas that will become part of the way in which they understand themselves and the world around them and the way they develop as individuals. In much the same way as we teach sex education and drug awareness to youths in all walks of life, we teach concepts intrinsic to the elimination of sexually aggressive and inappropriate behavior to juvenile sexual offenders as important building blocks in their development and thinking.

Cognitive-behavioral and psychoeducational work is a central component in an integrated treatment model and is considered key to success. In fact, many (nonintegrative) programs are built entirely on cognitive-behavioral and psychoeducational work alone. These ideas and tools for change are built largely on the three primary models of (1) thinking errors, (2) consistent and predictable patterns of dysfunctional behavior, and (3) relapse prevention plans and include ideas closely connected to these three essentials or variants on a theme. Although the three models are distinct in their own right, in a cognitive-behavioral or psychoeducational model they are almost inseparable, and ideas about patterned dysfunctional behaviors serve as the link between cognitive distortions and the relapse prevention plan.

PSYCHOEDUCATIONAL AND COGNITIVE-BEHAVIORAL FOCUS

In a pure cognitive-behavioral model built on a base of ideas common to cognitive therapy, ideas and cognitions are explored on a case-by-case basis, and treatment interventions are geared to each individual client. However, this is not the case in sexual-offender-specific treatment, in which cognitive concepts and behavioral techniques are taught uniformly to all clients, who are expected to learn and utilize them. Because these cognitive-behavioral ideas are closely linked to and taught through psychoeducation, they become part of a cognitive-behavioral and psychoeducational component.

In a well-developed treatment model, these ideas are explored further in individual and group therapy and are customized to each individual client to ensure their relevance. In addition, given the generally abstract notions involved, through individual therapy clinicians can ensure that their clients have the intellectual or age-developed cognitive capacity to understand the ideas or to recognize learning disabilities or learning differences that require a different approach to teaching these concepts. In fact, the greatest risk with either the psychoeducational or cognitive-behavioral model is that their methods will overestimate the ability of individual clients, miss differences in cognitive ability or learning needs, or mistake the mere repetition of ideas and the ability to complete workbook assignments for the genuine acquisition and integration of ideas.

Figure 16.1 breaks the psychoeducational and cognitive-behavioral component into four quadrants, each of which has a different focus in the way that it teaches these important concepts and tools:

1. The *psychoeducational instructional* quadrant emphasizes teaching the ideas and places less emphasis on describing the ideas in detail or exploring and measuring cognitive distortions.
2. The *psychoeducational cognitive* quadrant emphasizes both instruction and exploration.
3. The *psychoeducational workbook* quadrant places little emphasis on either instruction or cognitive exploration and depends instead on structured workbooks and other boilerplate materials to teach and test for concepts
4. The *cognitive-behavioral* quadrant minimally utilizes psychoeducational technique and emphasizes a therapeutic approach to recognizing and exploring cognitive-behavioral ideas through either individual or group treatment.

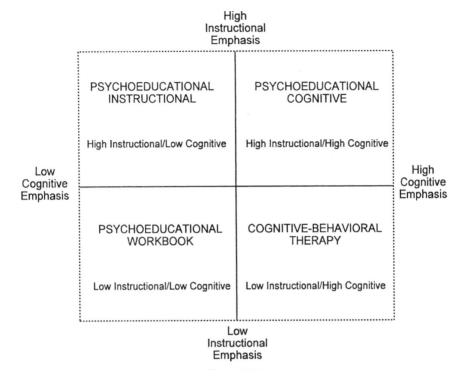

Figure 16.1
Types of psychoeducational-cognitive approaches.

THINKING ERRORS AND COGNITIVE DISTORTIONS

The thinking errors model is often attributed to Yochelson and Samenow (1976), who asserted that criminals base their behaviors on distortions in their thinking that allow them to behave in antisocial and self-serving ways. However, they described their model more in terms of thinking *patterns* than errors in thinking and noted that no single pattern or group of patterns is causal; their perspective is that these patterns represent features in criminal thinking that are often unrecognized as patterns or errors by those engaged in criminal behavior. Although 52 distinct thinking patterns emerge from their work, the model is essentially comprised of (a) patterned attitudes, (b) patterned and automatic responses, and (c) patterned ways in which thinking errors are transformed into action. Focused on a criminogenic model, the thinking error model is similar to a cognitive distortion model, which uses mental health as its frame of reference. Either way, the terms and ideas are largely interchangeable and describe the same cognitive process by which individuals build their attitudes, beliefs, and behaviors on irrational or inaccurate ideas (cognitions) and preconscious patterns of automatic thinking and schemata.

Blending the criminogenic thinking error model with the mental health–

based cognitive distortion model, automatic thoughts and negative internal scripts form the basis for negative and irrational thoughts that lead to self-defeating beliefs and ineffectual behaviors, inappropriate and antisocial thoughts that allow for the victimization of others, or both. In both cases, cognitive distortions are generated spontaneously and are the result of consistent and automatic irrational thinking, or negative internal scripts that are self-reinforcing and always have negative consequences. In the mental health model they have negative consequences for the individual; in the criminogenic model they have negative consequences for others. In the combined forensic mental health model, cognitive distortions have both self-defeating and antisocial consequences.

This process is described in Chapter 13 and essentially involves a linear connection between an initiating event (in sexual-offender-specific treatment, usually called a *trigger*), an automatic thought, and a subsequent behavior. In a thinking errors–cognitive distortions model, the middle step (automatic thought) involves a negative or irrational thought based on a negative internal script, which results in a negative behavior. In turn, the behavioral outcome serves to reinforce negative automatic thoughts and thus creates a dysfunctional cognitive-behavioral cycle. This sequence is illustrated in Figure 16.2, which depicts both the positive and negative cognitive-behavioral cycles.

Thinking errors allow the development of assumptions, beliefs, attitudes, relationships, and behaviors that are self-defeating, self-destructive, or destructive to others. They are built on feelings and ideas that are inaccurate, incomplete, or irrational or that in some way rationalize unhealthy and inap-

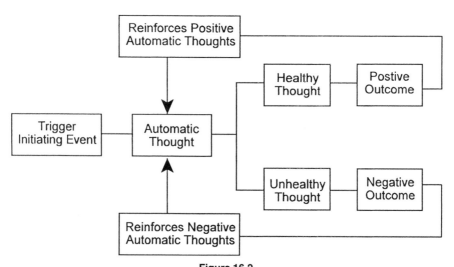

Figure 16.2
The cognitive-behavioral cycle.

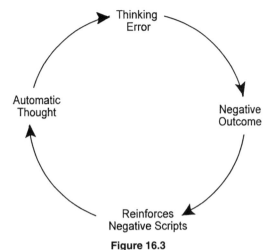

Figure 16.3
The self-reinforcing cycle of thinking errors.

propriate behaviors. As shown in Figure 16.2, like dysfunctional behavioral cycles, thinking errors are also cyclical and negatively self-reinforcing, often hampering the development of self-esteem. Thinking errors or cognitive distortions are built on *and* lead to misapprehension and misinterpretation, faulty assumptions and misbeliefs, inappropriate or poor decisions, and ultimately self-fulfilling prophecies of disappointment, personal failure, or the failure of others—thus recreating, reinforcing, and maintaining the experiences and feelings on which thinking errors are built in the first place. This specific cycle is shown in Figure 16.3. The cycle of thinking errors can be interrupted only when people understand how they respond to situations and learn how to recognize and change their irrational thoughts and beliefs to thoughts and beliefs that are more rational and realistic.

Juvenile sexual offender treatment helps clients understand the concepts of thinking errors and recognize cognitive distortions in their everyday thinking and provides tools for correcting thinking errors, replacing cognitive distortions with correct thinking and subsequently acting on rational, correct, and positive cognitions that are self-fulfilling and prosocial (or, at least, not self-defeating or harmful to others).

Types of Thinking Errors

There are many different ways to describe and understand thinking errors. However, in the forensic mental health model, thinking errors fuel both antisocial and self-defeating behaviors and fall into one of three groups:

- *Type 1 Thinking Errors: Unwilling to Accept Responsibility.* These cognitive distortions allow people to abdicate responsibility for their behaviors.

- *Type 2 Thinking Errors: Self-Defeating.* These cognitive distortions hamper personal growth and self-esteem.
- *Type 3 Thinking Errors: Narcissistic (or, "Me, Me, Me").* These cognitive distortions focus the attention of individuals solely onto themselves.

Combined, these thinking errors result in a series of highly interactive cognitions that include self-defeating, self-destructive, relationally disconnected, and antisocial thoughts, beliefs, and attitudes that lead directly to similarly negative behaviors. In turn, such behaviors negatively influence the experiences, beliefs, and ideas that reinforce and generate still more thinking errors. The object of treatment is to recognize and interrupt this sequence of negative thoughts and behaviors and help the juvenile replace them with rational and accurate ideas that lead to socially appropriate and self-potentiating behaviors and experiences and hence interrupt and escape the negatively self-reinforcing cycle.

Type 1 Thinking Errors: Unwilling to Accept Responsibility
- *Denial.* The individual pretends it did not happen and might even try to fool himself into thinking it did not happen. If he denies it ever happened, maybe it will go away.
- *Shifting the focus.* The individual tries to turn people's minds and attention onto something else to distract them from the real issue.
- *Blaming others.* The individual blames the problem and his own behavior on someone or something else.
- *Blaming the victim.* The individual blames the victim as though he were not at fault and somehow the victim brought it on him- or herself.
- *Intellectualization.* The individual tries to use ideas and intellect to sidetrack issues and out-think the opposition, finding excuses and explanations.
- *Innocence and playing dumb.* The individual acts as though he did not know it was wrong or against the rules or pretends that he did not know better.
- *Rationalization.* The individual finds reasons, explanations, and excuses for what he did.
- *Justification.* The individual finds reasons to explain the "correctness" of what he did, as though it were okay.
- *Minimization.* The individual downplays the importance of what happened or of its meaning.
- *Dismissal.* The individual disregards, ignores, or brushes aside what happened or other people's feelings as though they do not matter.
- *Angelic thinking.* This is a victim stance in which the individual portrays himself as a wonderful person incapable of breaking the rules or harming someone.

Type 2 Thinking Errors: Self-Defeating
- *Catastrophic thinking.* The individual magnifies the impact of negative experiences to extreme proportions.
- *Hopelessness.* The individual assumes that nothing will ever work out and that things will always go wrong.
- *Overgeneralization.* Something goes wrong in one situation, and the individual applies it to all situations.
- *Black-and-white thinking.* The individual sees things as all or nothing: Things are either one way or the other.
- *Oughts, shoulds, and musts.* The individual feels that life ought to be a certain way, that he should do something, or that things must go the way he wants them to.
- *Negative predictions and fortune-telling.* The individual predicts failure in situations yet to happen because things have gone wrong before.
- *Projection.* The individual makes negative assumptions about the thoughts, intentions, or motives of another person, which are often projections of his own thoughts and feelings about the situation.
- *Mind reading.* The individual feels that others should know how he feels or what he wants even though he does not tell them.
- *Labeling.* The individual labels himself or someone else negatively, which shapes the way he sees himself or that other person, often for simplistic reasons.
- *Personalization.* The individual treats a negative event as a personal reflection or confirmation of his own worthlessness.
- *Negative focus.* The individual focuses mainly on negative events, memories, or implications while ignoring more neutral or positive information about himself or about a situation.
- *Avoidance.* The individual avoids thinking about emotionally difficult subjects because they feel overwhelming or insurmountable.
- *Emotional misreasoning.* The individual draws an irrational and incorrect conclusion based on the way he feels at that moment.

Type 3 Thinking Errors: Narcissistic
- *Life is too hard.* The individual feels that life is just too unfair and that somehow owes him more.
- *Entitled.* The individual feels as though he deserves good things even if he does not have to work for them.
- *Victim stance.* The individual feels as though he is the victim of the whole world and as though he is the one who has been harmed.
- *Grandiose.* The individual feels as though he is better or more important than other people or as though others should and do look up to him.
- *Revenge.* The individual feels as though he has been wronged and is allowed (or entitled) to get his revenge.

- *Personalization.* The individual feels that the rules are applied only to him, instead of everyone, and that people and things are against him personally.
- *One-upsmanship.* The individual feels he has to do better than everyone else and show everyone that he is the best.

Cognitive Distortions as Errors in Ideas, Beliefs, and Attitudes

Cognition is not limited to ideas but also includes beliefs and attitudes. A thinking error model includes not only thoughts, ideas, and plans that enter someone's head but also beliefs about self and others and the way the world is or should be. Fitting with a model of thinking errors as self-defeating, antisocial, or both, these beliefs can be self-harming or harmful to others.

However, beliefs can be considered to be thinking errors only in light of the surrounding culture or subculture. Beliefs become thinking errors because they are out of sync with that culture and, more to the point, are judged by the culture to be out of sync. For instance, a belief that men are entitled to take what they want from women, or that they are in some way superior, is today considered to be incorrect thinking; if linked to male aggression against women, in a criminogenic model this belief would be considered and treated as a thinking error. This was not always the case, however, and in many circles today men are still considered dominant and entitled. Understanding cognitive distortions in the beliefs that lie beneath behavior is of enormous importance, as well as understanding the family, peer, community, and ethnic cultures to which the individual belongs and which have served both to shape beliefs and to lend validity to them. Here, we see a social psychology–anthropology approach to understanding the belief form of the cognitive distortion.

Attitudes are closely linked to beliefs. Attitudes may be more subtle than beliefs and are perhaps not capable of such clear distinction. Whereas beliefs can often be articulated and are a reflection of the things held to be true or false, attitudes are often more subtle. They include often-unstated perceptions about the world and people and a complex interaction among beliefs, values, and ideas, and a cognitive orientation toward particular things. We talk about good attitudes or bad attitudes, but when self-deprecating attitudes lead to self-defeating behavior or negative and hostile attitudes lead to aggression, we consider them to be another variant of a cognitive distortion. Ideas, beliefs, and attitudes are all cognitive mind-sets, or schemata, and these provide the material for the automatic thoughts behind the cognitive distortion and lend themselves toward the conditioned behavioral responses that result from such thinking errors.

Consequently, we want to help youths recognize errors not just in their thinking or their ideas but also in the beliefs and attitudes that accompany and frequently lead directly to those ideas. Most typically, scales and inventories (often nonpsychometric in design) are used to measure attitudes and beliefs, which can provide a useful feedback tool for juveniles in treatment. In their book on the assessment of sexual abuse, Prentky and Edmunds (1997) provided several examples of such instruments. However, many of these scales are designed for use with adults and cannot appropriately be applied to juveniles. This is particularly true for those instruments that were normed on an adult population.

THE COGNITIVE MAP AND COGNITIVE RESTRUCTURING

Cognitive distortions emerge from a deeper level of automatic thought. The cognitive map is the underlying preconscious schema that consists of interlocking sets of beliefs, ideas, and experiences about the world and on which ideas and action are built. At this level lie the cognitive scripts that define specific decisions and actions taken in response to different situations and stimuli. Part of the cognitive map that steers the juvenile sexual offender, these scripts represent built-in and implicit assumptions and theories about the world (Ward & Hudson, 2000a, 2000b). Decisions based on such implicit ideas are virtually automatic and are fast, effortless, and almost intuitive. They represent internal maps, or the bedrock of thinking errors.

This level of preconscious thought is the clear target in psychodynamic treatment but also exists as a target in cognitive-behavioral therapy. Here, the goal is to get beyond naming and identifying thinking errors to unlocking preconscious thoughts and bringing them to the surface, where they can be deconstructed and reconstructed. This is the process of *cognitive structuring*, in which the goal is to break down automatic ideas and behaviors, reframe them, and consequently restructure them in healthier and prosocial ways that empower the individual and, in the case of antisocial behavior, make the world safer for others.

COGNITIVE DISTORTIONS AND SEXUAL OFFENSES

In a more complex model that conceptualizes the interaction between thinking errors and sexually aggressive behavior, there are three stages of cognitive distortions, each of which is directly connected to the offense. In such a pathological cycle, cognitive distortions fuel and justify behavioral dysfunctions, which in turn support and maintain further cognitive distortions, as shown in Figure 16.4.

- *Stage 1. Preoffense Cognitive Distortions: Contributing and Leading.* Critical to the sexual offense are those thinking errors that contribute to a sexual offense. These are the ideas, beliefs, and attitudes that mix thoughts and feelings together and move the individual toward sexually aggressive

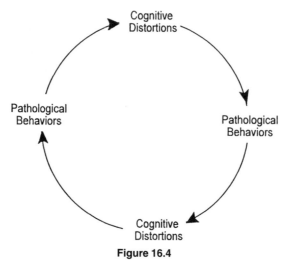

Figure 16.4
The cognitive distortion–pathological behavioral cycle.

behaviors, setting the groundwork for and justifying the movement toward sexually aggressive behavior.

- *Stage 2. In-Offense Cognitive Distortions: Allowing and Supporting.* In most cases, the mind does not switch off during the offense itself, with no recognition of right or wrong. Thinking errors not only drive the offense in the first place but also support the offense while it is occurring.
- *Stage 3. Postoffense Cognitive Distortions: Justifying and Strengthening.* These are the thinking errors that continue to develop and evolve after the offense. In any model where remorse, shame, or some other form of social conscience does not kick in to reshape the offender's experience of the offense, thinking errors serve to justify the offense, reinforce the behavior, and strengthen the offending behavior and, indeed, the thinking errors themselves.

These cognitive distortions derive from the same list of thinking errors but are qualitatively different based on the role they play in the various developmental stages of the sexual offense—from the development of an offense scenario, to the execution of the offense and maintaining offense behaviors during the assault, to justifying and further integrating an offending mind-set in the individual offender. This particular sequence of stages and the resulting self-reinforcing cycle are shown in Figure 16.5.

WORKING WITH COGNITIVE DISTORTIONS

The role of the treatment team is to teach these concepts and models to juvenile sexual offenders and test for their acquisition. Of greater importance,

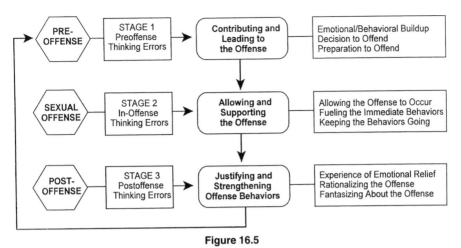

Figure 16.5
Stages of cognitive distortions in the sexual assault cycle.

though, is the therapeutic work done with individual youths and groups to ensure that clients understand these ideas, how they have developed within them and where they come from, and how to apply techniques and methods to recognize thinking errors and overcome them.

The aim of cognitive-behavioral treatment is to uncover the cognitive map, or implicit assumptions, on which cognitive distortions and antisocial behaviors are built. This is a difficult target to reach, however. The goal is not simply the rote memorization of ideas and terminology, but the actual unlocking (a rather abstract psychodynamic concept) of a preawareness level of automatic functioning, bringing it to a level of conscious awareness and reprogramming it. This requires a great deal of work, effort, repetition, and practice on the part of both the client and the clinician. The first task is to instill or activate in the juvenile a recognition of the harm caused and a genuine desire to want to change. This notion, or extratherapeutic client factor, is central to all treatment, including the psychoeducational or cognitive-behavioral aspect.

DYSFUNCTIONAL BEHAVIORS AND THE BEHAVIORAL CYCLE

Beyond thinking errors, there is a focus on dysfunctional behavioral patterns in juvenile sexual offenders in which cognitive distortions are thought to fuel the thoughts and ideas that lead to dysfunctional behavior. However, in a cyclical or linear model of behavioral dysfunction, thinking errors occur at a later point in the sequence that begins with an initiating event.

The belief that juvenile sexual offenders and other troubled children demonstrate patterns of dysfunctional behavior is neither new nor complex. Like the thinking errors model, these behavioral patterns can be seen as linear progressions in which one thing leads to another until a negative behavior occurs, or as repetitive cycles of behavior that persist until interrupted. This dysfunctional behavioral cycle is the most commonly accepted and typically used model in the treatment of juvenile sexual offenders and is also closely connected to the model of relapse prevention planning.

In sexual-offender-specific treatment, the dysfunctional behavioral cycle is often referred to as the sexual assault cycle, in which the negative behavior is the sexual offense. However, the model is limited, especially in cases where there has been only a single episode of sexually abusive behavior. A broader dysfunctional behavioral cycle is more adaptable to all forms of antisocial and negative behavior, and sexually abusive behavior fits easily into the model.

The Behavioral Cycle

The behavioral cycle provides a simple way to describe, illustrate, and teach the relationship between triggering events and interactions, feelings and emotions, thoughts and ideas, and behaviors (in this case, sexual offending behaviors). Although a behavioral cycle that focuses specifically on sexual offending provides more detail and distinct moments and opportunities to examine each step of the cycle and the elements that contribute and add up to sexual offending behavior, the cycle is a simple concept, illustrated in Figure 16.6:

- *Triggering event.* The behavioral cycle starts with a situation or an event that serves as a trigger to a feeling-thought-behavior sequence.
- *Feeling/emotional response.* The event triggers an emotional response.
- *Thoughts and ideas.* The feelings and emotions trigger a cognitive response, or thoughts, ideas, beliefs, or attitudes.

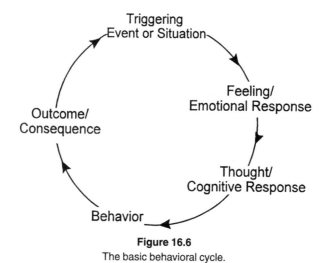

Figure 16.6
The basic behavioral cycle.

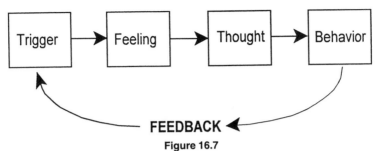

Figure 16.7
A linear model of the behavioral sequence.

- *Behavior.* Thoughts and ideas lead to a behavior or action of some kind.
- *Outcomes.* All behaviors have outcomes, results, and consequences .
- *New event.* Behavioral outcomes feed back into and help shape the next situation or event.
- *Triggering event.* The new event triggers a new cycle of event-feeling-thought-behavior-outcome-event.

Linear Steps in the Cyclical Behavioral Sequence

Although the behavioral cycle is most commonly used, it is just as relevant to describe the individual steps that make up the behavioral cycle in a linear, stepwise fashion. That is, the triggering event leads to a feeling, then a thought, and then a behavior. The response to the behavior, or the *feedback*, may turn the linear sequence into a cycle, as depicted in Figure 16.7. Certain types of feedback reinforce the linear steps (positive reinforcement) and lead to repetition of the behavior, turning the linear sequence into a cycle.

The Behavioral Cycle: A Warning

Cycles, of course, are only metaphors intended to clarify, simplify, and demonstrate the relationship among behaviors and behavioral reinforcers; mind-sets that accompany and lead to behavior; emotional responses that interact with and influence cognition; and environmental stimuli that initiate emotions and cognitions in the first place. They are a useful tool to help the treatment team and youths conceptualize behavioral chains and link them to events, feelings, and ideas. However, they lose their value when children and staff begin to depend on behavioral cycles as a way to explain all behavior at all times.

Furthermore, cycles are abstract interpretations of reality, and even a simple cycle model may be too complex for some youths. Consequently, cycle models are not for every juvenile, especially cognitively impaired children, younger children, or juveniles whose thinking is highly concrete and rigid. Cycles, as well as the cognitive processing work that often goes along with the model, also should not take the place of a more informed discussion of behaviors, behavioral motivators, and behavioral outcomes.

There are any number of variants on the behavioral cycle, published in various books and workbooks and in use in many programs. Some of these are particularly complex, whereas others that are quite simple nonetheless force fit every individual into the same sequence of events and outcomes. These cycle models not only assume the same process for every juvenile sexual offender but also use set labels and descriptions that may not fit a given situation. Moreover, highly defined cycles like this fail to make sense to many children who are required to describe and explain their behavior in terms of the cycle, and the intervention and learning opportunity becomes more an assignment than a meaningful treatment intervention. Staff who are exposed to these highly defined cycles may also start to think that behaviors can only be explained in the terms provided by the cycle template and therefore begin to forget that the cycle is merely a metaphor, thus losing or never developing their ability to use the cycle as a means to an end, and not the end itself.

The Dysfunctional Behavioral Cycle

Having warned that the model is a tool that is not intended to replace therapy, that has no value by itself, and that is contraindicated in some cases as too abstract or complex, it is also important to recognize that a behavioral cycle (or linear step sequence) is neither necessarily positive nor negative. It can just as easily be used to explain positive behavior. Cycles are only simplistic explanations of behaviors and behavioral influences and reinforcers. However, in our work with juvenile sexual offenders, we focus on negative behavioral cycles—that is, cycles of triggers and responses that lead to negative and acting-out behaviors. These are referred to as dysfunctional behavioral cycles.

Phases of the Dysfunctional Cycle

Despite cycle models that prescribe highly defined sequences, often clearly describing the experiences, emotions, thoughts, and intentions that sexual abusers are expected to pass through on their way to a reoffense (Carich, Gray Rombouts, Stone, & Pithers, 2001; Freeman-Longo, 1989; Lane, 1997b; G. Ryan, 1999a; Way & Spieker, 1997), it is very unlikely that most individuals pass through such a defined and uniform process. Even if it were true for most adult sexual offenders, it may not be true for juveniles. Although it is reasonably certain that all individuals pass through a sequence of emotional and cognitive experiences en route to a behavior, it is unwise to suggest that all individuals pass through the same sequence.

Instead, the cycle is one tool to help juveniles connect their history, triggers, feelings, thoughts, and behaviors. Every individual will pass through a behavioral cycle in a different way, unique to his particular circumstances and psychological makeup. Thus, it is useful to think of behavioral cycles as having definite phases through which individuals pass. A phase model allows for both *individuality* (the reality that juveniles have different experiences as they pass through their particular cycles) and *common experiences* (all cycles de-

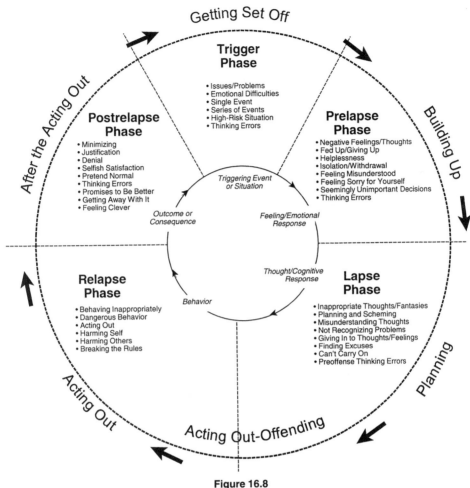

Figure 16.8

The phases of the dysfunctional behavioral cycle, with examples of feelings, thoughts, and behaviors within each phase.

velop essentially the same way, and all individuals pass through essentially the same phases of development).

Figure 16.8 shows a phased cycle with the basic cycle of event-feeling-thought-behavior-outcome-event at the center (Figure 16.6) and the phases attached to and surrounding each step in the process. Shown within each phase are the sorts of experiences and activities typical of that phase, although each individual has a different experience during each phase.

- *Phase 1: The Trigger Phase (Getting Set Off).* This phase represents the initiating event and can last for a moment or many weeks. The trigger is that thing, or series of things, that upsets or excites a youth and sets off a negative behavioral cycle.

- *Phase 2: The Prelapse Phase (Building Up).* During this phase things start to go wrong for the youth: negative thoughts or feelings, anger, self-doubt, depression, loneliness, or feeling misunderstood, frustrated, or self-pity. Things build up inside of the youth, and if not caught and interrupted, these thoughts and feelings can lead to the next phase of the cycle.
- *Phase 3: The Lapse Phase (Planning).* A lapse occurs when youths have inappropriate thoughts, urges, fantasies, and other ideas about behaving inappropriately. During this phase juveniles start to think about and plan negative or inappropriate behaviors. The lapse phase is that time soon or immediately before the youth's thinking turns into negative behavior, and it is critical that youths spot these lapses in their thinking because they signal the possibility of a relapse.
- *Phase 4: The Relapse Phase (Acting Out).* Acting out occurs when youths return to negative or problematic behaviors, and relapse occurs when they act out in old, familiar patterns. The relapse is a return to patterns of inappropriate or negative behaviors. In the case of sexual offending, a relapse means returning to sexual offending behaviors.
- *Phase 5: Postrelapse Phase (After the Acting Out).* After youths relapse, or act out, they enter the postrelapse phase, in which they experience many thoughts, feelings, and other things that keep the cycle going. Instead of interrupting the cycle before they behave dangerously again, they find all sorts of ways to avoid dealing with what they have done.

Interrupting and Escaping the Cycle

As youths are taught to recognize thinking errors and components and phases of the behavioral cycle, they are enabled to interrupt the progression and further development of the process and thereby escape the cycle. Like everything in the treatment of troubled children, of course, this is easier recognized, spoken about, and practiced in group and individual therapy. Actually escaping a behavioral cycle is carried out not in group, a workbook exercise, or a written relapse prevention, but in everyday application.

Juvenile sexual offenders experience and engage in far more general behavioral difficulties than they do sexual reoffenses. It is in this arena of their everyday lives that they can truly put into effect and practice the ideas learned in psychoeducational treatment, and through the application of these ideas that clinicians can judge how well their clients are learning the ideas and learning to use them. Practice makes perfect!

Processing the Behavioral Cycle

Youths in treatment who work with the behavior cycle are often expected to understand not just the cycle but also how it applies to them. This is especially true when they are expected to use the cycle model to work through and understand their problem behaviors. This is sometimes referred to as *processing the cycle,* in which youths are expected to use the cycle to describe and make

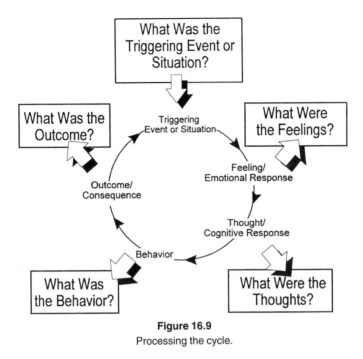

Figure 16.9
Processing the cycle.

sense of their emotions, thoughts, and behaviors by working through their cycle and its various components, as shown in Figure 16.9.

Cycle Work Materials

Any behavioral cycle model can be developed into workbooks or worksheets and used with great frequency. However, this makes it easy to depend on workbooks (the psychoeducational-workbook approach to treatment, shown in Figure 16.1) and risks turning treatment into the standardized completion of worksheets. Processing the cycle requires a clinical approach so that the experience is therapeutic and meaningful.

The advantage of using workbooks, however, is that treatment can be extended outside of individual and group treatment sessions, and juveniles can be held responsible for their own treatment. In addition, in residential programs in particular, nonclinical staff can work with juveniles on the materials, extending treatment to other members of the treatment team. In addition, workbook materials can be customized to meet the needs of individual treatment programs and the needs of individual youths in treatment.

Alternatives to the Cycle

The cycle should be used to enhance and supplement treatment work, rather than substitute for the clinical work, whether cognitive-behavioral or psychodynamic. In addition, the cycle model is not for everyone but should be re-designed for youths who have more concrete learning needs or who are too young to make use of the model, or avoided altogether.

It is possible to create a similar, but noncyclical, model that outlines the steps and sequences involved in dysfunctional behaviors and poor decision making in a more easily understood linear model. For instance, a stairway model or ladder is often employed with younger children or cognitively im-paired individuals to illustrate the sequential and progressive process of events, emotions, thoughts, and decisions that lead to action. Models like these may be more effective in teaching the concept that behavior is linked to triggers through the mediators of experience, emotion, and cognition. How-ever, a simpler diagram is not enough. The concepts, as well as the words and terms used to describe the concepts, must also be simpler, more concrete, and more direct.

OTHER RELATED TERMS AND CONCEPTS

Thinking errors, behavioral cycle, and relapse prevention models (Chapter 17) are closely related—and, in fact, interrelated. Thinking errors lead to dys-functional behavioral cycles and play a significant role throughout. Similarly, cognitive distortions themselves are cyclical in their self-reinforcement and replication. Relapse prevention plans are built on both recognizing and avoid-ing thinking errors and are intended as a method for escaping or interrupting dysfunctional behavioral cycles that otherwise lead to relapse.

In addition to thinking errors, cycles, and relapse prevention plans, there are a number of important and related terms and concepts. These contribute to understanding both the behavioral cycle or a linear behavioral model and the development of the relapse prevention plan. Although there are variants on these ideas, they generally have similar names and similar meanings. To-gether they add up to a language of shorthand markers that can help juveniles learn to recognize problem areas and how to avoid or negotiate them, thus either interrupting and escaping their cycle before it progresses too far or avoiding it completely. Accordingly, these few ideas are enormously useful tools for those juveniles who have the cognitive capacity to understand them (as well as recognize when and how to use them), the emotional and behav-ioral control required to apply them, and the desire and commitment to mo-tivate and ensure their use. The goal is to use the concepts to develop these skills, but youths must first be ready, willing, and able to use the tools before they can have value.

Lapses and Relapses. A lapse signifies a return to dysfunctional thinking and is a potential precursor to a relapse, or a return to the dysfunctional behavior. In a substance abuse model, a lapse includes thoughts or cravings for the substance or the actual acquisition of the substance. Relapse occurs when the substance is used. In reality, however, it is sometimes difficult to distinguish between a lapse and a relapse. For instance, is the actual purchase of drugs in itself a relapse, and does one sip of beer count as a lapse or a relapse? In sexual offending, lapse represents the urges and fantasies that edge juvenile sexual offenders toward a possible sexual offense. It also includes behaviors that may themselves be considered relapse, such as isolating a planned victim or preparing for a sexual assault. Lapse thinking and behavior are connected to and are precursors to relapse, and we want to help offenders recognize such thinking *before* they relapse.

Seemingly Unimportant Decisions (SUDs). Often important factors in dysfunctional behavioral cycles, these are the decisions that people make in the course of their daily lives that seem unimportant at the time but later add up to significant problems and steps along the dysfunctional cycle. These are also sometimes known as seemingly irrelevant decisions (SIDs) and apparently irrelevant decisions (AIDs).

Triggers, Dangerous Situations, and High-Risk Factors. Another critical element in any problematic behavioral cycle is the trigger. Triggers set off a problem sequence. These are the people, relationships, interactions, situations, or other things that trigger a problem sequence of events or begin a cycle. Triggers and dangerous situations (DSs) are similar. If the trigger is the thing that initiates an emotional response, the DS is the environment or circumstances in which the trigger occurs. Dangerous situations are also known as high-risk situations (HRSs), and the elements that can act as triggers or lead to trouble are referred to a high-risk factors (HRFs). Situations and circumstances that we know can initiate a series of emotions and thoughts can get out of control and lead to behaviors that are dangerous for the juvenile and others. Escape techniques are very important, but it is more important for the youth to recognize and avoid dangerous HRSs and HRFs *before* they trigger a dysfunctional behavioral cycle. Accordingly, we want to teach youths how to recognize their particular triggers and avoid those HRFs that put them in jeopardy of beginning a problematic behavioral cycle.

Escapes and Interruptions. In any model that includes a sequence of steps that pass from trigger to relapse, there is the opportunity to escape the sequence at any point by recognizing the dangerous path that is being followed. In effect, escaping the sequence amounts to the same thing as interrupting the sequence, in which the sequence is broken, thus avoiding the otherwise inevitable outcome of relapse, or behavioral dyscontrol.

Denial. Denial has many faces. Offenders can deny that the event occurred at all or deny their part in the offense. Other forms of denial are much more prevalent, however, especially in young offenders. These include playing

```
Denial of . . .
    Abuse . . . . . . . . . . . . . . . It was consensual; it wasn't abusive.
    Awareness . . . . . . . . . . . I didn't realize anyone would be hurt.
    Deviancy  . . . . . . . . . . . I only have appropriate sexual feelings and fantasies.
    Facts  . . . . . . . . . . . . . . I didn't do it; it wasn't me.
    Fantasies . . . . . . . . . . . I only fantasize to normative sexual fantasies.
    Frequency  . . . . . . . . . . It only happened once.
    Harm  . . . . . . . . . . . . . . No one got hurt; it was no big deal.
    Impact  . . . . . . . . . . . . . S/he's no worse for it; s/he'll get over it.
    Intensity . . . . . . . . . . . . I only did one thing.
    Intent  . . . . . . . . . . . . . . I didn't mean anything by it; I was just curious.
    Knowledge . . . . . . . . . . I didn't know it was wrong.
    Meaning   . . . . . . . . . . . It doesn't mean anything.
    Planning . . . . . . . . . . . . It just happened.
    Problem  . . . . . . . . . . . . It happened, but I don't really have a problem.
    Reality  . . . . . . . . . . . . . It won't happen again.
    Recollection . . . . . . . . . I don't remember.
    Responsibility   . . . . . . . It wasn't my fault.
    Seriousness . . . . . . . . . It wasn't such a bad thing.
    Significance   . . . . . . . . It didn't do much harm.
    Wrongdoing . . . . . . . . . There's nothing wrong with what happened.
```

Figure 16.10
Forms of denial.

down the significance of the offense, its reality, the intent, or the harm done. Here, there is an *emotional* level of denial in which the facts are not disputed but denial is an attempt to ward off the emotional reality of the behavior in terms of its impact on others or as a reflection on self or future behaviors. Sometimes, these forms of emotional denial are referred to as *pretend normal*. Examples of different types of denial are shown in Figure 16.10.

Denial in its most basic form—and the most critical form to overcome in treatment and the form on which treatment is then built—is probably best exemplified in the first step of any Alcoholics Anonymous–style 12-step model: "We admitted that our lives had become unmanageable." In the 12-step model for the treatment of juvenile sexual offenders described in Chapter 12, the first step for the youth is the ability and willingness to recognize and admit that he has a problem. Without such a recognition, treatment is built on some form of denial instead of on the groundwork provided by acknowledgment and personal responsibility.

With respect to the much discussed and rather confusing finding of the Hanson and Bussière (1998) meta-analysis that denial is not a critical factor in offense recidivism, Hanson (personal communication, April 11, 2002) reported that the term can be considered more appropriately to reflect minimization than categorical denial. In addition, Lund (2000) noted that most of the offenders in total denial were not included as subjects in the meta-analysis in the first place.

Although successful treatment is based on acknowledgment and the personal responsibility that accompanies acknowledgment and honesty and denial is antithetical to treatment, many variants on denial exist, as noted. In many ways, denial serves as an important defense mechanism for individuals, and perhaps especially for juveniles, in treatment. Although an important goal is to overcome denial, the goal is not to shame, confront, berate, or in any hostile manner force or drag the truth from the juvenile. Treatment is about engagement, interaction, and personal growth, not about interrogation and confession. The clinician must work with clients in individual and group therapy to help them overcome their denial, shame, and guilt and work through the process of accepting personal responsibility and engaging in deeper and more honest treatment.

Minimization. One way to deny the reality of a situation is to downplay or minimize its depth or breadth: It was no big deal; it didn't matter; it could've been worse. Minimizing is a way of avoiding the truth or the consequences, and as long as clients minimize, they are not only avoiding the consequences but also in a significant way failing to acknowledge the meaning of the behavior and hence failing to engage meaningfully in treatment. Denial and minimization are both ways to avoid pain, but treatment often requires that the juvenile sexual offender experiences deeply emotional pain, in part as the result of confronting both his own behaviors and treatment of others and his experience of how he has been treated by others, as well as self-image and sense of personal identity.

Abstinence Violation Effect. This is a complex way of saying that when someone in recovery engages in significant lapses or actual relapses, they give up. That is, the violation of abstinence leads to a deepening of relapse behaviors. Abstinence violation effect (AVE), also known as rule violation effect, is a potentially significant problem because once an offender gives up, he falls back into disturbed patterns of thinking and behaviors and perhaps decides that he is, indeed, an offender, that treatment does not work, and that he cannot succeed, and other forms of cognitive distortions that drive dysfunctional ideas and behaviors deepen and become more frozen. The antidote for AVE is teaching those in recovery that they may slip (major lapse or minor relapse) and even relapse but that escape or interruption is still possible in order to prevent still more relapses. This can be built into a relapse prevention plan. The difficulty is that in teaching this message, we do not want to suggest that relapse is acceptable or inevitable, because in the case of a sexual offender, relapse means a sexual assault. We do want to teach that regardless of future behaviors, some slips may be inevitable and all are recoverable—but they will also have consequences.

Figure 16.11
The reoffense chain. Reproduced with permission of Charlene Steen (1993).

The Reoffense Chain. SUDs, DSs, and HRFs add up to dangerous waters for children and adolescents who have already engaged in sexual offending behaviors. They represent the potential first steps to *re*offending and thus must be recognized and avoided. SUDs and DSs are dangerous because they put kids who have sexually offended into situations where they may have the opportunity to offend again or raise the temptation to engage in offending behaviors. This is the potential start of a relapse chain, or a series of linked events that could eventually result in a sexual offense. In an alternative to the dysfunctional behavioral cycle, Charlene Steen (1993) described this chain as a sequence of interrelated steps leading from abstinence (not offending) to sexual reoffense, as shown in Figure 16.11.

The Trauma Outcome Process. This model (Rasmussen, 2002; Rasmussen et al., 1992) is often cited and used in work with juvenile sexual offenders, although is intended for children ages 4 through 12 who are defined as sexually reactive. The trauma outcome process distinguishes among behavior that is self-destructive, abusive to others, healthy and adaptive, or recovery based.

The trauma outcome process is an integrated model blending psychodynamic ideas and processes with cognitive-behavioral concepts and methods. It is based on the idea that sexually reactive children who are themselves victims of abuse or maltreatment ultimately resolve the internal conflicts caused by trauma by (a) internalizing them and becoming self-destructive, (b) exter-

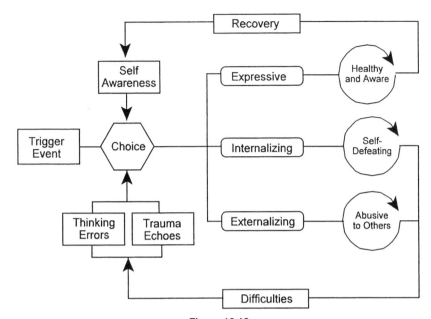

Figure 16.12
The trauma outcome process. Adapted from Rasmussen (2002).

nalizing and becoming abusive to others, or (c) expressing their emotions and becoming self-aware, thus finding a healthy path to emotional recovery. Each path itself leads to a mini self-reinforcing cycle and is precipitated by a choice made by the child to take one path or another. The goal of treatment is to use both psychodynamic and cognitive-behavioral therapy to teach awareness and help children recognize that unhealthy choices are based on thinking errors that justify negative choices and *trauma echoes,* or the emotional and cognitive vestiges of earlier trauma in the life of the child. The trauma echoes are internalized ideas about self and others, or implicit assumptions, embedded into preconsciousness by the trauma process. The model is summarized in Figure 16.12.

Four Factors–Four Preconditions Model. Finkelhor's (1984) description of the four factors and preconditions that determine child sexual abuse is another example of a model used to describe the specific behavior of one population (in this case, adult sexual offenders of children) applied to another (juvenile sexual offenders). The model was developed to explain adult and not juvenile behavior, and it is specifically directed toward adult child molesters and not adult rapists. Implicit in the model is that adults who offend children face and must overcome different obstacles to child abuse than juveniles who engage in similar behaviors. Nevertheless, it is often applied to juvenile offenders as well and is a useful way to conceptualize the pathway to sexual offending.

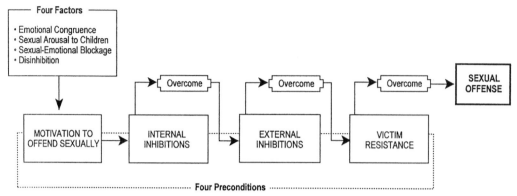

Figure 16.13
Four factors–four preconditions model of child sexual molestation.
Adapted from Finkelhor (1984).

As illustrated in Figure 16.13, in order for an adult sexual offense against a child to occur, four preconditions must be met; these are fueled by four factors that must also be present.

Four Factors

1. *Emotional Congruence.* There is a fit between the emotional needs of the offender and the sexual or other characteristics of the child that makes the act of child sexual molestation congruent and satisfying.
2. *Sexual arousal to children.* The offender must find the child or the idea of sexual contact with the child sexually arousing.
3. *Sexual-emotional blockage.* The offender is blocked from other means of sexual and sexual-emotional gratification.
4. *Disinhibition.* Conventional inhibitors against sexual arousal to or sexual contact with children are overridden or nonexistent, and sexual interest is thereby disinhibited.

Four Preconditions

1. *Motivation to offend sexually.* The offender must experience a level of motivation sufficient enough to consider sexually molesting the child.
2. *Overcoming internal inhibitors.* The offender must overcome internal inhibitors and barriers that would normally act to prevent him from contemplating and certainly from committing such crimes.
3. *Overcoming external inhibitors.* The offender must next overcome environmental inhibitors and barriers that serve to protect victims from abuse and crime.
4. *Overcoming the resistance of the child.* Finally, the offender must find a way to engage the child in the sexual act, using means that range from the use of force to manipulative and nonthreatening coercion and trickery.

It is easy to see how this model can be applied to any sexual offender, adult or juvenile, and any victim, child or adult. It describes a pathway to offending based on personal characteristics (factors) interacting with situational variables (preconditions) to create a sexual offense outcome, much as pathways were described in Chapter 5.

The model offers a simple and parsimonious approach to both conceptualizing sexual offending behaviors and teaching the ideas to sexual offenders in treatment, helping them to recognize how these factors apply (or do not) to them and how they managed to overcome these preconditions in their sexual offenses. The cautionary notes are (a) that this is a model used to describe adult sexual offenses against children and (b) that it is a model only, and it does not match the factors, preconditions, and course of sexually offending faced by every juvenile sexual offender in his particular circumstances and offense history.

CONCLUSION: TOWARD RELAPSE PREVENTION

Taken together, the concepts described in this chapter present a language for both treatment staff and juveniles that is itself instructive. In addition, they are central to understanding and developing a relapse prevention plan.

However, as is true also of the relapse prevention planning process described in the following chapter, there is a risk that clients in treatment will learn to mimic what they are being taught, sometimes even fooling themselves into believing that they have actually acquired and can apply new information and ideas about themselves, their behaviors, and the world in which they live. For these ideas to be taught effectively, clinicians must ensure that they are understood and can be applied, rather than simply memorized and answered correctly in a workbook or described in a group. As is true for all aspects of treatment, the instruction of these ideas must be individualized to meet the real-life needs, learning style, and cognitive skills of each individual client. This may mean teaching kids individually or in dyads or small groups rather than in a larger group setting, or developing special materials geared to individuals or special populations, rather than depending on a one-size-fits-all approach.

CHAPTER 17

The Relapse Prevention Plan

THE RELAPSE prevention plan is a psychoeducational and cognitive-behavioral tool designed to help the offender operationalize his learning about the sexual assault cycle, thinking errors, coping skills, and alternatives to offending. The relapse prevention plan

- Identifies high-risk situations and relationships
- Names overwhelming feelings that signal or lead to inappropriate or unhealthy thoughts
- Helps the offender and others spot and correct thinking errors and deviant thinking that may lead to inappropriate or dangerous behavior
- Lists desired behavioral outcomes
- Identifies the consequences of inappropriate or dangerous behaviors
- Lists healthy and appropriate behavioral strategies that serve as alternatives to unhealthy or destructive behavior
- Describes effective coping activities and relationships
- Binds the offender to the plan through a ritual involving a relapse prevention–behavioral contract signed by the offender and other people instrumental to the plan or serving as witnesses to the relapse prevention plan

Ultimately, the relapse prevention plan serves as a tool to interrupt the cycles of thinking errors and sexual offending described in the last chapter and as a contract that has both practical and symbolic meaning. A critical part of the treatment process, and usually the final step prior to discharge from treatment and re-engagement in the community, the relapse prevention plan represents a problem recognition and avoidance plan. It is no different in concept from a safety plan for suicidal patients, an anger management plan for those whose major problems are episodic rages, or a substance abuse relapse prevention plan for alcohol or drug abusers. The difference is that in the case of the juvenile sexual offender, relapse equals sexual offending.

THE IDEAS OF RELAPSE PREVENTION PLANNING

Much of what is written about the relapse prevention model addresses philosophy, application, and research outcomes, but the relapse prevention plan itself, in whatever form it takes, is a simple idea. The relapse prevention plan is a behavioral plan designed to avoid or escape the event-emotion-cognition-behavior cycle and based on the three primary components of cognitive awareness, emotional regulation, and behavioral control.

The relapse prevention process is utilized throughout treatment with juvenile sexual offenders and in many treatment programs represents the core approach to treatment (Association for the Treatment of Sexual Abusers, 1996). The goal of such a model is to help offenders recognize the factors that trigger and lead to relapse—built largely on a combined thinking errors and behavioral cycle model—and develop the motivation and skills required to avoid or escape the reoffense chain. Burton and Smith-Darden (2001) referred to this model as a subset of cognitive-behavioral theories in which the focus of treatment is on specifying and modifying the sexual abuse cycle and the emotional-cognitive-behavioral chain and reported that 79% of outpatient and residential treatment programs for male adolescent sexual offenders utilize this approach far more than any other ("multiple interventions" are the next closest choice at 10–13% of programs), and more frequently in the case of female juvenile sexual offenders.

Nevertheless, the emphasis on the relapse prevention plan is more commonsense and optimistic than proven, and no definitive evidence exists that it is effective in reducing sexual offense recidivism and supporting abstinence from sexual offending behaviors (Laws et al., 2000). The U.S. General Accounting Office (1996) reported that there is no consensus about what treatment works to reduce the recidivism, and little is certain about whether, and to what extent, any form of treatment works. For these reasons, Laws (2001) denounced the manner in which the relapse prevention model has been so uncritically accepted by the treatment community and considered this acceptance to be one the model's greatest shortcomings because it has not further developed and has become institutionalized.

If we fail to remember this when developing relapse prevention plans, we risk fooling ourselves and the community into thinking that the relapse prevention plan is a proven tool that will ensure community safety. Nevertheless, just as the safety contract is important in working with suicidal patients who agree to sign such a contract, a relapse prevention plan is important for similar reasons. Such plans represent (a) an acknowledgment of risk, (b) a plan and means to keep safe, (c) a commitment to safety, and (d) a symbolic agreement that in itself may fulfill a treatment need. In many ways, the plan encompasses the extratherapeutic factors that the client brings into and takes out of therapy: the factor of hope and expectancy represented by the plan and the therapeutic alliance of which it is an extension. The relapse prevention plan also represents a treatment technique and thus is associated with each of the four factors common to effective therapy. When the relapse prevention plan is successful, it is more likely due to a combination of these factors than any individual factor alone, although in keeping with the model of common factors, the most significant factor is that introduced by the client (i.e., the amount of importance and investment he places on the process).

A relapse prevention plan model is best suited for individuals committed to treatment and abstinence from harmful behaviors and is best described as a means to maintain recovery, beginning from a stage of abstinence. The intention is to help maintain treatment gains (Nelson, Miner, Marques, Russell, & Achterkirchen, 1989) and provide a structure to ensure that a step-by-step process is available and that ongoing intervention is provided to ensure that treatment does not fall apart (Laws, 2001; Laws et al., 2000). In the case of sexual offending, relapse prevention is both a self-directed approach to safety and a process for ensuring outside monitoring and intervention. Although optimistically aiming at abstinence (from sexual aggression), relapse prevention is also a harm-reduction model (Stoner & George, 2000), allowing us to recognize that reduction of harm is an important—if not more realistic—approach to the role of relapse prevention planning in community safety, even in the absence of abstinence.

DEVELOPING THE RELAPSE PREVENTION PLAN

In the final analysis, whatever the feared relapse (substance abuse, rage, self-harm, or, in our case, sexual offending), a relapse prevention plan is intended to help clients stay in appropriate control of their behavior. It is intended to help the client recognize and avoid the sorts of situations and interactions that may set off a sequence of feelings, thoughts, and behaviors that may finally result in a relapse, or a return to the offending behavior.

Carich, Gray, Rombouts, Stone, and Pithers (2001) described the goals of relapse prevention as

- Ensuring that offenders gain a thorough understanding of the key concepts in sexual offender treatment and recidivism
- Teaching offenders effective methods for self-monitoring
- Teaching offenders and others how to identify specific cues that signal potential risk or recidivism
- Teaching offenders how to employ specific interventions to disrupt the relapse process

- Informing individuals in the offender's daily life of the relapse prevention plan so that they can assist and monitor the relapse prevention plan

Relapse prevention plans recognize both relapse, or the behavior to avoid, and lapses, which are thoughts of returning or intentions to return to the offending behavior. In any relapse prevention plan the offender can return to a safe state at any time by recognizing dangerous situations, high-risk factors, and lapses and by employing the coping skills identified in the plan, thus breaking the reoffense chain that leads to relapse. A relapse prevention plan usually involves

- Identifying high-risk situations, people, interactions, and relationships
- Listing ways to avoid, reduce, or eliminate high-risk situations, people, interactions, and relationships
- Identifying and understanding urges or cravings to return to target behaviors (prelapse or lapse phase)
- Establishing ways to recognize slips and lapses and signs of pending relapse
- Recognizing thinking errors that contribute to the relapse sequence
- Describing self-monitoring skills and techniques
- Identifying effective coping strategies, alternative behaviors, and stress reduction techniques
- Identifying key people and resources to turn to in the event of pending or actual lapse or relapse
- Promising to use named coping strategies, alternative behaviors, and stress reduction techniques
- Naming the consequences of relapses
- Describing how to recover from a relapse

ABSTINENCE VIOLATION EFFECT

As described in Chapter 16, abstinence violation effect (AVE) is an important factor in the implementation of the relapse prevention plan and must be addressed in the development of the plan. AVE is undoubtedly a major reason why individuals in recovery from substance abuse, on diets, involved in exercise regimens, and so on drop out of the rehabilitation program once they have broken the rules. AVE is another way of describing *giving up,* which is itself based on any number of cognitive distortions that both fail to recognize the ability to recover once again and allow the failure to maintain abstinence to serve as a go-ahead for further relapse behaviors. It is essential that the juvenile be able to recognize that lapse and relapse are of great concern but that he can recover before further harm is caused.

BUILDING EFFECTIVE RELAPSE PREVENTION PLANS

Building an effective plan means understanding why relapse prevention plans do not always succeed. Relapse prevention plans often fail because juveniles do not:

- Place real meaning on the development of their relapse prevention plan
- See real value in the relapse prevention plan, often creating one as a requirement of treatment rather than a lifesaving tool
- Develop a comprehensive relapse prevention plan
- Include and invest important resources and people in the process of relapse prevention planning
- Work fully on developing each area of the plan
- Use their relapse prevention plan once completed
- Use their relapse prevention plan at critical times
- Use their relapse prevention plans for long enough or over an extended period of time
- See or experience the relapse prevention plan as a life saver

Accordingly, a meaningful and effective relapse prevention plan can be built only when the client is able to recognize the importance and significance of the plan and when the plan is adequate to the task of helping the youth maintain treatment gains and stay safe—not for one week but for many years. Accordingly, relapse prevention plans must be reviewed periodically and revised so that they become living tools, not simply relics or mementos of past treatment. In addition, both the therapist and the client often fail to recognize the complexity of that *particular* client, coming up with cookie-cutter relapse prevention plans instead of a plan custom built for that individual. Laws et al. (2000, p. xii) wrote that relapse prevention "is an individualized approach that varies from driver to driver. Although some 'core' competencies of [relapse prevention] can be taught in groups based on standardized treatment manuals, an individualized approach can help tailor the core elements to meet the individual differences of participants" (Laws et al., 2000, p. xii).

In order to build an effective plan, the recovering juvenile sexual offender must make a commitment to relapse prevention and must recognize and accept the reality and potential for relapse. Juveniles are usually unable either to see the necessity of commitment in the earliest stages of their treatment or to make an authentic commitment, and they are usually not willing or able to accept the possibility of relapse. For these reasons, pacing means accomplishing the necessary treatment groundwork before developing the final or detailed relapse prevention plan, or before expecting early relapse prevention plans to be meaningful. For a plan to stand a chance, it must:

- Be custom built for the individual client
- Be sufficiently comprehensive and detailed
- Be realistic and match the reality of the youth's life and environment
- Be built on the youth's ability to fully understand the plan and its meaning
- Have the youth's commitment to maintain the plan
- Identify established external resources and a support system
- Ensure that external parties are fully aware of every detail of the plan and of all risk factors
- Establish ongoing and periodic reviews of the plan
- Establish in the mind of the youth, his family, and external support system that the plan is critical to success

THE DEVELOPMENT AND PACING OF THE PLAN OVER TIME

The juvenile's first relapse prevention plan is not likely to be the effective and meaningful plan that he will need at discharge from a residential treatment setting. Youths engaged in outpatient treatment require a relapse prevention plan throughout treatment, as they continue to live and engage in community life outside of treatment sessions. Nevertheless, the initial plan will involve far more outside supervision and far less sophisticated expectations that the youth will self-monitor or be committed to abstinence. Over time, the relapse prevention plan for both outpatients and juveniles in residential treatment must develop to the point that it has meaning and commitment and contains a detailed and realistic plan for maintaining treatment growth and for recognizing, avoiding, and handling high-risk situations. Whether outpatient or residential, pacing means developing the final relapse prevention plan only when the youth has completed the work required for him and his family to see the relapse prevention plan as critical—in other words, when the client is able to invest in the plan. The following are necessary for this to occur:

- The groundwork must be built on which the juvenile will see the relapse prevention plan as important.
- A sense of the purpose of a relapse prevention plan must be instilled in the youth.
- Relapse prevention planning must begin early in the treatment, but the final plan is developed at the end of treatment.
- It must be clear when the final relapse prevention plan is actually needed.
- Interim relapse prevention plans must be developed while the individual is still in treatment.
- Interim relapse prevention plans must serve as experiments by which to learn about triggers, high-risk factors, and lapses while the individual is still in treatment.

- Through interim plans, youths must learn why and in what ways early relapse prevention plans are ineffective.
- Family members and other important community resources must be included in the development of the final relapse prevention plan

EXTERNAL PARTIES: MONITORING AND SUPPORT

The input of family members and other individuals who are or will be central in the life of the juvenile in the community where the relapse prevention plan is most critical is essential. Their input is valuable because these individuals know the youth and his environment well. Beyond this, their input not only rounds out the plan but also builds their commitment to it and supports the recovering juvenile sexual offender. It is important that parents and other significant and appropriate family members (often based on relationship and age) be actively involved in monitoring the plan and the youth, including his adherence to the plan; they are built into the plan as an active support system and are part of the youth's coping mechanism as in sharing with, talking to, or spending time with a particular family member. In this regard, family members serve as mentors and sponsors to good health in much the same way as sponsors serve this role in a substance abuse recovery model. In fact, this interaction and relationship element is probably one of the greatest strengths and most critical elements of an effective plan.

The same is true for other external parties, such as social workers, therapists, probation officers, and even teachers, whose roles can range from observers to active participants who provide support and mentoring. In all cases, whether family members or others, all parties involved in the plan must be familiar with and understand the plan. It is this support system, also, that is actively engaged in the process of reviewing and modifying the plan over time, thus keeping it alive and meaningful and keeping the youth and the community safe.

THE SYMBOLIC QUALITY

The final step in the final relapse prevention plan is the symbolic act of gathering together signatories to the relapse prevention plan. Their signatures bind them all—from the juvenile to members of his support system—to the plan and makes them all parties to the juvenile's success. The importance of rituals in this case should be neither overlooked nor overestimated.

That is, the ritual of signed and witnessed signatures to the contract is a process of binding together and working to support recovery. At the same time, the act alone will in no way guarantee success or even that the various signatories will provide the level of commitment and awareness promised. The act of signing the relapse prevention plan contract, then, like the plan itself, is the culmination of a process that has reached out to educate, make the need for relapse prevention known, and engage all parties in successful recovery during and beyond the active phases of treatment.

CONCLUSION: THE RELAPSE PREVENTION PLANNING PROCESS

The relapse prevention plan is both an outcome and a process. It is an outcome because it results in an actual relapse prevention plan. It is a process because the plan is merely the physical representation of the process by which the youth has learned about himself, engaged and developed a support system, and worked hard to develop a plan that is realistic, authentic, and meaningful, and to which he can commit himself.

The plan should be worked through many times before it is finalized, and although it may be as short and simple as one or two pages, the plan is merely the summary of a larger process. Plans that are developed without this process—even the completion of a relapse prevention planning workbook or curriculum such as that developed by Steen (1993) or Leversee (2002)—are only empty shells.

The relapse prevention model was transferred from the field of substance abuse treatment, where it has also proven to work only under the right kind of circumstances. Those circumstances include a client who wants to change and is ready to change, a meaningful plan that is realistic and appropriate for each individual client, and a support system that serves as an actual part of the plan. However, unlike the recovering alcohol or drug abuser, the recovering juvenile sexual offender does not have one feature that has proven highly effective for hundreds of thousands of substance abusers. For many in recovery from substance abuse, the ability to join and attend Alcoholics Anonymous (AA) or other support groups has been essential. Indeed, as so many substance abuse relapse prevention plans include AA as a central and daily component, it may be that recovery works *because* of AA rather than other components in the plan. In fact, AA itself works not because of relapse prevention plans, but because of the commitment made by the recovering substance abuser to relapse prevention and all it entails.

Of course, no such meetings or affiliations are possible for the recovering sexual offender. Thus, the relapse prevention plan must be built and developed over time to inculcate meaning and must have the understanding and commitment of the juvenile and his support system to help it fulfill its goal of both abstinence from sexually abusive behavior and the reduction of harm.

CHAPTER 18

Victim Clarification

VICTIM CLARIFICATION refers to the process of making amends and paying some form of restitution to the victims of sexual offending behaviors. Victim clarification, considered an important aspect of sexual-offender-specific treatment (Mussack & Stickrod, 2002), means eventually bringing the offender and the victim into direct contact in face-to-face clarification (victim-abuser) sessions for the express purposes of

- Addressing and resolving issues for the victim
- Confronting the offender with his behavior, as well as with the victim of his behavior
- Providing an opportunity to test empathy, remorse, and compassion in the offender and his ability and willingness to make amends for his behavior

As noted in previous chapters, the victim of juvenile sexual offending is frequently another family member, often a younger sibling. In these circumstances, the juvenile offender is usually removed from the home during treatment. When this is the case, successful victim clarification work is a prerequisite for both family reunification and family visits that include both the offender and the victim. Thomas (1997) considered victim clarification to be the first of three steps in the process of family reunification following sexual abuse (the other steps are reconciliation and reintegration), and she described this process as lengthy, intensive, and emotionally draining for all involved.

So that the groundwork for future reconciliation and reintegration can be carefully and thoroughly built, victim clarification work takes place later in treatment rather than earlier and should not be rushed or forced by the offender, by the offender's family if the victim is another family member, or even by the victim.

348

THE CONTEXT AND FUNCTION OF VICTIM CLARIFICATION

Victim clarification occurs within the broader process of sexual-offender-specific treatment. It is a facet of treatment important for the spiritual healing of both the victim and the perpetrator of the sexual abuse.

By *spiritual*, I mean a process by which individuals are connected to a larger and more meaningful reality and sense of connectedness, both within themselves and to people and things outside of themselves. Those who victimize others often feel a disconnection between themselves and their victims and not only objectify (turn into objects or things) other people but also, in some way, dissociate themselves from their own behaviors, at least when they are engaged in the abusive act. Following victimization, many victims become spiritually damaged, or lose a sense of connection to or trust in others, and doubt themselves and their surroundings. In this context, spiritual healing is often a symbolic process designed to restore (or build) a sense of connection and wholeness in both the perpetrator and the victim. Throughout treatment, in attempting to foster empathy, encourage a sense of remorse for behaviors that victimize others, build respect for others and self, and develop healthy relationships, the goal is to develop in the offender's personality a healthy connection with and link to others.

THE PURPOSE OF VICTIM CLARIFICATION

Another way to think of victim clarification is as victim *restitution*, or making amends. The term *victim clarification* means that the offender has clarified in his mind

- That there *is* a victim
- *Who* the victim is
- That there is likely more than one victim in every offense (e.g., the direct victim of the offense, the victim's family, the offender's family, and the community at large)

In addition, victim clarification refers to the process by which the perpetrator later clarifies or explains his new position with regard to his perpetration, his apologies, and his goal of making amends or providing restitution to the victim.

From this perspective, victim clarification is only a first step in the process of making amends and paying restitution. This process begins with clarification in the offender's mind and reality. Mussack and Stickrod (2002) described victim clarification as a three-step process that involves (a) clarification to self in which the offender undergoes a process of personal change and preparation for making amends; (b) clarification to the victim, involving indirect and direct apologies, victim-abuser sessions, and other forms of restitution made to the victim; and (c) clarification to others who also have been harmed.

For this reason, victim clarification can begin only after the offender has engaged in much reflective and honest soul searching and has become able to seek, accept, and use help. Victim clarification has no meaning if it is conducted too early, for the wrong reasons, or before the offender has come to realize why making amends is important.

VICTIM AWARENESS VERSUS VICTIM CLARIFICATION

The concepts of victim clarification and victim awareness go hand in hand. However, even though many young offenders engage in victim awareness projects, it is not clear whether such projects can accomplish true victim clarification. In fact, victim awareness projects are more likely to serve as groundwork for victim clarification sessions or as substitutes when victim-abuser sessions are not possible.

It is important that offenders grasp the meaning of being the perpetrator of a sexual offense and the full experience of their victims. This usually means that they must engage in face-to-face victim clarification work whenever possible, and especially when the victim is a family member. This should be a goal for all clinicians in their family work, unless contraindicated or disallowed by specific circumstances. In some cases, the victim is too young to participate in victim-abuser sessions, refuses to attend sessions, or is otherwise too emotionally unstable or troubled to participate in the process. There are also instances in which the parents do not want victim-abuser sessions to occur or the victim's therapist recommends against such sessions. If the family is unstable, the clinician treating the juvenile sexual offender may decide against the process. Additionally, victim clarification may not be possible if the victim is not a family member, often because the victim is not available or the victim's family does not want to engage in the process.

VICTIM-ABUSER SESSIONS

The victim-abuser session is the most active and obvious part of the victim clarification process, that is, the face-to-face contact between perpetrator and victim. Most of what happens in these sessions is symbolic: Although the actual damage cannot be undone, remorse can be shown, empathy demonstrated, apologies given, questions posed and answered, and other interactions undertaken that help heal the damage and allow the process of restoration to move on.

These sessions are potentially anxiety provoking and emotionally charged for both the victim and the offender. In some cases, this is because offenders and victims have been held apart for a lengthy period of time, and expectancies and uncertainties are high. In other cases, the victim has a considerable amount of fear, anxiety, anger, confusion, or other strong emotion as a result of being sexually abused by the offender. In either case, victim-abuse sessions are to be treated carefully. On this, the National Task Force on Juvenile Sexual Offending (1993, p. 71) noted,

> Bringing victims and the perpetrator of their abuse together in face-face sessions as an adjunct to treatment is clearly an area for caution and careful planning. The goals of such sessions should be clearly defined and all persons involved must feel both physically and psychologically safe. Since victims frequently blame themselves for their abuse, clarification sessions with the one who abused them . . . can reduce this self-blame. Abusers can hear the consequences of their behavior and its impact, in personal terms, on the lives of victims.

THE CLINICIAN'S ROLE IN VICTIM CLARIFICATION

Victim-abuser sessions can take many forms. However, as victim clarification is considered a clinical intervention, it requires that a clinician facilitate the process and run face-to-face sessions rather than other treatment staff, including those trained in other forms of offender-victim mediation. Because victims are so frequently younger siblings and because the families of non-family victims often do not wish to participate in victim clarification sessions for their child or are unavailable, victim clarification usually involves only family members and thus becomes an extension and facet of family therapy. In this light, clinicians bring into victim clarification sessions the same skills and perspectives they bring into any family therapy session.

Nevertheless, when the victim clarification process is extended to other family victims (such as cousins) and nonfamily victims (e.g., the child of a family friend or a neighbor), the same processes are applied and the same set of skills are required in the clinician. These skills involve great sensitivity toward the victim's experience and that of her or his family; the ability to structure the environment so that it is safe for all participants; the ability to foster a facilitative and healing environment; clinical judgment and decision-making skills that help clinicians decide how and when to apply interventions, as well as the interventions to apply; and adherence to defined processes and procedures by which victim-abuser sessions are implemented, one version of which is described in this chapter.

The victim-abuser session is only one part of the larger victim clarification process. Like all aspects of treatment, effective victim clarification requires preparation, formulation, timing, and clinical skills. Like many aspects of therapy, if victim-abuser sessions occur at the wrong time, under the wrong circumstances, or without adequate preparation, the chances are that they will simply fill a treatment checkpoint rather than necessarily prove meaningful or effective. To move into face-to-face sessions too quickly may reduce the effectiveness of this part of the healing process and damage the overall treatment process for both the offender and victim.

Victim Clarification

- It is designed to be in the victim's best interests.
- It is planned to meet the victim's needs and emotional readiness.
- Honesty, remorse, and sensitivity must be developed in the offender before victim clarification sessions are planned.
- Sessions occur only in a therapeutic setting.
- The victim is assessed by an independent clinician before clarification sessions begin in order to determine her or his emotional stability and readiness to participate.
- The victim is assessed by the same independent therapist after clarification sessions in order to assess her or his emotional stability and ability to continue or to determine that no further clarification sessions are required and that such work has been successful.
- The clinician treating the offender discusses the case with the victim's therapist in order to ensure effective and appropriate communication and that clarification work is proceeding in the best interests of the victim effectively and at the right pace.
- Clarification sessions involve the offender's therapist and the victim's therapist whenever possible.
- Clarification requires the agreement of both the offender's therapist and the victim's therapist prior to continuing clarification sessions or determining that no further clarification work is required.

Figure 18.1
Guidelines for the victim clarification process.

Using a 12-step process adapted to the treatment of juvenile sexual offenders, such as the model illustrated in Figure 12.1, allows a broad view of the preparation and sequencing work that must precede face-to-face victim-abuser sessions. As shown, it is not until Steps 8 and 9 that victim clarification work takes place, far into treatment and only when the appropriate groundwork has been laid.

ENSURING THE INTEGRITY OF VICTIM CLARIFICATION SESSIONS

Victim clarification sessions are potentially risky emotional propositions for both the victim and the perpetrator. As their purpose is to help promote the healing and treatment of both parties and all other parties directly involved, it is important to construct a clear framework to ensure that the process has integrity (is not damaged, compromised, or guided by nontherapeutic or inappropriate issues) and safeguards the emotional well-being of both the victim and the offender. Keeping such a framework in mind offers clear practice guidelines for the clinician, defines the goals of the sessions, and in the process defines and describes the purpose of victim clarification. Guidelines and key points are illustrated in Figure 18.1.

SAFEGUARDING THE VICTIM

The emotional safety and well-being of the victim is paramount during this process; the intention is to heal wounds, not open or deepen them. The National Task Force on Juvenile Sexual Offending (1993) described victim-abuser sessions as victim sensitive, meaning that all participants must consider the needs, values, safety, and rights of the victim above all else. Similarly, Umbreit and Greenwood (2000), writing about victim-offender mediation, an approach often adopted in restorative justice programs, noted that sensitivity to victim needs and safety are the first concern in all such work. Accordingly, it is usually necessary for the victim to be in individual therapy during the process of victim clarification, particularly during victim-abuser sessions.

The victim's therapist should work with the victim before, during, and after victim-abuser sessions and assess the impact of the victim clarification process on the victim and her or his emotional well-being during the process. The victim's therapist should consult with the offender's therapist throughout victim clarification and should be encouraged and welcomed to attend and participate in victim-abuser sessions, which can be held in the victim's therapist's office if appropriate.

Some parents may feel that the victim does not require individual therapy during the victim clarification process; nevertheless, victim clarification sessions should not be initiated unless the victim is seeing a therapist during victim-abuser sessions. Only a therapist is able to make an independent and trained judgment as to victim safety and well-being. There may be some exceptions to this condition, but these will be rare and determined on an individual basis and only under unusual circumstances. This might include a situation in which the victim has completed therapy and the offender's clinician is satisfied that the victim is emotionally able to engage in victim clarification; however, this will also require communication with the prior therapist or a review of prior clinical records. An additional circumstance might involve victim clarification many years after the sexual victimization occurred with the victim showing no emotional or behavioral difficulties at the time of the victimization or since. Other circumstances in which the victim is actively seeking clarification, refuses therapy, and is not demonstrating emotional or behavioral difficulties might prove an exception. It may also be important to provide victim clarification even without a victim therapist if the juvenile sexual offender is returning home, the family or victim is refusing therapy, and the only alternative is reunification without any victim clarification at all. As noted, however, these situations should be avoided whenever possible, and the clinician should insist that the victim be in treatment during the victim clarification to ensure her or his emotional well-being.

PARTICIPANTS IN VICTIM-ABUSER SESSIONS

It is not always clear who should be involved in victim-abuser sessions. Ideally, the victim will be present, as well as both parents (or custodial guardians). However, for many reasons, not all family members are always available (e.g., divorced parents, or one parent is unwilling or unable to attend). Victim-abuser sessions should also include other siblings when possible; however, some siblings may be too young, unavailable, or unwilling to attend. In some instances, grandparents or other close family members should be invited to attend.

In some cases, inviting the victim to victim-abuser sessions may be contraindicated. This depends on the victim's age, emotional stability, and desire to attend regardless of age or emotional stability. For example, even if the victim is currently emotionally well, if the victimization occurred several years ago when the victim was very young, is there a reason to reraise the experience and the memory for the victim? These questions and others should be explored in the stages of victim clarification work, described later in this chapter, specifically Stages 2 (Identifying Victims), 3 (Presession Work), 4 (Introduction to Apologies), and 5 (Listening to the Victim). Finally, if the victim is a nonsibling family member, such as a cousin, or if the victim is a neighbor or someone else likely to continue to be in the perpetrator's life, should face-to-face victim clarification sessions include that victim? In cases where the victim is *not* included in victim clarification sessions, it is still possible to conduct face-to-face sessions between the perpetrator and other family members, such as the parents, who are also victims of the abusive behavior.

In considering guidelines for victim inclusion, the victim should be

- Willing to engage in victim-abuser sessions
- In therapy throughout the victim clarification process
- Likely to participate actively in the offender's life once he is returned to the community
- Likely to remain in the offender's life well into the future, even if not immediately active in the offender's life
- Emotionally stable
- Old enough to interact in and understand the meaning and content of victim-abuser sessions
- Actively seeking or desiring the ability to confront the offender or to resolve issues arising from the abuse

In terms of which other family or community members should be included in victim-abuser sessions, clinicians should consider

- All custodial parents or guardians
- Other parents, stepparents, foster parents, and noncustodial guardians significantly affected by the abuse

- Nonvictim siblings, if old enough, cognitively able, and emotionally stable
- Other adult family members who are significantly affected by the abuse, such as grandparents, uncles, and aunts
- Other same- or near-age relatives, such as cousins, who are significantly affected by the abuse
- Other close members of the perpetrator's community who are significantly affected by the abuse, such as close family friends
- Other close members of the perpetrator's community who may serve as important safeguards and supports following the offender's return to the community (although this may be more appropriate during the relapse prevention planning phase of treatment, rather than victim clarification)
- The victim's therapist or other family therapist

PROCESS AND COMPONENTS OF VICTIM CLARIFICATION

When it is determined that victim clarification is an appropriate intervention, the clinician initiates the process. Victims are never contacted directly by the clinician, as they are usually children. Accordingly, the clinician will discuss victim work with the victim's parents or legal guardians. There are several stages to the process of victim clarification:

1. *Preclarification:* the clarifying work leading to the offender's readiness to engage in victim-abuser sessions
2. *Identifying Victims:* the offender's ability and willingness to identify and recognize the victims of abuse
3. *Presession Work:* the assessment of the victim's ability and willingness to engage in victim-abuser sessions
4. *Introduction to Apologies:* indirect victim contact establishing the clarification process
5. *Listening to the Victim:* actively seeking and understanding the victim's perspective and needs
6. *Face-to-Face Contact:* victim-abuser sessions intended to make amends, bring closure, and lead to reunification
7. *Assessment:* ongoing evaluation of the victim's and offender's emotional well-being throughout the clarification process
8. *Closure:* termination of the formal process of victim clarification and continuation, if necessary, of family therapy

Like most stage models, there is overlap between the stages of victim clarification. Any given stage usually contains some material and tasks from the stages on either side, and the length of each stage and the victim clarification process as a whole differ for each client. However, a stage model provides a means for clinicians, offenders, victims, families, and others to understand that the victim-abuser sessions represent only one stage in the larger victim clarification process.

Stage 1: Preclarification

This stage leads to the offender's ability to recognize that he has victimized others, sincerely believe that he has victims, and understand the possible impact of his behavior on victims. As noted earlier, the offender cannot meaningfully engage in victim work and restitution until the concept and meaning of victimization are fully clarified. During this stage, which can last many months, offenders learn about their own behaviors and the impact of sexual offending behaviors on their victims and can be helped to understand their victim's perspective through individual therapy, group therapy, family therapy (without the victim), verbal and nonverbal therapies, and workbook exercises and materials.

Stage 2: Identifying Victims

The victims of sexual abuse are clearly identified during this stage. This requires that the perpetrator is ready and able to think about his offenses and understand that they were offenses, and is able to identity his victims and *why* they were victims.

Stage 3: Presession Work

The clinician contacts the victim or the victim's family and assesses what they want, do not want, are ready for, and are not ready for. This phase of victim work prepares for direct contact and paves the way for making amends and paying restitution. During this stage, the clinician also contacts the victim's therapist to ensure that the therapist agrees that victim work is appropriate and that the victim is ready for the work. As described earlier, under most circumstances victim clarification work should not commence without an external therapist working with the victim.

The victim's parents must give consent for the offender's therapist to have open communication with the victim's therapist, and the victim's therapist must be willing and open to engage in such dialogue. This is the time to start assessing the wisdom and necessity of engaging the victim in face-to-face sessions and the ability or desire of the victim to engage in such sessions. It is also the time to discuss the role played by the victim's therapist in the victim-abuser sessions, even to the point of conducting the sessions in that therapist's office rather than at the residential treatment program.

Stage 4: Introduction to Apologies

This stage of the work often involves preliminary and tentative contact with the victim, including introducing the amends process to the victim, often through nondirect means such as letters that offer an apology, demonstrate interest in the victim's experience and feelings, show remorse and deep regret, and ask the victim if he or she will engage in the next stage, which involves face-to-face therapeutic contact to deepen the process. If the offender cannot express humility by this point, he is not ready to engage in meaningful victim work, as he is probably still more concerned with himself than with the actual process of making amends and helping heal the victim.

Written exercises may include *victim empathy essays,* in which the perpetrator describes his empathy and support for his victim; *victim letters,* in which the perpetrator writes a fictional letter to himself from his victim in which he imagines and describes what and how his victim might be feeling; and *apology letters,* in which the offender writes letters of apology to his victim and other family members (which may or may not be actually sent). All of these written exercises can be very powerful, and they require the clinician or group members to hold the offender responsible for working hard at his writing and injecting real meaning into it.

Victim Empathy Essays

Victim empathy essays may be written in any number of ways. They are intended to put the perpetrator into his victim's shoes and have him imagine (or have empathy with) the victim's experience then and now. Victim empathy letters are usually not intended to be mailed to the victim but are shared with the clinician and offender group. Victim empathy essays can also be directed toward the experience of the victim's family, which is often also the offender's family. One form of victim empathy essay describes the offender's thoughts about his victim and how he imagines he has affected that victim. Another form is written by the offender in the first person and describes how he imagines the experiences of his victim from the victim's perspective. Excerpted samples of victim empathy essays are shown in Figure 18.2, and depending on how the essay is written can include statements about

- How the victim might be feeling now
- What the victim might have felt during the sexual assault
- What the victim might have felt after the sexual assault
- How the sexual abuse might have changed the victim's life
- How the sexual abuse might have affected the way the victim sees him- or herself now
- How the offender would feel in the victim's position

Sample 1

Jimmy is my brother, and he's also my victim. I know I hurt him by what I did to him, and that he must have suffered then and now. I believe he must have been hurt by me, because I'm his big brother and I'm supposed to protect and help him, not hurt him. He's probably not sure what to think about me and what I did to him, and he probably doesn't know who he can trust now and who might hurt him like I did.

When I made him have sex with me the first time, I know he was afraid because he was asking me to stop and I knew that it wasn't what he wanted to do, and that he felt helpless because I was so much bigger than him. Although I never hit him, I know I hurt him because I held his arms really hard a couple of times, and he was crying. He must have been really scared, and angry and confused. I know I would be. Afterwards, I knew he was scared of me because he stayed away from me for a while, but I did it again. Each time it got easier for me, but now I know it got harder for him, and he must have really started to feel like garbage after a while. Maybe he felt like that after the first time, but each time it happened must have made him feel more and more helpless, and maybe hate me more and more.

Nowadays I know Jimmy wants to see me, because he asks about me and says he misses me. That's really amazing, because I caused him so much harm and I wonder if he really knows it. I think that maybe he thinks it was maybe his fault and not mine, or maybe that what I did doesn't really matter. If he does, that would be terrible.

Sample 2

Ever since my brother made me have sex with him, my life has changed. Although I feel alright a lot of the time, underneath I feel really angry and dirty and I'm afraid to tell people what happened to me. I see all this stuff on TV about people who get raped, and I know that happened to me, but I can't tell anyone about it. If I did, they'd think there was something wrong with me, or that I liked it. I can tell mom, but that's not the same and I don't want her to feel any worse than she did when she found out about it. Because I waited a long time to tell her, I know she felt even worse, and I wonder if she thinks it was my fault or something because I didn't tell her right away.

When Dave was doing the sex to me and making me have sex with him, it was horrible. I can still feel what it was like when he was on top of me, and his breath smelled and was all over me, and made me feel sick. When he put his thing in me it hurt and hurt, although he didn't care at all. I cried, but didn't want to make any noise because I didn't want to get into any trouble. Although I wished someone would walk in and help me, I was afraid they would and they'd blame me as well. I felt trapped, and it hurt, and I was trapped. After I thought and thought about what happened, and thought about those people on TV who get raped and now I was one of them.

We never talk about it at home, like it never happened, and I wonder if I've let everyone down. I'm not sure if my life has been ruined, but sometimes it feels that way.

Figure 18.2
Samples excerpts of victim empathy essays.

- How the victim might be feeling about the offender now
- How the victim was not at fault in any way, no matter what the circumstances of the sexual abuse
- How the victim's family might be feeling
- How the victim's family might be feeling about the offender
- What the offender can do for the victim in restitution for the sexual abuse
- What the offender is doing in restitution for his offense

Victim Letters

Victim letters are fictional letters written by the offender to himself. In a group setting, members can write victim letters to one another. Such letters are intended to help develop and drive empathy and understanding for the victim and again place the perpetrator into his victim's shoes. As with victim empathy essays, victim letters can also be directed toward the victim's family, which is often also the offender's family. The victim letter is written by the offender in the victim's voice as though the victim is writing a letter to the offender about her or his experiences. Figure 18.3 shows a sample of a victim letter, which can include

- How the victim is feeling about him- or herself now
- How the victim felt about the offense when it happened
- How the victim felt right after the offense
- How the sexual abuse changed the victim's life
- How the victim feels about his or her own future now
- How the victim feels about the offender
- What the victim would like to see happen to the offender
- Any questions that the victim may have about why this happened, why the offender chose her or him to offend against, or any other questions that the offender imagines his victim may have
- How the victim would like the offender to make amends for or pay restitution for the sexual abuse

---

Dear Mike:

Ever since you raped me and made me do what you wanted, I've been upset a lot and have had a difficult time with my life. I wonder why you did that to me, and if I hurt you or something? I really always looked up to you, even when you were mean to me, but then you really hurt me because you used me for sex, like I was your girlfriend or something. All those things you did to me and made me do to you were really horrible, and I feel like I know things that kids my age aren't supposed to. Now I think about things in a way that I never used to, and sometimes I wonder what sex would be like with other people. I don't want to be like that, but I am and that's your fault.

I don't feel like other kids, and I worry that if I say or do the wrong things people will think I want to have sex with them. I also feel like a lot of people and especially kids your age or grown-ups really secretly want to have sex with me, and might if they had the chance. I feel like I don't know what to do a lot of the time, and even though I see a therapist I don't really tell him what I'm really thinking because I don't want him to think there's something wrong with me, and sometimes I wonder if he'd like to have sex with me if he could. My life has been different since you did that to me, and I can't be the same as I was ever again. I hope you know that, and I hope the people who are working with you know that too.

I want you to say sorry, but I don't really care. How can saying sorry make me feel better or make things go back to the way they were?

Figure 18.3
Sample victim letter.

Apology Letters

Apology letters are the most direct and the least dependent on the offender's imagination. In these letters, the perpetrator is writing his own thoughts and feelings about what he did and what happened, and he is writing them directly to the victim or the victim's family (which, again, may be the offender's own family). Victim letters may or may not be sent, but it is unlikely that early versions of such letters will be sent. Under no circumstances should victim letters be sent to the victim or the victim's family without the express consent of the family and the victim ahead of time, and the victim's therapist must be consulted as to the appropriateness of sending such letters at that time. Additionally, letters must never be sent without the prior review and approval of the therapist, and letters can be read in group treatment so that other group members can give feedback as well.

It is also important to note that although these letters are by definition letters of apology, the victim should not feel compelled in any way to offer forgiveness. That is, the letter should offer a sincere and authentic apology but *not* ask for forgiveness, which is an action that only the victim can decide upon. Nor should the letter be written in any way that directly benefits the offender. That is, the fact that the offender has written an apology does not entitle him to feel that he has now apologized and can move on. A excerpted sample of an apology letter is shown in Figure 18.4, and content typically includes

Dear Tina:

I am writing because I want to tell you how sorry and terrible I feel about what I did to you, and how I know you must feel. What I did to you should never happen to anyone, and it's especially bad because I'm your brother and you should be able to trust and count on me to help you and always be your friend. Instead, I took advantage of you and used you to get my needs met, not because you did anything wrong but because I was selfish and didn't think about what you needed for a second. I know now that what I did was really bad, and that I must make it up to you if I can.

I want to tell you that I'm sorry for everything I did to you, and also for not being the big brother, friend, and protector you needed. I hope I can be a better person and want to one day become your friend again, but know I have to work hard to prove myself to you and mom and dad.

I really want to tell you that what happened was all my fault and all my responsibility. I've learned a lot about being responsible here, and want to make sure you know that it wasn't your fault at all—not one little bit. I was the one who did the wrong things, and only me. You may not really be sure of me or even believe what I'm saying is true, and you don't have to. I hope one day you will come to trust me again but you never have to, and you never have to tell me that what I did is behind us now because that's not your job. It's my job to say I'm sorry and prove that to you over time. What I will promise is that I'll never do that to you or anyone else again, and am going to be a person who's safe to be around.

Figure 18.4
Sample apology letter.

- An acknowledgment that a sexual assault occurred
- The offender's acceptance of full responsibility for the sexual abuse
- A clear statement that the victim is not responsible for any part of the sexual abuse, no matter what the circumstances under which the abuse occurred
- A clear expression of remorse for the sexual abuse
- A clear expression that the offender knows and believes he caused harm to his victim
- A direct, sincere, and authentic apology to the victim for the harm caused
- A statement that the victim does not have to forgive the offender, now or ever
- An explanation for why the offense happened
- A description of the emotions the offender imagines and expects the victim is feeling
- A promise that the offender will never again sexually assault the victim or any other person
- A promise that the offender will get help and continue to seek and accept help as he needs it to ensure that he keeps his promise never again to engage in sexual abuse

Stage 5: Listening to the Victim

Another important element in victim clarification work is that of listening to the victim's feelings, thoughts, and experiences. It is the offender's job to do the listening, even before face-to-face sessions, through letters, communication through parents, and other messages from the victim delivered indirectly to the offender. Equally important, it is the clinician's job also to listen to the wishes, needs, fears, hopes, and concerns of the victim and the victim's family.

Stage 6: Face-to-Face Contact: Victim-Abuser Sessions

Face-to-face therapeutic contact sets the pace for normalizing relationships after the victim clarification phase of treatment has been completed. Here, the focus continues to be on the process of offender humility, apology, making some form of amends and paying some form of restitution, and actively listening to the victim's feelings, thoughts, and experiences.

There are many variations in scenarios and enactments, all of which essentially focus around the clinician's techniques, beliefs, and experiences and are therefore idiosyncratic and variable based on the individual clinician rather than fixed and consistent from therapist to therapist. However, there are guidelines that can help the therapist consider the issues to be covered and content to be included in victim-abuser sessions, the structure of sessions and how to conduct them, and other elements important to the success of the process.

One guideline is to focus victim-abuser sessions strictly on the offense, the offender's ability and willingness to apologize and make restitution, and the relationship between offender and victim, rather than on broader and more general aspects of family therapy in a family in which incest has occurred.

Content of Victim-Abuser Sessions
The clinical content of each victim clarification is determined by the clinician, often in accordance with her or his training and experience. However, during the course of the victim-abuser sessions and based on the emotional and cognitive readiness of others participating in the session (most of all the victim), content should generally include

- A description and full disclosure of the offense by the offender
- Open discussion of the offense among all family members (taking into account the victim's age and emotional and cognitive level)
- Discussion of the impact of the offense on the victim
- Discussion of the impact of the offense on other family members
- Responses to any questions asked by the victim
- A forum for the victim to make statements, express feelings, or describe experiences
- The exposure of family secrets directly relevant or believed relevant to the sexual abuse
- Discussion of how sexual abuse was able to occur in the family and family patterns that may have allowed, supported, hidden, maintained, or otherwise allowed the abuse to occur
- A sincere and authentic apology by the offender
- A demonstration of empathy for the victim by the offender
- A demonstration of remorse by the offender for his behaviors
- A demonstration of understanding and support by all family members for the victim
- Any necessary apologies to the victim by other family members who may have intentionally or unintentionally allowed the abuse to occur or continue
- A statement and description by the offender of how he intends to make restitution to the victim
- Clear statements by all parties involved that the offending behavior was not the victim's responsibility in any way, regardless of the circumstances under which the sexual abuse occurred
- The opportunity for the victim to grant or offer forgiveness to the offender (although this is not required and certainly should not be the goal for these sessions)

Clinicians may decide to include other interventions such as repeated apologies by the offender, repeated and increasingly detailed disclosures by the offender, larger scale family apologies to the victim, or symbolic gestures or rituals, nonverbal exercises, or other interventions in victim-abuser sessions. Clinicians may also want other family members to describe what they know about the offenses or the victim to describe his or her experience and the details of the offense if the victim is willing and able. However, content of this sort is not necessary for victim-abuser sessions and is largely idiosyncratic to the style and approach of the therapists facilitating the session. Of equal and great importance are the following:

- Victim-abuser sessions, and the victim clarification process as a whole, are aimed primarily at the impact of the offense on the victim and on the well-being of the victim, the victim's family, and the relationship between the victim and the offender, in that order.
- Victim-abuser sessions, and the victim clarification process as a whole, are not intended to focus on the impact of the offense on the offender.
- It is not important or necessary for the victim to accept an apology or grant forgiveness.
- It is acceptable and appropriate for the victim to change his or her position from one session to the next, as well as to change his or her mind about anything that transpired during any previous victim-abuser session.
- Victim-abuser sessions must be canceled, postponed, or terminated if they appear to be causing any revictimization.
- Siblings should not attend victim-abuser sessions if there is a risk to their emotional well-being or if they begin to demonstrate trauma due to being exposed to the sessions or details discussed in them.
- The clinician must remain tuned into any subtle intimidation or pressure on the victim, whether intentional or unintentional, by the offender or other family members, including parents.

Structure of Victim-Abuser Sessions

Victim-abuser sessions must consider the needs and well-being of both victim and offender; nevertheless, face-to-face sessions should be first and foremost geared toward the victim's needs. The purpose of the session is to make restitution to the victim, with the resulting outcome resolution and reunification if victim clarification is successful. Accordingly, clinicians must ensure that

- The victim has the ability to end the session at any time
- Enough time is provided in each session to cover all material relevant to that session

- Sessions are scheduled frequently enough to ensure that the victim clarification process moves along smoothly without getting bogged down
- Victims meet with their individual therapists prior to the next victim-abuser session

Location of the Victim-Abuser Sessions

Sessions are typically held at the residential program but may be held at the office of the victim's therapist. The location should be planned to ensure the most effective process and outcome to victim clarification. Sessions held in the office of the victim's therapist may serve to reinforce the primacy of the victim in the process and the victim's sense of emotional comfort and support.

Number of Required Victim-Abuser Sessions

The number of victim-abuser sessions required to complete this stage of the victim clarification process depends on the circumstances, including the impact of the abuse on the victim and family, the age of the victim at the time of the sexual abuse, the current emotional condition of the victim, and the resilience of both the victim and the family, among other factors, as well as the events and course of each session. It is the job of both the offender's clinician and the victim's therapist to assess and determine when the victim-abuser sessions portion of victim clarification has reached a successful conclusion. Of course, the conclusion of formal victim-abuser sessions does not mean that victim clarification is over. In most cases victim clarification will transform into ongoing family therapy, including both the offender and the victim, and move into other areas of family life.

STAGE 7: ASSESSMENT

Stage 7 is a parallel process that occurs alongside Stage 6. To ensure that victim-abuser sessions are not causing emotional harm to either the victim or the offender, it is critical to evaluate both parties after face-to-face sessions, although it is the role of the victim's therapist to assess the victim.

STAGE 8: CLOSURE

The formal conclusion of victim clarification is an arbitrary point determined by the combined judgment of the offender's clinician and the victim's therapist and informed by the experience of the victim-abuser sessions and the experiences of the victim, the victim's family, and the offender.

After victim clarification is completed, family visits can be reinitiated, and family reunification, in one form or another, can proceed. Family therapy can begin or continue as well, now including all members of the family, if appropriate, whereas previctim clarification family therapy included only the offender and nonvictimized family members. Thus, victim clarification will transform from a specialized form of family therapy into a more general form. However, it is important to note that victim clarification has ended as a formal process, marking a symbolic reflection of spiritual healing. Some therapists may want to implement a more ritualized end to the victim clarification process, making a stronger point about healing within the family, whereas others may prefer to note that victim clarification has progressed into the broader goals of family therapy.

At all times, clinicians must remember that further sexual abuse or a return to previous family behaviors is always a possibility and will remain so for a long time. It is also possible that, despite best efforts, not all information about family sexual abuse has emerged. Important, then, is the clinician's continued vigilance and awareness of patterns of family communication and interaction, particularly between the offender and victim, rather than being lulled into a false sense of success and permanent change. The forensic mind-set must be maintained in seeking evidence of continued dysfunction, as well as increased normalcy and recovery within the family.

ON APOLOGIES, FORGIVENESS, AND SHAME

There are many controversies and concerns about victim clarification and family reunification. One particularly strong concern rests with the notion of seeking and granting forgiveness. Most models of victim clarification focus on the offender's ability to feel genuine remorse and offer an authentic and sincere apology, but not in the hopes of absolution or forgiveness. This is because the goal of forgiveness suggests that it is the victim's responsibility to forgive the offender for his behaviors and sexual assault, and hence free him from guilt. This process may serve the offender as much or more than the victim and pressure the victim to meet the needs of the offender, and even the family.

Accordingly, there should be little to no emphasis on forgiveness in victim clarification, and certainly no request made by the offender for absolution, although the choice to forgive is a choice the victim may make. "The notion that forgiveness is a prerequisite for reunification places an unreasonable burden on victims . . . and the risk of covert coercion within family relationships is increased by such expectations" (National Task Force on Juvenile Sexual Offending, 1993, p. 73).

Another area of concern involves shame and humiliation. The goal of victim clarification is to benefit both the victim and the offender, and although considering the victim's needs above all else, the intervention is clearly intended to promote the healing and rehabilitation of the offender as well. In her 16-step model of sexual abuse repentance and reparation, the equivalent of victim clarification, Madanes (1990) has the offender kneel down in front of his victim and apologize, and indeed has all other family members do the same in a powerful and highly ritualized model. One of Madanes' goals, described in Step 7, is to humiliate the offender in a highly dramatic show of repentence and thus disempower the offender while empowering and strengthening the victim. However, shame-based therapies are not considered appropriate in the treatment of juvenile sexual offenders, and in its recommendations for victim-abuser sessions the National Task Force on Juvenile Sexual Offending (1993) noted its opposition to such models, writing that "humiliating or degrading interactions are abusive and must be considered counterproductive to the goals of treatment" (p. 71).

CONCLUSION

In many ways, victim clarification is simply a variant of family therapy. It is a specialized form, however, with specific rules and protocols that serve to standardize, delineate, and contain the process in order to ensure that it is effectively implemented, that potentially volatile emotions are contained and channeled, and that it occurs in a therapeutic milieu that is safe for all parties concerned.

Victim clarification serves several purposes. It provides a forum for the healing of emotional wounds, self-expression, communication, understanding, and resolution, with an emphasis on the healing of the victim and the restitution of the offender. Under the best of circumstances, for the victim this process helps restore or build safety, control, and dignity; for the offender, it provides a means for developing empathy, expressing remorse, and making amends. For the family, victim clarification offers the opportunity for reunification.

However, despite the protocols and stages of victim clarification, there is no preferred method to provide or facilitate the victim clarification process. Different clinicians will use different favorite interventions and materials in the early stages of the process and will apply different techniques and interventions during the face-to-face victim-abuser sessions that mark the most significant test of victim clarification. Accordingly, victim clarification is best practiced by clinicians who understand its process and purpose, who are experienced in and familiar with the steps that precede face-to-face sessions, and who are experienced and comfortable in the family therapy environment in which victim-abuser sessions occur. The stages, tasks, and themes within each stage provide the backdrop and structure against which the therapeutic work takes place.

CHAPTER 19

Individual Therapy

THE THREE most central therapies in work with juvenile sexual offenders—as well as with troubled kids in general—are group, individual, and family therapies, utilizing both psychodynamic and cognitive-behavioral approaches. Other approaches, such as expressive and experiential therapies, may also be used, but treatment modes such as art, drama, or recreational therapy are rarely used as the primary source of treatment. The same is true also for the milieu therapy found in residential or inpatient (and sometimes day treatment) environments. Although important, the milieu provides the fabric against and into which group, individual, and family treatment are provided.

However, not all sexual-offender-specific treatment involves all primary modes of treatment, for several reasons. In some cases, resources limit availability, and in others treatment providers prefer one over another or believe that some modes are unnecessary or ineffective. In still other cases, providers may not recognize or overlook the importance of all three modes. In an integrated treatment model, especially a model aimed at treating adolescents and children, each of these modes will be woven into treatment. Together, these therapies treat the whole child as (a) an individual, (b) an interactional member of the peer group and the social environment, and (c) a member of a family in which the youth represents the identified patient. In employing all three treatment modes, strengths and weaknesses will become apparent, and clues and directions will emerge that will shape the individualized and comprehensive treatment required in the rehabilitation of the juvenile sexual offender. Figure 19.1 depicts each treatment mode incorporated into a larger whole-child model, showing also specific aspects related to each mode and the distinct differences that are unique to each treatment modality.

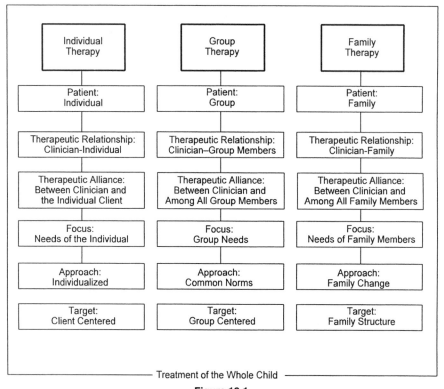

Figure 19.1

Individual, group, and family therapy as components of a whole-child treatment model.

INDIVIDUAL THERAPY

Individual therapy describes the way in which treatment is provided, through the one-on-one relationship between the clinician and the client. However, as previously described, some therapists do not provide individual treatment at all, and others consider individual therapy as a supplement to group treatment, serving to reinforce the ideas being taught, discussed, or processed in group sessions. More often than not, a treatment model in which individual therapy is seen as nonessential, secondary, or ineffective is likely to be cognitive-behavioral in orientation due to the thrust of cognitive-behavioral therapy in sexual-offender-specific treatment as instructive and prescriptive rather than exploratory and expressive.

However, this need not be. As described, a strong model of cognitive therapy emphasizes individual work, including the formulation, exploration, and engagement that take place within the therapeutic relationship, itself most strongly and typically experienced in individual and not group therapy.

Lundrigan (2001) wrote that a primary concern regarding the use of individual therapy is when it is used as a stand-alone technique rather than as part of an integrated and multimodal program of treatment. Here the issue is one of individual therapy serving as the only, or at the least the primary, mode of treatment. Given this book's emphasis on integrated treatment, Lundrigan's position is supported. In general, the thrust of treatment should be multimodal when dealing with complex issues in adolescent development, socialization, and juvenile sexual offending, with different treatment modalities and methods aiming at different targets within the treatment universe.

If faced with a choice of only one treatment modality due to scarce resources, group therapy is preferable over individual or family therapy because it allows participants to address peer and development issues that are not easily accessible to assessment or change through any other means. However, this is a choice one should hope to avoid. In such a case, the choice of a *single* therapy would be the problem, not the choice of choosing the *best* therapy. An alternative for the community treatment setting is multisystemic therapy (Henggeler, Schoenwald, Borduin, Rowland, & Cunningham, 1998), which is an integrated approach to the treatment of antisocial and troubled kids in the community that uses a variety of methods (not likely to provide group therapy directly, multisystemic therapy may refer to a group as part of an overall treatment strategy).

In general, individual therapy for juvenile sexual offenders is best utilized and constructed as part of multimodal treatment serving a distinct role that cannot be filled by any other form of therapy. On its own, individual therapy is too weak to rehabilitate the juvenile sexual offender adequately. The same is true, however, of both group and family therapy when used alone.

Lundrigan also asserted that "if individual therapy is properly utilized in careful coordination with the other [treatment] components, and if monitored with adequate clinical supervision, this mode can potentially be one of the most significant components of the program" (p. 162). G. Ryan and Lane (1997) concurred and noted that many juvenile sexual offenders can benefit from individual therapy, but they cautioned that individual therapy should be provided only by clinicians trained in sexual abuse issues and in the context of the larger and integrated treatment team.

CAUTIONS AND BOUNDARIES

Given the population and treatment issues associated with juvenile sexual offending, there are many potential pitfalls to the use of individual treatment, suggesting that the intimacy and one-on-one nature of the relationship may invite confused roles (Lundrigan, 2001). Nevertheless, with adequate training, supervision, and preparation, the clinician may avoid such pitfalls. In the specific case of the juvenile sexual offender, if the clinician is prepared and oriented to a forensic model of mental health and is aware of the issues and dynamics for the juvenile sexual offender, as well as operating within a structured clinical framework described in Chapter 15 (Day & Sparacio, 1989), these should be nonissues in individual therapy.

Intimacy and Sexual Risk

The key to individual therapy is the therapeutic relationship, or as Rollo May (1961) referred to it, "two-persons-existing-in a-world" (p. 73). Given the natural and intended therapeutic intimacy of this relationship, the transference and countertransference issues that are recognized in psychodynamic therapy and by many informed cognitive-behavioral therapists, and the nature of the client as sexually inappropriate and aggressive, the strength of the relationship requires caution.

Even under the best of conditions, transference and intimacy in therapy can arouse sexual feelings in the client. In the case of the juvenile sexual offender, this should be of special concern. Therapists should not overlook the fact that they may unconsciously send mixed messages. Even when messages are clear, sexual offenders may misconstrue them and inject meaning into the relationship that is not present. In juveniles, and especially those who are already confused about sex or highly sexualized and who have already crossed sexual boundaries, the intimacy of the therapeutic relationship can and is often likely to stimulate affectionate and sexual feelings. The therapist must be aware, then, that she or he may become a highly sexualized object for the client, or even someone whom the juvenile attempts to seduce or otherwise engage in a sexual relationship. Under such circumstances, aside from boundary confusion, the therapist must never overlook the possibility of personal danger, including physical or sexual assault, especially given the secure and closed environment in which individual therapy is conducted.

Boundaries

At the initiation of therapy, the therapist must establish clear boundaries and be alert to subtle shifts and overstepping of boundaries in both directions. Boundaries represent the distance between the client and the clinician within the therapeutic relationship and serve as the foundation that defines structure and upon which structure is built. The therapeutic alliance brings the therapist and client together in an intimate relationship; boundaries keep them apart and define their roles within this relationship.

Boundaries keep both the therapist and the client safe; therefore, boundary confusion and violations—even subtle violations—represent important issues to address in therapy, especially with developing young adults who are in therapy *because* of boundary violations.

CLINICIAN SELF-DISCLOSURE AND BOUNDARIES

Clinician self-disclosure is a complex concept that is closely related to boundaries. The clinician's ability to engage in an authentic and meaningful relationship and be genuine, open, and transparent is an important attribute in effective therapy. At the same time, the degree and nature of clinician self-disclosure is mediated by the nature of the work, professional ethics and rules of conduct that frown on dual relationships that by necessity involve a level of self-disclosure, or agency guidelines or policies if practicing within an agency, as well as a professional orientation. Highly defined nondirective therapies will include very little, if anything, in the way of clinician self-disclosure, even to the degree of a clinically sterile counseling office devoid of highly personal artifacts that are self-revealing. Other settings, such as substance abuse treatment centers, encourage clinicians to share their histories if relevant to treatment and often consider such clinician disclosure to be an integral aspect of treatment.

Treatment with juveniles is complex, especially in residential treatment programs where the clinician's professional life and the juvenile's daily life are often far more connected and intertwined than in the outpatient office or outreach environment. Working with sexual offenders means that boundaries have already been crossed and in many cases that the juvenile offender has misunderstood the nature of shared information or interactions and the purpose or context of the sharing and even built up a storehouse of information based on small facts about potential victims. Small self-disclosures may become part of a larger situation over which the clinician later loses control. In fact, one might argue that poor choices around clinician self-disclosure represent a series of seemingly unimportant decisions (SUDs) on the part of the clinician.

The sorts of self-disclosures generally referred to in a model of effective clinician attributes include openness, freedom of expression, a willingness to share ideas and perspective, clinician transparency, and a willingness to answer certain kinds of questions that clients may pose. To use extreme examples, it does not extend to the clinician sharing details of sexual behaviors or interests, family difficulties or problems, problems at work, substance use, and so forth. The guidelines for clinician self-disclosure are clearly bounded by treatment interventions that are in the best interests of the client, including self-disclosure as a treatment intervention only and not a clinician need. In a multidisciplinary or treatment team model, members of the treatment team must agree on the general level of self-disclosure and must approve specific and more detailed clinician self-disclosure, thus ensuring that the disclosure is an intervention, creating transparency around disclosures and hence protecting both the clinician and the client against boundary violations, either intentional or ill-informed. In the absence of a multidisciplinary team, the clinician is advised to avoid significant self-disclosure altogether or seek supervision.

Informed professional judgment must prevail at all times. The clinician must understand the meaning and limits of self-disclosure, and especially the risks of self-disclosure to the client, the clinician, and the therapeutic relationship.

THE FORENSIC MIND-SET

Recognizing the nature of the client; the nature of the circumstances that bring the client and clinician together; the often intense, graphic, and sexual discussions that occur as part of the work in individual therapy; personal and community safety; and the consequences of treatment failure, the therapist must maintain a forensic mind-set throughout treatment. Combined with the structured therapeutic environment, a forensic approach to treatment will keep the clinician aware, informed, and alert to shifts in direction that may mislead the clinician and take both the clinician and client down paths that are ineffective and counterproductive or, far worse, unsafe for both.

THE USE OF INDIVIDUAL THERAPY

Individual therapy fills a unique role and provides an intimate one-on-one treatment environment. Although public safety is implicit in this relationship in the forensic treatment model (Welldon, 1997), this one-on-one therapeutic relationship cannot be replicated in any other treatment approach.

Whether cognitive-behavioral or psychodynamic, individual therapy individualizes treatment and focuses only on the client without the distraction and draw of group dynamics, group management, and group goals. It provides the opportunity to understand the individual client and build a strong therapeutic alliance that allows the client to take chances and go to emotional and cognitive places that he might not otherwise consider. Individual therapy offers the client the opportunity to learn about himself and develop insight, explore what he is learning in other treatment modalities (e.g., group and family treatment), gather support for the work in which he is engaging, and have all attention focused on him and his needs. Individual therapy offers the therapist the opportunity to meaningfully assess the client and his progress in treatment, including the level at which he has integrated and can use the ideas and information that he is learning in treatment. Individual therapy is the treatment environment in which the therapist has the greatest opportunity to understand the juvenile sexual offender's world through his eyes.

In individual therapy, treatment goals are discussed and agreed upon; daily interactions are discussed and processed; transference issues and affectional bonds are experienced and played out; and direction and guidance are available to the juvenile client. Individual therapy includes customized techniques and therapeutic experiences that address the juvenile at his unique cognitive or emotional level, such as play therapy for younger juveniles, eye movement desensitization and reprocessing (EMDR), and dialectical behavior therapy (DBT). Through individual therapy, the therapeutic alliance is built and extended, and the role of the therapist as a central agent of hope and change is strengthened. These things are not secondary to other modes of therapy and in many cases cannot be undertaken or accomplished through other therapeutic means, but both are important in their own right and help bring together different modes of therapy in a blended and integrated multimodal treatment.

Case Study 19.1 describes the ability of individual therapy to help a deeply troubled adolescent offender begin to recognize and let go of patterns of sexually damaging attitudes and behaviors, through the development of alternative behaviors, insight, and the experience of success in treatment and in relationships.

INDIVIDUAL THERAPY AS A TALKING CURE

Clients can be verbally expressive in many different forms of therapy, but none more so than individual therapy. Although not every version of individual therapy involves extensive client talk, this is the most common venue for such self-expression. This talking-cure approach involves the client's ability to recognize, express, and sometimes vent thoughts and feelings, thus externalizing and discharging them. For many children and adolescents, especially troubled juveniles, feelings can sometimes be explosive. Whether feelings are negative or positive, expressing them usually has value. It is often the manner in which emotions are released or thoughts expressed that can be problematic.

Talk therapy is not the only means by which thoughts and feelings can be therapeutically expressed. Many treatment programs for juvenile sexual offenders provide expressive and experiential therapy as a forum for self-expression as well as skill development. Nevertheless, individual therapy in particular is focused on the client's ability to engage in self-revealing and self-exploratory conversation; accordingly, a central focus in individual therapy is on the juvenile's ability to engage with the therapist in discussion and self-expression. In addition to the opportunity for clients to experience emotional discharge and engage in self-exploration, talk therapy allows the clinician to learn more about the juvenile and the relevant dynamics at play.

Why talk therapy works is not clear. In fact, when it comes to the treatment of juvenile sexual offending, it is unlikely that talk therapy would work on its own. Nevertheless, for many people, simply talking about their day, their life,

Martin was a 15-year-old in residential treatment who between ages 12 and 13 raped his 6-year-old sister on multiple occasions. While in treatment, he participated in individual and group therapy and addressed a number of treatment questions, including factors that led to his sexual offenses, such as his parents' divorce, his distant relationship with his mother, his father's absence from his life, being bullied by his older brothers, having few friends, being picked on in school, and using pornography and sexual fantasy as an emotional escape and a way to feel normal. Martin discussed the progression in his sexual arousal pattern, beginning with fantasizing about women in soft pornography magazines and then pretending his sister was one of the sexual models, becoming aroused by his sister's clothing, dressing in her clothes and masturbating to sexual images of her, and eventually molesting and subsequently raping her. Martin explored the role that social isolation played in his offending pattern, and treatment frequently focused on the development of improved social skills. Martin's anxiety and hyperactivity were stabilized with medication, and he became a more active participant in therapy groups and in the social milieu. He began to exhibit greater empathy and patience and reported feeling better about himself, and in his last six months in residential care he began to develop closer relationships with peers and staff.

Martin actively engaged in individual therapy and identified and discussed factors leading to his offenses, future risk factors, and his relapse prevention needs. He discussed the development of his fetishistic and transvestic behavior and how his continued paraphilic interest might be a risk factor for reoffense. Martin explored how his offenses affected his sister, described his remorse for his behaviors with her and his oppositionality with his mother, and explored his relationships with other major family members. Martin also discussed his interactions with peers and staff and his evolving capacity to develop relationships and feel emotionally connected. He was aware that his social skills had improved and came to see himself as capable of change—unlike his father, who, while Martin was in treatment, was arrested and jailed for sexually assaulting a young girl.

Case Study 19.1

their feelings, or their problems is therapeutic and may also help them to identify solutions. To this degree, self-expression and self-disclosure are both psychologically and physically healing, serving as a mechanism (or relief valve) for cognitive and emotional release (Harvey, Orbuch, Chwalisz, & Garwood, 1991; Pennebaker, 1997; Pennebaker, Zech, & Rimé, 2001; Rich & Copans, 1998; Segal & Murray, 1994; Tallman & Bohart, 1999).

Talking gives meaning and adds clarity to feelings and thoughts. In a therapeutic environment talking can sometimes serve as a cathartic or abreactive experience in which difficult emotional experiences are discharged through the process of describing them. Although talk therapy and self-expression are hardly likely to be the key mechanism to behavioral improvement and reduced recidivism, through talk therapy juvenile sexual offenders can gain emotional relief, explore ideas, learn communication skills, and receive support and direction.

INDIVIDUAL THERAPY AS SUPPORTIVE

As described earlier, almost all individual therapy is built on the therapist-client relationship, the key to which is the support offered to the client by the clinician. However, some individual therapies are more supportive than others. Pinsker (1998) described supportive therapy as a model intended to overcome symptoms and prevent relapse but not necessarily to bring about personality change. In this regard, he described therapy that is more supportive than exploratory or prescriptive as a far less intense and less substantial therapy, but nonetheless a cornerstone of treatment.

Above all, the supportive component reflects and defines the therapeutic relationship itself. For Pinsker (1998), it is a two-way relationship involving two-way conversation, and it is thus highly interactive. In a supportive model of therapy, the clinician is engaged in the conversation and, hence, the relationship. In this regard, supportive techniques begin to include some of the directive techniques associated with cognitive-behavioral therapy, such as praise, encouragement, reassurance, advice, instruction, and guidance. As in client-centered psychodynamic therapy, such responses are sincere and pertinent. In a support mode, the client is treated and understood as a person rather than merely the subject of therapy to whom therapeutic technique is applied. However, support is clearly defined by the therapeutic process and does exceed that boundary. It is directed at and connected to the emotional, interactional, behavioral, or other adaptive issues that, for the juvenile sexual offender in treatment, are both the sexual offending itself and the psychological and life circumstances that surround the behavior. Helping the client to understand better and make better attributions, or *clarification,* is another tool employed in a model of supportive therapy, and this tool approximates some of the variables attached to the cognitive-behavioral genotype.

Case Study 2 describes a case in which the supportive power of therapy is instrumental in helping the juvenile sexual offender to emerge from behind denial, express real thoughts and feelings even though they are distressing to him and others, and begin to move beyond his difficulties without minimizing them.

THE DYNAMIC QUALITY OF INDIVIDUAL THERAPY

Chapter 14 presented the four common factors that contribute to treatment outcome and efficacy: (a) extratherapeutic client factors, (b) the therapeutic alliance, (c) expectancy and hope, and (d) the therapeutic model and technique. Whereas each factor can be considered independently, in actual practice they

Alan was a 17-year-old admitted into residential treatment at age 15 after engaging in sodomy with three boys aged 5 to 7. He did not have a history of being sexually or physically abused, but he grew up in a chaotic household never knowing his father and raised by a cocaine-addicted mother who had many short-term sexual relationships and multiple live-in boyfriends. Although his mother was in recovery during Alan's treatment and had married, it was difficult to engage her in family treatment, and his step-father remained distant.

After one year in treatment, Alan expressed an interest in disclosing more offenses but was afraid that he would get into more legal trouble. The court decided that no additional charges would be filed. Alan was eventually able to disclose 17 victims, all boys aged between 5 and 8, and came to recognize his sexual arousal to young boys, as well as his bisexuality. Although his mother was never able to accept Alan's disclosures and continued to dismiss or minimize them, Alan came to recognize his sexual interests as deviant and dangerous, and over time he shifted his focus from trying to demonstrate that he did not have a problem to identifying major and serious difficulties. Individual therapy allowed Alan to explore and discuss his thoughts and interests and understand the reality of his behaviors, the prognosis for his future, and the importance of stepping out of the offending closet so that he could get treatment.

During his last year in treatment, Alan began to engage in more prosocial and outgoing interactions with peers, became less dependent on his therapist, and in group and family therapy expressed himself more assertively, including more honest appraisals of himself. During his last six months, he disclosed several sexual encounters with animals, thus continuing to engage in self-initiated disclosures and demonstrating his desire to change. Individual therapy became a safe place for Alan to explore himself, including those things he did not like but initially pretended did not exist. He left treatment in a more positive and realistic state, recognizing that he was likely to continue for many years at a moderate to high risk to reoffend in the event that he did not maintain a high level of relapse prevention. Alan made a voluntary decision to remain in probation in order to receive external supervision and support.

Case Study 19.2

can more appropriately be considered to interact and influence one another. For instance, hope and expectancy are also features of the extratherapeutic factors that the juvenile brings into treatment. Yet, as indicated in the aforementioned list of therapist attributes and described by Marshall, Anderson, and Fernandez (1999), one function of the therapist (and hence the therapeutic alliance) is to influence and enhance favorable expectancy in the client. Thus, the therapeutic relationship has the capacity for improving the extratherapeutic elements introduced by the client, which in turn affect hope and expectation. Individual therapy, then, affects not only the development and application of the therapeutic relationship, but also the pattern of interactions among the common factors.

THE THERAPEUTIC ALLIANCE

Dryden's (1989) description of the therapeutic alliance provides an effective means for exploring the role of individual therapy. His description involves three components:

1. **Bonds.**
   - The interpersonal attitudes of the therapist and their impact on the client. In the client-centered tradition, when the therapist (a) is genuine in the therapeutic relationship, (b) shows unconditional acceptance of the client as a person, and (c) demonstrates empathy with the client, the client tends to move to a position of greater psychological growth.
   - The client's feelings and attitudes toward the therapist. This dimension includes concepts such as the client's trust in the therapist, feelings of safety in the relationship, and the degree of faith in the therapist as a change agent.
   - The fit between the interpersonal styles of both client and therapist, in which the focus is interactive. In this case, the therapeutic bond can be increased when the fit between the two is good and threatened when the fit is poor. An example of good fit may be found in a relationship where the therapist is dominant and the client submissive; conversely, a poor fit may be found in a relationship where the therapist is passive and the client hostile. Thus, the therapist may need to modify her or his style to initiate an effective therapeutic relationship.
   - Issues of transference and countertransference by which both client and therapist bring to the counseling relationship tendencies to perceive, feel, and act toward others in ways that are influenced by their prior interactions with significant others.
2. **Goals.** This area pertains to therapist and client objectives. A positive therapeutic outcome is facilitated when the therapist and client agree on the goals and agree to work on goal achievement. The therapeutic alliance is threatened when the therapist and client have different outcome goals in mind.
3. **Tasks.** These are the goal-directed activities carried out by both the client and the therapist and include several important dimensions:
   - Does the client understand the nature of the therapeutic tasks that he is being called on to execute?
   - If the client understands the tasks, does he see the importance of them?
   - Does the client have the capacity and skills to carry out the required therapeutic tasks?
   - Does the client have the confidence to undertake the tasks?

- If the client is willing and has the skills to undertake a particular task, does the task have sufficient value in accomplishing meaningful change in the client's life? In other words, is it actually a useful goal?
- Does the client understand the nature of the therapist's tasks and how these relate to his own tasks?

ROLE AND APPROACH OF THE THERAPIST

As described in Chapter 15, regardless of the therapeutic framework, individual therapy serves multiple purposes that meet the needs of both a cognitive and a psychodynamic model. Individual therapy is used to

- Recognize the juvenile's cognitive framework
- Understand the juvenile's phenomenological experience
- Understand how the juvenile relates to others
- Reframe the juvenile's experiences and events in his life
- Instruct the juvenile in new ideas and skills
- Understand and process emotional experiences
- Understand and explore cognitive themes, ideas, and beliefs
- Learn about and overcome psychological defensiveness
- Address patterns of avoidance
- Explore recurrent themes in the juvenile's experience
- Discuss and process current and recent experiences
- Form connections among current and past experiences
- Develop insight or new understanding
- Provide meaning and clarification
- Give explicit advice and direction
- Encourage the juvenile to try or adopt new behaviors
- Facilitate the juvenile's ability to communicate openly
- Ensure that the juvenile understands what is expected
- Ensure that the juvenile is committed to the work

In this approach to and use of individual therapy, particularly in the interactive and pragmatic approach (interpersonal functional therapy) described in Chapter 13, the therapist is highly interactive and engaged with the juvenile. Thus, the clinician is involved in the discovery and exploration of practical ideas that can help the juvenile accomplish the broad goals of sexual-offender-specific and holistic treatment. This is similar in principle to the model of client-centered facilitative therapy articulated by Carl Rogers (Rogers & Wood, 1974), who stated that "the first pre-requisite for doing therapy is not a theory . . . but a way of being with persons that is facilitative" (p. 213). In fact, Rogers' description of the attributes of the therapist remains the model for the effective therapist regardless of theoretical orientation: a sensitive and empathic understanding of the client's feelings and personal meanings, warm acceptance of the client, and unconditional regard in which the client is seen as an individual rather than as an object for diagnosis. In therapy inspired by this model, the therapist aims for the development of the facilitative treatment environment in which the juvenile can better understand himself, become more self-expressive and more self-confident, and learn how better to cope with life (Rogers, 1961). This idea is echoed by O'Brien, Pilowsky, and Lewis (1992), who wrote that "children conceive of the therapist as a real object in their lives, one who offers a viewpoint different from others and, above all, who allows the testing of new ideas and new ways of feeling and behaving in a supporting and supportive environment. Thus, therapy allows the children to experience and experiment" (p. xvi).

Marshall, Anderson, and Fernandez (1999) noted that the therapist's approach and the development of the therapeutic relationship contribute significantly to treatment outcomes regardless of treatment approach. They identified therapist features such as warmth, sincerity, support, and empathy as equally important to behavioral and cognitive therapists as to psychodynamic clinicians, and they described 25 specific attributes that they believe maximize therapeutic outcome. Combined with the integrated therapeutic prototype described in Chapter 15, as well as the client-centered ideas generally developed by Rogers (Rogers, 1961; Rogers & Wood, 1974), clinician attributes and behaviors employed in the practice of interpersonal functional therapy are described in Figure 19.2.

Attributes

- Accepting of the client
- Confident and self-assured
- Directive and reflective
- Emotionally responsive
- Encouraging
- Honest
- Noncollusive
- Nonjudgmental
- Professional
- Sincere and genuine
- Trustworthy

- Communicative and clear
- Demonstrating a belief in the client's capacity
- Emotionally neutral
- Empathic and sensitive
- Flexible
- Interested in the client
- Nonconfrontationally challenging
- Open and transparent
- Respectful
- Supportive
- Warm and friendly

Behaviors

- Clarifies and asks questions
- Creates favorable expectancies

- Defines and controls structure and content
- Discusses and defines treatment goals

- Creates a facilitative environment
- Deals appropriately with frustrations and problems

- Demonstrates belief in client capacity for growth
- Listens carefully and actively

Figure 19.2
Attributes and behaviors of the therapist in interpersonal functional therapy.

In keeping with Roger's (1961) model of self-actualization and belief in the client's ability to take increased personal responsibility and move toward greater efficacy, in her model of personal construct psychology, Houston (1998) asserted that explanations for behavior lie within each individual, that people are active in the world and not just passive recipients, and that change is always possible. This struggle to find explanations within the juvenile's individuality, to believe in the juvenile's capacity for self-efficacy, and to create the facilitative environment in which the client can change and is motivated to change is the work most evident in individual treatment. Not to believe in these capacities, and hence not to believe in the power of individual therapy, suggests that the model of treatment is more corrective and forensic than it is oriented toward mental health and personal growth. Whereas that may be an appropriate approach to take with adult sexual offenders, it is not the case with sexually reactive children and juvenile sexual offenders, who—as virtually everything in our literature tells us—do have the capacity to change.

Case Study 19.3 presents an adolescent offender who was able to recognize the meaning behind a lifetime pattern of self-defeating behavior that became sexually destructive to others, and through this recognition and the acquisition of new skills, he began to develop a new outlook and improved self-esteem.

GUIDELINES FOR INDIVIDUAL THERAPY

Given the many uses and approaches of individual therapy, from psychodynamic exploration to self-expression, the provision of support, the processing and reinforcement of group and family therapy content, cognitive reframing, and trauma reduction, individual therapy is too wide-ranging to apply a simple formula. However, there are some basic guidelines that underlie all applications and uses of individual therapy that can both instruct and keep the therapist on track and ensure that the therapy is individualized:

1. *Start where the client is.* The therapist must ensure that the client's needs, emotional level, cognitive skills, and interest and preparedness for therapy are known. Therapy must be aimed at the client's current level.
2. *Use appropriate techniques.* The therapist must apply the correct technique to each client and each treatment situation. Therapists limited to single approaches will miss the opportunity to help many clients who do not fit their approach. The technique should fit the client, rather than squeeze the client to fit the approach. Under such circumstances, failure is seen as client failure rather than as the failure of the technique, which cannot serve the desired outcome of helping the child.

Jose was a 16-year-old who had few social skills and had been ostracized by peers for most of his life. He was in treatment for sexual offenses against younger children and was able to disclose several more offenses against children during his first year in treatment. He had never had any friends, had never been invited to parties or peer social events, and was shunned by peers largely because of his behaviors and arrogance. However, he managed to form friendships with considerably younger family cousins and neighbors that eventually turned into sexual relationships, inappropriately meeting his needs for affiliation and social mastery. The issue for Jose was not one of pedophilia, however, but engagement and emotional comfort.

It became clear that Jose's arrogance and oppositionality were intended to prevent adults and peers from getting too close and thus learning about his social incompetency, as well as serving as a defense against any closeness that he had come to believe would result in later rejection and disappointment. His attitude and behaviors had developed into a near personality disorder built around his sense of failure with peers. Individual therapy, coupled with group and family work, allowed him to become increasingly aware of the role played by his oppositional and irritable behaviors and how they prevented his growth, thus keeping him isolated. Whereas group therapy focused on the development of appropriate self-expression, especially when scapegoated and verbally bullied by other group members, individual therapy helped Jose to see how his behaviors and interactions in group recreated the environment he was expecting to find and how he came to use sexual relationships with children as a means for self-fulfillment and social connection. Through individual work, Jose came to see the damage he had caused himself, his family, and his victims, and he began the process of making amends, victim awareness, and victim clarification.

Jose increasingly became more appropriately assertive, less oppositional, and able to speak directly and without hostility; developed his level of social comfort and social skills; and showed increasing comfort with himself and in his ability to be honest about his thoughts, feelings, and behaviors. By the time Jose entered a less restrictive and intense level of treatment, he was far more confident and socially skilled, self-expressive, and experiencing improved self-esteem and a stronger sense of accomplishment and hope.

Case Study 19.3

3. *Be interested.* Therapists not really interested in their clients, especially when the clients are kids who can sense authenticity in adults, are not likely to be successful. Children—including juvenile sexual offenders—are interesting people with interesting lives, ideas, and experiences. Therapists should foster genuine interest in their clients as they build and use the therapeutic relationship.

4. *Find things to like about clients.* Clinicians who do not like their clients (or, worse, find them heinous) will not be successful. The need is even more critical with children and adolescents who have often experienced many adults and peers who do not really like them. This does not mean liking or condoning all aspects of the client's personality and

behavior, but "hating the sin but not the sinner" will help to provide the corrective emotional experience.

5. *Be respectful.* No matter how assertive, forceful, challenging, or confrontive, clinicians do not own their clients and do not have the right to treat them with disrespect. In all cases, disrespect is unlikely to meet the goals of a positive therapeutic relationship or the rehabilitation of the juvenile and is antithetical to the treatment alliance.

6. *See the world through the client's eyes.* This relates to the juvenile's phenomenology but also deals with empathy and connection. Clinicians must be able to understand the client's world in the way that each client experiences it.

7. *Push clients further.* Pacing is essential, beginning with the first guideline in which the clinician works at the client's level. Nevertheless, clinicians must continue to assess clients throughout treatment and take them further, ensuring not only that they learn new ideas, acquire new information, develop new language, and experience insight and retain these things, but also that they go deeper and further until treatment is considered to be over.

8. *Take clients where they do not want to go.* Although potentially controversial, given the depth of the pathology in sexual offending and the goal of eliminating such behaviors before juvenile sexual offenders possibly evolve into adult sexual offenders, taking clients to uncomfortable emotional places is key.

9. *Help clients be uncomfortable.* The first part of this guideline is to encourage clients to go to emotionally charged places that they would rather avoid—and usually do avoid through some form of emotional numbing or distraction, such as oppositional behavior, substance abuse, aggression, dissociation, and even sexual aggression itself. The second part of the guideline is supporting juveniles when they get to those affectively laden places and helping them recognize that they *can* tolerate the discomfort and thus face and eventually overcome the emotional problem.

10. *Formulate the case.* Therapists should constantly think about the treatment they are providing and the client's changing treatment needs over time.

11. *Seek supervision.* Clinicians are well advised to get supervision, including peer supervision, to help them formulate and plan for treatment, especially when so much is at stake for the juvenile and potentially the community.

CONCLUSION

It is not possible to provide the treatment focus or interaction that can be achieved in individual therapy through any other form of treatment. Whether or not clinicians use individual therapy often has more to do with their own level of experience and comfort than with certain knowledge that individual therapy works or does not work. Regardless of empirical proof of the efficacy of individual therapy, a lack of evidence does not mean that something does not work or is not helpful. It merely means that it is not proved. In fact, as noted throughout this book, there is no empirical evidence that *any* form of treatment works for juvenile or adult sexual offenders, yet the alternative (to provide no treatment at all) is unthinkable.

Individual therapy is an important tool in the arsenal of treatment approaches available to rehabilitate juvenile sexual offenders. It should be employed as part of an integrated treatment strategy that also involves group and, whenever possible, family therapy.

CHAPTER 20

Group Therapy and Group Leadership

GROUP TREATMENT is likely the most prevalent form of treatment with sexual offenders, both adult and juvenile. Its prevalence can be attributed largely to the economy of treatment it provides (a single 45- to 90-minute therapy session can reach as many clients as are in the group) and to the widespread belief that it is an effective mode of treatment. In the group, clients can universally be exposed to the same messages and the same learning environment, demonstrate and learn social interaction skills, and show change over time through the level and quality of group participation. However, as noted in chapter 11, although group is commonly believed to be an effective treatment model, not all practitioners agree, and some believe that group treatment is contraindicated in some cases (Dishion, McCord, & Poulin, 1999).

An integrated and multimodal model of treatment for juvenile sexual offenders goes far beyond group work alone, including individual therapy and, where possible, family therapy. Nevertheless, it is clear to many clinicians that groups are among the most effective tools in treating sexual offending behavior and that they generally provide meaningful treatment for adolescents. In addition, within the group mode itself, group therapy can be broad and varied, providing a range of treatment focuses, inclusive of sexual-offender-specific treatment and collateral treatment aimed at the reduction of related pathologies and deficits, as well as the enhancement of social skills and mental health in general. In fact, the general clinical perspective is that group therapy as a specific treatment mode is of unquestionable value and is an effective and critical mode in the treatment of troubled children. Groups provide a powerful means for addressing both pathology through therapy groups and (non-pathological) life and skill enhancement in personal growth groups that are not aimed at rehabilitation at all, but simply greater self-efficacy. To this end, there is a long tradition of group work in all forms of human development and psychotherapy meeting many different needs. The economy of group is one such reason, but the more compelling and ethical reasons are treatment based because, like individual and family therapy, groups provide a treatment form and treatment environment that cannot be provided any other way.

However, it is the composite of treatment approaches and interventions, coupled with the central and organizing theme of sexual assaultive behavior, that makes individual or family treatment sexual offender specific. The same is true of sexual offender group therapy. Groups are sexual offender specific because the focus is on sexually aggressive and inappropriate behavior and because the themes and activities of such groups are directed toward the treatment of such behavior. The principles, interventions, and activities of group therapy are universal.

THE STRENGTHS AND GOALS OF GROUP THERAPY

First, the uses of group work are flexible and multiple. In the treatment setting, group work may be used for a range of purposes including psychotherapy, activity planning, problem solving and decision making, task accomplishment, or the development of individual skills. Of special importance, though, and not replicated by any other therapy medium, treatment in group occurs within the context of a social and interactional environment drawn from the backgrounds of diverse and otherwise unrelated individuals who come together solely for the purpose of treatment.

Group members have the opportunity to learn about themselves and others, express thoughts and share feelings, discover connections and similarities between themselves and other group members, realize that they are not alone in their experiences of the world, and recognize differences between themselves and others and thus their own uniqueness. In group, clients engage in social interactions in a therapeutically controlled and facilitative environment and can experiment with new roles and new ideas and be observed and redirected in a treatment environment capable of providing corrective emotional and cognitive experiences. In addition, in group the same messages and ideas are shared with and processed by all group members in a highly interactional process; group members can be observed by the therapist in the interactional environment; and group members stimulate, challenge, and support one another and can build a new peer culture. Finally, groups provide the medium through which to brainstorm ideas and work together as a team to complete tasks of all sorts.

Group therapists can learn a great deal about group members as both individuals and social beings, and—equally true—group members can learn a great deal about one another and themselves. Groups are a wonderful medium because they possess therapeutic, educational, interactional, and social components that do not exist in other therapeutic modalities. Group therapy is built on the idea that facilitated groups allow treatment interventions and opportunities for personal growth that are not present during interactions between two people (i.e., the therapist and the client). Groups present a fertile environment for self-expression and self-awareness, cohesion and cooperation, role modeling, feedback, and other experiences that allow the development of both social skills and individual reflection. Group therapy provides a therapeutic environment that encourages the open expression and sharing of thoughts, feelings, and experiences among group members.

THE THERAPEUTIC ENVIRONMENT

The objective of group therapy is to build a therapeutic environment in which group members are enabled to

1. Share and explore their personal experiences with peers in a safe and controlled setting
2. Recognize that their problems are not unique and that others may have found solutions to these or similar problems
3. Build a resource for self-help, thus achieving a sense of empowerment and self-efficacy
4. Provide feedback to other group members and thus facilitate the development of communication and other interpersonal skills
5. Receive feedback from other group members and thus develop both listening and learning skills
6. Explore and experiment with new roles and behaviors in an environment where they can receive input from other group members on the appropriateness of and their success in these roles
7. Build a sense of altruism, in which they are presented with the opportunity to put the needs of others ahead of themselves and to be helpful and important in the lives of others
8. Build cohesiveness with and a sense of belonging to a group that accepts and understands them and that fosters a feeling of common purpose and mutual support
9. Express negative and positive feelings appropriately and get things off their chest

Rounding out a description of the group treatment environment, Sawyer (2000) described seven factors that make the group both a rich corrective and rehabilitative experience and a treatment-enhancing environment:

1. In the social environment of the group, the interactional patterns of each group member are visible and can become targets for change if necessary.

2. Groups build on the strengths and healing powers of relationships among members.
3. Through group interactions, relationship skills and deficits become evident, as well as antisocial character traits and interactional tendencies.
4. The group interactional process allows emotional, cognitive, and behavioral changes to occur within a relationship-based environment and not simply within the client's own head.
5. Group treatment allows the development of multiple treatment relationships providing multiple sources for feedback and support.
6. Group members experience connection, commonality, and support when taking emotional risks.
7. Groups can produce direct, honest, supportive, and challenging pro-treatment cultures that assist and require members to become self-disclosive.

PRIMARY GROUP TREATMENT FACTORS

Yalom (1985) wrote that "the multiplicity of forms is so evident today that it is best not to speak of group therapy but of the many group therapies" (p. x). This is because group therapy is a fluid form of treatment. However, just as there appear to be common factors present in psychotherapy in general, there are also factors common to the group therapeutic process. Yalom's work distinguishes between the group's manifest (surface) content and its underlying core. He asserted that by separating the front of the group (i.e., its shape, techniques, form, and language), the core elements of the group are revealed, or those aspects of group work intrinsic to the therapeutic process within the group and across all groups: "Disregard the 'front,' consider only the actual mechanisms of effecting change in the patients, and we will find that these mechanisms of change are limited in number and remarkably similar across groups" (p. xi). Yalom's work gives shape to the group process, allows the development of a theory and language by which effective groups can be understood and described, and gives rise to 11 therapeutic factors (see Figure 20.1) described by Yalom as common to all effective groups.

Incorporating each of the aforementioned goals and factors, primary group treatment factors can be defined as

1. Social relatedness and connection
2. Acquisition of new information and ideas
3. Socialization and the development of social skills
4. Self-expression and emotional discharge
5. Corrective emotional experiences

- **Instillation of Hope.** New group members see other members recovering, improving, and overcoming difficulties, helping them to overcome feelings of hopelessness.

- **Universality.** Group members learn that their problems are not unique, and they are similar to others and share common experiences.

- **Information and Guidance.** Group members are provided the opportunity to learn through the instruction and advice of group leaders and other group members.

- **Altruism.** Group members are able to put the needs of others ahead of their own and to be helpful to others.

- **Corrective Recapitulation of the Family Experience.** Group members can relive and understand family patterns through the group experience, shed dysfunctional behavioral and attitudinal patterns learned in the family, and adopt and use new behaviors.

- **Socialization.** Group members develop increased social skills and are able to model advanced social skills to newer group members.

- **Identification and Imitative Behavior.** Group members observe and imitate other group members, in turn serving as role models for newer group members.

- **Interpersonal Learning.** Group members learn about themselves through the feedback of others in the group (learning <u>input</u>) and by adjusting and adapting their ability to engage actively with others in group (learning <u>output</u>).

- **Cohesiveness.** Group members experience a sense of belonging to a group that accepts and understands them, allows close contact with others, and provides a sense of common purpose and mutual support.

- **Catharsis.** Group members are able to express negative and positive feelings.

- **Existential Factors.** Group members recognize that there is no escape from some of life's unpleasant realities, but they must take responsibility for the way they live regardless of how much adversity they may face.

Figure 20.1
Group therapeutic factors. From Yalom (1985).

GROUP TYPE AND PURPOSE

Groups in sexual-offender-specific treatment take on many different shapes and forms, and through different types of groups it is possible to pursue a variety of goals using different types of groups.

Shaffer and Galinsky (1974) defined two types of groups: psychotherapy groups aimed at rehabilitation and the reduction of psychopathology, and skills training (or human relationships) groups aimed at enhancement of skills and efficacy. Smead (1995) defined four types of groups: (a) *work groups* that have a particular task to accomplish, (b) *psychoeducational groups* that serve an instructional and guidance function, (c) *counseling groups* aimed at interpersonal problem solving, and (d) *psychotherapy groups* directed toward rehabilitation and the reconstruction of personality. In a similar vein, Rose and Edleson (1987) described five categories of target skills pursued through group treatment: (a) the development of interpersonal and social skills; (b) the development of general problem-solving skills including alternative think-

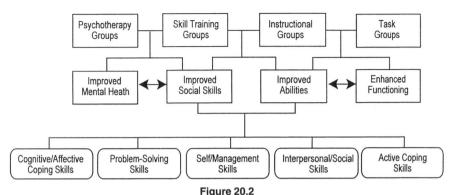

Figure 20.2
Group types and outcomes.

ing, consequential thinking, and means-end thinking; (c) cognitive and emotional coping skills that increase the client's capacity to deal with internal and external events; (d) active coping skills that incorporate skills such as problem solving but focus more on skills that allow clients actively to interrupt or escape problem situations; and (e) self-management skills by which adolescents and children may learn self-monitoring and self-regulation techniques and skills. These models are incorporated into the general model of group type and group outcome shown in Figure 20.2.

Although the subjects dealt with in group treatment can be limitless depending on the design of the treatment program, specific client needs, and the creativity of the clinician, groups typically center around one of two primary purposes and adopt one of three primary types, or alternatively one of two adjunctive group types.

PRIMARY GROUP PURPOSE

Group purpose can be considered either *exploratory* or *prescriptive*. In the exploratory group (sometimes referred to as process based), the primary purpose is the development of awareness and insight in which group members experience a sense of awareness about themselves, one another, their victims, their behaviors, their circumstances, and other matters related to treatment. In the prescriptive group (content based), the primary purpose is the development of cognitive and behavioral skills, including the ability of group members to correct dysfunctional thoughts and behaviors.

Such distinctions in describing group purpose are somewhat artificial, however. In reality, groups have more than one purpose, and the desired end product in all cases is change. Nonetheless, in most groups one purpose or focal point stands out more than the other, and thus the manner in which the goals of change are both envisaged and pursued. In the exploratory group the primary route to change is believed to be insightful self-awareness; thus,

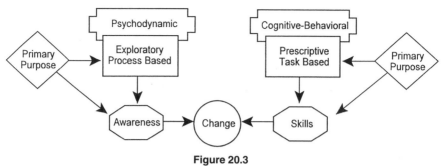

Figure 20.3
Primary group purpose and pathway to change.

the primary purpose becomes that of increasing *awareness* in group members, from which enhanced self-management and interactional skills can grow. In the prescriptive group change is conceptualized as the product of improved and more effective cognitive and behavioral skills; thus, the purpose becomes that of developing improved *skills* in group members, from which more effective and appropriate behavior will develop. In either case, the less dominant purpose serves only as a secondary vehicle that reinforces and meets the goals of the primary purpose. In the exploratory group, skill development is aimed at the capacity to experience increased awareness and insight. Conversely, in prescriptive groups, self-awareness is the means by which new skills are developed. Figure 20.3 shows primary group purpose and the route to client change.

Primary Group Type

The *psychodynamic* approach to groups always has an exploratory purpose, and because this approach is most commonly linked to the interactional process of the group, these groups are often referred to as *process groups*. Process groups are focused largely on the development of awareness and insight in group members and skills related to interpersonal relationships and interactions. They concentrate on the underlying and often invisible dynamics in group process; learning and the development of insight through the experience of being in the group; and the process of interaction, idea exchange, communication, and role modeling within the group. In the psychodynamic group, awareness is linked to insight, or a deeper and more penetrating level of awareness. Skill development is aimed at increasing self-knowledge, improving social interactions, increasing frustration tolerance, and enhancing insight and empathy.

The *cognitive-behavioral* group is the most common type of group in the treatment of juvenile sexual offenders, as well as the most commonly supported approach. These groups, also known as *content groups* because they are driven by the particular tasks (or content) of the group, focus on the development of both awareness and skills. However, in the cognitive group, awareness is not linked to insight but rather reflects the capacity to recognize cognitive distortions and high-risk situations. In this case, rather than an end state (as it is, to some degree, in the psychodynamic approach), awareness is a gateway skill that must be developed in order to lead to the more highly developed ability to change cognitive distortions and avoid risky circumstances. Cognitive-behavioral groups concentrate on the acquisition of thinking skills, the ability to recognize and correct cognitive distortions and dysfunctional behavioral cycles, relapse prevention planning, and the development of a broad awareness and recognition of these important concepts both in principle and in real-life application.

Psychoeducational groups focus on providing information to group members and developing skills connected to thinking, emotions, behavior, relationships, attitudes, beliefs, interactions, and other aspects of interpersonal and prosocial functioning. Accordingly, like cognitive groups, psychoeducational groups are primarily content oriented, concentrating on the tasks of instruction and skill acquisition. However, in the psychoeducational group, neither process nor awareness is the goal. Instead, the focus is squarely on content alone. Emphasis is on behavior more than cognition, and the aim is to teach skills and directly influence behavior. The operating principle in the psychoeducational group is that through learning new skills, inappropriate or unwanted behavior can be eliminated or modified. Psychoeducation is distinguished from education by its focus on behaviors that appear to be related to and influenced by emotions, thoughts, and feelings, although these thought processes are not necessarily central to the practice of psychoeducation.

ADJUNCTIVE GROUP TYPES

Adjunctive groups typically are not provided as primary groups. In many cases, adjunctive groups are not provided at all. However, these groups can be important components in a well-rounded group program. *Expressive* groups most typically include art, drama, music, or movement therapy groups and focus on the ability to express ideas, feelings, memories, experiences, and values in a largely nonverbal manner. *Experiential* groups usually involve therapeutic recreation, outdoor adventure, and physical challenge programs that focus on the ability to learn and develop insight and social skills through the experience of directly engaging in an activity or event. Activities promote group interactions and teamwork, healthy leisure, the release of energy through appropriate activity, and the appropriate and successful use of free and leisure time. Whereas expressive groups are more exploratory, experien-

Group Type	Brief Description	Primary Group Purpose	
		Exploratory (Awareness Based)	Prescriptive (Skill Based)
Cognitive-Behavioral	Correction of thinking errors and reduction of resulting negative behaviors		✓
Psychoeducational	Delivery of ideas and information about improved functioning		✓
Psychodynamic	Underlying dynamics in group process and the development of insight through the group experience	✓	
Expressive	Expression of ideas, feelings, experiences, and values in a largely nonverbal manner	✓	
Experiential	Developing insight and social skills through the experience of directly engaging in an activity or event		✓
Recreational	Recreational/leisure activities designed to promote group interactions, healthy leisure, energy release		✓
Skill Development	Acquisition of concrete social and personal skills		✓

Figure 20.4
Matrix of group type and purpose.

tial groups tend to be more oriented to skill development. Figure 20.4 provides a summary and overview of group types and their primary function as exploratory or prescriptive.

SEXUAL-OFFENDER-SPECIFIC GROUPS

Primary groups for juvenile sexual offenders are either content-focused cognitive-behavioral or psychoeducational groups or process-oriented psychodynamic groups. Content-based groups will teach ideas and ways to apply them, transforming ideas into attitudinal and behavioral change. These may include teaching basic ideas about behavioral cycles and thinking errors, the practical exploration and application of these ideas and how they play out in the lives of group members, the development of relapse prevention plans, and planning for discharge and aftercare. Content groups can also be topic or skill based, teaching or discussing items such as healthy sexuality, relationship skills, anger management, and social skills development. Such groups will typically use homework, didactic instruction, role modeling, instructional videos, discussion, and other methods to introduce and teach the concepts. In all sexual-offender-specific content groups, the topic is related to developing an understanding of appropriate and inappropriate sexual behaviors, pathways to and ways to avoid relapse, and the development of prosocial skills that enhance healthy sexual behaviors.

Process groups focus on the daily interactions and experiences of group members and are often indirectly connected to sexual behaviors. These groups are concerned with developing communication and interactional skills through the experience of being in the group and learning to be an effective group member, recognizing unhealthy ways of thinking through giving and receiving feedback in the group, and developing awareness of self and others through engagement and connection. Process groups depend on the group leader's ability to focus the group on interactions and help group members gain self-awareness through group participation. These groups are sexual offender specific because the underlying goal is to connect cognitive, interactional, and behavioral patterns to sexually inappropriate and aggressive behavior, thus providing both recognition and an emotionally corrective experience.

SEXUAL OFFENDER GROUP TYPES AND THEMES

Sexual-offender-specific groups can be designed in many ways to work on the identification, exploration, and discussion of sexual behavior and ways to avoid reoffending. Several primary themes are found in the treatment of the juvenile sexual offender, sometimes incorporated into broader groups and sometimes used to organize groups focused on a particular theme. In any case, varied group interventions can be used to introduce and process treatment themes, ranging from discussion and verbal processing to experiential activities intended to have significant impact on group members, including role playing, structured activities, watching and discussing videos, and introducing outside speakers into groups.

- *Discharge* groups focus on the discussion and acquisition of relapse prevention plans and skills and the development of aftercare plans.
- *Disclosure* groups are dedicated to sexual offense disclosures by group members. Sometimes several members make brief disclosures during any particular group session, but sessions may also focus on the detailed disclosures of a single member, allowing ample opportunity for questions, discussion, and processing.
- *Victim awareness* groups are focused on activities related to the experiences of victims and may include the reading of victim letters and stories, victim restitution projects, victim commemorations, and other activities designed to increase victim awareness in group members.
- *Focus* groups are based on a particular subject relevant to sexual offending and may involve events in the news, videos, guest speakers, or other relevant topics.
- *Psychoeducational* groups introduce, teach, and explore cognitive-behavioral ideas relevant to the elimination of sexual offending and the development of replacement behaviors.

- *Skill application* groups are closely related to psychoeducational groups and focus on the ability of group members to apply outside of group what they have learned, describe difficulties faced in the application of new ideas and behaviors, and find solutions to problems faced in applying new skills.
- *Expressive-experiential* groups use (often nonverbal) activities to build cohesion, create new understanding, or drive home group themes with the purpose of developing increased awareness in group members that will help them reshape their view of themselves and others.

Sexual Offender Group Techniques and Activities

Activity-based groups use structured activities or experiences to engage and teach group members. In some cases, activities are followed by verbal processing in order to help group members understand the purpose of the activity, process their experience, and reflect on what they learned. Other activities do not involve any processing but depend instead on the experience itself to teach and help group members see things differently. Either way, activities are usually structured, with a beginning and end, and often have a script for the therapist to follow in its application. However, techniques are not as defined as activities and are more typically used by therapists to organize and engage members and draw them out. Role plays, for instance, are often defined activities used to accomplish a particular task. A technique such as the hot seat (one group member occupies the chair while others give feedback) may have a less defined purpose, however, and be used to engage group members or help them deliver feedback to one another.

Both techniques and activities are aimed at experiential learning or self-expression. Often borrowed from family therapy, psychodrama, or other therapies, group techniques include hot seats, empty chairs (in which a victim or someone else is imagined to be sitting in an empty chair and the group engages that imaginary person in a conversation), doubling (one group member stands behind the chair of another and talks for that person), role play and role reversals, and so on. These can be powerful and effective means to engage and interest group members, and they are often as effective (if not more effective) as verbal processing in group.

Activities and techniques can easily be incorporated into group, from initial warm-up exercises to those designed to create opportunities for greater engagement, open group members up to new ideas, or use nonverbal means to experience and express ideas. Groups often start and end with a routine activity, and this may include a circle of shared ideas, expressions of how the day is going, description of feelings, some sort of positive statement, and even brief disclosures of sexual offenses. There is no set method or pattern for us-

Steve usually ran his groups as strictly talk groups, depending on verbal interactions and processes to engage group members and address and work through treatment tasks. However, he used different kinds of techniques and activities in groups when they seemed appropriate, usually to teach ideas more effectively that group members might not understand as deeply if he used discussion only. He also used activities to provide a level of variety to groups so that they did not become repetitive, and sometimes because as group membership changed or the group got stuck, activities could help quickly move things.

Steve sometimes used the goldfish bowl technique to help group members learn more about their process, and broke the group in two. One group sat in a circle and was surrounded by the other group members. The inner group engaged in the group process, while the outside group silently watched on with each member assigned the task of watching a particular inner circle group member or noting some particular process activity in the inner group, such as the way that people engaged in conversation. In shorter length groups, the outer group eventually began discussing with one another what they had observed in the group, while the inner group listened and learned about their process. In longer groups, Steve would have the two groups switch places and repeat the process, and eventually both groups would merge and share and process what they had observed and learned. Steve also sometimes used art and movement activities in group, role plays, and other activities designed to illustrate to group members how they were connected to one another and how their behaviors affected the community. On other occasions, he brought short videos clips into the group for focused discussion. Overall, he found that mixing activities with his usual discussion-based groups provided many ways to teach and engage group members and help them to learn experientially, as well as through words.

Case Study 20.1

ing activities and techniques, and group leaders learn by watching other group leaders, getting training, and delving into their own experiences. There are many excellent books that contain literally hundreds of group exercises and activities, many of which can be adapted for work in sexual-offender-specific groups.

Some activities particular to sexual-offender-specific groups are those associated with disclosures of sexual offenses, in which the youth describes his behaviors to other group members, and with the victim clarification process, in which group members begin and practice the process of restitution and making amends to victims. As with group activities and techniques in general, there is no set way to accomplish these tasks, and therapists learn by watching and talking to other therapists, by supervising and training, and by applying and experimenting with their own ideas. Case Study 20.1 provides an illustration of the use of structured activities in group treatment.

GROUP STRUCTURE

Groups are a wonderful medium because their therapeutic and educational component allows them to be very flexible. Nevertheless, regardless of purpose or flexibility, groups require planning and structure.

LEADERSHIP AND COTHERAPY

It is always preferable to have trained cotherapists in a group because there is often too much going on in the group for one clinician to spot and control. In addition, each therapist can play different roles, one focused on content and the other on process, for instance. Furthermore, when one therapist is more experienced than the other, the less experienced clinician has the opportunity to learn through observation, modeling, active supervision, and on-the-job training. However, although it is not always possible to have two therapists running groups, it is still important to have a coleader, such as trained paraprofessional staff. The goal is to have the coleader play a leadership role, however, and not sit quietly in the background or play the role of disciplinarian.

When cotherapy is possible, it is useful to have teams of male and female therapists. Having mixed-gender leadership adds a further dynamic to the group and the opportunity for group members to witness male and female staff working together, but this is a matter of philosophy more than necessity. When cotherapy occurs, it is important for clinicians to discuss and process the group with one another before and after the group.

GROUP SIZE

Typically, groups contain at least four members. Unless a group is didactic only, resembling a classroom more than a group, the upper limit to group size is about 10 members. No matter how many therapists are in the group, having 10 or more group members does not allow enough opportunity for all group members to participate fully in the group, and group dynamics become difficult to spot and control. The ideal group size in juvenile sexual offender groups is between six and eight. Adolescent groups with fewer than six members can strain a group, depending on the involvement of group members, their ability to participate, and their capacity to run a group themselves.

NORM

Norms are the behaviors, interactions, and attitudes expected of group members. Norms are expectations rather than rules or requirements, although adherence to defined rules may be a norm. Nonetheless, norms act like rules and often are more effective, especially in the well-defined and positive group culture. In fact, Shaw (1981) noted that norms outlast the group life of individual members and have an enduring and powerful effect on the group as a whole. In addition to norms about basic group participation and involvement, norms typically include things such as

- Respect for one another.
- The right of all group members to be heard.
- Safety from verbal and emotional aggression, hostility, and derision.
- Emotional responses are okay and encouraged.
- Everything reasonable is open for discussion.
- Behaviors, ideas, attitudes, and emotions can be challenged.
- Engagement in the group process and with one another is important for the whole group.
- The group supports all group members and not just some.
- Exploring issues and ideas with objectivity and thorough analysis is of importance.
- Success and accomplishment are the result of group effort.

GROUP RULES

Rules provide the basic structure for groups. Distinguished from norms, they nevertheless resemble norms because they allow group members to know what is expected, how to behave and interact, and the consequences for both positive and negative behaviors. Ferrara (1992) described the *Limit and Lead* model in group work, in which the therapist uses rules and structure to set limits, leading group members into therapeutically productive engagement. In his model Ferrara established clear, consistent, firm, and fair limits through which the goal is to lead group members to accomplish target behaviors through feedback, shaping and prompting behaviors, and fading the direct lead into the background in anticipation that behaviors will eventually be retained by group members.

However, there are no "correct" rules. These are set by each clinician, or perhaps mandated by the larger agency. Usually, rules set a tone for respect, how group members may respond to one another and interact in the group, when and if group members may leave the group for bathroom breaks or emotional time-outs, and under what conditions group members will be required to leave the group for inappropriate participation or nonparticipation. Rules become more complex when they shape how certain activities take place, such as expected level of participation, disclosures of sexual offenses, and participation in defined activities, and begin to resemble group norms. The clinician often establishes the rules, but some clinicians may allow group members to participate in rule development or set rules themselves. Rules are fluid and change over time. At all times it is important that the group

Receiving Feedback

Positive/Open Style

- Open. Listens without frequent interruption or objections.
- Responsive. Is willing to hear what's being said without turning the table.
- Accepting. Accepts the feedback without denial.
- Respectful. Recognizes the value of what is being said and the speaker's right to say it.
- Engaged. Interacts appropriately with the speaker, asking for clarification when needed.
- Active Listening. Listens carefully and tries to understand the meaning of the feedback.
- Thoughtful. Tries to understand the personal behavior that has led to the feedback.
- Interested. Is genuinely interested in getting feedback.
- Sincere. Genuinely wants to make personal changes if appropriate.

Negative/Closed Style

- Defensive. Defends personal actions and frequently objects to feedback given.
- Attacking. Verbally attacks the feedback giver and turns the table.
- Denies. Refutes the accuracy or fairness of the feedback.
- Disrespectful. Devalues the speaker, what the speaker is saying, or the speaker's right to give feedback.
- Closed. Ignores the feedback, listening blankly without interest.
- Inactive Listening. Makes no attempt to hear or understand the meaning of the feedback.
- Rationalizing. Finds explanations for the feedback that dissolve any personal responsibility.
- Patronizing. Listens but shows little interest.
- Superficial. Listens and agrees but gives the impression that the feedback will have little actual effect.

Giving Feedback

Effective/Positive Delivery

- Supportive. Delivered in a nonthreatening and encouraging manner.
- Direct. The focus of the feedback is clearly stated.
- Sensitive. Delivered with sensitivity to the needs of the other person.
- Considerate. Feedback is intended not to insult or demean.
- Descriptive. Focuses on behavior that can be changed, rather than personality.
- Specific. Feedback is focused on specific behaviors or events.
- Healthy Timing. Given as close to the prompting event as possible and at an opportune time.
- Thoughtful. Well considered rather than impulsive.
- Helpful. Feedback is intended to be of value to the other person.

Ineffective/Negative Delivery

- Attacking. Hard-hitting and aggressive, focusing on the weaknesses of the other person.
- Indirect. Feedback is vague and issues are hinted at rather than addressed directly.
- Insensitive. Little concern for the needs of the other person.
- Disrespectful. Feedback is demeaning, bordering on insulting.
- Judgmental. Feedback is evaluative, judging personality rather than behavior.
- General. Aimed at broad issues which cannot be easily defined.
- Poor Timing. Given long after the prompting event, or at the worst possible time.
- Impulsive. Given thoughtlessly, with little regard for the consequences.
- Selfish. Feedback meets the giver's needs, rather than the needs of the other person.

Figure 20.5
Rules of feedback.

therapist remain ultimately in charge of the rules and ready to pull the reins back in whenever necessary.

GROUP LEARNING ENVIRONMENT

Cohen and Smith (1976) stated that learning occurs in groups only when a number of conditions are present. Feedback between group members is of great value because it provides a means for members to help one another and to learn both to listen and to give feedback. It is important, then, to establish rules and norms governing feedback, as shown in Figure 20.5.

Self-disclosure is important also, both as a means for self-expression (and sometimes catharsis) and, in the sexual-offender-specific group, as a means to divulge and share information about sexual offending behaviors with other group members. Through disclosure, group members learn to share and listen, as well as learn from their own experiences and the experiences of others. A supportive group climate that includes emotional safety and mutual trust is central also, so that group members can jointly explore and experiment with new ideas and new roles. Finally, the ability to practice and apply new ideas and behaviors is critical in the effective learning environment and must become part of the group culture if the group is to be an effective means for therapy and rehabilitation. Figure 20.6 depicts the conditions for effective learning in group treatment.

- Feedback among group members
- Self-disclosure
- Self-expression
- Sharing of information
- Listening to others
- Being supportive
- Emotional safety
- Mutual trust
- Ability to practice new ideas and behaviors

Figure 20.6
Conditions required for learning in the group requirement.

ADAPTING GROUPS FOR SPECIFIC POPULATIONS

Despite descriptions of group types and purposes, in reality groups are not fixed entities that can be neatly categorized. Although it is possible to define primary group purposes and group types, the process of doing so is academic. It helps us to understand the underlying process and content of group therapy and to dissect groups for a better look and as a way to describe groups to others. In practice, groups are multifaceted and highly varied. In addition, groups are not limited in how they are designed and facilitated. Although there is an underlying theory to both group design and group leadership and although group therapy should be informed by empirical literature, groups can be run in many ways, largely defined by the experience, style, and approach of the group clinician. In fact, groups can be adapted to fit many purposes and should be designed or adapted to fit the specific client population for whom the group is intended.

Three obvious examples of special populations stand out. Groups for cognitively impaired clients should be directed toward the more concrete end of the conceptual and experiential spectrum, regardless of age. That is, whether cognitive-behavioral or psychodynamic in approach, group content is probably going to miss connecting with this population of kids if it is too abstract. It is possible that group members will be able to recite what they have learned in group, and particularly cognitive/skill-based groups, but this may reflect parroting, or the mere repetition of ideas and words, rather than the actual acquisition and integration of new ideas.

Groups for young children, too, should be especially designed in terms of length, content, structure, and activities. Group leaders should design these groups to be interactional, activity driven, and based on creative variants that are educational, engaging, fun, and designed for teaching and learning, and not simply toned-down replicas of adolescent groups. This is true of both process and cognitive groups, in which the age of the child is of paramount importance given the developmental lack of formal cognitive and abstract thinking skills in children, as well as their emotional rawness and sometimes primitiveness. In process groups, the development of interactional skills and empathy is a legitimate goal, but the development of insight is unlikely. For similar reasons, cognitive-behavioral groups for young children must be designed to meet the cognitive-developmental level of group members.

Thought-disordered or psychotic clients represent another special population that requires groups to be designed with their needs in mind, and with content and process elements that will work for them in group. Groups are intended to help kids succeed, grow, and develop new skills in groups, and those that are designed or operationalized for the wrong population are not likely to succeed. Groups should be designed and implemented for the population they intend to serve.

MIXED GROUPS

Custom designing groups does not mean that high-cognitive and low-cognitive clients, for example, should never be placed in the same group, or that psychotic-like clients should never mix in groups with nonpsychotic clients. The question of whether groups should be homogeneous or heterogeneous in nature cannot be answered here. Nevertheless, among the juvenile sexual offender population, children and adolescents should not be mixed into the same group, with the exception of older children and younger adolescents with an age difference of 2 years or less.

GROUP LEADERSHIP THEORY: ART INTO PRACTICE

Given the intensity and volume of interactions in group work and the need for the therapist to pay attention to and treat multiple clients at the same moment, group work is fast moving and more scattered than either individual or family work, requiring well informed and almost instinctive or habitual responses on the part of the group therapist. However, although there are endless ways to conceptualize and describe group therapy, including the role and function of the group leader, the participation and response of group members, and those attributes most important to group life, there is no step-by-step instruction manual that will allow for the effective facilitation of groups.

Like individual and family psychotherapy, group leadership is an art more than it is a science (Napier & Gershenfeld, 1983): It is learned through practice and active supervision rather than didactic instruction or academic review. Nevertheless, a theory of group dynamics, development, and leadership can help provide the practitioner with a framework against which to think about groups and develop the professional skills required to run effective groups and understand the life of the group. Transforming theory into working action is where art comes into play.

THE THERAPEUTIC RELATIONSHIP AND ALLIANCE IN GROUP THERAPY

One of the most obvious differences between group and individual therapy, as shown in Figure 19.1, is the nature of the therapeutic relationship. In group therapy the relationship is between the group therapist or group leader and the group *syntality*, or the equivalent of the ongoing and emerging group personality (Shaw, 1981), as well as among group members themselves. In effect, the group treatment milieu is the equivalent of the therapeutic relationship, in which the therapeutic alliance is cemented between and among the clinician and all group members. A successful alliance is the result of satisfying and productive interactions between the therapist and among all group members.

GROUP DYNAMICS: PROCESS AND CONTENT

Group dynamics is a term used to describe the interactions between group members—the movement of ideas, feelings, relationships, discussion, and so forth. Group dynamics represents the flow of group life and what is happening among group members at any given time. As is true in individual therapy as well, there are two aspects to group dynamics:

- *Group content* refers to the task of the group, or its goal. Content includes the aims, purpose, and overall goals of the group. Content is often the thing that is most easily recognized about a group, or *why* it exists.
- *Group process* is less visible and refers to the relationships among group members and how they interact with one another. Process includes the methods and style of group member communication, how people listen and speak to one another in the group, who gets to talk in the group and when, and other underlying aspects of group dynamics. Group process does not reflect or address the goals of the group, but rather the process of how those goals get achieved.

Content addresses *what* is being done by the group; process reflects *how* it is being done. Of this, MacKenzie (1990) wrote,

> The therapist must strive to understand the interactional process going on in the group. This involves a constant struggle to avoid being solely caught up in the content of the material. The therapist must practice moving in and out of the group process. At times, the therapist will be very much an interactional member of the group, but must be able to back out of the group and see it as an observer. . . . At one level, the therapist is attending to the words and the content themes while at the same time looking at the process through which the material is being presented or handled. (p. 205)

Case Study 20.2 describes the distinction between process and content material in groups and the difference between groups designed to address each type of treatment need.

THE DEVELOPMENTAL STAGES OF THE GROUP

There are a myriad of theories that explore the network and pattern of relationships among group members during the course of group life. In essence, these theories describe the ebb and flow of the group as it moves from formation to termination, and whereas some postulate a strictly linear flow and others a cyclical movement, the major theories hypothesize discrete stages within group development and growth.

In fact, every group has a beginning point and an end point, while in actual operation, groups are constantly in the "middle" state. This is most obvi-

In a psychoeducation group designed to teach and discuss cognitive-behavioral concepts, the group leader recognized significant tensions and negative interactions between Paul and Tom. These were interrupting their (as well as other group members') ability to engage in and learn from the group. The group leader knew that these issues were not appropriate material to be dealt with in the psychoeducation group, but also knew that the group could not accomplish its learning tasks if these process issues became too significant. She chose to call attention to the interactions, identifying them to the group as process issues, noting that they would be addressed and dealt with in the process (psychodynamic) group scheduled for the following day, or if the two group members could not contain the interactions, she would meet with them after the group. Had the situation been reversed and psychoeducation needs become apparent in the process group, she would have identified them to the group as psychoeducational needs, noting that the necessary education and discussion would be provided in the next psychoeducation group. The group leader recognized the difference between content and task and understood the necessary connection between them, but used different types of groups to address each type of treatment focus.

Case Study 20.2

ously true for closed-ended groups, or groups that have a definite start and end date or number of sessions. Unlike open-ended groups that have no end point, the life cycle of a closed-ended group is clear. The developmental cycle of open-ended groups is not as easy to see, and it may be assumed that once established, there is no further development or evolution. From this perspective, groups are seen as static entities, and there is no recognition that groups change and evolve, based largely on the discharge and admission of group members over time, as well as ongoing events in the lives of individual members.

Most theories of group therapy hold that groups pass through discrete stages of development, and such models provide a framework for understanding group practices and development, as well as for comparing the actual process and progress of the group to expectations about how the group should be developing. In group development models, groups move through a set of developmental processes that resemble stages. Cohen and Smith (1976), for instance, described group growth and development punctuated by a sequence of interrelated and orderly events, and Bennis and Shepard (1956), Schutz (1973), MacKenzie and Harper-Giuffre (1992), and Yalom (1985) also described the group process passing through a series of discrete stages. Each stage has specific developmental tasks, preparing and paving the way for the work to be accomplished in the following stage. Unlike a stage model of human development, however, groups that do not successfully negotiate or complete the tasks of one stage do not pass into the next stage. Instead, groups simply fail to progress at all and remain stuck in earlier stages where dissatisfaction or lack of focus is most evident, or they disband.

Group stage theory is useful because it helps the group clinician visualize the group as a dynamic process, regardless of the specific type of group or its task. In a developmental model, only in an advanced stage of productivity are group members able to work directly on the therapeutic issues that produce and support personal change. High-functioning and mature groups are characterized by their ability to reach and maintain such a stage. In a developmental model it is not possible to accomplish this condition without passing through prior developmental stages that build the groundwork for group cohesion and effectiveness. Shown in Figure 20.7, Lacoursiere's (1980) model of group development describes five stages that synthesize many of the general ideas of group development into a well-defined and useful conceptualization of group life.

A review of Lacoursiere's (1980) five stages shows that although both content/task and process/interaction are always present in group life, the first three stages focus on process rather than task, which cannot be effectively addressed or resolved until group process issues are recognized and resolved. Only in the fourth stage (production) is group work focused more on content than process. Groups must work on their process, or *how* they get things done, in order to be effective at content, or *what* gets done. Additionally, not every group reaches the more advanced stage of production, or even resolution.

Each time a new member enters the group, the group devolves or returns to an earlier stage of development as it accommodates and adjusts to the new member. Mature (i.e., well-developed and highly functioning) groups are able to assimilate and adjust to new members and quickly return to a higher developmental stage; nonetheless, they pass through the stages again. However, as each member shapes the personality and capacity of the group, the group is highly dependent on the contributions of each member. The inability to adjust to new members, pass along group norms, or respond to and address the needs and ideas of new members prevents groups from moving forward. Poor group leadership also will hold a group back, thus it is important that group therapists have a theory of group development and leadership to guide them.

GROUP STAGES DURING EACH GROUP SESSION

The group stage model can easily be applied, not only across the life of the group but also within each session. It can be seen that individual group sessions typically begin with an orienting process or exercise, move to Stage 2 issues and problems, address and resolve these, and spend the bulk of the group working on productive treatment issues before the session ends. In the high-functioning group, the group moves quickly to Stage 4 where the bulk of

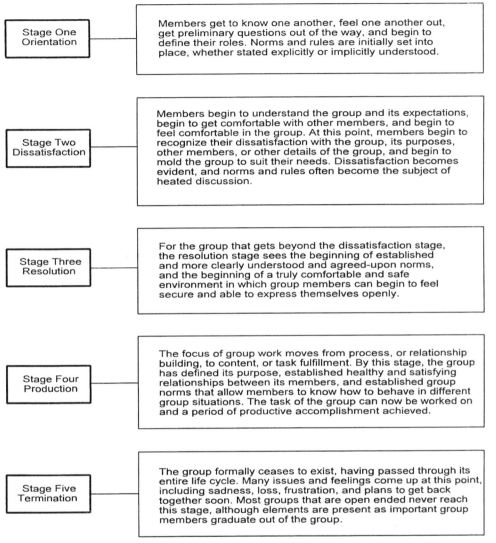

| Stage One Orientation | Members get to know one another, feel one another out, get preliminary questions out of the way, and begin to define their roles. Norms and rules are initially set into place, whether stated explicitly or implicitly understood. |

| Stage Two Dissatisfaction | Members begin to understand the group and its expectations, begin to get comfortable with other members, and begin to feel comfortable in the group. At this point, members begin to recognize their dissatisfaction with the group, its purposes, other members, or other details of the group, and begin to mold the group to suit their needs. Dissatisfaction becomes evident, and norms and rules often become the subject of heated discussion. |

| Stage Three Resolution | For the group that gets beyond the dissatisfaction stage, the resolution stage sees the beginning of established and more clearly understood and agreed-upon norms, and the beginning of a truly comfortable and safe environment in which group members can begin to feel secure and able to express themselves openly. |

| Stage Four Production | The focus of group work moves from process, or relationship building, to content, or task fulfillment. By this stage, the group has defined its purpose, established healthy and satisfying relationships between its members, and established group norms that allow members to know how to behave in different group situations. The task of the group can now be worked on and a period of productive accomplishment achieved. |

| Stage Five Termination | The group formally ceases to exist, having passed through its entire life cycle. Many issues and feelings come up at this point, including sadness, loss, frustration, and plans to get back together soon. Most groups that are open ended never reach this stage, although elements are present as important group members graduate out of the group. |

Figure 20.7

Lacoursiere's (1980) group developmental stage theory.

group time can be spent on treatment activities before wrapping up so that the group can end on a positive note. In groups that are moving toward effectiveness but not quite there, Stage 4 is reached but late in the group session with inadequate time available to address and process treatment issues, and the group either extends past its allotted time or ends on a difficult, tense, or unsatisfying note. Ineffective groups, on the other hand, never get past Stage 2, even within individual sessions. Figure 20.8 illustrates the developmental stages within a single group.

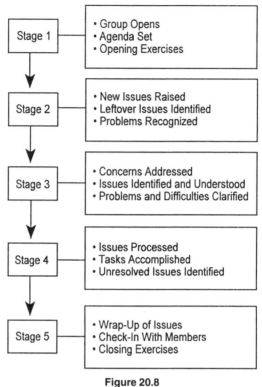

Figure 20.8
Group developmental stages in a single session.

THE FACILITATION OF GROUP CULTURE

Groups change and shift over time, especially in ongoing groups that routinely discharge old members and admit new members. In a stage model, every time a new member is admitted, the group returns to an earlier stage of development. The establishment of a group culture, or a well-defined set of expectations and methods for responding to the needs of each member, allows groups to maintain goals and standards and apply these to new group members. However, although group culture offers a language and set of expectations, they must also must remain flexible and adaptive. Groups based on a static culture become stagnant and fail to adjust to new members.

It is the group therapist's job to establish this culture, building the therapeutic milieu within which group treatment and the participation and growth of individual group members occurs. Pam and Kemker (1993) noted that in the *captive* group, or the group that requires participation (as is almost always the case in sexual-offender-specific treatment), clients often have to be socialized into learning how to be group members, and what the role entails. Often, new group members have goals that do not match the goals of the group leader or the group. It is the group culture that initially defines the group for the new members and socializes him. The role for the therapist in this case is to maintain a cohesive group identity, even as the group changes at both the level of individual membership and the group's developmental stage.

Pam and Kemker (1993) believe that all group members seek social acceptance at some level. They also believe that group members demonstrate their social problems at the here-and-now level, and it is the group leader's role, therefore, to catch on to and build on these tendencies of group membership. However, "in order for patients to tolerate the stresses of feedback [in the group setting], they must first feel cared about and secure. Interpersonal learning can only occur within the ongoing structure of a protective, supportive network" (p. 422). This job of developing the supportive group environment also falls to the group leader, whose task it is both to facilitate the opportunity for individual growth among group members and to mold the effective treatment milieu within the group.

Case Study 20.3 describes the manner in which a new member aggressively entered a well-defined group and how the group worked with him to introduce, socialize, and integrate him into the existing group culture without allowing him to destabilize the structure of the group.

Dave was a 16-year-old with a history of sexually abusing his two younger brothers, a lifetime history of conduct problems and social disconnection, and a highly dysfunctional family. He transferred from his previous therapy group into a well-established and higher functioning group, based on his progress in treatment. Dave entered the new group and almost immediately began to let the group know how important he had been in the other group, almost didactically offering advice to others group members, exhibiting a high need to be accepted into the group and recognized as mature.

His new group was highly developed, had established a format and means for recognizing and accomplishing tasks, and was sensitive to both process and content. The group had been effective at helping its members recognize and make important decisions, was clear and direct with its members about inappropriate behaviors and dishonesty, and provided a great deal of support and encouragement for members, allowing and encouraging them to experiment with new roles. The group had also learned how to recognize resistance in its members and not allow members to go unchallenged when behaving inappropriately. This group confronted Dave early on, demonstrating to him its norms and its culture and refusing to let him intimidate or dominate the group. At the same time, the group was able to welcome Dave as a new member, recognizing and addressing his anxiety, encouraged him to relax and be honest, and helped him understand expectations and how to develop into an effective group member, without allowing him to regress the group and keep it in a less functional or productive stage.

Case Study 20.3

THE DEVELOPMENTAL STAGES OF THE GROUP THERAPIST

Dies (1985) described some therapists who are unprepared for group work and others who fail to use group therapy techniques and instead attempt to provide individual therapy within the group setting, limiting interaction between group members and restricting group process. He referred to the problem of structure and activity within the group and the struggle to apply the correct blend of leadership style. Dies asserted that only the most skilled and experienced clinicians can competently lead certain kinds of therapy groups. In fact, many therapists experience anxiety and uncertainty in the leadership of groups, reducing their sense of enthusiasm to the task and leading them to feel ineffective.

Zaslav (1988) asserted that "hands-on clinical experience is at once the necessary and intimidating training tool in group therapy" (p. 511) and noted that "learning to harness the interpersonal process within a group in a skillful manner is generally a difficult endeavor for the neophyte therapist" (p. 512). He suggested that group therapy is particularly stressful because

- There is an abundance of stimuli and tasks within the group with which to contend
- The new group therapist will at times feel ineffective and intimidated
- The group process must often be managed under the eye of a supervisor, trainer, or cotherapist, which generates more stress for the new group therapist

Zaslav (1988) described the anxiety-reducing benefit of having a conceptual framework for understanding phenomena. This can be helpful to the inexperienced group therapist who may be feeling anxiety, self-doubt, and frustration. He suggested that group therapists also pass through stages of development, and he used the acronym GROUP to describe the process:

- *Stage 1:* **G**roup shock, in which the new group therapist feels threatened, overwhelmed, or confused by the abundance of stimuli.
- *Stage 2:* **R**eappraisal, in which the new group therapist retreats into a more comfortable but more inhibited (and even hostile) style of leadership. In this stage of development, the group therapist may attempt to pay more attention to group process but continue to feel frustrated or confused. In this stage the group therapist may feel inadequate or become angry with uncooperative group members.
- *Stage 3:* **O**ne step behind, in which, with supervisory support and adequate training, the new group therapist begins to identify and follow the interactive process in the group, especially when there is a more experienced coleader or trainer in the group to observe and work with. In this stage the trainee is beginning to understand process-oriented interventions as they occur and to anticipate some of them.

- *Stage 4:* Using the here and now, in which the group therapist begins to formulate and use interventions that focus on the interactive group process rather than content issues.
- *Stage 5:* Polishing skills, in which the group therapist begins to develop internalized templates that help to predict and recognize critical intervention points in group process, and the therapist also uses techniques that both highlight and intervene in the group process.

BEHAVIORS OF EFFECTIVE GROUP THERAPISTS

Napier and Gershenfeld (1983) identified several features of group leadership and corroborated the idea that the effective therapist must be skilled in both process and content areas. They noted that the focus is on leadership *behaviors* and not the personal traits of leaders and that diagnostic skills at both the individual and group level are imperative. It is important not only that group leaders have the skills to understand and enhance interpersonal relationships within the group and to bring about the fulfillment of task requirements, but also that they have the judgment and problem-solving skills that will guide the group in the appropriate direction. They noted that group leadership is an almost habitual process, in which the therapist is aware of the group at all times and constantly assesses and moves the group along as part of an ongoing process. Although they consider group leadership to be an art, Napier and Gershenfeld noted that the behaviors of effective leadership can be learned.

Lieberman, Yalom, and Miles (1973) described four primary leadership behaviors in the development and leadership of effective groups.

1. *Emotional stimulation* is considered the leadership behavior that includes revealing feelings; challenging, confronting, and expressing feelings and values; and the group therapist's active participation in the group. These therapist behaviors stimulate group members by asking questions, making direct interventions, and confronting and encouraging self-disclosure. Effective group leaders are moderate in their use of emotional stimulation.
2. *Caring* is constituted by the protecting of members, displays of affection and support, praise and encouragement, expressions of worth and concern for others, genuineness, modeling relationships, and encouraging feedback and mutual support from all group members. Caring alone is not enough to sustain an effective group, but effective group leaders ensure a caring approach in their work.
3. *Meaning-attribution* provides conceptual guidelines for the group to follow in understanding what's happening at any given moment, explanation, interpretation of reality, and a framework for recognizing change. Effective group leaders are high in their use of meaning attribution.

4. *Executive function* provides limit setting and rule establishment, procedures, pacing and sequencing, directing movement and managing time, goal development, interceding, decision making, and so forth. Effective group leaders are low to moderate in their use of executive function, using it when needed.

Whereas emotional stimulation and caring are maintenance functions that deal primarily with group process issues, executive function and meaning attribution focus on group task and create a set of therapist behaviors that address both aspects of group life. Lieberman et al. found that high levels of caring and meaning attribution, coupled with moderate amounts of both executive function and emotional stimulation, presented the most effective style of leadership.

Case Study 20.4 describes leadership style and approach and group stage, in which a new therapist entered an established group that had nevertheless not progressed far in its developmental life.

Alice stepped into the role of group therapist for a group that was long established but had not been worked hard by the previous group leader and was not an effective group. Alice quickly presented herself as a powerful force in the group, and the group quickly moved into a stage of dissatisfaction, actively attempting to demoralize and control her, thus rendering her helpless and maintaining the group status quo. The group adopted an oppositional stance, and several powerful members conspired against Alice within and outside of the group, challenging her role and attempting to demonstrate her inferiority and inability to lead them. The group struggled against her leadership, and some members passively refused to comply with directives and were dismissive of her. With supervisory support, Alice became more comfortable and stronger in her style and approach, put into place clear rules, and took charge of the group, in some cases temporarily removing members. She raised issues, challenged members directly in group, clarified group process, provided strong chairmanship, and generally modeled what she expected the group to look like, eventually helping the group get beyond active dissatisfaction and into a stage where treatment issues were being addressed and resolved.

The group increasingly accepted Alice's leadership, moving further into the process of learning how to be a group, and periodically was able to address individual treatment issues directly rather than simply fight Alice. The group continued to move back and forth from a stage of productivity to one of dissatisfaction, fueled largely by one or two angry group members, and Alice worked with these members both within the group and individually. The group generally became more focused on the work of treatment, coming to recognize that the conflicts and power struggles with the group leader mirrored the attitudes and behaviors of group members outside of the group and in many cases reflected issues of domination, control, manipulation, coercion, and conduct disorder that were part of their sexual offenses.

Case Study 20.4

STEERING THE GROUP: CRITICAL INCIDENTS

Leading a group is like rafting down a river. The group leader cannot easily move upstream and generally has to move with the current and flow of the river as it moves downstream. The skillful leader can see the river ahead, including its pitfalls and attributes, and can steer the group along so that it goes where the leader steers it. Critical incidents mark those events in the course of group life that allow a clear shift in group discussion or immediate purpose. They represent points at which the group leader can intervene if desired, and they are natural and effective steering points.

The critical incident model (Cohen & Smith, 1976) suggests that landmarks are available for leaders to follow in diagnosing situations and providing group interventions that shape and define the group. As a tool the model offers the therapist the option of different levels of intervention (aimed at group, interpersonal, or individual-level behaviors), different types of interventions (conceptual, experiential, or structured), and different intensities of intervention (on a continuum of intensity from low to high). It is an ideal model for recognizing and responding to group process and steering the group to, through, and sometimes around difficult task and process issues.

GROUP INTERVENTIONS

Therapist group interventions can be addressed to different targets within the group from the individual to the group as a whole and can be delivered at varying levels of intensity from mild to strong. Additionally, therapist interventions can take different forms.

Intervention Target. Interventions can be directed toward one of three group member levels:

- *Personal.* The intervention is directed toward a single group member.
- *Interpersonal.* The intervention is directed toward a subgroup of two or more people within the group.
- *Group.* The intervention is directed toward the entire group.

Intervention Intensity. The intervention can be made at one of three levels of intensity:

- *Low Intensity.* The intervention is mild and low-key.
- *Moderate Intensity.* The intervention is more direct and stronger than low-intensity interventions.
- *High Intensity.* The intervention is strong and powerful.

Intervention Form. In addition to the target and the level of intensity, intervention activities, or the form of the intervention, can be

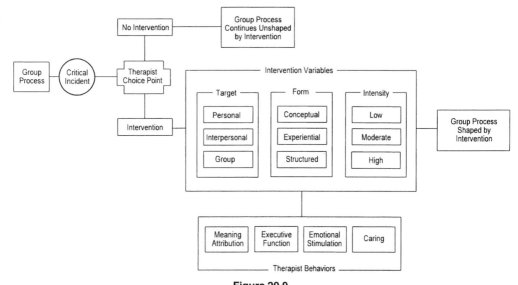

Figure 20.9
Critical incidents and therapist intervention targets and level of intensity.

- *Conceptual.* Intervention is verbal and interpersonal. Most often, this means that the intervention involves the therapist directly addressing the group members.
- *Experiential.* Intervention is experiential, using an activity or exercise that evokes an affective or cognitive response in group members. This might mean the use of drawings, psychodrama, movement, or other activities that are largely nonverbal.
- *Structured.* The intervention uses a structured activity such as role plays, workbook exercises, or other activities that are defined by the therapist.

Combinations of intervention target, intensity, and form are used in conjunction with the previously described leadership behaviors, offering the group therapist great range in the choice of interventions used to intervene, direct, focus, and reshape group process, using an intervention style that ranges from gentle and subtle to direct and assertive. Figure 20.9 shows the relationship among the target, intensity, and form of group interventions and the relationship between interventions and leadership style.

CONCLUSION

This chapter described group therapy for juvenile sexual offenders as a complex process that is no different in structure from any other form of group therapy. In fact, the differences between groups appear to be more differences in goals and objectives than essential and vastly distinct areas of practice. That is, all types of groups have task requirements, but whereas the actual task is distinctive depending on the nature of and reason for the group, the means for accomplishing tasks and effecting change remain essentially the same. Although there are common therapeutic factors that provide structure and meaning, there are no shortcuts or cookbook approaches to running effective groups and providing group members with opportunities for rehabilitation and self-improvement.

Although it is the group clinician's responsibility to run the group, the clinician alone does not create change. There are clear conditions necessary for the growth of group members and the effective development of the group itself. The actual role and behavior of the leader and the influence embedded in that position is one of these conditions, but there are several other important factors as well, including group norms, climate, and mechanisms for feedback; emotional expression; and other characteristics of interpersonal communication. Together, these represent the group therapeutic milieu, within which change occurs. It is the group leader's responsibility to build the therapeutic milieu and facilitate participation, learning, and growth within it, and it falls to the clinician to ensure that such conditions are fostered and developed within the early stages of group life.

Given the complexities of group therapy and the process of rehabilitation and change at which it is aimed, the group clinician can make informed decisions regarding the experiences provided for group members only when the process of change is well understood. Having a framework and a broad sense of group development allows the group therapist to practice the art of group leadership more securely, knowing where the group is heading and expecting the developmental pitfalls that are consistent with the process. Feeling more confident and secure, more in touch with the group's life, and more in control, the therapist has the freedom to test out new ideas and practices in the group and further expand his or her knowledge of group process and response.

CHAPTER 21

Family Therapy

ALTHOUGH LESS often applied, family therapy is nonetheless an important aspect of sexual-offender-specific treatment with juveniles. In most cases, the youth is still an active member of his family and is still under some form of parental control or guardianship, and in many instances the victim is a younger sibling or relative. In the case of outpatient treatment, the juvenile sexual offender is often living with or near his family during treatment, and in residential treatment the youth will sometimes return home to live with his family after treatment is complete. Even in cases where the juvenile is not living at home during treatment and will not return after treatment, the youth will remain a member of the family, and usually some type of family relationship will continue.

Contrasted to individual and group therapy, family therapy is the least frequently provided treatment approach often because of lack of resources, either in terms of time or cost. When therapists have limited time available for the provision of therapy sessions, they must choose between treatments competing for the same time slot; in many cases, family therapy falls by the wayside. In other cases, families are unwilling to engage in family therapy for a variety of reasons ranging from anger at the youth to a belief that the problem rests with the juvenile sexual offender and not with the rest of the family, denial of the problem, disinterest in treatment, or logistical reasons such as not being able to take time off from work to attend sessions or distance if the juvenile is receiving treatment far from home. In other cases, the juvenile has no family, or the clinician decides that the family is not ready for treatment or treatment is contraindicated or would otherwise be counterproductive. In still other cases, the clinician may not recognize the importance of family therapy or may not be trained in this approach. In some cases, family treatment is provided by clinicians inexperienced or untrained in family therapy, and sometimes it is provided in the form of family psychoeducation or family meetings, which are important extensions of treatment but are not family therapy.

In general, family therapy is important to strengthen the juvenile sexual offender and his family as a whole and ensure that family members can provide the support and supervision to ensure that there will not be a relapse. The family therapy model views the dysfunction of any individual family member as a problem for the entire family. This is especially evident when the sexual abuse is perpetrated against another family member.

FAMILY TREATMENT

Barnes and Hughes (2002) asserted that treatment programs for juvenile sexual offenders must develop methods to help families look at and understand how their beliefs and values have influenced the beliefs, behavior, and relationship of their child, which in turn contributed to the sexually abusive behavior. A primary goal of family treatment, then, is not only to help the parents understand their child's sexual behavior and help correct that behavior, but also to help families understand that the family itself is connected to the sexual behaviors of one of its children, and patterned family emotional, cognitive, and behavioral scripts may be partially responsible for the enactment of sexual offending behavior.

Family treatment has three specific forms: family meetings, family psychoeducation, and family therapy. Family meetings provide information, clarify and explain, and define expectations and requirements. For example, meetings usually take place to discuss treatment issues, progress, or problems; to define home contracts and expected behaviors; and to clarify general family issues and conditions. Family meetings may also be called to develop and review relapse prevention plans and get them into place. Psychoeducation is provided primarily to teach family members what they will need to know to be effective managers and helpers of their children, and it is thus often didactic. This type of treatment educates parents and other family members about the treatment of the child and empowers them to engage actively in treatment and aftercare plans. Family therapy seeks to address and resolve the most difficult issues, including the idea that the behavior of the juvenile sexual offender is intimately linked to and a by-product of family patterns and structures.

In family psychoeducation and meetings, family members retain their roles as parents, children, and siblings, and the family retains its overall structure. No effort is made to challenge or change these roles or structures, and family members are responded to in their respective roles as parents or children. Family therapy, however, is not concerned with setting or reviewing rules, except as a gateway to the relationships, roles, communication, and structural issues within the family—the family dynamics. These are unconscious factors at play within the interactions of family members that control and influence cognitions, emotions, behaviors, and the personality development of individual family members.

In family education and meetings, treatment providers need the skills of organization, communication, instruction, chairmanship, and facilitation. Family therapy requires skills based on therapeutic technique and design. As shown in Figure 19.1, family therapy is built on the therapeutic relationship between the clinician and all family members—the therapeutic alliance that forms between the clinician and family members—and among family members, and the focus of the treatment is the structure of the family and change within that structure.

THE FAMILY AS CLIENT

Many clinicians believe that many of the problems associated with adolescent pathology are systemic: Causes and resolution lie outside the client's control. In this model, assessment and treatment are directed toward understanding the client's psychological processes and external behavior; the family to which he or she belongs and its internal processes for communication, growth, and achievement; and the larger social environment, including the educational, peer, recreational, and other community systems in the client's life.

Specifically, in family treatment we see the family as a system in need of help, rather than a family suffering *because of* the client. Our role is to help open up or build new channels of communication, to identify or help the self-identification of dysfunctional patterns of family behavior, to empower individual members, and, in some instances, to educate and direct so that the family may become more effective and independent. In family therapy, the family—not the child—is the patient. Accordingly, the family is the focus of treatment, rather than the individual within the family. Of this, Stierlin (1974) asserted that the unit of treatment is "no longer the person, but a set of relationships" (p. 303).

FAMILY FUNCTION, STRUCTURE, AND SELFHOOD

Family function reflects the capacity of individual family members to engage in prosocial behaviors, accomplish personal goals, maintain meaningful relationships with other family members, and build meaningful and satisfying interpersonal relationships outside of the family. The ability of individual family members to meet such intra- and extrafamily goals thereby reflects the family's capacity to produce healthy family members and be considered a well-functioning family. A well-functioning family is one in which family members are personally successful and effective and hold themselves and other family members in high regard. In low-functioning families, life problems are evident among multiple family members, and there is either distance and separation among family members or a great deal of codependence. Function is a product of family structure.

Family structure can be considered the glue that holds the family together and the medium through which all interactions occur and functional ability is enhanced or diminished. In effect, the family structure represents the means by which the family functions, the family is held together as a whole group, and family members learn to engage with people outside of the family, basing their behaviors, interactions, and relationships on the family structure that they have internalized. Minuchin (1974) defined family structure as the invisible set of functional demands that organizes the ways and patterns by which family members interact with one another and individuals outside of the family. This structure comprises all aspects of family life, including

- Given roles, or manifest hierarchy, within the family, such as parent, child, son, oldest sibling, and so on
- Actual roles, or actual hierarchy, within the family, such as parentified child, domineering parent, organizer, and the like
- Relationships and interactions among family members, including alliances and conflicts among family members
- Explicit and clearly defined family rules for behavior and engagement
- Implicit and unstated family norms, attitudes, beliefs, and expectations
- Intrafamily communication, or communication among family members
- Extrafamily communication, or communication between the family and the outside world

Together, these and other interactional and patterned family expectations, beliefs, and behaviors constitute the family, which, in Minuchin's (1974) words, "imprints its members with selfhood" (p. 47). It is this family structure, or the functional family group itself, that is the target for treatment in family therapy.

Effective family structures are relationship enhancing and supportive, open in communication and free of confused or mixed messages, flexible and adaptable, transparent and honest, and constantly moving family members toward individuation and independence. In poorly structured families we find mixed and uncertain messages, relationships that are either distant or enmeshed and stifling, rigid and uncertain rules, family relationships and roles that are in conflict or skewed, in which the wrong roles are being played by the wrong family member or filled with role models for antisocial or self-destructive behaviors.

Fossum and Mason (1986, p. 86) asserted that dysfunctional families exhibit eight significant characteristics which are transmitted to and live on through family members as operational rules. Their perspective is both that individuals are unaware of these family-imprinted rules, but nonetheless perpetuate and live them out in their ongoing lives, presumably passing them on in turn to their own developing families.

- *Control:* Be in control of all behavior and interactions.
- *Perfection:* Always be right and always do the right thing.
- *Blame:* Blame others when things do not happen as planned.
- *Denial:* Deny feelings, especially negative or vulnerable feelings.
- *Unreliability:* Do not expect reliability or constancy in relationships.
- *Incompleteness:* Do not bring transactions to completion or resolution.
- *No Talk:* Do not talk openly or directly about shameful, abusive, or compulsive behavior.
- *Disqualification:* Discount, deny, or disguise shameful, abusive, or compulsive behavior.

Although family therapy targets the family as the patient and the subject for change, it nevertheless remains true that the basic effort of family therapy is to help each family member achieve a high level of differentiation of self (Bowen, 1971) and thus become healthy family members and high-functioning individuals. An important part of overcoming and changing behaviors in individuals, then, means recognizing family rules and characteristics that unconsciously influence the attitudes, beliefs, and behaviors of individuals and working to change them. In family therapy, the family and its members are helped to discover the current rules and characteristics and create new and healthy rules to live by and inject into their relationships and experiences.

Case Study 21.1 illustrates a family environment in which dysfunctional family structure, relationships, and communication played a significant role in the development and maintenance of sexually assaultive behavior.

THE TARGET OF FAMILY THERAPY

The basic unit for treatment in family therapy is the functional family group itself and not the single client in isolation (Ackerman, 1962), and symptoms of any particular family member are seen as reflective of the characteristics or dysfunction of the overall family (Satir, 1971). In this view, the locus of pathology is the family and not the individual, and all interventions are directed toward the family on the basis that beneficial changes in the larger family environment will have benefits for each individual family member as well. The dysfunctional behavior of any individual family member is entwined with the normative behavior and interactions of the family as a whole. The first goal in family therapy, then, is to shift the focus of treatment away from the family member identified as the patient and onto the family as a whole, thereby influencing change in the general system of family relations so that the behavior of its individual members will reflect that change.

Daryl was a 16-year-old who repeatedly sexually assaulted the 11-year-old daughter of his stepmother as a surrogate for her. His 30-year-old stepmother was physically unwell, requiring medical treatment, and had come to feel unattractive as well as neglected and uncared for by her husband (Daryl's father), who was often away from home due to work. The stepmother began to see her stepson as someone to feel close to, and indirectly as a surrogate object for both emotional comfort and as a means to feel attractive. She began to wear provocative clothing, often embraced him and sat next to him placing his arm around her, and acted in a subtly sexual manner around him, seeking his attention. No overt or conscious attempt was made to seduce Daryl, but at the same time as feeling she was attractive to a young man, the stepmother was able to make her husband jealous. Confused and already heavily into pornography that was present in the home, Daryl began to fantasize about his stepmother and wondered if she wanted to have sexual contact with him. He began a sexually assaultive relationship with her 11 year old daughter, which lasted for almost one year, while engaging in sexual fantasies about her mother.

These difficult issues were addressed in family therapy between father, stepmother, and Daryl, and the dynamics and patterns of family structure, roles, relationships, and communication were explored. The family began to understand the sexual tension and environment of sexual frustration that existed in the home, and that this environment, as well as the message that it was okay to engage in sexualized behaviors in the family, contributed to the sexual assaults.

Case Study 21.1

In the family of the juvenile sexual offender, this means discovering what elements in family life have contributed to the development of sexualized behaviors or the belief that one family member may sexually abuse another. Sometimes there are blatant family patterns that support sexual behaviors, such as sexually suggestive attitudes or behaviors in parents and, in some cases, the known use of pornography by one or both parents. In many cases, there is a lack of parental supervision for the children or an unwillingness to exert or even recognize the need to control behaviors. Roles can be confused also, in which children are given greater responsibility than they want or deserve, and they begin to fill roles that should be played by adults. Communication in many of these families is so poor that the victimized child feels unable to disclose the abuse, instead waiting for discovery and rescue. In these cases, the therapist helps the family to discover patterns that influence or enable sexual offending behavior and subsequently make changes in the family structure.

The second goal for the therapist is to recognize that the family is a system and that communication and effect flow in all directions. This means not only that the offender's behavior may have been influenced by family structures but also that the family is affected and permanently changed by the child's sexual behavior, particularly when the victim is another family member.

APPROACHES TO FAMILY THERAPY

Family therapy represents both a set of ideas about how individuals develop from childhood into adulthood in the family environment and an object relations theory about how family values, attitudes, interactional and communication patterns, and ways of experiencing the world and self are internalized into each family member. It also reflects a set of ideas about how to approach treatment, and well as an orientation to human functioning and problems. However, there are multiple approaches to family therapy that are broadly based on the two therapeutic genotypes of cognitive-behavioral and psychodynamic therapy.

A cognitive-behavioral approach to family therapy will focus largely on the symptoms of dysfunction within individuals and the family and will help family members quickly recognize shared cognitive distortions and negative values that undermine family success. Fossum and Mason (1986) referred to this sort of approach as seeking first-order change that is focused on symptom relief. However, most family therapy is practiced as a psychodynamic model in which hidden structural and interactional dynamics direct behavior and can be changed only after being brought to the surface, identified, and understood. Of this, Fossum and Mason wrote that the role of family therapy is to unlock the shared family unconscious, which they define as second-order change, thus bringing deeper and more enduring change to the rules and characteristics that govern family structure.

FOCUS OF FAMILY THERAPY

Important commonalities exist in most models of family therapy, which shape the process and targets of therapy. These commonalities are *all* treatment targets in family therapy, which like individual and group therapy is not a fixed or static entity but recognizes that various factors interact with and influence one another, creating unique treatment scenarios.

- *The family is the patient.* As stated earlier, the focus in family therapy is always on the family as a treatment unit, and not on any individual family member. Thus, the clinician must not become distracted or pulled into a view of the family problems that is centered on one individual (in this case, the juvenile sexual offender). Often, families have difficulty understanding and accepting this, as they typically come into therapy sessions to help (and sometimes attack) the identified patient, rather than seeing the whole family as the patient and the target for change. Rather, the juvenile sexual offender's behavior is understood and approached as an offshoot of family functioning, and the goal is to understand the impact of the behavior on the entire family and as a reflection of the entire family, or, more precisely, the way the family is structured and functions.

- *The orientation is in the present.* Family therapy is centered on *current* functioning, not past. Although it is important to gather family history in order to understand current family functioning and structure, only the family's immediate experience is important. History is significant only if it continues to influence current functioning. Applying this orientation to the juvenile sexual offender and his family, structural factors that were present in the family during the sexually abusive behavior must be understood if we are to recognize whether they still exist. In understanding the juvenile sexual offender as a family member, and often the victim as a family member as well, we must recognize what it was and perhaps still is about the family system that unintentionally failed to recognize, perhaps led or contributed to, or helped maintain or strengthen the sexual victimization.

- *The family is a system equally affected by all members.* The family is considered to be a system of interacting people and events, in which nothing occurs in a vacuum, and the development of attitudes, ideas, relationships, and behaviors is the product of the interactional system in which no family member stands alone or unaffected. Although the clinician and the therapy session respect the roles held by individuals within the family (i.e., the parents remain parents and the children remain children), family roles are dropped in the family therapy session in recognition that all family members have equally powerful, influential, and important roles within the family system; that all roles and family members are interdependent on all others; and that each family member is equally capable of transforming the dynamics and functioning of the entire family. This also means recognizing that the treatment issue can be conceptualized in any number of ways, including how the family affected the child's decision or capacity to sexually offend, how the child's sexual offense affected and altered the family, or how family structure continues to affect all family members, helping the family figure out how to be safe and maximize the functioning of each family member and the family as a whole.

- *Family systems interact with external systems.* Families do not exist in a vacuum and are in constant interaction with the larger neighborhood, community, and cultural systems of which they are a part. Ideas are passed or fail to pass back and forth between the family to the larger systems, and family members do not live or grow within closed systems that are isolated from the larger system. Understanding the relationship between the family and the larger system is central, including the manner in which material, ideas, and energy flow back and forth or are restricted, as well as the type and form of energy and material.

- *The family has its own culture which is transmitted through its generations.* Ideas, attitudes, beliefs, values, and behaviors are shared and transmitted through the family structure, or family culture. Through the overt modeling of these elements and the projection of emotional patterns and problems, parents with histories of antisocial or self-destructive behaviors risk unintentionally transmitting these values and behaviors to their children, who will in turn pass them along to later generations of children, creating a multigenerational culture.
- *Families are dynamic.* Families and internal and external relationships are constantly changing over time. Parental relationships mature and change over time, and children grow from infancy to adulthood and are decreasingly influenced by the immediate family and increasingly influenced by their external environment. Families that are rigid have great difficulty negotiating changes. By contrast, the open family, in which relationships between family members are close but are neither fixed nor fused, allows for the personal growth of its members, has rules by which it operates, and has the capacity to meet changes directly, clearly, and appropriately (Satir, 1971).
- *Individuation of family members.* In healthy families, members move constantly toward a state of differentiation and individuality without loss of family connection and closeness. The process of individuation does not stop at adulthood, and it applies equally to the children and parents in the family. Unhealthy family relationships are characterized by either distance, enmeshment, or codependence.

THE TREATMENT ENVIRONMENT AND THE THERAPEUTIC ALLIANCE

Family therapy is not individual therapy spread among different family members. Nor is it group therapy applied to a family, although there are similarities. Instead, family therapy occurs in a highly complex treatment environment made up of clearly hierarchical, extremely personal and private, and long-term, permanent, and emotionally joined relationships that are unlike any other form of relationship and in which the therapist is a complete outsider. These relationships existed before the clinician entered the picture and in most cases will continue long after the clinician leaves the picture. The therapist and the act of family therapy represent but a moment in the life of the family, and they are admitted to a highly personal zone into which few, if any, others are ever allowed. Accordingly, the therapist must remain cognizant of this treatment environment at all times, respectful of its boundaries and difficulties, and appreciative of the chance to help by entering the most secret and innermost world of the family. Even when mandated, as is frequently the case in the treatment of sexual offenses, the family treatment environment remains the same delicate and complex mix. The therapist's job is to understand, enter, and negotiate this world and find a means to join with the family, form a therapeutic relationship, and build the treatment alliance among all parties, including the clinician.

Minuchin (1974) described the therapeutic relationship in family therapy as a "joining operation" in which the clinician must accept the family's organization and style and blend with them: The therapist must "follow their path of communication, discovering which ones are open, which are partly closed, and which are entirely blocked" (p. 123). Bowen (1978) discussed the therapeutic process as one in which the clinician develops a relationship with the family while nevertheless remaining emotionally outside family relationships and not getting caught up in unhealthy and countertherapeutic alliances among family members. Bowen maintained that it is important that the therapist be a highly differentiated individual in order to remain an emotionally objective observer in the midst of an emotional system in turmoil while at the same time relating intimately to key people in the system.

In accord with a common factors model of treatment (Chapter 14), family therapy requires the development of a therapeutic alliance, which means that the clinician engages with the family's circumstances and its rules while maintaining a sense of self and distance. The clinician must form hypotheses, develop goals for treatment, and enter each session with a purpose and direction but remain open to the process of the family and the family circumstances, following the family's lead. Minuchin and Fishman (1981) asserted that as long as the clinician is aware of the family environment and field at that moment, therapeutic spontaneity becomes shaped by the field, allowing the therapist to act freely and comfortably in the knowledge that nothing is "correct" in such an environment, but only approximate. The therapist can probe, knowing that, at worst, the probing will yield important and useful information.

The goal of family therapy is to analyze family dynamics and introduce necessary change. In order to accomplish this task, the clinician must first process relationships with the family in order to create the therapeutic environment and alliance that will facilitate change. Following Minuchin (Minuchin, 1974; Mincuhin & Fishman, 1981), several clear and primary tasks emerge for the family therapist:

- *Joining,* or the process by which the therapist engages with the family, forms the therapeutic relationship, and creates a therapeutic system in which the clinician is positioned as the leader in the system
- *Accommodation,* or the process by which the clinician is able to adjust to family dynamics and the family is able to adjust to the clinician's role and method
- *Maintenance,* in which the clinician recognizes and provides support for the family's current structure

- *Tracking*, in which the clinician observes and follows the family's methods of interactions and communication and is able to recognize critical moments or incidents (Chapter 20) and select treatment interventions

As much as goals to be accomplished, these tasks represent techniques. In family therapy, this involves adopting a perspective that informs the therapist and ensures attention to detail. However,

> If the therapist becomes wedded to technique, remaining a craftsman . . . contact with patients will be objective, detached, and clean, but also superficial, manipulative, . . . and ultimately not highly effective. Training in family therapy should therefore be a way of teaching technique whose essence is mastered then forgotten. . . . Only a person who has mastered technique and then contrived to forget it can become an expert therapist. (Minuchin & Fishman, 1981, p. 1)

PROVIDING FAMILY THERAPY

Family therapy occurs in either the outpatient or residential treatment environment, two very different conditions. For the juvenile living at home during treatment, there are many factors to consider, including whether the victim is also living in the home. If the victim is a family member still living at home (most likely a younger sibling), an assessment must be made regarding the physical and emotional safety and comfort of the victim, and the victim should be engaged in treatment with an independent clinician who can draw conclusions about and make recommendations regarding the victim's needs.

If the juvenile sexual offender is living at home during treatment, an immediate goal will be to develop improved means for monitoring, supervising, and communicating; a behavioral contract of some sort; and an early version of a relapse prevention plan. In such cases, early family therapy is more pragmatic and resembles family meetings more than family therapy. After safety and supervision issues have been addressed and plans put into place, family therapy can begin to take on a more process-oriented tone.

For the youth in outpatient treatment and living at home or in the community, family therapy will occur in the context of real and active family relationships and should be geared toward these interactions. This is in distinct contrast to family therapy provided for juveniles in residential treatment, who are engaged in a completely different relationship with their parents during treatment and do not interact heavily with their families between family therapy sessions. In the residential environment, family therapy is substantially different in both its context and focus because it explores past interactions and future relationships rather than the interactions, communication experiences, and issues that result from daily contact. In addition, in the residential treatment environment parents are visitors more than they are guardians, and treatment staff instead serve as the child's custodians. These changes

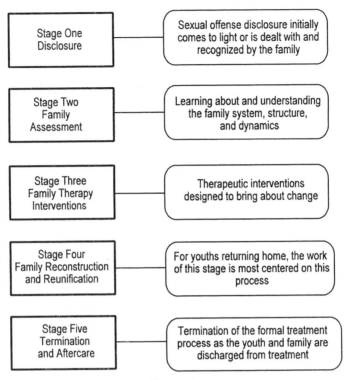

Figure 21.1
Five stages of family treatment. (From Thomas (1997).

in living arrangements and roles significantly affect the tone and content of family therapy. Nevertheless, there are basic elements common to all forms and contexts of family therapy for juvenile sexual offenders, including decisions about treatment planning, recognizing and working with dynamics specific to each family, and the structure and provision of family therapy.

Thomas's (1997) five-stage model of family treatment provides a clear overview of the process from initiation to closure. Although her model is linear, in reality family therapy is not at all linear; facets described in the Thomas model occur simultaneously, and families move back and forth in treatment. Nevertheless, the model (Figure 21.1) offers a clear and direct way to view the process of family therapy.

FAMILY TREATMENT GOALS

Treatment goals form the basis for treatment interventions and tasks in any given session. Consequently, after an initial exploration and assessment of family dynamics and structure, it is important for the family therapist to develop family goals. In sexual-offender-specific treatment, the goals are always going to be centered on the sexual aggression of the juvenile sexual offender, and if the victim is another family member, family treatment must also take into account victimization. Typically, all family work is going to center on understanding family factors that contributed to, helped to maintain, or failed to recognize or prevent the offense, but specific goals will vary widely.

For the most part, based on an understanding of family patterns, goals will include improved communication, relationships, and interactions, as well as the expression of emotions, conflict resolution and problem-solving skills, boundary development, the development of prosocial family values and attitudes, and individuation for adolescent family members. Goals will also invariably include the juvenile's disclosure of sexual behaviors to his parents and perhaps other family members (age of other family members is a significant consideration here), parent participation in the development and application of relapse prevention plans, and victim clarification work if the victim is another family member (Chapter 18). In addition, goals must be based on the age of the juvenile sexual offender and his approach into adulthood, whether the juvenile is living at home during treatment or will be returning home after residential treatment, and generally whether family reunification is expected for the juvenile and his family. Finally, special considerations based on family dynamics always exist in family work with juvenile sexual offenders that often form the basis for particular goals that are significant for that family.

The availability of family therapy is often limited in one way or another, and family therapy is best envisioned as a short-term process that works episodically (4 to 8 sessions rather than open-ended). Accordingly, family goals should always be focused on the most pressing issues: those most central to family functioning, most easily accessible and subject to achievement, and providing the greatest base for the development of later family goals if family therapy is continued. Above all, family therapists must form some sense of the family structure and changes necessary to improve functioning and create a healthy environment and have a clear sense of where they are taking family therapy and why.

SEXUAL-OFFENSE-SPECIFIC FAMILY DYNAMICS

Clinicians will uncover many variations on family structure and dynamics in the families of juvenile sexual offenders, each of which may serve as the basis for family therapy goals or as issues to be otherwise addressed in treatment. However, of particular note are the dynamics that often appear in the interactional patterns of the families of juvenile sexual offenders. In some cases, working on these sexual-offense-specific issues may be better suited for a limited form of family therapy initially concentrated on only the parental subset of the family, paving the way for later work involving more family members. Therapists should make this decision after assessing each particular family situation.

The dynamics at work in how the parents process and make sense of the offense are not isolated and at work only in the situation created by the sexual offense. Instead, they are almost certainly representative of dynamics constantly at play in the family, and they may have contributed to the situation that gave rise to the sexual offense in the first place. Dynamic factors do not operate in isolation from one another; frequently, multiple dynamics are evident, more often than not interacting with and cross-fertilizing one another.

- *Denial.* Denial encompasses many variants, from situations in which the family does not believe the offenses occurred (sometimes even after the child admits to the offenses) to varying forms of dismissal or minimization, including the belief that no harm was done or that it will not happen again. Here, the family therapist must question whether treatment can begin or prove effective with a family in some form of denial. In general, denial is a force to be reckoned with, but it is far from a reason not to engage in therapy. In fact, as part of the process of accommodation and joining, the family therapist may have to accept the family's perception and beliefs and find a way to later break through denial once a therapeutic relationship has been formed.
- *Minimization.* Minimization usually means that the family fails to recognize the significance of the problem or the pathology for the offender or perhaps for the victim. This is often a matter of education and support. Again, accommodation and joining are the way to accomplish treatment goals, not fighting with the family or trying to convince them that they are wrong.
- *Blame.* Here, the family is looking for someone other than the juvenile offender to blame or share the blame. Under the worst of circumstances, they blame the victim in some way that ranges from directly to indirectly blaming the victim, even if the victim is their own child. In other circumstances, parents find other people, situations, or circumstances that are somehow responsible for the offenses. Projecting blame onto others not only diverts responsibility from the offender but also, in a family therapy model, displaces the offender's own sense of responsibility for the offense.
- *Passive conspiracy.* There are many instances in which the family was aware of the sexual behavior, or at least some version of it, but passively conspired with the child by covering up the behavior in the hope that once discovered, it would not continue. Another version of the passive conspiracy occurs when the family suspects sexual misconduct but chooses not to confront it, hoping it is not so or will simply go away.
- *Guilt and shame.* In the first case the parents are dealing with their guilt for allowing the abuse to occur or not catching it, and in the second they are feeling shame about themselves, their child, or their family. Whereas

guilt can be a useful emotion (or cognition, depending on how you view it) and can help families learn to be more proactive and responsive, shame is a damaging and self-defeating emotion-cognition that serves little positive purpose in treatment. In either case, the route to resolution involves exploring the pathway and steps along the way that led to the offense and establishing new pathways that improve relationships and communication and establish supervision for the offender and safety for the victims.

- *Stigmatization.* The parents feel that they, their child, or their family is tainted, and they feel unable to face or seek help from other family members, friends, or others in the community. Here, the treatment issues are about hope and the ability to get beyond a bad situation, recognize how to get help, and recognize that one way to accomplish health is through reparation and making amends, a process that helps heal the victim, the community, the offender, and the family.

- *Helplessness.* The parents feel helpless about the situation, apparently unable to understand how their child could have engaged in a sexual offense, or why. They appear hapless and unable, but underlying their passivity, more intense and active feelings are dormant, such as anger, shame, and guilt. It is important for the family therapist to have families recognize this dynamic of helplessness in which they see themselves as victims, rather than active players, waiting for rescue from outside rather than taking responsibility and learning ways to recognize problems and take more control.

- *Family splits and divided loyalties.* When the victim is also a family member, the parents are not always sure how to offer support to both of their children or whether they can offer support to both without letting one or the other down. Alternatively, parents may clearly align with and offer greater support to either the victim or the offender at the expense of the other child. In such a case, when alignment is with the offender, it suggests that the parents do not understand or correctly estimate the potential damage caused to the victims. When parents align with the victim, it suggests a great deal of anger directed toward the offender, who is also their child and in need of their help, or their confusion about how to support the offender as well as the victim.

- *Failure to treat victim.* Another variant of minimization occurs when the parents do not place their victimized child into treatment or even have the child assessed by a clinician. The assumption is that parents simply do not recognize the potential or actual emotional issues faced by the victim.

- *Mixed messages.* Here, the parents give the offender two or more messages that appear to conflict with one another or a single message that has a different and contradictory underlying tone that also presents a confusing and uncertain message to the offending child and probably to other family members. These include messages such as how did we let you down/how could you let us down, we'll always stand by you/we don't know if we can support you, and why didn't you tell us/we don't want to hear. In all cases, the clinician's role is to help family members recognize the confusion and ambivalence, and sometimes dishonesty, embedded in messages and work toward improved and clearer communication. However, it is also very important to help family members and the juvenile offender recognize that contradictions do exist in the real world and need not and cannot always be resolved, and that we must work toward tolerating situations that do not always fit our needs.

THE THREADS OF DYSFUNCTION

Family therapy involves exploring the details of how the sexual offenses could have occurred and how so many major barriers were crossed or proved ineffective in preventing the behavior. In particular, the focus is on the factors present in family life that indirectly or directly led or contributed to the offenses, served as maintenance factors, or interfered with the family's ability or willingness to see what was going on for their child or children. The idea is that the family carries the threads of dysfunction later enacted by its members.[1]

Case Study 21.2 describes a juvenile's sexual offenses against his younger brother in the context of a pathologically disturbed family and captures his ability to move forward in treatment only after family therapy addressed and helped rehabilitate the problem.

DISCLOSURES

In sexual-offender-specific family therapy, the juvenile invariably discloses his sexual offenses to his parents and perhaps other family members as well. In addition to figuring out when and how to introduce this component into family therapy, and how often it needs to occur, there is also the element of deciding which family members need to hear the disclosures. The argument against disclosure to other siblings is that they do not necessarily need to know the details or themselves be potentially traumatized, especially when they do not want to know. The argument in favor of full disclosure to parents and other teenage siblings aged 14 and above is that disclosures to family members hold the juvenile offender fully responsible for his behavior and require him to face and openly admit to his behaviors in front of the people most

---

[1]My thanks to Rebecca Steil-Lambert for her ideas and succinct wording.

Mark was a 17-year-old intelligent but emotionally disturbed adolescent with poor social skills and a pathology that resembled borderline personality disorder. Individual and group therapy addressed his mood, behavior, and social interactions, but in family therapy the focus was on his feeling cheated by his mother, who had never been available to him. He had been born out of wedlock and never knew his father; during his childhood his mother had been in prison for substance abuse. She gave birth to his younger brother, Jon, while there, and Mark was left with a surrogate father who was verbally and physically abusive to him. Even after release from prison, Mark's mother remained emotionally and physically distant. In the ensuing years, Mark came increasingly to resent his younger brother, feeling that Jon had a closer relationship with their mother, and sexually offended Jon several times, as well as being physically and emotionally cruel to him.

Family therapy focused on similarities between Mark and his mother, including rationalizations and justifications made by both and the emotional distance they maintained from others. Mark learned that his mother was only superficially close with most people, including his brother, and began to recognize that this was not a rejection of him but more a reflection of his mother's style and character. Through mutual discovery, both mother and son came to feel more connected to one another, and Mark began increasingly to individuate from his mother and more comfortably accept the distance between them as he came to feel loved by her. The mother remained somewhat distant but also reported feeling closer and became more physically present and active in Mark's life. She was also able to discuss more honestly her boundaries and inability to go beyond them, even for her children. As Mark came to feel more connected to his mother, he became more able to work on his own issues, recognizing how much his relationship with his mother had affected him. He became more comfortable for staff and peers to be with, improved group interactions, was less emotionally reactive, began to feel more connected to his brother, who was in residential treatment, and for the first time began to recognize his responsibility to his brother.

Case Study 21.2

important in his life, and bring the full impact of his behavior and the family problem directly to other family members. In addition, where the victim was another child in the family, the disclosure makes the victim's pain and abuse known to all other family members who are old enough to understand what happened. However, when to disclose and to whom can be decided by the family therapist in the context of the family work with each particular family.

VICTIM CLARIFICATION

As described in Chapter 18, when sexual victimization has occurred within the family, victim clarification is a particular form of family therapy that addresses the relationship between the offender, the victim, and the family.

ADDITIONAL TREATMENT NEEDS OF FAMILY MEMBERS

During the course of family therapy, it may become evident that other family members require additional treatment, ranging from individual mental health or substance abuse treatment for a parent or a sibling to marriage therapy for the parents. In the case of family therapy for juveniles in residential treatment, it may become apparent that the rest of the family can benefit from family therapy in their home community. The role of the therapist in these cases is not to blur boundaries by providing or attempting to provide such treatment, but instead to strongly recommend treatment needs to other family members.

It also sometimes becomes apparent that one or more parents was sexually victimized as a child or teenager. If this material is introduced into family therapy, it must be under the clinician's direction based on the assessment that such material is important and useful for both family health and the treatment of the juvenile sexual offender. It is not unusual for parents to play out their own issues in family therapy, which is sometimes appropriate; however, it is frequently not appropriate and part of a family pathology in which boundaries become blurred and parents seek to inappropriately meet their own needs, treating their children as peers rather than children. Case Study 21.3 describes multigenerational sexual abuse in a family and the ability to engage in meaningful individual and family treatment only after parental sexual assault was revealed.

NONTHERAPEUTIC CONTACT BETWEEN FAMILY MEMBERS

Contact between the juvenile sexual offender and his parents and other family members should be nontherapeutic outside of treatment. That is, they should address difficult issues related to the offending behaviors only in the context of family therapy. For example, disclosures of sexual offenses should not be addressed outside of family therapy or without the direction of the clinician. The same is true for victim clarification, which should only occur under the direction of the therapist and in specifically designated victim clarification sessions. Although this is difficult to monitor, especially when the youth is living at home, it should be a goal and expectation of family therapy that the family will bring therapeutic issues into treatment. Part of the clinician's work in this case is to establish rules and guidelines about what therapeutic issues should not be discussed outside of therapy and how to address and discuss them if they do arise. In addition, family therapy should move forward rapidly so that families can acquire the skills needed to address and resolve these issues outside of therapy sessions. It is, after all, a goal of all therapy to make individuals—or families—self-sufficient.

Barry was a 17-year-old in residential treatment due to extensive sexual assaults against his 11-year-old sister. He was sexually active while in treatment, engaging in illicit sexual relationships in his prior residential treatment program and his current program. Although receiving individual, group, and family therapy, Barry was not able to engage actively in treatment, often appearing flat and dysthymic and showing no change in behaviors or interactions. Soon after the peer sexual relationship was discovered, Barry become more depressed but in individual therapy announced that his father had sexually abused him for many years, and as recently as several weeks prior had urged him not to disclose the offenses, saying they could get family treatment when Barry turned 18. In fact, he had reported his sexual victimization at the time of its occurrence several years earlier but recanted after his father told him his disclosure would destroy the family. Family therapy had been taking place throughout Barry's treatment but had been ineffective. His family had wanted the family therapist to begin victim clarification work within weeks of Barry's entering treatment and had consistently tried to rush therapy and quickly move Barry and his sister through the treatment process. Family therapy now took an important turn.

The father was removed from the home by court order, but charges were not filed. Family therapy continued with Barry and his mother with an immediate focus about decisions regarding the father who wanted to reunify, reporting he had now entered his own treatment. Barry had to decide whether to press charges, and his mother had to decide whether to readmit her husband back into family life. Questions were also raised about the possibility that Barry's father may have sexualized his daughter (Barry's sister) as well. Family therapy focused on patterns of multigenerational sexual abuse, deceit perpetrated in the family for many years, the conspiracy of silence between Barry and his father, and the mother's inability or unwillingness to see the multiple sexual abuse that had existed, and that Barry had previously reported. Family therapy was now able to address issues openly and honestly, and both Barry and his mother were able to form a closer relationship. Both took more responsibility for their own actions and their inactions and felt empowered to move through life more honestly and make stronger and more independent decisions. After leaving residential care, Barry moved into a transitional independent living program, where he reported additional sexual offense against nonfamily members (younger children) and actively sought ongoing treatment.

Case Study 21.3

CONFIDENTIALITY AND MANDATED REPORTING

Issues of confidentiality should be discussed with the family before family therapy begins. Indeed, confidentiality issues should always be discussed with the parents ahead of time if they are the legal guardians of the juvenile sexual offender. That is because many programs do not hold disclosures of sexual offenses as confidential, and this information must be shared with the juvenile offender and his legal guardians before and during assessment and treatment (Chapters 8 and 10).

In addition to work with the juvenile offender himself, in family therapy it sometimes becomes evident or seems likely that additional child abuse or neglect has occurred within the family. As most, if not all, family clinicians are mandated reporters, (i.e., they are legally required to report child abuse and neglect), such conditions must be reported to the appropriate authorities. This can represent a significant block to family therapy and the therapeutic relationship and alliance. Nevertheless, in these instances the clinician is not permitted to maintain confidentiality. Many states allow child care and protection reports to be filed anonymously, and in those cases the clinician can file without notifying the parents, hoping that they will not realize it is the clinician who has filed. However, in many cases, the family will probably figure it out anyway, and any breach in the therapeutic relationship caused by the report will probably only be deepened. The preferred alternative is to inform the family of the need and decision to report, based on earlier descriptions of confidentiality limits, and explore and work through the issues therapeutically.

STRUCTURE OF FAMILY THERAPY

After the clinician decides that family therapy is an important and viable treatment option, several other decisions need to be made about the structure and provision of therapy, most notably participation and duration.

FAMILY SESSION PARTICIPATION

Who will participate in the sessions, and can family therapy be provided without all family members? In two-parent families, sometimes only one parent is available and the other parent never attends family sessions or is inconsistent in attendance or participation. This is sometimes the result of work schedules and other times the result of a lack of interest, failure to recognize the importance of family therapy, or the nature of family relationships. The clinician must also decide whether all siblings should attend, teenage siblings only, or no siblings at all. Even then, the siblings may not want to attend or may be unable to attend because of their schedules. These factors are of special significance when treatment is away from home.

Some family therapists may decide that both parents and all siblings must attend. For any number of reasons, however, it may not be viable to have all family members attend, and the therapists's insistence may lead the family to feel controlled and become oppositional or may limit the family's sense of trust in the therapist or ability to feel supported and understood. A rigid position regarding attendance may kill any chance that family therapy can prove effective and negate the accommodation and joining principles of family therapy. In all likelihood, the therapist is going to have to work with the availability of family members and their willingness to attend and find ways to engage all relevant family members increasingly, or eventually decide that family therapy cannot proceed due to the inability to gather and engage the necessary family members in treatment. The clinician must also decide if there is an age limit below which siblings need or should not attend. In addition, during disclosures of sexual offenses, a decision must be made about which, if any, siblings should be there to hear the disclosures, which are likely to be graphic and disturbing.

Divorced and blended families raise additional questions. Which set of parents and family members should engage in family therapy? Should family therapy be held as separate sessions for each side of the divorced family, or should blended sessions be held for all family members? Much of this depends on the relationship of the divorced parents, as well as on the pragmatic reality of the family situation and the availability of family therapy. Furthermore, the clinician must decide whether holding separate family therapy sessions is useful or whether it maintains the disconnection and animosity between parents and helps foster a dysfunctional family system. Although decisions must be made based on both case-by-case needs and the pragmatics of treatment, some general guidelines may prove useful:

1. Both custodial parents should attend family therapy sessions, including the stepparent or live-in surrogate parent in the event of remarriage or repartnering.
2. In the case of divorced families, family therapy should be aimed at the parent most involved in the youth's life and most likely to provide living resources or support in the future.
3. In divorced families where both parents are actively involved in parenting, family therapy should be offered to both sets of families when therapeutic resources allow.
4. If family therapy is offered to both sets of parents in broken families, divorced parents should be encouraged to attend blended family sessions, rather than separate sessions that enable their inability to work together or communicate with one another, and stepparents should attend also. In cases when blended sessions are not possible, the therapist must decide about separate family sessions for both parents (Guidelines 2 and 3).
5. Siblings should be cognitively able and mature enough to be privy to and engage in discussions about sexual behaviors and sexual abuses within the family.
6. Participating siblings should be present for disclosures if it appears that they can be of help to either family victims or the offender or if they want to be present.
7. Victims should not engage in family therapy sessions until the sessions are geared toward victim clarification and such work has been completed.

8. Extended family members such as grandparents and uncles and aunts should attend family meetings if they play a significant role in parenting and raising the children in the family or are actively involved in the family and the sexual offense.

9. The clinician should begin therapy with whichever parents are available and willing to engage in family therapy and then, through joining and accommodation and the development of the therapeutic relationship, should engage other appropriate and necessary family members in family therapy.

Timing, Length, and Frequency of Family Therapy

The issues of when to begin family therapy, as well as how often to provide it and for how long, are clearer and more certain in outpatient treatment when the youth is living at home and much less clear for kids in residential or other out-of-home treatment. For the most part, family therapy should be designed to fit and become integrated into the larger treatment picture of individual and group treatment, as well as other treatment that is being provided, which will vary depending on treatment venue and overall length of time in treatment. General guidelines for length, frequency, and duration include the following:

1. Family therapy should begin when the family seems ready to attend family sessions and enough assessment and individual work have been completed to allow the family sessions to have meaning for the therapist.

2. Family sessions should be 90 minutes in length in order to allow adequate time for the processing of therapeutic interactions during each sessions and for resolution prior to ending the session. Sixty-minutes sessions are appropriate only when just two family members are in session (the youth and one parent).

3. In the outpatient setting in which the youth is at home and interacting daily with family members, family sessions should occur weekly or every other week in order to address real-life treatment issues. In the residential setting, sessions can occur on alternate weeks or once each month. However, in either case, the work going on in family sessions during any case should dictate how often sessions should be held.

4. Family therapy should be planned as short-term and focused interventions, initially based on four to eight sessions. Time-limited family work can thus be more focused, can reduce the anxiety of family members who otherwise face the idea and uncertainty of endless sessions, and sessions can always be extended beyond the initially allotted number of sessions, remaining time limited.

5. Family sessions can be continued at a later point in the youth's treatment and can be used to assess and gauge change and movement in family life and structure.

6. Family sessions should be goal based but can shift and change over time to reflect changes in family structure, as well as changes in treatment focus.

PRAGMATICS

Like all other aspects of treatment, family therapy occurs within a real environment that is filled with factors that both drive and limit treatment. Weighed against treatment needs considered to be essential, pragmatic factors must ultimately shape family therapy. This includes and informs decisions regarding the number of family therapy sessions, the number and nature of participating family members, and the frequency and duration of family therapy.

TO TREAT OR NOT TO TREAT

There are cases in which family therapy is an obvious choice, such as when the juvenile is living at home during outpatient treatment or will be returning home after residential treatment and discharge is pending. It is also indicated when the victim is another family member and family work represents an important aspect of his or her treatment, when there are clear and pressing family issues which when resolved will benefit the juvenile and his family, or when the family is seeking family therapy (even so, in some cases the family therapist may decide that family therapy is contraindicated).

However, sometimes it is not clear whether family therapy is necessary or should be provided, especially when treatment resources are scarce. This is particularly true for juvenile sexual offenders in residential treatment or not otherwise living at home or in cases where family reunification is not a goal. Examples include the following:

- The youth is in residential treatment or foster care and will not be returning home after treatment, and treatment resources are scarce.
- The youth is in residential treatment or foster care and will not be returning home for a long time, and family therapy should take place closer to the point of reunification.
- The youth is not living at home during treatment, and family issues among other family members extend far beyond the sexual offenses—and far beyond the capacity of sexual-offender-specific family therapy. In such cases, the clinician should consider recommending that the remainder of the family seek family therapy in their own communities.

- The youth is not living at home during treatment, and family treatment issues that include the youth are far too complex to be addressed while he is living away from home. Here, the recommendation may be that family therapy continues more intensively after the juvenile offender returns home or moves to a treatment facility closer to his family.
- Family therapy requires an interactional family life and active family interactions. Youths in treatment away from home do not have a family life filled with active and ongoing interactions, and family therapy is more appropriate after the youth has returned home or to the community.
- There are so many difficulties in parent behaviors, or family patterns are so dysfunctional and caustic that family therapy is considered not in the best interests of the juvenile sexual offender, family reunification is not recommended, and the clinician recommends that the juvenile sexual offender separate completely from the family.
- Parental involvement in treatment for youths in treatment away from home is so sporadic, disconnected, or remote that family therapy cannot be reasonably considered an effective means of treatment. The same is true when families decline, are actively resistant to the idea of family therapy, or are passively resistant and consistently fail to engage in treatment.

Balanced against these reasons not to provide family therapy, as well as the availability of therapy resources, there are nonetheless compelling reasons to provide family therapy in all cases, even when the child is not living at home during treatment and is not expected to return home in the future.

- The family remains a family whether reunited or not, and family members will continue to have relationships with one another throughout their lives.
- Family issues will still require resolution, and family therapy can help smooth the way for improved relationships in the present and future.
- Family therapy can help the family improve overall functioning.
- Family therapy can help all family members accept the juvenile's disengagement from the family.
- Family therapy can help heal the juvenile in treatment, as well as other family members.
- Family therapy can aid the process of offender restitution and victim recovery.
- Family therapy can assist differentiation and individuation of family members, including the juvenile sexual offender.

A variant exists in terms of divorced families and blended families (i.e., one or both parents have remarried). In such cases, assuming that the youth will be returning to live with one parent, should family therapy involve only that parent and the stepparent, or should it involve both sets of parents, who, after all, are both still the juvenile's parents? In these cases, the victim may reside with one parent while the offender resides with the other. Sometimes the question of family therapy in split families is resolved because the custodial parent refuses to have the other parent involved, but this is an unsatisfactory and destructive resolution to a treatment issue; it may only contribute to the family's problem. There are no universal answers about when, how, and to whom family therapy should be provided, and directions and answers can be found only in the specific situation.

TIPS FOR FAMILY THERAPY

Many parents have difficulty with family treatment. However, treatment providers sometimes assume the worst about some families, especially those who are contentious or hostile. Although this is understandable, it serves no productive purpose for clinicians or programs to engage in either judgments of or power plays with parents. In fact, if clinicians recognize that families are often clients as well (especially after they enter family therapy), then clearly family members must be treated with the same level of respect and support offered to the children with whom clinicians work, and who are their children. Figure 21.2 offers useful guidelines for the family therapist, with particular respect to those things to avoid in family therapy.

Clinicians must also recognize that most parents love their children and want the best for them. The fact that parents cannot always live up to these worthy values or follow through on their interest in their children does not

---

- Don't negatively label families.
- Don't create an environment that replicates a family's poor experience with the system.
- Don't help parents feel incapable.
- Don't become an adversary to the family.
- Don't make unnecessary value judgments about families.
- Don't become frustrated with parents.
- Don't personalize your experiences with the family.
- Don't display frustrations or hostility.
- Don't treat the parents as idiots.
- Don't assume you know best.

Figure 21.2
Tips for family therapy: 10 things to avoid.

- Recognize that most parents love and want the best for their children.
- Recognize that many parents have had poor and frustrating experiences with the educational, social services, mental health, court, and other systems that are meant to help them.
- Recognize that most parents want to become competent and effective.
- Get to know how a family works, and find a way to join therapeutically with that family.
- See beyond the negative or frustrating qualities of a family.
- Understand what it must be like for those parents.
- Feel the family's pain.
- Help the family achieve competence.
- Never forget multicultural issues.
- Try to understand why the family minimizes and denies.

Figure 21.3
Tips for family therapy: 10 things to accomplish.

lessen this fact even if they cannot provide what is needed and, in many instances, are responsible for the troubles experienced by their children. Figure 21.3 highlights those things that clinicians should aim to accomplish in their work as family therapists.

Finally, as illustrated in Figure 21.4, one important goal for family therapists is to learn about the family and how it works structurally, behaviorally, and dynamically, and what drives its structure.

THE PARENT EDUCATION AND SUPPORT GROUP: MULTIFAMILY WORK

The multifamily group, composed of three or more families, can be considered either a facet of family therapy or a treatment mode that falls more into the area of parent education and support. The equivalent of group treatment for juvenile sexual offenders, it can be either more psychotherapeutic or educational and supportive. Typically, the multifamily group is used for the purpose of parent education and support, as it can be difficult to provide therapy to multiple families at the same time.

In cases where family therapy is also provided for individual families, the role of parent education is to supplement the therapy and provide a means for general communication, relationship building, and self-help. In the event that family therapy is not provided, the multifamily group often serves as a surro-

- *Family Roles:* What roles do different family members play, and why?
- *Family Communication:* How do family members communicate with one another, and how open is communication?
- *Family Relationships:* What is the quality of relationships and interactions among family members?
- *Family Structure:* How are family members connected to one another, and what configurations exist between family members?
- *Family Functioning:* How well does this family function internally and in relationship to the external world?
- *Family Secrets:* What secrets or unstated history exists within the family, and why?
- *Family Rules:* What are the stated and unstated rules in this family, and how do they contribute to functional or dysfunctional patterns in the family as a whole and as individual family members?
- *Family Stress:* What pressures, internal and external, are affecting this family, and why?
- *Family Needs:* Do family members get their needs met in the family, and if so, how?
- *Family Flexibility:* How flexible and adaptable is this family, internally and externally, to past situations and currently developing situations and changes?

Figure 21.4
Tips for family therapy: 10 things to learn.

gate, reaching multiple families at the same time. In the parent education and support group, change comes through skill and the development of knowledge more than it does affective experience or insight, and the group focuses on the acquisition of communication and problem-solving skills in parents and other family members. Figure 21.5 describes the purpose of a parent education and support group.

CONCLUSION

Thomas (1997) noted that "every adolescent enters treatment with a family attached" (p. 360), which, of course, is the reason to provide family therapy. Although treatment is influenced by pragmatic realities, to miss the opportunity for family therapy is to miss filling an important treatment need in the lives of juvenile sexual offenders. In terms of the family's needs, Thomas wrote that "more than anything else, the family will need the treatment provider to be able to put all the pieces together, to make the chaos in their lives comprehensible, to show that control is possible, and to facilitate healing changes" (p. 363).

Purpose

- Help participants learn how families function
- Provide participants with an understanding of principles that can be used to help in family situations
- Provide participants with the opportunity to learn about themselves and their own families through sharing with and observing other families
- Provide feedback to all participants from other participants
- Stimulate communication across families
- Build a model for communication and explore methods for problem solving

Role of the Therapist or Group Leader

- Enhance clear communication
- Help define a healthy family system
- Help consolidate gains and review and reinforce lessons learned

Figure 21.5
Parent and education support (multifamily) groups.

Following Lundrigan's (2001) broad model of family treatment, which incorporates many individual facets of treatment, a compete program of family treatment will include

- Ongoing general communication
- Ongoing general support
- Family meetings with and without the youth
- Family psychoeducation
- Family education and support group
- Family therapy

Through providing a sophisticated and comprehensive approach to family treatment, we cover much ground. We strengthen the family through education and skill development and offer opportunities for increased family awareness and the restructuring of the family environment. Through family therapy interventions, we reduce the incidence of family risk factors and increase the number and quality of protective factors that often can only be provided in the family environment—not just for the juvenile sexual offender but also for other children within the family—in a true model of rehabilitation and growth.

CHAPTER 22

Treating the Whole Child in a Whole-Minded Manner

THE WORK of treating juvenile sexual offenders is difficult in most respects. Fully understanding what is meant by sexual-offender-specific treatment is complex also, and the term is often an empty shell to be filled in by individual practitioners, including those tasks, functions, and interventions that are provided within the practice of that model. This book has provided a comprehensive look at the work of JSO treatment and an integrated model by which to understand and practice the work. It has presented an overview of information and perspectives, as well as ideas and methods by which to understand and apply those ideas, transforming them into the practice of treatment and rehabilitation. This final chapter summarizes and overviews key points and provides some final ideas and suggestions.

A SIX-POINT APPROACH TO FORENSIC TREATMENT

In forensic treatment there are at least six ways to understand and approach the problem of juvenile sexual offending as well as identifying targets for intervention, as shown in Figure 22.1. Although each may direct a different approach to treatment, none are mutually exclusive or incompatible with the others. In an integrated and comprehensive treatment model, each approach complements and enhances the other, leading to a sophisticated understanding of the dynamics of juvenile sexual offending and the development of each juvenile sexual offender.

1. The public health approach identifies issues in the larger community and intervenes at the macro level first and individually at the tertiary

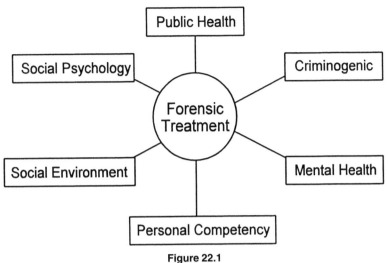

Figure 22.1
A six-point approach to forensic treatment.

level. This approach is of particular importance in treatment because it recognizes risk and protective factors in the juvenile's living environment and aims at making the community a safer and less risky environment in which to grow and develop into adulthood.

2. The criminogenic approach recognizes its primary targets as criminality, dangerousness, forensic factors, and public safety.

3. The mental health approach recognizes the problem existing within the psychology of the individual and aims primary interventions at that level first, incorporating secondary and tertiary treatments at the group and family, followed by the larger social environment.

4. The personal competency approach considers the juvenile's cognitive style and social skills and the ability to negotiate the social world successfully as central targets for treatment.

5. The social environment (social learning) approach seeks to understand the immediate social environment in which the child or adolescent was raised and lived, in which the offenses occurred, and in which the underlying motivators for the offenses developed.

6. The social psychology approach considers and assesses in the individual the impact and effect of the larger social context and understands and defines individual and group treatment in this context.

There are doubtless many other ways to conceptualize a treatment framework, but in forensic mental health and the treatment of the whole child, each of these approaches factors into development and provision of treatment.

THE TASKS OF THE TREATMENT

Even though we can break treatment into its constituent components for the purposes of description and analysis, and even define stages of treatment, it is important to keep in mind that treatment is neither component driven nor sequential. It is instead holistic and simultaneous, often moving back and forth and built on combinations of disparate and sometimes contradictory ideas.

Clinicians, for instance, must recognize that juvenile sexual offenders as a group are heterogeneous yet share many features; that treatment constantly explores new ground yet continually returns to the same ideas; and that treatment is highly individualized yet general in content. Similarly, youths in treatment must recognize that accepting a higher risk for sexually reoffending (when appropriate) often helps them remain safe and thus lowers their risk level; that learning how to trust and feel vulnerable makes them less vulnerable and more trustworthy; that struggling to gain control often means remaining out of control; and that accepting loss of control can help them to gain real control. Part of the therapist's job is to recognize these seeming paradoxes and synthesize them into a greater whole, thus helping the juvenile to develop into a healthier and more capable individual.

The clinician also must build the therapeutic structure and alliance within which personal change may occur for the juvenile sexual offender. In a common factors model, much of this work has to do with the client's motivation to change, the development of the therapeutic relationship, and the interaction between these two factors. One way to picture the clinician's job, however, is to imagine the task as that of creating a fertile environment in which prosocial growth can occur and a healthy personal identity can emerge.

Whether provided in the community or in residential care, treatment essentially aims at 20 primary goals that, if accomplished, leave the youth in a position to continue to grow in a prosocial direction. These goals provide a clear description of the ideal outcomes of sexual-offender-specific treatment:

1. Appropriate boundaries
2. Awareness of others
3. Emotional regulation
4. Engagement and attachment
5. Enhanced support network
6. Healthy sexual development
7. Increased responsibility
8. Improved family functioning
9. Impulse deferment
10. Internalized behavioral control
11. Moral development
12. Prosocial attitudes

13. Prosocial behaviors
14. Remission of psychiatric comorbidity
15. Resolution of sexual deviancy
16. Retention and transfer of skills
17. Self-esteem
18. Skill enhancement
19. Social competency
20. Tolerance for emotional distress

KEEPING IT SIMPLE: SIMPLE RULES FOR TREATMENT

Treatment is a complex undertaking, but the simpler we make it for our youthful clients—and ourselves—the simpler it is to keep a focus on the goals of treatment. This is especially true for younger and more cognitively limited children and adolescents. Five behaviors describe virtually every sexual offender, not only in their sexual offenses but in many other areas of their lives as well. Turning the behaviors into proactive rules can help kids understand their behaviors in a simple context and thus help them become more aware and remain safe, as well as framing treatment and providing opportunities for the exploration of attitudes, ideas, and behaviors.

Five Behaviors[1]
1. Taking something that's not yours. Sexual offenders use the bodies of other people and take from them their freedom, privacy, safety, and often innocence.
2. Not asking permission. Sexual offenders do not ask permission for what they take.
3. Invading space. Sexual offenders invade the physical, emotional, and sexual space of others.
4. Keeping a secret. Sexual offenders keep secrets and force others to keep secrets as well.
5. Taking it out on someone else. Sexual offenders take out their frustrations and get their needs met literally by taking advantage of another person.

Five Proactive Rules
1. Don't take things that don't belong to you.
2. Always ask permission.
3. Respect boundaries.
4. Don't keep secrets.
5. Don't take things out on other people.

---

[1]My thanks to Cathy Sickles, who devised this clever and simple perspective on the behaviors of juvenile sexual offenders.

CONDITIONS FOR SUCCESS

Success in treatment is difficult to measure. However, there are two key ingredients. The first involves factors related to a therapist's own work and the second to the therapist's view of clients and the therapeutic work.

FACTORS PERTAINING TO THERAPIST PRACTICE

One key to effective treatment is the way in which clinicians perceive themselves in relationship to their work and the way in which they conduct their clinical practice.

- *Professional preparation.* Clinicians should not engage in the practice of therapeutic work for which they are not trained or adequately prepared, unless they will be provided with specific training and close supervision on the job by experienced supervisors.
- *Supervision.* Clinicians who undertake this work must ensure that adequate supervision is available. For some clinicians, this means supervision and sometimes direction by an experienced senior clinician. For clinicians already experienced and able to practice independently, supervision may take the form of collegial consultation. Whether provided by clinical supervisors or clinical peers, supervision offers perspective, the opportunity to think through and discuss a case out loud, direction, and support.
- *Professional development.* Clinicians must continue to engage in the activities of professional development and continuing education in order to enhance and expand their skills and exposure to new ideas. This means attending seminars and conferences, reading books and journals, and ideally joining a professional organization that focuses on the treatment of juvenile sexual offenders and related topics, linking the clinician to the larger field and its practitioners, providing current and ongoing education, and forming and sealing professional identity.
- *Self-care.* Most of the training that clinicians undertake, including ongoing professional development and continuing education, is naturally directed at developing a better understanding of their work and learning new skills. However, it is equally as important for clinicians also to engage in development that is perhaps more personally renewing than it is focused on skill development. The ability to come into the work refreshed, relaxed, and revitalized is essential if clinicians are to engage in energetic, enthusiastic, and creative work.

  Work with juvenile sexual offenders is often high-speed, multifocused, and energy-consuming. In all this, it is easy for clinicians to lose sight of the need for self-care. The work is difficult, and clinicians often hear tragic and sometimes heinous stories about offenses committed by their youthful clients or offenses perpetrated against their clients at some earlier time. Forensic mental health clinicians are charged with the task and responsibility of trying to help the juvenile sexual offender while protecting individuals from him in the event that he does not change. For most people, this is a draining task. In many cases, change is not evident in the juvenile, or not evident enough, and the work can feel like—and indeed often is—an uphill struggle. Clinicians who do not take care of their needs outside of their work, including personal relationships, relaxation, and spiritual refreshment, risk not only burnout but also the quality and effectiveness of their work and their ability to help the juvenile and society.

- *Maintaining personal safety.* Clinicians must not underestimate the possibility that they may be harmed. Although rare, the risk exists. Clinicians must know their clients well and must take precautions to avoid becoming a victim of the sexual offenders they are treating. This is particularly true in the case of older adolescent and adult sexual offenders, but precautions must be taken in work with all individuals, of any age, who have already engaged in sexually assaultive behavior. Clinicians who do not think about personal safety or assume that they are somehow immune from being sexually or physically assaulted by their clients are naive and are placing themselves in harm's way. In crime statistics, women are sexually assaulted far more frequently than men and are at far greater risk for sexual assault. The same is true for female clinicians working with male clients.

FACTORS PERTAINING TO THERAPIST PERSPECTIVE

The way that clinicians view their clients and the provision of treatment is significant to the effectiveness and success of treatment.

- *Building strengths.* Clinicians should remember that juvenile sexual offenders not only are a heterogeneous group in terms of background and developmental paths, but also are diverse in that as individuals, each child or adolescent has different interests, skills, strengths, and things to offer. Treatment and rehabilitation built on correcting deficits is not likely to be as successful or affirming as treatment built on highlighting and reinforcing strengths.
- *Risk and protective factors.* In a similar vein, although we need to identify and eliminate risk factors, and in many ways that is what sexual-offender-specific treatment is about, treatment must focus also on developing and reinforcing protective factors.

- *Denial and responsibility.* The best place to start in treatment is at the point where the juvenile recognizes that there is a problem that cannot be denied. This point is represented as the first step in a 12-step program.
- *Motivation.* An important prerequisite for success is that the youth *wants* to change. In part, one of the therapist's jobs is to help the youth reach this place in his life, but the juvenile who is able to say he does not want to be that kind of person anymore, or the type of person who hurts others, is on the right track.[2]
- *One step forward, one step back.* Juveniles in treatment are always going to regress in treatment. Remember that the idea of one step forward, one step backward is just a metaphor. In reality, juveniles who move forward in treatment do not lose what they have gained when they regress; nor should they be expected to move only forward. Clinicians should expect clients to slip and slide, recognizing that they have not really lost ground. If the therapist falls into the trap of believing this to be true, then the therapist is suffering, along with the client, from abstinence violation effect (Chapters 16 and 17).
- *Insight and awareness.* Children and adolescents in treatment are always able to develop some form of insight linked to their age and cognitive level. Improved awareness of self and others is both a worthy goal and a goal that can be accomplished to some degree.

TIPS FOR FORENSIC PRACTICE

Forensic clinicians are focused on the criminal aspects of their client's behaviors, the knowledge that most juvenile sexual offenders are in treatment because of external requirements, and the reality that in sexual-offender-specific treatment, the truth often has to be discovered through investigative clinical work rather than something that easily emerges through the voluntary cooperation of juvenile sexual offenders.

- *Have a healthy skepticism.* Forensic work requires an investigative mind. Clinicians should maintain a healthy sense of doubt and questioning. Clinicians should not accept answers or explanations that do not seem fully to fit the facts, and they should not assume that the information they are getting from juveniles is necessarily honest or straightforward. To this end, clinicians should even question new disclosures of sexual offenses that juveniles sometimes later make in treatment, asking why the new disclosure and why now?
- *Look for clues.* Forensic clinicians seek answers and clues that can shed light, provide new information, fill in the gaps, and sometimes prompt more honesty and engagement in treatment.

---

[2]Thanks to Siri Khalsa for his simple way of phrasing a complex idea, and for making clear this important st in treatment.

- *Stay focused.* Clinicians should remain focused on the object and course of treatment and not get sidetracked by other issues or directions that arise. Clinicians who lose focus invite the possibility of not getting the full picture and allow juveniles to slip through the cracks.

- *Expect more.* Clinicians should be aware that juvenile sexual offenders have often not revealed the entire truth, and clinicians should continue to expect more information and details, often far into treatment. It is not always the case that juveniles have more to offer, but combined with healthy skepticism, clue seeking, and focus, clinicians will have a sense of whether the juvenile is being forthcoming and whether there is more that the client has yet to disclose.

- *Keep close records.* Clinicians should maintain careful and detailed records that protect them and their clients and allow themselves and others to understand the course of treatment and the work that has been accomplished, including the details of their work.

- *Stay in control.* Clinicians should remain in control and not engage in power plays that clients sometimes invite or attempt to force on the clinician. Supervision can be vital here to help clinicians recognize power plays and remain unentangled.

- *Build an alliance.* The therapeutic relationship is no less important in work with juvenile sex offenders than with any other treatment population. It is critical to effective treatment.

- *Formulate an understanding.* Clinicians should avoid getting caught up in cookbook approaches to treatment and common language and ideas about causality. Understand the individual juvenile in your care. As Cordess (2001) pointed out understanding the dynamics of each case is critical precisely because it captures the individuality of each offender and the reasons for his particular behaviors.

CONCLUSION: TREATING THE WHOLE CHILD IN A WHOLE-MINDED MANNER

In the final analysis, treating the whole child means treating different aspects of the pathology presented by the juvenile in treatment, but it also means recognizing the array of forces at play in the lives of each individual child or adolescent. Treatment of the whole child, then, means viewing the problem of juvenile sexual offending from many angles and attacking through treatment and rehabilitation as many of those problems as possible, or at least identifying them as significant factors to be addressed. As we must build protective factors, we must also weaken and eliminate risks.

Finally, the clinician can neither do it all nor be all things. There will always be too many things to address in treatment, and too few resources. There will always be things we miss, and we will keep learning. There will also be children and adolescents so damaged that we will wonder how or if we can help undo the damage. Nevertheless, our goal is to prevent our youthful clients from growing into adults like those described by Shaw (1999), who wrote, "in spite of our best efforts, there will be individuals who are so psychologically and neurologically damaged and without social conscience or respect for others that they will not respond to our treatment armamentarium as it now exists. These individuals will continue to be a threat to society, and it will be necessary to incarcerate them for the protection of the community" (p. 188).

References

Abel, G. G., Osborn, C. A., & Twigg, D. A. (1993). Sexual assault through the life span: Adult offenders with juvenile histories. In H. E. Barbaree, W. L. Marshall, & S. M. Hudson (Eds.), *The juvenile sex offender* (pp. 104–117). New York: Guilford Press.

Abel Screening. (2001). *Discoveries* [Electronic version]. Retrieved May 2002 from www.abelscreen.com/aboutasi.htm

Ablon, J. S., & Jones, E. E. (1998.). How expert clinicians' prototypes of an ideal treatment correlate with outcome in psychodynamic and cognitive-behavioral therapy. *Psychotherapy Research, 8*, 71–83.

Ackerman, N. W. (1962). Family psychotherapy and psychoanalysis: The implications of a difference. *Family Process, 1*, 30–43.

American Academy of Child and Adolescent Psychiatry. (1999). Practice parameters for the assessment and treatment of children and adolescents who are sexually abusive of others. *Journal of the American Academy of Child and Adolescent Psychiatry, 38:12* (Suppl.), 55–76.

American Academy of Pediatrics. (2001a). Children, adolescents, and television. *Pediatrics, 107*, 423–426.

American Academy of Pediatrics. (2001b). Media violence. *Pediatrics, 108*, 1222–1226.

American Academy of Pediatrics. (2001c). Sexuality education for children and adolescents. *Pediatrics, 108*, 498–502.

American Psychiatric Association. (1996). *Committee on the Practice of Psychotherapy: Resource document on medical psychotherapy.* Washington, DC: Author.

American Psychiatric Association. (2000). *Diagnostic and statistical manual of mental disorders* (4th ed., text revision). Washington, DC: Author.

Arnett, J. J. (1999). Adolescent storm and stress, reconsidered. *American Psychologist, 54*, 317–326.

Asay, T. P., & Lambert, M. L. (1999). The empirical case for the common factors in therapy: Quantitative finding. In M. A. Hubble, B. L. Duncan, & S. D. Miller (Eds.), *The heart and soul of change: What works in therapy* (pp. 23–55). Washington, DC: American Psychological Association.

Association for the Treatment of Sexual Abusers. (1996). *Reducing sexual abuse through treatment and intervention with abusers* [Position paper]. Beaverton, OR: Author.

Association for the Treatment of Sexual Abusers. (1997). *Ethical standards and principles for the management of sexual abusers.* Beaverton, OR: Author.

Association for the Treatment of Sexual Abusers. (2000). *The effective legal management of juvenile sexual offenders* [Position paper]. Beaverton, OR: Author.

Association for the Treatment of Sexual Abusers. (2001). *Practice standards and guidelines for members of the Association for the Treatment of Sexual Abusers.* Beaverton, OR: Author.

Bachelor, A., & Horvath, A. (1999). The therapeutic relationship. In M. A. Hubble, B. L. Duncan, & S. D. Miller (Eds.), *The heart and soul of change: What works in therapy* (pp. 133–178). Washington, DC: American Psychological Association.

Bailey, S. (2000). Sadistic, sexual, and violent acts in the young. (2000). In C. Itzen (Ed.), *Home truths about child sexual abuse: Influencing policy and practice* (pp. 200–221). London: Routledge.

Baker, A. J. L., Tabacoff, R., Tornusciolo, G., & Eisenstadt, M. (2001). Calculating number of offenses and victims of juvenile sexual offending: The role of posttreatment disclosures. *Sexual Abuse, 13,* 79–90.

Barbaree, H. E. & Cortoni, F. A. (1993). Treatment of the juvenile sexual offender within the justice and mental health systems. In H. E. Barbaree, W. L. Marshall, & S. M. Hudson (Eds.), *The juvenile sex offender* (pp. 243–263). New York: Guilford Press.

Barbaree, H. E., Hudson, S. M., & Seto, M. C. (1993). Sexual assault in society: The role of the juvenile sexual offender. In H. E. Barbaree, W. L. Marshall, & S. M. Hudson (Eds.), *The juvenile sex offender* (pp. 1–24). New York: Guilford Press.

Barker, R. L., & Branson, D. M. (2000). *Forensic social work: Legal aspects of professional practice* (2nd ed.). New York: Haworth Press.

Barnes, C., & Hughes, G. (2002). Family work with adolescent sexual offenders. In M. C. Calder (Ed.), *Young people who sexually abuse: Building the evidence base for your practice* (pp. 231–240). Dorset, England: Russell House.

Bateman, A. W. (2002). Integrative therapy from an analytic perspective. In J. Holmes & A. Bateman (Eds.), *Integration in psychotherapy: Models and methods* (pp. 12–25). Oxford, England: Oxford University Press.

Beck, A. T. (1979). *Cognitive treatment and the emotional disorders.* New York: Meridian.

Beck, J. S. (1995). *Cognitive therapy: Basics and beyond.* New York: Guilford Press.

Becker, J. V., Johnson, B. R., & Hunter, J. A. (1996). Adolescent sex offenders. In C. R. Hollin & K. Howells (Eds.), *Clinical approaches to working with young offenders* (pp. 183–195). Chichester, England: Wiley.

Becker, J. V., & Kaplan, M. S. (1988). The assessment of sexual offenders. *Advances in Behavioral Assessment of Children and Families, 4,* 97–118.

Beckett, R. (1999). Evaluation of adolescent sexual abusers. In M. Erooga & H. Masson (Eds.), *Children and young people who sexually abuse others: Challenges and responses* (pp. 204–224). London: Routledge.

Bennis, W. G., & Shepard, H. A. (1956). A theory of group development. *Human Relations, 9,* 415–437.

Bentovim, A. (2002). Research on the development of sexually abusive behaviour in sexually abusive males: The implications for clinical practice. In M. C. Calder (Ed.), *Young people who sexually abuse: Building the evidence base for your practice* (pp. 345–354). Dorset, England: Russell House.

Berger, P. L., & Luckmann, T. (1967). *The social construction of reality: A treatise on the sociology of knowledge.* Garden City, NY: Anchor Books.

Beutler, L. E. (2000a). David and Goliath: When empirical and clinical standards of practice meet. *American Psychologist, 55,* 997–1007.

Beutler, L. E. (2000b). Empirically based decision making in clinical practice. *Prevention and Treatment, 3,* Article 27. Retrieved July 2002 from http://www.journals.apa.org/prevention/volume3/pre0030027a.html

Bilchik, S. (1998). Mental health disorders and substance abuse problems among juveniles. *OJJDP Fact Sheet, 82.* Washington, DC: U.S. Department of Justice, Office of Juvenile Justice and Delinquency Prevention.

Blanchard, G. T. (1998). *The difficult connection: The therapeutic relationship in sexual offender treatment.* Brandon, VT: Safer Society Press.

Bluglass, R. (1990). The scope of forensic psychiatry. *Journal of Forensic Psychiatry, 1, 7.*

Boer, D. P., Hart, S. D., Kropp, P. R., & Webster, C. D. (1997). *Manual for the Sexual Violence Risk–20.* Burnaby, British Columbia, Canada: Mental Health, Law, and Policy Institute, Simon Fraser University.

Boeringer, S. B. (2001). Rape and sexual coercion: A social learning model. *Sex Offender Law Report, 2,* 49–59.

Borum, R., Bartel, P., & Forth, A. (2002). *Manual for the Structured Assessment of Violence in Youth (SAVRY):* Tampa, FL: Department of Mental Health Law and Policy, University of South Florida.

Borum, R., Fein, R., Vossekuil, B., & Berglund, J. (1999). Threat assessment: Defining an approach for evaluating risk of targeted violence. *Behavioral Sciences and the Law, 17,* 323–337.

Bowen, M. (1971). The use of family therapy in clinical practice. In J. Haley (Ed.), *Changing families: A family therapy reader* (pp. 159–192). New York: Grune and Stratton.

Bowen, M. (1978). *Family therapy in clinical practice.* Northvale, NJ: Aronson.

Bowlby, J. (1979). *The making and breaking of affectional bonds.* London: Routledge.

Brown, E. J., & Kolko, D. J. (1998). Treatment efficacy and program evaluation with juvenile sexual abusers: A critique with directions for service delivery and research. *Child Maltreatment, 3,* 362–373.

Brown, J. D., & Keller, S. N. (2000). Can the mass media be healthy sex educators? *Family Planning Perspectives, 32,* 255–256.

Bumby, K. M. (2000). Empathy inhibition, empathy deficits, and attachment difficulties in sexual offenders. In D. R. Laws, S. M. Hudson, & T. Ward (Eds.), *Remaking relapse prevention with sexual offenders: A sourcebook* (pp. 143–166). Thousand Oaks, CA: Sage.

Burton, D. L. (2000). Were adolescent sexual offenders children with sexual behavior problems? *Sexual Abuse: A Journal of Research and Treatment, 12,* 37–48.

Burton, D. L., & Smith-Darden, J. (2001). *North American Survey of Sexual Abuser Treatment Models: Summary Data 2000.* Brandon, VT: Safer Society Press.

Cade, B., & O'Hanlon, W. H. (1993). *A brief guide to brief therapy.* New York: Norton.

Calder, M. C. (Ed.). (1999). *Working with young people who sexually abuse: New pieces of the jigsaw puzzle.* Dorset, England: Russell House.

Calder, M. C. (2000a). The comprehensive assessment of juveniles who sexually abuse. In M. C. Calder (Ed.), *The complete guide to sexual abuse assessments* (pp. 73–88). Dorset, England: Russell House.

Calder, M. C. (Ed.). (2000b). *The complete guide to sexual abuse assessments.* Dorset, England: Russell House.

Calder, M. C. (2001). *Juveniles and children who sexually abuse: Frameworks for assessment* (3rd ed.). Dorset, England: Russell House.

Campbell, T. W. (2000). Sexual predator evaluations and phrenology: Considering issues of evidentiary reliability. *Behavioral Science and the Law, 18,* 111–130.

Cantwell, H. B. (1995). Sexually aggressive children and societal response. In M. Hunter (Ed.), *Child survivors and perpetrators of sexual abuse: Treatment innovations* (pp. 79–107). Thousand Oaks, CA: Sage.

Carich, M. S., Gray, A., Rombouts, S., Stone, M., & Pithers, W. D. (2001). Relapse prevention and the sexual abuser cycle. In M. S. Carich & S. E. Mussack (Eds.), *Handbook for sexual abuser assessment and treatment* (pp. 77–103). Brandon, VT: Safer Society Press.

Carnes, P., Delmonico, D. L., & Griffin, W. (2001). *In the shadows of the Net: Breaking free of compulsive online sexual behavior.* Center City, MN: Hazelden Foundation.

Castonguay, L. G., Goldfried, M. R., Wiser, S., Raue, P. J., & Hayes, A. M. (1996). Predicting the effect of cognitive therapy for depression: A study of unique and common factors. *Journal of Consulting and Clinical Psychology, 64,* 497–504.

Center for Sex Offender Management. (1999a). *Glossary of terms used in the management and treatment of sexual offenders.* Silver Spring, MD: Author.

Center for Sex Offender Management. (1999b). *Understanding juvenile sexual offending behavior: Emerging research, treatment approaches and management practices.* Silver Spring, MD: Author.

Center for Sex Offender Management. (2000). *Myths and facts about sex offenders.* Silver Spring, MD: Author.

Chaffin, M., & Bonner, B. (1998). Don't shoot, we're your children: Have we gone too far in our response to adolescent sexual abusers and children with sexual behavior problems? *Child Maltreatment, 3,* 314–316.

Chambless, D. L., Baker, M. J., Baucom, D. H., Beutler, L. E., Calhoun, K. S., Crits-Cristoph, P., Daiuto, A., DeRubeis, R., Detweiler, J., Haaga, D. A. F., Johnson, S. B., McCurry, S., Mueser, K. T., Pope, K. S., Sanderson, W. C., Shoham, V., Stickle, T., Williams, D. A., & Woody, S. R. (1998). Update on empirically validated therapies, II. *The Clinical Psychologist, 51,* 3–16.

Cocozza, J. J., & Skowyra, K. R. (2000). Youth with mental health disorders: Issues and emerging responses. *Juvenile Justice, 7*(1), 3–13.

Cohen, A. M., & Smith, R. D. (1976). *The critical incident in growth groups: Theory and technique.* San Diego, CA: University Associates.

Cooke, D. J., & Philip, L. (2001). To treat or not to treat? An empirical perspective. In C. R. Hollin (Ed.), *Handbook of offender assessment and treatment* (pp. 17–34). Chichester, England: Wiley.

Cordess, C. (2001). Forensic psychotherapy. In C. R. Hollin (Ed.), *Handbook of offender assessment and treatment* (pp. 309–329). Chichester, England: Wiley.

Craissati, J., McGlurg, G., & Browne, K. (2002). Characteristics of perpetrators of child sexual abuse who have been sexually abused as children. *Sexual Abuse: A Journal of Research and Treatment, 14,* 225–239.

Davis, G. E., & Leitenberg, H. (1987). Adolescent sex offenders. *Psychological Bulletin, 101,* 417–427.

Day, R. W., & Sparacio, R. T. (1989). Structuring the counseling process. In W. Dryden (Ed.), *Key issues for counselling in action* (pp. 16–25). London: Sage.

de Anda, D. (2002). *Stress management for adolescents: A cognitive-behavioral program.* Champaign, IL: Research Press.

Dies, R. R. (1985). Leadership in short-term group therapy: Manipulation or facilitation? *International Journal of Group Psychotherapy, 35*, 435–455.

Dishion, T. J., McCord, J., & Poulin, F. (1999). When interventions harm: Peer groups and problem behavior. *American Psychologist, 54*, 755–764.

Doren, D. M. (2001). Ironies involving actuarial risk instrumentation use in civil commitment assessments. *Sex Offender Law Report, 2*, 35–48.

Doren, D. M. (2002). *Evaluating sex offenders: A manual for civil commitments and beyond.* Thousand Oaks, CA: Sage.

Dryden, W. (1989). The therapeutic alliance as an integrating framework. In W. Dryden (Ed.), *Key issues for counselling in action* (pp. 1–15). London: Sage.

Duncan, B. (2001). The future of psychotherapy. *Psychotherapy Networker, 25*(4), 24–33, 52–53.

Duncan, B., Miller, S., & Sparks, J. (2000). Exposing the mythmakers. *Family Therapy Networker, 24*(2), 24–33, 52–53.

Eldridge, H. (2000). Patterns of sexual offending and strategies for effective assessment and intervention. In C. Itzen (Ed.), *Home truths about child sexual abuse: Influencing policy and practice* (pp. 313–334) London: Routledge.

Elkin, I., Shea, M. T., Watkins, J. T., Imber, S. D., Sotsky, S. M., Collins, J. F., Glass, D. R., Pilkonis, P. A., Leber, W. R., Docherty, J. P., Fiester, S. J., & Parloff, M. B. (1989). National Institute of Mental Health Treatment of Depression Collaborative Research Program: General effectiveness of treatments. *Archives of General Psychiatry, 46*, 971–982.

Ellis, A. (1993). *How to stubbornly refuse to make yourself miserable about anything—Yes, anything!* New York: Lyle Stuart.

Ellis, A. (1995). *Better, deeper, and more enduring brief therapy: The Rational Emotive Behavioral Therapy approach.* New York: Brunner/Mazel.

Epps, K. J. (1997). Managing risk. In M. S. Hoghughi (Ed.), *Working with sexually abusive adolescents* (pp. 35–51). Thousand Oaks, CA: Sage.

Epps, K. J. (1999). Filling the theoretical reservoir. In M. C. Calder (Ed.), *Working with young people who sexually abuse: New pieces of the jigsaw puzzle* (pp. 8–26). Dorset, England: Russell House.

Erikson, E. H. (1963). *Childhood and society* (2nd ed.). New York: Norton.

Everstine, D. S., & Everstine, L. (1993). *The trauma response: Treatment for emotional injury.* New York: Norton.

Faulkner, A., & Thomas, P. (2002). User-led research and evidence-based medicine. *British Journal of Psychiatry, 180*, 1–3.

Fehrenbach, P. A., Smith, W., Monastersky, C., & Diesher, R. W. (1986). Adolescent sex offenders: Offenders and offense characteristics. *American Journal of Orthopsychiatry, 56*, 225–253.

Ferrara, M. L. (1992). *Group counseling with juvenile delinquents: The limit and lead approach.* Newbury Park, CA: Sage.

Finkelhor, D. (1979). *Sexually victimized children.* New York: Free Press.

Finkelhor, D. (1984). *Child sexual abuse: New theory and research.* New York: Free Press.

Finkelhor, D., Mitchell, K. J., & Wolak, J. (2000). *Online victimization: A report on the nation's youth.* Alexandria, VA: National Center for Missing and Exploited Children.

First, M. B., Spitzer, R. L., Gibbon, M., & Williams, J. B. W. (1997). *Structured clinical interview for DSM-IV Axis I disorders.* Washington, DC: American Psychiatric Press.

Fisher, S., & Greenberg, R. P. (1997). *From placebo to panacea: Putting psychiatric drugs to the test.* New York: Wiley.

Fossum, M. A., & Mason, M. J. (1986). *Facing shame: Families in recovery.* New York: Norton.

Freeman-Longo, R. (1989). *Why did I do it again? Understanding my cycle of problem behaviors.* Holyoke, MA: NEARI Press.

Frick, P. J. (2002). Juvenile psychopathy from a developmental perspective: Implications for construct development and use in forensic assessments. *Law and Human Behavior, 26,* 247–253.

Furby, L., Weinrott, M. R., & Blackshaw, L. (1989). Sex offender recidivism: A review. *Psychological Bulletin, 105,* 3–10.

Garfield, S. L. (1996). Some problems associated with "validated" forms of psychotherapy. *Clinical Psychology: Science and Practice, 3,* 218–229.

Gilgun, J. F. (1999). CASPARS: Clinical assessment instruments that measure strengths and weaknesses in children and families. In M. C. Calder (Ed.), *Working with young people who sexually abuse: New pieces of the jigsaw puzzle* (pp. 50–58). Dorset, England: Russell House.

Gilgun, J. F., Klein, C., & Pranis, K. (2000). The significance of resources in models of risk. *The Journal of Interpersonal Violence, 14,* 627–646.

Glasser, M., Kolvin, I., Campbell, D., Glasser, A., Leitch, I., & Farrelly, S. (2001). Cycle of child sexual abuse: Links between being a victim and becoming a perpetrator. *British Journal of Psychiatry, 179,* 482–494.

Goldfried, M. R., & Wolfe, B. E. (1998). Toward a more clinically valid approach to therapy research. *Journal of Consulting and Clinical Psychology, 66,* 143–150.

Goldstein, A. P., Glick, B., & Gibbs, J. C. (1998). *Aggression replacement training: A comprehensive intervention for aggressive youth* (Rev. ed.). Champaign, IL: Research Press.

Graham, F., Richardson, G., & Bhate, S. (1997). Assessment. In M. S. Hoghughi (Ed.), *Working with sexually abusive adolescents* (pp. 52–91). Thousand Oaks, CA: Sage.

Greenberg, S. A., & Shuman, D. W. (1999). Irreconcilable conflict between therapeutic and forensic roles. In D. N. Bersoff (Ed.), *Ethical conflicts in psychology* (2nd ed., pp. 513–520). Washington, DC: American Psychological Association.

Greenwald, R. (1999). *Eye Movement Desensitization and Reprocessing (EMDR) in child and adolescent psychotherapy.* Northvale, NJ: Jason Aronson.

Gretton, H. M., McBride, M., Hare, R. D., O'Shaughnessy, R., & Kumka, G. (2001). Psychopathy and recidivism in adolescent sex offenders. *Criminal Justice and Behavior, 28,* 427–449.

Grisso, T. (1998). *Forensic evaluation of juveniles.* Sarasota, FL: Professional Resource Press.

Grisso, T., & Barnum, R. (2000). Massachusetts Youth Screening Instrument–Second Version: User's Manual and Technical Report. Worcester, MA: University of Massachusetts Medical School.

Grisso, T., Barnum, R., Fletcher, K. E., Cauffman, E., & Peuschold, D. (2001). Massachusetts Youth Screening Instrument for Mental Health Needs of Juvenile Justice Youths. *Journal of the American Academy of Child and Adolescent Psychiatry, 40,* 541–548.

Grossman, L. S., Martis, B., & Fichtner, C. G. (1999). Are sexual offenders treatable? A research overview. *Psychiatric Services, 50,* 349–361.

Grove, W. M., & Meehl, P. E. (1996). Comparative efficiency of informal (subjective, impressionistic) and formal (mechanical, algorithmic) prediction procedures: The clinical-statistical controversy. *Psychology, Public, Policy, and Law, 2,* 229–323.

Grove, W. M., Zald, D. H., Lebow, B. S., Snitz, B. E., & Nelson, C. (2000). Clinical versus mechanical procedures: A meta-analysis. *Psychological Assessment, 12,* 19–30.

Hall, G. S. (1970). *Adolescence: Its psychology and its relation to physiology, anthropology, sociology, sex, crime, religion, and education.* Manchester, NH: Ayer.

Hanson, R. K. (1997). *The development of a brief actuarial risk scale for sexual offense recidivism.* Ottawa, Ontario, Canada: Department of the Solicitor General of Canada.

Hanson, R. K. (1998). What do we know about sexual offender risk assessment? *Psychology, Public Policy, and Law, 4,* 50–72.

Hanson, R. K. (2000). *Risk assessment.* Beaverton, OR: Association for the Treatment of Sexual Abusers.

Hanson, R. K. (2001). Sexual offender risk assessment. In C. R. Hollin (Ed.), *Handbook of offender assessment and treatment* (pp. 84–96). Chichester, England: Wiley.

Hanson, R. K. (2002, June). *Sexual offender recidivism: What we know and what we need to know.* Poster session presented at the New York Academy of Sciences conference on Understanding and Managing Sexually Coercive Behavior, Washington, DC.

Hanson, R. K., & Bussière, M. T. (1998). Predicting relapse: A meta-analysis of sexual offender recidivism studies. *Journal of Consulting and Clinical Psychology, 66,* 348–362.

Hanson, R. K., & Scott, H. (1995). Assessing perspective taking among sexual offenders, nonsexual criminals, and nonoffenders. *Sexual Abuse: A Journal of Research and Treatment, 7,* 259–277.

Hanson, R. K., & Thornton, D. (1999). *Static 99: Improving actuarial risk assessment for sex offenders.* Ottawa, Ontario, Canada: Department of the Solicitor General of Canada.

Hanson, R. K., & Thornton, D. (2000). Improving risk assessments for sex offenders: A comparison of three actuarial scales. *Law and Human Behavior, 24,* 119–136.

Hare, R. D. (1999). *Without conscience: The disturbing world of psychopaths among us.* New York: Guilford Press.

Hart, S. D. (1998). The role of psychopathy in assessing risk for violence: Conceptual and methodological issues. *Legal and Criminological Psychology, 3,* 123–140.

Hart, S. D., Watt, K. A., & Vincent, G. M. (2002). Commentary on Seagrave and Grisso: Impressions of the state of the art. *Law and Human Behavior, 26,* 241–246.

Harvey, J. H., Orbuch, T. L., Chwalisz, K. D., & Garwood, G. (1991). Coping with sexual assault: The roles of account-making and confiding. *Journal of Stress Management, 4,* 515–531.

Hawkes, C., Jenkins, J. A., & Vizard, E. (1997). Roots of sexual violence in children and adolescents. In V. Varma (Ed.), *Violence in children and adolescents* (pp. 84–102). London: Kingsley.

Heilbrun, K., Nezu, C. M., Keeny, M., Chung, S., & Wasserman, A. L. (1998). Sexual offending: Linking assessment, intervention, and decision making. *Psychology, Public Policy, and Law, 4,* 138–174.

Hellerstein, D. J., Rosenthal, R. N., Pinsker, H., Samstag, L. W., Muran, J. C., &

Winston, A. (1998). A randomized prospective study comparing supportive and dynamic therapies. *Journal of Psychotherapy Practice Research, 7,* 261–271.

Henggeler, S. W., Schoenwald, S. K., Borduin, C. M., Rowland, M. D., & Cunningham, P. B. (1998). *Multisystemic treatment of antisocial behavior in children and adolescents.* New York: Guilford Press.

Hodgins, S. (2001). Offenders with major mental disorders. In C. R. Hollin (Ed.), *Handbook of offender assessment and treatment* (pp. 434–451). Chichester, England: Wiley.

Hoge, R. D., & Andrews, D. A. (1996). *Assessing the youthful offender: Issues and techniques.* New York: Plenum Press.

Hollin, C. R. (2001). To treat or not to treat? An historical perspective. In C. R. Hollin (Ed.), *Handbook of offender assessment and treatment* (pp. 3–15). Chichester, England: Wiley.

Holmes, J., & Bateman, A. (Eds.). (2002). *Integration in psychotherapy: Models and methods.* Oxford, England: Oxford University Press.

Houston, J. (1998). *Making sense with offenders: Personal constructs, therapy and change.* Chichester, England: Wiley.

Hubble, M. A., Duncan, B. L., & Miller, S. D. (1999). *The heart and soul of change: What works in therapy.* Washington, DC: American Psychological Association.

Hudson, S. M., & Ward, T. (2001). Adolescent sexual offenders: Assessment and treatment. In C. R. Hollin (Ed.), *Handbook of offender assessment and treatment* (pp. 363–377). Chichester, England: Wiley.

Hunter, J. A. (2000). Understanding juvenile offenders: Research findings and guidelines for effective management and treatment. *Juvenile Justice Fact Sheet.* Charlottesville, VA: Institute of Law, Psychiatry, and Public Policy, University of Virginia.

Hunter, J. A., Figueredo, A. J., Malamuth, N. M., & Becker, J. V. (in press). Developmental pathways in youth sexual aggression and delinquency: Risk factors and mediators. *Journal of Family Violence.*

Hunter, J. A., Figueredo, A. J., Malamuth, N. M., & Becker, J. V. (2003). Juvenile sexual offenders: Towards the development of a typology. *Sexual Abuse: A Journal of Research and Treatment.*

Hunter, J. A., & Lexier, L. J. (1998). Ethical and legal issues in the assessment and treatment of juvenile sexual offenders. *Child Maltreatment, 3,* 339–348.

Huston, A. C., Wartella, E., & Donnerstein, E. (1998). *Measuring the effects of sexual content in the media: A report to the Kaiser Family Foundation.* Menlo Park, CA: Henry J. Kaiser Family Foundation.

Itzen, C. (2000). Child protection and child sexual abuse prevention: Influencing policy and practice. Understanding and treating the effects of childhood abuse and neglect. In C. Itzen (Ed.), *Home truths about child sexual abuse: Influencing policy and practice* (pp. 405–448). London: Routledge.

Jensen, P. S., Kettle, L., Roper, M. T., Sloan, M. T., Dulcan, M. K., Hoven, C., Bird, H. R., Bauermeister, J. J., & Payne, J. D. (1999). Are stimulants overprescribed? Treatment of ADHD in four U.S. communities. *Journal of the American Academy of Child and Adolescent Psychiatry, 38,* 797–804.

Johnson, T. C. (1999). *Understanding your child's sexual behavior: What's natural and healthy.* Oakland, CA: New Harbinger.

Johnson, T. C. (2000). Sexualized children and children who molest. *Siecus Report, 29*(1), 35–39.

Johnson, T. C., & Feldmeth, J. R. (1993). Sexual behaviors: A continuum. In E. Gil & T. C. Johnson (Eds.), *Sexualized children: Assessment and treatment of sexualized children and children who molest* (pp. 41–52). Rockville, MD: Launch Press.

Kafka, M. P. (1995). Current concepts in the drug treatment of paraphilias and paraphilia-related disorders. *CNS Drugs, 3,* 9–21.

Kafka, M. P. (2001). Paraphilias and paraphilia-related disorders. In G. O. Gabbard (Ed.), *Treatments of psychiatric disorders* (3rd ed., Vol. 2, pp. 1951–1979). Washington, DC: American Psychiatric.

Kafka, M. P., & Hennen, J. (2000). Psychostimulant augmentation during treatment with selective serotonin reuptake inhibitors in men with paraphilias and paraphilia-related disorders: A case series. *Journal of Clinical Psychiatry, 61,* 664–670.

Kahn, T. J., & Chambers, H. J. (1991). Assessing reoffense risk with juvenile sexual offenders. *Child Welfare, 70,* 333–345.

Kann, L., Kinchen, S. A., Williams, B. I., Ross, J. G., Lowry, R., Hill, C. V., Grunbaum, J. A., Blumson, P. S., Collins, J. L., & Kolbe, L. J. (1998). Youth Risk Behavior Surveillance: United States, 1997. *CDC Surveillance Summaries, MMWR 1998, 47*(No. SS-3), 1–89.

Kavoussi, R. J., Kaplan, M., & Becker, J. V. (1988). Psychiatric diagnoses in adolescent sexual offenders. *Journal of the American Academy of Child and Adolescent Psychiatry, 27,* 241–243.

Kazdin, A. E., & Bass, D. (1989). Power to detect differences between alternative treatments in comparative psychotherapy outcome research. *Journal of Consulting and Clinical Psychology, 57,* 138–147.

Keijsers, G. P. J., Schaap, C. P. D. R., & Hoogduin, C. A. L. (2000). The impact of interpersonal patient and therapist behavior on outcome in cognitive-behavior therapy: A review of empirical studies. *Behavior Modification, 24,* 264–297.

Kenny, D. T., Keogh, T., & Seidler, K. (2001). Predictors of recidivism in Australian juvenile sexual offenders: Implications for treatment. *Sexual Abuse, 13,* 131–148.

Kerr, S., Goldfried, M. R., Hayes, A. M., Castonguay, L. G., & Goldsamt, L. A. (1992). Interpersonal and intrapersonal focus in cognitive-behavioral and psychodynamic-interpersonal therapies: A preliminary analysis of the Sheffield Project. *Psychotherapy Research, 4,* 266–276.

Kirby, D. (2001). Understanding what works and what doesn't in reducing adolescent sexual risk-taking. *Family Planning Perspectives, 33,* 276–281.

Kirby, J. (2001). *Emerging answers: Research findings on programs to reduce teen pregnancy (summary).* Washington, DC: National Campaign to Prevent Teen Pregnancy.

Knight, R. A., & Prentky, R. A. (1993). Exploring characteristics for classifying juvenile sexual offenders. In H. E. Barbaree, W. L. Marshall, & S. M. Hudson (Eds.), *The juvenile sex offender* (pp. 45–83). New York: Guilford Press.

Knight, R. A., & Sims-Knight, J. E. (in press). The developmental antecedents of sexual coercion against women in adolescents. In G. O'Reilly, W. L. Marshall, R. Beckett, & A. Carr (Eds.), *Handbook of clinical interventions with juvenile sexual offenders.* London: Routledge.

Kohlberg, L. (1976). Moral stages and moralization: The cognitive-developmental approach. In T. Lickona (Ed.), *Moral development and behavior* (pp. 31–53). New York: Holt, Rinehart, and Winston.

Kunkel, D., Cope-Farrar, K., Biely, E., Farinola, W. J. M., & Donnerstein, E. (2001). *Sex on TV (2): A biennial report to the Kaiser Family Foundation.* Menlo Park, CA: Henry J. Kaiser Family Foundation.

Lacoursiere, R. L. (1980). *The life cycle of groups: Group developmental stage theory.* New York: Human Sciences Press.

Lambert, M. J. (1992). Implications of outcome research for psychotherapy integration. In J. C. Norcross & M. R. Goldstein (Eds.), *Handbook of psychotherapy integration* (pp. 94–129). New York: Basic Books.

Lambert, M. J., & Bergin, A. E. (1993). The effectiveness of psychotherapy. In A. E. Bergin & S. L. Garfield (Eds.), *Handbook of psychotherapy and behavior change* (4th ed., pp. 143–189). New York: Wiley.

Lane, S. (1997a). Assessment of sexually abusive youth. In G. Ryan & S. Lane (Eds.), *Juvenile sexual offending: Causes, consequences, and correction* (Rev. ed., pp. 219–263). San Francisco: Jossey-Bass.

Lane, S. (1997b). The sexual abuse cycle. In G. Ryan & S. Lane (Eds.), *Juvenile sexual offending: Causes, consequences, and correction* (Rev. ed., pp. 77–121). San Francisco: Jossey-Bass.

Laumann, E. O. (1996). *Early sexual experiences: How voluntary? How violent?* Menlo Park, CA: Henry J. Kaiser Family Foundation.

Laws, D. R. (2001). Relapse prevention: Reconceptualization and revision. In C. R. Hollin (Ed.), *Handbook of offender assessment and treatment* (pp. 297–307). Chichester, England: Wiley.

Laws, D. R., Hudson, S. M., & Ward, T. (Eds.). (2000). *Remaking relapse prevention with sexual offenders: A sourcebook.* Thousand Oaks, CA: Sage.

Lee, J. K. P., Jackson, H. J., Pattison, P., & Ward, T. (2002). Developmental risk factors for sexual offending. *Child Abuse and Neglect, 26,* 73–92.

Leversee, T. F. (2002). *Moving beyond sexually abusive behavior: A relapse prevention curriculum.* Holyoke, MA: NEARI Press.

Levin, B. L., Hanson, A., Coe, R. D., & Taylor, A. (1998). *Mental health parity: 1998 National and state perspectives.* Tampa, FL: Louis de la Parte Florida Mental Health Institute.

Lewis, D. O., Shanok, S. S., & Pincus, J. H. (1981). Juvenile male assaulters: Psychiatric, neurological, psychoeducational, and abuse factors. In D. O. Lewis (Ed.), *Vulnerabilities to delinquency* (pp. 89–105). Jamaica, NY: Spectrum.

Lexcen, F., & Redding, R. E. (2000). Mental health needs of juvenile offenders. *Juvenile Justice Fact Sheet.* Charlottesville, VA: Institute of Law, Psychiatry, and Public Policy, University of Virginia.

Lichter, S. R., Lichter, L. S., & Amundson, D. R. (2000). *Sexual imagery in popular entertainment.* Washington, DC: Center for Media and Public Affairs.

Lieberman, M. A., Yalom, I. D., & Miles, M. B. (1973). *Encounter groups: First facts.* New York: Basic Books.

Litwack, T. R. (2001). Actuarial versus clinical assessments of dangerousness. *Psychology, Public Policy, and Law, 7,* 409–443.

Longo, R. E. (2002). A holistic approach to treating young people who sexually abuse.

In M. C. Calder (Ed.), *Young people who sexually abuse: Building the evidence base for your practice* (pp. 218–230). Dorset, England: Russell House.

Loss, P., & Ross, J. E. (1988). *Risk assessment/interviewing protocol for adolescent sexual offenders.* New London, CT: Author.

Luborsky, L., Rosenthal, R., Diguer, L., Andrusyna, T. P., Berman, J. S., Levitt, J. T., Seligman, D. A., & Krause, E. D. (2002). The dodo bird verdict is alive and well—Mostly. *Clinical Psychology: Science and Practice, 9,* 2–12.

Luborsky, L., Singer, B., & Luborsky, L. (1975). Comparative studies of the psychotherapies: "Everybody has won and all must have prizes." *Archives of General Psychiatry, 32,* 995–1008.

Lund, C. A. (2000). Predictors of sexual recidivism: Did meta-analysis clarify the role and relevance of denial? *Sexual Abuse: A Journal of Research and Treatment, 12,* 275–287.

Lundrigan, P. S. (2001). *Treating youth who sexually abuse: An integrated multi-component approach.* New York: Haworth Press.

Lynam, D. R. (2002). Fledgling psychopathy: A view from personality theory. *Law and Human Behavior, 26,* 255–259.

MacKenzie, K. R. (1990). *Introduction to time-limited group psychotherapy.* Washington, DC: American Psychiatric Press.

MacKenzie, K. R., & Harper-Giuffre, H. (1992). Introduction to group concepts. In H. Harper-Giuffre & K. R. MacKenzie (Eds.), *Group psychotherapy for eating disorders* (pp. 29–51). Washington, DC: American Psychiatric Press.

Madanes, C. (1990). *Sex, love, and violence: Strategies for transformation.* New York: Norton.

Maione, P. V., & Chenail, R. J. (1999). Qualitative inquiry: Research on the common factors. In M. A. Hubble, B. L. Duncan, & S. D. Miller (Eds.), *The heart and soul of change: What works in therapy* (pp. 57–88). Washington, DC: American Psychological Association.

Malamuth, N. M. (2002, June). *Integrating etiological models of sexual coercion.* Poster session presented at the New York Academy of Sciences conference on Understanding and Managing Sexually Coercive Behavior, Washington, DC.

Margison, F. (2002). Psychodynamic interpersonal therapy. In J. Holmes & A. Bateman (Eds.), *Integration in psychotherapy: Models and methods* (pp. 107–124). Oxford, England: Oxford University Press.

Marshall, W. L., Anderson, D., & Fernandez, Y. (1999). *Cognitive-behavioural treatment of sexual offenders.* Chichester, England: Wiley.

Marshall, W. L., & Eccles, A. (1993). Pavlovian conditioning processes in adolescent sex offenders. In H. E. Barbaree, W. L. Marshall, & S. M. Hudson (Eds.), *The juvenile sex offender* (pp. 118–142). New York: Guilford Press.

Marshall, W. L., Hudson, S. M., & Hodkinson, S. (1993). The importance of attachment bonds in the development of juvenile sexual offending. In H. E. Barbaree, W. L. Marshall, & S. M. Hudson (Eds.), *The juvenile sex offender* (pp. 164–181). New York: Guilford Press.

Marshall, W. L., Hudson, S. M., Jones, R., & Fernandez, Y. M. (1995). Empathy in sex offenders. *Clinical Psychology Review, 15,* 99–113.

Marshall, W. L., Serran, G. A., & Franca, A. C. (2000). Childhood attachments, sexual abuse, and their relationship to adult coping in child molesters. *Sexual Abuse: A Journal of Research and Treatment, 12,* 17–26.

Masson, H., & Erooga, A. (1999). Children and young people who sexually abuse others: Incidence, characteristics and causation. In M. Erooga & H. Masson (Eds.), *Children and young people who sexually abuse others: Challenges and responses* (pp. 1–18). London: Routledge.

May, R. (1961). *Existential psychotherapy.* New York: Random House.

McCann, J. T. (1998). *Malingering and deception in adolescents: Assessing credibility in clinical and forensic settings.* Washington, DC: American Psychological Association.

McCann, J. T. (2002). *Threats in schools: A practical guide for managing violence.* New York: Haworth Press.

McIvor, G. (2001). Treatment in the community. In C. R. Hollin (Ed.), *Handbook of offender assessment and treatment* (pp. 551–565). Chichester, England: Wiley.

Mediascope Press. (1997). *Issue briefs: National Television Violence Study.* Studio City, CA: Author.

Mediascope Press. (2001). *Issue briefs: Teens, sex, and the media.* Studio City, CA: Author.

Meehl, P. E. (1996). *Clinical versus statistical prediction: A theoretical analysis and a review of the literature.* Northvale, NJ: Aronson.

Meichenbaum, D. (1977). *Cognitive-behavior modification: An integrative approach.* New York: Plenum Press.

Meichenbaum, D. (1985). *Stress inoculation training.* New York: Pergamon Press.

Melton, G. B., Petrila, J., Poythress, N. G., & Slobogin, C. (1997). *Psychological evaluation for the courts* (2nd ed.). New York: Guilford Press.

Mental health: Does therapy help? (1995). *Consumer Reports,* 734–739.

Miller, R. C., & Berman, J. S. (1983). The efficacy of cognitive-behavioral therapies: A quantitative review of the research evidence. *Psychological Bulletin, 94,* 39–53.

Miller, W. R., & Rollnick, S. (Eds.). (2002). *Motivational interviewing* (2nd ed.). New York: Guilford Press.

Millon, T. (1996). Foreword. In J. T. McCann & F. D. Dyer. (Eds.), *Forensic assessment with the Millon inventories* (pp. vii–ix). New York: Guilford Press.

Minne, C. (1997). Forensic psychotherapy assessments and the legal system. In E. V. Welldon & C. Van Velsen (Eds.), *A practical guide to forensic psychotherapy* (pp. 246–252). London: Jessica Kingsley.

Minuchin, S. (1974). *Families and family therapy.* Cambridge, MA: Harvard University Press.

Minuchin, S., & Fishman, C. H. (1981). *Family therapy techniques.* Cambridge, MA: Harvard University Press.

Miranda, A. O., & Corcoran, C. L. (2000). Comparison of perpetration characteristics between male juvenile and adult sexual offenders: Preliminary results. *Sexual Abuse: A Journal of Research and Treatment, 12,* 139–188.

Monahan, J. (1995). *The clinical prediction of violent behavior.* Northvale, NJ: Aronson.

Monahan, J., Steadman, H. J., Silver, E., Appelbaum, P. S., Robbins, P. C., Mulvey, E. P., Roth, L. H., Grisso, T., & Banks, S. (2001). *Rethinking risk assessment: The MacArthur study of mental disorder and violence.* New York: Oxford University Press.

Mossman, D. (1994). Assessing predictions of violence: Being accurate about accuracy. *Journal of Consulting and Clinical Psychology, 62,* 783–792.

Murlow, C. D., Williams, J. W. Jr., Trivedi, M., Chiquette, E., Aguilar, C., Cornell, J. E., Badgett, R., Noel, P. H., Lawrence, V., Lee, S., Luther, M., Ramirez, G., Richardson, W. S., & Stamm, K. (1999, February). *Treatment of depression: New pharmacotherapies.* Evidence Report/Technology Assessment Number 7. AHCPR Publication No. 99-E014. Rokville, MD: U.S. Department of Health and Human Services, Agency for Health Care Policy and Research.

Murphy, W. D., DiLillo, D., Haynes, M. R., & Steere, E. (2001). An exploration of factors related to deviant sexual arousal among juvenile sexual offenders. *Sexual Abuse: A Journal of Research and Treatment, 13,* 91–103.

Mussack, S. E., & Carich, M. S. (2001). Sexual abuser evaluation. In M. S. Carich & S. E. Mussack (Eds.), *Handbook for sexual abuser assessment and treatment* (pp. 11–36). Brandon, VT: Safer Society Press.

Mussack, S. E., & Stickrod, A. (2002). *The clarification process for sexual offenders.* Retrieved May 2002 from http://www.choicesoforegon.com/clarification.htm

Napier, R. W., & Gershenfeld, M. K. (1983). *Making groups work: A guide for group leaders.* Boston: Houghton Mifflin.

National Task Force on Juvenile Sexual Offending. (1993). The Revised Report on Juvenile Sexual Offending 1993 of the National Adolescent Perpetration Network. *Juvenile and Family Court Journal, 44,* 1–120.

Nelson, C., Miner, M., Marques, J., Russell, K., & Achterkirchen, J. (1989). Relapse prevention: A cognitive-behavioral model for treatment of the rapist and child molester. In J. S. Wodarksi & D. L. Whitaker (Eds.), *Treatment for sexual offenders in social work and mental health settings* (pp. 125–155). New York: Haworth Press.

Norcross, J. C. (2000). Toward the delineation of empirically based principles in psychotherapy: Commentary on Beutler (2000). *Prevention and Treatment, 3,* Article 28. Retrieved July 2002 from http://www.journals.apa.org/prevention/volume3/pre0030028c.html

O'Boyle, K., Lenehan, K., & McGarvey, J. (1999). Developing groupwork with young people who sexually abuse. In M. C. Calder (Ed.), *Working with young people who sexually abuse: New pieces of the jigsaw puzzle* (pp. 207–224). Dorset, England: Russell House.

O'Brien, J. D., Pilowsky, D. J., & Lewis, O. W. (1992). *Psychotherapies with children and adolescents: Adapting the psychodynamic process.* Washington, DC: American Psychiatric Press.

O'Brien, M. J., & Bera, W. (1986). Adolescent sexual offenders: A descriptive typology. *Preventing Sexual Abuse, 1*(3), 1–4.

O'Connell, M. A., Leberg, E., & Donaldson, C. R. (1990). *Working with sexual offenders: Guidelines for therapist selection.* Newbury Park, CA: Sage.

O'Donohue, W., Penix, T., & Oksol, E. (2000). Behavioral economics: Understanding sexual behavior, preference, and self-control. In D. R. Laws, S. M. Hudson, & T. Ward (Eds.), *Remaking relapse prevention with sexual offenders: A sourcebook* (pp. 123–139). Thousand Oaks, CA: Sage

Office of Juvenile Justice and Delinquency Prevention. (2000b, May). *OJJDP Research 2000.* Washington, DC: Author.

Office of Juvenile Justice and Delinquency Prevention. (2000a, May). *Children as victims* [1999 National Report Series Bulletin NCJ 180753]. Washington, DC: Author.

Ogles, B. M., Anderson, T., & Lunnen, K. M. (1999). The contributions of models and techniques to therapeutic efficacy: Contradictions between professional trends and clinical research. In M. A. Hubble, B. L. Duncan, & S. D. Miller (Eds.), *The heart and soul of change: What works in therapy* (pp. 291–225). Washington, DC: American Psychological Association.

Olfson, M., Marcus, S. C., Weissman, M. M., & Jensen, P. S. (2002). National trends in the use of psychotropic medications by children. *Journal of the American Academy of Child and Adolescent Psychiatry, 41*, 514–521.

O'Neill, J. V. (2002, March). Therapy technique may not matter much. *NASW News, 47*(3), 3.

Pam, A., & Kemker, S. (1993). The captive group: Guidelines for therapists in the inpatient setting. *International Journal of Group Psychotherapy, 43*, 419–438.

Pennebaker, J. W. (1997). Writing about emotional experiences as a therapeutic process. *Psychological Science, 8*, 162–166.

Pennebaker, J. W., Zech, E., & Rimé, B. (2001). Disclosing and sharing emotion: Psychological, social and health consequences. In M. S. Stroebe, R. O. Hansson, W. Stroebe, & H. Schut (Eds.), *Handbook of bereavement research: Consequences, coping, and care* (pp. 517–544). Washington, DC: American Psychological Association.

Perkins, D., Hammond, S., Coles, D., & Bishop, D. (1998). *Review of sex offender treatment programmes*. Review prepared for the High Security Psychiatric Services Commissioning Board, United Kingdom National Health Service. Retrieved July 2002 from http://www.ramas.co.uk/report4.pdf

Perry, G. P., & Orchard, J. (1992). *Assessment and treatment of adolescent sex offenders*. Sarasota, FL: Professional Resource Press.

Pinsker, H. (1998). The supportive component of psychotherapy. *Psychiatric Times, 15*(11). Retrieved July 2002 from http://www.psychiatrictimes.com/p981160.html

Pithers, W. D., Gray, A., Busconi, A., & Houchens, P. (1998). Children with sexual behavior problems: Identification of five distinct child types and related treatment considerations. *Child Maltreatment, 3*, 384–406.

Power, M. J. (2002). Integrative therapy from a cognitive-behavioral perspective. In J. Holmes & A. Bateman (Eds.), *Integration in psychotherapy: Models and methods* (pp. 27–47). Oxford, England: Oxford University Press.

Prendergast, W. E. (1993). *The merry-go-round of sexual abuse: Identifying and treating survivors*. New York: Haworth Press.

Prentky, R., & Burgess, A. W. (2000). *Forensic management of sexual offenders*. New York: Kluwer Academic.

Prentky, R., Harris, B., Frizzell, K., & Righthand, K. (2000). An actuarial procedure for assessing risk with juvenile sexual offenders. *Sexual Abuse, 12*, 71–93.

Prentky, R. A., & Edmunds, S.B. (1997). *Assessing sexual abuse: A resource guide for practitioners*. Brandon, VT: Safer Society Press.

Print, B., & Morrison, T. (2000). Treating adolescents who sexually abuse others. In C. Itzen (Ed.), *Home truths about child sexual abuse: Influencing policy and practice* (pp. 290–312). London: Routledge.

Print, B., & O'Callaghan, D. (1999). Working in groups with young men who have sexually abused others. In M. Erooga & H. Masson (Eds.), *Children and young people who sexually abuse others: Challenges and responses* (pp. 124–145). London: Routledge.

Quinsey, V. L., Harris, G. T., Rice, M. E., & Cormier, C. A. (1998). *Violent offenders: Appraising and managing risk.* Washington, DC: American Psychological Association.

Rasmussen, L. A. (2002). An integrated systemic approach to intervention with children with sexually abusive behavior problems. In M. C. Calder (Ed.), *Young people who sexually abuse: Building the evidence base for your practice* (pp. 61–175). Dorset, England: Russell House.

Rasmussen, L. A., Burton, J. E., & Christopherson, B. J. (1992). Precursors to offending and the trauma outcome process in sexually reactive children. *Journal of Child Sexual Abuse, 1,* 33–48.

Reddy, M., Borum, R., Berglund, J., Vossekuil, B., Fein, R., & Modzeleski, W. (2001). *Pyschology in the Schools, 38,* 157–172.

Regier, D. A., Hirschfeld, R. M., Goodwin, F. K., Burke, J. D., Jr., Lazar, J. B., & Judd, L. L. (1988). The NIMH Depression Awareness, Recognition, and Treatment Program: Structure, aims, and scientific basis. *American Journal of Psychiatry, 145,* 1351–1357.

Reppucci, N. D., & Redding, R. E. (2000). Screening instruments for mental illness in juvenile offenders: The MAYSI and the BSI. *Juvenile Justice Fact Sheet.* Charlottesville, VA: Institute of Law, Psychiatry, and Public Policy, University of Virginia.

Rich, P. (2001a, May). *Clinical assessment of juvenile sexual offenders and risk for reoffending.* Workshop session presented at the 3rd annual regional joint conference of Massachusetts Association for the Treatment of Sexual Abusers/Massachusetts Adolescent Sexual Offender Coalition, Marlboro, MA.

Rich, P. (2001b, May). *The role, utility, and critical nature of clinical evaluation in assessing risk for sexual re-offending.* Plenary panel session presented at the 16th national annual conference of the National Adolescent Perpetration Network, Kansas City, MO.

Rich, P. (2002). *Survey results: Student self reports of sexually aggressive behaviors, 2002.* (Available from Stetson School, Inc., 455 South Street, Barre, MA 01005).

Rich, P., & Copans, S. A. (1998). *The healing journey: Your journal of self-discovery.* New York: Wiley.

Righthand, S., & Welch, C. (2001). *Juveniles who have sexually offended: A review of the professional literature.* Washington, DC: Office of Juvenile Justice and Delinquency Prevention, U.S. Department of Justice.

Roberts, E. J. (1982). Television and sexual learning in childhood. In D. Pearl (Ed.), *Television and behavior: Ten years of scientific progress and implications for the 80s* (pp. 209–223). Washington, DC: U.S. Government Printing Office.

Rogers, C. R. (1961). *On becoming a person: A therapist's view of psychotherapy.* Boston: Houghton Mifflin.

Rogers, C. R., & Wood, J. K. (1974). Client-centered therapy. In A. Burton (Ed.), *Operational theories of personality* (pp. 211–258). NY: Bruner/Mazel.

Rose, S. D., & Edleson, J. L. (1987). *Working with children and adolescents in groups.* San Francisco: Jossey-Bass.

Rösler, A., & Witztum, W. (2000). Pharmacotherapy of paraphilias in the next millennium. *Behavioral Sciences and the Law, 18,* 43–56.

Ross, J., & Loss, P. (1991). Assessment of the juvenile sexual offender. In G. D. Ryan & S. L. Lane (Eds.), *Juvenile sexual offending: Causes, consequences, and correction* (pp. 199–251). Lexington, MA: Lexington Books.

Ryan, E. P. (2001). Mood disorders in juvenile offenders. *Juvenile Justice Fact Sheet.* Charlottesville, VA: Institute of Law, Psychiatry, and Public Policy, University of Virginia.

Ryan, G. (1997a). Phenomenology: A developmental-contextual view. In G. Ryan & S. Lane (Eds.), *Juvenile sexual offending: Causes, consequences, and correction* (Rev. ed., pp. 122–135). San Francisco: Jossey-Bass.

Ryan, G. (1997b). Sexually abusive youth: Defining the population. In G. Ryan & S. Lane (Eds.), *Juvenile sexual offending: Causes, consequences, and correction* (Rev. ed., pp. 3–9). San Francisco: Jossey-Bass.

Ryan, G. (1997c). Theories of etiology. In G. Ryan & S. Lane (Eds.), *Juvenile sexual offending: Causes, consequences, and correction* (Rev. ed., pp. 19–35). San Francisco: Jossey-Bass.

Ryan, G. (1999a). Recent developments and conclusions. In G. Ryan and Associates, *Web of meaning: A developmental-contextual approach in sexual abuse treatment* (pp. 133–151). Brandon, VT: Safer Society Press.

Ryan, G. (1999b). Treatment of sexually abusive youth: The evolving consensus. *Journal of Interpersonal Violence, 14,* 422–436.

Ryan, G., Miyoshi, T. J., Metzner, J. L., Krugman, R. D., & Fryer, G. E. (1996). Trends in a national sample of sexually abusive youths. *Journal of the American Academy of Child and Adolescent Psychiatry, 35,* 17–25.

Salter, A. C. (1988). *Treating child sex offenders and victims: A practical guide.* Newbury Park, CA: Sage.

Satir, V. M. (1971). The family as a treatment unit. In J. Haley (Ed.), *Changing families: A family therapy reader* (pp. 127–132). New York: Grune and Stratton.

Sawyer, S. (2000). Some thoughts about why we believe group therapy is the preferred modality for treating sex offenders. *Forum, 12*(2), 11–12.

Schram, D. D., Milloy, C. D., & Rowe, W. E. (1991). *Juvenile sex offenders: A follow up study of reoffense behavior.* Olympia, WA: Washington State Institute for Public Policy, Urban Policy Research and Cambie Group International.

Schutz, W. (1973). *Elements of encounter.* Big Sur, CA: Joy Press.

Seagrave, D., & Grisso, T. (2002). Adolescent development and the measurement of juvenile psychopathy. *Law and Human Behavior, 26,* 219–239.

Segal, D. L., & Murray, E. J. (1994). Emotional processing in cognitive therapy and vocal expression of feeling. *Journal of Social and Clinical Psychology, 13,* 189–206.

Seligman, M. E. P. (1995). The effectiveness of psychotherapy: The *Consumer Reports* study. *American Psychologist, 50,* 965–974.

Shaffer, J. B. P., & Galinsky, M. D. (1974). *Models of group therapy and sensitivity training.* Englewood Cliffs, NJ: Prentice-Hall.

Shapiro, F. (1995). *Eye Movement Desensitization and Reprocessing: Basic principle, protocols, and procedures.* New York: Guilford Press.

Shaw, J. A. (1999). Male adolescent sex offenders. In J. A. Shaw (Ed.), *Sexual aggression* (pp. 169–193). Washington, DC: American Psychiatric Press.

Shaw, M. E. (1981). *Group dynamics: The psychology of small group behavior* (3rd ed.). New York: McGraw-Hill.

Silverman, W. H. (1996). Cookbooks, manuals, and paint-by-numbers: Psychotherapy in the 90's. *Psychotherapy: Theory, Research, Practice, Training, 33,* 207–215.

Sirles, E. A., Araji, S. K., & Bosek, R. L. (1997). Redirecting children's sexually abusive and sexually aggressive behaviors: Programs and practices. In S. K. Araji (Ed.), *Sexually aggressive children: Coming to understand them* (pp. 161–192). Thousand Oaks, CA: Sage.

Skuse, D., Bentovim, A., Hodges, J., Stevenson, J., Andreou, C., Lanyado, M., New, M., Williams, B., & McMillan, D. (2000). Risk factors for development of sexually abusive behavior in sexually victimized adolescent boys. In C. Itzen (Ed.), *Home truths about child sexual abuse: Influencing policy and practice* (pp. 222–231). London: Routledge.

Smallbones, S. W., & Dadds, M. R. (2000). Attachment and coercive sexual behavior. *Sexual Abuse: A Journal of Research and Treatment, 12,* 3–15.

Smead, R. (1995). *Skills and techniques for group work with children and adolescents.* Champaign, IL: Research Press.

Smith, M. L, Glass, G. V., & Miller, T. I. (1980). *The benefits of psychotherapy.* Baltimore: Johns Hopkins University Press.

Smith, W. R., & Monastersky, C. (1986). Assessing juvenile sexual offenders risk for re-offending. *Criminal Justice and Behavior, 13,* 115–140.

Snyder, H. N. (2000a). *Sexual assault of young children as reported to law enforcement: Victim, incident, and offender characteristics* (NCJ 182990). Washington, DC: Bureau of Justice Statistics.

Snyder, H. N. (2000b). *Juvenile arrests 1999.* Washington, DC: Office of Juvenile Justice and Delinquency Prevention.

Steadman, H. J., Silver, E., Monahan J., Appelbaum, P. S., Robbins, P. C., Mulvey, E. P., Grisso, T., Roth, L. H., & Banks, S. (2000). A classification tree approach to the development of actuarial violence risk assessment tools. *Law and Human Behavior, 24,* 83–100.

Steele, B. F., & Ryan, G. (1997). Development gone wrong. In G. Ryan & S. Lane (Eds.), *Juvenile sexual offending: Causes, consequences, and correction* (Rev. ed., pp. 59–76). San Francisco: Jossey-Bass.

Steen, C. (1993). *The relapse prevention workbook for youth in treatment.* Brandon, VT: Safer Society Press.

Stetson School. (2000a). *The assessment of student assets and vulnerabilities.* (Available from Stetson School, Inc., 455 South Street, Barre, MA 01005).

Stetson School. (2000b). *The Interim Modified Risk Assessment Tool.* (Available from Stetson School, Inc., 455 South Street, Barre, MA 01005).

Stetson School. (2000c). *The Juvenile Risk Assessment Tool.* (Available from Stetson School, Inc., 455 South Street, Barre, MA 01005).

Stierlin, H. (1974). Family theory: An introduction. In A. Burton (Ed.), *Operational theories of personality* (pp. 278–307). New York: Bruner/Mazel.

Stiles, W. B., Shapiro, D. A., & Elliott, R. (1986). Are all psychotherapies equal? *American Psychologist, 41,* 165–180.

Stoner, A. A., & George, W. H. (2000). Relapse prevention and harm reduction. In D. R. Laws, S. M. Hudson, & T. Ward (Eds.), *Remaking relapse prevention with sexual offenders: A sourcebook* (pp. 56–75). Thousand Oaks, CA: Sage.

Tallman, K., & Bohart, A. C. (1999). The client as a common factor: Clients as self-healers. In M. A. Hubble, B. L. Duncan, & S. D. Miller (Eds.), *The heart and soul of change: What works in therapy* (pp. 91–131). Washington, DC: American Psychological Association.

Tangney, J. P., & Dearing, R. L. (2002). *Shame and guilt.* New York: Guilford Press.

Thase, M. E., & Beck, A. T. (1993). An overview of cognitive therapy. In J. E. Wright, M. E. Thase, A. T. Beck, & J. W. Ludgate (Eds.), *Cognitive therapy with inpatients* (pp. 3–34). New York, Guilford Press.

Thomas, J. (1997). The family in treatment. In G. Ryan & S. Lane (Eds.), *Juvenile sexual offending: Causes, consequences, and correction* (Rev. ed., pp. 360–403). San Francisco: Jossey-Bass.

Thomas, J., & Viar, C. W. (2001). Family treatment of adult sexual abusers. In M. S. Carich & S. E. Mussack (Eds.), *Handbook for sexual abuser assessment and treatment* (pp. 163–192). Brandon, VT: Safer Society Press.

Umbreit, M. S., & Greenwood, J. (2000). *Guidelines for victim-sensitive victim-offender mediation: Restorative justice through dialogue.* St. Paul, MN: Center for Restorative Justice and Peacemaking, University of Minnesota.

U.S. Department of Health and Human Services. (1999). *Mental health: A report of the Surgeon General.* Rockville, MD: Author.

U.S. Department of Health and Human Services. (2001a). *Child Maltreatment 1999.* Washington, DC: Administration on Children, Youth, and Families.

U.S. Department of Health and Human Services. (2001b). *Youth Violence: A report of the Surgeon General.* Rockville, MD: Author.

U.S. Department of Health and Human Services. (2002). *The Surgeon General's call to action to promote sexual health and responsible sexual behavior.* Rockville, MD: Author.

U.S. Federal Trade Commission. (2000). *Marketing violent entertainment to children: A review of self-regulation and industry practices in the motion picture, music recording, and electronic game industries.* Washington, DC: Author.

U.S. General Accounting Office. (1996a). *Cycle of sexual abuse: Research inconclusive about whether child victims become adult abusers* (GAO/GGD-96-178). Washington, DC: Author.

U.S. General Accounting Office. (1996b). *Sex offender treatment: Research results inconclusive about what works to reduce recidivism* (GAO/GGD-96-137). Washington, DC: Author.

Vernon, A. (1998). *The PASSPORT program: A journey through emotional, social, cognitive, and self-development.* Champaign, IL: Research Press.

Vizard, E. (1997). Adolescents who sexually offend. In E. V. Welldon & C. Van Velsen (Eds.), *A practical guide to forensic psychotherapy* (pp. 48–55). London: Kingsley.

Vizard, E. (2002). The assessment of young sexual abusers. In M. C. Calder (Ed.), *Young people who sexually abuse: Building the evidence base for your practice* (pp. 176–195). Dorset, England: Russell House.

Wampold, B. E., Mondin, G. W., Moody, M., Stich, F., Benson, K., & Ahn, H. (1997). A meta-analysis of outcome studies comparing bonafide psychotherapies: Empirically, "all must have prizes." *Psychological Bulletin, 122,* 203–215.

Ward, T., & Hudson, S. M. (2000a). A self-regulation model of relapse prevention. In D. R. Laws, S. M. Hudson, & T. Ward (Eds.), *Remaking relapse prevention with sexual offenders: A sourcebook* (pp. 79–101). Thousand Oaks, CA: Sage.

Ward, T., & Hudson, S. M. (2000b). Sexual offenders' implicit planning: A conceptual model. *Sexual Abuse: A Journal of Research and Treatment, 12,* 189–202.

Waters, R. (2000). Generation Rx. *Family Therapy Networker, 24*(2), 34–43.

Watkins, B., & Bentovim, A. (1992). The sexual abuse of male children and adolescents: A review of current research. *Journal of Child Psychology and Psychiatry, 33,* 197–248.

Way, I. (2002). Childhood maltreatment histories of male adolescents with sexual offending behaviors: A review of the literature. In M. C. Calder (Ed.), *Young people who sexually abuse: Building the evidence base for your practice* (pp. 26–55). Dorset, England: Russell House.

Way, I. F., & Spieker, S. D. (1997). *The cycle of offense: A framework for treating adolescent sexual offenders.* Notre Dame, IN: Jalice.

Webster, C. D., Douglas, K. S., Eaves, D., & Hart, S. D. (1997). *HCR-20: Assessing risk for violence* (Version 2). Burnaby, British Columbia, Canada: Mental Health, Law, and Policy Institute, Simon Fraser University.

Weinrott, M. R. (1996). *Juvenile sexual aggression: A critical review* (Center Paper 005). Boulder, CO: University of Colorado, Center for the Study and Prevention of Violence.

Welldon, E. V. (1997). Forensic psychotherapy: The practical approach. In E. V. Welldon & C. Van Velsen (Eds.), *A practical guide to forensic psychotherapy* (pp. 13–19). London: Kingsley.

Weller, E. B., Weller, R. A., Fristad, M. A., & Rooney, M. T. (1999). *Children's Interview for Psychiatric Syndromes.* Washington, DC: American Psychiatric Press.

Wieckowski, E., Hartsoe, P., Mayer, A., & Shortz, J. (1998). Deviant sexual behavior in children and young adolescents: Frequency and patterns. *Sexual Abuse: A Journal of Research and Treatment, 10,* 293–303.

Will, D. (1999). Assessment issues. In M. Erooga & H. Masson (Eds.), *Children and young people who sexually abuse others: Challenges and responses* (pp. 86–103). London: Routledge.

Witt, P. H. (2000). A practitioner's view of risk assessment: The HCR-20 and the SVR-20. *Behavioral Sciences and the Law, 18,* 791–798.

Wood, R. M., & Cellini, H. R. (1999). Assessing risk of recidivism in adult male sexually violent offenders. *Offender Programs Report, 3,* 49–61.

Woody, S. R., & Sanderson, W. C. (1998). Manuals for empirically supported treatments: 1998 update. *Clinical Psychologist, 51,* 17–21.

Worling, J. R. (2001). Personality-based typology of adolescent male sexual offenders: Differences in recidivism rates, victim-selection characteristics, and personal victimization histories. *Sexual Abuse, 13,* 149–166.

Worling, J. R. (2002). Assessing risk of sexual assault recidivism with adolescent sexual offenders. In M. C. Calder (Ed.), *Young people who sexually abuse: Building the evidence base for your practice* (pp. 365–375). Dorset, England: Russell House.

Worling, J. R., & Curwen, T. (2000). Adolescent sexual offender recidivism: Success of specialized treatment and implications for risk prediction. *Child Abuse and Neglect, 24,* 965–982.

Worling, J. R., & Curwen, T. (2001). *The "ERASOR:" Estimate of Risk of Adolescent Sexual*

Recidivism (Version 2.0). Toronto, Ontario, Canada: Safe-T Program, Thistletown Regional Centre.

Wyre, R. (2000). Paedophile characteristics and patterns of behaviour. In C. Itzen (Ed.), *Home truths about child sexual abuse: Influencing policy and practice* (pp. 49–69). London: Routledge.

Yalom, I. D. (1985). *The theory and practice of group psychotherapy* (3rd ed.). New York: Basic Books.

Yochelson, S., & Samenow, S. E. (1976). *The criminal personality: Vol. 1. A profile for change.* Northvale, NJ: Aronson.

Zametkin, A. J., & Ernst, M. (1999). Problems in the management of attention-deficit-hyperactivity disorder. *New England Journal of Medicine, 340,* 40–46.

Zaslav, M. R. (1988). A model of group therapist development. *International Journal of Group Psychotherapy, 38,* 511–519.

Author Index

Subject Index